Perceptual constancy
Why things look as they do

Perceptual Constancy examines a group of long-standing problems in the field of perception and provides a review of the fundamentals of the problems and their solutions. Experts in several different fields – including computational vision, physiology, neuropsychology, psychophysics, and comparative psychology – present their approaches to one of the fundamental problems of perception: How does the brain extract a stable world from an ever-changing retinal input? How do we achieve color constancy despite changes in the wavelength content of daylight? How do we recognize objects from different viewpoints? And how do we know the sizes of those objects?

The contributors deal with the perception of color, size, shape, and speed from the perspectives of developmental, clinical, and comparative psychology, psychophysics, physiology, and computational modeling. But constancy comes at a price, and the final chapters address how the visual system must retain the ability to learn and also how the errors we make reveal the mechanisms we use. This important volume will appeal to researchers and graduate students in perceptual psychology, neurophysiology, and computer modeling.

Dr. Vincent Walsh is Research Psychologist in the Department of Experimental Psychology at Oxford University.
Dr. Janusz Kulikowski is Professor of Visual Neuroscience in the Visual Sciences Laboratory at UMIST, Manchester, UK.

Perceptual constancy

Why things look as they do

Edited by

VINCENT WALSH

JANUSZ KULIKOWSKI

PUBLISHED BY THE PRESS SYNDICATE OF THE UNIVERSITY OF CAMBRIDGE
The Pitt Building, Trumpington Street, Cambridge CB2 1RP, United Kingdom

CAMBRIDGE UNIVERSITY PRESS
The Edinburgh Building, Cambridge CB2 2RU, UK   http://www.cup.cam.ac.uk
40 West 20th Street, New York, NY 10011-4211, USA   http://www.cup.org
10 Stamford Road, Oakleigh, Melbourne 3166, Australia

© Cambridge University Press 1998

First published 1998

Printed in the United States of America

Typeset in Times Roman and Century Schoolbook 10/12.5 pt., in Penta [RF]

Library of Congress Cataloging-in-Publication Data
Perceptual constancy : why things look as they do / edited by Vincent
Walsh, Janusz Kulikowski.
p.   cm.
Includes bibliographical references and indexes.
ISBN 0-521-46061-1 (hardcover)
1. Visual perception.   I. Walsh, Vincent, 1961–   .
II. Kulikowski, J. J.
BF241.P437   1998
152.14 – dc21   97-6655
                                                                CIP

A catalog record for this book is available from the British Library.

ISBN 0 521 46061 1 hardback

Contents

Contributors   *page* vii

Introduction: What you see is not what you get   1
Vincent Walsh and Janusz Kulikowski
1   Visual organization and perceptual constancies in
    early infancy   6
    Alan Slater
2   The McCollough effect: Misperception and reality   31
    G. Keith Humphrey
3   Perception of rotated two-dimensional and three-
    dimensional objects and visual shapes   69
    Pierre Jolicoeur and G. Keith Humphrey
4   Computational approaches to shape constancy   124
    Shimon Edelman and Daphna Weinshall
5   Learning constancies for object perception   144
    Peter Földiák
6   Perceptual constancies in lower vertebrates   173
    David Ingle
7   Generalizing across object orientation and size   192
    Elisabeth Ashbridge and David I. Perrett
8   The neuropsychology of visual object constancy   210
    Rebecca Lawson and Glyn W. Humphreys
9   Color constancy and color vision during infancy:
    Methodological and empirical issues   229
    James L. Dannemiller
10 Empirical studies in color constancy   262
    Jimmy M. Troost
11 Computational models of color constancy   283
    A. C. Hurlbert

12 Comparative aspects of color constancy   323
    Christa Neumeyer
13 The physiological substrates of color constancy   352
    Hidehiko Komatsu
14 Size and speed constancy   373
    Suzanne P. McKee and Harvey S. Smallman
15 Depth constancy   409
    Thomas S. Collett and Andrew J. Parker
16 The perception of dynamical constancies   436
    Mary K. Kaiser
17 Perceptual learning   455
    Merav Ahissar and Shaul Hochstein
18 The history of size constancy and size illusions   499
    Helen E. Ross and Cornelis Plug

    Author index   529
    Subject index   539

Contributors

Merav Ahissar   Department of Psychology, Hebrew University, Jerusalem, Israel

Elisabeth Ashbridge   School of Psychology, University of St. Andrews, St. Andrews, UK

Thomas S. Collett   School of Biological Sciences, University of Sussex, Brighton, UK

James L. Dannemiller   Department of Psychology, University of Wisconsin, Madison, Wisconsin, USA

Shimon Edelman   School of Cognitive and Computing Sciences, University of Sussex, Brighton, UK

Peter Földiák   Psychological Laboratory, University of St. Andrews, St. Andrews, UK

Shaul Hochstein   School of Cognitive and Computing Sciences, University of Sussex, Falmer, Brighton, UK

G. Keith Humphrey   Department of Psychology, The University of Western Ontario, London, Ontario, Canada

Glyn W. Humphreys   Cognitive Science Research Centre, School of Psychology, University of Birmingham, Edgbaston, Birmingham, UK

A. C. Hurlbert   Physiological Sciences, Medical School, University of Newcastle-upon-Tyne, UK

David Ingle   Brain and Cognitive Sciences, Massachusetts Institute of Technology, Cambridge, Massachusetts, USA

Pierre Jolicoeur   Department of Psychology, University of Waterloo, Waterloo, Ontario, Canada

Mary K. Kaiser   NASA Ames Research Center, Moffett Field, California, USA

Hidehiko Komatsu Neuroscience Section, Electrotechnical Laboratory, Ibaraki, Japan

Janusz Kulikowski Visual Sciences Laboratory, UMIST, Manchester, UK

Rebecca Lawson Department of Psychology, University of Waterloo, Waterloo, Ontario, Canada

Suzanne P. McKee Smith-Kettlewell Eye Research Institute, San Francisco, California, USA

Christa Neumeyer Institut für Zoologie III, J. Gutenberg-Universität, Mainz, Germany

Andrew J. Parker University Laboratory of Physiology, Oxford, UK

David I. Perrett School of Psychology, University of St. Andrews, St. Andrews, UK

Cornelis Plug Department of Psychology, University of South Africa, Pretoria, South Africa

Helen E. Ross Department of Psychology, University of Stirling, Scotland

Alan Slater Department of Psychology, Washington Singer Laboratories, University of Exeter, Exeter, UK

Harvey S. Smallman Department of Psychology, University of Durham, Durham, UK

Jimmy M. Troost Nijmegen Institute for Cognition and Information, University of Nijmegen, The Netherlands

Vincent Walsh Department of Experimental Psychology, University of Oxford, Oxford, UK

Daphna Weinshall Department of Computer Science, The Hebrew University, Jerusalem, Israel

Introduction: What you see is not what you get

Vincent Walsh and Janusz Kulikowski

The last half century has seen a continuing acceleration in our knowledge of basic mechanisms underlying visual processing. We now know a great deal about human psychophysical performance at the limits of detection and discrimination of luminance, wavelength, contrast, orientation, and motion. The neuronal substrates for these functions have also been the subject of an electrophysiological onslaught that began with the studies of Hubel and Wiesel. These two branches inform each other and serve to place constraints on the kinds of theories that can be generated from one or other data set – a particularly good example being the recent interplay between psychophysics and physiology in unpacking the perceptual significance of Parvo and Magno pathways. The success in describing low-level visual processes is reflected in almost every textbook in the area of vision in which detection and discrimination mechanisms are given most of the page space. In addition, if we are lucky, there is a chapter on recognition, constancy, or illusions at the end of the book.

But most of the daily work of the visual system is carried out well above levels of detection, and although "threshold measurements have been enormously useful in theoretical and clinical work . . . by definition . . . they tell us little about seeing" (Georgeson, 1991, p. 106). In other words, one cannot simply transfer the rules we have learned from studying threshold vision to studies of suprathreshold vision. Nor do the wealth of data on discrimination appear to tell us much about seeing: There are so many differences between most objects that there is probably great redundancy in the ability of the visual system to see two things as different – an ability of little use if one doesn't know what the different objects *are*.

A less obvious but perhaps more fundamental problem in studying vision is to ask how, given very different retinal inputs, the visual system ever manages to recognize an object or a color. This is not a new problem. It is over 200 years since Monge noted that perceived color is to some extent dependent on illumination. This means that color vision departs from Newton's articulation of the – by now commonsense – notion that "Every Body reflects the rays of its own Color more copiously than the rest." The colors we see, then, are not merely the wavelengths we get. This much is agreed on by all those studying constancy. The agreement ends there.

In this book we have tried to bring together authors from different disciplines to provide a coherent view from the different approaches that can be taken to address the problems of perceptual constancies. The debates will sound familiar: How much do retinal mechanisms contribute to constancy? What role do cognitive factors play? What is the time course of the phenomena? Also familiar will be the observation that coherence is not always the result! One might be surprised to learn that the question itself is sometimes the subject of disagreement. For example, there is no agreed standard for the measurement of color constancy and different workers use different methods. The result is that some would argue that human color constancy is "a non-existent phenomenon" (Valberg & Lange-Malecki, 1990), whereas others would argue that it is very robust (Troost & De Weert, 1991). The difference is instructive. Valberg and Lange-Malecki approached the problem using traditional psychophysical techniques, measuring departures from exact matches, whereas Troost and De Weert adopted a naming paradigm that took account of the categorical organization of higher-level color processes. The measurement of color constancy is also susceptible to the effects of instruction (Arend, Reeves, Schirillo, & Goldstein, 1991); what we see is influenced by what we are doing.

Perhaps some would prefer to stay away from a field that disputes both what is being measured and how to measure it, but as the authors in this book demonstrate, it is possible to determine how color constancy differs during the development of the visual system (Dannemiller), how it is affected by the figural content of a scene (Troost), and what are the constraints on developing computational models (Hurlbert).

It is 20 years since a volume was dedicated to perceptual constancies (Epstein, 1977), so perhaps it is worthwhile to consider what is new to this volume as a measure of how far we have come. Several major advances are evident in this new volume. The most salient of these is in the neurophysiology of perception. In 1977 Gross's program of recording from the inferotemporal cortex was still completely novel, but at the time of publication of this book there are at least a dozen laboratories around the world devoted to studying the responses of inferotemporal neurons to complex features of objects. Similarly, in 1977, Zeki had not yet demonstrated the importance of area V4 in color constancy, and Yoshioka had not provided the important demonstration of the ability of neurons in areas V1 and V2 to encode some aspects of surface color rather than wavelength. Two chapters reflect these advances: Ashbridge and Perrett discuss the role of the temporal visual cortex in the perception of objects from different views, and Komatsu provides an up-to-date account of the contribution made by cortical visual areas to color constancy.

Advances are also reflected in the computational chapters in this volume. In

1977 computational approaches to vision were few and usually uninformed by physiology; Epstein's book does not contain a chapter on computational models of vision. The intellectual legacy of Marr is represented here in several chapters. The computational approach is not only articulated in the chapters by Edelman and Weinshal, Hurlbert, and Földiák but also permeates the other approaches. The work reported in Ashbridge and Perrett's chapter, for example, is driven almost entirely by hypotheses generated from a knowledge of computational models of perception. Jolicoeur and Humphrey also use the explicit predictions of computational models to test how it might be possible for the human visual system to recognize an object when it is rotated to give a new retinal image.

One thing that emerges from these pages is that the visual system does not trouble itself to give a perfect description of the world. Indeed, mechanisms that provided absolute constancy would risk losing valuable information (Jameson & Hurvich, 1989). As Földiák puts it, "The goal of perception is to give a useful description of the world," which fortunately is "far from random." From this perspective, the answer to Koffka's question "Why do things look as they do?" might be "Because they are as they are," and the visual system makes use of the regularity of the world in order to recognize the old and detect the new. The utilitarian approach of the brain is seen in McKee and Smallman's chapter on size and speed constancy. How do we perceive the size of an object when it is 2 feet away and when it is 200 feet away? In this case, as in others, the visual system does not make life easy for the psychophysicist: Information about both the angular subtense and the true distance and size of an object is available, and which one dominates may depend on what the visual system is doing.

The third strand of research represented here, which was not available, or at least not addressed in 1977, is the comparative approach. The human visual system has evolved from systems that must have looked a lot like some of the simpler visual systems of animals alive today, and from considering the abilities of animals, we can develop a picture of the constraints imposed on human vision. These simpler systems, however, can spring some surprises on us. Goldfish, for example, have color constancy, but it seems that the function for which we certainly require a secondary visual cortex may be performed by retinal mechanisms in the goldfish.

The final area unavailable in 1977 is that of neuropsychology. Although the effects of right parietal lesions on recognition of objects from different views were reported in 1973 (Warrington & Taylor), a full analysis of the effects of brain damage on constancy began only with the advent of computational theories. One will thus find here a good degree of correspondence between computational (Edelman & Weinshall), human experimental (Jolicoeur & Humphrey), and neuropsychological (Lawson & Humphreys) approaches.

The majority of the chapters take the problem of constructing a stable or useful visual world as one of responding to changes in the visual world in order to be able to see things as the same when their viewing angle or other conditions are changed. The visual system cannot survive merely by solving problems and fielding its best algorithms when there are changes in distance, illumination angle, speed of presentation, or other factors. Some problems need intermediate or longer-term solutions, and this requires great plasticity from the adult visual system. One strategy is to recalibrate the system. Ahissar and Hochstein give several examples of perceptual learning, the ability of the visual system to change its responses as a consequence of experience. The upshot is twofold: What you see depends on what you've seen but also on what you did with what you saw. In other words, task demands have an effect on learning in perceptual tasks (Ellison & Walsh, 1997).

Perhaps the best case study of how far we have come in understanding constancy and plasticity in the visual system is to be found in our understanding of the McCullough effect. Humphrey shows how the relatively low-level effect, itself an expression of adaptive plasticity in the visual system, can be understood with reference to physiological data – neurons with the required color/orientation properties are evident in V1 and V2; neuropsychological data – patient DF, who has extensive extrastriate cortex damage and cannot discriminate orientation, nevertheless reports perceived color changes after adaptation to the McCullough gratings; and computational theories – the McCullough effect has proved to be a useful test case for different models of adaptation in the visual system.

Whatever the discipline of the individual reader of this volume, it is hoped that the breadth of approaches represented will offer some new and unexpected insights and generate new experimental hypotheses. Those who are unfamiliar with the material may find a new branch of vision science opened to them; those already in the field may find something new in the book or allow it to serve as a useful reference; and those who already know it all should begin to put another volume together – advice we give because we know that trying to keep nearly two dozen researchers to a publication deadline will keep them quiet for some time.

References

Arend, L. E., Reeves, A., Schirillo, J., & Goldstein, R. (1991). Simultaneous colour constancy: Papers with diverse Munsell values. *Journal of the Optical Society of America A*, 8, 661–672.

Ellison, A., & Walsh, V. (1997). Perceptual learning in visual search: Some evidence for specificities. *Vision research*, in press.

Epstein, W. (1977). *Stability and constancy in visual perception*. London: Wiley.

Georgeson M. (1991) Over the limit: Encoding contrast above threshold in human vision. In J. J. Kulikowski, V., Walsh, & J. J. Murray (Eds.), *Limits of Vision*. London: Macmillan.

Jameson, D., & Hurvich, L. M. (1989) Essay concerning color constancy. *Annual Review of Psychology, 40*, 1–22.

Troost, J. M., & de Weert, C. M. M. (1991). Naming versus matching in color constancy. *Perception & Psychophysics, 50*, 591–602.

Valberg, A., & Lange-Malecki, B. (1990) "Colour constancy" in Mondrian patterns: A partial cancellation of physical chromaticity shifts by simultaneous contrast. *Vision Research, 30*, 371–380.

Wandell, B. A. (1995) *Foundations of vision*. Sunderland, Mass.: Sinauer.

Warrington, E. K., & Taylor, A. M. (1973). The contribution of the right parietal lobe to object recognition. *Cortex, 9*, 152–164.

1   Visual organization and perceptual constancies in early infancy

Alan Slater

1. Introduction

Speculation about the origins and development of various organizational principles has been around for hundreds of years, and these speculations gave rise to one of the longest-running debates in psychology and vision research, concerning whether perception is innate or learned. The nativist view that perceptual abilities are unlearned and may be present at birth had fewer adherents than the opposing empiricist assertion that perception is exceptionally impoverished at birth and that its development is a consequence of learning. The oldest empiricist theory of perceptual learning was put forward by the philosopher George Berkeley in *A New Theory of Vision*, published in 1709. He claimed that the distance of objects, or "distance of itself," cannot be perceived directly because the image on the retina is flat and two-dimensional. Given that the retinal image of an object changes "as you approach to, and recede from the tangible object" such that "it has no fixed or determinate greatness," it follows that the sense of vision provides constantly changing and ambiguous information both about distance and about an object's true size. Therefore, the argument continues, "the judgement we make of the distance of an object, viewed with both eyes, is entirely the result of experience."

More recent theorists, who similarly emphasized the extreme perceptual limitations of infants, were Hebb and Piaget. Hebb (1949) acknowledged that "The idea that one has to learn to see a triangle must sound extremely improbable" (p. 31) but argued that perception of even such simple shapes is the result of complex learning. Piaget said of the young infant, "The world is a world of pictures, lacking in depth or constancy, permanence or identity which disappear or reappear capriciously" (1954, p. 3) and, with respect to vision, "Perception

The author's research, described here, was supported by the following grants from the Economic and Social Research Council: C00230028/ 2114/ 2278; RC00232466. My thanks to Liz Brown, Anne Mattock, and Victoria Morison, who collected most of the data, and to the subjects' mothers and the staff of the Maternity Unit, Royal Devon and Exeter Hospital, Heavitree, Devon, for their help and cooperation.

of light exists from birth and consequently the reflexes which insure the adaptation of this perception (the pupillary and palpebral reflexes, both to light). All the rest (perception of forms, sizes, positions, distances, prominence, etc.) is acquired through the combination of reflex activity with higher activities'' (1953, p. 62).

The obvious alternative to a perceptual learning account of visual development is to adopt a nativist view that the ability to perceive a stable, organized world is an innate property of the visual system and to claim that babies perceive the world in much the same way that adults do. One of the first researchers to carry out scientific investigations into perceptual organization in infancy was Bower (1966), and he concluded ''that infants can in fact register most of the information an adult can register but can handle less of the information than adults can'' (p. 10).

Answers to the many questions about the origins and development of visual organization awaited the development of procedures and methodologies to test infants' perceptual abilities, and in the last 30 years a large number of relevant infant studies have been reported. In general, these studies have given rise to conceptions of the *competent infant* because the perception of young infants has been found to be surprisingly well organized. Although we can now reject extreme empiricist views of perceptual development, the picture of infant visual perception that is emerging is more complex than any of the early theories would have claimed: Some aspects of perceptual organization are present at birth, whereas others show considerable development throughout infancy. Several types of perceptual organization that are found in early infancy are discussed here, and the chapter is divided essentially into two parts. In ''Visual Organization in Early Infancy,'' a number of organizational principles are discussed under the headings of form perception, stimulus compounds and spatial relationships, subjective contours, biomechanical motion, categorization and prototypes, and intermodal peception. The purpose of this section is to emphasize the point that many types of visual organization, in addition to those usually referred to as the perceptual constancies, contribute to the perceived stability, coherence, and meaningfulness of visual perception. The second major section, ''The Visual Constancies,'' describes research relating to the presence of a number of constancies in infancy: shape, size, feature, and identity constancies.

2. Visual organization in early infancy

Organizational principles are essential for visual perception to be meaningful, and it is therefore important to ask whether, and in what ways, the perception of young infants is organized. A number of different ways in which visual input is organized early in life are discussed here.

2.1 Form perception

The newborn infant can discriminate between a range of stimuli that differ in pattern or form. The typical procedures used to demonstrate these abilities use habituation to one pattern and subsequent dishabituation (recovery of visual attention) to a novel pattern, or familiarization to a series of stimuli that have one invariant property in common, followed by the presentation of a pattern that is novel in the sense of not possessing the invariant property. Three of the findings from the use of these procedures with newborns are the following: (1) discrimination between the simple outline shapes of a square, triangle, cross, and circle, and between complex abstract shapes (Slater, Morison, & Rose, 1983, 1984); (2) discrimination between gratings that differ only in their orientation (Atkinson, Hood, Wattam-Bell, Anker, & Tricklebank, 1988; Slater, Morison, & Somers, 1988); and (3) discrimination between acute and obtuse angles, which may be the basic "building blocks" of form perception (Slater, Mattock, Brown, & Bremmer, 1991a).

There is evidence that infants discriminate between significant objects that they encounter in their real worlds very soon after birth. Field, Cohen, Garcia, and Greenberg (1984) and Bushnell, Sai, and Mullin (1989) reported that infants showed reliable preferences for their mother's face, compared with that of a female stranger, at 45 and 49 hours after birth, respectively. In a recent study, Walton, Bower, and Bower (1992) reported that infants 12 and 36 hours after birth produced more sucking responses in order to see a videotaped image of their mother's face as opposed to an image of a stranger's face.

Of course, we do not know exactly what aspects of the face the babies were using in order to make the face discriminations. The results of the experiments described here might argue for some degree of form perception at birth, but it is difficult to provide unambiguous evidence of such an ability: Perception of form in the sense of perceiving wholes rather than parts (e.g., the perception of a triangle as a triangle rather than a collection of lines and angles) is extremely difficult to demonstrate in young infants. The problem is the following: When the newborn baby reliably discriminates, say, a circle from a cross, it is possible that the baby may be making the discrimination on the basis of detecting the different orientations of the lines that make up the stimuli rather than by seeing the circle and cross as whole figures. Nevertheless, the several findings previously described suggest that newborn infants possess at least sufficient rudimentary form perception to respond to, and learn about, objects on the basis of their form properties.

2.2 Stimulus compounds and spatial relationships

All nondeforming objects contain a number of features that stand in a constant or invariant relationship to each other. For example, in the human face the hairline is at the top, the eyes are horizontal and above the nose and mouth, the ears are at the sides, and so on, and the precise combinations of these features are the same for any one face but differ between faces. Even a very simple line stimulus has the several features of length, width, orientation, and chromaticity. In order to be able to perceive stimuli as wholes or patterns, the perceiver has to do at least two things: (1) to "bind together" those combinations of features that occur together, that is, to perceive stimulus compounds rather than encoding or processing the separate elements or components, and (2) to detect the invariant relationships between the elements. There is evidence for the presence of both of these abilities at birth.

2.2.1 Perception of stimulus compounds.   In an experiment to test whether newborn babies have the ability to process and remember stimulus compounds, the babies (who averaged 2 days of age) were familiarized, on successive trials, to two separate stimuli (Slater et al., 1991). An achromatic representation of the chromatic stimuli shown can be seen in Figure 1.1. For half of the infants the stimuli were a green diagonal (GD) stripe and a red vertical (RV) stripe; the other babies were familiarized to GV and RD. In the former case there are two novel compounds of these elements, RD and GV. On test trials the babies were shown one of the familiar compounds paired with one of the novel ones (Figure 1.1 shows the four possible test pairings), and they showed strong novelty preferences – that is, they looked longer at the novel compounds. Note that the novel compounds consisted of stimulus properties (color and orientation) that had been seen before. The novelty preferences are therefore clear evidence that the babies had processed, and remembered, the simple stimulus compounds that they had seen on the familiarization trials.

2.2.2 Spatial relationships.   Antell and Caron (1985) showed newborns two simple stimuli, which varied in their absolute locations across the familiarization trials but maintained a constant spatial relationship with each other. A black cross was always above (or, for half of the subjects, below) a black square. On test trials the subjects showed a novelty preference where the novel stimulus was the same two stimuli, but with the up/down order reversed. From these findings, the investigators argued that newborns are sensitive to relative location and that they "are capable of detecting an invariant spatial relation between two elements and of using that information to discriminate a novel arrangement of the same elements" (p. 21). One criticism of this study is that the babies could have shown these novelty preferences if they had attended to only one of the

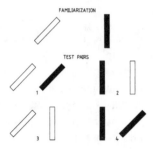

Figure 1.1. Following familiarization (above) to two stimuli that differ in color and orientation, there are four possible test pairings of familiar and novel compounds (below).

stimuli (either the top or bottom one) because this changed from familiarization to test trials. These findings are therefore suggestive, rather than conclusive, evidence for the detection of spatial relationships between stimulus elements at birth.

These studies suggest that the ability to organize the features of objects into coherent wholes, and to detect the relationships between the features of separate objects, is present at or close to birth.

2.3 Subjective contours

One type of perceptual organization that relates to form perception, and that is found with artificial stimuli, is the perception of subjective contours and their organization into unitary patterns. Subjective contours are illusory contours that are perceived "in the absence of any physical gradient of change in the display" (Ghim, 1990; Kanizsa, 1979). An example of this illusion is pattern A in Figure 1.2, and most adults see the contours of a real square despite the fact that the contours are absent. Perception of subjective contours is dependent on the alignment of the inducing elements, and when this alignment is altered the subjective contour of the square is not perceived, as is apparent by looking at patterns B, C, and D in Figure 1.2.

Convincing evidence that 3- and 4-month-old infants perceive subjective contours was provided in a series of experiments by Ghim (1990). In one experimental condition the infants were familiarized, or habituated, either to a pattern containing a subjective contour (SC, pattern A, Figure 1.2) or to a nonsubjective contour (NSC, pattern B, C, or D). Following this, the infants in the SC group discriminated SC from one of the NSC patterns, but infants in the NSC groups did not discriminate between the familiarized pattern and a different NSC pattern. This leads to the conclusion that the infants were perceiving subjective contours, the inference being that "the differences between patterns with and without subjective contours is greater than the differences between patterns without subjective contours'' (p. 225). In another condition, infants were familiarized to an outline of a *real* square. Subsequently they perceived an NSC pattern as more novel than the SC pattern, again suggesting that they perceived the ''squareness'' of the SC pattern.

Ghim's fourth experiment is particularly revealing with respect to early form perception, as well as telling us more about detection of subjective contours. Infants were familiarized to the SC pattern, and on the test trials they were shown patterns E and F of Figure 1.2. They showed a strong novelty preference for the incomplete diamondlike pattern, indicating that the incomplete squarelike pattern was seen as being similar to the SC pattern. Note that this novelty preference would not have resulted if the infants had attended only to the corners of the previously seen SC pattern because there are no corners in either pattern E or pattern F (Figure 1.2). Ghim suggested that the results ''support contentions that the infants filled in the gaps among the aligned elements in the SC pattern, and . . . add to our belief that infants have knowledge of the complete form and its components after viewing patterns that produce forms with subjective contours'' (pp. 243, 244).

2.4 Biomechanical motion

Many of the studies described so far have shown infants stimuli that are static and unchanging, and we have learned a considerable amount about visual perception from the use of such stimuli. However, it is clear that many aspects of perceptual organization require integration of information over space and time, and an understanding of these aspects requires the use of dynamic stimuli. One such aspect of organization is the ability to detect the information contained in changing point-light displays.

Biomechanical motions are the motions that correspond to the movements of a person, and a point-light display to depict such motion is usually produced by filming a person in the dark who has some 11 points of light attached to the major joints (ankles, knees, hip, shoulder, etc.) and the head. In part A of Figure 1.3 a display corresponding to a single, static frame is shown, and observers shown such static frames are usually unaware that it represents a human form. However, if the displays are moving (as depicted in part B of Figure 1.3), an impressive range of discriminations is easily made: Adult observers perceive the human form, and from displays with durations as short as 200 msec they can specify its actions (press-ups, walking, running, dancing, etc); adults are also capable of recognizing friends and detecting gender and other characteristics of a person (Bertenthal, 1992; Cutting & Proffitt, 1981; Johansson, 1977).

Adults' discriminations and recognitions from such point-light displays are typically made effortlessly, despite the fact that the motions presented are ac-

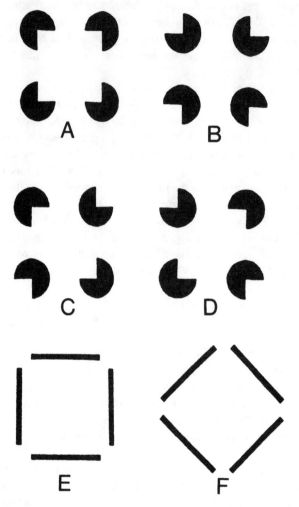

Figure 1.2. Stimuli used by Ghim (1990). Pattern A (SC) produces subjective contours forming a square. Patterns B, C, and D (NSC) do not produce subjective contours. The incomplete lines (E and F) were used in the test phase of an experiment following habituation to pattern A. Reprinted with permission.

tually very complex. For example, as a person walks, the hips, shoulders, head, and arms change height during the gait cycle; the wrists, elbows, ankles, and knees produce rigid pendulum motions relative to the movement of the joints at the next level of the hierarchy. Thus, the ankle describes a pendular motion relative to the knee, and the knee describes a pendular motion relative to the hip, whereas the hip describes a translatory motion relative to the ground. Similar considerations apply to the wrist, elbow, and shoulder, although this could

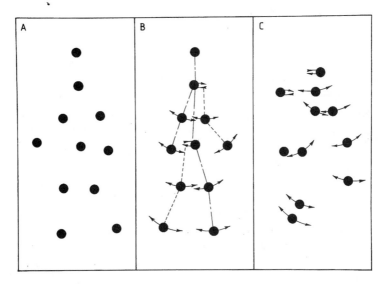

Figure 1.3. Three possible point-light displays. (A) A static display is not usually seen as representing a human form. (B) When the display is in coherent motion, as depicted here, it is easily seen as a person walking. (C) If the same point lights move in an incoherent or random motion, perception tends to be of a swarm of bees. Derived from Bertenthal (1992).

be more complex if the walker shrugs his or her shoulders. The displays become considerably more complex if the person walks on uneven ground or, say, there are point-light displays of two people dancing and spinning around. Nevertheless, these displays, too, are recognized effortlessly by adults.

A variety of evidence suggests that babies are sensitive to the biomechanical motions specified by the dynamic transitions of point-light displays. Three-month-old infants can discriminate between upright and inverted point-light displays of a person walking, but only if the displays are moving; there is no discrimination between two static versions of the displays (Bertenthal, Proffitt & Cutting, 1984). In many studies, computer-generated displays are produced in which the points of light either mimic an upright walker with the lights at the major joints (a "coherent" display), or with the lights moving "off the joint," or randomly, or in a less coherent fashion than that of a real walker: Random patterns often suggest a moving swarm of bees. With these sorts of displays, it has been found that young infants prefer to look at a coherent display rather than a random one, and that 3-month-olds encode coherent displays more rapidly than incoherent ones, implying that they are detecting the organizational structure of the coherent one (Bertenthal, Proffitt, Spetner, & Thomas, 1985; Fox & McDaniels, 1982). Bertenthal (1992), discussing infants' awareness of the processing constraints that allow perception of biomechanical displays, suggests that "there is no clear lower-bound on the age at which they are first implemented. It is therefore quite reasonable to propose that these constraints are part of the intrinsic organization of the visual system" (p. 209).

There is an intriguing age change between 3 and 5 months in infants' responses to these displays. Babies 3 months of age discriminate between an upside-down point-light walker and a random pattern of lights, but 5- and 7-month-olds do not (Bertenthal & Davis, 1988). Bertenthal and Davis's interpretation of this apparently paradoxical age change is that by 5 months infants are responding to the perceived familiarity of the displays, that is, as a result of experience and accumulated knowledge they recognize the upright display as a human walker, whereas the inverted and random displays are perceived equivalently because they are both unfamiliar. By 5 months of age, therefore, infants respond to these sorts of displays at a higher level of perceptual processing: Perception interacts with prior knowledge to affect what is perceived. Familiarity certainly affects adults' perception of such displays: An inverted display is often seen as several objects in motion, whereas an upright one is invariably seen as a moving person.

Bertenthal (1992) cites two additional studies in support of the claim that knowledge affects infants' perception of biomechanical motion. In the first, Fox and McDaniels (1982) found that 6-month-olds discriminated a point-light display of moving hands from an incoherent or perturbed display, but neither 2- nor 4-month-olds did so. Bertenthal points out that visually guided reaching appears at around 5 months of age, so that only the 6-month-olds would have sufficient familiarity with the hands to allow the displays to be discriminated on the basis of familiarity. In the second study, Bertenthal (1992) showed 3- and 5-month-olds point-light displays of a person producing different types of walking (walking, marching, walking while waving arms above the head) and found that the older, but not the younger, infants generalized to a different display of an upright walker. This suggests that the 5-month-olds had extracted some *general* property of human gait that was not specific to any individual display.

Thus, it seems that very young infants distinguish between biological and nonbiological motion on the basis of the *perceptual* information, or perceptual processing constraints, contained in the former; and that by 5 months of age knowledge, or *conceptual* information, constrains the interpretation of point-light displays of the human gait, and by 6 months of age of the movement of the hands. That is to say, as infants gain experience of the world, they begin to respond to perceptual displays on the basis of their *meaning* in addition to (and sometimes in opposition to) their perceptual structure. These knowledge-based constraints, which by definition are dependent on experience, will emerge at different ages, depending on the ways in which infants interact with, learn about, and accumulate knowledge about the perceptual information they encounter. As Bertenthal (1992) comments: "there is no reason to think that (a) particular age possesses some unique status. Some percepts will not interact with age until later ages, whereas others might be constrained at (very early) ages. The deciding factor is the relevance and accessibility of the stored knowledge'' (p. 210).

2.5 Categorization and prototypes

Perceptual categorization occurs whenever two or more perceptually discriminable stimuli are responded to equivalently. This type of organization of the perceptual input allows us to organize, make sense of, and thereby reduce the otherwise overwhelming variation in the appearance of stimuli, both people and objects. A number of researchers have begun to study infants' abilities to categorize their perceptual environments and to extract prototypical representations from category exemplars. A few illustrative studies are described here under the headings of orientation, form and prototypes, and prototypes for faces.

2.5.1 Orientation. Newborn infants discriminate between stimuli that differ only in orientation: They distinguish between vertical and horizontal and between mirror-image oblique stripes (Slater, Morison & Somers, 1988; Slater & Sykes, 1977). Bomba (1984) reported that 4-month-olds who had been familiarized to a number of oblique striped patterns that differed in orientation generalized what they had seen to a differently oriented oblique pattern (in the sense that they perceived a vertical pattern as novel and a new oblique one as familiar). This oblique category includes obliques that are either side of vertical (i.e., clockwise and anticlockwise: Quinn & Bomba, 1986). Bomba demonstrated that the infants could discriminate between the orientations of the different oblique patterns used, which suggests that their generalization reflects categorization behavior. He also found that this categorization behavior improved with age, in that younger infants showed both a poorer ability to discriminate between obliques and a poorer ability to generalize from one discriminable oblique to another. Taken together these results suggest that orientation detection is present from birth but that the ability to treat different oblique orientations as members of the same category improves over the first few months.

2.5.2 Form and prototypes. When we as adults categorize our perceptions and experiences, we allocate them to particular categories in terms of their possession (or absence) of invariant features or information that define the category. For most perceptual categories we can define a *prototype*, which is an ideal or average member, and the prototypical member is used both to organize and define other members of the population and to select new members from incoming stimuli. An ideal perceptual prototype might be, for example, a perfect square, with equal-length lines and right angles: The category ''dog'' does not have an ideal prototype, but something like a mongrel would be closer to an

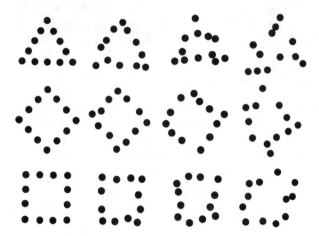

Figure 1.4. Examples of the stimuli used by Bomba and Siqueland (1983). The proto-typical triangle, diamond, and square are on the left, and from left to right are distortions of each. © 1983 Academic Press. Reprinted with permission.

average prototypical member of the class than some of the more exotic subspe-cies. Categorization and generation of prototypes go hand in hand: It is not possible to categorize stimuli unless one has some idea of what the defining characteristics of the category are.

Bomba and Siqueland (1983) investigated infants' categories based on form: The types of stimuli they used are shown in Figure 1.4. The triangle, diamond, and square on the left of the figure are the ideal prototypes, or good examples of the categories, and when 3- and 4-month-olds were familiarized to the dis-tortions of one of the patterns (A, B, and C, Figure 1.4), their learning gener-alized to the category prototype that they had not previously seen. Thus, having been familiarized, for example, to distortions of the triangle, they subsequently gave a novelty response to the (preferred) prototypical square or diamond when this was paired with the prototypical triangle. A further experiment demonstrated that the infants could discriminate between the prototypes and their within-category distortions, suggesting that the infants categorized the prototype as a new instance of the familiar category despite the ability to discriminate between it and its distorted versions.

A further experiment demonstrated that their prototypical forms had the spe-cial status of prototypes: That is, they were more squarelike, diamondlike, and trianglelike than their distortions. In this experiment, each infant was familiar-ized to a number of distorted exemplars of one of the categories. Then after a delay period intended to induce some loss of memory about the characteristics of the specific exemplars, the babies were tested for recognition by being shown

one of the previously seen exemplars paired with the previously unseen prototype. This resulted in an apparently paradoxical novelty preference for the "old"
(previously seen) exemplar. Bomba and Siqueland call this a *prototype effect*,
and their interpretation is as follows: The infants categorize the previously unseen prototype as the best examplar of the recently acquired form category, and
it is therefore more easily recognized (more familiar) than the distorted exemplar, although the latter had been seen earlier.

2.5.3 Prototypes for faces.   The human face is one of the most frequently encountered stimuli in the infant's world, and it is not surprising to find that information about individual faces is learned early in life: As discussed earlier, infants
discriminate their mother's face from that of a stranger as early as 12 hours after
birth. Such early learning testifies to the importance of the face in the baby's
world, and further evidence suggests that babies quickly form a prototype, or averaged version, of the face. Samuels and Ewy (1985) showed pairs of black and
white slides of same-gender faces (equal numbers of male and female faces were
used) to 3- and 6-month-old infants. The slides were constructed so that each of
the members of a pair were as similar as possible in gross physiognomic appearance, but they differed in attractiveness as rated by adults: Attractive and unattrac-
tive faces were paired together. Both age groups looked longest at the attractive
faces used, and this was true for all of the 12 facial pairings. The preference was
extremely strong, with the attractive faces eliciting 70% of the total looking. This
finding was replicated with slightly younger infants (2- and 3-months-olds) by
Langlois et al. (1987), who used as their stimuli color slides of female faces. It
seems unlikely that there is an unlearned aesthetic preference for faces, and the
most likely interpretation of the results is the following.

   If two faces are shown together in a stereoscope, so that one is presented to
the left eye, the other to the right, the two images will often fuse so that the
observer sees only one face. When this happens, it is invariably the case that
observers report that the fused face is more attractive than either of the original
faces. Similarly, if faces are computer generated to produce averaged features,
the results are seen as attractive, and such averaged faces become even more
attractive as more faces are added (Langlois & Roggman, 1990). Thus an averaged or prototypical face, resulting from combining features from many faces,
would be perceived as being physically attractive, and the babies' preferences
for attractive faces can therefore be interpreted as a prototype effect.

2.6 Intermodal perception

Most of the objects and events we perceive are intermodal. For example, the
shape of an object is the same whether we see it or touch it, lip movements are
synchronized with the sound of the voice, and dropping a rigid object on a hard

surface will cause a sharp, banging sound. The ability to detect and learn about intermodal relationships is an important organizational property of our perceptual system, and many researchers have investigated the origins and development of intermodal perception (Spelke, 1987).

Several types of intermodal perception can be distinguished, most of which are present, albeit in primitive form, at birth. As adults we tend to look in the direction of a sound and to reach for things we see – that is, sounds specify and give the location of visual stimuli, and visually perceived objects inform haptic perception. With respect to the first of these abilities, newborn infants also look in the direction of a sound source. One of the earliest studies to show this was by Wertheimer (1961), who reported that his baby daughter, when she was only 8 minutes old, turned her eyes toward a sound played softly in one ear or the other. Butterworth (1983) found that this orienting tendency was stronger if the sound-producing object was visually present (as opposed to being artificially produced with the use of tape recorders and earphones), leading him to the conclusion that newborns *expect* to see the thing that produced the sound. Visually directed reaching first appears at around 4½ months after birth. From this time babies will reach for near by but not for out-of-reach objects, and they will adjust their reaches to take into account the object's size, distance, direction, and movement (Spelke, 1987).

In one type of intermodal coordination, two (or more) sensory modalities give equivalent or matching information. Meltzoff and Borton (1979) gave 1-month-olds either a smooth or a nubby nipple (dummy or pacifier) to suck, and they were not allowed to see the nipple. On the later test trials the infants looked longer at a picture of the *familiar* nipple, giving evidence that the infants were matching the texture of the nipple across the two modalities of vision and touch. In a later study, Gibson and Walker (1984) had 1-month-olds explore either a rigid or flexible object in their mouths; subsequently they looked at a *novel* pattern of movement. It is not clear why a familiarity preference should be found in one study and a novelty preference in the other, but these studies demonstrate that cross-modal matching of texture and substance/movement is perceived soon after birth.

In another type of intersensory perception, events specified by different modalities are temporally linked by a contingency relationship: As an example, a ball makes a sound at the precise moment it hits the ground. Infants as young as 3 months of age (younger infants have not been tested) will look longer at a face that has a synchronized voice accompanying it than at a nonsynchronized pairing (Dodd, 1979), and 4-month-olds will look longer at objects that are dropped when a sound occurs when the object hits the ground if this is shown paired with a nonsynchronized event (Spelke, 1979).

Many intersensory relationships are quite arbitrary. We know that cows "moo," sheep "baa," and pigs "oink," and that a friend's voice uniquely belongs to her face. These associations are clearly a product of learning, and the acquisition of such knowledge begins in early infancy. In a study by Spelke and Owsley (1979), 3½-month-old infants were sat between their mother and father, and they heard the (nonsynchronized) voice of one parent presented between the parents' faces. The infants looked longer at the parent whose voice was played. In a recent study, we (Slater, Brown, Nicholas, & Lee, in preparation) have found that newborn infants associate arbitrary pairings of simple visual stimuli with sounds. The stimuli presented were a green diagonal line accompanied by a male voice repeating the word *teat* and a red vertical line accompanied by a female voice repeating the word *mum*. On the test trials, the infants looked longer at unfamiliar combinations (such as the green diagonal accompanied by *mum*) than at familiar ones. Clearly, infants learn to associate sounds and sights (and probably other intermodal associations) from birth.

Intermodal perception is critical to perception of a stable world: If the different modalities gave rise to unrelated and uncoordinated perceptions, then the infant's perceived world would be bewildering in ways that we (and infants!) could not comprehend. Fortunately, and perhaps not surprisingly, intermodal perception is present from birth: "The same sensations, actions, and mechanisms for perceiving objects that are said to underlie intermodal perception are thought to underlie perception of all kinds" (Spelke, 1987, p. 264).

2.7 Overview

The several lines of evidence presented in the previous sections suggest that from an early age infants are able to organize the components of objects into coherent wholes, and are able to organize featural information into higher-level relations and into meaningful and organized perceptions. Many organizational abilities are present at birth – perhaps some degree of form perception, sensitivity to biomechanical motion, detection of depth and size information, intermodal perception, and so on – but will almost certainly improve in their level of functioning postnatally. Other perceptual abilities, including the classification of stimuli, the formation of perceptual prototypes, and the interaction of perception with prior knowledge, develop after birth.

In short, perception is organized at birth, but many organizational abilities either improve or develop postnatally. This means that we cannot speculate with any certainty on whether the various abilities that are called the visual constancies are functioning at birth or what the course of their postnatal development is. These are empirical questions, and the findings relating to their development are discussed in the next section.

3. The visual constancies

We have seen that the newborn baby has sufficient prerequisite visual abilities to allow of the possibility that some of the visual constancies may be present at or soon after birth. In the last 30 years a large number of relevant infant studies have been reported, so that it is now possible to outline the development of several of the constancies. Some of these studies are described here under the headings of shape and size constancy and identity and existence constancy.

3.1 Shape and size constancy

Perception of an object's real shape, regardless of changes to its orientation, or slant, relative to the observer, is called *shape constancy. Size constancy* refers to the fact that we see an object as the same size, regardless of its distance from us: a person 60 feet away from us subtends an image on the retina that is one-sixth of that person 10 feet away, but we see the person as being the same size. Experimental evidence for the presence of these constancies in early infancy has accumulated over the last 30 years. This evidence is reviewed here, beginning with Bower's early conditioning experiments.

3.1.1 Bower's early experiments.   The first researcher to report systematic ex-perimental evidence for the presence of constancies in infant perception was Tom Bower (1966). He used conditioning procedures to suggest that shape and size constancy are present by about 2 months of age. His conditioning proce-dures were designed to discover whether or not young infants could perceive the true or real shapes and sizes of stimuli, independently of changes to their orientation or retinal sizes. In brief, infants were conditioned to give a head-turn response in the presence of one stimulus (the conditioned stimulus), and then they were tested for their responses to stimuli that differed in their orien-tations, distances, and retinal and real shapes and sizes from the conditioned stimulus: The stimuli that elicited the most head-turn responses on these test trials should be those that appeared to the infants to be most like the conditioned stimulus. Thus, if the infants had been basing their conditioned head-turn re-sponses on the objects' *real* shapes and sizes, then on the test trials they should give more responses to the *same* objects, even though these were now shown in different orientations or at different distances. Alternatively, if the infants had been basing their head-turn responses on the conditioned objects' *retinal* pro-jections, or their distance from the infants, the test-trial responses should be most readily elicited by those stimuli that were closest in retinal shape or size, or viewing distance.

In Bower's shape constancy experiment, 2-month-old infants were condi-tioned to respond to a wooden rectangle that was turned 45° away from the fronto-parallel plane (a plane at right angles to their line of sight). On the test trials they gave more responses to the *same* rectangle, this time in the parallel line of sight, than either to a trapezoid shape that gave the same retinal image as the conditioned stimulus or to a trapezoid shape that was in the same right angle plane as the conditioned stimulus. That is, the infants had clearly learned to respond to the conditioned stimulus's *real* shape, and not its retinal shape or its orientation.

A similar finding resulted from Bower's size constancy experiment. Two-month-olds were trained to respond to a 1-foot cube located 3 feet away from them. Subsequently, they gave more head-turn responses to the same-size cube at a distance of 9 feet, whose retinal image size was one-third the size of the training stimulus, than to a 3-foot cube at 9 feet, whose retinal size was the same as that of the training stimulus.

These conditioned responses to the objects' real rather than retinal shapes and sizes suggest that shape and size constancy are present by 2 months of age. However, Bower's experiments left two unanswered questions. First, can other researchers, using different methodologies, confirm his findings? Second, does this mean that these constancies are present at birth? E. J. Gibson expressed the latter question succinctly with respect to size constancy, and her remarks are equally applicable to shape constancy: "Does this mean that *no* learning is involved in the development of size constancy? Definitely not, since even eight weeks gives a lot of opportunity for visual experience" (1970, p. 104). These two questions are considered in detail in the following sections.

3.1.2 Shape constancy and slant perception. The first experimenters to use a different method than Bower's conditioning procedure, and to find similarly convincing evidence for the presence of shape constancy in early infancy, were Caron, Caron, and Carlson (1979). The method they used was habituation or familiarization, followed by tests with novel and familiar shapes. Three-month-old infants were shown one of two stimuli, either a square or a trapezium, for an average of about eight trials. On each trial the familiarized stimulus was shown in a different slant in order to desensitize the infants to changes in slant prior to the test trials. Following the familiarization trials, there was considerably greater recovery of attention to a different shape than to the same shape when the same (familiarized) shape was in a different slant than any seen earlier. This finding indicates "that the constant real shape of the habituated figure had been perceived across rotational transformations" (p. 716).

The results of Caron et al., like those of Bower, leave open the question of whether maturation and/or learning make a contribution to the development of shape constancy and do not indicate when this ability first emerges. Slater and Morison (1985) used the visual preference method (preferential looking, or PL) and habituation/dishabituation procedures to investigate whether slant perception and shape constancy are present at birth (the babies tested averaged just over 2 days from birth). In the PL study it was found that looking at (i.e., preference for) one stimulus (a square) changed in a consistent manner with changes in slant when it was paired with one of two trapeziums that remained in a constant slant (the two trapeziums were constructed such that the larger one, when it was slanted 60° from the frontal plane, gave the retinal image of the square, and the smaller one, in the frontal plane, or flat, gave the retinal image of the square at a slant of 60°). A highly systematic effect was found such that the more the square was oriented away from the frontal plane, the less time the babies spent looking at it. These findings are shown in Figure 1.5: Slant changes of 15° caused reliable changes in newborns' preferential looking, suggesting that newborns detect fine variations in slant. In the second experiment of Slater and Morison, familiarization trials, similar to those used by Caron et al. with 3-month-olds, were given with one stimulus (either a square or a trapezium) that, on successive trials, was at different slants to the eye. On the test trials that followed, the square and trapezium were paired together, the familiar shape being in a different slant than any shown earlier, and every one of the 12 newborns tested looked more at the novel shape. These results demonstrate that newborn babies have the ability to extract the constant, real shape of an object that is rotated in the third dimension: that is, they have shape constancy.

3.1.3 Size constancy and response to retinal size. In the 1970s and 1980s, McKenzie and Day reported several experiments on size constancy and related issues. They worked on the reasonable assumption "that the consistent outcomes of Bower's experiments ... would be sustained using alternative methods" (Day, 1987, p. 78) and used habituation/dishabituation procedures. In their first experiment (McKenzie & Day, 1972), they habituated infants in the age range 6 to 20 weeks to one stimulus and then looked for recovery to several test stimuli, these differing from the familiarized one in size and distance. They were unable to get a response that could be interpreted in terms of size constancy but found that their infants' looking on the test trials was exclusively determined by viewing distance: The babies simply looked more at the nearer stimuli, whether they were large or small.

This is an important finding in that it tells us that distance per se affects infants' looking but does not clarify the position with respect to the development of size constancy. However, two of their later experiments demonstrated that size constancy is present in infant perception at least by 4 months of age. In the first of these experiments, McKenzie, Tootell, and Day (1980) habituated infants aged 18, 26, and 33 weeks to a colored realistic model of a human head, and on test trials the 26- and 33-week-olds (but not the 18-week-olds) treated the same-sized head as equivalent to the original (i.e., they showed no recovery of visual attention to it), even when it was shown at a different distance from the eyes, and hence gave a different retinal image size. In the second experiment (Day & McKenzie, 1981), 18-week-olds only were tested, and they were habituated to a model head that moved toward and away from them. On the test trials they were shown another head of a different size, which moved through

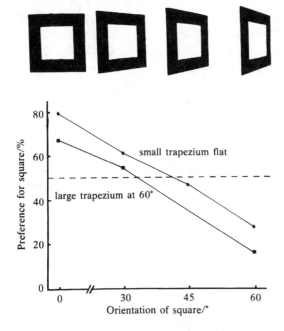

Figure 1.5. As the orientation of the square shifted away from the frontal plane (0°), it became increasingly less preferred when paired with either a large or a small trapezium. The retinal images of the square in its four slants are shown at the top of the figure.

the same range of distance and visual angles as that of the habituated stimulus. The rationale underlying the experiment was that recovery from habituation in the test phase, were it to occur, must result from detection of the real size of the object independently of its distance or visual angle. This recovery, in fact, was what was found, indicating "that the infants perceived and responded to the invariant size of the object as its visual angle varied. That is to say, visual size constancy obtained" (Day, 1987, p. 83).

In his excellent review of the literature on size constancy in infancy, Day (1987) concludes that "size constancy is operative at 18 weeks" (p. 85) but leaves open the question of whether it is present in earlier infancy. His caution is reflected by others, and it is commonly stated that shape constancy is present at birth but that, in contrast, "size constancy does not emerge until 4 to 6 months of age" (Berk, 1991, p. 157). Actually, there seems to be no obvious or logical reason why size constancy should make a later appearance than shape constancy because both require appreciation of depth and the third dimension; in fact, two studies give convincing evidence that size constancy, too, is present at birth.

In the first of these studies, Granrud (1987) tested newborn infants in either a Constant-Size or Variable-Size condition. In the Constant-Size condition the infants were shown a 6-cm-diameter sphere at three distances: 16, 24 and 32 cm. The Variable-Size group was shown (separately) three different-sized spheres, 3, 6, and 12 cm in diameter, presented, respectively, at distances of 16, 24, and 32 cm. The spheres shown to the infants in the two groups subtended identical retinal images, and there were two 20-sec trials for each stimulus, giving six trials for each group of infants. The Constant-Size group showed a significant decline in looking time over the trials but the Variable-Size group did not, suggesting that the former group was seeing a same-sized sphere over trials, which caused them to lose interest as the trials progressed, whereas the latter group perceived that there were different-sized spheres on the successive trials. These results suggest that newborn infants possess some degree of size constancy.

Converging results to support this conclusion were provided in the second study, by Slater, Mattock, and Brown (1990), who also used newborn babies (averaging less than 3 days of age) as their subjects, but with a different experimental design. The stimuli they used were cubes, one being half the size of the other (see Figure 1.6). In the first experiment a preferential looking procedure was used, and the infants were shown several pairings of cubes that varied in their sizes and distances from them: In different pairings, identical-sized cubes were shown at different distances or different-sized cubes were shown, either at the same viewing distance or at different distances from each other; in the latter pairings, the small cube was either closer to or farther away than the large one. Highly consistent preferences were found, which could be described in terms of a simple rule: "Look longest at the cube that gives the largest retinal size, regardless of its distance or its real size." One pairing in which neither stimulus was preferred is shown in Figures 1.6 and 1.7. In this pairing the large cube was presented at 61 cm from the eyes and the small one at half the distance, 30.5 cm, as Figure 1.7 shows, their retinal images were identical. These findings are convincing evidence that newborns can base their responding on *retinal* size alone.

However, in the second experiment of Slater et al., newborns were shown one of the cubes at different distances on each of six familiarization trials: The purpose of this experiment was to desensitize the infants to changes in the distance (and hence to changes in retinal image size) of the familiarized cube. A similar desensitization procedure was also used in the shape constancy experiments of Caron et al. (1979) and Slater et al. (1985), described earlier. On the test trials the infants were shown the large and small cubes, paired together but at the different distances shown in Figure 1.6, and hence subtending identical retinal images (Figure 1.7). They strongly preferred the different-sized cube to the familiarized one: That is, they were responding on the basis of the objects' *real* sizes and hence were displaying size constancy.

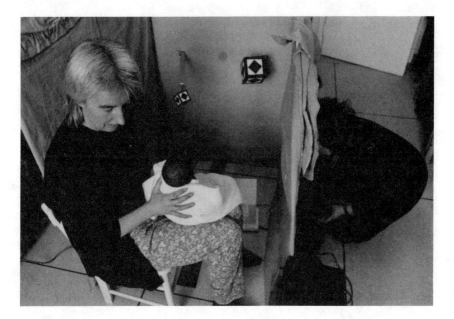

Figure 1.6. A newborn baby being tested in a size constancy experiment.

3.1.4 Conclusion. The findings described in this section support and extend Bower's claim, made nearly 30 years ago, that shape and size constancy are present in early infancy. It has now been firmly established that the basic perceptual processes underlying these constancies are present at birth: Newborn infants (about 2 days after birth) show consistent changes in their looking behavior as stimuli change in their slants, orientations, and retinal image sizes relative to their viewing perspective; however, the same babies also show consistent responses indicating that they detect and discriminate objects' *real* shapes and sizes. As young infants often refuse to look at objects that are more than 2 or 3 feet away from them, these findings demonstrate shape and size constancy for near distances, although there seems to be no reason to believe that additional perceptual mechanisms need to develop in order for them to be operative for farther distances.

In his review of size constancy in early infancy, Day (1987) discusses research with children and adults that has found that in size-matching tasks the instructions given to the subjects "play a major role in determining whether objects are responded to in terms of their 'projective' (retinal) or 'real' size" and suggests that "This observation indicates a measure of cognitive control over the perceptual processes involved in size constancy" (p. 68). Although this may be the case, we should note that the "instructions" given to newborn

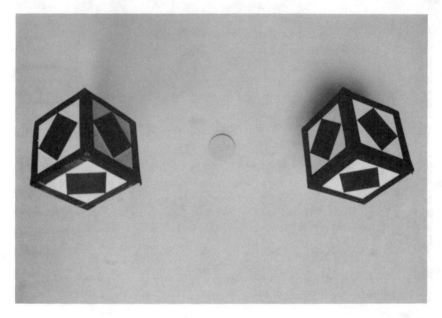

Figure 1.7. The stimuli shown to the infants. This photograph, taken from the baby's viewing position, as seen in Figure 1.6, shows the small cube on the left at a distance of 30.5 cm and the large cube on the right at a distance of 61 cm.

babies, in the form of preferential looking studies that elicit responses to the retinal cues of slant and retinal image size, and desensitization to these cues that elicit responses to objects' real shapes and sizes, indicate that newborns also detect and respond both to projective and to real shapes and sizes. It seems likely that, with respect to shape and size constancy, children's and adults' *cognitive control* serves primarily to direct their attention to different aspects of the basic perceptual information that is detected and responded to at birth.

3.2 Identity and existence constancy

The term *perceptual constancy* can be used to refer to any situation in which the infant or adult subject extracts some invariant (constant) property from a changing stimulus array and treats those objects that contain this property in the same way. We can also talk of constancy when the subject recognizes that an object retains an important property or characteristic across some transformation or change. In this section two other "constancies," which are found in young infants, are discussed: identity and existence constancies.

Identity constancy is the ability to recognize an object as being the *same* object across some transformation. This ability is very difficult to demonstrate, and Burnham (1987) argues that it is "difficult to envisage how such a conclusion (the presence of identity constancy) . . . could ever be reached from the behavior of preverbal infants" (p. 15). That is, how could we ever know that an infant perceives the unique identity of individual objects rather than simply being aware of featural similarities across transformations? One study that perhaps comes closest to demonstrating identity constancy in infants was described by Bower (1971). Infants were seated in front of mirrors that could produce several images of their mother. Babies younger than 20 weeks happily smiled, cooed, and waved their arms to each of these multiple mothers, whereas older babies became upset at seeing more than one mother: The older babies seemed to be aware that they had only one mother, and they might therefore be said to have identity constancy.

Existence constancy refers to the belief that objects continue to exist even though they are no longer available to the senses. Several eminent researchers, among them Piaget, have argued that the expression "Out of sight, out of mind" literally captures the young infant's understanding of objects. However, it seems that existence constancy makes its appearance in early infancy. In an early experiment, Bower (1971) reported that babies as young as 3 weeks of age expressed "surprise" (as measured by heart rate changes) if an object they had seen being hidden by a screen failed to reappear when the screen was removed. In a later study, Baillargeon, Spelke, and Wasserman (1985) reported that 5-month-old infants were able to appreciate the continued existence of a completely invisible object: The babies were familiarized to a "drawbridge" that moved back and forth through a 180° arc in front of them; a block was then placed behind the drawbridge such that it should have impeded its full 180° movement. When the drawbridge was raised and the block went out of view, the babies were "surprised" (as indexed by increased looking) when the drawbridge went through an "impossible" 180° arc, indicating that they were puzzled about how the screen could pass through the (now invisible) solid object.

Clearly, both identity and existence constancy are more sophisticated than shape and size constancy, but they are present in early infancy. Burnham (1987) raises the possibility that a proper understanding of the world of objects, what is known as the *object concept*, of which identity and existence constancy are part, arises out of the "basic" constancies, such as shape and size.

4. Conclusions

This chapter has focused on the theoretical debates and presented some of the experimental evidence relating to the organization of visual perception in early infancy. The perceptual world of the newborn baby is surprisingly well organized. Newborns respond to movement and distinguish between two- and three-dimensional stimuli; they discriminate between objects in terms of their size;

their acuity is sufficient to allow them to learn about objects, such as faces, that are important in their worlds. Several types of visual organization are found at birth, including at least rudimentary form perception, response to spatial relationships and to stimulus compounds rather than separate elements, orientation detection, intersensory perception, and, perhaps particularly important, shape and size constancy. Sensitivity to, and detection of, subjective contours and biomechanical motion are present in early infancy and may indeed be present close to birth.

The infant's visual world becomes enriched in at least two ways as development proceeds. First, maturation and/or early learning permit basic capacities and various organizational abilities to improve and develop. The newborn displays some competence in structuring the visual world, but of course, their world is very different from ours. As one authority speculates: "Perhaps their experience is like ours during those first few moments when we awake in a strange room: we see everything, but nothing makes sense" (Gordon, 1989, p. 70). This illustrates the second way in which the visual world becomes enriched: although the newborn's world may be organized, it lacks familiarity, meanings, and associations. Infants begin the vital task of learning about their visual world from birth. They quickly learn to recognize familiar faces, they can associate apparently arbitrary combinations of multimodal stimuli (e.g., they soon learn to associate the mother's face with her voice and her smell), and they readily learn to classify and to form prototypes of frequently encountered objects. The newborn's visual world is structured as a result of the intrinsic organization of the visual system. As development proceeds, the innate and developing organizational mechanisms are added to by experience, which furnishes the familiarity, meanings, and associations that assist the infant in making sense of the perceived world.

References

Antell, S. E., & Caron, A. J. (1985). Neonatal perception of spatial relationships. *Infant Behavior and Development, 8*, 15–23.

Atkinson, J., Hood, B., Wattam-Bell, J., Anker, S., & Tricklebank, J. (1988). Development of orientation discrimination in infancy. *Perception, 17*, 587–595.

Baillargeon, R., Spelke, E. S., & Wasserman, S. (1985). Object permanence in 5-month-old infants. *Cognition, 20*, 191–208.

Berk, L. (1991). *Child development* (2nd ed.). London: Allyn & Bacon.

Bertenthal, B. I. (1992). Infants' perception of biomechanical motions: Intrinsic image and knowledge-based constraints. In C. Granrud (Ed.), *Visual perception and cognition in infancy*. Hillsdale, N.J.: Erlbaum.

Bertenthal, B. I., & Davis, P. (1988). *Dynamical pattern analysis predicts recognition and discrimination of biomechanical motions*. Paper presented at the annual meeting of the Psychonomic Society, Chicago.

Bertenthal, B. I., Proffitt, D. R., & Cutting, J. E. (1984). Infant sensitivity to figural coherence in biomechanical motions. *Journal of Experimental Child Psychology, 37*, 213–230.

Bertenthal, B. I., Proffitt, D. R., Spetner, N. B., & Thomas, M. A. (1985). The development of infant sensitivity to biomechanical motions. *Child Development, 56*, 531–543.

Bomba, P. C. (1984). The development of orientation categories between 2 and 4 months of age. *Journal of Experimental Child Psychology, 37*, 609–636.

Bomba, P. C., & Siqueland, E. R. (1983). The nature and structure of infant form categories. *Journal of Experimental Child Psychology, 35*, 294–328.

Bower, T. G. R. (1966). The visual world of infants. *Scientific American, 215*(6), 80–92.

Bower, T. G. R. (1971). The object in the world of the infant. *Scientific American, 225*, 30–38.

Burnham, D. K. (1987). The role of movement in object perception by infants. In B. E. McKenzie & R. H. Day (Eds.), *Perceptual development in early infancy: Problems and issues*. Hillsdale, N.J.: Erlbaum.

Bushnell, I. W. R., Sai, F., & Mullin, T. (1989). Neonatal recognition of the mother's face. *British Journal of Developmental Psychology, 7*, 3–15.

Butterworth, G. (1983). Structure of the mind in human infancy. In L. P. Lipsitt & C. K. Rovee-Collier (Eds.), *Advances in infancy research* (Vol. 2, pp. 1–29). Norwood, N.J.: Ablex.

Caron, A. J., Caron, R. F., & Carlson, V. R. (1979). Infant perception of the invariant shape of objects in slant. *Child Development, 50*, 716–721.

Cutting, J. E., & Proffitt, D. R. (1981). Gait perception as an example of how we may perceive events. In H. Pick & R. Walk (Eds.), *Perception and perceptual development* (Vol. 2. New York: Plenum.

Day, R. H. (1987). Visual size constancy in infancy. In B. E. McKenzie and R. H. Day (Eds.), *Perceptual development in early infancy: Problems and issues*. Hillsdale, N.J.: Erlbaum.

Day, R. H., & McKenzie, B. E. (1981). Infant perception of the invariant size of approaching and receding objects. *Developmental Psychology, 17*, 670–677.

Dodd, B. (1979). Lip reading in infants: Attention to speech presented in- and out-of-synchrony. *Cognitive Psychology, 11*, 478–484.

Field, T. M., Cohen, D., Garcia, R., & Greenberg, R. (1984). Mother–stranger face discrimination by the newborn. *Infant Behavior and Development, 7*, 19–25.

Fox, R., & McDaniels, C. (1982). The perception of biological motion by human infants. *Science, 218*, 486–487.

Ghim, H.-R. (1990). Evidence for perceptual organization in infants: Perception of subjective contours by young infants. *Infant Behavior and Development, 13*, 221–248.

Gibson, E. J. (1970). The development of perception as an adaptive process. *American Scientist, 58*, 98–107.

Gibson, E. J., & Walker, A. (1984). Development of knowledge of visual and tactual affordances of substances. *Child Development, 55*, 453–460.

Gordon, I. E. G. (1989). *Theories of visual perception*. New York: Wiley.

Granrud, C. E. (1987). Size constancy in newborn human infants. *Investigative Ophthalmology and Visual Science, 28*, (Suppl), 5.

Hebb, D. O. (1949). *The organization of behavior*. New York: Wiley.

Johansson, G. (1977). Visual perception of biological motion and a model for its analysis. *Perception and Psychophysics, 14*, 201–211.

Kanizsa, G. (1979). *Organization in vision: Essays on gestalt perception*. New York: Praeger.

Langlois, J. H., & Roggman, L. A. (1990). Attractive faces are only average. *Psychological Science, 1*, 115–121.

Langlois, J. H., Roggman, L. A., Casey, R. J., Ritter, J. M., Rieser-Danner, L. A., & Jenkins, V. Y. (1987). Infant preferences for attractive faces: Rudiments of a stereotype? *Developmental Psychology, 23*, 363–369.

McKenzie, B. E., & Day, R. H. (1972). Object distance as a determinant of visual fixation in early infancy. *Science, 178*, 1108–1110.

McKenzie, B. E., Tootell, H. E., & Day, R. H. (1980). Development of visual size constancy during the 1st year of human infancy. *Developmental Psychology, 16*, 163–174.

Meltzoff, A., & Borton, R. W. (1979). Intermodal matching by human neonates. *Nature (London)*, *282*, 403–404.

Piaget, J. (1953). *The origins of intelligence in the child*. London: Routledge and Kegan Paul.

Piaget, J. (1954). *The construction of reality in the child*. New York: Basic Books.

Quinn, P. C., & Bomba, P. C. (1986). Evidence for a general category of oblique orientations in four-month-old infants. *Journal of Experimental Child Psychology, 42*, 345–354.

Samuels, C. A., & Ewy, R. (1985). Aesthetic perception of faces during infancy. *British Journal of Developmental Psychology, 3*, 221–228.

Slater, A. M., Mattock, A., & Brown, E. (1990). Size constancy at birth: Newborn infants' responses to retinal and real size. *Journal of Experimental Child Psychology, 49*, 314–322.

Slater, A. M., Mattock, A., Brown, E., & Bremner, J. G. (1991a). Form perception at birth: Cohen and Younger (1984) revisited. *Journal of Experimental Child Psychology, 51*, 395–405.

Slater, A. M., Mattock, A., Brown, E., Burnham, D., & Young, A. W. (1991b). Visual processing of stimulus compounds in newborn babies. *Perception, 20*, 29–33.

Slater, A. M., & Morison, V. (1985). Shape constancy and slant perception at birth. *Perception, 14*, 337–344.

Slater, A. M., Morison, V., & Rose, D. (1983). Perception of shape by the new-born baby. *British Journal of Developmental Psychology, 1*, 135–142.

Slater, A. M., Morison, V., & Rose, D. (1984). Habituation in the newborn. *Infant Behavior and Development, 7*, 183–200.

Slater, A. M., Morison, V., & Somers, M. (1988). Orientation discrimination and cortical function in the human newborn. *Perception, 17*, 597–602.

Slater, A. M., Morison, V., Town, C., & Rose, D. (1985). Movement perception and identity constancy in the new-born baby. *British Journal of Developmental Psychology, 3*, 211–220.

Slater, A. M., Rose, D., & Morison, V. (1984). Infants' perception of similarities and differences between two- and three-dimensional stimuli. *British Journal of Developmental Psychology, 2*, 287–294.

Slater, A. M., & Sykes, M. (1977). Newborn infants' visual responses to square wave gratings. *Child Development, 48*, 545–554.

Spelke, E. S. (1979). Perceiving bimodally specified events in infancy. *Developmental Psychology, 15*, 626–636.

Spelke, E. S. (1987). The development of intermodal perception. In P. Salapatek & L. Cohen (Eds.), *Handbook of infant perception* (Vol. 2, pp. 233–273).

Spelke, E. S., & Owsley, C. J. (1979). Intermodal exploration and knowledge in infancy. *Infant Behavior and Development, 2*, 13–28.

Walton, G. E., Bower, N. J. A., & Bower, T. G. R. (1992). Recognition of familiar faces by newborns. *Infant Behavior and Development, 15*, 265–269.

Wertheimer, M. (1961). Psychomotor coordination of auditory and visual space at birth. *Science, 134*, 1692.

2   The McCollough effect: Misperception and reality

G. Keith Humphrey

If you gaze at a waterfall for a minute or so and then look at the rocks beside the waterfall, the rocks will appear to be moving in the opposite direction to the motion of the water. This is an example of a visual aftereffect called the *motion aftereffect*. Visual aftereffects have been known since at least the time of Aristotle, who is often credited with the first description of the motion aftereffect. Other aftereffects, sometimes called *figural aftereffects*, are based on properties of static patterns such as their spatial frequency, orientation, or curvature. For example, after viewing a high-contrast grating that is tilted slightly to the right of vertical, a grating that is oriented vertically will appear to be tilted slightly to the left of vertical (e.g., Blakemore, 1973). This aftereffect is called the *tilt aftereffect*. Motion and figural aftereffects are generated by activity on a single stimulus dimension such as motion, orientation, curvature, or spatial frequency.

In 1965, Celeste McCollough described an aftereffect that explicitly paired two stimulus dimensions – orientation and color. Subjects viewed patterns of black and orange vertical stripes alternating with black and blue horizontal stripes[1] for 2 to 4 minutes. After such induction, subjects reported color aftereffects on black and white versions of the induction patterns that were determined by the orientation of the patterns. The colors of the aftereffects seen on each pattern were desaturated but were approximately complementary to the color in which the pattern was presented during induction. Vertical black and white stripes appeared bluish, and horizontal black and white stripes looked orange. If, however, the black and white stripes were oriented at 45°, no color aftereffect was seen. If induction was monocular, the aftereffect appeared only in the induced eye; it did not transfer to the noninduced eye. Further, the after-

Preparation of this chapter was supported by a grant from the Natural Sciences and Engineering Council of Canada to G. K. Humphrey, no. A1643. Thanks to Andy Herbert and Larry Symons for helpful comments on a early draft of the chapter. I am also grateful to Peter Dodwell, Diane Skowbo, and Celeste McCollough Howard, who provided insightful comments on and germane criticisms of a draft of the chapter and saved me from many errors and oversights. Thanks also to Jack Broerse and Celeste McCollough Howard for sending me descriptions of some of their recent, as yet unpublished research. Of course, I am fully responsible for all remaining errors, both large and small.

effect could still be detected more than an hour later after 2–4 minutes of induction. The reader can experience the aftereffect by following the instructions accompanying Figure 2.1.

The aftereffect discovered by McCollough is a perceptual distortion that involves two stimulus dimensions – the color appearance of achromatic test contours, which is contingent on the orientation of the test contours. Subsequent research showed that such contingent aftereffects can be established not only between orientation and color but also between, for example, spatial frequency and color or movement and color. For economy of expression, I refer to all such contingent color aftereffects as MEs (in reference to McCollough effects). There is a large literature[2] concerned not only with the properties of the effects, but also with what they may tell us at a theoretical level about the mechanisms of spatial vision. Although some of the literature on the ME will be reviewed here, the reader should consult the excellent and detailed reviews of Skowbo, Timney, Gentry, and Morant (1975), Stromeyer (1978), and Harris (1980) for more discussion, particularly of the older literature.

This chapter concentrates on recent research and theoretical proposals. Specifically, we are concerned with four interrelated issues: (1) At what level in the visual system are MEs produced? (2) What pattern processing mechanisms are involved in producing the effects? (3) What is the nature of the adaptation, that is, how is it best conceptualized? and (4) Do such aftereffects serve a functional role?

At what level in the visual system are MEs produced?

Results suggesting that the ME is a low-level phenomenon

In many ways, the study of the ME, like much of vision research, is concerned with the mind–brain problem. That is, how sensations – a property of mind – are connected to the functioning of underlying brain mechanisms. Numerous research results suggest that the ME reflects changes in mechanisms at an early or low level in the primary visual pathway. Although there is no universal agreement on what constitutes a low level in the visual system, many visual neuroscientists would accept that the structures up to and including the striate cortex (area VI) are low level. In fact, much of the relevant research suggests that the ME is a low-level phenomenon in this sense. For example, the effect tends to be fairly local and specific to *retinal* area, orientation, and size (e.g., Bedford & Reinke, 1993; Ellis, 1976; Lovegrove & Over, 1972; McCollough, 1965; Stromeyer, 1972a, 1972b). Because neurons in area V1 of the visual cortex of the cat and monkey are the first to show orientation selectivity, the effect may involve these structures. Also, because cells in area V1 have smaller receptive fields than those at subsequent stages of processing, they code more

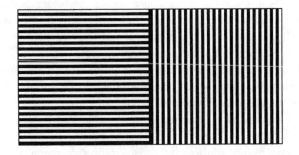

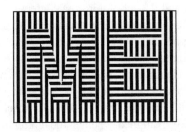

Figure 2.1. The McCollough effect can be experienced using the two colored gratings on the book cover and the test patterns shown above. In good lighting, look alternately at one colored grating and then the other for about 5 seconds each for a total time of approximately 2 minutes. You can move your eyes about on each grating as you look at it. After 2 minutes of induction, wait a few moments and then look at the black and white test patterns. The horizontal lines should look greenish, while vertical lines should appear pink.

locally than cells further on in the visual system (e.g., Buser & Imbert, 1992). Research has shown that the wavelength of the induction patterns, and not their perceived color, determines the aftereffect hue (Thompson & Latchford, 1986; Webster, Day, & Willenberg, 1988). Again, some research suggests that color sensitive cells in area V1 respond to the wavelength characteristics of a stimulus, whereas those further along in the visual system, such as in area V4, respond to more complex aspects of a color display and appear to be associated with color constancies (Zeki, 1990). As noted previously, McCollough (and many others, e.g., Murch, 1972; Savoy, 1984) found that the effect does not transfer from one eye to the other under typical conditions for assessing interocular transfer, although there is evidence of selective adaptation of binocular mechanisms (Seaber & Lockhead, 1989; Vidyasagar, 1976; White, Petry, Riggs, & Miller, 1978). Figural and motion aftereffects do show substantial interocular transfer (e.g., Blake, Overton, & Lema-Stern, 1981; Moulden, 1980), indicating that they are cortical in origin. The lack of interocular transfer of the ME suggests that the effect is produced at a site that precedes the emergence of binocular units or that some of the component mechanisms involved in the ME may not be cortical. It is also possible, of course, that the effect involves only cortical mechanisms that are monocular.

Research on the role of attention in the ME (described later) is consistent with the proposal that the effect occurs at an early stage of visual processing. Neurophysiological studies with primates show that response properties of cells in area V1 are not modulated by attentional manipulations, whereas those at higher levels, such as area V4, can be modulated by attentional demands (Desimone, 1992). Psychophysical studies divide visual processes operationally into high and low levels based, to some extent, on the role of focal attention. In particular, it has been suggested that low-level visual processes are those that can be carried out in parallel and do not require focal attention (e.g., Treisman, 1988) or that can operate at extremely brief presentations (e.g., Julesz, 1984). Detecting a green dot among red dots would be an example of a task requiring only low-level processing. High-level processing, such as is involved in identification of complex spatial relationships, is slower, is serial, and requires focal attention. If the ME results from adaptation of low-level mechanisms, one might expect that attentional manipulations would have little or no effect on it.

Houck and Hoffman (1986) examined whether focal attention was a necessary condition for producing MEs. They showed that even when attention was directed to an unrelated task during the induction period, the aftereffects were similar in strength to those found when attention was focused on the inducing patterns. Earlier research by White et al. (1978; Experiment 1) makes a related point. In one condition, White and his colleagues presented the induction patterns to one eye and a black and white checkerboard-like pattern to the other eye. In this condition the induction patterns were not even seen, at least for part of the induction period, because of binocular suppression by the checkerboard-like pattern. Nevertheless, the MEs in the rivalrous condition were of the same strength as those obtained in nonrivalrous conditions.[3] This result indicates that the site of the ME precedes the site of binocular rivalry. It has been argued on various grounds that the site of binocular suppression is after the striate cortex (Blake & Overton, 1979).

It is clear that attention to the induction patterns is not necessary for *induction* of the ME. It has also been suggested that attention is not required for the *perception* of the ME either. Thompson and Travis (1989) showed (following Mayhew & Frisby, 1978) that it took subjects several seconds to discriminate textures comprising compound, sinusoidal gratings oriented 0°, 60°, and 120° from compound gratings comprising sinusoids oriented 30°, 90°, and 150°. However, after inducing with the 0°, 60°, and 120° gratings presented in green light alternating with the 30°, 90°, and 150° gratings in red light, the same texture discrimination was performed much more quickly. Hence it could be argued that

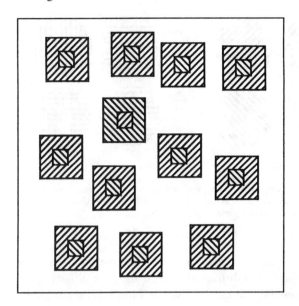

Figure 2.2. An example of the displays in the visual search task used by Humphrey, Gurnsey, and Fekete (1991) to study "pop-out" of the McCollough effect.

the ME emerges *preattentively*, prior to the (attentive) detection of the involved orientation.

Thompson and Travis (1989) argue that adaptation occurs at a stage in visual analysis before information in orientation and spatial frequency selective channels is lost due to further processing (see the later discussion of such channels). Because cells that are orientation and scale (size) selective are first located in area V1, this area could be the locus for the ME.

Recently, we also examined the role of attention in the detection of the ME (Humphrey, Gurnsey, & Fekete, 1991). We first investigated whether aftereffect colors could act like a simple "feature" in a visual search task. In these tasks a target item, for example a red disc, can be detected in a time that is independent of the number of background items, such as green discs (e.g., Treisman, 1988). This result suggests that the simple features can be detected in parallel without focal attention. The targets and distractors we used consisted of two concentric square regions in which, for the target, the outer square contained a black and white, left oblique grating and the inner square contained a right oblique grating. The distractor items had the right oblique grating on the outside and the left oblique grating on the inside (see Figure 2.2). Like the stimuli used by Thompson and Travis (1989), these displays were very difficult to discriminate before ME induction. Without ME induction, the time taken to detect a target among distractors increased substantially as the number of dis-

A   **B**

Figure 2.3. Examples of (A) oblique and (B) horizontal/vertical discrimination trials in
the four-alternative forced-choice task used by Humphrey, Gurnsey, and Fekete (1991)
and Humphrey, Goodale, and Gurnsey (1991).

tractors increased. After induction, however, detection time was essentially independent of the number of distractors because the color difference between the
target and distractors popped out. The subjects had parallel access to the aftereffect colors and didn't have to attend to any particular region or item in the
displays to ''bind'' the colors to the patterns.

We also conducted other experiments using a difficult four-alternative forced-
choice procedure in which subjects were required to discriminate a briefly presented (67–333 ms) monochromatic patch of square-wave grating oriented at
45° from three others oriented at 135° (and vice versa) (see Figure 2.3). Within
the task, subjects also discriminated between horizontal and vertical gratings.
Subjects performed the task before and after ME induction. Before induction,
discrimination between the obliques was very difficult. After induction with
colored oblique gratings, however, performance was strikingly better, indicating
that the color aftereffect functioned as a physically present color difference even
at exposure durations as short as 67 ms. Again, as in the visual search task, the
color aftereffect difference popped out of the display even at very brief exposure
durations. The mechanisms responsible for the detection of differences in the
orientation of oblique gratings obviously must be operative both with and without ME induction. However, it was only after ME induction that differences in
the orientation of obliques were tagged with a color difference. Without this
color difference, the differential signals that come from some presumably low-
level orientation selective mechanisms are not readily accessed in making discriminations between oblique gratings (see also Blake, 1979; Over, Blackwell,
& Axton, 1984; Thompson & Travis, 1989).

The results we have reviewed so far all suggest that the neural substrate for
the ME is at a low level of visual processing. Research conducted with brain-
damaged subjects is consistent with this view. We have studied two patients

with brain damage who experience the ME. One patient, DF (Humphrey, Goodale, & Gurnsey, 1991), has a diffuse pattern of brain damage due to anoxia, but damage in the posterior regions is confined mainly to the circumstriate belt. The primary visual cortex appears to be largely intact. DF has a profound impairment in form and orientation perception (Goodale, Milner, Jakobson, & Carey, 1991; Humphrey, Goodale, Jakobson, & Servos, 1994; Milner et al., 1991; Servos, Goodale, & Humphrey, 1993). She also has relatively good color vision (Milner & Heywood, 1989). Despite her inability to perform simple orientation discrimination tasks, after induction with colored vertical and horizontal gratings, DF experienced the ME and retained it for at least 20 hours.

We also examined DF's performance on the four-alternative forced-choice task, although at much longer exposure durations than used in the research described above with normal subjects. She performed at a chance level in discriminating between 45° and 135° oblique gratings, as well as between horizontal and vertical gratings before induction. However, after induction with one oblique grating in red and the other in green, her performance improved markedly, but only for the oblique gratings. After induction she performed the oblique discrimination trials by relying on the difference in aftereffect colors. In contrast, her performance on the horizontal–vertical discriminations was still at a chance level.

More recently, we tested another brain-damaged individual, PB, who, like DF, cannot discriminate even simple differences in form but has relatively good color vision (Humphrey, Goodale, Corbetta, & Aglioti, 1995). PB is a 36-year-old man who suffered extensive brain damage as a result of accidental electrocution. Like DF, he showed evidence of diffuse brain damage but again, like DF, the damage was more pronounced in the posterior region of the cortex. PB's visual abilities remain severely disturbed. He is unable to identify forms or perform simple grating orientation discrimination tasks. He does, however, experience the ME, but he may not retain it for very long. After an initial 15-minute induction session with colored gratings, he did not report a ME. When he was next seen, 2 months later, we used a 25-minute induction session. He clearly experienced the ME when he was tested immediately after induction, but the effect dissipated rapidly and was not reported 15 minutes later. We believe that the effect could not have entirely dissipated, however, because after only 10 additional minutes of reexposure to the adapting stimuli, appropriate color reports were reinstated.

The results of a study by Savoy and Gabrieli (1991) of patients with Alzheimer's disease are also consistent with an early locus for the generation of the effect. The patients showed a normal ME after 5 minutes of induction and retained the effect for at least 1 hour. Anatomical studies of patients with Alzheimer's disease have suggested that area V1 of the visual cortex is spared relative to area V2 and more central cortical areas (Lewis, Campbell, Terry, &

Morrison, 1987). As Savoy and Gabrieli argue, albeit speculatively because of the lack of anatomical information on the brains of their subjects, the patients they tested may have had more damage to V2 than to V1 and thus V1 may be a critical locus for the ME.

Collectively, these studies of brain-damaged patients are all consistent with the proposal that the ME occurs at an early stage of visual processing. Of course, further studies of patients with discrete brain damage to other visual areas, including the primary visual cortex, are necessary before firm conclusions can be drawn. Mel Goodale and I have conducted some very preliminary work with a cortically blind patient with bilateral occipital infarcts. Despite her ability to discriminate between red and green in a forced-choice paradigm, she shows no evidence of a ME. Although by no means conclusive, this result again points to the role of the primary visual cortex in the generation of the ME.

Results that question whether the ME is a purely
low-level phenomenon

The research just reviewed indicates that the ME reflects changes in mechanisms at an early stage of visual processing. There are research results, however, that question such an account and suggest that higher-level interpretive processes are involved. For example, MEs dependent on imagery have been reported by Finke and Schmidt (1977, 1978) and others (Kaufman, May, & Kunen, 1981; Kunen & May, 1981). Finke and Schmidt reported that imagining alternating vertical and horizontal gratings while viewing alternating green and red fields induced an ME. An imagery condition in which subjects viewed gratings but imagined colors did not produce a ME. The induction of MEs contingent on imagined gratings has, however, not been replicated by others, and the research has been criticized on several grounds (Broerse & Crassini, 1981b, 1984; Zhou & May, 1993). Indeed, Finke himself has suggested that such effects are likely due to associations at higher levels in the visual system than that at which the ME occurs (Finke, 1989).

It has also been claimed that MEs may depend on the subjective organization of a pattern. Uhlarik, Pringle, and Brigell (1977) induced a ME with colored gratings and tested with a pattern that had two different perceptual organizations. As can be seen in Figure 2.4, in one organization the vertical and horizontal bars appear clearly segregated and the pattern looks like a diamond of horizontal bars on a background of vertical bars; in the other organization, it appears to be a set of nested *U*'s, with each *U* having both vertical and horizontal components. The authors reported that subjects experienced the ME only when they saw the diamond and concluded that cognitive organizational factors can influence the ME. Thus, according to this account, adaptation of low-level stimulus-bound mechanisms cannot provide a complete account of the ME. Others have

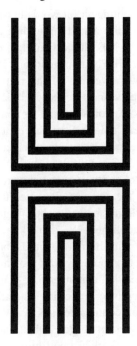

Figure 2.4. The type of test pattern used by Uhlarik, Pringle, and Brigell (1977) to study the influence of perceptual organization on the McCollough effect.

reported similar findings (Jenkins & Ross, 1977; Meyer & Phillips, 1980), but these studies are not without problems (Broerse & Crassini, 1981a, 1986). Broerse and Crassini (1986) found that when complementary colors (either real or ME colors) were superimposed on a test pattern like that used by Uhlarik et al. (1977), the perceived organization of the pattern never changed – it was always seen as a diamond of horizontal stripes on a vertical background. Thus, as Broerse and Crassini point out, if there are no changes in perceptual organization after ME induction, the claim that changes in perceptual organization cause changes in the appearance of MEs is empty.

Watanabe, Zimmerman, and Cavanagh (1992) have examined the influence of the perception of transparency on the ME. They devised a series of test patterns that differed in terms of whether they were perceived as a transparent overlay of horizontal and vertical stripes or not. After ME induction, the ME was greater in the condition that supported the perception of transparency than in similar conditions that did not lead to this subjective organization. The results suggest that a high-level factor such as transparency can influence the ME.

One of the most surprising studies is that of Allan, Siegel, Collins, and McQueen (1989), who reported text-contingent color aftereffects. Specifically, they found weak but reliable color aftereffects contingent on words but not on nonwords composed of the same letters. This is truly a startling finding in that it suggests that linguistic factors can influence the ME. Subjects in their experiments were induced with pairs of words such as SIREN in magenta and RINSE in green. After induction they were tested with a version of the method of constant stimuli devised by Allan, Siegel, Toppan, and Lockhead (1991) as a sensitive measure of the ME. They found MEs to words but not to nonwords such as ENSRI and RENSI. We have found weak color aftereffects contingent on both words and nonwords using the Allan et al. (1991) measurement procedure (Humphrey, Skowbo, Symons, Herbert, & Grant, 1994). This occurred, however, only if the central letter of the each of the words or nonwords was fixated during both induction and test trials. If the subjects alternated fixation between the first and last letters of the words during induction but fixated the central letter during test trials, the effect was abolished. We don't know why Allan et al. (1989) did not obtain aftereffects contingent on nonwords, but one speculation is that nonwords may have promoted more eye movements and hence disrupted the local color and contour orientation contingencies. It appears that the ME to words is not dependent on linguistic properties but rather is based on adaptation to local color and orientation contingencies.

Similar criticisms apply to some recent research of Siegel, Allan, and Eissenberg (1992). They have claimed, contrary to an earlier report by Foreit and Ambler (1978), that MEs can be induced with different geometric forms such as a square and a cross. In my lab we have been able to replicate the finding of Siegel et al., but only when subjects fixated the same point on the forms during induction and test trials (Humphrey, Herbert, Symons, & Kara, 1994). If subjects changed the loci of fixation between induction and test, color aftereffects were not obtained. Similar results have been found by Broerse and Grimbeek (1994). Thus, as with color aftereffects contingent on words, MEs to forms appear to be based on local orientation and color contingencies.

It appears that, perhaps with the exception of the recent results of Watanabe et al. (1992), the ME is not subject to the influence of high-level factors. Thus, the ME can be explained in terms of the adaptation of low-level mechanisms in the visual system, and this adaptation is not modulated by higher-level perceptual and cognitive factors. We turn now to some more specific proposals about the nature of these low-level mechanisms.

The nature of the mechanisms involved in generating the ME

McCollough (1965) suggested that MEs are caused by the color adaptation of neurons in the visual cortex that code the local orientation of bars or edges. Much of the early theorizing following Hubel and Wiesel's discoveries in the 1960s suggested that such units were the fundamental elements of early visual perception. The responses of cortical cells were seen as being specific to bars and edges and were often referred to as bar or edge *detectors*. A second approach to neural contour processing, beginning with the classic studies of Enroth-Cugell and Robson (1966) and Campbell and Robson (1968), applied linear systems, or Fourier, analysis to the problem of describing early processing of spatial patterns. The response of cortical cells was described in terms of their spatial frequency characteristics, and the cortex was seen to perform a spatial Fourier analysis on the incoming image. Edge detector models were seen as being in opposition to spatial frequency analysis in the 1960s and 1970s. This either-or position has now given way to a view of the striate cortex as consisting of arrays of neurons selective to local regions of space, spatial frequency, and orientation. The responses of cortical neurons have been seen to approximate Gabor-type functions (for a review, see Kulikowski & Kranda, 1986) or other types of function (e.g., see Field, 1993). These responses can be described either as a spatial receptive field or, in the Fourier domain, as a sensitivity to sine and cosine gratings that vary in spatial frequency, orientation, and phase. According to this approach, a spatial pattern will be analyzed by a series of local filters acting in parallel that are differentially sensitive to different orientations and spatial frequencies.

The linear systems approach has also been applied to the study of the ME where it has been suggested that spatial frequency selective mechanisms are being adapted during ME induction. Recall that Thompson and Travis (1989) suggested that ME adaptation occurs at a stage in visual analysis before information available in spatial frequency channels has been lost in further visual processing. More direct support for this position comes from the finding that the ME can be induced with gratings differing in color and spatial frequency at the same orientation. The results of studies differ, however, in terms of the magnitude of spatial frequency difference needed to produce the ME. Some researchers have found MEs to gratings separated by one octave (Haapasalo, 1982; Lovegrove & Over, 1972), but others have not found the effect unless the gratings were separated by two octaves or more (Breitmeyer & Cooper, 1972). Recent results suggest that a one-octave difference in spatial frequency is not enough to produce the ME, suggesting that the ME is broadly tuned for spatial frequency (Day, Webster, Gillies, & Crassini, 1992).

Further support for the notion that the ME results from changes in spatial frequency analyzers tuned to different orientations comes from studies in which checkerboards have been used as the induction patterns. Gratings can be thought of as one-dimensional stimuli in that the luminance variation occurs in only one direction – orthogonal to the orientation of the grating. Most visual patterns, including checkerboards, vary in two spatial dimensions. Kelly (1976) showed that the fundamental spatial frequency components in a checkerboard are oriented at $\pm 45°$ relative to the orientation of the edges defining the checks.

Higher harmonics are located at other orientations from the edges. For example, the third harmonics are oriented at 18° and 72° with respect to the orientation of the edges. Psychophysical (Kelly, 1976) and neurophysiological research (DeValois, DeValois, & Yund, 1979) using checkerboards has found that both psychophysical thresholds and responses of single cells were determined by the spatial frequency components rather than by the checkerboard edges. These results are consistent with the notion that the visual system is performing a type of two-dimensional spatial frequency analysis on its input.

If the ME results from adaptation of spatial frequency mechanisms, one would expect that it would be associated with the orientation and spatial frequency of the components of checkerboards rather than with the orientation of the edges. Several studies have found just this result. After induction with upright and diagonally oriented checkerboards in different colors, MEs occurred on gratings oriented 45° from the orientation of the edges of the checks rather than on gratings at the same orientation as the check edges (Green, Corwin, & Zemon, 1976; May & Matteson, 1976; Zhou & May, 1993). If the fundamental frequency was filtered out of the induction patterns, MEs aligned with the orientation of the edges were found (Zhou & May, 1993). These MEs were weaker, however, than those found to the fundamental using unfiltered checkerboards as induction stimuli.

Webster, Day, Gillies, and Crassini (1992) have recently examined this issue further. Unlike some of the earlier investigators, they did not find MEs at either the orientation of the edges or the fundamentals when both an upright and a 45° checkerboard were induced in different colors. They did obtain MEs when only one checkerboard was induced in a single color. In the latter case, MEs occurred on sine-wave gratings aligned with the fundamental frequency and, in some cases, with third harmonics of the checkerboard spectrum. As Webster et al. point out, the production of MEs aligned with the third harmonics is an important finding for the spatial frequency approach (see also DeValois et al., 1979). Smith (1977) and Tyler (1977; see also MacKay, 1981) have criticized studies using checkerboards on the grounds that the diagonals of the checks in a checkerboard fall on a common line that is oriented at 45° with respect to the orientation of the edges of the checks. Such alignment could adapt edge detecting mechanisms. This argument cannot account for the results obtained on grating patterns aligned with the third harmonics of the checkerboard patterns. These patterns do not align with the edge orientation or with a common line through the diagonals of the checks. It should be noted, however, that the MEs obtained by Webster et al. to the patterns aligned with the third harmonic were weak and were not found consistently in all induction conditions.

The studies just reviewed used checkerboard patterns with a spatial frequency above 1.0 cycle per degree. If checkerboard gratings with a spatial frequency less than about 1.0 cycles per degree are used, MEs associated with the orientation of the check edges do occur (May, Agamy, & Matteson, 1978; May, Matteson, Agamy, & Castellanos, 1978; Webster et al., 1992). Webster et al. (1992) found MEs to the frequency components and to the edges at low spatial frequencies but only to the frequency components at higher spatial frequencies. Based on these results, they suggested that spatial frequency mechanisms are operating at both high and low spatial frequencies but that an edge mechanism is also operative at low spatial frequencies.

The view that the visual system performs the initial encoding of patterns by means of localized orientation and spatial frequency selective mechanisms has led to considerable insight into the nature of early visual processing. Such encoding is local – the receptive fields of the mechanisms are responsive to only a circumscribed retinal area. Some recent research challenges the claim that the ME is due only to adaptation of purely local mechanisms, whether these are conceived of as bar and edge detectors or oriented spatial frequency analyzers. We now consider that research.

Evidence for MEs based on global pattern properties

We know a great deal about the local coding properties in the early stages of visual analysis, but without some way of integrating these local signals, the system appears to be a mere "bag of marbles" (to use a phrase of Koenderink, 1988). Thus, one of the outstanding problems in pattern and form perception is how the local elements of form are integrated into a unified percept. This process of integration was, of course, a central concern of the Gestalt psychologists. Because of recent neurophysiological discoveries, it is also currently a topic of interest in neurophysiology (e.g., Engel, König, Kreiter, Schillen, & Singer, 1992). Most of the evidence reviewed earlier indicates that the ME is a local phenomenon – this is consistent with most contemporary views of early visual processing. Some of our research, however, has challenged that view in suggesting that global organizational factors influence the ME (Dodwell & Humphrey, 1990). This places the generation of the ME at a level of visual processing where such organizational factors operate.

The research was guided by a theory of spatial vision developed by the mathematician W. C. Hoffman (1966, 1978; Hoffman & Dodwell, 1985). One major concern of the theory is to explain how the discrete and local processes of early vision give rise to global percepts. Hoffman's theory is called the *Lie Transformation Group Theory of Neuropsychology (LTG/NP)*. A nontechnical introduction to LTG/NP is given by Dodwell (1983; see also Dodwell, 1991), who gives, taking some cues from Gibson (1950, 1966), an "ecological" interpretation of the theory. Gibson emphasized that observers in the natural environment are continually moving and that this movement produces changes in the visual input. Such movement produces various flow patterns that observers use to guide themselves and perceive the structure of the layout. As we move about, patterns projected on the retina undergo translation (both horizontal and vertical), rotation, expansion/contraction, and shear (Koenderink, 1985), and yet, to a large extent, we perceive invariant or stable features of the environment. LTG/NP is concerned with how this stability comes about, and proposes that the visual system embodies mechanisms attuned to these transformations that can annul their effects and maintain perceptual constancy.

LTG/NP suggests that the local cortical mechanisms that code orientation at various positions of the retinotopic map provide the visual system with vector-field information. A vectorfield can be considered to be a rule or set of rules that associates a specific orientation or direction with each position in the field. According to LTG/NP, certain visual forms are primitives because they are static representations (orbits) of the transformations a mobile visual organism continually encounters. For example, as we move our heads and/or eyes from side to side, the visual field translates, or as we move forward, the field undergoes transformations of expansion. Nevertheless, the perception of patterns and objects is stable. To maintain such stability or constancy, the visual system must have mechanisms capable of compensating for these transformations of the retinal image (Dodwell, 1983). It has been argued that certain mathematical operators, called *Lie operators,* are represented in the vectorfield structure of the visual cortex, and these operators could accomplish the task (Dodwell, 1983).

Lie operators are differential operators that take continuous derivatives of an image with respect to different coordinate systems. Repeated application of a Lie operator generates orbits. For example, the operator for horizontal translation generates a series of horizontal lines as an orbit, whereas that for vertical translation generates a series of vertical lines. Similarly, the operator for rotational transformations generates a series of concentric circles, whereas that for dilation generates a series of lines radiating from a point. Under some interpretations, there could also be operators of various forms of shear (see Dodwell, 1991; Dodwell & Humphrey, 1990).

If it is true that the operators postulated by LTG/NP are fundamental to the functioning of the visual system, then the primitive patterns that represent the orbits of such operators could be of basic importance in pattern recognition. These patterns are shown in Figure 2.5. They are the most elementary patterns processed by the cortical vectorfields. As shown in Figure 2.5, there are three basic pattern pairs or orbits according to the primitive model of LTG/NP, with the two patterns in each pair being locally and globally orthogonal (Dodwell, 1983).

Dodwell and Humphrey (1990) postulated that the local vectors are the seat of generation of MEs, and because they are organized into structured vectorfields, the latter play a fundamental role in the production of MEs. Because the patterns of Figure 2.5 are the ones most readily processed by the vectorfields in

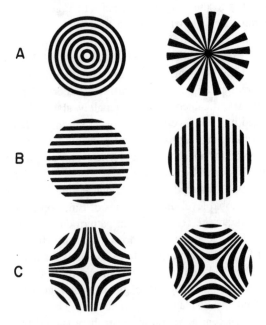

Figure 2.5. The three pairs of patterns used in the McCollough effect studies based on LTG/NP. The patterns are based on the orbits of 1-parameter transformation groups as described in LTG/NP. They are: (a) radial lines and concentric circles, derived from dilation/contraction and rotation in the frontal plane respectively; (b) vertical and horizontal grids, derived from translations and (c) oblique and upright rectangular hyperbolae, derived from rotation and shear in three dimensions.

question, they should be the ones that display robust MEs. It should be noted that the model does not preclude the color biasing of local processing elements. It does suggest, however, that to the extent that these are local elements in structured vectorfields, robust MEs will be induced at the vectorfield level.

The pattern pair of Figure 2.5b are the stimuli that have traditionally been used to create MEs. According to the theory, MEs should be induced with any patterns that belong to the basic set. Emerson, Humphrey and Dodwell (1985) found MEs to the patterns shown in Figure 2.5a, as have others (Cavill & Robinson, 1976; Humphrey, Dodwell, & Emerson, 1985, 1989; Yasuda, 1978), and to patterns shown in Figure 2.5c, as has Yasuda (1978). Emerson et al. did note, however, that the gratings were more effective in inducing MEs than were the other basic Lie pattern pairs. More important was the finding that MEs could be generated to all three pairs of patterns simultaneously in the same observer (Emerson et al., 1985; Walker, 1985). This result suggests that the three orbit pairs of Figure 2.5 address somewhat independent processing mechanisms in the visual system.

Inducing independent MEs to the three pattern pairs of Figure 2.5 suggests that the effects are generated at a global level and this level is the vectorfield level, according to LTG/NP. Emerson et al. (1985; see also Humphrey et al., 1985) claim that this result argues against a purely local site for ME generation because one and the same local element, a contour at a particular position and orientation, can in this paradigm be paired with different colors. For example, a mechanism selective to a vertical contour immediately above the point of fixation could be stimulated by both a vertical grating in red and radial lines in green. If local pattern-color contingency is solely responsible for the ME, there should be no perceived color on an achromatic vertical contour in the given position as the two local MEs cancel each other.

Dodwell and O'Shea (1987) reported further evidence supporting the view that MEs are generated at a global level. In the studies of Emerson et al. (1985), subjects were instructed to fixate the center of each pattern during induction. It is well known, however, that eye movements do not disrupt MEs to grating patterns. Dodwell and O'Shea examined the role of eye movements using the nongrating Lie patterns. They induced with, for example, red radial lines and green concentric circles but had their subjects change fixation regularly between four noncentral positions on the display during induction. They arranged the fixation locations such that, in central vision at least, there should be no local orientation-color contingencies because both the oblique directions, diagonal left and diagonal right, were seen equally in red and green. Nevertheless, MEs were reported and indicated that the effects were spatiotopic (dependent on the position of the pattern in space) rather than retinotopic (dependent on the position of the pattern on the retina).

Most of the results described thus far were obtained with induction patterns that were locally and globally orthogonal. It is possible, however, that the effects observed were not due to the global structure in the pattern, but rather to local orthogonality. To evaluate this possibility, Dodwell and O'Shea (1987) induced observers with patterns composed of short red horizontal and vertical lines alternating with a green figure composed of the same elements, but with each rotated through 90° (see Figure 2.6). Under strict fixation, the patterns were locally orthogonal but lacked global organization. Despite the local orthogonality, no MEs were reported in naive observers. If, however, patterns were constructed of the same elements but displayed more coherence or organization, then strong MEs were found. Dodwell and O'Shea concluded that local color orientation contingency is not sufficient to generate MEs.

One further finding is particularly relevant to the LTG/NP approach to MEs. As Figure 2.5 illustrates, the basic patterns come in three orthogonal pairs. As mentioned earlier, the orthogonal nature of the basic pattern pairs is a fundamental property of LTG/NP (Dodwell, 1983; Hoffman & Dodwell,

A   B

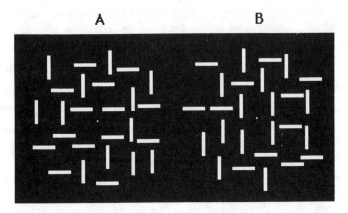

Figure 2.6. A pattern pair, similar to that used by Dodwell and O'Shea (1987; Experiment 2), in which the pattern elements in one pattern are oriented at 90° with respect to the elements in the other pattern. The white bars in pattern A were in one color, such as red, during induction, whereas the bars in pattern B were green. Under central fixation the patterns are locally orthogonal, but there is no global organization of the oriented elements in the patterns.

1985). An unanticipated finding of Humphrey et al. (1985) was that after induction with a pair of nonorthogonal patterns in complementary colors, such as red concentric circles and a green horizontal grating, a number of observers reported the expected MEs on the inducing patterns, but they also reported MEs on the noninduced orthogonal pairmates. For example, subjects reported that concentric circles appeared green and horizontal gratings appeared red, but also that radial line patterns appeared red and vertical gratings appeared green. Humphrey et al. (1989) followed up on this result that we have since referred to as the *indirect ME* (Dodwell & Humphrey, 1990). A similar effect was reported earlier by Stromeyer (1969) and has also been found by others (Allan & Siegel, 1991; Shute; 1979; Wolfe & Roorda, 1990; but see MacKay & MacKay, 1977).

We argued that the indirect ME is due to some property of the visual system that organizes the processing of pattern and color along contrasting, probably orthogonal, and seemingly bipolar dimensions (Dodwell & Humphrey, 1990; Humphrey et al., 1989). The pattern aspects of the indirect ME follow naturally from the cortical vectorfields of LTG/NP and their orthogonal "control structures" (Hoffman & Dodwell, 1985) and are consistent with some earlier observations of MacKay (1957, 1961). It is interesting to note that in 1937 Gibson and Radner reported aftereffects (what are now called *tilt aftereffects*) to *both* vertical lines and horizontal lines after adapting to a line slightly off vertical (similar results have since been reported by Campbell & Maffei, 1971; Heeley,

1979; and Morant & Mistovich, 1960). Gibson and Radner say, "an aftereffect on one axis is accompanied by an indirect after-effect on the other axes" (p. 464).

Problems with the LTG/NP account of global MEs

Having made a case for the relevance of LTG/NP to the understanding of MEs that appear to depend on global pattern structure, considerable caution is in order. First, although we have been able to induce MEs with all three pattern pairs of the primitive model of LTG/NP, the gratings, the classic ME stimuli, are the most effective patterns (see also Walker, 1985). There are several ways of trying to account for this difference. Even within the basic model of LTG/NP (Dodwell, 1983), it could be argued that the linear gratings are simpler or more basic than the others. Perhaps because only one partial differential operator is necessary to specify their orbits, they could be seen as simpler than the other two pairs of basic patterns that are specified by two such operators. This suggestion, however, is very speculative in its direct linking of an aspect of perceptual performance and "mathematical simplicity."[4]

A second speculative possibility is that mechanisms at a lower level of visual processing are addressed more effectively by the gratings than by the other patterns, and adapting lower-level mechanisms produces stronger MEs. It is well known that neurons in area V1 respond to stimulus dimensions such as orientation and spatial frequency. Recent research by Gallant, Braun, and Van Essen (1993), which was motivated in part by LTG/NP, has found cells in area V4 of macaque monkeys that are selective to some of the nongrating patterns, particularly the concentric circles. Perhaps, then, the nongrating patterns are adapting systems at a higher level than the grating patterns, and this may produce weaker MEs. If this is true, one might expect that the brain-damaged individuals, DF and PB, would not experience MEs with the nongrating Lie patterns. This is a researchable issue. Another possibility is that if MEs to the nongrating patterns are produced at a higher level in the visual system, they would show some degree of interocular transfer. We, however, have not been able to attain interocular transfer of MEs to concentric circles and radial line patterns (Humphrey, Gurnsey, & Bryden, 1994).

A third explanation for the greater effectiveness of gratings in inducing MEs could be that small eye movements made during "fixation" disrupt local contour orientation and color contingencies in the nongrating patterns but not in the grating patterns. This account is consistent with the notion that all MEs depend on local orientation and color contingencies.

Another caution concerns the local MEs obtained in our studies. Although we have emphasized the fact that there were many reports indicating MEs to the global aspects of the pattern, we also had many reports of partial MEs on

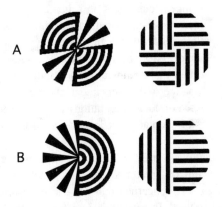

Figure 2.7. (A) Examples of the test patterns composed of four quadrants used by Emerson et al. (1985) and Humphrey et al. (1985) in their studies using the multiple induction procedure. (B) Examples of the bipartite test patterns used in some studies that reexamined some of the findings of Humphrey et al. (1985). See text for further details.

the test patterns (Emerson et al., 1985; Humphrey et al., 1985) These partial reports likely indicate the influence of local color and contour contingencies. Our theory of the ME (Dodwell & Humphrey, 1990) certainly does not deny local MEs, but it emphasizes that the strongest MEs are generated by coherent patterns, particularly those of the primitive model of LTG/NP. Given the great potential for interference in the multiple-pattern induction regimes if the ME is a purely local phenomenon, it is surprising that we obtained *any* reports indicating global MEs. This was particularly true when MEs were induced with all three pattern pairs (Emerson et al., 1985). In this condition, over the course of the multiple induction sessions, any small retinal area received many orientation and color pairings. It would be expected, on a purely local account, that only partial "patchwork-like" reports would be given.

Some recent unpublished research in my lab questions some of our earlier results using the multiple induction procedure. I reexamined the induction of multiple MEs in the same observer in conditions similar to some of those of Humphrey et al. (1985). As in our earlier studies, subjects were induced in two separate sessions separated by a few minutes. For example, induction with a red vertical grating and a green horizontal grating would be followed by induction with red concentric circles and green radial lines. As in Emerson et al. (1985) and Humphrey et al. (1985), "complete" reports were taken as evidence that the effects were global in nature. The test patterns used in our early reports were composed of four quadrants, as shown in Figure 2.7A. A color report was counted as a "complete ME" if a subject indicated that both quadrants in a test pattern representing a single inducing pattern appeared to be completely colored. Any response in which a smaller area was indicated as being colored was considered a partial ME. This rather stringent classification scheme was used because we wished to ascertain whether whole-field, pattern-specific MEs could be obtained with all the induced patterns and whether the patterns were addressing different and independent "channels" for the processing of pattern information in the visual system. We argued that complete reports indicated global MEs and would be evidence for separate and independent channels, whereas partial reports could indicate MEs based on local orientation-color contingencies and could be accounted for in terms of adaptation of local orientation selective mechanisms.

In my reexamination of these findings, I used bipartite test patterns like those shown in Figure 2.7B, as well as full test patterns – that is, black and white versions of the induction patterns. I was concerned that our earlier results were a function of the test patterns we had used. In particular, I wished to see whether the quartered test patterns might have inflated the number of complete reports because of the possibility that local MEs could "spread" more readily over bounded, quartered sections than over a half or full test pattern. Shallow color gradients can spread (Krauskopf, 1967), and Murch (1969) and Walker (1985) have reported that the ME can spread over test patterns that are larger than the induced area of the retina.

For the bipartite test patterns, indicating an aftereffect on one full half of the test pattern was considered a complete ME report, whereas indicating any smaller area was considered to be a partial report. For the full patterns, the subject had to indicate that the whole pattern appeared pink or green for a report to be considered a complete ME; indicating a ME on any smaller region was considered a partial report. As we found previously (Emerson et al., 1985; Humphrey et al., 1985), there was a mixture of both partial and complete reports. The results for the bipartite test patterns were comparable to the results we found earlier using similar induction conditions in that I found more complete than partial reports (Humphrey et al., 1985). It should be noted, though, that more of the complete MEs were reported on grating patterns than on the concentric circles and radial lines.[5]

On the full test patterns, however, more of the reports were partial (50%) than complete (33%); the remaining 17% of the reports were of no color. This result suggests that our earlier findings depended mainly on the test patterns used. The results, however, were a little more complicated. Of the complete reports given, more occurred if subjects were induced with one pair of orthogonal patterns in complementary colors in one session (e.g., green horizontal grating and red vertical grating), followed by induction with the other pair in complementary colors (i.e., red concentric circles and green radial lines). In this condition, more of the reports were complete (47%) than partial (34%). In contrast, if the patterns within each of the two induction sessions were not orthogonal, such as first adapting to a green horizontal grating and red concentric circles, followed by induction with a red vertical grating and green radial lines, there were far more partial (66%) than complete reports (19%). This finding suggests the possibility that in adapting to multiple patterns, induction with nonorthogonal patterns within each induction session may create more interference in the production of complete MEs than induction with orthogonal patterns within induction sessions.

An examination of the nature of the partial reports is instructive. Of the partial reports, more were given to the concentric circle and radial line test patterns (66%) than to the grating test patterns (34%). Consider a partial report to the concentric circle test pattern in the condition in which a subject was induced with a red vertical grating, a green horizontal grating, green concentric circles, and red radial lines. The reports tended to indicate that the more horizontally oriented contours in the test pattern were seen as pink, whereas the more vertically oriented sections were seen as white. This finding is what would be expected on a local account given the colors of the inducing gratings. The green horizontal grating would reinforce the ME to the horizontal sections of the green concentric circles, whereas the red vertical grating would interfere with the ME on the vertical sections of the concentric circles.

Celeste McCollough Howard (personal communication, June 1993; see also McCollough, 1994) has also examined MEs in a multiple induction regime using vertical and horizontal gratings, concentric circles, and radial line patterns. When she used test patterns composed of quadrants and our criteria for counting a ME report as complete, she obtained a large proportion of complete reports. When she used full test patterns, however, most of the reports were partial. The partial reports were similar to those described earlier and could be explained by the addition and competition of local effects.

It appears that whether one obtains local or global effects depends to a great extent on the test patterns used. These results suggest that an examination of the factors controlling color spreading of the ME could provide important information about the nature of the ME. Grossberg (1987) has a model of the ME that posits color spreading along but not across contours. As mentioned earlier, Murch (1969) and Walker (1985) have reported that the ME can spread over test patterns that are larger than the induced area of the retina, but detailed quantitative studies are lacking. A recent report by Broerse and O'Shea (1995) discusses the role of color spreading in the ME.

The results of Dodwell and O'Shea (1987) showed that making controlled eye movements while inducing MEs with nongrating patterns did not disrupt the MEs. Other research questions their results. Yasuda (1978) reported that when subjects were instructed to move their fixation point once a second, but without specifying where to look, very few MEs were reported to concentric circle and radial line patterns. Emerson et al. (1985; note 1) noted that in a pilot study in which subjects' gaze wandered over the nongrating patterns, very few

MEs were reported. It appears that eye movements in which the fixation points are uncontrolled disrupt the ME on nongrating patterns. More recently, however, Humphrey et al. (1994) have found that even with controlled eye movements similar to those used by Dodwell and O'Shea (1987), very few MEs were induced with concentric circles and radial line patterns (see also Broerse & O'Shea, 1995).

Dodwell and O'Shea (1987) also concluded that MEs depend on global pattern organization because random patterns with locally orthogonal elements (Figure 2.6) did not induce MEs in naive observers. They did comment in a footnote, however, that experienced observers could detect faint MEs following induction with the nonstructured patterns. Recently, Broerse and O'Shea (1995) examined the influence of pattern coherence systematically. They were able to induce MEs, under central fixation, that were contingent on randomly organized and locally orthogonal orientation components. This result is inconsistent with Dodwell and O'Shea's general conclusion that global organization is necessary for MEs. The MEs induced with randomly organized components, however, were weaker than those induced with globally organized components, suggesting some role for global organization. However, Broerse and O'Shea argue, based on the results of further experiments, that MEs involve only separate, localized, edge- and color-spread mechanisms.

As should be clear from the preceding discussion, there are many problems with the vectorfield approach to the ME developed by Dodwell and Humphrey (1990). Clearly, our earlier research overstated the case for global MEs and the independence of the MEs induced in the multiple-induction regime. More research on the role of test patterns in the ME is needed. It appears too that the factors underlying the effects of pattern coherence may not be as simple as we thought. Research like that of Broerse and O'Shea (1995) has begun to define more precisely the roles of local and global factors in the generation of MEs. Such research is particularly timely given recent neurophysiological research showing that even in the primary visual cortex, cells are capable of integrating information across large regions of visual space and the filtering properties of single cells can be modified by various contextual influences (reviewed in Gilbert 1992). It remains to be seen whether the ME is subject to any contextual and global influences or whether it can be fully accounted for in terms of local adaptation and color spreading (see Broerse and O'Shea, 1995).

Despite all of the problems with the application of LTG/NP to an explanation of the ME, there are some significant aspects of the approach that should not be overlooked. First, although the recent results question the approach, they would not likely have been discovered without it. At the very least, then, the approach has served an important heuristic function. It has also provided a general framework that led to novel interpretations of extant findings, as well as suggesting new experiments that predicted novel results. This is clear in the interpretation of the orthogonal, indirect ME. Further results on indirect MEs and the "vector addition" of MEs contingent on the direction of movement have also been discovered as a result of some predictions of LTG/NP (described in Dodwell, 1992). The theory motivated experiments, but new results now indicate that the LTG/NP account of the pattern processing mechanisms underlying the ME does not appear to be correct. Even if the LTG/NP approach hasn't supplied the definitive explanation of the pattern aspects of the ME, it has suggested some very provocative questions, and asking such questions is a crucial first step in understanding. Further, LTG/NP reminds us that a theory of vision must provide a link between the local mechanisms of early vision and the stable world of objects and events that we perceive (Broerse, Shaw, Dodwell, & Muir, 1994; Dodwell, 1994).

What is the nature of the adaptation underlying McCollough effects?

McCollough's (1965) original explanation was that MEs are caused by the color adaptation of neurons in the visual cortex that code local orientation in the form of bars or edges. The hypothesis proposes that ME induction distorts the wavelength-response functions of edge detectors that normally respond to a broad band of wavelengths. Another hypothesis relies on the notion that repeated stimulation with a particular pattern can "fatigue" neural mechanisms that code for that pattern type – that is, its value along a particular stimulus dimension (for discussion, see Mollon, 1977). In the case of the ME, it is proposed that the effects are caused by the fatiguing of "double-duty" units that code simultaneously for orientation and color, as found in monkey striate cortex (e.g., Hubel & Wiesel, 1968; Leventhal, Thompson, Liu, Zhou, & Ault, 1995; Michael, 1978). Such units would normally respond best to a particular combination of color and orientation.

Models based on fatiguing of simple neural elements have been criticized on several grounds. First, MEs last far longer than could be expected from what is known of the physiology of single cells in the visual system. MEs can last for hours, days or weeks without complete dissipation (Jones & Holding, 1975; Riggs, White & Eimas, 1974). This is generally considered to be much longer than the fatiguing and recovery times of simple neural processes. A second criticism is that the rate of decay depends on the conditions of stimulation. The ME is preserved in the absence of stimulation (Jones & Holding, 1975; MacKay & MacKay, 1975), and the form of decay can be modified to some extent by pre- and postinduction exposure to achromatic gratings (Skowbo, 1988). A third criticism is that because there are many different types of contingent aftereffects, the number of such detectors would have to be very large. Contingent aftereffects have been found in which color and spatial frequency are linked (e.g.,

Breitmeyer & Cooper, 1972; Day et al., 1992; Lovegrove & Over, 1972; Stromeyer, 1972b); color and movement are linked (e.g., Broerse et al., 1994; Favreau, 1979; Favreau et al., 1972; Heppler, 1968; Mayhew & Anstis, 1972); and when brightness or lightness and orientation are linked (Allan & Tirimacco, 1987; Mikaelian, Linton & Phillips, 1990; Over, Broerse, Crassini & Lovegrove, 1974). Contingent aftereffects have also been found in hearing (Allan, 1984; Marks, 1992; Walker & Irion, 1979; Walker, Irion, & Gordon, 1981) and in the tactile modality (Walker, 1977, 1978; Walker & Shea, 1974). If all such contingent aftereffects are based on fatigue of the appropriate double-duty detectors, the number of such mechanisms will increase with the discovery of each new contingent aftereffect. Despite these problems, researchers still argue that fatigue of double-duty detectors is a reasonable explanation for contingent aftereffects (e.g., Houck & Hoffman, 1986; Sharpe, Harris, Fach, & Braun, 1992).

Because of the problems with fatigue of double-duty detector accounts of contingent aftereffects, others have suggested that the ME involves separate mechanisms that code for color and orientation or other dimensions. One such explanation for MEs holds that they result from a form of classical conditioning. Such a view was proposed by several researchers, perhaps first by Viola (1966; see also Kohler, 1962), although she did not believe it could account for her results. Others have made similar proposals (e.g., Mayhew & Anstis, 1972; Skowbo, Gentry, Timney, Morant, 1974), and Murch (1976) presented a particular model of a classical conditioning account of the ME. In Murch's formulation, a grating serves as the conditioned stimulus and the color as the unconditioned stimulus. During induction, the color of the grating, red say, leads to an unconditioned response, green, that becomes associated with the grating. The classical conditioning account of the ME, although not strictly Murch's formulation of it, has been developed extensively by Allan and Siegel (1986, 1993; Siegel & Allan, 1993).

Besides the problems with the fatigue account, another reason for proposing a conditioning model is the belief that contingent aftereffects always last much longer than simple aftereffects, themselves usually attributed to a form of fatigue or desensitization. Most MEs are long-term aftereffects in that the aftereffect lasts much longer than the duration of the inducing period. Simple aftereffects are often believed to be short term in that they last for a duration that is similar to their inducing period. However, there is accumulating evidence that simple aftereffects of motion (Favreau, 1979; Hershenson, 1985; Kalfin & Locke, 1972; Masland, 1969), spatial frequency (Blakemore, Nachmias, & Sutton, 1970; Heggelund & Holman, 1976), tilt (Wolfe & O'Connell, 1986), and size (Frome, Harris & Levinson, 1975; Fromme, Levinson, Danielson, & Claudetscher, 1979) can last for several hours or days. As Harris (1980; see also Siegel & Allan, 1993) observed, it is possible that these simple aftereffects are also contingent effects, but they are contingent on some unknown attribute of the stimulus or experimental arrangement. If they are not, the longevity of MEs itself cannot be taken as evidence for a conditioning model.

The issue of whether the ME is a result of classical conditioning or not has been debated extensively at a variety of levels (Allan & Siegel, 1986, 1993; Dodwell & Humphrey, 1990, 1993; Harris, 1980; McCarter & Silver, 1977; Murch, 1977; Skowbo, 1984, 1986). One level is concerned with the empirical results that can or cannot be accommodated by the classical conditioning account. Researchers have presented evidence to show that manipulations that produce clear behavioral changes in conditioning produce analogous changes in the ME. Much of this research has been discussed critically and insightfully by Skowbo (1984, 1986, 1988; see also Allan & Siegel, 1986, 1993; Dodwell & Humphrey, 1993; Siegel & Allan, 1993). One problem with the debate is that it appears that the terms and concepts of the conditioning account are quite flexible and seemingly can be accommodated to diverse findings. Such flexibility makes it very difficult to propose crucial experiments that could potentially show the account to be false. It seems that some features of ME generation are suggestive of classical conditioning, but others are not (Dodwell & Humphrey, 1990, 1993). However, even if there is a classical conditioning component to the ME, this surely does not take us very far in understanding the particular visual mechanisms underlying the effect and how the effect is constrained by these mechanisms (Dodwell & Humphrey, 1993).

Classical conditioning is not the only associative model to have been proposed for MEs (e.g., Creuzfeldt, 1973; Grossberg, 1987). Some associative accounts propose an increase in excitation between between units coding for color and orientation (Montalvo, 1976), whereas others propose an increase in inhibition between such units (Barlow, 1990a, 1990b; Barlow & Földiák; 1989; Creuzfeldt, 1973; Savoy, 1984; Shute, 1979). The latter models differ in whether they propose unidirectional or bidirectional inhibition. Most of the models propose that inhibition is unidirectional – from form to color. Barlow and Földiák (1989; Barlow, 1990a, 1990b) propose a bidirectional inhibitory account – from form to color as well as from color to form. Barlow and Földiák propose that the strengthening of inhibition between color and orientation coding mechanisms that occurs during ME induction serves to decorrelate them. This decorrelation is implemented in an "anti-Hebbian" fashion. The purpose of such decorrelation by inhibition is to keep the elementary dimensions of perception separate, thereby making various types of learning possible. According to the model, it is necessary to keep perceptual dimensions separate because the nervous system will not be able to establish new associations if the independent probabilities of the elements separately (i.e., color and orientation) involved in the association cannot be known or represented. In effect, decorrelation increases the ease with which the cortex can detect new associations (see also Atick, 1992; Barlow, 1990b).

The issue of whether the ME is based on changes in excitation or inhibition is difficult to decide on present evidence, although there is research consistent with the notion of an increase in inhibition underlying the ME. Certain aspects of the ME are enhanced by drugs that heighten inhibition in the central nervous system or block excitation (Byth, Logue, Bell, Best, & King, 1992; Shute, 1979; see also Logue & Byth, 1993). Indirect evidence that lower than normal levels of excitatory neurotransmitters do not disrupt the ME comes from the research of Savoy and Gabrieli (1991) with Alzheimer's disease. These patients have a deficiency in acetylcholine (e.g., Terry & Katzman, 1983), an excitatory transmitter in much of the brain, including the primary visual pathway (e.g., Spehlmann & Downes, 1974). The patients studied by Savoy and Gabrieli nevertheless had normal MEs.

If the ME is based on an increase in inhibition, there is still the issue of whether the inhibition is unidirectional or bidirectional. There are some suggestive results supporting the idea that ME induction increases mutual or bidirectional inhibition between mechanisms coding for color and orientation or other stimulus dimensions. Not only have researchers found that ME induction produces color aftereffects contingent on form or motion, the usual ME, but there is also some evidence for aftereffects of form dependent on color (Dawson & Stromeyer, 1978; Haapasalo, 1982; Held & Shattuck, 1971; Humphrey et al., 1994; & Virsu Haapasalo, 1973), although they are weak (Timney, Gentry, Skowbo, & Morant, 1976), and motion aftereffects contingent on color (Favreau, 1979; Favreau et al., 1972; Mayhew & Antis, 1972; Sharpe et al., 1992).

As reviewed earlier, many researchers have suggested that the ME results from a modification of connection strength between mechanisms that code for color and separate achromatic systems that code for form. On the basis of present evidence, however, it is unclear just where the color and form mechanisms underlying the ME reside. I have argued that the ME reflects changes at a low level of the visual system and have suggested that area V1 has the requisite properties. It could be that the "blobs" of area V1 that, according to some accounts, contain a high proportion of color-selective cells that are monocular and contain unoriented receptive fields (Livingstone & Hubel, 1984; Ts'o & Gilbert, 1988; but see Leventhal et al., 1995) serve as the color component, whereas other cells in area V1 that are orientation and spatial frequency sensitive, but show a broadband response to wavelength, subserve the form component (Savoy & Gabrieli, 1991). This would place the locus for the production of the effect entirely in area V1. Other possibilities, however, cannot be ruled out on the basis of the evidence presently available. For example, it is possible that the color component is generated in the lateral geniculate nucleus, with the form component being cortical, perhaps in area V1. It is also possible, although perhaps less likely given much of the evidence reviewed here, that the effects may be produced at higher stages of visual processing (Livingstone & Hubel, 1987; see also Seaber & Lockhead, 1989).

Do such aftereffects serve a functional role?

Why do long-term aftereffects exist? Do they have a purpose? According to fatigue accounts, such aftereffects do not have a function, but rather reflect the fact that certain neural mechanisms have been desensitized or "used up" by overstimulation (Ullman & Schectman, 1982). The effects could be seen to have a function according to conditioning accounts (Allan & Siegel, 1993), but we have argued that there is another way to view such aftereffects that gives more insight into their adaptive significance (Dodwell & Humphrey, 1990, 1993). We view aftereffects and other adaptation phenomena as the reflection of certain functional processes that are involved in a continuous calibration and adjustment of the visual system. Our proposal owes much to the theorizing of Helson (1964) and Andrews (1964; see also Gibson, 1937).

Both Helson (1964) and Andrews (1964) noted that perceptual systems are sensitive to the statistical properties of sensory input and adjust their output based on the statistical distribution of the input. Helson postulated that, in making psychophysical judgments, the observer sets up an implicit scale based on the statistical properties of the set of objects being judged. The most important idea in his adaptation level theory is that there is a "neutral point," or adaptation level, that is in some sense the "centroid" of psychophysical judgments. Perceptual judgments are made in relation to this neutral point. Changes in adaptation level occur in response to particular perceptual "diets."

What useful function do such changes in adaptation level serve? Andrews (1964), building on Helson's ideas, suggests a function. He was concerned particularly with the question of matching the internal representation of the world to external properties. Some of these external properties are statistical in nature and reflect properties of the world that occur in the long run. Consider an example given by Andrews (1964). On average, movement of elements in the visual field is zero in all directions. This is a long-range statistical property of the world but it is violated all the time in the short run, so to maintain stability, such short-term fluctuations are ignored. If, however, the criterion is consistently violated in the diet of stimulation applied to the visual system, the discrepancy between the general statistical property of zero motion and its local perturbation will be detected. The long-range criterion could be violated by, for example, imposing linear motion in one part of the field over a substantial period of time. Andrews proposes that in response to this input, the visual system, through an error correction device (ECD), changes the internal representation to attempt to reduce the discrepancy. Generally speaking, this device will impose an inverse

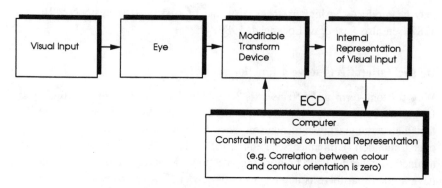

Figure 2.8. A schematic model of an error-correcting mechanism that explains the McCollough effect. The eye receives correlated color and contour information. The modifiable transform device is essentially an alterable transfer function that changes the appearance or internal representation of the visual input in accord with instructions from the error-correcting device (ECD). The ECD contains information about the long-term correlations between color and orientation and alters the transfer function when there is a significant departure from this long-term correlation. During ME induction, the ECD changes the transfer function to maintain an appropriate neutral point in the adaptation level for orientation-contingent color. (Based on Andrews, 1964, and Dodwell & Humphrey, 1990.)

transformation on its input. The internal representation of movement will *oppose* the externally detected motion, so that when the latter ceases, the internal representation exhibits movement in the opposite direction, as in the motion aftereffect. Applying these ideas to MEs, we have argued that they are due to changes in adaptation level, but changes that are *contingent on other stimulus features* (Dodwell & Humphrey, 1990). Changes in the contingent adaptation levels are controlled by ECDs that are sensitive to average contingencies in the external world that are violated in the course of experimental generation of MEs.

Setting up a contingent aftereffect violates a statistical characteristic that is true of the world in the long run. We suggested that MEs are generated because the zero correlation that exists in the long run, and on average, between color and contour orientation is violated during the induction period. In a ME induction regime, a particular color and an orientation are highly correlated. To maintain the internal representation of the long-run zero correlation between a particular color and an orientation in the presence of the artificially high induced correlation during ME generation, the system recalibrates and, in effect, decorrelates color and orientation (see Figure 2.8).

How does this generate a ME? If red is appearing too frequently in conjunction with verticals, the neutral point for red in the presence of verticals is shifted, according to adaptation-level theory, toward the overrepresented end of the color continuum, that is, red. Likewise, the neutral point for the correlation of horizontal contours with green has to be shifted toward green in order to reduce the imposed bias. Because the neutral point for vertical has been shifted toward red, achromatic vertical contours will have a greenish tinge, and similarly, horizontal contours will have a neutral point shifted toward green, so that achromatic horizontals will appear reddish.

Our theory suggests that MEs play a useful role in that they adjust the internal representation of the world to conform with the long-run statistical properties of the external environment. Our proposal is "ecological" in that it considers aspects of the statistical structure of the world, and posits a mechanism that represents this structure and recalibrates if the input deviates too far from it. Although our theory was developed in relation to the ME, it can apply to other simple aftereffects, not just contingent aftereffects (see Andrews, 1964). Our proposal has certain affinities with other theories in proposing a function for various adaptation phenomena (Anstis, 1975; Barlow, 1990a; Barlow & Földiák, 1989; Harris, 1987; Roorda & Wolfe, 1990; Ullman & Schechtman, 1982). In particular, the account of aftereffects and other adaptation phenomena by Barlow and Földiák (1989; Barlow, 1990a) as involving anti-Hebbian learning that implements decorrelation is consistent with much of our theory.

Conclusion

Although MEs seem to represent an inconstancy in perception, our approach suggests that they are an attempt by the visual system to overcome distortions and aberrations of its input, that is, to reestablish the normal zero correlation between color and certain basic pattern properties. On our interpretation, MEs and other aftereffects show that the visual system strives to represent the constant or invariant properties of the world, and if the visual input deviates significantly from these properties, the system attempts to recalibrate itself. Aftereffects are not just perceptual laboratory curiosities. They reveal some of the purposeful, dynamic means that the visual system uses to stay in touch with enduring properties of the world.

It has been more than 30 years since McCollough (1965) first reported the intriguing visual aftereffect that now bears her name. Three decades of research and more than 200 research papers on the topic have certainly added to our knowledge of the ME and related contingent aftereffects. The results are quite strong in supporting the view that the ME is a low-level visual phenomenon that, to use Pylyshyn's (1984) phrase, is "cognitively impenetrable." There are, however, many areas where there are conflicting results and interpretations and where our understanding is very inadequate. The underlying physiology of the ME is not understood and perhaps requires a more direct approach in which recordings are made in the monkey visual system. We know that rhesus monkeys experience the ME (Maguire, Meyer, & Baizer, 1980), so the study of its physiological basis could be pursued in such animals, as has the physiological basis of other adaptation phenomena (e.g., Saul & Cynader, 1989). It is also unclear just how local or global the effect is and how this depends on various induction and test pattern properties. Recent neurophysiological research has suggested that even area V1 has considerably more adaptive and integrative properties than were suspected less than a decade ago (e.g., Engel et al, 1992). Further studies of the effect of pattern organization factors on the ME could be motivated and guided by this research. Until very recently, with the exception of Montalvo (1976), there were no computational simulations of the ME. This is now changing as researchers are developing computer models of the ME and other adaptation effects (Barlow & Földiák, 1989; Broerse & Shaw, 1993; Grossberg, 1987; McLoughlin & Savoy, 1993). It is hoped that future findings from neurophysiology, psychophysics, and computer simulations will deepen our understanding of this fascinating visual aftereffect.

Notes

1. Most research since the time of McCollough's original report has used various reds and greens as the induction colors rather than orange and blue or other color combinations. Reds and greens generally produce strong aftereffects, whereas those produced by yellows and blues are usually weaker (Stromeyer, 1969), although the strength of the aftereffect produced by different induction hues varies with spatial frequency (Stromeyer, 1972b). Afterimage colors can also be used to induce MEs (Day, Webster, Gillies, & Crassini, 1989; Humphrey et al., 1989; Murch, 1969).
2. A reasonable estimate is that, as of 1994, approximately 200 papers have been published on the ME and variations of the effect since the time of McCollough's original report. I owe this estimate to Diane Skowbo and Celeste McCollough Howard.
3. Rivalry does not interfere with the production of simple aftereffects either (e.g., Blake & Fox, 1974; Blake & Overton, 1979; Lehmkule & Fox, 1975).
4. There are some results that could be seen to contradict this suggestion. In LTG/NP, diagonal gratings involve a linear combination of two simple operators for their generation. According to the argument then, they should be less effective than the horizontal and vertical gratings in generating MEs. Research by Fidell (1970), however, does not support this prediction in that induction with diagonal gratings (separated by 90°) produced MEs as strong as induction with horizontal and vertical gratings. It was true in general, however, that induction with orthogonal gratings (separated by 90°) produced stronger MEs than did induction with non-orthogonal gratings (separated by less than 90°).
5. This result prompted me to re-examine the results of Humphrey et al. (1985). There too more complete reports were given to the grating patterns than to the concentric circle and radial line patterns.

References

Allan, L. G. (1984). Contingent aftereffects in duration judgements. In J. Gibbon & L. Allan (Eds.), Timing and time perception. *Annals of the New York Academy of Sciences, 423,* 116–130.
Allan, L. G., & Siegel, S. (1986). McCollough effects as conditioned responses: Reply to Skowbo. *Psychological Bulletin, 100,* 388–393.

Allan, L. G., & Siegel, S. (1991). Characteristics of the indirect McCollough effect. *Perception & Psychophysics, 50*, 249–257.

Allan, L. G., & Siegel, S. (1993). McCollough effects as conditioned responses: Reply to Dodwell and Humphrey. *Psychological Review, 100*, 342–346.

Allan, L. G., Siegel, S., Collins, J. C., & MacQueen, G. M. (1989). Color aftereffect contingent on text. *Perception & Psychophysics, 46*, 105–113.

Allan, L. G., Siegel, S., Toppan, P., & Lockhead, G. (1991). Assessment of the McCollough effect by a shift in psychometric function. *Bulletin of the Psychonomic Society, 29*, 21–24.

Allan, L. G., & Tirimacco, N. T. (1987). An orientation-contingent achromatic aftereffect. *Bulletin of the Psychonomic Society, 29*, 21–24.

Andrews, D. P. (1964). Error-correcting perceptual mechanisms. *Quarterly Journal of Experimental Psychology, 16*, 104–115.

Anstis, S. M. (1975). What does visual perception tell us about visual coding? In M. S. Gazzaniga & C. Blakemore (Eds.), *Handbook of psychobiology* (pp. 269–323). New York: Academic Press.

Atick, J. J. (1992). Could information theory provide an ecological theory of sensory processing? *Network, 3*, 213–251.

Barlow, H. B. (1990a). A theory about the functional role and synaptic mechanism of visual aftereffects. In C Blakemore (Ed.), *Vision: Coding and efficiency* (pp. 363–375). Cambridge: Cambridge University Press.

Barlow, H. (1990b). Conditions for versatile learning, Helmholtz's unconscious inference, and the task of perception. *Vision Research, 30*, 1561–1571.

Barlow, H., & Földiák, P. (1989). Adaptation and decorrelation in the cortex. In R. Durbin, C. Miall, & G. Mitchison (Eds.), *The computing neuron* (pp. 54–72). New York: Addison-Wesley.

Bedford, F. L., & Reinke, K. S. (1993). The McCollough effect: Dissociating retinal from spatial coordinates. *Perception & Psychophysics, 54*, 515–526.

Blake, R., & Fox, R. (1974). Adaptation to invisible gratings and the site of binocular rivalry suppression. *Nature, 249*, 488–490.

Blake, R. & Overton, R. (1979). The site of binocular rivalry suppression. *Perception, 8*, 143–152.

Blake, R., Overton, R., & Lema-Stern, S. (1981). Interocular transfer of visual aftereffects. *Journal of Experimental Psychology: Human Perception and Performance, 7*, 367–381.

Blake, T. (1979). Internally augmented displays: Contingent aftereffects as performance aids. *Journal of Experimental Psychology: Human Perception and Performance, 5*, 420–425.

Blakemore, C. (1973). The confounded brain. In R. L. Gregory & E. H. Gombrich (Eds.), *Illusion in nature and art* (pp. 8–47). London: Duckworth.

Blakemore, C., Nachmias, J., & Sutton, P. (1970). The perceived spatial frequency shift: Evidence for frequency-selective neurons in the human brain. *Journal of Physiology, 210*, 727–750.

Breitmeyer, B. G., & Cooper, L. A. (1972). Frequency-specific color adaptation in the human visual system. *Perception & Psychophysics, 11*, 95–96.

Broerse, J., & Crassini, B. (1981a). Comments on the use of perceptually ambiguous figures as McCollough-effect stimuli. *Perception & Psychophysics, 30*, 339–402.

Broerse, J., & Crassini, B. (1981b). Misinterpretations of imagery-induced McCollough effects: A reply to Finke. *Perception & Psychophysics, 30*, 96–98.

Broerse, J., & Crassini, B. (1984). Investigations of perception and imagery using CAEs: The role of experimental design and psychophysical method. *Perception & Psychophysics, 35*, 155–164.

Broerse, J., & Crassini, B. (1986). Making ambiguous displays unambiguous: The influence of real colors and colored aftereffects on perceptual alternation. *Perception & Psychophysics, 39*, 105–116.

Broerse, J., & Grimbeek, P. (1994). Eye movements and the associative basis of contingent color aftereffects: A comment on Siegel, Allan, and Eisenberg (1992). *Journal of Experimental Psychology: General, 123*, 81–85.

Broerse, J., & O'Shea, R. P. (1995). Local and global factors in spatially-contingent coloured aftereffects. *Vision Research, 35,* 207–226.

Broerse, J., & Shaw, C. (1993). *The long and short of sensory adaptation in the human visual system.* Paper presented at the third annual meeting of the Canadian Society for Brain, Behaviour and Cognitive Science, Toronto, Ontario.

Broerse, J., Shaw, C., Dodwell, P., & Muir, D. (1994). Colored aftereffects contingent upon global transformations? *Spatial Vision, 8,* 95–117.

Buser, P., & Imbert, M. (1992). *Vision* (R. H. Kay, Trans.). Cambridge, Mass.: MIT Press. (Original work published 1987).

Byth, W., Logue, N. A., Bell, P., Best, S. J., & King, D. J. (1992). The McCollough effect as a measure of central cholinergic activity in man. *Psychopharmacology, 106,* 75–84.

Campbell, F. W., & Maffei, L. (1971). The tilt after-effect: A fresh look. *Vision Research, 11,* 833–840.

Campbell, F. W., & Robson, J. G. (1968). Application of Fourier analysis to the visibility of gratings. *Journal of Physiology, 197,* 551–556.

Cavill, J., & Robinson, J. O. (1976). A color aftereffect contingent on complex pattern features. *Perception & Psychophysics, 19,* 454–459.

Creuzfeldt, O. D. (1973). Some neurophysiological considerations concerning "memory." In H. P. Zippel (Ed.), *Memory and transfer of information* (pp. 293–302). New York: Plenum Press.

Dawson, B. M., & Stromeyer, C. F., III. (1978). Form aftereffect contingent upon a colour shift. *Perception, 7,* 417–421.

Day, R. H., Webster, W. R., Gillies, O., & Crassini, B. (1992). Spatial-frequency-contingent color aftereffects: Adaptation with one-dimensional stimuli. *Perception & Psychophysics, 51,* 57–65.

Desimone, R. (1992). Neural circuits for visual attention in the primate brain. In G. A. Carpenter & S. Grossberg (Eds.), *Neural networks for vision and image processing* (pp. 343–364). Cambridge, Mass.: MIT Press.

De Valois, R. L., & De Valois K. K. (1990). *Spatial vision.* New York: Oxford University Press.

De Valois, K. K., De Valois, R. L., & Yund, E. W. (1979). Responses of striate cortex cells to grating and checkerboard patterns. *Journal of Physiology, 291,* 483–505.

Dodwell, P. C. (1983). The Lie transformation group model of visual perception. *Perception & Psychophysics, 34,* 1–16.

Dodwell, P. C. (1991). Transformations after Gibson: Biological and ecological constraints on vision. In J. R. Cronly-Dillon, & R. J. Watt (Eds.), *Pattern recognition by man and machine. Vision and visual dysfunction* (Vol. 14, pp. 19–29). London: Macmillan.

Dodwell, P. C. (1992). Perspectives and transformations. *Canadian Journal of Psychology, 46,* 510–538.

Dodwell, P. C. (1994). On raising our sights. *Spatial Vision, 8,* 9–17.

Dodwell, P. C., & Humphrey, G. K. (1990). A functional theory of the McCollough effect. *Psychological Review, 97,* 78–89.

Dodwell, P. C., & Humphrey, G. K. (1993). What is important about McCollough effects? A reply to Allan and Siegel. *Psychological Review, 100,* 347–350.

Dodwell, P. C., & O'Shea, R. P. (1987). Global factors generate the McCollough effect. *Vision Research, 27,* 569–580.

Ellis, S. R. (1976). Orientation constancy of the McCollough effect. *Perception & Psychophysics, 19,* 183–192.

Emerson, V. F., Humphrey, G. K., & Dodwell, P. C. (1985). Colored aftereffects contingent on patterns generated by Lie transformation groups. *Perception & Psychophysics, 37,* 155–162.

Engel, A. K., König, P., Kreiter, A. K., Schillen, T. B., & Singer, W. (1992). Temporal coding in the visual cortex: New vistas on integration in the nervous system. *Trends in Neurosciences, 15,* 218–226.

Enroth-Cugell, C., & Robson, J. G. (1966). The contrast sensitivity of retinal ganglion cells of the cat. *Journal of Physiology, 187,* 517–552.

Favreau, O. E. (1979). Persistence of simple and contingent motion aftereffects. *Perception & Psychophysics, 26*, 187–194.

Favreau, O. E., Emerson, V. F., & Corballis, M. C. (1972). Motion perception: A color-contingent aftereffect. *Science, 176*, 78–79.

Fidell, L. S. (1970). Orientation specificity in chromatic adaptation of human "edge-detectors." *Perception & Psychophysics, 8*, 235–237.

Field, D. J. (1993). Scale-invariance and self-similar "wavelet" transforms: An analysis of natural scenes and mammalian visual systems. In M. Farge, J. Hunt, & Vassilicos (Eds.), *Wavelets, fractals and fourier transforms: New developments and new applications* (pp. 151–193). Oxford University Press.

Finke, R. A. (1989). *Principles of mental imagery*. London: MIT Press.

Finke, R. A., & Schmidt, M. J. (1977). Orientation-specific color aftereffects following imagination. *Journal of Experimental Psychology: Human Perception and Performance, 3*, 599–606.

Finke, R. A., & Schmidt, M. J. (1978). The quantitative measure of pattern representation in images using orientation-specific color aftereffects. *Perception & Psychophysics, 23*, 515–520.

Flanagan, P., & Dodwell, P. (1991). Pattern-specific contrast threshold elevation. *Spatial Vision, 5*, 159–187.

Frome, F., Harris, C. S., & Levinson, J. Z. (1975). Extremely long-lasting shifts in perception of size after adaptation to gratings. *Bulletin of the Psychonomic Society, 6*, 433.

Fromme, F., Levinson, J. Z., Danielson, J. T., & Claudetscher, J. E. (1979). Shifts in perception of size after adaptation to gratings. *Science, 206*, 1327–1329.

Foreit, K. G., & Ambler, B. A. (1978). Induction of the McCollough effect I: Figural variables. *Perception and Psychophysics, 24*, 295–302.

Gallant, J. L., Braun, J., & Van Essen, D. C. (1993). Selectivity for polar, hyperbolic, and cartesian gratings in macaque visual cortex. *Science, 259*, 100–103.

Gibson, J. J. (1937). Adaptation with negative after-effect. *Psychological Review, 44*, 222–244.

Gibson, J. J. (1950). *The perception of the visual world*. Boston: Houghton Mifflin.

Gibson, J. J. (1966). *The senses considered as perceptual systems*. Boston: Houghton Mifflin.

Goodale, M. A., Milner, A. D., Jakobson, L. S., & Carey, D. P. (1991). A neurological dissociation between perceiving objects and grasping them. *Nature, 349*, 154–155.

Green, M., Corwin, T., & Zemon, V. (1976). A comparison of Fourier analysis and feature analysis in pattern-specific color aftereffects. *Science, 192*, 147–148.

Grossberg, S. (1987). Cortical dynamics of three-dimensional form, color, and brightness perception: II. Binocular theory. *Perception & Psychophysics, 41*, 117–158.

Haapasalo, S. (1982). Relationships between perceptual mechanisms for color and pattern in human vision. In Y. B. Kramertint (Ed.), *Dissertations humanarum litterarum* (Vol. 33, pp. 311–425). Helsinki: Suomalainen Tiedeakatemia.

Harris, C. S. (1980). Insight or out of sight? Two examples of perceptual plasticity in the human adult. In C. S. Harris (Ed.), *Visual coding and adaptability* (pp. 95–149). Hillsdale, N.J.: Erlbaum.

Harris, J. P. (1987). Contingent perceptual aftereffect. In R. L. Gregory (Ed.), *The Oxford companion to the mind* (pp. 166–168). New York: Oxford University Press.

Heeley, D. W. (1979). A perceived spatial frequency shift at orientations orthogonal to adapting gratings. *Vision Research, 19*, 1229–1236.

Heggelund, P., & Holman, A. (1975). Long-term retention of the "Gilinsky-Effect." *Vision Research, 16*, 1015–1017.

Held, R., & Shattuck, S. R. (1971). Color and edge-sensitive channels in the human visual system: Tuning for orientation. *Science, 174*, 314–316.

Helson, H. (1964). *Adaptation-level theory: An experimental and systematic approach to behavior*. New York: Harper & Row.

Heppler, N. (1968). Color: A motion-contingent aftereffect. *Science, 162*, 376–377.

Hershenson, M. (1985). Thirty seconds of adaptation produce spiral aftereffects three days later. *Bulletin of the Psychonomic Society, 23*, 122–123.

Hoffman, W. C. (1966). The Lie algebra of visual perception. *Journal of Mathematical Psychology,* *3,* 65–98; errata, *Journal of Mathematical Psychology,* 1967, *4,* 348–349.

Hoffman, W. C. (1978). The Lie transformation group approach to visual perception. In E. J. L. Leeuwenberg & H. F. M. J. Buffart (Eds.) *Formal theories of visual perception* (pp. 27–66). New York: Wiley.

Hoffman, W. C., & Dodwell, P. C. (1985). Geometric psychology generates the visual gestalt. *Canadian Journal of Psychology, 39,* 491–528.

Houck, M. R., & Hoffman, J. E. (1986). Conjunction of color and form without attention: Evidence from an orientation-contingent color aftereffect. *Journal of Experimental Psychology: Human Perception and Performance, 12,* 186–199.

Hubel, D. H., & Wiesel, T. N. (1968). Receptive fields and functional architecture of monkey striate cortex. *Journal of Physiology, 195,* 215–243.

Humphrey, G. K., Dodwell, P. C., & Emerson, V. F. (1985). The roles of pattern orthogonality and color contrast in the generation of pattern-contingent color aftereffects. *Perception & Psychophysics, 38,* 343–353.

Humphrey, G. K., Dodwell, P. C., & Emerson, V. F. (1989). Pattern-contingent color aftereffects on noninduced patterns. *Perception & Psychophysics, 45,* 97–109.

Humphrey, G. K., Goodale, M. A. G., Corbetta, M., & Aglioti, S. (1995) The McCollough effect reveals orientation discrimination in a case of cortical blindness. *Current Biology, 5,* 454–551.

Humphrey, G. K., Goodale, M. A., & Gurnsey, R. (1991). Orientation discrimination in a visual form agnosic: Evidence from the McCollough effect. *Psychological Science, 5,* 331–335.

Humphrey, G. K., Goodale, M. A., Jakobson, L. J., & Servos, P. (1994). The role of surface information in object recognition: Studies of a visual form agnosic and normal subjects. *Perception, 23,* 1457–1481.

Humphrey, G. K., Gurnsey, R., & Bryden, P. J. (1994). An examination of colour-contingent pattern aftereffects. *Spatial Vision, 8,* 77–94.

Humphrey, G. K., Gurnsey, R., & Fekete, E. (1991). Rapid discrimination of McCollough effects. *Perception, 20,* 467–482.

Humphrey, G. K., Herbert, A. M., Symons, L. A., & Kara, S. (1994). McCollough effect to "form": A local phenomenon. *Journal of Experimental Psychology: General, 123,* 86–90.

Humphrey, G. K., Skowbo, D., Symons, L. A., Herbert, A. M., & Grant, C. (1994). Text-contingent color-aftereffects: A re-examination. *Perception & Psychophysics, 56,* 405–413.

Jenkins, B., & Ross, J. (1977). McCollough effect depends upon perceived organizations. *Perception, 6,* 399–400.

Jones, P. D., & Holding, D. H. (1975). Extremely long-term persistence of the McCollough effect. *Journal of Experimental Psychology: Human Perception and Performance, 1,* 323–327.

Julesz, B. (1984). Toward an axiomatic theory of preattentive vision. In G. Edelman, W. Einar, and W. Cowan (Eds.), *Dynamic aspects of neocortical function* (pp. 585–612). New York: Wiley.

Kalfin, K., & Locke, S. (1972). Evaluation of long term visual motion after-image following monocular stimulation. *Vision Research, 12,* 359–361.

Kaufman, J. H., May, J. G., & Kunen, S. (1981). Interocular transfer of orientation-contingent color aftereffects with external and internal adaptation. *Perception & Psychophysics, 30,* 547–551.

Kelly, D. H. (1976). Pattern detection and the two-dimensional Fourier transform: Flickering checkerboard and chromatic mechanisms. *Vision Research, 16,* 277–289.

Koenderink, J. J. (1985). Space, form and optical deformations. In D. J. Ingle, M. Jeannerod, & D. N. Lee (Eds.), *Brain mechanisms and spatial vision* (pp. 31–58). Boston: Martinus Nijhoff.

Koenderink, J. J. (1988). Operational significance of receptive field assemblies. *Biological Cybernetics, 58,* 168–171.

Kohler, I. (1962). Experiments with goggles. *Scientific American, 206,* 62–72.

Krauskopf, J. (1967). Heterochromatic stabilized images: A classroom demonstration. *American Journal of Psychology, 80,* 634–637.

Kulikowski, J. J., & Kranda, K. (1986). Image analysis performed by the visual system: Feature versus Fourier analysis and adaptable filtering. In J. D. Pettigrew, K. J. Sanderson, & W. R. Levick (Eds.), *Visual neuroscience* (pp. 381–404). New York: Cambridge University Press.

Kunen, S., & May, J. G. (1981). Imagery-induced McCollough effects: Real or imagined? *Perception & Psychophysics, 30*, 99–100.

Lehmkuhle, S. W., & Fox, R. (1975). Effect of binocular rivalry suppression on the motion aftereffect. *Vision Research, 15*, 855–859.

Leventhal, A. G., Thompson, K. G., Liu, D., Zhou, Y., & Ault, S. J. (1995). Concomitant sensitivity to orientation, direction, and color of cells in layers 2, 3 and 4 of monkey striate cortex. *The Journal of Neuroscience, 15*, 1801–1818.

Lewis, D. A., Campbell, M. J., Terry, R. D., & Morrison, J. H. (1987). Laminar and regional distributions of neurofibrillary tangles and neuritic plaques in Alzheimer's disease: A quantitative study of visual and auditory cortices. *Journal of Neuroscience, 7*, 1799–1808.

Livingstone, M. S., & Hubel, D. (1984). Anatomy and physiology of a color system in the primate visual cortex. *Journal of Neuroscience, 4*, 309–356.

Livingstone, M. S., & Hubel, D. H. (1987). Psychophysical evidence for separate channels for the perception of form, color, movement, and depth. *The Journal of Neuroscience, 7*, 3416–3468.

Logue, N. A., & Byth, W. (1993). Extraversion and the McCollough effect. *British Journal of Psychology, 84*, 67–84.

Lovegrove, W. J., & Over, R. (1972). Color adaptation of spatial frequency detectors in the human visual system. *Science, 176*, 541–543.

MacKay, D. M. (1957). Moving images produced by regular stationary patterns. *Nature, 180*, 849–850.

MacKay, D. M. (1961). Interactive processes in visual perception. In W. A. Rosenblith (Ed.), *Sensory communication* (pp. 339–355). Cambridge, Mass.: MIT Press.

MacKay, D. M. (1981). Strife over visual cortical function. *Science, 289*, 117–118.

MacKay, D. M., & MacKay, V. (1975). What causes decay of pattern-contingent chromatic aftereffects? *Vision Research, 15*, 462–464.

MacKay, D. M., & MacKay, V. (1977). Multiple orientation-contingent chromatic after-effects. *Quarterly Journal of Experimental Psychology, 29*, 203–218.

Maguire, W. M., Meyer, G. E., & Baizer, J. S. (1980). The McCollough effect in rhesus monkey. *Investigative Ophthalmology and Visual Science, 19*, 321–324.

Marks, L. E. (1992). The contingency of perceptual processing: Context modifies equal-loudness relations. *Psychological Science, 3*, 285–291.

Masland, R. M. (1969). Visual motion perception: Experimental modification. *Science, 165*, 819–821.

May, J. G., Agamy, G., & Matteson, H. H. (1978). The range of spatial frequency contingent color aftereffects. *Vision Research, 18*, 917–921.

May, J. G., & Matteson, H. H. (1976). Spatial frequency-contingent color aftereffects. *Science, 192*, 145–147.

May, J. G., Matteson, H. H., Agamy, G., & Castellanos, P. (1978). The effects of differential adaptation on spatial frequency-contingent color aftereffects. *Perception & Psychophysics, 23*, 409–412.

Mayhew, J. E. W., & Anstis, S. M. (1972). Movement aftereffects contingent on color, intensity, and pattern. *Perception & Psychophysics, 12*, 77–85.

Mayhew, J. E. W., & Frisby, J. P. (1978). Texture discrimination and Fourier analysis in human vision. *Nature, 275*, 438–439.

McCarter, A., & Silver, A. (1977). The McCollough effect: A classical conditioning phenomenon? *Vision Research, 17*, 317–319.

McCollough, C. (1965). Color adaptation of edge-detectors in the human visual system. *Science, 149*, 1115–1116.

McCollough, C. (1994). *Do McCollough effects provide evidence of global pattern-processing?* Paper presented at the annual meeting of the Association for Research in Vision and Ophthalmology, Sarasota, Florida.

McLoughlin, N. P., & Savoy, R. L. (1993). *Modelling monocular and binocular properties of the McCollough effect.* Poster presented at the annual meeting of the Association for Research in Vision and Ophthalmology, Sarasota, Florida.

Meyer, G. E., & Phllips, D. (1980). Faces, vases, subjective contours and the McCollough effect. *Perception, 9,* 603–606.

Michael, C. R. (1978). Color vision mechanisms in monkey striate cortex: Simple cells with dual opponent-color receptive fields. *Journal of Neurophysiology, 41,* 1233–1241.

Mikaelian, H. H., Linton, M. J., & Phillips, M. (1990). Orientation-specific luminance aftereffects. *Perception & Psychophysics, 47,* 575–582.

Milner, A. D., & Heywood, C. A. (1989) A disorder of lightness discrimination in a case of visual form agnosia. *Cortex, 25,* 489–494.

Milner, A. D., Perrett, D. I., Johnston, R. S., Benson, P. J., Jordan, T. R., Heeley, D. W., Bettucci, D., Mortara, F., Mutani, R., Terazzi, R., & Davidson, D. L. W. (1991). Perception and action in visual form agnosia. *Brain, 114,* 405–428.

Mollon, J. D. (1977). Neural analysis. In K. Von Fieandt & I. K. Moustgaard (Eds.), *The perceptual world* (pp. 71–97). New York: Academic Press.

Montalvo, F. S. (1976). A neural network model of the McCollough effect. *Biological Cybernetics, 25,* 49–56.

Morant, R. B., & Mistovich, M. (1960). Tilt aftereffects between vertical and horizontal axes. *Perceptual and Motor Skills, 10,* 75–81.

Moulden, B. (1980). Aftereffects and the integration of neural activity within a channel. *Philosophical Transactions of the Royal Society of London B, 290,* 39–55.

Murch, G. M. (1969). Size judgements of McCollough afterimages. *Journal of Experimental Psychology, 81,* 44–48.

Murch, G. M. (1972). Binocular relationships in a size and color orientation specific aftereffect. *Journal of Experimental Psychology, 93,* 30–34.

Murch, G. M. (1976). Classical conditioning of the McCollough effect: Temporal parameters. *Vision Research, 16,* 615–619.

Murch, G. M. (1977). A reply to McCarter and Silver. *Vision Research, 17,* 321–322.

Over, R., Blackwell, A., & Axton, C. (1984). Confusable gratings selectively elicit orientation-contingent colour aftereffects. *Australian Journal of Psychology, 36,* 337–342.

Over, R., Broerse, J., Crassini, B., & Lovegrove, W. (1974). Orientation-specific aftereffects and illusions in the perception of brightness. *Perception & Psychophysics, 15,* 53–56.

Pylyshyn, Z. W. (1984). *Computation and cognition: Toward a foundation for cognitive science.* Cambridge, Mass.: MIT Press.

Riggs, L. A., White, K. D., & Eimas, P. D. (1974). Establishment and decay of orientation-contingent aftereffects of color. *Perception & Psychophysics, 16,* 535–542.

Roorda, J., & Wolfe, J. M., (1990). *The McCollough effect is a byproduct of internal error-correcting mechanisms.* Paper presented at the annual meeting of the Optical Society of America, Boston.

Saul, A. B., & Cynader, M. (1989). Adaptation in single units in visual cortex: The tuning of aftereffects in the spatial domain. *Visual Neuroscience, 2,* 593–607.

Savoy, R. L. (1984). "Extinction" of the McCollough effect does not transfer interocularly. *Perception & Psychophysics, 36,* 571–576.

Savoy, R. L., & Gabrielli, J. D. E. (1991). Normal McCollough effect in Alzheimer's disease and global amnesia. *Perception & Psychophysics, 49,* 448–455.

Seaber, J. H., & Lockhead, G. R. (1989). McCollough aftereffects in strabismus and amblyopia. *Vision Research, 29,* 609–617.

Servos, P., Goodale, M. A., & Humphrey, G. K. (1993). The drawing of objects by a visual form agnosic: Contribution of surface properties and memorial representations. *Neuropsychologia, 31,* 251–259.

Sharpe, L. T., Harris, J. P., Fach, C. C., & Braun, D. I. (1992). Contingent aftereffects: Lateral interactions between color and motion. *Perception & Psychophysics, 49,* 434–447.

Shute, C. C. D. (1979). *The McCollough effect.* Cambridge: Cambridge University Press.

Siegel, S., & Allan, L. G. (1993). Pairings in learning and perception: Pavlovian conditioning and contingent aftereffects. In D. Medin (Ed.), *The psychology of learning and motivation* (Vol. 28, pp. 127–160). New York: Academic Press.

Siegel, S., Allan, L. G., & Eissenberg, T. (1992). The associative basis of contingent color aftereffects. *Journal of Experimental Psychology: General, 121,* 79–94.

Skowbo, D. (1984). Are McCollough effects conditioned responses? *Psychological Bulletin, 96,* 215–226.

Skowbo, D. (1986). McCollough effects as conditioned responses? Reply to Allan and Siegel. *Psychological Bulletin, 100,* 394–397.

Skowbo, D. (1988). Interference with McCollough effects via pre- and postinduction exposure to achromatic gratings: Time course and magnitude of aftereffect decrement. *Perception & Psychophysics, 44,* 295–303.

Skowbo, D., Gentry, T. A., Timney, B. N., & Morant, R. B. (1974). The McCollough effect: Influence of visual stimulation on decay rate. *Perception & Psychophysics, 16,* 47–49.

Skowbo, D., Timney, B. N., Gentry, T. A., & Morant, R. B. (1975). McCollough effects: Experimental findings and theoretical accounts. *Psychological Bulletin, 82,* 497–510.

Smith, F. D. (1977). Checkerboards and color aftereffects. *Science, 198,* 207–208.

Spehlmann, R., & Downes, K. (1974). The effects of acetylcholine and of synaptic stimulation on the sensorimotor cortex of cats.1. Neuronal responses to stimulation of the reticular formation. *Brain Research, 74,* 229–242.

Stromeyer, C. F. (1969). Further studies of the McCollough effect. *Perception & Psychophysics, 6,* 105–110.

Stromeyer, C. F., III. (1972a). Contour contingent color aftereffects: Retinal area specificity. *American Journal of Psychology, 85,* 227–235.

Stromeyer, C. F., III. (1972b). Edge-contingent aftereffects in human vision: Spatial frequency specificity. *Vision Research, 12,* 717–733.

Stromeyer, C. F., III. (1978). Form-color aftereffects in human vision. In R. Held, H. W. Leibowitz, & H. L. Teuber (Eds.), *Perception: Handbook of sensory physiology* (Vol. 8, pp. 97–142). New York: Springer-Verlag.

Terry, R., & Katzman, R. (1983). Senile dementia of the Alzheimer type: Defining a disease. In R. Katzman & R. Terry (Eds.), *The neurology of aging* (pp. 51–84). Philadelphia: F. A. Davis.

Thompson, P., & Latchford, G. (1986) Colour-contingent after-effects are really wavelength-contingent. *Nature, 320,* 525–526.

Thompson, P., & Travis, D. (1989). Making Mayhew and Frisby effortlessly discriminable. *Perception, 18,* 231–235.

Timney, B. N., Gentry, T. A., Skowbo, D., & Morant, R. B. (1976). Threshold elevation following adaptation to coloured gratings. *Vision Research, 16,* 601–607.

Treisman, A. (1988). Features and objects: The fourteenth Bartlett Memorial Lecture. *Quarterly Journal of Experimental Psychology, 40A,* 201–237.

Ts'o, D. Y., & Gilbert, C. D. (1988). The organization of chromatic and spatial interactions in the primate striate cortex. *Journal of Neuroscience, 8,* 1712–1727.

Tyler, C. W. (1977). Checkerboards and color aftereffects. *Science, 198,* 208–209.

Uhlarik, J., Pringle, R., & Brigell, M. (1977). Color aftereffects contingent on perceptual organization. *Perception & Psychophysics, 22,* 506–510.

Ullman, S., & Schechtman, G. (1982). Adaptation and gain normalization. *Proceedings of the Royal Society of London B, 216,* 299–313.

Vidyasagar, T. R. (1976). Orientation specific colour adaptation at a binocular site. *Nature, 261*, 39–40.

Viola, M. (1966). *Color adaptation contingent upon the geometry of the inducing stimulus.* Senior honors thesis, Smith College.

Virsu, V., & Haapasalo, S. (1973). Relationships between channels for colour and spatial frequency in human vision. *Perception, 2*, 31–40.

Walker, J. T. (1977). Orientation-contingent tactual size aftereffects. *Perception & Psychophysics, 22*, 563–570.

Walker, J. T. (1978) Simple and contingent aftereffects in the kinesthetic perception of length. *Journal of Experimental Psychology: Human Perception and Performance, 4*, 294–301.

Walker, J. T., & Irion, A. L. (1979). Two new contingent aftereffects: Perceived auditory duration contingent on pitch and on temporal order. *Perception & Psychophysics, 26*, 241–244.

Walker, J. T., Irion, A. L., & Gordon, D. G. (1981). Simple and contingent aftereffects of perceived duration in vision and audition. *Perception & Psychophysics, 29*, 475–486.

Walker, J. T., & Shea, K. S. (1974). A tactual size aftereffects contingent on hand position. *Journal of Experimental Psychology, 103*, 668–674.

Walker, W. D. (1985). *Quantitative profiles of Lie pattern McCollough effects generated through the use of a computer-controlled hue matching technique.* Honours thesis, Queen's University at Kingston.

Watanabe, T., Zimmerman, G. L., & Cavanagh, P. (1992). Orientation-contingent color aftereffects mediated by subjective transparent structures. *Perception & Psychophysics, 52*, 161–166.

Webster, W. R., Day, R. H., Gillies, O., & Crassini, B. (1992). Spatial-frequency-contingent color aftereffects: Adaptation with two-dimensional stimulus patterns. *Perception & Psychophysics, 51*, 66–78.

Webster, W. R., Day, R. H., & Willenberg, K. (1988). Orientation-contingent color aftereffects are determined by real color, not induced color. *Perception & Psychophysics, 44*, 43–49.

White, K. D., Petry, H. M., Riggs, L. A., & Miller, J. (1978). Binocular interactions during establishment of McCollough effects. *Vision Research, 18*, 1201–1215.

Wolfe, J. M., & O'Connell, K. M. (1986). Fatigue and structural change: Two consequences of visual pattern adaptation. *Investigative Ophthalmology and Visual Science, 27*, 538–543.

Wolfe, J. M., & Roorda, J. E. (1990). *Long-term visual aftereffects: The by-products of error-correcting mechanisms?* Unpublished manuscript.

Yasuda, K. (1978). Color aftereffects contingent on MacKay complementary regular patterns. *Japanese Psychological Research, 20*, 115–123.

Zeki, S. (1990). Parallelism and functional specialization in human visual cortex. In *The Brain, Cold Spring Harbor Symposia on Quantitative Biology* (Vol. LV, pp. 651–661). London: Cold Spring Harbor Laboratory Press.

Zhou, H., & May, J. G. (1993). Effects of spatial filtering and lack of effects of visual imagery on pattern-contingent color aftereffects. *Perception & Psychophysics, 53*, 145–149.

3   Perception of rotated two-dimensional and three-dimensional objects and visual shapes

Pierre Jolicoeur and G. Keith Humphrey

Much of the empirical work focusing on the perception of rotated visual shapes has centered on resolving an ongoing theoretical debate in which there have been two poles. At one extreme is the position that representations of visual shape are essentially viewpoint independent. In this view, regardless of the orientation, size, or location of the shape with respect to the viewer, the visual system constructs or activates the same underlying representation. Object constancy is achieved by virtue of the nature of the underlying representation (e.g., Corballis, 1988; Marr, 1982). At the other extreme is the position that representations of shape are viewpoint specific, with different representations resulting from changes in the orientation or size of the form (although translation invariance – invariance across different retinal locations – is usually assumed) (e.g., Kolers & Perkins, 1969a, 1969b; Tarr & Pinker, 1989). In this view, object constancy is achieved in two ways: by the storage of multiple representations and, in some accounts, by the use of transformation or normalization processes. Recent theoretical work has included various hybrid notions, but the distinction between orientation- and size-invariant representations versus representations with viewpoint specificity has remained as a central issue that still provides the impetus for contemporary research on object and form perception. In this chapter, we provide an overview of work on form and object perception, much of which bears on the theoretical debate just outlined.

Memory: Two-dimensional shapes

Most of the early work on the perception of rotated shape focused on two-dimensional shapes and used methodologies based on memory and on transfer of learning. The most well-known work of this type is probably that of Rock (see Rock, 1956, 1973; Rock & Heimer, 1957). This type of experiment has two phases: a learning phase and a testing phase. In the learning phase, subjects were shown drawings of simple two-dimensional forms. In the testing phase, the subjects were asked to discriminate between forms that were presented in the learning phase (usually called *old forms*) and forms that had never been seen before (usually called *new forms*). In addition, some of the old forms were

69

Table 3.1. *Mean percentage of "old" responses in Dearborn's shape recognition experiment for repeated shapes, depending on the orientation of the test figure, and for "new" figures.*

	Orientation of test figure					
	0°	± 90°	180°	180° flip	Mirrored	New
N = 9	59%[a]	38%	51%	32%	46%	30%
N = 7	53%	28%	43%	30½%	42%	22%

[a]The percent correct at the bottom of column A of Dearborn's Table II (70%) does not correspond with the results in that column. We assume that the data in the column were correct and that the average percent listed at the bottom of his table was an error.
Source: These results were derived from Tables II and III of Dearborn (1899).

transformed from one view to another across the learning and recognition phases. For example, many of the experiments reviewed in Rock (1973) involve experiments in which the transformation is a rotation of the form on the page (or tachistoscope card). Several interesting results have been obtained using this general procedure. The most relevant for our present purposes was that the recognition accuracy (percent correct recognition of old forms) was significantly lower for forms that were rotated than for forms that were presented at the same orientation as in the learning phase. This general finding is quite robust and has been reported by several other researchers (e.g., Braine, 1965; Dearborn, 1899; Gibson & Robinson, 1935).

Consider the experiment described by Dearborn (1899). In the learning phase, ink blots (never seen before) were shown to subjects. In the test phase, old and new ink blots were presented and subjects were asked to decide whether they had been seen before or not. The old ink blots were presented in a number of different conditions: Some were presented at the same orientation as in the learning phase (0°), some were rotated 90° clockwise or counterclockwise (±90°), some were rotated 180°, some were flipped 180° (rotated out of the page, which is equivalent to a 180° rotation in the image plane plus a left–right reversal), and some were left-right mirror reversed. The results are shown in Table 3.1. Two of Dearborn's nine observers had high false alarm rates (they frequently responded "old" to new shapes). The results without these two observers (N = 7) are also displayed in Table 3.1.

The results have several interesting characteristics. First, any transformation of the shape between the learning phase and the testing phase resulted in a drop in recognition memory. Second, the effect of rotation in the image plane was nonmonotonic. Memory was better for a 180° rotation than for a 90° rotation, although a 180° flip did produce the worst performance. Third, left–right mirror reversal also produced an appreciable decrement in recognition memory. It is clear that both rotations and mirror imaging had large effects on memory.

The main empirical conclusion from these experiments is that usually there is a memory decrement when the orientation of the shape shown at the time of the memory test is different from that shown in the learning phase. The weakest theoretical implication that necessarily follows from these results is that some part of the memory system or of the perceptual system must be sensitive to the orientation of visual shapes. On the other hand, performance is well above chance, even when there is a decrement in performance. Thus, theories of object and form perception must account for both the failures to recognize and the reduced but successful recognition following transformations.

Further experiments by Rock and Heimer (1957), in which the tilt of the subject's head was manipulated, are consistent with the view that the orientation of the shape relative to the environmental upright is an important determinant of the representation of the shape. In one experiment, for example, subjects viewed shapes with the head upright in the learning phase and with the head tilted 90° (clockwise, for example) during the testing phase. At the time of the test, some shapes were presented rotated 90° (also clockwise) and some were presented in the same orientation as during the learning phase. Because of the subject's head tilt, shapes tested environmentally upright were now rotated 90° (counterclockwise) relative to retinal directions. The results depended on whether the subjects were informed that some shapes had been rotated from the environmental upright. If the subjects were uninformed, recognition was better for environmentally upright (but retinally rotated) shapes, 51% correct old responses, than if the shapes were retinally upright (but rotated in the environment), only 37% correct. In contrast, if the subjects were informed that the shapes could be rotated, the recognition of environmentally upright (but retinally rotated) shapes was 57% correct, but the recognition of retinally upright shapes (rotated in the environment) was now 69% correct, which was significantly better than 57%.

Rock and Heimer (1957) argued that shapes were encoded in the visual system at two different levels of representation. One level was postulated to preserve a description of the shape encoded in retinal coordinates. Rock (1974) calls this the *retinal factor*. The other level was believed to encode the phenomenal appearance of the shape, which, according to Rock, critically depends on the relationship between the shape and a perceptual frame of reference. Rock calls this aspect of shape perception the *assignment-of-direction factor*. According to Rock, the frame of reference (usually the environmental upright) defines the directions of the top and bottom of visual shapes (in the absence of knowledge to the contrary). Furthermore, visual shapes are described relative to these special directions (top and bottom). If a shape is encoded while viewed for the first time in a particular orientation, the portion of the shape that is near the top of the frame of reference will be considered the top of the shape, which will result in a particular description (or phenomenal appearance) of the shape. If, at a later time, the same shape is shown, but rotated with respect to the frame of reference, a different part of the shape will be taken as the top and a different perceptual description of the shape will be constructed. This new description will be more likely to mismatch with the previously stored representation than if the shape had been presented in the same orientation, which results in a decrement in memory performance (Rock, 1973). In this view, the perception of a shape is not simply a function of the internal geometry of the shape. It is a joint function of that geometry and of the relationship between the shape and a perceptual frame of reference.

More recently, Rock and Nijhawan (1989) have demonstrated that memory for rotated shapes (subjects not informed) is superior when there is a match in retinal orientations if the shapes were encoded under conditions of divided attention, in contrast to the results of Rock and Heimer (1957). When the shapes were attended during the learning phase, however, the results paralleled those of Rock and Heimer (1957) described earlier. These results are consistent with Rock's claim that there are two levels of representation, one of which is tied to retinal coordinates (see also Steinfeld, 1970).

Interestingly, similar results have been obtained with a manipulation of size between the learning and memory testing phases of a recognition memory experiment (Jolicoeur, 1987). Subjects were shown shapes (abstract line drawings and line drawings of objects) that differed in size across the learning and testing phases of a recognition memory experiment. Recognition memory was faster and more accurate when the test shapes matched the size of the shapes, as shown in the learning phase (see also Biederman & Cooper, 1992). These effects are based on memory for the perceived size of the object rather than on retinal size (Milliken & Jolicoeur, 1992). The perceived size is close to the objective size when there are sufficient cues to perceive the distance between the viewer and the shape. This evidence converges with that from experiments in which orientation was manipulated in suggesting that some aspect of memory for shape is sensitive to the size and orientation in which shapes have been learned.

Recognition of objects rotated in depth

The experiments discussed in the preceding section on memory for two-dimensional shapes examined two-dimensional shapes rotated in the image plane. Several similar experiments have since been conducted using three-dimensional forms. Furthermore, in most cases, the three-dimensional forms were rotated about the vertical axis rather than along the line of sight (two-dimensional shapes are usually rotated in the image plane or about the line of sight). One important reason for investigating rotations in depth about the vertical axis is that although such rotations change the retinal image, they do not alter the top-to-bottom ordering of the parts and attributes of the form, nor do they alter the top-bottom spatial relations between the parts and attributes of the form. For example, Rock (e.g., 1973) argued that the top–bottom directions are most important in influencing the phenomenal appearance of the shape (i.e., the nature of the internal representation leading to the perception of shape). Biederman (1985, 1987, 1988) proposed a similar idea, but he went further and suggested that changes in viewpoint that leave the top–bottom spatial relations between object parts intact should have no effect on perceptual identification.

A large proportion of the research on the representation and recognition of three-dimensional transformations of objects have used objects that the subjects have not seen before. The use of unfamiliar objects allows one to manipulate the characteristics of the objects and to control the subject's experience with the objects. In particular, unlike work involving natural objects, work with artificial materials allows one to control the views that are shown to the subjects during the learning phase of the experiments. Rock and his colleagues (Rock & DiVita, 1987; Rock, DiVita, & Barbeito, 1981) performed some of the first research on the recognition of novel three-dimensional objects that were rotated in depth between learning and testing. They examined recognition using three-dimensional wire-frame objects. The objects were randomly curved wires. Such wire-frame objects allow one to study three-dimensional shape recognition with very limited self-occlusion of object parts as they are presented in different views. The objects were viewed binocularly during learning and test. During test trials the subjects indicated whether they recognized the object from the learning phase. In these experiments it was shown that when the objects were seen from different orientations (Rock et al., 1981) or positions (Rock & DiVita, 1987), they were readily recognized if they had the same retinal projection. If, however, the retinal projection was altered by a change in three-dimensional orientation or position, there was an appreciable drop in recognition accuracy.

The results indicated that representation of three-dimensional novel objects is viewer centered in that recognition is a function of the match between the retinal projection of an object when it is first encountered and when it is seen again. In another study (Rock, Wheeler, & Tudor, 1989), subjects were asked to imagine how unfamiliar wire-frame objects would look from different positions and were required to recognize them. Subjects reported being unable to perform this task unless they used analytic strategies such as isolating features and basing recognition on these features. It was concluded that object-centered representations of unfamiliar objects were not spontaneously achieved.

Research by Bülthoff and Edelman (1992; Bülthoff, Edelman, & Sklar, 1991; Edelman & Bülthoff, 1992) has also examined generalization to novel views of novel objects rotated in depth. Most of this research used three-dimensional tubelike objects (Bülthoff & Edelman, 1992; Edelman & Bülthoff, 1992), although similar results have been reported for three-dimensional "amoeba-like" objects (Bülthoff et al., 1991). As with wire-frame objects used by Rock and his colleagues, there is very limited self-occlusion of the tubelike objects as they are presented in different views. In one set of experiments (Bülthoff & Edelman, 1992), subjects were trained with two different views of an object and tested for recognition of novel views of the trained objects among new objects. Some of the novel views were within the range of the two trained orientations, and others were outside this range. Views within the range could be achieved by rotating the object from one of the trained orientations to the other. Views outside the range could not be achieved this way. Recognition accuracy was much better for novel views within the range of the trained views than for those outside this range. Bülthoff and Edelman argued that new views of objects can be recognized by an "interpolation" process, but only if they can be generated from a linear combination of the stored two-dimensional views. In addition, views outside the range but along a trajectory that extrapolated linearly from the trained views were recognized with higher probability than views that deviated along a path orthogonal to the set of views that could be generated by linear combinations of the stored views. The results provided support for Bülthoff and Edelman's interpolation model. Other research on generalization to novel views shows that even with rich surface, motion, and stereo information, recognition is strongly viewpoint dependent (Edelman & Bülthoff, 1992).

Edelman and Bülthoff (1992; see also Cavanagh, 1991) suggest that, at least for subordinate-level object recognition (see the later discussion), three-dimensional objects are represented as a collection of specific views where each view corresponds to a snapshot of the object taken from a particular perspective. The whole collection of views has a structure because the views that belong together, presumably as a result of being seen in close temporal succession, are more closely associated with each other (see Edelman & Weinshall, 1991).

The research results just reviewed provide evidence for viewpoint-dependent frameworks for three-dimensional object recognition. Other research, however, suggests that three-dimensional object recognition performance depends on viewpoint to a much lesser extent (Biederman, 1987; Biederman & Gerhardstein, 1993; Gerhardstein & Biederman, 1991). One difference between the experiments purporting to show viewpoint dependence and those purporting to show viewpoint independence concerns the objects used as stimuli. One question we can ask about the objects used in the studies showing viewpoint dependence is as follows: Are the objects used in these studies representative of the objects we normally recognize in daily life? Do they activate our normal encoding and recognition strategies? On a global scale, the objects used by these experimenters had an unusual structure lacking symmetry and other regularities. Also, the wire objects of Rock and his colleagues had no extended surfaces, thereby depriving the observer of information such as that obtained from shading and other sources of surface information, which, according to Marr and Nishihara (1978), may be vital to the formation of an object-centered representation. Rock and DiVita (1987) have argued that we encounter such objects as clouds and rocks that are similar in geometric properties to their wire objects. But we are rarely required to recognize different rocks or clouds; therefore, the results obtained by Rock and his associates may not be indicative of how we recognize objects with a more readily representable structure.

In addition to the problems mentioned in the preceding paragraph, a crucial aspect of the studies showing viewpoint dependence is that the objects used in each study were very similar to each other in their basic "part-structure." Biederman and Gerhardstein (1993) have pointed out that many of the studies that have obtained strong view-dependent results have used objects in which the stimuli are not distinguishable by basic object part type or by first-order relations such as "top-of" or "side-connected." They suggest that to recognize objects in these studies, one must make difficult subordinate-level distinctions (see Jolicoeur, Gluck, & Kosslyn, 1984; Rosch, Mervis, Gray, Johnson, & Boyes-Braem, 1976) similar to discriminating among different kinds of sparrows, for example. Such distinctions may depend on attention to small details that change appearance or become occluded with depth rotations (Edelman, 1992). A viewpoint-invariant theory such as Biederman's (1987) deals with entry-point level categorizations (Jolicoeur et al., 1984; Rosch et al., 1976), such as distinguishing between a cup and a telephone or between a sparrow and a penguin, in which the object parts and global shape differ. According to this approach, a more appropriate test of orientation invariance for the recognition of novel objects would employ a set of objects that are readily distinguishable by their parts and do not depend on local features or details.

Humphrey and Khan (1992) addressed the issues of object selection discussed in the preceding paragraphs. Their study used a large set of novel objects. The objects were constructed using a heterogeneous set of parts. The parts were simple, regular volumes similar to Biederman's (1987) geons and Marr and Nishihara's (1978) generalized cones. Overall, the objects were regular in shape; most were symmetrical about the major axis and possessed an axis of elongation. The objects were made of clay and were painted matte white. Some examples are shown in Figure 3.1. In several experiments, the subjects were trained with one view of the objects and then tested for their recognition of familiar and novel views produced by rotating the objects about the y-axis. One experiment used slide projections of the objects. The results indicated that the representation of the objects seen during training was viewpoint specific, as recognition of objects in novel orientations 40° or 80° from the trained orientation was relatively poor. The error rate increased markedly as the objects were rotated in depth away from the trained orientation. In another experiment, subjects were shown the real objects under monocular or binocular viewing. Again there was

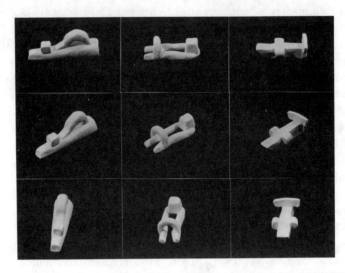

Figure 3.1. Examples of the stimuli used by Humphrey and Khan (1992). After Humphrey and Khan (1992).

a high error rate indicating limited generalization to novel views, although in some respects performance was better under binocular than monocular viewing (see also Edelman & Bülthoff, 1992). Overall, the results indicated that subjects formed viewpoint-specific representations of the objects during training. These results are shown in Figure 3.2. In the top panel, response times are shown to be an increasing monotonic function of the angular difference between the view shown at the time of testing and the view shown in the training phase. The accuracy scores shown in the bottom panel have the same general pattern, with smaller angular differences associated with higher accuracy.

The results of Humphrey and Khan (1992) question the argument that viewpoint-specific representations depend on the subject's ability to make subordinate-level distinctions, as the objects used were quite dissimilar. Gerhardstein and Biederman (1991), however, have found results differing from those of Humphrey and Khan. They found that the effects for depth rotation of "nonsense" objects constructed of geons were very small. Example stimuli are shown in Figure 3.3. The most likely account of the differences across studies is that Gerhardstein and Biederman measured effects on repetition priming rather than direct identification time. A detailed discussion of priming measures is reserved for a later section in this chapter (titled "Priming"). It is possible, however, that the difference in results also depended on stimulus differences. The objects created by Biederman and Gerhardstein were line drawings with very distinctive geons. Humphrey and Khan used gray-scale images or real objects, and it is

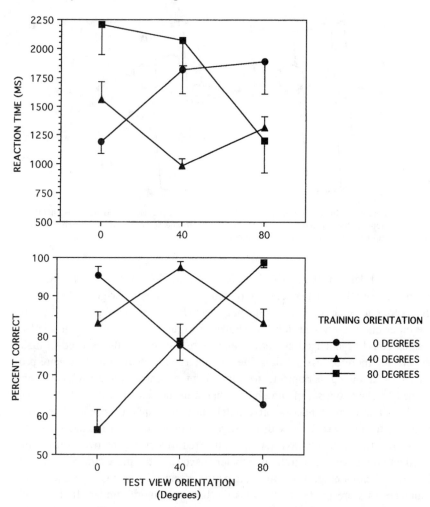

Figure 3.2. Results of Humphrey and Khan (1992). After Humphrey and Khan (1992).

possible that the geonlike parts were more uniform than those used by Gerhardstein and Biederman. Furthermore, Gerhardstein and Biederman's results
were obtained for rotations in which the part descriptions were the same after
rotation but not when the part descriptions differed. That is, for some objects,
a rotation in depth caused a change in the parts that were visible, and for these
objects naming time did increase.

Edelman (1992) has approached the issue of subordinate- versus basic-level
distinctions in terms of the similarity of objects at the two levels. In general,
objects at a subordinate level are more visually similar than those at a basic

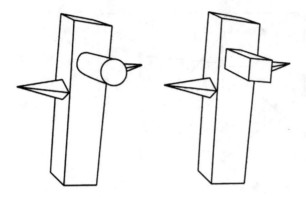

Figure 3.3. Illustration of the type of stimuli used by Biederman and Gerhardstein (1993). Some stimuli differed only by rotation in depth and some, as shown here, by a change in one of the smaller parts of the object.

level (see Edelman 1991, 1992, for discussion). In psychophysical research, Edelman (1992) used two classes of animal-like, computer-generated objects that belong to separate basic-level categories: One class resembled monkeys and the other class resembled dogs, as shown in Figure 3.4. The objects in the two classes could be changed smoothly, and these changes could be used to make the classes more or less similar. The exemplars of objects in a class were produced by allowing parameters to vary about a central value. Subjects were trained to classify a set of the objects that were presented in a limited number of views that corresponded approximately to a three-quarter frontal view. After training, testing was done with the objects rotated in depth around either the vertical or the horizontal axis. As hypothesized, the closer the two distributions for the two classes were in the parameter space (i.e., the more similar they were by the measures employed), the greater the effect of a change in view in that more errors were made for the classes that were more similar. If the object classes were far apart in the parameter space, the effect of depth rotation on the classification task was reduced even if the two object classes had the same parts (geons). Thus a part difference is not necessary for such generalization if the object classes are widely separated in the space. A further experiment showed that the use of different parts did not guarantee viewpoint-independent classification if the two object classes were close in the parameter space. Simulations using an interpolating classifier that represents three-dimensional objects by a collection of two-dimensional views (see also Poggio & Edelman, 1990) produced many results similar to those obtained psychophysically.

The type of experiment conducted by Edelman (1992) is very promising in that one might be able to carry out more controlled psychophysical research on object recognition than has been done in the past given the possibility of

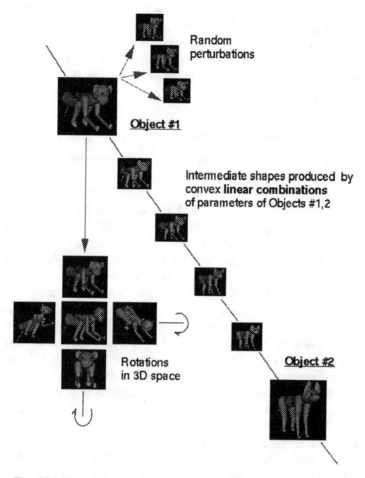

Figure 3.4. Illustration of the stimuli created by Edelman (1992) showing a prototypical monkey (upper left) and a prototypical dog (lower right), along with several exemplars along the diagonal that have parameter values between the two prototypes. Courtesy of Shimon Edelman.

smoothly varying objects and classes. Edelman (1992) cautions, however, that the results were obtained with only two artificially created stimulus classes. Thus, it is unclear how the results will generalize to other object classes. There are many other issues discussed by Edelman concerning, for example, the nature of the psychological space used to represent objects.

Much recent research on the recognition of unfamiliar views of novel three-dimensional objects demonstrates consistently that the representation of these objects is viewpoint dependent. There is some question, however, about the dependency of the results on using objects that are structurally similar. This is an issue that clearly warrants further investigation. It should be noted that even if strong viewpoint dependency is found only when the objects to be discriminated are similar, this is still an important issue in object perception. As has been pointed out before (e.g., Marr & Nishihara, 1978), any adequate model of object recognition must account for object discrimination both within and between classes of objects.

Identification time: Two-dimensional objects

Another way to study the nature of the process and representations involved in the perception of rotated shapes is to measure the time required to achieve recognition at the time of testing. Many experiments of this sort have been used to argue that the representation of simple shapes is orientation invariant and probably based on feature extraction (Corballis, Macadie, Crotty, & Beale, 1985; Corballis & Nagourney, 1978; Corballis, Zbrodoff, Shetzer, & Butler, 1978; Eley, 1982; Koriat & Norman, 1989b; White, 1980; Young, Palef, & Logan, 1980). In the experiments of Corballis and his colleagues, subjects were asked to name or to make simple decisions requiring identification (e.g., letter-digit categorization). Typically, the stimulus set had a small number of stimuli, often consisting of three letters and three digits. The stimuli were presented multiple times to each subject, in different orientations, and the main dependent variable was the time required to perform the task, measured from the presentation of the target stimulus until the subject's response. The finding across most of these experiments is that orientation effects on identification time are either quite small or nil, although there is sometimes a significant effect (e.g., see Corballis et al., 1978).

Results such as those of Eley, or of Young et al., demonstrate that subjects are able to learn to extract orientation-invariant attributes that can distinguish between a small set of repeated stimuli. As such, these results show that the human visual system can perform discriminations based on a small set of orientation-invariant features and use this approach to achieve object constancy. Given that we are able to see the simpler constituents of more complex shapes, it is to be expected that subjects would make use of this ability when possible. What is less clear, however, is the degree to which we use orientation-invariant features or attributes in less constrained situations in which there are more stimuli and less opportunity to learn the distinguishing attributes necessary for successful discrimination of one stimulus from the others.

It is easy to show that the orientation-invariant feature route cannot be the whole solution even for stimuli as simple as letters and digits. For example, Jolicoeur, Snow, and Murray (1987) demonstrated that the time needed to identify alphanumeric characters in fact does vary systematically with greater rotations of the character from its usual (upright) orientation. Jolicoeur et al. asked subjects to name rotated uppercase letters as quickly as possible. The time needed to name the characters increased approximately linearly as the orientation of the letters departed more from zero degrees (upright). The magnitude of the effect was on the order of 50 to 75 ms.

Why is there a discrepancy between the results of Jolicoeur et al. (1987) and those of many previous researchers? One answer is that Jolicoeur et al. did not preexpose the experimental stimuli to the subjects (during practice trials, for example), and the stimuli were repeated only a small number of times during the course of the experiment. In contrast, previous experiments in which small or null results were reported typically displayed the small number of stimuli used before the experiment proper and/or displayed them numerous times during the experimental trials. Thus, subjects had an opportunity to learn which attributes could be used to discriminate the shapes from one another. In the absence of this specific learning experience, easily measurable orientations effects are observed. Thus, although subjects can quickly learn to rely on orientation-invariant attributes (especially when the stimulus set is very small), one should not conclude that the results provide a general characterization of the nature of the internal representations of visual shape or of the perceptual processes that support visual recognition. Additional evidence for the orientation-sensitive nature of the representation of alphanumeric characters is presented in the section titled "Perceptual Identification."

The results from experiments showing null effects of orientation demonstrate the opportunistic nature of human pattern recognition. When a small stimulus set is used and when the stimuli are repeated, subjects tend to focus on a small set of distinguishing attributes, which often leads to orientation invariance. A similar phenomenon occurs with more complex forms, such as line drawings of objects (Snodgrass & Vanderwart, 1980). For example, Jolicoeur (1985) demonstrated that the time needed to name rotated line drawings is sharply affected by the orientation of the object. The function relating naming time to rotation, however, was not linear over the whole range of orientations. Subjects were tested with stimuli at 0°, 60°, 120°, 180°, 240°, and 300° of clockwise rotation in the image plane. Between 0° and ± 120°,[1] naming times increased linearly and the magnitude of the effect was between 100 and 200 ms. Between ± 120° and 180°, however, the results were variable, sometimes showing a reduction in naming times, sometimes showing only a small increase. An example of such results can be seen in Figure 3.5. It was clear that the observed naming times for upside-down objects were less than what would have been expected from a linear extrapolation of the results obtained for the other orientations. Similar results have been reported by Maki (1986). These results were obtained for trials in which the object was displayed for the first time.

Both Jolicoeur (1985) and Maki (1986) found that naming times became less strongly affected by misorientation of the objects on subsequent trials. This at-

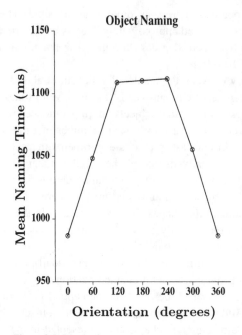

Figure 3.5. Results from experiments of Jolicoeur, Keillor, and Ingleton (1992) based on naming responses of 288 subjects for 120 objects drawn from the Snodgrass and Vanderwart (1980) set.

tenuation of the orientation effect with repeated presentation was found to be specific to the objects shown rather than due to a growing general ability to identify rotated objects (Jolicoeur, 1985). Now the question arose as to what was mediating the attenuation of the orientation effect. Phrased another way, what was producing increasing degrees of object constancy across changes in orientation? Two possibilities were considered by Jolicoeur (1985), but the results at that time were not sufficient to decide the issue one way or the other. One possibility was that subjects learned to associate particular orientation-invariant attributes or features with some of the objects and later came to rely on these attributes in order to name the objects in subsequent blocks of trials. Another possibility was that subjects were storing multiple views of the object as they were presented from block to block in the experiment (each object was seen in a different orientation in each new block). In subsequent blocks, according to this model, subjects could normalize the input stimulus to any one of the previously stored representations rather than to a representation of the upright object.

Tarr and Pinker (1989; see also Tarr, 1989 described later) have demonstrated the viability of the second possibility in a number of elegant experiments. In their experiments, subjects first learned to identify a small number of stimuli (i.e., three). The stimuli had very similar features, but they were nonetheless clearly discriminable. The stimuli were initially learned in a small set of fixed orientations. Errors were infrequent, and the main dependent variable was identification time. With practice, identification time at all original orientations became equivalent. Then subjects were tested with a much larger set of orientations, with a fine sampling of the range of possible orientations. In a nutshell, the results were that identification times were fast with the originally learned orientations and increased (approximately linearly) as the orientation of the test stimulus departed further from one of the learned orientations. The magnitude of the orientation effects was not out of range plausibly to be due to a mental rotation process (Shepard & Cooper, 1982; see also the section titled "Normalization Operations").

There is abundant, clear-cut evidence that the time needed to identify objects often increases sharply with rotation from upright (e.g., Jolicoeur, 1985, 1988; Jolicoeur & Milliken, 1989; McMullen & Jolicoeur, 1990). Furthermore, the results of Tarr and Pinker (1989) demonstrate that human pattern recognition can use multiple orientation-dependent representations plus transformations to achieve object constancy. On the other hand, the results of Corballis and his colleagues, White, Eley, and others demonstrate that shapes are sometimes discriminated by relying on a small number of distinguishing features.

What needs to be established, then, are the conditions under which each of these different sets of mechanisms and representations are used. Murray, Jolicoeur, McMullen, and Ingleton (1993) tackled the issue of the mechanism mediating the attenuation of the effects of orientation with repeated naming of objects. The logic of the experiments was as follows: If the attenuation is mediated by the storage of a viewpoint-dependent representation corresponding to a particular prior stimulus, then the relationship between the orientation of the test stimulus and that of the prior stimulus should determine how much attenuation is observed. Consider a specific example. Suppose that the first presentation of an object is one that is rotated 60°. Furthermore, suppose that the second presentation of the object is at either 120° or at 240°.[2] Now consider the predictions made by the hypothesis that the attenuation is due to normalization to a previous view. The rotational distance of the object from 0° is the same in both cases (e.g., 120°). However, the stimulus shown at 120° is only 60° away from the postulated representation stored following the first presentation of the object, whereas the stimulus shown at 240° is 120° away. The prediction is clear-cut: The stimulus at 120°, which has a potential representation 60° away along the path of rotation toward the upright, should be named more quickly than the stimulus shown at 240°. The results were equally clear-cut: There was no difference in naming time for these two types of trials. However, in both cases, there was a substantially reduced orientation effect compared with that of objects that had not been seen before. The conclusion is that, for these stimuli, the attenuation in the magnitude of the orientation effect was not due to the prior storage of an orientation-specific representation. Although such a mechanism is clearly possible, given the demonstrations of Tarr and Pinker (1989), it is not the mechanism that mediates the attenuation observed when subjects name rotated common objects.

The suggestion is that the attenuation is mediated by attributes or features that are either orientation invariant or, at least, are less affected by orientation than the original stimulus. This line of reasoning led Jolicoeur (1990) to suggest that there are two routes to object recognition (see also Humphreys & Riddoch, 1984). One route was postulated to rely on orientation-specific representations, plus normalization processes, and another route to rely on feature-based mechanisms in which the features are relatively orientation invariant. In this view, in the absence of context or prior knowledge about the stimuli, the representations used for identification are orientation dependent. Most objects have a predominant orientation in the environment (Biederman, 1987). These objects are likely to have a principal representation that corresponds with the usual orientation of the object. When a test stimulus departs significantly from the usual orientation, a normalization process is required to achieve a match between the input and the memory representation. There is reasonable evidence that mental rotation (Shepard & Cooper, 1982) may be the process of normalization (e.g., Jolicoeur, 1985, 1987; Tarr & Pinker, 1989; see also the section titled "Normalization Operations").

Alternatively, because common objects will have been seen from a variety of vantage points, it is likely that there are a number of representations in memory. If so, it is likely that the representations corresponding with the upright views are more easily accessible than those for other views. However, the existence of additional representations could account for the fact that the magnitude of the orientation effect is sometimes slightly smaller for the identification of rotated objects relative to that observed in tasks requiring left–right discriminations (and which presumably require mental rotation on most trials; see Jolicoeur, 1988).

Perceptual identification

Further evidence for the orientation-sensitive nature of the representation of letters and digits can be found in the results of Jolicoeur and Landau (1984). In these experiments, letters were exposed briefly, followed immediately by a pattern mask. The dependent measure was the error rate in the unspeeded naming of the letter following the trial. The error rate increased sharply and linearly as the letters were rotated from 0° to 180°. Furthermore, unlike the results of experiments in which identification time is the dependent variable, there was no reduction in the magnitude of the orientation effect with additional practice. Similar results (unpublished) have been obtained recently in Jolicoeur's laboratory with masked presentations of rotated Snodgrass and Vanderwart (1980) line drawings. Both sets of results show that the representations mediating perceptual identification under data-limited conditions are sensitive to rotation in the image plane for both simple and more complex stimuli.

What is less clear, however, is why practice effects are substantial in experiments measuring identification time under unlimited viewing conditions, whereas practice effects are negligible in experiments measuring error rates under limited viewing conditions. One possibility is that the brief and masked presentations of the stimuli make it especially difficult for subjects to encode both the features of the stimuli and the spatial relation between features. Perhaps the reduced viewing conditions force the subjects to rely on a feature-based strategy from the start, which results in little or no change across trials, in contrast to what is found in response time paradigms. More research will be required to understand these differences between reaction time and masking experiments.

Identification time: Three-dimensional shapes

Other research is also consistent with the formation of a viewer-centered representation of novel three-dimensional objects. Tarr (1989) used computer-generated shapes rotated in depth about the x, y, and z axes. The objects were composed of cubes formed into arms of varying length at right angles to each other. In many respects, the objects were three-dimensional versions of those used by Tarr and Pinker (1989) and were similar to the objects used by Shepard and Metzler (1971) in their initial mental rotation research. As in the research of Tarr and Pinker (1989), subjects first learned names for a small set of objects seen in specific orientations and then, during testing, named the objects as quickly as possible. The results replicated Tarr and Pinker's (1989) results in that the time needed to name unfamiliar orientations increased with the distance from the nearest familiar orientation. Tarr concluded, like Tarr and Pinker (1989), that the results support the notion that the visual system stores multiple view-specific representations of objects, and that novel views are normalized by a mental rotation process.

Humphrey and Khan (1992) also found that as the views of the objects presented during testing deviated from the trained depth orientation, there was not only an increase in error rate (described earlier) but also a reliable increase in recognition time for those objects that were correctly recognized as having been seen during training. For the conditions in which subjects viewed real objects (not slide projections) during training and testing, there was a monotonic increase in recognition latency with increasing misorientation of the object relative to the trained view.

Canonical views

Some views of three-dimensional objects are better for recognition than others. The term *canonical view* was introduced by Palmer, Rosch, and Chase (1981) to refer to views that were somehow the best or most representative views of objects. In a series of experiments they showed the importance of canonical views for three-dimensional object perception and recognition. Palmer and colleagues found that for many everyday objects such as a horse, a shoe, or a car, the canonical view was approximately a three-quarter view. In one experiment, subjects were shown 12 photographs of objects in 12 perspective views. They were required to judge how good or typical the pictures were of the objects. In another experiment, subjects were asked to imagine objects and to report the amounts of front, back, side, and top surfaces that were visible in the mental image. A further experiment required subjects to become familiar with the objects, then to imagine each object and to photograph it in the view that best depicted the image. Correlations among all of the tasks in the study were quite high and indicated that these various tasks measured the same underlying variable related to canonicalness. This hypothesis was supported further by an identification task in which subjects named objects more quickly and accurately when the objects were in their canonical view than when they were in noncanonical views.

The finding that everyday objects are recognized more readily when seen from a canonical viewpoint, and that this viewpoint is stable and consistent across subjects, is important. It suggests that the long-term representation of objects is not view independent and that there may be properties of objects that are naturally emphasized in long-term representations. According to Palmer et al. (1981), an object's canonical perspective provides better access to the internal representation of the object than do other perspectives because it is the view that contains the most salient information about the object. On this account, the surface visibility of an object is maximized in the canonical perspective and is consequently critical to object recognition.

Cutzu and Edelman (1992) have suggested that a canonical view is a "minimally deformed view." Their idea is similar to that of Palmer et al. (1981) but has been developed more formally. One can consider an object to be a set of points in three-dimensional space. This set of points can define a set of interfeature distances in three-dimensional space. Any projection of a three-dimensional object onto a two-dimensional surface will necessarily deform some of these interfeature distances. Cutzu and Edelman suggest that the "goodness" of a two-dimensional projection of a three-dimensional object can be interpreted in terms of the amount of deformation in the image. The smaller the amount of deformation in the interfeature distances, the better the view is. The canonical view, according to this account, is the least deformed view, which corresponds with the projections identified as canonical by Palmer et al. (1981) in most cases.

One potential problem with the Palmer et al. (1981) study, however, is the use of familiar objects. Familiar objects may be encountered frequently in a limited number of perspectives because of the way they are used or seen. Tarr and Pinker (1989) have hypothesized that the storage of an object in a particular orientation depends on the frequency of encounter. That is, the more often an object is seen in a certain orientation, the more likely it is to be stored in long-term memory in that orientation. It follows that the use of familiar objects could confound the results such that orientations in which familiar objects are best recognized may be those that contain the most surface information, but these orientations may be also the ones most frequently encountered. It is difficult to determine which of the two variables contributes most to recognition. Thus Palmer et al.'s results may reflect the frequency of encounter of a given object in a particular view. Indeed, Palmer et al. suggest that familiarity of different views and the relation of these views to function may play a substantial role in determining the importance of different views.

Evidence that canonical views arise with unfamiliar objects has been reported in the face recognition literature. Thomas, Perrett, Davis, and Harries (1991) exposed subjects to videotapes of model clay heads undergoing rotation about the y axis. In a recognition task, they found that subjects responded fastest to heads presented in a 45° view (three-quarter profile). An advantage for the three-quarter view in recognition of unfamiliar faces has also been found in other studies (Bruce, Valentine, & Baddeley, 1987; Harries, Perrett, & Lavender, 1991; Logie, Baddeley, & Woodhead, 1987).

Although the finding that a 45° orientation of the face leads to more rapid recognition of unfamiliar faces is consistent with the findings of Palmer et al. (1981) and could be taken to indicate that such views of faces are canonical, this is true only for unfamiliar faces. There is no advantage for a three-quarter profile over frontal views of familiar faces, although both of these views are better than full-profile views (Bruce, 1988). Perhaps familiar faces are encountered more frequently in frontal views than in profile. Faces as a class of stimuli are very familiar, and because all faces are structurally similar, they may invoke encoding strategies that may not be used in encoding other objects. For example, identifying faces likely requires subordinate-level discrimination in which metric properties of features and the relations among features may be crucial. We should be cautious, then, in generalizing results obtained with faces to other objects, particularly when entry-point level or basic level distinctions are involved.

Edelman and Bülthoff (1992) studied the emergence of canonical views using unfamiliar tubelike objects. They first exposed their subjects to a moving sequence of the objects and then tested their recognition of static views of the objects seen during training among a set of similar nontarget objects. All of the test views of the target objects had been seen in the training sequence equally often. Nevertheless, they found that canonical views of novel three-dimensional objects evolved. The canonical views were views that yielded faster response times and lower error rates than other views. Because all test views had been seen equally often, the emergence of the canonical views could not be attributed to the amount of prior exposure to specific views of the objects. Repeating the experiment such that the same views were seen again and again eliminated much of the variation in ease of recognition of different views of the objects, demonstrating that frequency of exposure is also an important determinant of speed of recognition.

Cutzu and Edelman (1992) also examined the emergence of canonical views with tubelike objects. They used training and testing methods similar to those used by Edelman and Bülthoff (1992) and found that subjects did form canonical views of objects. The particular views that were canonical, however, varied to a great extent among the subjects. This contrasts with the wide agreement among subjects on the canonical view of everyday objects found by Palmer et al. (1981). Cutzu and Edelman suggested that the subjects in their experiment tended to remember best those views of objects in which they perceived relatively invariant shapes that were similar to familiar objects such as geometric figures or characters. The particular features that reminded the subjects of such shapes varied across the subjects in the study.

Another approach to the nature of representative or canonical views has been used by Perrett and his colleagues (Perrett & Harries, 1988; Perrett, Harries, & Looker, 1992). In their research, subjects are free to explore an object from different viewpoints and the time spent inspecting different views is measured. For example, Perrett et al. (1992) showed subjects an arbitrary machine tooled object and instructed them to view the object so as to form a clear understanding of its shape and structure. The time spent in looking at different views was recorded. Interestingly, more time was spent in looking at the plan views in which the line of sight was approximately perpendicular to the surfaces or faces of the object (see also Harries et al., 1991; Perrett & Harries, 1988). One might have predicted, based on the research of Palmer et al. (1981), that the object would be inspected from a view in which the major axes were 45° to the line of sight. Perrett et al. found, however, that such views were inspected at a low rate. Also, in a mental imagery task in which subjects were to call to mind a mental image of the object and then rotate the object to that view, the plan views were usually chosen. In contrast, however, when subjects were asked to indicate the view that they considered to be structurally most informative, they chose a three-quarter view, similar to the canonical views of Palmer et al. Thus measures of visual inspection and the views most readily imagined seem to converge on plan views. The views most efficiently recognized or providing maximal structural information also seem to be the same, but in this case it is three-quarter views (for discussion, see Perrett et al., 1992).

If canonical views lead to good performance in identification and other tasks, then there must be views of objects that lead to relatively poor performance. One type of depiction that affects recognition adversely is one in which a major axis of an object is foreshortened. Such views could occlude parts or features, as well as obscure an object's main axis of elongation. Following the suggestion of Cutzu and Edelman (1992), such foreshortened views would be deformed because points or features that are relatively far apart in three-dimensional space would be close together in the depiction.

Research on the recognition of noncanonical or unconventional views of objects was conducted on brain-damaged people by Warrington and Taylor (1973, 1978). They found that patients with damage to the posterior regions of the right hemisphere were selectively impaired in the identification of "unusual view" photographs of objects compared to "conventional view" photographs of the same objects. Also, patients with right hemisphere damage were impaired on a same/different matching task in which one conventional view photograph was paired with an unusual view photograph of the same object or with a different object. Since the time of Warrington and Taylor's (1973, 1978) research, a number of studies have shown that patients with right hemisphere damage have difficulty recognizing unconventional views of objects but generally perform well with conventional views of the same objects (Humphreys & Riddoch, 1984; Landis, Regard, Bliestle, & Kleihues, 1988; Layman & Greene, 1988; Ratcliff & Newcombe, 1982; Warrington & James, 1986, 1988).

Many of the unusual view photographs used in these studies were views in which the longest dimension of the object was foreshortened. The findings of Warrington and Taylor (1973, 1978) appear to have been an important factor in the development of Marr's theory of object recognition (Marr, 1982; Marr & Nishihara, 1978) in which the axis (or axes) of elongation or symmetry plays a crucial role. Marr suggested that an object-centered description can be based on some axis (or axes) determined by salient geometric characteristics of the shape. The location and orientation of the parts can then be described in relation to this axis. For many objects the intrinsic or principal axis will be defined by elongation or symmetry. For views of objects that do not foreshorten the elongation, the longest axis in the image will correspond to the longest axis in the object. Selecting this axis will yield a description based on the proper object-centered coordinate frame. If the major axis of elongation is foreshortened in the image, however, then selecting the longest image axis may not produce a description based on the object's natural axis and object identification may be disrupted. Alternatively, determining which direction corresponds with the direction of the main axis may be more difficult for a foreshortened view. Normally, in everyday life, the analysis of the image could make use of depth information that could help in the selection of the axis of elongation.

The principal axis was not well represented and difficult to obtain from the pictures in the unconventional view photographs of Warrington and Taylor (1973, 1978; for discussion, see Shallice, 1988). Marr suggested that the errors made by patients with right hemisphere damage occurred because of difficulty in extracting the principal axis (but see Warrington & James, 1986). Marr's suggestion was studied by Humphreys and Riddoch (1984). They, like Warrington and Taylor, found that patients with right hemisphere damage had difficulty recognizing foreshortened view of everyday objects. Further, the naming responses of the brain-damaged individuals suggested that they often interpreted the form information as an object oriented in the plane of the photograph rather than as an object oriented in depth. Humphreys and Riddoch found, however, that if the objects were photographed resting on graph paper that added linear perspective cues, performance on the foreshortened views improved. It may be that the presence of these depth cues assisted in the selection of the appropriate principal axis, which, according to Marr, plays a central role in object identification.

Humphrey and Jolicoeur (1988, 1993) followed up on the research of Humphreys and Riddoch (1984) but with normal subjects. They produced a series of line drawings of common objects in which the major axis of the objects were foreshortened and contrasted identification of these drawings with views in which this axis was less foreshortened. Specifically, they used views in which the major axis was at an 80° or 45° angle to a view in which the major axis was perpendicular to the viewing direction. All major features and parts were visible in both views of the objects, as can be seen in Figure 3.6. Despite the availability of the major features and parts in both views, the 45° views were identified much more rapidly and with fewer errors than were the 80° views. If, however, as in Humphrey and Riddoch (1984), the objects were presented on a background with strong monocular depth cues, performance on the foreshortened views improved, although it still was not as good as with the 45° views. This latter result suggests that some of the effects of foreshortening may occur because of difficulty in locating the principal axis of elongation of the objects, as suggested by Marr (1982). The depth background could be supplying a visual reference frame that assists in the selection of the principal axis and the construction of an object-centered representation. That is, the monocular depth cues could help to establish a three-dimensional reference frame that is used to encode the foreshortened views.

Given the consistent finding of problems in recognizing foreshortened views

A   B

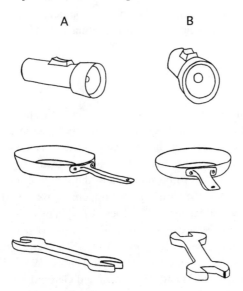

Figure 3.6. Examples of the stimuli used by Humphrey and Jolicoeur (1988, 1993) in non-foreshortened and foreshortened views.

in patients with right hemisphere damage, it might be that normal subjects would show a left visual field advantage in identifying foreshortened views. Humphrey and Jolicoeur (1993), however, found no evidence for a left visual field advantage for the identification of either the 80° or the 45° views of the objects, despite the clear difficulty in recognizing the foreshortened views. Their results are consistent with a large body of evidence indicating no hemifield effects for object identification tasks in normal subjects (Biederman & Cooper, 1991c; Kimura & Durnford, 1974; Levine & Banich, 1982; Paivio & Ernest, 1971; Young & Bion, 1981; Young, Bion, & Ellis, 1980) and extend this lack of a hemifield difference to views of objects in which the principal axis is foreshortened.

The research just reviewed shows that some views of both common and unfamiliar objects rotated in depth lead to much more efficient identification and recognition than do other views. The formation and nature of canonical views clearly need more research. Just how the canonical view depends on the geometry of the object and whether the deformation model of Cutzu and Edelman (1992) can predict canonical views of regular, solid objects should be investigated. It is also possible, as Newell and Findlay (1992) suggest, that there may not be any underlying general rules used by the visual system in forming canonical views; instead, the rules may be object specific. Despite some lack of understanding of how canonical views are formed, the abundant evidence for their existence is problematic for models postulating that rotations in depth have no consequence for object identification (e.g., Biederman, 1987; Corballis, 1988).

Priming

Recently, a number of researchers have used experiments in which priming was the main dependent variable to study the nature of the underlying representations of visual shapes. One group of researchers has argued that there is a dissociation between two memory systems for visual shape. One system, mediating explicit memory, is postulated to encode and to be sensitive to the size and orientation of visual shapes, as expected from the earlier work on memory for visual shape (e.g., Humphrey & Khan, 1992; Jolicoeur, 1987; Rock, 1973). The other system, mediating implicit memory, has been claimed to be insensitive to size and orientation (Cooper, Schacter, Ballesteros, & Moore, 1992; Schacter, Cooper, & Delaney, 1990; Schacter, Cooper, Delaney, Peterson, & Tharan, 1991). Biederman and Cooper (1991a, 1991b, 1992) and Biederman and Gerhardstein (1993) have also proposed a dissociation between two types of visual representations of objects, one of which is postulated to be sensitive to size and orientation, and the other of which is claimed to be size, location, and orientation invariant. If we could be confident about these results, they would be some of the most exciting, provocative, and profound results in the area of visual pattern recognition obtained in the last two decades. Because of the potential theoretical importance of these results, we examine them in detail here, along with the methods and logic used to relate results to theory.

Consider first the experiments of Biederman and Cooper (1992). In these experiments, subjects were asked to name drawings of objects in two blocks of trials. The first block of trials acts as a learning phase in which the subjects are given an opportunity to encode the particular visual depictions of the objects used in the study. In the second block of trials, the objects are shown a second time, some of them in a depiction identical to that used in the first block of trials, some of them transformed in size. In addition, some objects are replaced by another one that has the same generic name (e.g., upright piano changed to grand piano, with both of them named piano). Denote objects shown at the same size across the two blocks ss (small-small) and LL (large-large); objects shown at a different size as sL (small-large) and Ls (large-small); replaced objects as R; naming times in Block 1 as N (new objects). The pattern of naming times in the second block was as follows: $(ss = LL) \equiv (sL = Ls) < R < N$. That is, naming times in the second block were fastest for objects repeated exactly as shown in the first block, which were similar in magnitude to these found for objects that were transformed in size. Both were faster than the times observed for replaced objects, with all times in the second block being faster than those in the first block in which subjects were naming objects for the first time.

The greater speed of naming in the second block relative to the first block can be considered as a measure of priming. The results were clear-cut in demonstrating significant amounts of priming. What is less clear, however, is what representations mediated the observed priming. Biederman and Cooper were sensitive to this issue, which is why they included the condition in which objects were replaced by objects with the same name. Their argument is that the difference between the naming times for replaced objects from that found for naming in the first block represents an exhaustive measure (see Reingold & Merikle, 1988, 1990) of the nonvisual components of priming. If so, any difference between priming in this condition and priming in another condition must represent the visual component of priming. Thus, they argue the difference in priming between the replaced condition and the identical condition $(R - (ss,LL))$ represents the visual component of priming. Because $(ss,LL) \equiv (sL,Ls)$, it follows that $(R - (ss,LL)) \equiv (R - (sL,Ls))$, Biederman and Cooper concluded that the visual component of priming was not affected by changes in the size of the object across the first and second presentations of the objects. Using this logic, they conclude that there must be a representation that mediates the visual component of priming and that this representation is size invariant. Biederman and Cooper (1992) also replicated the size-congruency effect on the speed of recognition memory reported by Jolicoeur (1987; Milliken & Jolicoeur, 1992). The difference in the effects of changes in pattern size from the first to the second presentation across tasks (repetition priming versus recognition memory) is what supports Biederman and Cooper's proposed dissociation between memory systems.

The logic of the Biederman and Cooper experiment hinges on the assumption that all of the difference between the R condition (replaced) and the same-view conditions (LL,ss) is due to visual differences between the stimuli, with none of the effect due to differences in meaning. It is likely that the R condition (replaced) reflects more than one of the nonvisual components of priming in the (LL,ss) conditions (identical repetitions). The same name is used in both cases, and because some of the priming effect will be associated with greater ease in retrieving this name, some of the priming effect will be due to a facilitation in name retrieval. Although the items in the R condition do differ from the items in the identical conditions in visual terms, and although they match on the names, it is likely that the R condition differed in more than simply the visual component of the task. For example, the semantic representations of upright piano and of grand piano are not identical. In fact, they are quite different, being associated with different uses (e.g., concert versus school), different contexts (home versus symphony hall), different sound qualities, and so on. It is likely that some of the reduction in priming across the R and (LL,ss) conditions is due to differences in meaning associated with the depicted objects. Thus, at least some of the R − (LL,ss) difference probably reflects the difference between the repetition of identical semantic representations (leading to a faster activation time) versus the activation of a close (but different) semantic associate (leading to a slower activation time). It is even possible that all of the R − (LL,ss) difference is due to differences at the semantic level. Thus, it is not clear what the procedure used by Biederman and Cooper (1992) actually measures. It could represent purely differences in semantic priming (possible), purely differences in visual priming (unlikely), or some unknown mixture of the two (most likely). If the priming measure represents differences in semantic-level representations, then it is not surprising that there was no effect of size congruency. Given the problems associated with the interpretation of these methods, we believe that the results of this procedure must be viewed with caution and are in need of evidence from converging operations. These converging operations should rule out the possibility that the observed priming does not reflect purely the influence of visual representations. If the measure is not a pure measure of visual priming, additional research aimed at estimating the portion of the measure that is purely visual would be useful.

Next, consider the result of Schacter et al. (1990, 1991). The goal of these articles was to demonstrate a distinction between explicit and implicit memory for visual shapes and to document differences between the nature of the under-lying representations supporting the two postulated kinds of memory. In most experiments supporting the distinction, there were two phases: a learning phase and a testing phase. In the learning phase, subjects were asked to examine two-dimensional drawings of possible or impossible three-dimensional objects. The objects remained in view for several seconds (5 s in most experiments). The possible objects resembled what a mechanical engineering student might be asked to produce in a drafting class. The impossible objects were locally similar to the possible objects, but the entire combinations of lines and angles could not be interpreted as a view of a possible object. The typical task during the learning phase was to decide whether the object faced predominantly toward the left or toward the right (e.g., imagine a stapler drawn in perspective, as if on a desk, seen in prototypical view slightly from above). There were two possible tasks in the testing phase. One task, which the authors believe reveals the prop-erties of implicit memory, consisted of deciding whether a drawing exposed for 100 ms depicted a possible or an impossible object. The items included new and old possible and impossible objects. The other task was a yes-no recognition memory experiment in which the original objects were embedded in a list con-taining an equal number of new items. The objects usually remained in view for 5 s during the recognition memory test.

Consider first the results from the object-decision task. Old possible objects were reported as possible more often (about 12% more frequently) than new possible objects. In contrast, there was no significant effect for impossible objects (performance was not superior for old impossible objects than for new impossible objects). The encapsulated summary of these results given by the authors is that priming is observed for possible objects but not for impossible objects. In general, across the experiments, encoding manipulations thought to be associated with explicit memory (e.g., what category of objects are you reminded of when you look at this stimulus?) have a significant effect on recognition memory performance but little or no effect on the performance in the object-decision task.

Now consider the more pertinent (for our purposes) experiments of Cooper et al. (1992). In Experiment 1, they manipulated the size of the objects between the learning and testing phases. The magnitude of priming in the object-decision task for possible objects was not affected by this manipulation. Subjects correctly said that a drawing depicted a possible object about 77% of the time for old possible objects shown at the same size versus about 65% of the time for new objects. For objects that changed in size, performance was about 77% for old objects versus about 60% for new objects. There were no significant differences across the same-size and different-size conditions. In contrast, as found by Jolicoeur (1987), recognition memory was superior when size remained constant than when size changed across the learning phase and the testing phase.

The results deserve closer scrutiny, however, because there were a number of curious trends that suggest that we should be cautious in accepting them at face value. A more complete picture of the results is shown in Table 3.2. Consider the results for impossible objects in the object decision task. In every size-combination condition, the measured score was higher for new objects than for old objects. That is, there was a tendency for stimuli that had been seen before to be called possible. These results are consistent with a bias to respond possible to old objects (for both possible and impossible objects). For possible objects, this bias increases the apparent magnitude of priming. For impossible objects, it may have masked positive priming to such an extent as to reverse the effect and produce a net negative priming. This possible bias was discussed at some length in Schacter et al. (1990, 1991) and in Cooper et al. (1992). The authors performed an analysis using Yule's Q, a statistic that provides a measure of priming that is not contaminated by the kind of response bias that concerns us here. Based on this statistic, however, one can only argue that the overall results (for both possible and impossible objects) show significant priming, independent of response bias. That is, the tests using Yule's Q demonstrated that not all the apparent priming was due to bias. Thus, the authors concluded that there was true net priming over and above any possible response biases. We have no difficulty with this conclusion. However, this test does not clarify whether or

Table 3.2. *Results of Experiment 1 in Cooper et al. (1992)*

	Possible objects				Impossible objects			
Item type	ss	LL	sL	Ls	ss	LL	sL	Ls
				Object decision				
Old	.78	.75	.77	.78	.58	.73	.73	.66
New	.66	.65	.58	.63	.66	.81	.78	.68
				Recognition memory				
Old	.78	.88	.68	.66	.78	.82	.66	.69
New	.31	.13	.23	.15	.26	.24	.23	.26

Note: ss = studied small, tested small; LL = studied large, tested large; sL = studied small, tested large; Ls = studied large, tested small. In the object decision task, the results are the proportions correct. In the recognition memory task, the results are the proportions of "old" responses for both old and new objects (i.e., hits for old items and false alarms for new items).

not the results for possible or impossible objects taken separately are interpretable independently of possible response bias. The fact that subjects responded possible more often to old impossible objects than to new impossible objects in every size-combination condition (Cooper et al., 1992, Experiment 1) is strong evidence that there was a sizable bias influencing the results. This bias makes it difficult to accept the claim that only possible objects produced priming. The analyses using Yule's Q are not relevant to this issue.

In Experiment 2, the repeated stimuli in the test phase were shown either without change or with a left–right mirror-image reversal. In the object decision task, in the same-orientation condition, subjects said that a stimulus was an object 89% of the time when an object was seen in the same left–right orientation as in the study phase compared with 71% for new possible objects. For left–right reflected old objects, performance was at 82% for old objects compared with 72% for new objects. The results are shown in more detail in Table 3.3.

Although the magnitude of priming was 18% for same-view objects and only 10% for mirrored views, which is a substantial reduction in the amount of priming, this difference was not significant and the authors concluded that there is no difference in priming as a function of changes in left–right orientation. In contrast, a 9% change in recognition memory (using hits minus false alarms as the measure) was taken as evidence that explicit memory does code for left–right parity.

It seems to us that the pattern of results obtained for possible objects in

Table 3.3. *Results of Experiment 2 in Cooper et al. (1992)*

Item type	Possible objects		Impossible objects	
	Same	Mirror	Same	Mirror
	Object decision			
Old	.89	.82	.70	.70
New	.71	.72	.77	.68
	Recognition memory			
Old	.83	.78	.77	.63
New	.12	.16	.22	.27

Note: In the object decision task, the results are proportions correct. In the recognition memory task, the results are the proportions of "old" responses for both old and new objects (i.e., hits for old items and false alarms for new items).

Experiment 2 of Cooper et al. (1992) suggests that the magnitude of priming was reduced when the patterns were mirror-imaged, but the priming measure used was not sensitive enough to produce a statistically significant difference. In fact, this brings us to a concern we have about all of the priming experiments we have considered so far (those from the Biederman group and those from the Schacter/Cooper group). This concern is that these experimenters set out to measure potentially small modulations in the observed amount of priming, but their experiments were not designed to measure such small effects.

How much change in priming would one expect, assuming that representations mediating priming were orientation and size sensitive? There is no particular reason to expect that all of the priming observed for an exact replication would disappear after a transformation of the image. What we expect is a reduction in the amount of priming, but by how much? This question is difficult to answer in the absence of fully worked-out computational models of priming. However, we suspect that a reasonable answer is somewhere between 10% and 20% of the total amount of priming due to visual representations. One way to justify this effect size is to consider how much recognition memory is affected by the change in view across the learning phase and the testing phase. Consider the recognition memory results from Cooper et al. (1992), Experiment 1. For possible objects shown at the same size, the hits minus false-alarms score was .61. For possible objects shown at a different size, the score was .48. Thus, changing size resulted in a reduction of .13 relative to a memory level of .61, or a 21% change. Now consider the priming results. For possible objects shown at the same size, the total amount of priming is about 11% (averaging the difference between old and new objects across ss and LL trials in Table 3.2). Thus, 11% is the total effect size we have to work with. This value is likely to be inflated by the bias effect discussed earlier.

Assuming a 20% effect of changing the size of the stimuli across learning and testing, it is reasonable to expect a 2% change in the amount of priming. We do not believe that the experiments that we are examining now had the power to detect effects of this size. This is reasonably evident, for example, by perusing the baseline scores displayed in Table 3.2 (scores in the object decision task for new stimuli). For possible objects, the baseline varied from .58 to .66, which is about four times as much as the expected effect size. For impossible objects, the baselines ranged from .66 to .81, which is more than seven times the magnitude of the expected effect. The suggestion is simply that these experiments had the power to detect some effects, such as the overall amount of priming, but they did not have enough power to measure reliably the effects of modulations in the amount of priming of the size that would be expected from changes in image size or orientation.

Similarly, in the experiments of Biederman and Cooper (1991b), the three experiments in which the position of an object was changed between the first and second blocks in a transfer-of-learning paradigm showed a small advantage for objects shown in the same position. On average, the effect size was 6 ms. In two of their experiments, they estimated the visual component of priming to result in a 35 ms effect (Experiment 2) in one case and a 44 ms effect in the other (Experiment 4). Assuming that a change in position would result, say, in a 20% change in the magnitude of priming, we expect an effect of about 8 ms, which is remarkably close to the observed (but not significant) 6 ms effect.[3] According to the authors' own power analysis, they did not have the power to detect effects of this magnitude.

In contrast to the results just presented, in which priming measures were found to be insensitive to changes in viewpoint and viewing conditions between learning and testing, a number of results have purported to demonstrate viewpoint specificity. First, consider the results of Srinivas (1993). Her experiments used the two-phase transfer-of-learning paradigm in which the main dependent measure was subjects' ability to identify (by name) objects that were presented briefly on a computer screen (i.e., a perceptual identification task). Consider Experiments 3 and 4 in her 1993 article. The stimuli were drawings of objects in a usual prototypical view (see Palmer et al., 1981) or in an unusual view (somewhat foreshortened but clearly recognizable). For each object there was a drawing from a usual view and one from an unusual view. During the study phase, the objects were shown in a usual view, an unusual view, or not shown. The task during the learning phase was to type the name of the object into the computer that was displaying the drawings following a 2 s exposure. During the test phase the objects were exposed for 50 ms, followed by a 500 ms pattern mask. The main dependent measure was the percent correct identification of the displayed object. In general, there was significantly more priming when the view presented in the test phase was the same as that shown in the learning phase. However, there was no difference between the usual-usual and unusual-usual conditions. That is, there was poor transfer from usual to unusual views but good transfer from unusual to usual views. These results (and others in Srinivas, 1993) suggest that the representations mediating priming in perceptual identification have a higher degree of viewpoint specificity than is suggested by the results of Biederman and his colleagues or of Cooper and her colleagues.

Bartram (1976) had subjects judge whether sequentially presented pairs of pictured objects had the same name. The pairs could be the same object from identical viewpoints (what we will call the *identity* condition), the same object from different viewpoints (the *rotated* condition), or two different objects with the same name. The disparate views of the same objects differed by a rotation in depth of about 45°. When line drawings of familiar objects were used with a 500 ms interstimulus interval (ISI), Bartram reported an apparently significant 37 ms difference between the identity and rotated conditions. (In Bartram's experiments the first picture was always presented for 500 ms.) When photographs were used with both 250 ms and 2 s ISIs, there was an even larger difference between these two conditions. Bartram noted, however, that this latter difference may have been due to a subset of his stimuli that were all visibly similar to one another and thus that could be confused with one another. The other stimuli showed a much smaller effect. Thus, the status of this effect with photographs was somewhat unclear. With both types of stimuli, however, there was a clear advantage of the rotated condition over the condition in which the stimuli were different pictures with the same name.

Bartram (1976) argued that his experiments provided evidence for the operation of three different levels of representation: a *picture* code, which would be viewer centered; an *object* code, which could be considered to be viewpoint independent; and a *semantic* code. He suggested that the picture code might be used only for line-drawn stimuli and not for photographs. Alternatively, he suggested that there may be only an object code and a semantic code for both types of stimuli, and that the differences between the identity and rotated pairs with line drawings may have occurred because of the time taken to align, via mental rotation, the rotated pictures.

Ellis and Allport (1986; see also Ellis, Allport, Humphreys, & Collis, 1989) conducted experiments similar to those of Bartram (1976). They were particularly interested in the temporal decay rates of putative visual codes. They argued that the stimuli used by Bartram (1976) and others (e.g., Kelter, Grvtzbach, Freiheit, Hvhle, Wutzig, & Diesch, 1984) may have been problematic. The different views of the same objects in these studies were produced by rotating objects in depth by about 45° (i.e., out of the picture plane). Because such a rotation very often results in different features being visible in the two views, any performance differences between the identity and rotated conditions could have resulted from the fact that the rotated images actually had somewhat different visual features than the identical, nonrotated images. Ellis and Allport also used objects that were photographed rotated in depth, but they ensured that no major feature was obscured, nor was a major axis foreshortened for different views of the same object.

Ellis and Allport (1986) also used the matching task in which subjects had to decide if successively presented photographs had the same name. Four trial types were used. *Same* trials included identical views of the same objects (the identity condition), the same object photographed from different angles (the rotated condition), and different objects with the same name. On *different* trials two different objects were presented. The first picture in the pair to be matched was presented for 500 ms and was followed, after an ISI of 100 ms, 500 ms, or 2 s, by the second picture. At the two short ISIs, same decision latency was fastest for the identity condition, next fastest for the rotated condition, and slowest for the name matches. However, at the 2 s ISI, the identity and rotated conditions did not differ, although both were faster than the same name condition. Additional results relevant to this issue were that the advantage of the identity condition over the rotated condition was eliminated when a pattern mask was shown between the picture pairs even at the 100 ms ISI (Ellis & Allport, 1986) and was significantly reduced when the first and second pictures were of different sizes (Ellis et al., 1989).

Based on their results, Ellis and his colleagues proposed a three-level representational system for picture matching. One level was called *view* to emphasize that it is viewpoint specific or viewer centered, although it is nonretinotopic (Ellis et al., 1989). Representations at this level account for the advantage of the identity condition over the rotated condition. A second level was called *object*, and this level was claimed to be based on object-centered object codes. Ellis et al. (1989) report results suggesting that representations at the object level require more time to be generated than representations at the view level and that object-level representations are not disrupted by masking. In addition, object-level representations were claimed to be more enduring than those at the view level. Finally, they proposed another level of internal code, *model*, to account for the matching of physically different objects that have the same name. Like Marr (1982; Marr & Nishihara, 1978), Ellis and his colleagues emphasized the distinction between viewer-centered and object-centered representations.

Humphrey and Lupker (1993) examined the proposal of Ellis and Allport

(1986) that viewer-centered representations of objects decay rapidly, whereas object-centered or semantic-level representations do not. A picture-matching task was used in which subjects decided whether successively presented line drawings of objects rotated in the frontal plane had the same name. The pictures were either identical pictures, pictures of different objects with the same name, or pictures of objects with different names. The two successive pictures could be in the same or a different orientation. In one experment, two orientations (0° [upright] and 120°) and two ISIs were examined (100 ms and 2 s). In a second experiment, two orientations (0° and 60°) and three ISIs were examined (100 ms, 2 s and 5 s). In neither experiment was there any evidence that viewpoint-specific representations disappeared at longer ISIs. These results did not replicate those of Ellis and Allport (1986), and they are inconsistent with their model.

Lawson and Humphreys (1993) have also conducted picture-matching tasks in which they observed substantial view specificity for line drawings of depth-rotated objects. In these tasks, subjects were presented two pictures sequentially and had to judge whether the second picture showed the same object as the first. The time between presentation of the first and second pictures was either 595 or 2510 ms. The first picture was presented for 100 ms, and the second was presented until the subject responded. Lawson and Humphreys argued that such a task does not require access to semantic information, as in naming tasks, and is a more direct measure of the perceptual processing required for object recognition. Also, matching tasks of this sort may be more sensitive to the effects of visual similarity than naming or identification tasks that may reflect postperceptual processes such as the frequency of object names. These postperceptual processes are likely to add variability to the results, making it more difficult to detect effects of small magnitude.

In the experiments of Lawson and Humphreys, the second picture could be identical to the first picture or a depth-rotated version (around the y axis) of the first picture or a picture of a different object. Although they performed several experiments, for our purposes we will emphasize only some of their results. First, they replicated the identity benefit found by others, as reviewed earlier. They found that if the first picture was identical to the second, matching was more rapid than if the second picture was a rotated version of the first. This result could have been due to the matching of transient, low-level image descriptions. These low-level descriptions underlying the identity benefit appeared to be transient because the benefit decreased with a longer interval between the presentation of the first and second pictures. They did not find, unlike Ellis and Allport (1986), that an intervening mask between the two pictures disrupted the view-specific representation underlying the identity benefit.

Lawson and Humphreys also found a reliable visual similarity effect for matching of nonidentical views. That is, matching was faster for visually similar than for visually dissimilar nonidentical views. In other words, picture priming was maximized when the two pictures were very similar. Generally, the visually similar objects were separated by a smaller rotation in depth than the visually dissimilar objects. Such results suggest that the representations of the objects are view specific and provide evidence against the notion that such representations are object centered. Further, at least for nonforeshortened views, the main components of the objects were salient in all depicted views. Despite the clear visibility of these components, matching was not equally efficient for all nonforeshortened target views. This result suggests that matching was not made on the basis of component parts without concern for the metric relations among components, as some theorists suggest (Biederman, 1987); rather, the representation of the objects did preserve component parts and metric relations among the parts. The result also qualifies the proposal of Ellis and colleagues (Ellis & Allport, 1986; Ellis et al., 1989) in that Lawson and Humphreys argue that the postulated object-level code is relatively abstract but is nevertheless view specific.

Lawson and Humphreys also found some effects of foreshortening in that if relatively nonforeshortened views were seen first, followed by foreshortened views, matches were slow. They qualified this latter result by showing that the disadvantage for foreshortened views disappeared if the first picture was a foreshortened view and it was matched to an identical or a similar foreshortened view. The result with the foreshortened views was not due to difficulty in encoding foreshortened views, but rather was due to the general difficulty in matching visually dissimilar views of the same object. Foreshortened views, relative to nonforeshortened views, obscured component parts and metric relations among the parts.

Recent research by Stephen and Parker (1993) has found different results for interclass (entry-point level and basic level) and intraclass (subordinate level) matching of common objects. In their experiments subjects were shown a grayscale photograph of one object briefly, and 800 ms later they were shown a second photograph. The object in the second photograph could be the same object in the same orientation as the first, the same object in a different orientation (at a 45° or 90° rotation about the y-axis from the orientation of the first object) or a different object. The subject's task was to decide if the second object presented was the same as the first, regardless of orientation. They found that when the set of objects to be matched was from clearly different categories, there was no effect of orientation. In contrast, when the set of objects to be matched was from the same category, and thus the objects were structurally similar, there was a reliable effect of orientation. With same category objects, it took longer to decide if the objects were the same if the orientation was different between the first and second pictures than if the two views of the object were in the same orientation. Further, the greater the difference in orientation, the longer it took to decide. These results indicate that similar objects are more likely to yield viewpoint-dependent results (see also Cutzu & Edelman, 1992).

Structural representations and priming

We have devoted a substantial portion of this chapter to a detailed review of some recent work on priming because the first articles to appear using this approach claimed to have demonstrated the existence of viewpoint-invariant visual structural representations. We reviewed the experiments claiming to demonstrate viewpoint invariance quite critically. Here we wish to emphasize something that may have been lost in the foregoing discussions. Namely, we believe that it is possible to obtain recognition performance that is essentially orientation invariant, given the right context. For example, in the experiments of Murray et al. (1993), the reduction in the magnitude of the usual orientation effect obtained by rotating stimuli in the image plane was found to be independent of which particular views had been seen in the learning phase. They argued that their results ruled out an account of the reduction of orientation effects with practice in terms of a model based on multiple representations plus transformations (e.g., Tarr & Pinker, 1989). However, the fact that transfer was not orientation specific is not sufficient grounds to claim that transfer was mediated by an orientation-invariant structural representation of the objects. In fact, it is possible for transfer to be mediated by "free-floating" features or attributes of the objects rather than by integrated structural representations. In the experiments of Biederman and Gerhardstein (1993), for example, the stimulus set consisted of drawings of 24 three-dimensional objects. These objects were selected to be quite distinctive from each other, such that a unique description of the objects could be given in terms of their parts. It is possible that transfer of learning in this kind of experiment could be mediated by the association of one or two distinctive parts with particular objects. If so, it would not be surprising to observe viewpoint invariance, to the extent that the parts or attributes mediating transfer are themselves orientation invariant (see Biederman & Gerhardstein, 1993, Experiment 4, for evidence that the parts advocated by Biederman, 1987, may be able to tolerate a substantial amount of rotation in depth). What is more difficult to demonstrate, however, is that the representations mediating the observed transfer were full-fledged structural descriptions of objects. The experiments of the Schacter-Cooper group are interesting for this reason. They argued that the presence of priming for possible objects and the absence of priming for impossible objects were due to subjects' ability to construct an integrated structural representation of possible objects but not of impossible objects. However, the evidence for response biases in their results prevents us from interpreting performance for impossible objects, as discussed at length in the previous section. We conclude that their results could have been mediated by representations based on free-floating features rather than by fully elaborated structural representations.

The evidence from studies based on the results of priming experiments is mixed. Some studies found no significant effects (e.g., Biederman & Cooper, 1992; Cooper et al., 1992). These studies were criticized earlier, however, on logical and methodological grounds. Other studies have reported significant viewpoint specificity in priming (e.g., Lawson & Humphreys, 1993; Srinivas, 1993). We find the demonstrations of significant results more convincing than arguments that depend on accepting the null hypothesis. Thus, we are not yet prepared to accept claims for the existence of orientation-invariant structural descriptions distinct from the representations that must mediate orientation- or size-dependent results observed in recognition memory tasks (e.g., Jolicoeur, 1987; Rock, 1973).

Normalization operations

It has often been suggested, as we have noted many times, that normalization operations are used to recognize objects when input representations deviate in orientation from long-term representations (e.g., Jolicoeur, 1985; Tarr & Pinker, 1989; Ullman, 1989). Such operations serve to "align" the input representation of a viewed object with a stored model (or stored models) of the object (or vice versa). Although there may be several types of normalization processes, we will confine our discussion to processes that may be responsible for orientation normalization. The main finding supporting the existence of such a process is that there is generally a monotonic increase in recognition or naming latency with increasing rotation of the input object away from familiar orientations. This process is often considered to be an incremental, analog transformation process and has often been referred to as *mental rotation* (for a review, see Shepard & Cooper, 1982).

In support of the analog nature of mental rotation, Shepard (e.g., 1984) has suggested that there is a similarity between that process and some aspects of apparent motion. For example, Shepard and Judd (1976) found that the critical onset asynchrony needed to produce a percept of rigid motion between two depictions of objects was linearly related to the depicted angular disparity between the objects. Further, the variation in critical time was similar for two-dimensional and three-dimensional rotations. Research on mental rotation conducted by Shepard and his colleagues (for a review, see Shepard & Cooper, 1982) has also shown that reaction times are linearly related to the angular disparity between depicted objects, and generally similar results were found for depth and picture-plane rotations. The similarity in results of both apparent motion and mental rotation tasks has led Shepard to suggest that at some level the processes underlying mental rotation are similar to those underlying the perception of motion (but see Friedman & Harding, 1990). Such an argument is consistent with the supposed analog nature of mental rotation.

Before we discuss empirical support for a mental rotation process in object recognition, we discuss briefly an important point made by Edelman and Bülthoff (1992). Most studies of object recognition find that not only is reaction time linearly related to the angular disparity between familiar and novel views, but so is the error rate. This finding is also true of the classic mental rotation literature (e.g., see Shepard & Cooper, 1982). Edelman and Bülthoff (1992) have suggested that a dependence of error rate on orientation is not consistent with a normalization approach. A normalization approach, they argue, should predict a uniformly low error rate regardless of stimulus orientation. That is, if the information is available in the stimulus for computing a normalizing transformation (see Ullman, 1989), error rate should not be dependent on orientation. Because they have found an increasing error rate in their research (Edelman & Bülthoff; 1992; Bülthoff & Edelman, 1992), as have others (e.g., Humphrey & Khan, 1992; Palmer et al., 1981), as the view deviates from the learned or canonical view, they argue that the normalization approach is suspect. Instead, they suggest that the view-interpolation approach can better account for such errors, as well as some of the results usually explained by mental rotation (Edelman & Weinshall, 1991).

Edelman and Bülthoff (1992) do point out, however, that their argument applies only to a perfect normalization device. They acknowledge that error rates may not be diagnostic in distinguishing between an imperfect normalization mechanism in which larger transformations increase the noise and the view-interpolation approach. Indeed, Kosslyn (1980) has proposed that noise accumulates with greater degrees of rotation away from a target orientation. Given that the assumption of a completely error-free normalization process is not plausible in the context of human vision, normalization operations cannot be dismissed as possible mechanisms involved in human pattern recognition.

Tarr and Pinker (1989) presented strong evidence consistent with the use of mental rotation to align an input shape with a stored orientation. In their experiments, subjects were first trained on two-dimensional shapes in a single canonical orientation. The shapes were novel and had similar local features but different global configurations. Subjects learned to identify three such shapes by an arbitrary name during the learning phase. Following training, subjects named the objects in new "practice" orientations. It was found that the time needed to name the shapes in practice orientations increased monotonically as the shapes were rotated from the orientation at which they had been learned. Tarr and Pinker attributed this dependency of naming latency on misorientation to the time it took to perform mental rotation. This orientation effect diminished with practice so that naming latency became roughly equivalent at all of the practiced orientations, a finding consistent with that of Jolicoeur (1985). Following the practice trials, subjects were tested on new "surprise" orientations. Reaction time again increased linearly with differences between stimulus orientation and the nearest familiar orientation. Tarr and Pinker also attributed this reemergence of the orientation effect to mental rotation. The practice effect did not transfer to new orientations because subjects stored multiple viewpoint-specific representations during practice. When subjects were presented with novel orientations, no direct match between the input and stored orientations was found; therefore, subjects were required to rotate the input mentally to match one of the stored familiar orientations.

Normalization: Mental rotation

Evidence that mental rotation may be used as a normalization mechanism in the identification of familiar rotated objects can be found in the experiments of Jolicoeur (1985, 1988). These experiments used line drawings of objects (Snodgrass & Vanderwart, 1980) rotated in the image plane. Performance was compared across two tasks: naming and left–right decisions. As in other studies, the naming task was used to estimate the effects of rotation on the time needed to identify the objects. The left–right task was used to estimate the rate of mental rotation for the particular stimuli used in the naming task.

In the left–right task, an object was presented on the screen and a timer was started when the stimulus appeared. The task was to decide whether the object faced to the left or to the right, for upright objects, or whether the object would have faced to the left or to the right if it had been presented upright, for objects presented at nonzero orientations. The subject was to press a telegraph key with the left index finger if the object faced left or to press a telegraph key with the right index finger if the object faced right. Subjects were asked to respond as quickly as possible while keeping errors to a minimum. Response time was measured from the onset of the object to the subject's response.

The left–right task produced a large orientation effect on response times in which response times became increasingly longer as the objects were rotated further from upright. This pattern of results is consistent with the notion that visual representations of the objects are mentally rotated until upright before the left–right decision is made. In fact, the magnitude of the orientation effect was very similar to that found in other experiments that have been taken as evidence for a process of mental rotation (e.g., see Corballis, 1982; Shepard & Cooper, 1982). This pattern of results was found in both articles (Jolicoeur, 1985, 1988).

The effects of orientation on object naming, overall, were different from those observed in the left–right task. In particular, whereas response times increased monotonically from 0° to 180° in the left–right task, the increase in response times in the naming task was linear from 0° to ± 120° but then decreased from ± 120° to 180° in the naming task. However, the slopes of the orientation effect on response times were similar across the two tasks between 0° and ± 120°. Overall, the results suggest that two mechanisms are involved in the naming task, one of which is more sensitive to orientation effects than the other.

The similarity of the slopes across the left–right task (presumed to reflect primarily a process of mental rotation) and the naming task for stimuli between 0° and ± 120° is consistent with the possibility that mental rotation was the mechanism responsible for the increase in identification time observed in the naming task.

The discrepancy between the two tasks for stimuli at 180° suggests that a second mechanism has a strong influence on performance in the naming task. Jolicoeur (1990) suggested a dual-systems theory of object identification. According to this theory, object identification is mediated by two underlying sets of mechanisms that operate in parallel. One set of mechanisms implements a normalization plus multiple representations system in which visual input is normalized to a viewpoint-specific representation that corresponds with an orientation that is closest to the visual input. Often, the most easily accessible representation will be that for an object at 0° (upright). The other set of mechanisms implements a feature-based system in which object representations in memory are tagged by a list of features and attributes. The first set of mechanisms is based on representations that retain information about the spatial relations between the parts and attributes of the object, whereas the feature-based system is thought to operate based on incomplete representations in which the spatial relations between the features and parts are not preserved. Thus, these features could be thought of as free-floating.

Koriat and Norman (1989b) provided evidence that orientation effects are particularly large when the spatial relations between the elements of a complex pattern are crucial for success in the task. In contrast, when knowledge of the elements alone is sufficient, orientation effects are small (see also, Takano, 1989). These results support the view that tasks that can be performed on the basis of free-floating features are not likely to be affected strongly by the orientation of the stimuli. In contrast, when spatial relations are important, some form of normalization appears to be required. The most likely candidate mechanism is mental rotation. In this view, at least some representations of visual shapes must be orientation specific; otherwise, there would be no need for normalization. These representations appear to be particularly important when the spatial relations between the elements of the shape must be maintained.

Normalization: Other mechanisms

Simion, Roncato, Bagnara, and Umiltà (1982) suggested that there may be two types of normalization mechanisms. One mechanism was postulated to operate on images, producing slow normalization with large effects of orientation, which is usually called mental rotation. The second mechanism was postulated to operate directly on visual input (the *visual code*). This mechanism was postulated to be much faster than mental rotation, but nonetheless to operate in analog fashion and to produce monotonic effects of orientation. These proposals were designed to account for results of experiments in which subjects matched two alphanumeric characters that could differ in orientation. Given that the same stimuli were repeated several times during the course of the experiments, however, it is likely that feature-based mechanisms could have had a large impact on the observed performance. Nonetheless, the suggestion that there may be more than one type of normalization mechanism is worthy of future consideration.

In fact, Koriat and Norman (1988, 1989a) argued for a special type of normalization mechanism, which they called *backward alignment*, which they believe may be distinct from the process of mental rotation postulated by several researchers to account for effects of orientation in tasks requiring left–right (or mirror–normal) decisions (e.g., Shepard & Cooper, 1982). Koriat and Norman required subjects to perform various tasks involving rotated letters, digits, and words. In many tasks there were significant effects of orientation, with orientation defined relative to the usual upright. They refer to these effects as effects of *angular deviation from upright* (*ADU*). Their experiments often involved the rapid presentation of a second stimulus following a response to a previous stimulus. The relationship between the orientation of the second stimulus relative to that of the first stimulus defines a second orientation, which they call *angular deviation from the previous stimulus* (*ADP*). Their main result is that effects of ADP are most consistent and strongest when a stimulus is repeated in exactly the same form (i.e., same mirror–normal version and same order of constituents for stimuli with multiple parts), and effects of ADP are very small or nonexistent when there is a change in version, in order of constituents, or a complete change in stimulus.

When effects of ADP are found, however, they can be substantial (more than 100 ms), and they are monotonic and sometimes linear. Koriat and Norman argued that the necessity for an exact match between the first and second stimuli suggests strongly that this normalization process is holistic in nature. Interestingly, the rate of normalization for backward alignment appeared to be affected by complexity of the visual patterns in that the rate of normalization was slower for stimuli with two characters than for stimuli with a single character (Koriat & Norman, 1989a). Koriat and Norman argue that this complexity effect is due to slowing of a unitary and holistic process of normalization.

The elegant experiments of Koriat and Norman have provided strong evidence for the existence of a distinct process of backward alignment. This mechanism brings a visual stimulus into alignment with the memory trace of a previous stimulus. From the point of view of object identification, this evidence raises the question of whether a mechanism like backward alignment could be involved in object recognition, where a correspondence is sought between a visual input and a previously stored representation of the stimulus. The relationship between this type of alignment and the correspondence mechanisms that mediate apparent motion also is not known. These questions seem worthy of future study.

Normalization: Conclusions

There is considerable evidence suggesting the involvement of normalization operations in the process of object identification. The experiments of Tarr and Pinker (e.g., 1989) provide convincing demonstrations that mental rotation can be used to map visual input to stored representations of previously seen objects and that these representations are viewpoint specific. The experiments of Jolicoeur (1985, 1988; see also Jolicoeur & Milliken, 1989; Maki, 1986; McMullen & Jolicoeur, 1990) suggest that mental rotation is in fact a likely candidate operation when objects are identified for the first time during a particular experiment. However, Murray et al. (1993) found evidence suggesting that transfer of learning for complex natural objects is mediated by a feature-based system rather than by multiple representations.

Overall, the suggestion is that some representations mediating object identification are orientation specific and that normalization aligns visual inputs to these stored representations. Given a restricted context, subsequent identification can be mediated by orientation-invariant representations, probably by means of free-floating features.

Frames of reference

By a *frame of reference* we refer to a means of specifying locations in space. Usually, locations are specified relative to a single fixed point or origin. That is, the location of one point is given in terms of another point, which in some sense is known (as in the location of one's head or eyes) or strategically useful (e.g., a fixed, stationary point may be useful when trying to describe the path of a moving object). Once we have a means of representing the relative positions of two points in space, we can represent simple spatial relations between object parts and spatial patterns. The richness and flexibility of the representational power of the human visual system suggests that some means of specifying the locations of points in space is necessary for representations of visual shape and objects.

Frames of reference often involve the notion of *axes*, which correspond to particular directions in space. There are many different types of reference frames that differ along a number of dimensions, and different types of frames have been proposed implicitly and explicitly by several researchers studying the representation of visual form. One important distinction is whether a reference system is viewer centered or object centered (Marr & Nishihara, 1978). These types of frames differ in the location of the origin of the coordinate system. In a viewer-centered system the origin is located on (or in) the viewer. In an object-centered system the origin is on (or in) the viewed object.

Another distinction between types of reference frames is whether the directions labeled by the frame (the axes) are fixed or adjustable. Results from head-tilt experiments have demonstrated that left–right and mirror–normal discriminations tend to induce the spontaneous use of a mental rotation process that uses the environmental vertical as a principal direction (as opposed to the retinal vertical). Thus, for these tasks, the direction defined by the frame is adjustable (probably in a continuous way) relative to retinal directions as the observer's head is tilted relative to vertical (e.g., Corballis, Nagourney, Shetzer, & Stefanatos, 1978; McMullen & Jolicoeur, 1990).

Further distinctions can be made depending on how frame orientations are adjusted or selected. One view is that the visual system can rotate a global frame of reference in a manner analogous to the mental rotation process proposed by Shepard and Cooper (1982) for the normalization of disoriented images. In this model, the time needed to adjust the orientation of a frame would be proportional to the angle of rotation between the original and terminal frame orientations. Another possibility is that several frames exist in parallel and compete for activation, and that perceptual identification is achieved when one frame becomes dominant over the others (e.g., Hinton, 1981).

It is usually assumed that the earliest stages of visual representation take place within a frame of reference based on retinal coordinates (Feldman, 1985). Many basic mechanisms are confined to fixed retinal coordinates, such as the McCollough effect (e.g., Humphrey, 1994).

A considerable amount of research has focused on determining the conditions under which visual information is not represented within a fixed retinal system. Much of this research has been devoted to isolating conditions that lead a perceptual frame with principal directions that deviate from retinal directions (e.g., Corballis & Roldan, 1975; Corballis, Zbrodoff, & Roldan, 1976).

The concept of reference frame has played an important theoretical part in the study of many issues in visual perception and visual cognition, for example, line orientation discrimination (Attneave & Olson, 1967; Attneave & Reid, 1968), perceived relative orientation (Haller, 1981), the perception of symmetry (Corballis & Roldan, 1975; Fisher & Bornstein, 1982), perceived motion (e.g., Cutting, 1982; Duncker, 1929; Mori, 1984), pattern matching (Bagnara, Simion, & Umiltà, 1984; Humphreys, 1983, 1984; Simion et al., 1982), the perception of multistable figures (Attneave 1968; Palmer, 1980; Palmer & Bucher, 1981), spatial stimulus–response compatibility effects (Ladavas & Moscovitch, 1984), memory for visual shape (Hock & Sullivan, 1981; Rock, 1973; Rock & Heimer, 1957; Wiser, 1980), mental rotation (Carpenter & Eisenberg, 1978; Cooper & Shepard, 1973; Corballis & McLaren, 1984; Corballis et al., 1976; Corballis, Nagourney et al., 1978; Just & Carpenter, 1985; Koriat & Norman, 1984, 1988; McMullen & Jolicoeur, 1990; Robertson, Palmer, & Gomez, 1987), theoretical representations for visual shape (Feldman, 1985; Hinton, 1981; Hinton & Parsons, 1981; Marr, 1982; Marr & Nishihara, 1978; Pinker, 1984), word recognition (Monk, 1985), perceived similarity among three-dimensional objects (Jolicoeur & Kosslyn, 1983), perceived directions (Attneave & Curlee, 1977), and the study of cognitive maps (Levine, Jankovic, & Palij, 1982; Shepard & Hurwitz, 1984).

Several observations highlight the importance of the concept of reference frame in the perception of visual shape. The observations of Mach (1886) on the perceived orientation of squares and diamonds (see Palmer, 1992) suggested early on that the notion of reference frame would play an important part in theories of form perception. This notion has been reinforced by the experiments of Rock and his colleagues (see the section on "Memory: Two-Dimensional Shapes"). One particular demonstration highlights the importance of reference frames and spatial directions in the representation of visual form. Rock (1973) showed subjects the outline of Africa rotated 90° on the page. Most subjects failed to spontaneously recognize the shape as that of Africa. In contrast, when it was viewed in its usual orientation, most subjects spontaneously said "Africa." This simple demonstration suggests strongly that visual shapes are encoded relative to a frame of reference and that different descriptions result when a subject adopts different frames to encode the same shape. This result is sufficient to cast doubt on Corballis's (1988) proposal that representations of visual shape are based on frame-free descriptions because this theory is ill equipped to account for Rock's African demonstration.

The importance of frames is also suggested by experiments in which one observes an orientation effect where orientation is defined relative to that of one or more shapes. Jolicoeur (1990) demonstrated what he called an *orientation-congruency effect* by showing that our ability to identify rotated uppercase letters is affected systematically by the orientation of a target letter relative to the orientation of other letters in a display. When the orientations were congruent (all letters had the same orientation), performance in identifying brief masked presentations was superior to that observed when the orientations were incongruent. Superior identification performance was observed in simultaneous and in sequential displays. Jolicoeur (1992) extended this result by demonstrating a similar effect on the time needed to find a rotated target in a visual search paradigm.

Very strong evidence for models in which shapes are represented in a frame of reference with directions that can be dissociated from retinal directions has been produced by experiments in which the orientation of the subject's head has been tilted clockwise or counterclockwise from vertical. In one set of articles, subjects performed normal–mirror or left–right discriminations with the head either upright or tilted. The common finding using this procedure is that the frame of reference used by subjects lies somewhere between the environmental upright and the retinal upright but is closer to the environmental upright (Corballis et al., 1976; Corballis, Zbrodoff, et al., 1978; McMullen & Jolicoeur, 1990). For example, a subject with the head rotated 60° clockwise from vertical takes significantly less time to decode whether an object faces left or right (e.g., a profile view of an elephant) when the object is shown at 0° (which is at −60° relative to the retina) than when it is shown at 60° (which is retinally upright) (McMullen & Jolicoeur, 1990). These results suggest the adoption of an environmental frame of reference when subjects must make left–right discriminations. In contrast, however, subjects spontaneously adopt a retinal frame of reference when the task is simply to name a rotated object, demonstrating that the identification of a rotated pattern is performed in a retinally aligned reference frame (McMullen & Jolicoeur, 1990).

The different alignment of the perceptual frame of reference for pattern recognition (retinal) as opposed to left–right decisions (environmental) shows that the visual system can adopt different sets of directions, depending on the task that must be performed. The results of head-tilt studies suggest that left–right directions in space are maintained relative to an external environmental frame, making it advantageous to align representations of objects with this frame before making left–right judgments. In contrast, pattern recognition, which generally does not require left–right discriminations (Corballis & McLaren, 1984), can be made without external reference, leading to the adoption of a retinal frame.

Rock (e.g., 1973) suggested that shapes are represented as descriptions within an extrinsic frame of reference. The reference frame, or coordinate system, that he proposed as being crucial is one aligned with the environmental vertical. When describing a shape within such a reference frame, there is an automatic assignment of a top and a bottom to the image. If, however, a shape is presented in an unfamiliar orientation, it may not be recognized because the description of the shape in terms of its top and bottom will change. In the absence of knowledge to the contrary, subjects assume that shapes are upright in the environment (Rock & Heimer, 1957; Rock & Nijhawan, 1989). However, the most easily accessible representations of objects appear to be encoded relative to retinal coordinates (McMullen & Jolicoeur, 1990). Much of the time, these two sets of directions are coincident. It is possible that most representations are encoded in a retinal frame, but that these representations can be rotated or remapped to coincide with environmental directions. However, at any one moment, the phenomenal appearance of the shape depends on which frame is active at that moment. The representations created when subjects have their heads tilted but expect shapes upright in the environment may be different from those encoded when the head is upright. More work will be required to resolve the apparent discrepancies between Rock's work on memory and the results of the on-line naming head-tilt experiments reported by McMullen and Jolicoeur (1990).

What is quite clear from all of the experiments examining orientation effects on the identification of objects rotated in the image plane is that such rotations disrupt object recognition. Even those espousing a viewpoint-invariant approach, such as Biederman (1987), have recognized the deleterious effects of such perturbations of top–bottom relationships. Indeed, the performance of the simulation of RBC by Hummel and Biederman (1992) decreases in a regular manner as objects are rotated in the frontal plane away from their familiar orientation.

The research of Humphreys and Riddoch (1984) and Humphrey and Jolicoeur (1988, 1993) points to the usefulness of external reference frames in recognizing foreshortened views of familiar three-dimensional objects. Research by Humphreys and Riddoch showed that right hemisphere–damaged patients had difficulty recognizing photographs of objects in which the major axis was foreshortened. They suggested that this was because the patients may have imposed a two-dimensional frame of reference on the foreshortened views. Humphreys and Riddoch found that if the objects were photographed on a surface supplying strong pictorial depth cues, the patients' performance improved, presumably because these cues helped the patients impose a three-dimensional reference frame on the object depictions. Humphrey and Jolicoeur found a similar result with normal subjects. The latency to name foreshortened views of common objects was decreased if the objects were presented on a background supplying depth cues congruent with the orientation of the objects. They argued that the depth cues assisted in locating the major axis of the object in the image, leading to faster recognition. Together the results suggest that selecting an appropriate reference frame is an important step in constructing a representation of visual form and that appropriate depth cues can support this process, leading to improved performance with identifying objects rotated in depth.

The reference frame or coordinate system used to build the description of an object in some models is extrinsic to the object (Rock, 1973). Others, perhaps most influentially Marr and Nishihara (1978), have argued for the importance of a coordinate system based on the object – that is, an intrinsic system. Such a system is defined with respect to the geometry of the shape being viewed. The description of the object is then built around the coordinate system defined by the object. Marr and Nishihara suggested that a principal axis could be based on image properties such as elongation and symmetry. The principal axis will define the main axis of the object, and the position of object parts can be described in relation to this axis. Such axis finding and description can be carried out at a number of scales, leading to a hierarchical decomposition of the object into its parts and their relations.

There is some experimental support for the use of intrinsic reference frames in human vision. Wiser (1981) conducted some experiments similar to those of Rock (1973). However, rather than using shapes without an obvious axis of elongation or symmetry, as Rock had done, Wiser used simple two-dimensional shapes that were clearly elongated and symmetrical about the axis of elongation. She used a learning and recognition paradigm in which subjects were familiarized with the shapes in which the axis of elongation and symmetry was oriented vertically, obliquely, or horizontally. During recognition testing, the shapes were presented in the familiar orientation or in one of the other orientations. Recognition for the shapes presented vertically was faster than recognition at other orientations, regardless of the orientation seen at learning. Wiser argued that the simple shapes were represented in relation to their intrinsic axis. Further, she suggested that during recognition the vertically oriented shapes should be recognized most rapidly because, based on demonstrations of Julesz (1971; see also, e.g., Barlow & Reeves, 1979), symmetry is most salient around a vertical axis.

When the results of Wiser (1981) and Rock (1973) are compared, it appears that whether intrinsic axis-based descriptions or descriptions based on extrinsic frames are used depends on the objects (see also Wiser, 1980). If the geometric characteristics of the shape yield a good axis, then intrinsic descriptions will probably be used. Other shapes may encourage the use of extrinsically based descriptions or descriptions based on local features (Humphreys & Quinlan, 1987). Research by Humphreys (1983; see also Humphreys & Quinlan, 1988) supports this proposal. Subjects had to decide if two sequentially presented shapes that could be in the same or different orientations were the same shape or not. The finding that is most relevant to the present discussion was that if the shape to be matched was, for example, a square, then matching was disrupted if it was rotated 45°. Such a rotation aligned different axes with the extrinsic vertical and produced a different description – a diamond. Humphreys suggested that shapes such as squares have ambiguous model axes and that the axis used to describe such shapes is determined by its alignment with the vertical reference frame (retinal and environmental directions were coincident in their experiments). This disruption in shape matching was not found for shapes such as isosceles triangles or elongated pentagons that have an intrinsic model axis.

Conclusions

In this chapter we performed a selective review of several areas of research and examined how results and theories of visual shape and object recognition bear on the problem of object constancy. In particular, we focused on the issue of whether representations of objects and visual shapes are best understood as orientation specific or as orientation free. The theories and models we reviewed fall on both ends of this continuum, as often did the data. Evidence for specificity under some conditions is uncontroversial, however, and acknowledged by almost everyone. The effects of rotations in the image plane on memory and on identification time for all but the most simple stimuli are robust and substantial. These effects are also found for memory and identification time for many types of three-dimensional stimuli rotated in depth.

The debate continues, however, with some scientists theorizing and gathering evidence in support of a viewpoint-invariant form of representation (e.g., Biederman, 1987; Cooper, et al., 1992; Corballis, 1988; Hummel & Biederman, 1992; Schacter et al., 1990, 1991), although some in this camp actually include hybrid representations that have a strong dependence on orientation of the top–bottom axis (e.g., Biederman, 1987). The most interesting recent evidence of this type has used priming as the main dependent measure. However, results in this area have been mixed, with several experiments demonstrating viewpoint specificity (Lawson & Humphreys, 1993; Srinivas, 1993), which calls into question the null findings in earlier reports. Our interpretation of these results is that we have technical reasons for remaining skeptical of demonstrations of viewpoint invariance from measures of priming. These reasons were discussed in depth in the earlier section titled "Priming."

Many chapters on pattern recognition in humans found in introductory texts of cognitive psychology emphasize the inadequacy of simple template models and suggest that recognition is mediated by a system based on orientation-invariant features (e.g., Juola, 1979). We believe that there is now an abundance of evidence suggesting that pattern recognition in humans is often much more viewpoint specific than might be construed from such chapters. Interestingly, increasing attention has been given to the exploration of viewpoint-dependent models of object recognition in the computer science literature (e.g., Bülthoff & Edelman, 1992; Edelman & Bülthoff, 1992; Ullman, 1989). The work of Edelman and his colleagues on interpolation between two-dimensional views, for example, shows how one of the classic arguments against viewpoint-dependent representations – the potential need for a very large number of specific representations – can be overcome. This elegant theoretical work, as well as that of Ullman (1989), dovetails nicely with the mounting evidence in the psychological literature in support of viewpoint-dependent representations and transformation mechanisms.

Evidence for orientation invariance under some conditions also abounds (e.g., Biederman & Cooper, 1991b, 1992; Biederman & Gerhardstein, 1993; Eley, 1982; White, 1980; see also Murray et al., 1993). At present, demonstrations of viewpoint invariance may reflect an opportunistic reliance on free-floating features. If so, these experiments may, in fact, not be very informative in terms of furthering our understanding of how the visual system represents the structure of visual shapes. Thus, an important goal for future experimentation is to isolate the nature of the representations that mediate performance in these studies so as to show that the representations are indeed more than a loose collection of features or attributes.

We conclude that the existence of viewpoint-dependent representations is well established. Evidence for viewpoint invariance is on less secure ground, and it remains to be seen whether or not the visual system relies on fully articulated viewpoint-invariant structural representations of visual shapes for object recognition. One thing is certain: The active search for viewpoint-invariant representations will continue, and the distinction between viewpoint specificity and viewpoint invariance is likely to remain an important one for the foreseeable future.

Notes

1. The results showed equivalent effects of rotating clockwise or counterclockwise.
2. Assume clockwise rotations in the image plane.
3. If we suppose that some fraction of the priming difference between the identical condition and the replaced condition was due to something other than visual priming (say, semantic priming), then the 6 ms may be closer to what we should expect.

References

Attneave, F. (1968). Triangles as ambiguous figures. *American Journal of Psychology, 81*, 447–453.

Attneave, F., & Curlee, T. E. (1977). Cartesian organization in the immediate reproduction of spatial patterns. *Bulletin of the Psychonomic Society, 10*, 469–470.

Attneave, F., & Olson, R. K. (1967). Discriminability of stimuli varying in physical and retinal orientation. *Journal of Experimental Psychology, 74*, 149–157.

Attneave, F., & Reid, K. W. (1968). Voluntary control of frame of reference and slope equivalence under head rotation. *Journal of Experimental Psychology, 1*, 153–159.

Bagnara, S., Simion, F., & Umiltà, C. (1984). Reference patterns and the process of normalization. *Perception & Psychophysics, 35*, 186–192.

Barlow, H. B., & Reeves, B. C. (1979). The versatility and absolute efficiency of the detection of mirror symmetry in random dot displays. *Vision Research, 19*, 783–793.

Bartram, D. J. (1976). Levels of coding in picture-picture comparison tasks. *Memory & Cognition, 4*, 593–602.

Biederman, I. (1985). Human image understanding: Recent research and a theory. *Computer Vision, Graphics, and Image Processing, 32*, 29–73.

Biederman, I. (1987). Recognition-by-components: A theory of human image understanding. *Psychological Review, 94*, 115–147.

Biederman, I. (1988). Aspects and extensions of a theory of human image understanding. In Z. W. Pylyshyn (Ed.), *Computational processes in human vision: An interdisciplinary perspective* (pp. 370–428). Norwood, NJ: Ablex.

Biederman, I., & Cooper, E. E. (1991a). Priming contour-deleted images: Evidence for intermediate representations in visual object recognition. *Cognitive Psychology, 23*, 393–419.

Biederman, I., & Cooper, E. E. (1991b). Evidence for complete translational and reflectional invariance in visual object priming. *Perception, 20*, 585–593.

Biederman, I., & Cooper, E. E. (1991c). Object recognition and laterality: Null effects. *Neuropsychologia, 29,* 685–694.

Biederman, I., & Cooper, E. E. (1992). Size invariance in visual object priming. *Journal of Experimental Psychology: Human Perception and Performance, 18,* 121–133.

Biederman, I., & Gerhardstein, P. C. (1993). Recognizing depth-rotated objects: Evidence and conditions for 3D viewpoint invariance. *Journal of Experimental Psychology: Human Perception and Performance, 19,* 1162–1182.

Braine, L. G. (1965). Disorientation of forms: An examination of Rock's theory. *Psychonomic Science, 3,* 541–542.

Bruce, V. (1988). *Recognizing faces* Hillsdale, NJ: Erlbaum.

Bruce, V., Valentine, T., & Baddeley, A. (1987). The basis of the ¾ view advantage in face recognition. *Applied Cognitive Psychology, 1,* 109–120.

Bülthoff, H. H., & Edelman, S. (1992). Psychophysical support for a two-dimensional view interpolation theory of object recognition. *Proceedings of the National Academy of Sciences, 89,* 60–64.

Bülthoff, H. H., Edelman, S., & Sklar, E. (1991). *Mapping the generalization space in object recognition.* Presented at the annual meeting of the Association for Research in Vision and Ophthalmology, Sarasota, Florida.

Carpenter, P. A., & Eisenberg, P. (1978). Mental rotation and the frame of reference in blind and sighted individuals. *Perception & Psychophysics, 23,* 117–124.

Cavanagh, P. (1991). What's up in top-down processing? In A. Gorea (Ed.), *Representations of vision: Trends and tacit assumptions in vision research* (pp. 295–304). Cambridge: Cambridge University Press.

Cooper, L. A., Schacter, D. L., Ballesteros, S., & Moore, C. (1992). Priming and recognition of transformed three-dimensional objects: Effects of size and reflection. *Journal of Experimental Psychology: Learning, Memory, and Cognition, 18,* 43–57.

Cooper, L. A., & Shepard, R. N. (1973). Chronometric studies of the rotation of mental images. In W. G. Chase (Ed.), *Visual information processing* (pp. 75–176). San Diego, CA: Academic Press.

Corballis, M. C. (1982). Mental rotation: Anatomy of a paradigm. In M. Potegal (Ed.), *Spatial abilities: Development and physiological foundations* (pp. 173–198). Orlando, FL: Academic Press.

Corballis, M. C. (1988). Distinguishing clockwise from counterclockwise: Does it require mental rotation? *Memory & Cognition, 16,* 567–578.

Corballis, M. C., Macadie, L., Crotty, A., & Beale, I. L. (1985). The naming of disoriented letters by normal and reading disabled children. *Journal of Child Psychology & Psychiatry, 26,* 929–938.

Corballis, M. C., & McLaren, R. (1984). Winding one's Ps and Qs: Mental rotation and mirror-image discrimination. *Journal of Experimental Psychology: Human Perception and Performance, 10,* 318–327.

Corballis, M. C., & Nagourney, B. A. (1978). Latency to categorize disoriented alphanumeric characters as letters or digits. *Canadian Journal of Psychology, 32* (3), 186–188.

Corballis, M. C., Nagourney, B. A., Shetzer, L. I., & Stefanatos, G. (1978). Mental rotation under head tilt: Factors influencing the location of the subjective reference frame. *Perception & Psychophysics, 24,* 263–273.

Corballis, M. C., & Roldan, C. E. (1975). Detection of symmetry as a function of angular orientation. *Journal of Experimental Psychology: Human Perception and Performance, 3,* 221–230.

Corballis, M. C., Zbrodoff, N. J., & Roldan, C. E. (1976). What's up in mental rotation? *Perception & Psychophysics, 19,* 525–530.

Corballis, M. C., Zbrodoff, N. J., Shetzer, L. I., & Butler, P. B. (1978). Decisions about identity and orientation of rotated letters and digits. *Memory & Cognition, 6,* 98–107.

Cutting, J. E. (1982). Blowing in the wind: Perceiving structure in trees and bushes. *Cognition, 12,* 25–44.

Cutzu, F., & Edelman, S. (1992). *Viewpoint-dependence of response time in object recognition.* Technical Report CS92-10. Rehovot, Israel: Weizmann Institute of Science.

Dearborn, G. V. N. (1899). Recognition under objective reversal. *Psychological Review, 6,* 395–406.

Duncker, K. (1929). Uber induzierte Bewegung. *Psychologishe Forschung, 12,* 180–259. (Condensed in W. Ellis [Ed. and trans.], *Source book of Gestalt psychology.* New York: Humanities Press, 1950.)

Edelman, S. (1991). *Features of recognition.* Technical Report CS91-10. Rehovot, Israel: Weizmann Institute of Science.

Edelman, S. (1992). Class similarity and viewpoint invariance in the recognition of 3D objects. Technical Report CS92-17. Rehovot, Israel: *Weizmann Institute of Science.*

Edelman, S., & Bülthoff, H. H. (1992). Orientation dependence in the recognition of familiar and novel views of three-dimensional objects. *Vision Research, 32,* 2395–2400.

Edelman, S., & Weinshall, S. (1991). A self-organizing multiple-view representation of 3D objects. *Biological Cybernetics, 64,* 209–219.

Eley, M. G. (1982). Identifying rotated letter-like symbols. *Memory & Cognition, 10,* 25–32.

Ellis, R., & Allport, D. A. (1986). Multiple levels of representation for visual objects: A behavioural study. In A. G. Cohn & J. R. Thomas (Eds.), *Artificial intelligence and its applications* (pp. 245–257). New York: Wiley.

Ellis, R., Allport, D. A., Humphreys, G. W., & Collis, J. (1989). Varieties of object constancy. *Quarterly Journal of Experimental Psychology, 41A,* 775–796.

Feldman, J. A. (1985). Four frames suffice: A provisional model of vision and space. *The Behavioral and Brain Sciences, 8,* 265–289.

Fisher, C. B., & Bornstein, M. H. (1982). Identification of symmetry: Effects of stimulus orientation and head position. *Perception & Psychophysics, 32,* 443–448.

Friedman, A., & Harding, C. A. (1990). Seeing versus imagining movement in depth. *Canadian Journal of Psychology, 44,* 371–383.

Gerhardstein, P. C., & Biederman, I. (1991). *3D orientation invariance in visual object recognition.* Presented at the annual meeting of the Association for Research in Vision and Ophthalmology, Sarasota, Florida.

Gibson, J. J., & Robinson, D. (1935). Orientation in visual perception: The recognition of familiar plane forms in differing orientations. *Psychological Monographs, 46,* 39–47.

Haller, O. (1981). Spontaneous reference systems in individuals. *Perceptual and Motor Skills, 53,* 591–603.

Harries, M. H., Perrett, D. I., & Lavender, A. (1991). Preferential inspection of views of 3-D model heads. *Perception, 20,* 669–680.

Hinton, G. E. (1981). A parallel computation that assigns canonical object-based frames of reference. In *Proceedings of the Seventh International Joint Conference on Artificial Intelligence* (Vol. 2, pp. 683–685). Los Altos, CA: Kaufman.

Hinton, G. E., & Parsons, L. M. (1981). Frames of reference and mental imagery. In A. Baddeley, J. Long (Eds.), *Attention and performance* (Vol. IX, pp. 261–277). Hillsdale, NJ: Erlbaum.

Hock, H. S., & Sullivan, M. (1981). Alternative spatial reference systems: Intentional vs. incidental learning. *Perception & Psychophysics, 29,* 467–474.

Hummel, J. E., & Biederman, I. (1992). Dynamic binding in a neural network for shape recognition. *Psychological Review, 99,* 480–517.

Humphrey, G. K. (1994). The McCollough effect: Misperception and reality. In Vincent Walsh & Janusz Kulikowski (Eds.), *Visual constancies: Why things look as they do.* (pp. 47–98). Cambridge: Cambridge University Press.

Humphrey, G. K., & Jolicoeur, P. (1988). Visual object identification: Some effects of foreshortening and monocular depth cues. In Z. W. Pylyshyn (Ed.), *Computational processes in human vision: An interdisciplinary perspective* (pp. 429–442). Norwood, NJ: Ablex.

Humphrey, G. K., & Jolicoeur, P. (1993). An examination of the effects of axis foreshortening, monocular depth cues, and visual field on object identification. *Quarterly Journal of Experimental Psychology, 46A,* 137–159.

Humphrey, G. K., & Khan, S. C. (1992). Recognizing novel views of three-dimensional objects. *Canadian Journal of Psychology, 46,* 170–190.

Humphrey, G. K., & Lupker, S. (1993). Codes and operations in picture matching. *Psychological Research, 55,* 237–247.

Humphreys, G. W. (1983). Reference frames and shape perception. *Cognitive Psychology, 15,* 151–196.

Humphreys, G. W. (1984). Shape constancy: The effects of changing shape orientation and the effects of changing the position of focal features. *Perception & Psychophysics, 36,* 50–64.

Humphreys, G. W., & Quinlan, P. T. (1987). Normal and pathological processes in visual object constancy. In G. W. Humphreys & M. J. Riddoch (Eds.), *Visual object processing: A cognitive neuropsychological approach* (pp. 43–105). Hillsdale, NJ: Erlbaum.

Humphreys, G. W., & Quinlan, P. T. (1988). Priming effects between two-dimensional shapes. *Journal of Experimental Psychology: Human Perception and Performance, 14,* 203–220.

Humphreys, G. W., & Riddoch, M. J. (1984). Routes to object constancy: Implications from neurological impairments of object constancy. *Quarterly Journal of Experimental Psychology, 36A,* 385–415.

Jolicoeur, P. (1985). The time to name disoriented natural objects. *Memory & Cognition, 13,* 289–303.

Jolicoeur, P. (1987). A size-congruency effect in memory for visual shape. *Memory & Cognition, 15,* 531–543.

Jolicoeur, P. (1988). Mental rotation and the identification of disoriented objects. *Canadian Journal of Psychology, 42,* 461–478.

Jolicoeur, P. (1990). Identification of disoriented objects: A dual-systems theory. *Mind and Language, 5,* 387–410.

Jolicoeur, P. (1992). Orientation congruency effects in visual search. *Canadian Journal of Psychology, 42,* 280–305.

Jolicoeur, P., Gluck, M. A., & Kosslyn, S. M. (1984). From pictures to words: Making the connection. *Cognitive Psychology, 16,* 243–275.

Jolicoeur, P., Keillor, J., & Ingleton, M. (1992, July). *Characteristics of objects and effects of orientation on the recovery of identity and top–bottom information.* Paper presented at the XXV International Congress of Psychology, Brussels.

Jolicoeur, P., & Kosslyn, S. M. (1983). Coordinate systems in the long-term memory representation of three-dimensional shapes. *Cognitive Psychology, 15,* 301–345.

Jolicoeur, P., & Landau, M. J. (1984). Effects of orientation on the identification of simple visual patterns. *Canadian Journal of Psychology, 38,* 80–93.

Jolicoeur, P., & Milliken, B. (1989). Identification of disoriented objects: Effects of context of prior presentation. *Journal of Experimental Psychology: Learning, Memory, and Cognition, 15,* 200–210.

Jolicoeur, P., Snow, D., & Murray, J. (1987). The time to identify disoriented letters: Effects of practice and font. *Canadian Journal of Psychology, 41,* 303–316.

Julesz, B. (1971). *Foundations of cyclopean perception.* Chicago: University of Chicago Press.

Juola, J. F. (1979). Pattern recognition. In R. Lachman, J. L. Lachman, & E. C. Butterfield (Eds.), *Cognitive psychology and information processing: An introduction* (pp. 489–523). Hillsdale, NJ: Erlbaum.

Just, M. A., & Carpenter, P. A. (1985). Cognitive coordinate systems: Accounts of mental rotation and individual differences in spatial ability. *Psychological Review, 92,* 137–172.

Kelter, S., Grvtzbach, H., Freiheit, R., Hvhle, B., Wutzig, S., & Diesch, E. (1984). Object identification: The mental representation of physical and conceptual attributes. *Memory & Cognition, 12,* 123–133.

Kimura, D., & Durnford, M. (1974). Normal studies on the function of the right hemisphere in vision. In S. J. Dimond & J. G. Beaumont (Eds.), *Hemispheric function in the human brain* (pp. 25–47). London: Paul Elek.

Kolers, P. A., & Perkins, D. N. (1969a). Orientation of letters and errors in their recognition. *Perception & Psychophysics, 5,* 265–269.

Kolers, P. A., & Perkins, D. N. (1969b). Orientation of letters and their speed of recognition. *Perception & Psychophysics, 5,* 275–280.

Koriat, A., & Norman, J. (1984). What is rotated in mental rotation? *Journal of Experimental Psychology: Learning, Memory, and Cognition, 10,* 421–434.

Koriat, A., & Norman, J. (1988). Frames and images: Sequential effects in mental rotation. *Journal of Experimental Psychology: Learning, Memory, and Cognition, 14,* 93–111.

Koriat, A., & Norman, J. (1989a). Establishing global and local correspondence between successive stimuli: The holistic nature of backward alignment. *Journal of Experimental Psychology: Learning, Memory, and Cognition, 15,* 480–494.

Koriat, A., & Norman, J. (1989b). Why is word recognition impaired by disorientation while the identification of single letters is not? *Journal of Experimental Psychology: Human Perception and Performance, 15,* 153–163.

Kosslyn, S. M. (1980). *Image and mind.* Cambridge, MA: Harvard University Press.

Ladavas, E., & Moscovitch, M. (1984). Must egocentric and environmental frames of reference be aligned to produce spatial S–R compatibility effects? *Journal of Experimental Psychology: Human Perception and Performance, 10,* 205–215.

Landis, T., Regard, M., Bliestle, A., & Kleihues, P. (1988). Prosopagnosia and agnosia for noncanonical views. *Brain, 111,* 1287–1297.

Lawson, R., & Humphreys, G. W. (1993). *View-specificity in object processing: Evidence from picture matching.* Unpublished manuscript, University of Birmingham, Birmingham, United Kingdom.

Layman, S., & Greene, E. (1988). The effect of stroke on object recognition. *Brain and Cognition, 7,* 87–114.

Levine, C., & Banich, M. T. (1982). Lateral asymmetries in the naming of words and corresponding line drawings. *Brain and Language, 17,* 34–45.

Levine, M., Jankovic, I. N., & Palij, M. (1982). Principles of spatial problem solving. *Journal of Experimental Psychology: General, 111,* 157–175.

Logie, R. H., Baddeley, A. D., & Woodhead, M. M. (1987). Face recognition, pose and ecological validity. *Applied Cognitive Psychology, 1,* 53–69.

Mach, E. (1886/1959). *The analysis of sensations.* (Translated from the German edition, 1886). New York: Dover.

Maki, R. H. (1986). Naming and locating the tops of rotated pictures. *Canadian Journal of Psychology, 40,* 368–387.

Marr, D. (1982). *Vision.* San Francisco: Freeman.

Marr, D., & Nishihara, H. K. (1978). Representation and recognition of the spatial organization of three-dimensional shapes. *Proceedings of the Royal Society of London, Series B, 200,* 269–294.

McMullen, P. A., & Jolicoeur, P. (1990). The spatial frame of reference in object naming and discrimination of left–right reflections. *Memory & Cognition, 18,* 99–115.

Milliken, B., & Jolicoeur, P. (1992). Size effects in visual recognition memory are determined by perceived size. *Memory & Cognition, 20,* 83–95.

Monk, A. F. (1985). Theoretical note: Coordinate systems in visual word recognition. *Quarterly Journal of Experimental Psychology, 37A,* 613–625.

Mori, T. (1984). Change of frame of reference with velocity in visual motion perception. *Perception & Psychophysics, 35,* 515–518.

Murray, J. E., Jolicoeur, P., McMullen, P. A., & Ingleton, M. (1993). Orientation-invariant transfer of training in the identification of rotated objects. *Memory & Cognition, 21,* 604–610.

Newell, F., & Findlay, J. M. (1992). Viewpoint invariance in object recognition. *Irish Journal of Psychology, 13,* 494–507.

Paivio, A., & Ernest, C. H. (1971). Imagery ability and visual perception of verbal and nonverbal stimuli. *Perception & Psychophysics, 10,* 429–432.

Palmer, S. E. (1980). What makes triangles point: Local and global effects in configurations of ambiguous triangles. *Cognitive Psychology, 12,* 285–305.

Palmer, S. E. (1992). Modern theories of Gestalt perception. In G. W. Humphreys (Ed.), *Understanding vision. An interdisciplinary perspective* (pp. 39–70). Oxford: Blackwell.

Palmer, S. E., & Bucher, N. M. (1981). Configural effects in perceived pointing of ambiguous triangles. *Journal of Experimental Psychology: Human Perception and Performance, 7,* 88–114.

Palmer, S. E., Rosch, E., & Chase, P. (1981). Canonical perspective and the perception of objects. In J. Long & A. Baddeley (Eds.), *Attention and performance* (Vol. IX, pp. 135–151). Hillsdale, NJ: Erlbaum.

Perrett, D. I., & Harries, M. H. (1988). Characteristic views and the visual inspection of simple faceted and smooth objects: Tetrahedra and potatoes. *Perception, 17,* 703–720.

Perrett, D. I., Harries, M. H., & Looker, S. (1992). Use of preferential inspection to define the viewing sphere and characteristic views of an arbitrary machine tool part. *Perception, 21,* 497–515.

Pinker, S. (1984). Visual cognition: An introduction. *Cognition, 18,* 1–63.

Poggio, T., & Edelman, S. (1990). A network that learns to recognize three-dimensional objects. *Nature, 343,* 263–266.

Ratcliff, G., & Newcombe, F. (1982). Object recognition: Some deductions from the clinical evidence. In A. W. Ellis (Ed.), *Normality and pathology in cognitive function* (pp. 147–171). New York: Academic Press.

Reingold, E. M., & Merikle, P. M. (1988). Using direct and indirect measures to study perception without awareness. *Perception & Psychophysics, 44,* 563–575.

Reingold, E. M., & Merikle, P. M. (1990). On the inter-relatedness of theory and measurement in the study of unconscious processes. *Mind and Language, 5,* 9–28.

Robertson, L. C., Palmer, S. E., & Gomez, L. M. (1987). Reference frames in mental rotation. *Journal of Experimental Psychology: Learning, Memory, and Cognition, 13,* 368–379.

Rock, I. (1956). The orientation of forms on the retina and in the environment. *American Journal of Psychology, 69,* 513–528.

Rock, I. (1973). *Orientation and form* (pp. 81–159). Orlando, FL: Academic Press.

Rock, I. (1974). The perception of disoriented figures. *Scientific American, 230,* 78–85.

Rock, I., & DiVita, J. (1987). A case of viewer-centered object perception. *Cognitive Psychology, 19,* 280–293.

Rock, I., Di Vita, J., & Barbeito, R. (1981). The effect on form perception of change of orientation in the third dimension. *Journal of Experimental Psychology: Human Perception and Performance, 7,* 719–732.

Rock, I., & Heimer, W. (1957). The effects of retinal and phenomenal orientation on the perception of form. *American Journal of Psychology, 70,* 493–511.

Rock, I., & Nijhawan, R. (1989). Regression to egocentrically determined description of form under conditions of inattention. *Journal of Experimental Psychology: Human Perception and Performance, 15,* 259–272.

Rock, I., Wheeler, D., & Tudor, L. (1989). Can we imagine how objects look from other viewpoints? *Cognitive Psychology, 21,* 185–210.

Rosch, E., Mervis, C. B., Gray, W. D., Johnson, D. M., & Boyes-Braem, P. (1976). Basic objects in natural categories. *Cognitive Psychology, 8,* 382–439.

Schacter, D. L., Cooper, L. A., & Delaney, S. M. (1990). Implicit memory for unfamiliar objects depends on access to structural descriptions. *Journal of Experimental Psychology: General, 119,* 5–24.

Schacter, D. L., Cooper, L. A., Delaney, S. M., Peterson, M. A., & Tharan, M. (1991). Implicit memory for possible and impossible objects: Constraints on the construction of structural descriptions. *Journal of Experimental Psychology: Learning, Memory, and Cognition, 17,* 3–19.

Shallice, T. (1988). *From neuropsychology to mental structure.* Cambridge: Cambridge University Press.

Shepard, R. N. (1984). Ecological constraints on internal representation: Resonant kinematics of perceiving, imagining, thinking, and dreaming. *Psychological Review, 91,* 417–447.

Shepard, R. N., & Cooper, L. A. (1982). *Mental images and their transformations.* Cambridge, MA: MIT Press.

Shepard, R. N., & Hurwitz, S. (1984). Upward direction, mental rotation, and discrimination of left and right turns in maps. *Cognition, 18,* 161–193.

Shepard, R. N., & Judd, S. A. (1976). Perceptual illusion of rotation of three-dimensional objects. *Science, 191,* 952–954.

Shepard, R. N., & Metzler, J. (1971). Mental rotation of three-dimensional objects. *Science, 171,* 701–703.

Simion, F., Bagnara, S., Roncato, S., & Umiltà, C. (1982). Transformation processes upon the visual code. *Perception & Psychophysics, 31,* 13–25.

Snodgrass, J. G., & Vanderwart, M. (1980). A standardized set of 260 pictures: Norms for name agreement, image agreement, familiarity, and visual complexity. *Journal of Experimental Psychology: Human Learning and Memory, 6,* 174–215.

Srinivas, K. (1993). Perceptual specificity in nonverbal priming. *Journal of Experimental Psychology: Learning, Memory, and Cognition, 19,* 582–602.

Steinfeld, G. J. (1970). The effect of retinal orientation on the recognition of novel and familiar shapes. *Journal of General Psychology, 82,* 223–239.

Stephen, D., & Parker, D. (1993). *The role of alignment in object processing.* Unpublished manuscript.

Takano, Y. (1989). Perception of rotated forms: A theory of information types. *Cognitive Psychology, 21,* 1–59.

Tarr, M. J. (1989). *Orientation dependence in three-dimensional object recognition.* Unpublished doctoral thesis, Department of Brain and Cognitive Sciences, Massachusetts Institute of Technology.

Tarr, M. J., & Pinker, S. (1989). Mental rotation and orientation-dependence in shape recognition. *Cognitive Psychology, 21,* 233–282.

Thomas, S., Perrett, D. I., Davis, D. N., & Harries, M. H. (1991). *Effect of perspective view on recognition of faces.* Unpublished manuscript.

Ullman, S. (1989). Aligning pictorial descriptions: An approach to object recognition. *Cognition, 32,* 193–254.

Warrington, E. K., & James, M. (1986). Visual object recognition in patients with right hemisphere lesions: Axes or features? *Perception, 15,* 355–366.

Warrington, E. K., & James, M. (1988). Visual apperceptive agnosia: A clinico-anatomical study of three cases. *Cortex, 24,* 13–32.

Warrington, E. K., & Taylor, A. M. (1973). The contribution of the right parietal lobe to object recognition. *Cortex, 9,* 152–164.

Warrington, E. K., & Taylor, A. M. (1978). Two categorical stages of object recognition. *Perception, 7,* 695–705.

White, M. J. (1980). Naming and categorization of tilted alphanumeric characters do not require mental rotation. *Bulletin of the Psychonomic Society, 15,* 153–156.

Wiser, M. A. (1980). *The role of intrinsic axes in the mental representation of shapes.* Unpublished doctoral dissertation, Massachusetts Institute of Technology.

Wiser, M. A. (1981). The role of intrinsic axes in shape recognition. *Proceedings of the third annual meeting of the Cognitive Science Society* (pp. 184–186). San Mateo, CA: Kaufman.

Young, A. W., & Bion, P. J. (1981). Identification and storage of line drawings presented to the left and right cerebral hemispheres of adults and children. *Cortex, 17,* 459–464.

Young, A. W., Bion, P. J., & Ellis, A. W. (1980). Studies toward a model of laterality effects for picture and word naming. *Brain and Language, 11,* 54–65.

Young, J. M., Palef, S. R., & Logan, G. D. (1980). The role of mental rotation in letter processing by children and adults. *Canadian Journal of Psychology, 34,* 265–269.

4 Computational approaches to shape constancy

Shimon Edelman and Daphna Weinshall

1. Classification of computational approaches to shape constancy

Computational approaches to geometric shape constancy can be classified according to their stance on two major issues: degree of reliance on reconstruction and availability of object models.

1.1 Shape reconstruction

Assuming that constancy involves the comparison of the stimulus to some immutable ideal (leading to a realization that the former is an instance of the latter), it is possible to distinguish between two stages in the computation leading to constancy: representation and matching. Different approaches to constancy call for a different distribution of the processing load between these two stages. On the one hand, there are approaches that depend on a reconstruction (leading to a quasi–three-dimensional representation) of the stimulus. The comparison between the recovered representation and the internal model in such a scheme may be quite simple (a kind of template matching), although the reconstruction itself is computationally challenging. On the other hand, there are approaches that employ rather simple representations (e.g., two-dimensional image-based measurements or features), for which they compensate by having to rely on complicated matching decision procedures. Examples of these two classes of approaches will be discussed in sections 2 and 3.

1.1.1 The availability of a model. We assume that constancy is achieved via a comparison between the input and a model. In fact, the involvement of a well-defined model is not a prerequisite for constancy (consider the drawing in Figure 4.1, devised by Biederman (1987) as an example of the ability of human observers to assign a correct three-dimensional interpretation to a novel view of an arbitrary object). In the following two sections, we will show how, by relaxing the assumption of the availability of a model, one can affect the conceptual underpinnings and the computational properties of constancy algorithms, both of the reconstruction and of the feature variety.

124

Figure: 4.1: A do-it-yourself object. There is a strong consensus in the reception of the three-dimensional structure of this object. Adapted with permission from Biederman (1987).

2. Constancy via reconstruction

Assuming that the goal is to reconstruct the shape of a three-dimensional object from a two-dimensional image or images, the issue still remains of whether and how to compute the pose of the object (its orientation with respect to the camera). Knowledge of the pose is usually not necessary for the recognition of the object. However, separating the pose from the shape may be difficult, and the ability to do that may be equivalent to the ability to perceive shape constancy. One may compare this ambiguity to the problem of color constancy, where the color of an object may be due to its surface pigmentation or to the spectral composition of the illumination source. Similarly, the shape of an image of an object may be due to the object's geometric structure or to the particular viewpoint from which it is observed. The issue here is whether to reconstruct shape and pose together or only shape. In the color analogy, the issue is whether to compute the color of the object and the color of the light source or just the color of the object.

2.1 Model-based approaches

Information about the three-dimensional shape of the target object can be put to use in the recognition[1] process in a number of ways. We consider here two possibilities: methods that involve alignment between an internal three-dimensional model and the input, and methods that operate directly on two-dimensional images, without explicit reconstruction of a three-dimensional model.

The approaches discussed in section 2.1.1 use knowledge of pose, whereas the approaches discussed in section 2.1.2 use partial reconstruction, namely, reconstruction of the shape parameters only (as opposed to complete reconstruction, which seeks to compute the parameters of the shape and the pose).

2.1.1 Normalization via pose. Our first example of the normalization approach is the alignment method (Fischler & Bolles, 1981; Rivers, Bouthemy, Prasada, & Dubois, 1981; Ullman, 1989). A generic alignment algorithm proceeds as follows. First, for each model available to the system, a viewing transformation is computed, subject to the requirement that the image and the appropriate view of the model match (i.e., become aligned) if the input view indeed belongs to the model. Second, the hypothesized transformation is carried out, and the degree of the resulting match is used to confirm or to refute the attribution of the input view to the model. The model that yields the best fit following alignment is declared the outcome of the recognition process.

As just formulated, the alignment approach appears to require an exhaustive search of all the space of all possible transformations of each model, so that the optimal combination of model and transformation can be found. In fact, Ullman's alignment method actually obviates the need to search through all transformations by specifying an algorithm for computing the aligning transformation given the correspondence between a small number of *anchor* image points and points in the model. Thus, the only search that remains to be done is over the possible models. Later in this section we discuss a related approach, recognition by geometric hashing, which seeks to eliminate the need for this search as well, at the cost of using a large database.

A slightly different formulation of the basic idea behind the normalization approach – recovery and use of explicit information about the viewpoint – can be found in Lowe's (1987) notion of viewpoint consistency constraints. In Lowe's method, locations of a few key points in the image lead to a hypothesis regarding the viewing transformation, which is then used to predict iteratively the locations of additional object points in the image. An advantage of this method is the possibility of aborting processing of a given model in the presence of growing evidence against its suitability, provided by the incremental evaluation process.

The third approach of this variety that we mention is Lamdan and Wolfson's (1988) geometric hashing. Here, several of the object's features are chosen to serve as a linear basis in terms of which the locations of all other features are encoded. For any choice of the basis features, it is possible to express all the other features of the object relative to the basis, that is, in transformation-invariant coordinates. Accordingly, in the preprocessing step of the geometric hashing method, the coordinates of all the feature points of the object are pre-computed for every possible choice of the basis feature set and are used to construct a hash table that associates the pair (model, basis) with the set of coordinates.[2] Recognition then proceeds in several steps. First, features of interest are extracted. Second, a basis set is chosen, and the coordinates of all other features in this basis are computed. A counter associated with the hash table entry corresponding to the set of computed coordinates is then incremented, in a process that resembles ''voting'' for the appropriate (model, basis) pair. Finally, the pair with the most votes is chosen, the transformation between the model thus retrieved and the image is computed (as in the alignment scheme), and the transformed model is verified against the image.

An important advantage of geometric hashing over straightforward alignment is in its lower computation complexity (Lamdan & Wolfson, 1988). The reduction in complexity is achieved in a trade-off against potentially heavy memory usage dictated by the storage requirements of the hashing scheme. It should be noted, however, that a heavy reliance on memory, in conjunction with a relatively simple computation process (such as voting), may be considered an advantage rather than a handicap in a scheme that aims at modeling recognition in biological vision.

2.1.2 Normalization via formal invariance. The normalization methods just discussed either align the image with the model, a process equivalent to pose computation (where the transformation of the object with respect to the camera is computed), or use the pose of the object in a voting scheme. However, neither alignment nor geometric hashing (or generally any indexing technique) needs to use the pose for recognition. To avoid pose dependency, it is necessary to use a representation of three-dimensional shape that does not depend on its orientation with respect to the camera or, equivalently, that is invariant to the transformation of the camera (or the eye).

Koenderink and van Doorn (1991) described a hierarchy of representations determined by the particular selection of the group of three-dimensional transformations of the camera, with respect to which invariance is sought:

Complete: The complete representation of the scene includes the three-dimensional coordinates of each point, possibly as a depth map, and the pose of the camera relative to the object. This representation is typically sought in reconstruction algorithms in computer vision.

Euclidean invariant: A description of the three-dimensional shape of objects that is invariant to the action of the group of similarity transformations in three-dimensions, which includes rotations, translations, and isotropic scaling.

Affine invariant: A description of the three-dimensional shape of objects that is invariant to the action of the group of linear transformations in three dimensions and of translations. The group of affine transformations includes the group of similarity transformations.

A *complete* representation describes uniquely the object and its orientation relative to the camera. It includes the largest possible amount of information concerning the scene, and therefore, not surprisingly, it is the most difficult one to compute. A *Euclidean* representation is unique for every general three-dimensional object, but different scenes (where the same object is observed from different orientations) may have the same representation. This is a desirable ambiguity. An *affine* representation is not unique: Objects that are related by a linear transformation have the same affine representation. For example, in two dimensions, all squares and parallelograms have the same affine representation because they can be obtained from each other by a linear transformation (namely, by stretch and shear). This ambiguity is less desirable: The cost of using an affine representation is an increased number of false-positive matches. On the other hand, affine three-dimensional shape representations are easier to compute because they can be computed from a sequence of two-dimensional images by a linear algorithm (Shashua, 1991; Weinshall, 1993).

The normalization methods described in the previous section can be implemented without computing pose, using such invariant representations. Alignment of an image can be done with an invariant representation of the object, in which case there is no need to search the transformation space, although there is still a need to search the model space (Weinshall, 1993). Geometric hashing already relies on an affine-invariant representation and uses the pose only in the voting scheme. This involvement of the pose can be eliminated and an object invariant quantity, such as the location of the center of gravity of the object, can be used instead during the voting (Mohan, Weinshall & Sarukkai, 1993).

2.1.3 Direct methods equivalent to reconstruction.   In all the examples of normalization, the achievement of constancy hinges on the availability of an explicit three-dimensional model of the object in question, which is used to relate different views to each other via viewpoint consistency constraints of some kind. A recent work by Ullman and Basri (1991) demonstrated that one need not represent the model of an object explicitly to determine whether an input image belongs to the object. Let each view of a three-dimensional object be represented by a list of x,y coordinates of the orthographic projections of certain object features onto the image plane. Ullman and Basri showed that in this case the representation of any view of the object can be written down as a linear combination (weighted sum) of the representation of a small number of fixed views of the same object.

A practical recognition scheme based on this result can be obtained, for example, as follows (Ullman & Basri, 1991): First, the fixed views of an object are used to precompute a matrix specific for that object. That matrix, when multiplied by the vector representing a novel view, yields a vector whose norm (magnitude) can be thresholded to decide whether the novel view belongs to the given object. Note that in this case the shape of the object (i.e., its model) is represented implicitly in the elements of the matrix. Indeed, according to the structure from motion theorems (Ullman, 1979), the shape can be recovered from the set of given views used to construct the matrix. Therefore, the linear combination scheme belongs properly to the class of model-based reconstructive approaches.

2.2 Model-free approaches

In all the model-based approaches discussed in the preceding section, constancy is essentially a matter of deciding which of a number of competing objects provides the best account of the structure of the input view. This notion of object constancy, although computationally powerful, seems to run counter to the intuition of what constancy is supposed to be about: perceiving the right shape of a not necessarily familiar object from an arbitrary viewpoint. It should be realized that it does not make sense to speak about *the* right shape if the object is indeed unfamiliar to the observer: In that case, the loss of information in the process of imaging ensures the existence of an infinity of solutions to the problem of recovery of the object's shape from the image.[3] Because of the infinite number of solutions, the problem of model-free shape recovery from a single image is mathematically ill-posed (Poggio, Torre, & Koch, 1985).

2.2.1 Assumptions regarding shape.   Despite the ill-posed nature of model-free shape recovery, people do tend to agree on the shape of the object depicted in Figure 4.1. Computational accounts of this feat of shape constancy are usually formulated in terms of the invocation of prior constraints on the solution. A classical example of such a prior is the recovery of the correct interpretation of an ellipse as the image of a tilted circle. Brady and Yuille (1984) showed that the circle is obtained in this case by requiring that the solution maximize the ratio between area and squared perimeter, a common simple shape descriptor in computer vision.

In the more complicated example involving polyhedral scenes, one may assume that the two-dimensional angles between edges belonging to the same face in the shape to be recovered are all straight (as in many artificial objects) or, more generally, that the angles are such that their variance is minimal (Marill, 1989). Algorithms based on constraints of this kind, when applied to line drawings of polyhedral scenes, arrive at solutions that frequently are intuitively satisfying.

An interesting variation on the theme of prior constraints on the sought shape is the assumption of bilateral symmetry. This assumption, which seems to be true of many natural objects as well as artificial ones, allows the recovery of an object's shape from a single view (Poggio & Vetter, 1992). This scheme can be seen as a development of the linear combination approach, in which one view is given and another view, necessary for constructing a model of the object, is obtained by an essentially geometric procedure based on a plane symmetry constraint (Mitsumoto, Tamura, Okazaki, Kamiji, & Fukui, 1992).

2.2.2 Assumptions regarding viewpoint.

In the theory of ill-posed problems, the imposition of constraints intended to make the problem well posed (e.g., have a unique solution) is called *regularization*. In the recovery of object shape, regularization amounts to constraining the possible shapes so that the indeterminacy associated with the unknown viewpoint is reduced. An alternative approach is to make assumptions regarding the viewpoint itself. Probably the least exacting assumption of this kind is that of generic or nonaccidental viewpoint (Binford, 1971; Lowe, 1986; Witkin & Tenenbaum, 1986).

To illustrate this concept, consider an image consisting of a single point. This could be the projection onto the image plane of a pointlike object or of a straight line seen end on. Note that the second interpretation involves a (rather unlikely) condition on the viewpoint, whereas the first one does not. Thus, by a simple probabilistic argument, the first interpretation – that of a pointlike object – is to be preferred (unless prior information is available that can bias the relative likelihood of the two interpretations; see Richards & Jepson, 1992). In other words, one is advised to favor the interpretations that do not presuppose an accident of viewpoint (such as seeing a line end on, something that happens for a set of viewpoints whose measure relative to the set of all possible viewpoints is zero).

The notion of generic viewpoint can be defined more formally and more precisely (Weinshall & Werman, 1997). As the camera is rotated around an object, its image changes. From some viewpoints it changes slowly, whereas from other viewpoints the change is much more rapid. Depending on how the image is represented, it is possible to compute these changes. We may then refer to the viewpoints where the image changes the fastest as *nongeneric views*. Viewpoint where the image changes the least may be called *generic views*. More generally we have here a continuous quantitative measure of viewpoint *genericity*, or the likelihood of seeing the object as it appears from a given viewpoint.

A quantitative probabilistic framework for exploiting the notion of generic views has been proposed by Freeman (1993). This framework applies Bayesian tools to estimate the relative likelihood of various possible interpretations of the input scene. A number of previously developed Bayesian approaches to shape recovery and scene understanding expressed the likelihood of a solution – a description of the geometry of a scene – in terms of fidelity to the observed image and prior probability of that scene. Freeman's formulation adds a third term to the scene probability equation: the generic view term, which quantifies how accidental the observed view of the scene is. This is done by introducing generic variables, such as viewpoint, object pose, and illumination direction, and considering the image as a function of these variables. The main idea that leads to the scene probability equation is that large values of the derivatives of the image with respect to the generic variables correspond to unlikely scenes. Although some initial experiments with applying this insight to the recovery of shape from shading (Horn & Brooks, 1989) seem promising (Freeman, 1993), it is not clear whether this approach can be made general enough to help solve the model-free version of the shape constancy problem in its full scope, including the recovery of shape from line drawings.

2.2.3 Nonaccidental properties.   The idea of nonaccidental shape properties (i.e., image features from which three-dimensional properties of objects can be safely inferred, barring the unlikely accident of a viewpoint), which originated in the work of Binford and was developed by Lowe and others (Binford, 1971; Lowe, 1986), serves as a foundation to Biederman's theory of object recognition by components (Biederman, 1987). Some of the nonaccidental properties of contour segments considered by this theory are straightness, sense of curvature, parallelism, and cotermination (e.g., two segments with endpoints near each other are to be interpreted as touching in three dimensions).

From a list of such properties, Biederman composes a small set of generic shape primitives (which he calls *geons*), which (1) can be readily detected in single images of objects, including line drawings, and (2) can be combined to form a faithful description of three-dimensional objects at the basic level of categorization. According to this theory, the drawing in Figure 4.1 is perceived as a composition of simple volumetric parts, which, along with their specified spatial relationships, give rise to the perception of three-dimensional shape that does not depend on the viewpoint.

3. Constancy without reconstruction

Recent developments in computer vision indicate that it may be possible to come up with a viable alternative to the reconstructionist approach to constancy. In this section, we survey the major computational approaches to shape constancy that do not require three-dimensional reconstruction of the shape. One way to avoid the need to reconstruct the viewed shape in three dimensions before recognizing it is by characterizing the shape in terms of a set of measurements or features that are provably invariant with respect to viewpoint changes (or any other factor that may affect the appearance of the shape in the observed image). As in the discussion of the reconstructionist theories, we classify the various approaches as model-based or model-free.

3.1 Model-based invariants

In section 2.1.2 we described representations that are invariant to changes of the viewing position. Any object can be represented in such a way. As the representation is invariant to the viewing position, it relates to all the images of the object in an inherently similar way. We can therefore take an object and one of its invariant representations and define an operator that acts on the image and performs verification: it returns one value (say, zero) if the image is an instance of the invariant model and another value otherwise. A verification operator of this sort is called a *model-based invariant operator*. Model-based invariant functions, for objects composed of n fiducial points, were described in Weinshall (1993). The question remains as to which features should be used in the description of the object, a question discussed subsequently.

The main drawback of this approach is that it is not very different from the reconstruction approach. Although no shape is reconstructed, not much saving is obtained either, because the image still needs to be compared sequentially to the different models in the database via the model-based invariant operators.

3.2 The model-free case

Ideally, a recognition operator is desirable that would operate on an image, and return a certain fixed value for all the views of the same object and different values for views of other objects. Such a model-free operator would be much more powerful, and more useful, than the model-based invariant function. For example, such an operator could be applied to an image to produce an index into a database, thereby identifying the object (or set of objects) present in the image.

Such operators can be defined only if there exist measurable quantities in the image that are invariant to changes in the orientation of the camera with respect to the object. Unfortunately, it has been shown that such invariants do not exist for general objects (Burns, Weiss, & Riseman, 1990; Moses & Ullman, 1992). This fact makes intuitive sense if one realizes that achieving shape constancy with unknown generic objects must necessarily involve classification (as opposed to the case when the objects have known models, which, as we pointed out earlier, may be properly termed *recognition*). In classification, the image is assigned to a family of objects. If model-free invariants exist for this family,[4] then identification may be attempted. In many situations, however, identification is unnecessary or meaningless (cf. Figure 4.1), and a general and qualitative description of the object's shape will suffice.

What would it mean for three-dimensional model-free invariant operators to exist? Despite the loss of information in projecting a three-dimensional object onto a two-dimensional image, there would have to be still enough information left to identify *any* possible object. The following argument shows that the requirement of identifiability of any possible object is too strong. A model-free invariant function must return the same value for any two objects composed of the same number of features, say, all objects with 10 features. Let us choose two objects comprising 10 points each. Either these two objects have one image

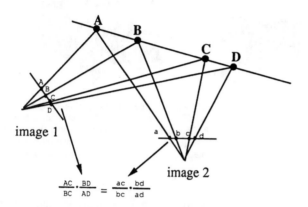

Figure 4.2. The cross-ratio remains constant for any image of the four coplanar space points *A, B, C, D*.

(projection) in common or there exists a sequence of fewer than 10 objects linking one of them to the other, such that each of two consecutive objects on the list have an image in common. A model-free invariant function would have to return the same value for all the objects on the list, and therefore it would not be able to discriminate between the original two objects.

If we know that the image cannot be an image of just anything, by virtue of certain conditions on the class of permitted objects, then restricted model-free invariant functions may exist. Projective invariant functions of planar objects have been discussed in the classical literature on projective geometry. One well-known example of such an invariant is the cross-ratio. For simplicity, we shall describe the cross-ratio of four collinear points (but this can be generalized to five coplanar points). Let *A, B, C, D* denote four such points (see Figure 4.2), and let $\bar{PQ}$ denote the length of the segment between points *P* and *Q*. Then the following cross-ratio of the four points remains the same for all their images:

$$\frac{\bar{AB}}{\bar{BC}} \cdot \frac{\bar{BD}}{\bar{AD}}$$

4. Computational models of shape constancy in human vision

4.1 Background

To what extent can the computational schemes for shape constancy discussed in the preceding sections serve as models of visual object perception and rec-

Figure 4.3. Canonical views: Certain views of three-dimensional objects are consistently easier to recognize or process in a variety of visual tasks. For example, a three-quarters view of an animal-like shape (left) is bound to yield a lower response time and a lower error rate and to receive a higher subjective "goodness" score than other views of the same object, such as the view on the right. Such differences may exist even among views that are seen equally often.

ognition in humans? The first thing to note about shape constancy in human vision is that it is far from perfect. To provide a background for discussion, we list here the major manifestations of the imperfections of shape constancy (see also Chapter 3 in this volume).[5]

- *Canonical views.* Perceiving the shape of an object irrespective of the viewing conditions such as its orientation in space and its distance from the observer frequently incurs a certain information processing cost over and above what it takes to recognize the same object in its most familiar appearance (see Figure 4.3). This additional processing cost is reflected in longer response times and in higher error rates evoked by randomly chosen views of the object, as compared to certain so-called canonical views (Palmer, Rosch, & Chase, 1981).
- *Mental rotation.* Transition from a canonical to a noncanonical view of an object does not merely increase the expected recognition time: Response latency depends on the viewpoint in an orderly fashion, growing monotonically with misorientation relative to the nearest canonical view (Edelman & Bülthoff, 1992; Tar & Pinker, 1989). This dependency of response time on misorientation resembles the celebrated finding by Shepard and Metzler (1971) of a class of phenomena that became known as *mental rotation.*
- *Limited generalization.* When asked to give a relatively broad classification of an object seen from an odd viewpoint (i.e., when the task requires basic-level categorization), people virtually never err, except when the object appears severely foreshortened (see Biederman (1987). In comparison, when the task can only be solved through relatively precise shape matching, the error rate reaches chance level at misorientation of about 40° relative to a familiar attitude (Edelman & Bülthoff, 1992; Rock & DiVita, 1987; Edelman, 1995).

4.2 Computational models of recognition in human vision

We now discuss three recognition schemes that were explicitly advanced by their proponents as models of human performance. The particular choice of models, although necessarily incomplete, has been dictated by the extent to

Figure 4.4. Generalization to novel views: People have great difficulty recognizing a novel view of an object if the contrast set consists of similar objects. In this example, the left and central images are two views of the same wirelike object, but the right image is not.

which they explicitly address the relevant computational issues and by their success in accounting for human performance in different shape constancy tasks.

4.2.1 Normalization to multiple stored views.   The dependence of naming time for novel objects on their orientation with respect to the observer was interpreted in the past as evidence for the involvement of mental rotation in recognition (Tarr & Pinker, 1989). According to one version of the alignment theory (see section 2.1.1), the human visual system tries to attain a match between the input and a model by a normalizing transformation that would align the input with the nearest stored view of the model. Presumably, the normalization process consumes time, and this is reflected in the dependence of the response time on the misorientation between the input and the nearest stored view. At some stage, the system may decide that it is worthwhile to adjoin the current view to the set of stored views, in which case subsequent responses to this view would become faster.

Can alignment constitute a viable model of shape constancy in human vision? The answer to this question would have been positive were the constancy perfect. Indeed, the technique of alignment is so powerful that it is difficult to see how it could be made to account for recognition response time data without giving up some of its central characteristics. Once a rotation angle has been computed on the basis of the hypothesized match, the normalization process can, in principle, be carried out in a single step (the complexity of this step, which amounts to matrix multiplication, may depend on the complexity of the object, but it certainly need not depend on the rotation angle). Furthermore, storing more and more views confers no computational advantage on the system (on the contrary, it taxes the system's memory requirements). Thus, alignment predicts neither the dependence of response time on misorientation nor the need to store multiple views of the object beyond the small number that is strictly necessary for representing its three-dimensional structure (as mentioned in section 2.1.1). Finally, the alignment theory cannot be easily brought to bear on the error rate data because it does not constrain possible sources of errors, either in the normalization stage or during matching.

It may be possible to reconcile the alignment theory with the experimental data on recognition if one is prepared to make assumptions regarding the mechanism of the normalization. Suppose that the hardware limitations of the system are such that only rotations by a fixed discrete amount are supported and, furthermore, that these rotations can only be carried out with respect to a few special axes.[6] Larger rotations will then take longer because of required iteration of the elementary rotation step. Moreover, rotation time will depend on the orientation of the axis (as it indeed does in the human data; see Shepard & Metzler, 1988). We note that such stepwise alignment in effect gives up the main computational advantage of the original theory, namely, freedom from the need to search exhaustively the space of all possible aligning transformations. Still, a recent development of the idea of alignment (Ullman, 1995) suggests that an appropriately distributed architecture and a combined bottom-up and top-down control structure may make alignment a useful model of the kind of shape constancy one finds in human vision.

Another way to reconcile the predictions of alignment with the human data is to give up the assumption that the recognition mechanism has access to precise three-dimensional models of objects. A likely alternative is for the alignment process to use three-dimensional models that are themselves computed from observed images of objects and that are updated when additional images become available. One should therefore expect imperfect performance, which improves with the availability of additional images of the target. Moreover, one should expect fewer errors when the model is compared with images that were used to build the model (as opposed to novel images), as indeed happens in the human data. This point is illustrated in Weinshall and Tomasi (1993).

4.2.2 Recognition by components.   Hummel and Biederman (1992) developed a detailed model of the phenomenon of constancy, as illustrated in Figure 4.5. Their model is based on Biederman's theory of recognition by components (RBC). This detailed implementation of RBC attempts to address most of the computational issues involved in the perception of constant shape in simple cartoonlike line drawings of three-dimensional objects. The processing stages that are explicitly modeled are as follows:

1. Grouping of contour fragments according to the long-established principles of perceptual organization (Lowe, 1986; Witkin & Tenenbaum, 1986);
2. Grouping of entire segments into geons (generic volumetric primitives postulated by RBC), based on the nonaccidental properties (see section 2.2.3);

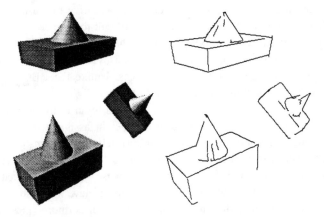

Figure 4.5. *Left*: The RBC model is designed to detect the constancy of objects such as this one across different views, even though they are unfamiliar. The implemented model deals not with shaded images but with line drawings. Adapted with permission from Hummel and Biederman (1992). *Right*: Reliable and consistent recovery of a representation resembling a line drawing from a gray-level image is by itself a most challenging computational problem (as noted in Hummel & Biederman, 1992, p. 514). The edge map shown here was obtained with an edge detection program that is part of a standard image-processing software package, using its default parameter settings.

3. Determination of the spatial relationships among geons and the formation of an appropriate shape representation.

The various intermediate representations employed by the model are distributed. For example, the presence of a contour in the input image is coded by a distribution of activities of units whose oriented receptive fields approximately match the location and orientation of the contour. At a higher stage, units responsible for certain contour configurations, such as the two ends of a partially occluded line, cooperate to produce the representation of the entire line. Finally, at the top stage, simultaneous activation of appropriate geon and spatial relation units signals the perceived shape.

When tested on a set of 10 objects, the model exhibited shape constancy by responding in an invariant manner to shapes undergoing translation, scaling, mirror reflection, and rotation (Hummel & Biederman, 1992). More important, the model represents one of the first attempts to address issues of object constancy computationally, on a level that is more concrete than the qualitative arguments normally employed by cognitive psychologists in the discussion of recognition.

4.2.3 Multiple-view interpolation. The distributed RBC model described in the preceding section relies, on the one hand, on graded-response mechanisms (e.g., receptive fields), which are perfectly credible both biologically and computationally. On the other hand, it postulates detectors sensitive to various configurations of line and curve segments, which are difficult to extract reliably from natural images (Hildreth, 1987; see Figure 4.5). The multiple-view interpolation model, described next, is more consistent, in that it uses receptive fieldlike mechanisms that operate directly on gray-level images. Unlike the RBC model, it concentrates on discrimination among similar objects.

Consider a receptive fieldlike structure, connected to an array of image elements, that is capable of rapidly adjusting the weight assigned to each input element according to an activity-dependent rule (Edelman & Weinshall, 1991). It appears that such a structure can be made into a ''detector'' selective for a particular view of a three-dimensional object. Because of the graded nature of the weight distribution, the receptive field for a given view will also exhibit a certain degree of generalization to similar views. Furthermore, providing a mechanism that incorporates several latent detectors of this kind with a sufficient number of training views would allow one to control the degree of generalization (Edelman, 1993). This control allows one to replicate the pattern of limited generalization to novel views exhibited by human subjects under conditions of high target-foil similarity (Bülthoff & Edelman, 1992). Moreover, if the representations of the stored views are linked to each other by an associative learning rule (cf. Sakai & Miyashita, 1992), the resulting structure will also replicate central features of the time course of recognition in humans, namely, canonical views and mental rotation.[7]

The computational rationale behind the multiple-view approach is derived from treating the problem of generalizing recognition across views as an instance of a standard problem in approximation theory – learning a function from examples (Poggio & Girosi, 1990). Clearly, the problem of shape constancy would be solved if it were possible to map any view of an object into a standard (constant) view, that is, to determine the function from any view to the standard one. Given a number of known views of an object as examples, it is possible to learn such a function only if its choice is properly constrained. Specifically, if it is assumed that the target function is smooth (changing the input view slightly will not change its classification), then regularization theory dictates a solution that is an interpolation of the example views. Moreover, an interpretation of this solution in terms of receptive fields yields exactly the mechanism outlined in the previous paragraph (Poggio & Edelman, 1990).

The multiple-view interpolation model combines psychophysical support with a solid computational grounding in recent developments in function approximation and in learning theory. However, this model will not be complete until it replicates the entire spectrum of human performance characteristics in recognition, from the strong viewpoint effects in the case of discrimination among highly similar objects to the complete constancy in the case of simple, easily distinguished shapes. One possibility of extending the multiple-view model in this manner is outlined in the next section.

4.2.4 Features of recognition.   Does the visual system rely on distinct sets of representations and processes for subordinate and basic levels of recognition? A recent proposal (Edelman, 1991a) outlined a possible approach to the understanding both of shape constancy and of its failures. On the one hand, like the multiple-view model, the proposed approach requires neither three-dimensional reconstruction of the stimulus, nor the maintenance of a library of three-dimensional models of objects. On the other hand, the proposed model is related to the RBC theory in that its representation of object views is allowed to include nonaccidental features similar to those used to detect the presence of geons in the image. The choice of features and their complexity presumably vary among objects: Recognition may start with the extraction of a large variety of image-based features, followed by an application of a recognition procedure appropriate for the given object set and for the required category level. Such procedures may be synthesized at need and optimized with practice (e.g., compound features may be formed out of simpler ones and subsequently relied on).

This approach predicts a trade-off between the viewpoint invariance of a feature and its diagnosticity or the degree of discrimination among object instances that it affords. Consider, for instance, a domain of objects composed of geon-like parts. To recognize such objects, a visual system can use local features such as image-plane positions of object corners or edges, as well as extended features such as patterns of shading over object surfaces. The two types of features will, in general, lead to different performances. When the pose of the object relative to the viewer changes, the projected locations of the corners will shift. Unless this shift is compensated for (e.g., by pose recovery and model alignment), recognition of unfamiliar views of the object will be poor. In comparison, the shape of a shaded patch can in principle be extracted, regardless of the pose of the object to which it belongs (as long as the patch is visible). At the same time, if the pose is fixed, projected corners, edges, or other localized features offer better discrimination among similar shapes than shading (cf. Bülthoff & Mallot, 1988). The foregoing considerations suggest that different patterns of performance emerge in response to the different levels of detail that must be addressed in subordinate and basic-level recognition. If this is true, then one would expect the extent of viewpoint invariance in subjects' performance to be affected by a manipulation of the relevant level of detail, determined by interobject similarity. This effect was indeed reported by Edelman (1995).

5. Conclusions

5.1 Constancy, representation, and reconstruction

The central role of the choice of representation in computational approaches to problems such as recognition and constancy is by now generally accepted, largely due to the intellectual legacy of Marr (1982). Unfortunately, a lack of distinction between the concept of *representation* and the admittedly related, but rather more restricted, concept of *reconstruction* is nearly as general.

This lack of distinction characterizes well the approach taken by the mainstream of computer vision research in the past 15 years. The importance of choosing the right representation for a given computational problem is widely acknowledged and has been most forcefully argued for by Marr. However, many vision researchers, including Marr, essentially ignored the possibility that the best representation of the visual world may not be the same as the visual world reconstructed in full three-dimensional detail.

In the philosophy of mind, the equation of representation with reconstruction is in the spirit of a tradition dating back to Aristotle (see Cummins, 1989). Computationally, a representation that is, in a sense, a geometrical replica of the thing being represented must be considered adequate for any visual task. From a pragmatic perspective, however, representation by reconstruction appears to be a poor choice for several reasons. First, experience in computer vision shows that such a representation is very difficult to recover from real, unconstrained data. Second, even though all the information necessary for solving a given visual task is present in the geometrically reconstructed scene, it is not necessarily encoded there in the optimal form.[8] Moreover, a reconstructed scene would require a homunculus to make sense of it (Pylyshyn, 1973): Of all possible approaches to scene interpretation, the one that starts with reconstruction is the most roundabout because reconstruction per se contributes nothing to interpretation. Third, as we mentioned in section 4, psychophysical evidence indicates that the human performance in recognition is in many cases inconsistent with the reconstructionist hypothesis.

5.2 Feature detectors and shape constancy

The roots of the alternative approach to representation taken by the multiple-views models can be traced back to Locke's *Essay Concerning Human Understanding*. In the part that addressed the problem of semantics of mental representations, Locke suggested that an idea represents a thing in the world if it is naturally and predictably evoked by that thing, and not necessarily, as the Aristotelians would have it, if the idea resembles the thing in any sense. According to this suggestion, and using a standard terminology of vision research, the activity of a sufficiently reliable *feature detector* constitutes a representation of the presence of an appropriate feature out there in the visual world.[9] Representations of entire objects can then be built out of the available primitives following simple principles of association if the repertoire of features is sufficiently rich (in particular if, at some stage in the system, features correspond to entire views of objects). Shape constancy, therefore, may be a combined effect of knowing what the relevant objects look like from different vantage points, of internalized knowledge concerning what happens to a view of an object that undergoes a certain transformation in space (Shepard, 1984), and of judicious selection of just the right things about the appearance of a three-dimensional object that had better be ignored.[10]

Notes

1. In the model-based case, the term *recognition* may be freely substituted for *constancy*.
2. A hash table is a data structure that allows efficient access to information identified by the key associated with it. In the present case, the key is the set of coordinates of object features, and the information to be retrieved is the identity of the object and the basis features.
3. Loss of geometric information; confounding between surface reflectance, surface orientation, illumination direction, and illumination intensity.
4. As they do for special kinds of objects, such as planar (flat) (Forsyth, Mundy, Zisserman, & Brown, 1990), or symmetrical ones (Moses & Ullman, 1992).
5. Failures of object constancy are particularly revealing as test cases for various theories of recognition, because a model based on any such theory, if it can be made to fail at all, is likely to do so in a peculiar way that can be compared to human performance in an appropriately designed experiment. Moreover, the human performance can also be manipulated so as to reveal as much as possible about the processes involved in recognizing objects under changes in viewpoint.
6. A suggestion for a simple connectionist implementation of a rotation module satisfying similar requirements can be found in Churchland (1987).
7. Which is then seen to be merely a reflection of a step-by-step spread of activation throughout the web of view detectors exciting each other (see Edelman, 1991b; Edelman & Weinshall, 1991).
8. Marr, in his book, makes a very similar argument a mere 14 pages before he discusses the work of Warrington (Warrington & Taylor, 1973) that swayed him in favor of the reconstructive approach.
9. Cf. Putnam's dictum on the meaning of a representation being in the world, not in the head (Putnam, 1988).
10. The choice of whether to ignore a troublesome aspect of the stimulus or try to make sense of it has been given an illuminating treatment in the section on "Filling in versus finding out" in Dennett (1991, p. 344). The problem of filling in the visual input across the blind spot or a scotoma (which, instead, may be merely labeled as being "the same" as the surrounding area), discussed by Dennett, corresponds in our case to the problem of reconstructing the three-dimensional shape of the object, an alternative to which has been outlined in section 4.2.3.

References

Biederman, I. (1987). Recognition by components: A theory of human image understanding. *Psychological Review, 94*, 115–147.

Binford, T. O. (1971). Visual perception by computer. In *IEEE Conference on Systems and Control*, Miami Beach, FL.

Brady, M., & Yuille, A. (1984). An extremum principle for shape from contour. *IEEE Transactions on Pattern Analysis and Machine Intelligence, 6*, 288–301.

Bülthoff, H. H., & Edelman, S. (1992). Psychophysical support for a 2-D view interpolation theory of object recognition. *Proceedings of the National Academy of Science, 89*, 60–64.

Bülthoff, H. H., & Mallot, H. A. (1988). Interaction of depth modules: Stereo and shading. *Journal of the Optical Society of America, 5*, 1749–1758.

Burns, J., Weiss, R., & Riseman, E. (1990). View variation of point-set and line segment features. In *Proceedings of the Image Understanding Workshop* pp. 650–659.

Churchland, P. S. (1987). *Neurophilosophy.* Cambridge, MA: MIT Press.

Cummins, R. (1989). *Meaning and mental representation.* Cambridge, MA: MIT Press.

Dennett, D. C. (1991). *Consciousness explained.* Boston: Little, Brown.

Edelman, S. (1991a). *Features of recognition.* Technical Bulletin CS-TR 91–10. Rehovot, Israel: Weizmann Institute of Science.

Edelman, S. (1991b). A network model of object recognition in human vision. In H. Wechsler (Ed.), *Neural networks for perception* (Vol. 1, pp. 25–40). New York: Academic Press.

Edelman, S. (1993). On learning to recognize 3D objects from examples. *IEEE Transactions on Pattern Analysis and Machine Intelligence, 15,* 833–837.

Edelman, S. (1995). Class similarity and viewpoint invariance in the recognition of 3D objects. *Biological Cybernetics 72,* 207–220.

Edelman, S., & Bülthoff, H. H. (1992). Orientation dependence in the recognition of familiar and novel views of 3D objects. *Vision Research, 32,* 2385–2400.

Edelman, S., & Weinshall, D. (1991). A self-organizing multiple-view representation of 3D objects. *Biological Cybernetics, 64,* 209–219.

Fischler, M. A., & Bolles, R. C. (1981). Random sample consensus: A paradigm for model fitting with applications to image analysis and automated cartography. *Communications of the ACM, 24,* 381–395.

Forsyth, D., Mundy, J. L., Zisserman, A., & Brown, C. M. (1990). Invariance – a new framework for vision. In *Proceedings of the 3rd International Conference on Computer Vision* (pp. 598–605). Washington, DC: IEEE Press.

Freeman, W. T. (1993). Exploiting the generic view assumption to estimate scene parameters. In *Proceedings of the 3rd International Conference on Computer Vision* (pp. 347–356). Washington, DC: IEEE Press.

Hildreth, E. C. (1987). Edge detection. In S. Shapiro (Ed.), *Encyclopedia of artificial intelligence,* (pp. 257–267.) New-York: Wiley.

Horn, B. K. P., & Brooks, M. (1989). *Seeing shape from shading.* Cambridge, MA: MIT Press.

Hummel, J. E., & Biederman, I. (1992). Dynamic binding in a neural network for shape recognition. *Psychological Review, 99,* 480–517.

Koenderink, J. J., & van Doorn, A. J. (1991). Affine structure from motion. *Journal of the Optical Society of America, 8* (2), 377–385.

Lamdan, Y., & Wolfson, H. (1988). Geometric hashing: A general and efficient recognition scheme. In *Proceedings of the 2nd International Conference on Computer Vision* (pp. 238–251). Washington, DC: IEEE Press.

Lowe, D. G. (1986). *Perceptual organization and visual recognition.* Boston: Kluwer.

Lowe, D. G. (1987). Three-dimensional object recognition from single two-dimensional images. *Artificial Intelligence, 31,* 355–395.

Marill, T. (1989). *Recognizing 3D objects without the use of models.* A. I. Memo No. 1157. Cambridge, MA: Artificial Intelligence Laboratory, Massachusetts Institute of Technology.

Marr, D. (1982). *Vision.* San Francisco; W. H. Freeman.

Mitsumoto, H., Tamura, S., Okazaki, K., Kajimi, N., & Fukui, Y. (1992). 3D reconstruction using mirror images based on a plane symmetry recovering method. *IEEE Transactions on Pattern Analysis and Machine Intelligence, 14,* 941–946.

Mohan, R., Weinshall, D., & Sarukkai, R. R. (1993). 3D object recognition by indexing structural invariants from multiple views. In *Proceedings of the 4th International Conference on Computer Vision* (pp. 264–268). Washington, DC: IEEE Press.

Moses, Y., & Ullman, S. (1992). Limitations of non model-based recognition schemes. In G. (Ed.), *Sandini Proceedings of the 2nd European Conference on Computer Vision, Lecture Notes in Computer Science* (Vol. 588, pp. 820–828). Berlin: Springer-Verlag.

Palmer, S. E., Rosch, E., & Chase, P. (1981). Canonical perspective and the perception of objects. In J. Long, & A., Baddeley (Eds.), *Attention and performance* (Vol. IX, pp. 135–151). Hillsdale, NJ: Erlbaum.

Poggio, T., & Edelman, S. (1990). A network that learns to recognize three-dimensional objects. *Nature, 343,* 263–266.

Poggio, T., & Girosi, F. (1990). Regularization algorithms for learning that are equivalent to multilayer networks. *Science, 247,* 978–982.

Poggio, T., Torre, V., & Koch, C. (1985). Computational vision and regularization theory. *Nature, 317,* 314–319.

Poggio, T., & Vetter, T. (1992). *Recognition and structure from one 2D model view: Observations on prototypes, object classes, and symmetries.* A. I. Memo No. 1347. Cambridge, MA: Artificial Intelligence Laboratory, Massachusetts Institute of Technology.

Putnam, H. (1988). *Representation and reality.* Cambridge, MA: MIT Press.

Pylyshyn, Z. (1973). What the mind's eye tells the mind's brain: A critique of mental imagery. *Psychological Bulletin, 80,* 1–24.

Richards, W., & Jepson, A. (1992). *What makes a good feature?* A. I. Memo No. 1356. Cambridge, MA: Artificial Intelligence Laboratory, Massachusetts Institute of Technology.

Rives, P., Bouthemy, B., Prasada, B., & Dubois, E. (1981). *Recovering the orientation and the position of a rigid body in space from a single view.* Technical Report. Quebec, Canada: INRS Telecommunications.

Rock, I., & DiVita, J. (1987). A case of viewer-centered object perception. *Cognitive Psychology, 19,* 280–293.

Sakai, K., & Miyashita, Y. (1992). Neural organization for the long-term memory of paired associates. *Nature, 354,* 152–155.

Shashua, A. (1991). *Correspondence and affine shape from two orthographic views: Motion and recognition.* A.I. Memo No. 1327. Cambridge, MA: Artificial Intelligence Laboratory, Massachusetts Institute of Technology.

Shepard, R. N. (1984). Ecological constraints on internal representation: resonant kinematics of perceiving, imagining, thinking, and dreaming. *Psychological Review, 91,* 417–447.

Shepard, R. N., & Metzler, J. (1971). Mental rotation of three-dimensional objects. *Science, 171,* 701–703.

Shepard, S., & Metzler, D. (1988). Mental rotation: Effects of dimensionality of objects and type of task. *Journal of Experimental Psychology: Human Perception and Performance, 14,* 3–11.

Tarr, M., & Pinker, S. (1989). Mental rotation and orientation-dependence in shape recognition. *Cognitive Psychology, 21,* 233–282.

Ullman, S. (1979). *The interpretation of visual motion.* Cambridge, MA.: MIT Press.

Ullman, S. (1989). Aligning pictorial descriptions: An approach to object recognition. *Cognition, 32,* 193–254.

Ullman, S. (1995). *Sequence-seeking and counter-streams: A model for information flow in the cortex.* Cerebral Cortex 5, 1–11.

Ullman, S., & Basri, R. (1991). Recognition by linear combinations of models. *IEEE Transactions on Pattern Analysis and Machine Intelligence, 13,* 992–1005.

Warrington, E. K., & Taylor, A. M. (1973). The contribution of the right parietal lobe to object recognition. *Cortex, 9,* 152–164.

Weinshall, D. (1993). Model-based invariants for 3D vision. *International Journal of Computer Vision, 10,* (1), 27–42.

Weinshall, D., & Tomasi, C. (1993). Linear and incremental acquisition of invariant shape models from image sequences. In *Proceedings of the 4th International Conference on Computer Vision* (pp. 675–682). Washington, DC: IEEE.

Weinshall, D., & Werman, M., (1997). On view likelihood and stability. *IEEE Transactions on Pattern Analysis and Machine Intelligence, 19,* 97–108.

Witkin, A. P., & Tenenbaum, J. M. (1986). On perceptual organization. In *From Pixels to Predicates* (pp. 149–169). Norwood, NJ: Ablex.

5   Learning constancies for object perception

Peter Földiák

Introduction

Regularities in the external world cause special, nonaccidental properties of the sensory signals (Barlow, 1959, 1972). They constrain the patterns of natural stimulation to a very small part of the space of all possible stimuli. This is indicated by the fact that in a set of images generated by assigning pixels at random, it is very unlikely that we will ever find one resembling a natural image. The structure of the external world is not often reflected in a simple way in the structure of the direct sensory measurements. The goal of the sensory system must be to transform the raw signals into a form in which the structure of the external environment corresponds well to the structure of the internal representation. Our perceptual system achieves this goal. To illustrate this, Figure 5.1a. shows four random dot patterns, two of which are identical. It is much harder, if not impossible, for us to say which two are the same without focusing on small details than to say which of the four images in Figure 5.1b are the same. Our ability to discriminate and generalize is based on our perceptual representations, which are matched to the pattern of natural stimulation.

Concentrating information

Cues about the presence of an object are spread out throughout the array of physical measurements. These clues must be combined, as none of them alone is likely to indicate uniquely the presence of an object. For instance, if you have been stung by a wasp, you should try to avoid the wasp, not just its sound or stripes or feel (Barlow, 1993). You don't want to take evasive action whenever you see yellow, or stripes, or even yellow stripes. On the other hand, the wasp sound alone, if it is specific enough, should alert you even if you cannot see the wasp, and you should react to the feel of a wasp on the skin even if the wasp is silent. In order to generalize correctly, the perceptual system must recognize that the characteristic appearance, sound, and feel of the wasp belong together, and the same is true for all other objects with which we can potentially

I would like to thank Chip Levy for his comments on biological plausibility and David Perrett and Mike Oram for their valuable comments on the manuscript.

144

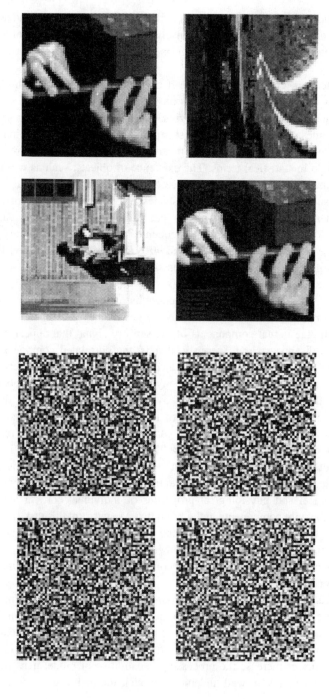

Figure 5.1(a: left; b: right). Two of both sets of images are identical. It is much harder to discriminate random dot patterns than natural stimuli.

form associations (Barlow, 1993). Note that the component features, such as the wasp noises and wasp shapes, are themselves special combinations of more elementary features, which already suggests that sensory analysis must be hierarchical.

Object detection will be most reliable if all the signals caused by an object are combined while all unrelated signals are excluded. As the physical signals carry no authentic labels about their origins, the sensory system must resort to heuristics, or rules of thumb, based on past experience about which combinations of the physical signal are likely to be meaningful. These heuristics are often well expressible in statistical terms. The existence of objects, such as wasps, in the world causes the simultaneous presence of sensory features associated with the objects, such as wasp noises, wasp shapes, wasp sizes, wasp colors, and wasp movements. Statistically, this means that the conjunction of these features (e.g., A and B) is present much more frequently than it would be simply by chance if there were no animals like wasps: $p(A\&B) \gg p(A)p(B)$ (Barlow, 1972, 1991). The sensory system should find these suspicious coincidences or sensory clichés in the stream of sensory data.

How could such nonaccidental conjunctions be detected? There are several clues in the structure of the input that may suggest what these sensory clichés are. One such clue is that components of the sensory signal that appear simultaneously and disappear simultaneously, that is, the correlated components of the signal, are likely to be related or have a common cause. Another observation about objects is that they tend to keep many of their properties relatively constant or that they change only gradually over time. Objects generally do not randomly vanish, appear, or suddenly turn into other, unrelated objects. Conservation laws and inertia, for instance, guarantee the continuity and relative constancy of objects and their properties. This structure or coherence in time can also be utilized to extract the relevant components of the sensory signals.

The physical task of information concentration in the brain is ideally suited to the anatomical and physiological properties of individual cortical neurons. Neurons are the only components in the brain that can perform this task (Barlow, 1994a). The structure of dendritic trees and axonal arbors seems well adapted to collecting information from a large number of very specific sources and sending the elementary decision based on the combined signal to a large number of specific targets.

The models to be discussed use greatly simplified neural units. These models, while ignoring several known properties of neurons, still capture important functional aspects of neural processing and demonstrate the power of even such simple principles. Incorporating additional functionally relevant details into the models may further increase the processing capabilities of model networks. In the simplest and relatively well-understood model, the neural unit sums all its synaptic input activities, each one weighted by the corresponding synaptic connection strength. Following summation, a simple nonlinearity, such as some kind of threshold function, is usually applied to this sum. Although the assumption of linear summation may be an oversimplification, it captures an important property of real neurons in that it is the precise synaptic pattern that determines what kind of activity pattern will activate or "match" a neuron, whereas the threshold determines how good this match has to be before the neuron is triggered. In the extreme cases of a very high threshold, the neuron can act approximately as a logic AND gate, requiring all its inputs, or, with a very low threshold, as a logic OR gate, requiring just one of them to match. Both model and real neurons function in the range between these two extremes, requiring a certain fraction of their effective inputs to be active. Learning in these networks takes place by the modification of the weight or strength of the synaptic connections.

Clue 1: Co-occurrence

The first clue to finding structure in the input is the co-occurrence of the component of the signal. This can easily be learned by both real and simulated neurons. The simplest kind of synaptic modification rule, put forward by Hebb (1949), suggests that a synapse should be strengthened when the two neurons it connects are both activated simultaneously. (Figure 5.2a shows a single unit of a neural network receiving input through connections of modifiable strengths.)

For the purposes of this example, let us assume that the random initial connection from input 1 is strong and the others are weak. Consider the case where the structure of the input patterns is such that input 1 and input 2 are almost always either both active or both inactive, that is, they are highly correlated. If the connection from input 1 (which in reality may correspond to a group of inputs) is initially strong enough, this input may activate the unit. As inputs 1 and 2 are always active at the same time, this means that input 2 and the unit will also be always active at the same time. According to Hebb's rule, this will cause the synaptic connection between input 2 and the unit to become gradually stronger (Figure 5.2b). As a result, the unit will eventually come to respond to this pairing even more strongly in the future, and eventually input 2 alone will be capable of activating the unit.

The various wasp features, for instance, show positive correlations between each other across time. If input 1 is active when there is a wasp sound and input 2 is active when a wasp shape is present, then the unit becomes a generalized "wasp detector" that can be activated even if only some (in this example, one) of these wasp features are present. If the activity of input 3 is uncorrelated with inputs 1 and 2, then the connection between input 3 and the unit will stay weak.

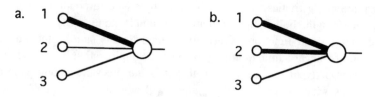

Figure 5.2(a,b). Illustration of the Hebbian mechanism of detecting co-occurrences.

For uncorrelated inputs, the initially random, nonzero weight from input 3 can even be made to disappear completely by specifying a weakening of a synapse between an inactive input and an active unit.

Competitive learning

This simple mechanism forms the basis of the network algorithm called *competitive learning* (Grossberg, 1976a,b, 1987; Malsburg, 1973; Rumelhart & Zipser, 1985). A competitive network has several units of the kind described above, each with connections from a set of inputs. The strengths of the initial connection are usually chosen randomly or determined by other (e.g., anatomical) constraints. The units compete with each other in the sense that only one of the output units is allowed to be active at any time. The interaction between the units, which is assumed to be a strong mutual inhibition, ensures that the unit with the largest weighted input (i.e., the unit whose connection pattern matches the input pattern best) wins the competition (Kaski & Kohonen, 1994; Lippmann, 1987; Yuille & Geiger, 1995). The outputs of all the other units will be suppressed by this unit. This competitive interaction makes it possible for different units to become selective to different frequently occurring input patterns. The algorithm, in its simple form, is equivalent to the statistical method of *k-means clustering* (Hertz, Krogh, & Palmer, 1991). Each input pattern is assigned to a single category corresponding to the unit that wins the competition for that pattern. The weight pattern of each output unit will approach the center of the cluster of input patterns for which that unit wins the competition. (This is a circular definition, however, as this set of patterns depends, in turn, on the weight pattern. Competitive learning is a kind of "bootstrapping" process with local optima). Simple competitive learning therefore divides the space of input patterns into distinct regions, each unit corresponding to a region. The units maximize a simple kind of similarity, the overlap, between the patterns to which they respond while at the same time maximizing the dissimilarity between patterns that are represented by different units (Hertz et al., 1991).

Figure 5.3 shows a competitive network with 16 (= 4 × 4) inputs and eight

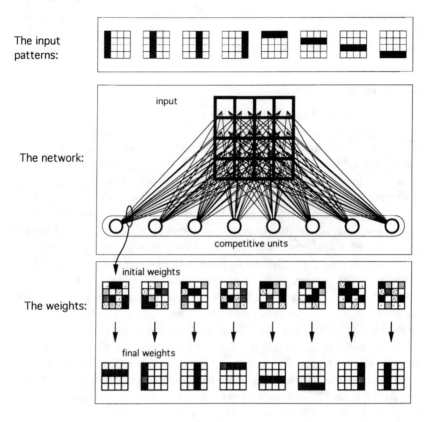

Figure 5.3. Illustration of competitive learning. Units become tuned to different frequently occurring patterns in the input.

competitive units. The input here was chosen to be a small subset of the 2^{16} possible binary input patterns: It consisted of four vertical and four horizontal lines presented repeatedly in random order. Hebbian learning on the weights of the winning unit causes the pattern of weights to match, in this example, one of the input patterns. The set of inputs to which any individual unit becomes selective is determined by the initial, possibly random, weight pattern of that unit and the particular sequence of input patterns.

Observe that these competing units behave highly nonlinearly even if the units themselves are linear, as a small change in the input pattern can change the winner of the competition. This nonlinearity makes it possible for the units to become selective to interesting (higher-order) structure, not simply correlations. Even if all pairwise correlations are removed from the set of input patterns, the competitive units can still discover structure, as each unit is adapted by only a subset of input patterns. This subset, the one for which the given unit is the winner, may still have nonzero correlations.

Cooperative representations

Although competitive learning is capable of discovering simple clusters in the input, the kind of categorization it performs is not quite suitable for sensory processing. The main problem is that a competitive network assigns each complete input pattern to a single category corresponding to the single winning unit. In such a "local" representation, only one of the units is active at any time; the number of categories is limited to the number of mutually exclusive units. This is clearly insufficient compared to the huge number of potential feature combinations that we can discriminate (e.g., Feldman, 1988). The resulting local representation is also unsuitable for the representation of similarities between patterns. As a result, associations to previously experienced patterns will not generalize to new patterns that can be discriminated from the old ones.

Several "soft" competitive schemes have been proposed to solve this problem by allowing several units to be active for each input (Nowlan, 1991). These soft competitive models still suffer from the same problem, however, that the units are trying to match the whole input pattern with a stored typical instance of the category. The activity of the units will reflect the goodness of match between the complete input and a complete exemplar or *prototype* pattern. Radial basis function networks, for instance, make this assumption quite explicit (e.g., Poggio & Girosi, 1990). This class of algorithms is sometimes referred to as *single-cause* classification models, as the model is trying to account for the data as a result of one predetermined pattern. This is still an unsatisfactory solution, as the units are not allowed to represent only certain aspects or features of the input and they are not allowed to properly share the job of representing the pattern. What is needed is a description of the input not in terms of units each trying to match the whole input to a single category, but rather in terms of units each of which represents some relevant aspect or feature of the input, encoding the input cooperatively, accounting for it by multiple causes. In a hypothetical example, if the input pattern is a "yellow Volkswagen," then units in a single-cause model representing different, previously stored yellow object prototypes will be competing with (i.e., inhibiting) units representing different kinds of previously stored car prototypes. The problem with this scheme is that a unit that matches neither aspect of the input very well (such as an "orange Renault" unit) may be activated more than any of the units that match only one aspect of the input but ones that match that aspect precisely (e.g., "yellow" or "Volkswagen" units). The valid generalizations, however, are most likely to be linked to these independent aspects of objects. The top speed of the car, for instance, will generalize correctly along the "car type" aspect rather than the overall similarity across all attributes (e.g., it will be independent of color).

A modified version of competitive learning attempts to represent such independent aspects of the input on separate units (Barlow & Földiák, 1989; Földiák, 1990, 1992). Instead of winner-take-all competition, the units here are forced to represent uncorrelated features of the input. A simple synaptic learning rule may be sufficient to enforce this constraint. The "anti-Hebb" rule (opposite of the usual Hebb rule) specifies a decrease in the total connection weight between two simultaneously active neurons (by either decreasing an excitatory weight or increasing an inhibitory weight). If two units are highly correlated, inhibition gradually builds up between them until the correlation is decreased and the units are forced to represent more distinct but not mutually exclusive aspects of the input.

If units represent uncorrelated aspects of the input, such as the color and make of a car in the previous example, then inhibition will not build up between them. Therefore, they are not forced to compete with each other and can be fully active in the representation simultaneously. As units representing different aspects of the stimulus are not in competition, they can represent a large variety of possible objects by their combinations. The main difference here is that units can signal the presence of a feature or aspect of a new situation even if the complete input pattern on the whole is very different from the previously experienced patterns containing that feature. In a prototype model, an input pattern may be a very poor match to any relevant prototype.

Instead of dividing the space of inputs into mutually exclusive regions, the multiple categorization scheme would generate overlapping, nonexclusive categories that cooperatively describe the input pattern. Instead of clustering, this corresponds more to the method of *clumping* (Everitt, 1974). Similar ideas involving neural network models have been put forward, such as *multiple cause clustering* (Dayan & Zemel, 1995; Saund, 1994), and *cooperative vector quantization* (Hinton & Zemel, 1994; Hinton & Ghahramani, 1997).

Specialization and generalization

Observe the two processes taking place in competitive networks: specialization and generalization. Networks show specialization by responding only when a special subset of input patterns is present. This may lead to a competing unit being active less frequently than an input unit, resulting in a sparse code in which each discriminable input pattern is represented by a different but relatively small subset of active cells from a large population of mostly silent cells (Barlow, 1972, 1994a; Földiák & Young, 1995). Such sparse codes are highly efficient if the constraints of local processing are taken into account

(Barlow, 1994b; Barlow & Gardner-Medwin, 1993; Gardner-Medwin & Barlow, 1992).

At the same time, a network can generalize in the sense that it is capable of recognizing inputs as members of a category even when a fraction of input components are either missing or imprecise, that is, different from the original set of patterns. This similarity, based simply on the number of common stimulus features or "overlap," can be sufficient to explain certain kinds of generalizations, such as the generalization to object parts (Kovács, Vogels, & Orban, 1995; Wachsmuth, Oram, & Perrett, 1994) and to cue invariance (Sáry, Vogels, & Orban, 1993). In most other cases, however, the changes that the stimulus undergoes require more complex kinds of generalization.

Invariance

Neurophysiological studies are often aimed at the exploration of the selective properties of sensory neurons. These studies raise questions about how neurons respond more to one particular set of patterns than to others. An equally puzzling but less well studied question, however, is how neurons' responses remain unaffected by stimulus changes that radically alter the low-level receptor signals out of which the responses of higher neurons must be constructed. A full description of the response properties of sensory neurons should therefore include their generalization properties (or abstract *generalization field*), as well as their selective properties (or abstract *receptive field*).

To obtain a useful sensory representation, similar external items need to be mapped to similar internal representations. The meaning of similarity, however, is different in these two domains. Similarity in the external world can be usefully defined by causal relationships and their predictors. Items that seem to result in similar outcomes are considered similar. Internal similarity, on the other hand, is a function of the neural representations and their transformations. The output of a simple neural unit is likely to remain unchanged if only a small number of its inputs change. The more inputs change, the more dissimilar the output becomes. This means that the measure of similarity for a simple neural unit is defined simply by the overlap between activity patterns. Even a simple change to a pattern, such as a slight shift, which does not affect our subjective judgment of similarity, can destroy this very simple kind of "bitwise" similarity in the input activities (Figure 5.4). For a simple neural unit, the two A's on the left in Figure 5.4 are less similar to each other than the A and B on the right, as there is less overlap between them.

More complex transformations, such as changes in size, lighting, three-dimensional viewpoint, orientation, changes in the shape of an object itself (e.g., of a book opening or of a cat stretching, curling up, or jumping), or even more abstract changes of objects can cause similarly drastic changes to the direct

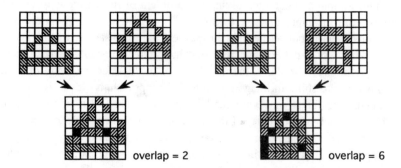

Figure 5.4. A simple shift in the position of a pattern can reduce the overlap between even identical shapes to a random level. Simple overlap between patterns does not capture our notion of similarity.

sensory measurements. An additional mechanism is therefore needed to handle the similarities not detectable as simple overlap between patterns.

The visual system must contain knowledge about these transformations in order to be able to generalize correctly. It is likely that the visual system learns from its sensory experience, which contains plenty of examples of such transformations.

Approaches to invariant recognition

Several computational schemes with varying degrees of complexity have been proposed to solve the invariance problem based, for instance, on elastic graph matching (Bienenstock & Malsburg, 1987; Buhmann, Lange, & Malsburg, 1989), Hebbian learning in a Hopfield network (Coolen & Kuijk, 1989), object-centered canonical frames of reference (Hinton, 1987; Zemel, Mozer, & Hinton, 1988), the computation of inner geometric pattern relations, size invariance by scale attention mechanism (Gochin, 1994; Olshausen, Anderson & Van Essen, 1993), shifter circuits (Anderson & Van Essen, 1987), higher-order networks, the alignment of object models (e.g., Ullman, 1989), or view interpolation (Bülthoff, 1994; Edelman & Poggio, 1992; Logothetis, Pauls, Bülthoff, & Poggio, 1994, chapter 4, this volume). Most of these models are based on stored complete prototype models of individual objects, and some of them require quite complicated control mechanisms for selection and matching. A problem with such control mechanisms is that they either have to test many alternatives or they need to know rather well what the object to be recognized is before they can control the recognition process. In either case, such a recognition process is likely to require more time than has been observed for the onset of firing of highly shape-selective neurons in the temporal cortex (Oram & Perrett, 1994).

One simple approach to solving the problem of invariance is to extract features from the input that are themselves invariant to the appropriate transformations. The output of the filter in Figure 5.5a, for instance, will be insensitive to rotations of a pattern, whereas that in Figure 5.5b will not be affected by changes in size. Similarly, the amplitude of the Fourier transform of an image is invariant to shifts in image position. This approach, however, is usually very limited. The filters in Figure 5.5, for instance, are invariant to rotation and expansion only if the center of the transformations is coincident with the center of the filters. The Fourier spectrum is invariant to shifts only as long as the complete input pattern shifts as a whole; shifts of only parts of the pattern do not leave the amplitude spectrum invariant.

Minsky and Papert (1969) have shown that, except for a few trivial cases, no single layer of *perceptron* units can extract features that are invariant in general to, for example, shifts in the position of the input patterns. A limited amount of invariance, however, may still be achieved by a single layer. A unit with connection weights that change only smoothly across space, for instance, will be less sensitive to small displacements of the input patterns than one with discontinuous weights. The requirement of smoothness, however, is a constraint on the possible weighting functions, which means that the stronger this constraint is, the smaller the number of possible filters and lower their selectivity becomes. With a single layer of units, this trade-off between discrimination power and invariance is usually inevitable.

A simple solution that gets around this trade-off uses multiple layers of units. A lower layer can have arrays of units, each having highly specific response properties. This layer performs the selective operation. Generalization is carried out by a following, separate layer by combining the response of a well-defined set or pool of selective units in a way similar to a logical OR operation. When the responses of a set of units with identical selectivity to one stimulus parameter but with differing selectivity to another parameter are pooled, the pooled response remains selective to the first parameter but becomes more invariant to the second.

Limited invariance to shifts in the position of a feature, for instance, could be achieved by pooling the responses of a sufficient number of units selective to the same feature in different positions within some region (see Figure 5.6). The number of inputs necessary to build such a generalization field depends on the size of the field over which the generalization is required and the shift tolerance of the individual inputs. The more shift tolerant each input is, the less frequently the shifts need to be replicated in space or the larger the area they can cover. The process of pooling the selective responses of units does not "blur" the input; the detailed selectivity of the low-level units is preserved in the higher-layer generalizing unit, except for the selectivity to the parameter being pooled (position, in this case).

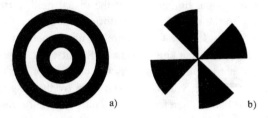

Figure 5.5. Receptive fields with simple invariance properties (rotation and size).

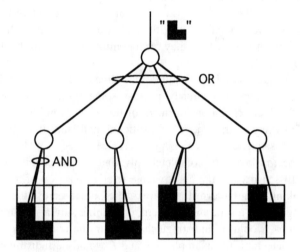

Figure 5.6. Invariance by pooling of the responses of the appropriate selective units.

This way of breaking down the problem into (at least) two stages achieves generalization across one aspect of the stimulus without loss of specificity to the other. This dual process of specializing and generalizing can be repeated several times, each time achieving selectivity across different ranges of a parameter or to new kinds of relationships between the components discovered by the previous layer. Generalization may be achieved not only to larger areas of the input (e.g., visual) field but also to other, more complex kinds of transformations.

The first detailed demonstration of the *invariance by pooling* idea was on the problem of shift-invariant handwritten digit recognition by Fukushima (1980, 1990; Fukushima & Miyake, 1982). His hierarchical, multilayer network (called the *Neocognitron*) consists of pairs of layers. Each pair of layers consists of an S (or simple) and a C (or complex) layer. Features are combined by units in the S layers. An S unit detecting a particular feature combination is replicated in many different positions in some limited part of the visual field, forming a "bank" of units responding to the same feature in different positions. Connections from the units in the S layers to the C units are set up in such a way that each C unit receives input from only a single bank of S units, and any single S unit within this bank can activate its C unit. As the position of the feature changes, the response of one of the S units is taken over by the response of another unit within the same bank. Therefore, the C unit pooling the response of the given bank would remain active in spite of the shift in position.

Units in each layer receive inputs from a limited region of the preceding layer (its receptive field) in such a way that lower-level units receive information from only a small part of the "retina" (i.e., they have small receptive fields). Units in higher layers have gradually larger fields, but only units in the highest layers have connections through which they receive information from the whole visual field (Figure 5.7).

Units in higher S layers combine features that already represent combinations of lower-level features and already possess some limited tolerance to shifts in position. The hierarchical arrangement of the network gradually gives rise to more selectivity and a larger range of positional invariance in higher layers. An important consequence of achieving invariance only gradually is that although units in the top layer are completely invariant to the position of the pattern, they are still sensitive to the approximate relative position of the component features making up a pattern. If features were pooled across the whole visual field in a single step, a scrambled pattern, containing similar features but in the wrong positions, would be indistinguishable from the correct one based on only orientation detectors; for example, a T and L would be indistinguishable. This is a kind of "binding problem." With multiple layers and gradual generalization, however, the T could be detected at a point where the tolerance to the position of the components is small relative to the size of the complete pattern, and these units would still be sensitive for the relative position of the two segments. The responses of these T-junction detectors with a relatively small range of invariance could be pooled over a somewhat larger area that, in turn, provides inputs to units with more complex pattern selectivity. In the top layer, units are completely indifferent to the position of the pattern, although they are still sensitive to the approximate relative position of its components. This is because if the relative positions of two components change beyond the range of invariance of an intermediate-level unit, this unit would no longer supply input to the high-level unit (Figure 5.8). A scrambled input would activate low-level detectors that fall outside the limited generalization field of the intermediate-level units, and therefore the scrambled pattern would not be confused with the original. This solution of the binding problem could be called *spatial binding*.

An alternative or additional mechanism for the solution of this problem is

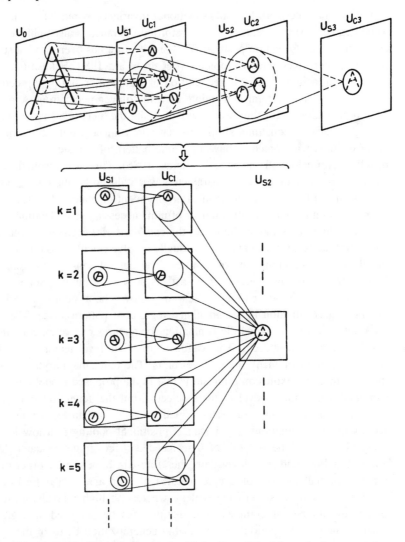

Figure 5.7. The hierarchical network of Fukushima. Selectivity and tolerance are increased simultaneously and gradually.

based on the existence of cells in the visual system inherently sensitive to those features that depend on relative position or configuration. Scrambling components removes and adds several of these features. This mechanism would rely not on the relative positions of the horizontal and vertical segments in the letters T and L but on the ability of the corner or T-junction features to differentially activate neurons. Such neurons, such as end-stopped complex cells, are known to exist already in primary visual cortex (Kato, Bishop, & Orban, 1978).

Fukushima's network has only positional invariance wired into it; however, some degree of size, orientation, and distortion tolerance is also achieved based on the tolerance to feature position. This architecture has been applied success-fully in pattern recognition problems (LeCun et al., 1989; Fukushima, 1980). LeCun et al. achieved reliable recognition of handwritten digits (zip codes) by using similar architectural constraints in a multilayer perceptron. A modified back-propagation algorithm was used to train the network that enforced a "weight-sharing" constraint similar to that wired into the Fukushima network: A set of units was forced to have the same pattern of connections in different positions (Rumelhart, Hinton, & Williams, 1986). This also resulted in faster learning, as the number of free parameters was reduced by the constraint.

Any model based on a hierarchical arrangement of feature detectors is open to criticism on the basis of the number of units necessary (e.g., Feldman, 1988). In a Fukushima-type model, however, the *combinatorial explosion* is moderated by several factors. Critical arguments usually involve calculations on the number of all possible combinations of features. The natural sensory environment is highly structured, and therefore the vast majority of stimulus parameter com-binations are likely never to arise. Learning allows the system to tune itself to optimize discrimination in the populated regions of pattern space. The system does not need to have good discrimination for features or feature combinations that in practice never occur. The useful intermediate-level features can also be shared or reused by many higher-level units. The other main argument against the combinatorial explosion criticism is that in the proposed model not only are combinations of lower-level features detected, but the generalizing stages lose selectivity to irrelevant parameters, which are therefore no longer multiplying factors in the calculations. For instance, positional pooling at a low level sig-nificantly reduces the number of units needed to cover the visual field. The number of low- and high-level units therefore can be a similar order of mag-nitude. A small number of simple features may be analyzed (e.g., in a large number of spatial positions and scales), whereas at higher levels, a gradually increasing number of complex combinations can be analyzed at a gradually smaller number of positions, as the spatial generalization fields of these higher units are much larger and a smaller number can cover the visual field.

Fukushima's model has helped to point out the importance of hierarchy and has demonstrated the idea of achieving invariance by pooling the responses of specific units. It has also demonstrated the possibility of achieving invariance to absolute position while still retaining sensitivity to the relative positions of the component features. Other aspects of Fukushima's model, however, make it less appropriate as a model of cortical pattern recognition. The main problem lies in the way the network learns. As it is necessary for the C units to receive input from only those S units that extract the same feature, and as the pooling connections between the S and C units are fixed, if the selectivity of one of the S units changes, it is necessary to change the selectivity of all the other S units

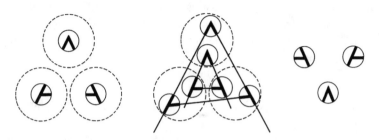

Figure 5.8. Intermediate-level units in the Fukushima network can become selective, for example, to line junctions with limited regions of tolerance (dotted circles). Such tolerance allows a slightly deformed pattern to be recognized, but scrambling the features will not activate the unit selective for the original pattern.

connected to the same C unit in the same way. Such a weight-sharing or weight-transport mechanism assumed by both the Fukushima's and the LeCun's model could not be easily implemented in a biological system.

Clue 2: Temporal coherence

An arrangement is needed in which units selective to the same feature all connect to the same complex unit. Instead of requiring simple units anatomically prewired to a complex unit (a "family") to develop in an identical way (as in the Fukushima model), the suggested alternative is that simple units can develop independently and then adaptively connect ones with similar selectivity to a complex unit (forming "clubs"). A learning rule is therefore needed to specify these modifiable, simple-to-complex connections. The Hebb rule, which depends only on instantaneous correlations, does not work here, as it would only detect overlapping patterns in the input. If the input to the simple layer contains an example of the feature at only one spatial position at any moment, then there will never be significant correlation between units selective to the same feature in different positions. The absence of positive correlations would prevent those units from being connected to the same output.

The proposed solution (Földiák, 1991) is a modified Hebbian rule in which the modification of the synaptic strength (Δw) at time step t is proportional not to the instantaneous pre-and postsynaptic activity, but instead to a time average (a *trace*) of either the presynaptic activity ($\bar{x}$) or the postsynaptic activity ($\bar{y}$). A decay term is added in order to keep the weights bounded. The version with a postsynaptic trace is:

$$\Delta w_{ij}^{(t)} = \alpha \, \bar{y}_i^{(t)} [x_j^{(t)} - w_{ij}^{(t)}]$$

where $\bar{y}_i^{(t)} = (1 - \delta) \, \bar{y}_i^{(t-1)} + \delta \, y_i^{(t)}$, α is the learning rate, and δ is the constant determining the decay rate of the trace.

An alternative, presynaptic trace version of the algorithm achieves the same goal, with similar results. The learning rule in this version contains a trace of the simple units rather than of the complex ones:

$$\Delta w_{ij}^{(t)} = \alpha \, y_i^{(t)} \, [\bar{x}_j^{(t)} - w_{ij}^{(t)}]$$

where $\bar{x}_j^{(t)} = (1 - \delta) \, \bar{x}_j^{(t-1)} + \delta \, x_j^{(t)}$.

This presynaptic version of the trace learning rule may be physiologically more plausible, as will be discussed.

Similar trace mechanisms have been used in models of classical conditioning by Sutton and Barto (1981). A trace has the effect that activity at one moment will influence learning at a later moment. This temporal low-pass filtering of the activity embodies the assumption that the desired features are stable over time in the environment. As the trace depends on the activity of only one unit, the modified rule is still local.

Simulation

The development of the connections between the S and C units (simple and complex in the sense used by Fukushima) was simulated in an example in which the goal is to learn shift invariance (Földiák, 1991). In the simple layer, there were position-dependent oriented line detectors, one unit for each of four orientations in the 64 positions on an 8×8 grid. There were only four units in the C layer, fully connected to the S units (Figure 5.9).

During training, moving lines covering the whole array are selected at random from four orientations and two directions. These lines are swept across the visual field, giving rise to activation of the simple units of the appropriate orientation but in different positions at different moments in time (Figure 5.10). The activation of these simple units is the input to the simulated network. Using the postsynaptic trace rule, if an active simple unit succeeds in exciting one of the four complex units, then the trace of that complex unit is enhanced for a period of time comparable to the duration of the sweep. Therefore, all the connections from the simple units that are activated during the rest of that sweep are strengthened according to the modified Hebb rule. Simple units of only one orientation are activated during a sweep, making it more likely that simple units of only one orientation will connect to the given complex unit (Figure 5.11).

To prevent more than one complex unit from responding to the same orientation, some kind of competitive, inhibitory interaction between the complex units is necessary. For the sake of clarity, the simplest possible competitive scheme (Rumelhart & Zipser, 1985) was used in the simulation described here. Alternatively, decorrelating connections could also be used here (unpublished results). Each unit took a sum of its inputs weighted by the connection strengths;

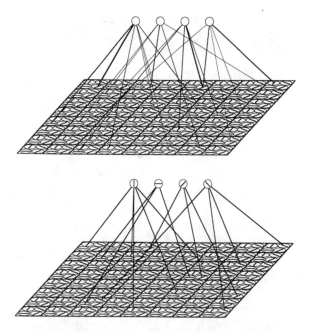

Figure 5.9. Architecture of the simple invariance learning network before and after training. Input units are selective to one of four orientations in a given position. The output units are initially connected randomly to the inputs (top). The goal is to connect the input units of the same orientation tuning to the same output unit (bottom).

the output y_k of the unit with the maximal weighted sum was set to 1, and the outputs of the rest of the units were set to 0.

The application of this learning rule in a multilayered hierarchical arrangement has also been studied (Wallis, Rolls, & Földiák, 1993; Wallis, 1996). Units in higher layers of this network learned to discriminate various complex stimuli (e.g., faces), regardless of position. It has been shown that competition in space can be combined with invariance learning (Oram & Földiák, 1995). Similar temporal smoothness constraints have also been applied with success (Stone, 1996).

The algorithm illustrated in the preceding example is not limited to learning to pool orientations across position. The pooling of any parameter of the stimulus that is selectively represented on a set of neurons for which the appropriate pattern of stimulation is available can be learned. The application of this algorithm to more complicated or abstract invariances (e.g., three-dimensional rotations or deformations) may be even more interesting, as it is even harder to

Figure 5.10. Seven consecutive frames from one of the sequences used as input (from Földiák, 1991). The four segments at each position in the figure represent the activation of a simple unit of the corresponding orientation and position. Thick segments are active units ($x_j = 1$), and thin ones are inactive units ($x_j = 0$). The trace is maintained between sweeps.

see how they could be specified without some kind of learning; the way such invariance properties could be wired in is much less obvious than it is in the case of positional invariance in Fukushima's or LeCun's models. All that would be required by the proposed algorithm is that the transformation-dependent units be available from previous stages of processing and that the environment generate sequences of the transformation, causing the activation of sequences of these transformation-dependent units within a short period of time. For instance, generalization across a three-dimensional viewing position can be learned as both conditions seem to be met. There is evidence for the existence of view-specific complex feature analyzers in the temporal cortex of the monkey visual system (Logothetis, 1994; Oram & Perrett, 1994; Perrett et al., 1991; Perrett, Rolls, & Caan, 1982; Tanaka, 1993). The normal visual environment contains many examples of objects undergoing continuous perspective transformations. Further examples may be the learning of generalization over different facial expressions by pooling cells selective for particular facial expressions or body postures of an individual (Figure 5.12). Neurons selective for particular body views, as well as ones that generalize across different postures, are known to exist (Perrett et al., 1992).

Discrimination versus invariance

Information about parameters that one set of neurons generalizes over need not be lost for higher levels of processing. Other sets of neurons can still retain selectivity for those parameters and generalize over other parameters. Absolute positional information, for instance, may be generalized over in neurons involved in object identification, and this information may be preserved in neurons performing spatial or motor tasks.

Generalization over object identity in such a spatial stream, however, need not be complete, which would help avoid the binding problem. A small amount of remaining selectivity to position in the "what" pathway or a small amount of selectivity to stimulus shape in the "where" pathway can resolve the correspondence problem. For instance, some of the neurons in area MT of the

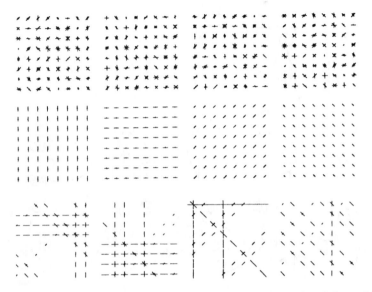

Figure 5.11. Connection patterns of the four complex units (a) random, before training, and (b) after training on 500 line sweeps across the visual field. The length of each segment indicates the strength of the connection from the simple unit of the corresponding position and the orientation to the complex unit. Initial weights were chosen from a uniform distribution on [0,0.1]. α; eq 0.02, δ = 0.2. (c) The result of training without a trace (δ = 1). The result and the speed of convergence are relatively insensitive to δ. Too short time constants (δ near 1), however, are not enough to link different phases of the transformation, and the results are similar to those demonstrated (e.g., c). Too long time constants (small δ), on the other hand, lead to confusion between the subsequent sweeps, as the trace does not decay sufficiently between two different patterns.

macaque, which is specialized in processing motion information, are also sensitive to the wavelength of the stimulus (Gegenfurtner et al., 1994).

The apparent antagonism between the ability to discriminate and the ability to generalize is therefore resolved by cooperative distributed representations. Similarity on only a small subset of the representation units of two patterns is sufficient to allow generalization between them along the specific aspect represented by that subset. The color of a car, for instance, may remind you of the color of someone's hair, even though the hair and the car on the whole are very different. This is in sharp contrast to the single-cause, or prototype, theories of classification, in which the hair and the car, whatever color they are, would never match each other's prototype (Földiák, 1998). In a cooperative representation, discrimination and generalization are not conflicting requirements, as similarity on one part of the representation can result in generalization without losing the ability to discriminate based on the dissimilar parts of the representation.

164   PETER FÖLDIÁK

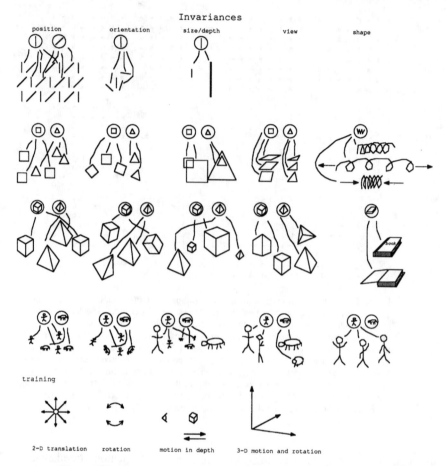

Figure 5.12. Some of the possible training stimuli for learning invariance to different transformations.

Biological relevance

The idea that invariant properties are achieved by the convergent pooling of the appropriate transformation-dependent cells is consistent with both anatomical and physiological data. The computational architecture necessary for this operation is far simpler than that required by most alternative models.

Single-cell electrophysiological experiments suggest that the invariance properties of perception are due to the receptive field characteristics of individual cells in the visual system. Complex cells in the primary visual cortex exhibit approximate invariance to position within a limited range (Hubel & Wiesel,

1962), whereas cells in higher visual areas in the temporal cortex exhibit more complex forms of invariance to the size, color, contrast, orientation, and retinal location of the stimulus; they also have much larger receptive fields (Bruce, Desimme, & Gross, 1981; Gross, 1992; Gross & Mishkin, 1977; Ito, Tamura, Fujita, & Tanaka, 1995; Miyashita & Chang, 1988; Perrett et al., 1982, 1989; Rolls & Baylis, 1986; Sakai & Miyashita, 1994; Schwartz, Desimone, Albright, & Gross, 1983; Tovee, Rolls, & Azzopardi, 1994).

The invariance learning model just presented makes three fundamental assumptions.

The first one is about the form of the synaptic learning rule: It is assumed that a synapse is strengthened not only when the activations of the pre- and postsynaptic cells are coincident, but also when they are both activated within a relatively short period of time. The trace mediating this memory for recent activity could have many possible biological implementations, as all biochemical processes have a nonzero extent in time. Obvious candidates are the membrane and synaptic mechanisms that have significant time constants. As cortical pyramidal cells may have much longer membrane time constants than previously estimated (possibly 100 ms or more), the simplest possibility is that the membrane could retain an electrical trace of past synaptic activity (Stratford, Mason, Larkman, Major, & Jack, 1989). Alternatively, the trace can be independent of the electrical activation of the neuron. The running average may be kept by a chemical concentration (e.g., calcium; Holmes & Levy, 1990) that is gradually changed by neural activity. Another implementation may involve the activation time constants of synaptic receptor channels (Rhodes, 1992). N-methyl-D-aspartate (NMDA) receptors, which are believed to be involved in the long-term potentiation of synapses, have relatively slow kinetics. NMDA receptor channels have relatively long opening times, desensitize slowly and incompletely, and can result in large, long-lasting synaptic currents (Lester, Clements, Westbrook, & Jahr, 1990; Mayer, Vyklicky, Benveniste, Patneau, & Williamson, 1991). NMDA currents can therefore last for approximately 200 ms. The neurotransmitter released at an earlier presynaptic activation may still be bound to the receptor at the time of a subsequent postsynaptic depolarization (Holmes & Levy, 1990). Such a mechanism would require the presynaptic activation to precede the postsynaptic activation for potentiation to occur. This condition was in fact required for long-term potentiation in the hippocampus (Levy & Steward, 1983). Because it is the presynaptic activity that is preserved in the state of the receptors, this mechanism would implement the alternative learning rule involving the presynaptic trace presented in the previous section, in spite of the postsynaptic location of the membrane channels that may be involved in this process. Experiments to determine the precision of the synchrony of binocular activation necessary for the development of binocularity showed that if the two eyes are stimulated in alternation, only alternation rates slower than 500 ms prevent the development of normal depth discrimination in kittens (Altmann, Lukmann, Yrevel, & Singer, 1987). Even longer time constants, up to 1–5 s, could be achieved by the metabotropic glutamate system (Levy, personal communication). An alternative to utilizing the single-unit properties of individual neurons for preserving information in neurons across time is to make use of network properties due to recurrent interconnections between neurons (Amit, 1994). The attractor states and hysteresis observed in such networks can be used to drive invariance learning, as was demonstrated in a model of chick imprinting (O'Reilly, 1992; O'Reilly & Johnson, 1994).

The second assumption is that units selective for different transformation phases are available in the network, so that the C or (complex) cells can learn to combine their activations. This assumption was first made in models of complex cells of the primary visual cortex (Hubel & Wiesel, 1962), where it was assumed that complex cells receive their major inputs from simple cells for the same orientation in different positions. Some complex cells are now known to receive direct input from the lateral geniculate nucleus (Bullier & Henry, 1979; Hoffman, 1971), and the simple model of Hubel and Wiesel turned out to be insufficient to explain all the properties of complex cells (Stone, Dreher, & Leventhal, 1979). Simple-cell-like subunits are still assumed as components of complex cell responses (Spitzer & Hochstein, 1985), and at least some of complex cells (e.g., those of layer 2) do not receive direct thalamic input (Gilbert et al., 1988). These cells probably receive their inputs from simple cells. The previously described mechanisms could be used to connect to a complex unit only the simple cells with the same orientation and spatial frequency tuning but with different spatial positions and phase tuning.

Another example of achieving transformation-invariant responses by combining transformation-specific units may come from the face-selective neurons found in monkey temporal cortex. Some of these face-selective neurons respond selectively to only one view of faces (e.g., the right profile), whereas the response of a smaller number of other neurons are invariant to head rotation and respond to all views of the face. The average response latencies of view-independent cells are slightly longer than those of view-dependent ones (130 vs. 119 ms) (Perrett et al., 1992), which is consistent with the assumption that the view-dependent cells may provide input to the invariant cells.

A further consideration is whether there are enough transformation-sensitive cells to cover the total range of the transformations. This problem is especially obvious when invariance to more than one transformation is required simultaneously. The need for an excessively large number of simple units can be avoided if their transformation tuning is sufficiently broad. This does seem to be the case with visual simple cells, whose receptive fields are fairly smooth. A receptive field with a large number of discontinuities would be much more sensitive to shifts of only a fraction of the width of the receptive field. The view-dependent, face-selective cells also show a relatively broad (approximately 60°) tuning to head rotation (Perrett et al., 1991).

The third important assumption is that the environment provides examples of the transformation. In the case of learning shift invariance, object motion or eye movements constantly provide the necessary transformations. The necessary sweeping activations may even be present before the start of normal visual stimulation during early development, as there is evidence of intrinsically generated waves of activity in the developing mammalian retina (Meister, Wong, Baylor, & Shatz, 1991; Wong, Meister, & Shatz, 1993). Forward motion in three-dimensional space, for instance, would provide ideal training for the size invariance property, and a more general form of motion would be able to train invariance to perspective transformations of objects. Other kinds of invariances, and the transformations necessary for their training, are shown in Figure 5.12.

A biologically plausible alternative or addition to the present algorithm would be to use back-projections from higher visual areas as "unsupervised teaching inputs" to bias Hebbian mechanisms toward invariant representations (Rumelhart & Zipser, 1985). Such a mechanism could help learn invariant categories whose members are not related to each other by sequences of commonly occurring transformations. These back-projecting connections would be a different way of introducing correlations between stimuli with no correlations in the forward stream, perhaps using information from other sensory modalities (Rolls, 1989; DeSa, 1994). Such a "top-down" biasing teaching signal would also provide a possible role for the large number of cortical axons projecting back from higher to lower visual areas.

As an interesting side effect, the proposed trace mechanism could help explain results by Miyashita (1988; Sakai & Miyashita, 1991; Stryker, 1991), who repeatedly presented a set of randomly generated fractal images to monkeys in a particular order. When they measured the responses to these images from cells in the temporal cortex, they found similarities in the responses to patterns that were presented close to each other in time in the training sequence. A trace mechanism would explain these temporal associations, as a trace that has no time to decay completely between stimulus presentations would have the effect of making the representation of these successively presented stimuli similar (Wallis, 1998).

Although achieving a transformation-independent representation would certainly be useful in recognizing patterns, the information that these invariance stages throw away may be vital in performing visual tasks. A separate system for detecting the time-variant components of the stimuli, such as a motion detection (or "where") system, would probably have to supplement and cooperate with such a "what" system in complex ways.

References

Altmann, L., Luhmann, H. J., Greuel, J. M., & Singer, W. (1987). Functional and neuronal binocularity in kittens raised with rapidly alternating monocular occlusion. *Journal of Neurophysiology, 58*(5), 965–980.

Amit, D. J. (1994) Persistent delay activity in cortex – a Galilean phase in neurophysiology. *Network, 5*(4), 429–436.

Anderson, C. H., & Van Essen, D. C. (1987). Shifter circuits: A computational strategy for dynamic aspects of visual processing. *Proceedings of the National Academy of Sciences of the USA, 84*, 6297–6301.

Barlow, H. B. (1959). Sensory mechanisms, the reduction of redundancy, and intelligence. In *The mechanisation of thought processes* (pp. 535–539). London: Her Majesty's Stationery Office.

Barlow, H. B. (1972). Single units and sensation: A neuron doctrine for perceptual psychology? *Perception, 1*, 371–394.

Barlow, H. B. (1993). Object identification and cortical organisation. In B. Gulyás, D. Ottoson, & P. E. Roland, (Eds.), *Functional organisation of the human visual cortex* (pp. 75–100). Oxford: Pergamon Press.

Barlow, H. B. (1994a). The neuron doctrine in perception. In M. Gazzaniga (Ed.), *The cognitive neurosciences,* (pp. 415–435). Boston: MIT Press.

Barlow, H. B. (1994b). What is the computational goal of the neocortex? In C. Koch & J. L. Davis (Eds.), *Large-scale neuronal theories of the brain.* Cambridge, MA: MIT Press.

Barlow, H. B., & Földiák, P. (1989). Adaptation and decorrelation in the cortex. In R. Durbin, C. Miall, & G. Mitchison, (Eds.), *The computing neuron* (pp. 54–72). Workingham, England: Addison-Wesley.

Barlow, H. B., & Gardner-Medwin, A. R. (1993, August). Sensory representations suitable for learning. In *Proceedings of the 32nd International Congress of Physiological Sciences, Glasgow*, 355.8. London.

Bienenstock, E., & Malsburg, C. V. D. (1987). A neural network for invariant pattern recognition. *Europhysics Letters, 4*, 121–126.

Bruce, C. J., Desimone, R., & Gross, C. G. (1981). Visual properties of neurons in a polysensory area in superior temporal sulcus of the macaque. *Journal of Neurophysiology, 46*, 369–384.

Buhmann, J., Lange, J., & Malsburg, C. V. D. (1989). Distortion invariant object recognition by matching hierarchically labeled graphs. In *IEEE/INNS International Joint Conference on Neural Networks* (Vol. 1, pp. 155–159). Washington, DC: IEEE Press.

Bullier, J., & Henry, G. H. (1979). Ordinal position of neurons in the cat striate cortex. *Journal of Physiology, 42*, 1251–1263.

Bülthoff, H. H. (1994). Image-based object recognition: Psychophysics. *Abstracts of the 17th Annual Meeting of the European Neuroscience Association* (p. 67).

Coolen, A. C. C., & Kuijk, F. W. (1989). A learning mechanism for invariant pattern recognition in neural networks. *Neural Networks, 2*, 495–506.

Dayan, P., & Zemel, R. S. (1995). Competition and multiple cause models. *Neural Computation, 7*(3), 565–579.

DeSa, V. R. (1994). Learning classification with unlabelled data. In J. D. Cowan, G. Tesauro, & J. Alspector (Eds.), *Advances in neural information processing systems* (Vol. 6, pp. 112–119). San Francisco: Morgan Kaufmann.

Edelman, S., & Poggio, T. (1992). Bringing the grandmother back into the picture: A memory-based view of object recognition. *International Journal of Pattern Recognition and Artificial Intelligence, 6*, 37–61.

Everitt, B. (1974). *Cluster analysis.* Aldershot, U.K.: Gower.

Feldman, J. A. (1988) Connectionist representation of concepts. In D. Waltz & J. A. Feldman (Eds.), *Connectionist models and their implications: Readings from cognitive science* (pp. 341–363). Norwood, NJ: Ablex.

Földiák, P. (1990). Forming sparse representations by local anti-Hebbian learning. *Biological Cybernetics, 64*(2), 165–170.

Földiák, P. (1990). Learning invariance from transformation sequences. *Neural Computation, 3*(2), 194–200.

Földiák, P. (1992). *Models of sensory coding*. Technical Report No. CUED/F-INFENG/TR 91. Cambridge: Department of Engineering, University of Cambridge.

Földiák, P., & Young, M. P. (1995). Sparse coding in the primate cortex. In M. A. Arbib, (Ed.), *The handbook of brain theory and neural networks* (pp. 895–898). Cambridge, MA: MIT Press.

Földiák, P. (1998). What is wrong with prototypes. *Behavioral & Brain Sciences*, in press.

Fukushima, K. (1980). Neocognitron: A self-organising neural network model for a mechanism of pattern recognition unaffected by shift of position. *Biological Cybernetics, 36*, 193–202.

Fukushima, K. (1990). Alphanumeric character recognition by the neocognitron. In R. Eckmiller (Ed.), *Advanced neural computers* (pp. 263–270). Amsterdam: North-Holland: Elsevier.

Fukushima, K., & Miyake, S. (1982). Neocognitron: A new algorithm for pattern recognition tolerant of deformations and shifts of position. *Pattern Recognition, 15*(6), 455–469.

Gardner-Medwin, A. R., & Barlow, H. B. (1992). The effect of sparseness in distributed representations on the detectability of associations between sensory events. *Journal of Physiology, 452*, 282.

Gegenfurtner, K. R., Kiper, D. C., Beusmans, J. M. H., Carandini, M., Zaidi, Q., & Movshon, J. A. (1994). Chromatic properties of neurons in macaque MT. *Visual Neurosciences, 11*, 455–466.

Gilbert, C. D., Bourgeois, J. -P., Eckhorn, R., Goldman-Rakic, P. S., Jones, E. G., Krüger, J., Luhmann, H. J., Lund, J. S., Orban, G. A., Prince, D. A., Sillito, A. M., Somogyi, P., Toyama, K., & Van Essen, D. C. (1988). Group report. Neuronal and synaptic organization in the cortex. In P. Rakic & W. Singer (Eds.), *Neurobiology of neocortex* (pp. 219–240). Chichester, England: Wiley.

Gochin, P. M. (1994). Machine shape recognition modeled after the visual system of the primate. In S. T. Venkataraman & S. Gulati (Eds.), *Perceptual robotics* (pp. 112–137). New York: Springer.

Gross, C. G. (1992). Representation of visual stimuli in inferior temporal cortex. *Philosophical Transactions of the Royal Society of London, B335*, 3–10.

Gross, C. G., & Mishkin, M. (1977). The neural basis of stimulus equivalence across retinal translation. In S. Harnad (Ed.), *Lateralization in the nervous system* (pp. 109–122). New York: Academic Press.

Grossberg, S. (1987) Competitive learning: From interactive activation to adaptive resonance. *Cognitive Science, 11*, 23.

Hebb, D. O. (1949). *The organisation of behavior*. New York: Wiley.

Hertz, J. A., Krogh, A. S., & Palmer, R. G. (1991). *Introduction to the theory of neural computation*. Redwood City, CA: Addison-Wesley.

Hinton, G. E. (1987). Learning translation invariant recognition in a massively parallel network. In G. Goos, & J. Hartmanis (Eds.), *PARLE: Parallel architectures and languages of Europe* (pp. 1–13). Berlin: Springer-Verlag.

Hinton, G. E., & Ghahramani, Z. (1997). Generative models for discovering sparse distributed representations. *Philosophical Transactions of the Royal Society B, 352*, 1177–1190.

Hinton, G. E., & Zemel, R. S. (1994). Autoencoders, minimum description lengths and Helmholtz free energy. In J. D. Cowan, G. Tesauro, & J. Alspector (Eds.), *Advances in neural information processing systems* (Vol. 6, pp. 3–10). San Francisco: Morgan Kaufmann.

Hoffman, K.-P. (1971). Conduction velocity of afferents to cat visual cortex: Correlation with cortical receptive field properties. *Brain Research, 32*, 460–466.

Holmes, W. R., & Levy, W. B. (1990). Insights into associative long-term potentiation from computational models of NMDA receptor-mediated calcium concentration changes. *Journal of Neurophysiology, 63*(5), 1148–1168.

Hubel, D. H., & Wiesel, T. N. (1962). Receptive fields, binocular interaction and functional architecture in the cat's visual cortex. *Journal of Physiology, 160*, 106–154.

Ito, M., Tamura, H., Fujita, I., & Tanaka, K. (1995). Size and position invariance of neuronal responses in monkey inferotemporal cortex. *Journal of Neuroscience, 73*(1), 218–266.

Kaski, S., & Kohonen, T. (1994) Winner-take-all networks for physiological models of competitive learning. *Neural Networks, 7*(6/7), 973–984.

Kato, H., Bishop, P. O., & Orban, G. A. (1978) Hypercomplex and simple/complex cell classifications in the cat striate cortex. *Journal of Neurophysiology, 41*, 1071–1095.

Kovács, Gy., Vogels, R., & Orban, G. A. (1995). Selectivity of macaque inferior temporal neurons for partially occluded shapes. *Journal of Neuroscience, 15*(3/1), 1984–1997.

LeCun, Y., Boser, B., Denker, J. S., Henderson, D., Howard, R. E., Hubbard, W., & Jackel, L. D. (1989). Backpropagation applied to handwritten zip code recognition. *Neural Computation, 1*, 541–551.

Lester, R. A. J., Clements, J. D., Westbrook, G. L., Jahr, C. E. (1990). Channel kinetics determine the time course of NMDA receptor-mediated synaptic currents. *Nature 346*, 565–567.

Levy, W. B., & Steward, O. (1983). Temporal contiguity requirements for long-term associative potentiation/depression in the hippocampus. *Neuroscience, 8*, 791–797.

Lippmann, R. P. (1987). An introduction to computing with neural nets. *IEEE ASSP Magazine, 4*(2), 4–22.

Logothetis, N. K., Pauls, J., Bülthoff, H. H., & Poggio, T. (1994) View-dependent object recognition by monkeys. *Current Biology, 4*,(5), 401–414.

Malsburg, C. V. D. (1973). Self-organisation of orientation sensitive cells in the striate cortex. *Kybernetik, 14*, 85–100.

Mayer, M. L., Vyklicky, L., Benveniste, M., Patneau, D. L., & Williamson, L. (1991). In H. V. Wheal, & A. M. Thomson (Eds.), *Excitatory amino acids and synaptic transmission* (pp. 123–140).

Meister, M., Wong, R. O. L., Baylor, D. A., & Shatz, C. J. (1991). Synchronous bursts of action-potentials in ganglion-cells of the developing mammalian retina. *Science 252*(5008), 939–943.

Minsky, M., & Papert, S. (1969). *Perceptrons.* Cambridge, MA: MIT Press.

Miyashita, Y. (1988). Neuronal correlate of visual associative long-term memory in the primate temporal cortex. *Nature, 335*, 817–820.

Miyashita, Y., & Chang, H. S. (1988). Neuronal correlate of pictorial short-term memory in the primate temporal cortex. *Nature, 331*, 68–70.

Nowlan, S. J. (1991). *Soft competitive adaptation: Neural network learning algorithms based on fitting statistical mixtures.* Technical Report No. CMU-CS-91-126. Pittsburgh: Carnegie Mellon University.

Olshausen, B. A., Anderson, C. H., & Van Essen, D. C. (1993). A neurobiological model of visual-attention and invariant pattern recognition. *Journal of Neuroscience, 13*(11), 4700–4719.

Oram, M., & Földiák, P. (1996). Learning generalisation and localisation: Competing for stimulus type and receptive field. *Neurocomputing, 11*, 297–321.

Oram, M. W., & Perrett, D. I. (1994) Modeling visual recognition from neurobiological constraints. *Neural Networks, 7*(6/7), 945–972.

O'Reilly, R. C. (1992). *The self-organisation of spatially invariant representations. Parallel distributed processing and cognitive neuroscience.* Technical Report No. PDP.CNS.92.5. Pittsburgh: Department of Psychology, Carnegie Mellon University.

O'Reilly, R. C., & Johnson, M. H. (1994). Object recognition and sensitive periods: A computational analysis of visual imprinting. *Neural Computation, 6*(3), 357–389.

Perrett, D. I., Harries, M. H., Bevan, R., Thomas, S., Benson, P. J., Mistlin, A. J., Chitty, A. J., Hietanen, J. K. & Ortega, J. E. (1989). Frameworks of analysis for the neural representation of animate objects and actions. *Journal of Experimental Biology, 146*, 87–113.

Perrett, D. I., Oram, M. W., Harries, M. H., Bevan, R., Hietanen, J. K., Benson, P. J. & Thomas, S.

(1991). Viewer-centered and object-centred coding of heads in the macaque temporal cortex. *Experimental Brain Research, 86,* 159–173.

Perrett, D. I., Rolls, E. T., & Caan, W. (1982). Visual neurons responsive to faces in the monkey temporal cortex. *Experimental Brain Research, 47,* 329–342.

Poggio, T., & Girosi, F. (1990). Networks for approximating and learning. *Proceedings of the IEEE, 78,* 1481–1497.

Rhodes, P. A. (1992). The long open time of the NMDA channel facilitates the self-organisation of invariant object responses in cortex. *Society for Neuroscience Abstracts, 18*(1), 740.

Rolls, E. T. (1989). The representation and storage of information in neuronal networks in the primate cerebral cortex and hippocampus. In C. Miall, R. M. Durbin, & G. J. Mitchison (Eds.), *The computing neuron* (chap. 8, pp. 125–159). Wokingham, England: Addison-Wesley.

Rolls, E. T., & Baylis, G. C. (1986). Size and contrast have only small effects on the responses to faces of neurons in the cortex of the superior temporal sulcus of the monkey. *Experimental Brain Research, 65,* 38–48.

Rumelhart, D. E., Hinton, G. E., & Williams, R. J. (1986). Learning internal representations by error propagation. In D. E. Rumelhart & J. McClelland (Eds.), *Parallel distributed processing* (pp. 318–362). Cambridge, MA: MIT Press.

Rumelhart, D. E., & Zipser, D. (1985). Feature discovery by competitive learning. *Cognitive Science, 9,* 75–112.

Sakai, K., & Miyashita, Y. (1991). Neural organisation for the long-term memory of paired associates. *Nature, 354,* 152–155.

Sakai, K., & Miyashita, Y. (1994). Neuronal tuning to learned complex forms in vision. *Neuroreport, 5,* 829–832.

Sáry, Gy., Vogels, R., & Orban, G. A. (1993) Cue-invariant shape selectivity of macaque inferior temporal neurons. *Science, 260,* 995–997.

Saund, E. (1994) A multiple cause mixture model for unsupervised learning. *Neural Computation, 7*(1), 51–71.

Schwartz, E. L., Desimone, R., Albright, T. D., & Gross, C. G. (1983). Shape recognition and inferior temporal neurons. *Proceedings of the National Academy of Sciences of the USA, 80,* 5776–5778.

Spitzer, H., & Hochstein, S. (1985). A complex-cell receptive-field model. *Journal of Neurophysiology, 53,* 1266–1286.

Stone, G. V. (1996). Learning perceptually salient visual parameters using spatiotemporal smoothness constraints. *Neural Computation, 8,* 1463–1492.

Stone, J., Dreher, B., & Leventhal, A. (1979). Hierarchical and parallel mechanisms in the organization of visual cortex. *Brain Research Review, 1,* 345–394.

Stratford, K., Mason, A., Larkman, A., Major, G., & Jack, J. (1989). The modelling of pyramidal neurones in the visual cortex. In R. Durbin, C. Miall, & G. J. Mitchison, (Eds.), *The computing neuron* (pp. 71–93). New York: Addison-Wesley.

Stryker, M. P. (1991) Temporal associations. *Nature, 354,* 108–109.

Sutton, R. S., & Barto, A. G. (1981). Towards a modern theory of adaptive networks: Expectation and prediction. *Psychological Review, 88,* 135–170.

Tanaka, K. (1993). Neuronal mechanisms of object recognition. *Science, 262*(5134), 685–688.

Tovee, M. J., Rolls, E. T., & Azzopardi, P. (1994). Translation invariance in the responses to faces of single neurons in the temporal visual cortical areas of the alert macaque. *Journal of Neurophysiology, 72*(3), 1049–1060.

Ullman, S. (1989) Aligning pictorial descriptions: An approach to object recognition. *Cognition, 32,* 193–254.

Wachsmuth, E., Oram, M. W., & Perrett, D. I. (1994). Recognition of objects and their parts: Responses of single units in the temporal cortex of the macaque. *Cerebral Cortex, 5,* 509–522.

Wallis, G. (1996). Using spatio-temporal correlations to learn invariant object recognition. *Neural Networks 9,* 1513–1519.

Wallis, G. (1998). Time to learn about objects. In *Information Theory and the Brain*, eds. R. Baddeley, P. Hancock, & P. Földiák, Cambridge Univ. Press. In press.

Wallis, G., Rolls, E. T., & Földiák, P. (1993). Learning invariant responses to the natural transformations of objects. *Proceedings of the International Joint Conference on Neural Networks, Nagoya, Japan* (Vol. 2, pp. 1087–1090).

Wong, R. O. L., Meister, M., & Shatz, C. J. (1993). Transient period of correlated bursting activity during development of the mammalian retina. *Neuron 11*(5), 923–938.

Yuille, A. L., & Geiger, D. (1995). Winner-take-all mechanisms. In M. A. Arbib (Ed.), *Handbook of brain theory and neural networks* (pp. 1056–1060). Cambridge, MA: MIT Press.

Zemel, R. S., Mozer, M. C., & Hinton, G. E. (1988) TRAFFIC: A model of object recognition based on transformations of feature instances. In D. S. Touretzky, G. E., Hinton, & T. J. Sejnowski (Eds.), *Proceedings of the 1988 Connectionist Summer School* (pp. 21–27). Los Angeles: Morgan Kauffmann.

6   Perceptual constancies in lower vertebrates

David Ingle

Introduction

This chapter reviews some constancy abilities (and failures) of lower vertebrates – the fishes and amphibians – in the hope of elucidating how well constancies can be expressed by animals that lack a cerebral cortex. Although recording and lesion experiments in primates suggest that some constancy operations (e.g., color and shape) depend on the so-called association cortices (see chapters 7 and 13), we do not yet know the extent to which simpler brains harbor mechanisms for the expression of familiar constancies: color, shape, size-distance, and space. I examine relevant performances of teleost fishes and of anuran amphibians (frogs and toads) on all but color constancy, which is reviewed in chapter 12. These questions may be seen as part of a wider inquiry into the functional advantages of evolving a visual cortex, as discussed earlier by Ingle and Shook (1984).

Size-distance constancy in frogs and toads

The ability of an organism to discriminate the actual size of prey objects is of such great ecological significance that highly visual predators might be expected to develop a constancy mechanism to determine an object's real size over a range of distances. In my first study of size-dependent prey selection in frogs (Ingle, 1968), I measured the frequencies with which frogs oriented or snapped at moving dummy prey of different sizes. I found that a wormlike dark shape 1.2° high was strongly preferred to a similar shape 3.6° high when both were seen at a 9-inch distance, but that the opposite preference was obtained when these two stimuli were compared at a 3-inch distance. This finding – that the frog's size preference peaked at a standard real size – was confirmed in more extensive tests of toads by Ewert and Gebauer (1973) and of frogs by Ingle and Cook (1977). Both studies agreed, however, that this mode of size constancy operates only up to about 6 inches because the viewing angle determines preferences for more distant stimuli (Figure 6.1). Because frogs and toads strike at objects only up to 6 or 7 inches away, it seems that the size-constancy rule

173

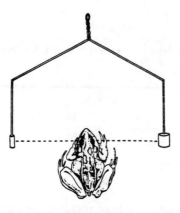

Figure 6.1a. Size-preference is measured in frogs in terms of the percentatge choice of a variably sized stimulus versus a standard stimulus presented simultaneously on opposite sides of the animal. These yellow cylinders are moved back and forth on a dark slate floor by means of a wire handle that imparts the same motion to each stimulus. The length of each stimulus is constant; only the height varies systematically on each trial.

operates to determine prey "value" only within that zone where a decision to catch the prey is required. When the prey is further away, the frog can hop closer before making that choice.

In frogs and toads, single-cell recordings and selective lesions within the visual system have both provided insights from which a model of size-distance constancy has been fashioned (Ingle, 1983a; see Figure 6.2). To begin with, the classic study of Lettvin, Maturana, McCulloch, and Pitts (1959) revealed that retinal fibers terminating within the superficial layer of the frog's optic tectum (a structure required for visually elicited feeding behavior of all nonmammalian vertebrates) had small visual receptive fields (3° to 4° wide) and were thus best excited by movement of small, dark spots (4° to 6° wide) moving through these fields. These visual units were popularly called *bug detectors* (although not by Lettvin) and were invoked to explain the frog's typical preference for small, dark objects (Ingle, 1968). However, other visual inputs to the tectum are required to explain the frog's (or toad's) preference for 20°-wide stimuli that move only 2 inches from the eye. I proposed that deeper retino-tectal fibers (the *changing contrast* fibers of Lettvin) mediate the frog's preference for nearby large objects because these fibers are best excited by large stimuli subtending angles of 10° to 30°. The question remains as to how tectal cells could switch their dominance from small-field to large-field retinal inputs during changes of prey distance.

A major clue to this explanation came from the discovery of Ewert (1968) that toads with lesions of the pretectum (just anterior to the tectum) pursued very large stimuli as prey, even when viewed at a 6-inch distance. In this respect,

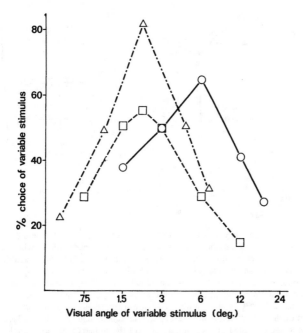

Figure 6.1b. Three size-preference curves were determined for each of three stimulus distances: 7.5, 15.0, and 22.5 cm. Ten frogs were tested 10 times with each size comparison at each of the two nearer distances, providing 100 data points to be averaged for each point depicted on the curves in this figure. Note that the preference for size of prey seen at 15 cm peaks at about half the visual angle peak as that for trials with prey seen at 7.5 cm. This size preference is therefore related to the real size of the objects, and not to their respective visual angles as subtended at the frog's eye. However, when tested 10 new frogs in the same manner with stimuli placed at a 22.5-cm distance, the peak preference was about 2°, the same as that obtained with prey at the 15-cm distance. We conclude that size constancy for these stimuli breaks down beyond 15 cm.

they behaved as if they has lost normal size-distance constancy and were sensitive only to inputs from large-field retinal fibers. In fact, Ewert (1984) showed that a single tectal neuron with a normal preference for moving disks of 6° to 8° width began to respond preferentially to a 30° disk immediately following injection of the chemotoxin kainic acid into the ipsilateral pretectum. Thus, pretectal modulation of tectal cells plays a key role in the adjustment of size preference to distance.

My unpublished studies of axonal transport of horseradish peroxidase (HRP) from the lateral pretectum into the adjacent tectum revealed that these fibers terminate mainly within the layer of tectal cell dendrites where one records terminals of the retinal large-field fibers. Figure 6.2 depicts a model that shows how high pretectal activity during viewing of distant prey inhibits large-field input and allows the tectal "feeding cells" to be driven mainly by small-field

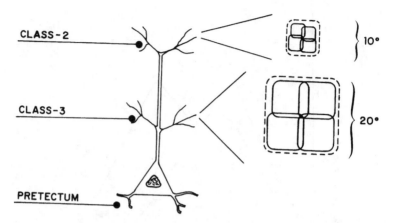

Figure 6.2. A schematic model of inputs to "feeding cells" in layer 6 of the frog's optic tectum, designed to account for modulation of size preference with viewing distance. Many cells in this layer, with long axonal projections to the medulla, have dendrites with terminals in both the small-field (class-2) retinal fiber layer and the large-field (class-3) layer. We assume that these tectal cells can be activated either by small moving objects within a region about 10° wide (shown on the upper right) or by large moving objects within a region 20° to 30° wide (shown on the lower right). However, because inhibitory inputs from the lateral pretectum are presumed to terminate mainly on dendrites receiving class-3 fibers, the activated pretectum can shut off the influence of larger-angle stimuli (when presented at a greater distance) and switch feeding preference to smaller objects seen at the same distance. Conversely, if pretectal inhibition relaxes during near viewing, the class-3 inputs dominate tectal cells and the preference among near stimuli switches to larger stimuli.

fibers. Relaxation of this pretectal inhibition during near viewing would allow the input from large-field retinal fibers to drive the feeding system. Other arguments in favor of this model are listed by Ingle (1983a). Because Collett (1977) showed that distance estimation is linked to accommodative state in toads, we propose that a corollary discharge from the accommodation system to the pretectum could "reset" the size filter inherent in the tectum. Further, because Collett and Harkness (1982) have reported that the African chameleon also uses its accommodative mechanism to determine prey distance, we suggest that our model applies to size constancy in reptiles as well as amphibians.

Failure of size constancy in the estimation of aperture width

Just as the tectum is the critical relay between the frog's eye and the motor apparatus for prey catching, the medial pretectum appears to be a critical visual relay for detouring around solid barriers as the frog pursues prey or leaps away from an approaching threat (see the review by Ingle, 1983b). Ingle (1980) first described the "barrier blindness" resulting from ablation of the frog's pretectum, and Ewert (1971) described single cells within the toad's pretectum that responded better to large, stationary edges than to moving objects. My own unpublished studies showed that many frog pretectal cells are best activated by vertical edges but that none recorded were better activated by horizontal edges. That result probably accounts for the finding that frogs readily avoid collision with vertically striped barriers (when pinched from behind) but typically collide with the same barriers rotated by 90° (Ingle, 1983b and unpublished studies). Finally, we found that frogs are more sensitive to the space between vertical edges than to the space between horizontal apertures when the aperture is just large enough for an escaping frog to negotiate. Thus frogs escape through horizontal rectangular apertures with a 2:1 length ratio but turn away from vertical apertures of the same dimensions.

We used this sensitivity to horizontal width of apertures to test the frog's ability to rescale the critical angular width of "just negotiable" apertures with varying distances (Ingle & Cook, 1977). We found that this sensitivity was rather finely tuned such that frogs were willing to jump only through apertures slightly wider than their own head width (Figure 6.3), but that they showed the same dependence on visual angle whether the barriers were 3 inches or 9 inches away in the frontal field. Unlike the case for prey-width discrimination, judging the minimal negotiable width of apertures does not obey the size-distance constancy rule. Although it is obviously important for the frog to avoid jumping between a too narrow aperture seen 3 inches away, it does not seem to matter that it makes an overly conservative choice in avoiding a 22° wide aperture seen 9 inches away.

The epistemological status of size-constancy laws

Although we take for granted that a monkey "knows" that the same object is the same size over a range of viewing distances, we may not extend that supposition to the frog. One reason is that the frog's (or toad's) expression of size constancy is limited to relatively nearby stimuli; it breaks down outside the snapping zone, even though Grobstein, Reyes, Vigzwanviger, and Kostyk (1985) have observed that frogs discriminate larger distances, as judged by their scaling their initial hop distance to prey distance. Second, frogs failed to exhibit size constancy for aperture width discrimination. The mechanisms operating for food evaluation (based on size) do not apparently operate for inter-edge width evaluation, indicating that visual filters for food-sized objects differ in fundamental ways from those used for larger objects and reinforcing a hypothesis (developed later) about size-dependent recognition in fishes. For the frog, the meaning of "size" of prey may be attractiveness of a bite-sized object to be caught in one leap and not to be extended to more distant objects. For a monkey, by contrast, size may be experienced as "which finger or hand shaping is needed to grasp

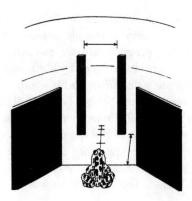

Figure 6.3a. We tested for size constancy in aperture discrimination by noting the direction of jumps between two frontal barriers as the frog avoided a pinch of the dorsum. When the aperture was easily negotiated, the frogs jumped forward between these edges, but as the width narrowed, the tendency to jump sideways substantially increased. By comparing behaviors with barriers set at distances ranging from 3.0 to 7.5 cm from the frog, we asked whether frogs modified their responses to critical aperture widths as a function of viewing distance.

that object,'' a motor equivalent that remains constant as the animal either reaches for a nearby object or walks and reaches for a more distant object. From this action-oriented view of perception, we can compare operational constancies in vertebrate groups without having to refer to the "knowing" of size as a geometrical abstraction.

Spatial constancy in frogs

When a human briefly views a target on the floor and then closes the eyes, he or she retains a robust mental image of the size and location of that object long after details of color and shape have faded in the "mind's eye." Moreover, as the human walks around the room without vision, he or she vividly imagines the object's location as fixed in space although continuously changing its relationship to the person's own body frame. Such spatial constancy of location memory seems to demand unconscious updating of each step and body rotation (without the conscious computation of angles and distances) in order to compensate memory for one's own locomotion. In humans, the storage and updating mechanism must involve the cerebral cortex, since the so-called split-brain subject (with the corpus callosum absent or cut) fails to retain accurate memory of target location while blindfolded after rotating the body such that the remembered target ''moves'' across the frontal midline into the opposite hemifield (Ingle, 1992; Ingle, Jacobson, Lassonde, & Sauerwein, 1990). We wondered whether a frog – without benefit of a cerebral cortex – would be capable of a

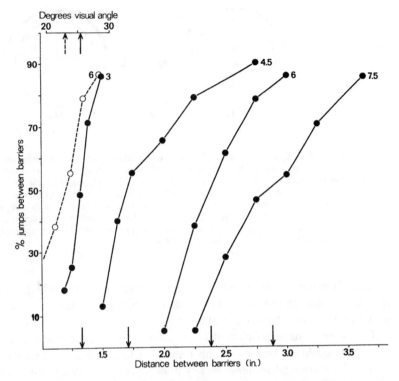

Figure 6.3b. The four curves obtained for 3.0-, 4.5-, 6.0-, and 7.5-cm widths are nearly identical when widths are converted to visual angles. On the left, the 6.0-cm curve is similar to the 3.0-cm curve in terms of visual angle (with the scale shown on the upper left). The 50% intercept on the 3-cm curve is 26°, and the 50% intercept on the 6-cm curve is 23° (not 13°, as constancy would predict). Note that each curve itself is rather finely tuned, such that frogs strongly discriminate 23° versus 26° widths at the 3-cm distance.

similar memory feat, and then of updating spatial memory while its body was rotated.

We found it relatively simple to assess this kind of memory without having to darken the room or blindfold a frog. We merely placed a vertically striped barrier near the frog for 10 s and then whisked it away (via a long handle), leaving the animal in an empty, homogeneous white arena for an additional interval. On moving a 4-inch-wide black disk directly toward the frog, we found that its escape direction was now modified to avoid just that area recently subtended by the barrier. Figure 6.4 shows one variant of this experiment using a 150° wide barrier: In all test trials, the frog turned 75° or more to clear the remembered barrier edge. Its elicited turns were nearly all greater than any turns elicited by the same 90° threat direction in the absence of a prior barrier pres-

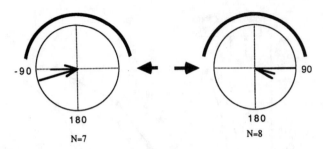

Figure 6.4. A typical example of threat-elicited detours around remembered barrier locations from a normal frog. After a vertically striped frontal barrier (subtending 150°)
has been removed for 10s, the frog jumps far to the left (clearing the remembered edge)
when the threat approaches from the left. Both of these sideways escape patterns are
very different from the 45° turns elicited by lateral threats on control trials (not preceded
by a barrier presentation). Such memory cannot be an artifact of an asymmetrical body
posture during the delay interval because the side toward which the frog escapes depends
on the side from which the threat approaches.

entation. Because the direction turned depends on the side from which the threat
approaches, such memory cannot be explained simply as a residual postural bias
set up by the earlier barrier presentation.

Following bilateral ablation of the striatum (in the ventrolateral telencepha-
lon), frogs could no longer remember such barrier locations, and they jumped
in directions identical to those on test trials without barrier presentations. Yet
each of these "amnesiac" frogs avoided visible barriers as well as did intact
frogs, presumably using their intact pretectum. Moreover, after unilateral striatum ablation, frogs accurately remembered barrier loci seen ipsilaterally but
forgot about barriers previously seen on the contralateral side of the midline.
The frog's striatum may function in a manner similar to that of the monkey
because single neurons in the striatum (caudate nucleus) of that species can
discharge prior to eye saccades toward remembered targets in a particular direction while remaining silent during saccades toward visible targets. Such neural discharge during the delay period may represent a preparatory response set
to "look there" that is analogous to that of the frog in remembering "don't
jump there."

Despite large cognitive differences between the frog and the monkey, we
have demonstrated the frog's ability to compensate its short-term spatial memory
for body rotation – that is, to show spatial constancy. After barrier presentation,
we passively rotated frogs on a plastic "lazy susan" disk (as shown in Figure
6.5) so that they faced in a direction 45° from their original alignment. Despite
this displacement, their threat-elicited escape directions (in 85% of 140 test trials
given to seven frogs) just cleared the real-world location of the terminal barrier

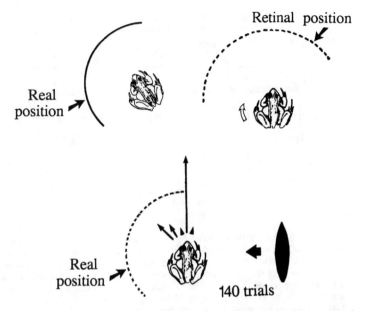

Figure 6.5. The adjustment of barrier location memory during passive rotation is shown here. On the upper left, the frog views a real barrier like that used in Figure 6.4. After the barrier is removed and the frog is rotated by 45° to the right, one can ask whether memory for barrier direction has maintained the same body-centered coordinates (indicated by the dashed line in the upper right figure) or has remained fixed in the same real-world location. When the looming disk approaches from the right (below), 85% of the frog's escape jumps narrowly bypass the real-world location of the formerly seen barrier edge (the dashed curve on the frog's left). This result contradicts the hypothesis that barrier location memory is stored in body-centered coordinates.

edge, as seen 15 s earlier. For this moderate rotation, at least, their barrier memory was coded in real-world rather than body-centered coordinates. Figure 6.6 depicts a simple neural network model that holds barrier edge memory in a maplike system. Rotation – via vestibular afference – modifies the standing pattern of excitation such that the largest excitation actually "slides" laterally within the map.

Although the idea that a neural representation of an object's location can actually move in the brain smacks too much of isomorphism for some tastes, remember that our study of split-brain people (Ingle et al., 1990) did support that conclusion. Unfortunately, one weakness in our attempt to compare spatial constancy mechanisms in humans and frogs is that we have not yet determined whether frogs (without the equivalent of a corpus callosum) are able to transfer barrier memory between opposite brain halves as they are rotated past a remembered barrier.

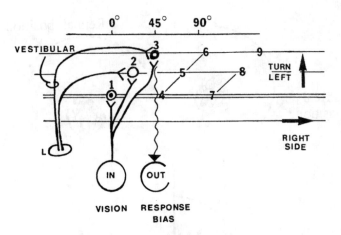

Figure 6.6. A simple network model designed to explain how vestibular afference during passive rotation can shift the peak excitation of so-called memory cells within a maplike storage system in the frog's brain – perhaps the striatum itself. The main assumption is that stimulus edge location is multiply represented within the brain's spatial map. Thus a barrier edge on the frog's midline (0°) activates the 0° locus within the lowest layer and the 45° locus in the upper layer. If the frog remains still, the activated cells in the bottom layer remain most active, and their dominant output will signal "barrier edge straight ahead" to lower brain centers. But when the frog is rotated 45° to the left, vestibular input will facilitate memory cells in the upper layer so that their output will now dominate, changing the effective memory signal to "barrier edge at 45° on the right."

The problem of shape invariance

An essential problem of shape recognition concerns the mechanism by which the shape of a particular object can be recognized after size changes, after rotations in depth, after rotations within the frontal plane, or after shifts of retinal image locus. Ingle (1976) reviewed existing studies of rotational invariance among various vertebrates, concluding that rotational constancy for geometric shapes is good among primates, rather poor in cats and rats, and apparently absent among the fishes. More recent work by Delius and Hollard (1987) and by Lombardi (1987) demonstrates good rotational invariance for shape recognition in pigeons comparable to that reported for monkeys. In the following section I review evidence for failure of rotational constancy in fish, plus additional experiments on shape invariance with changes in size or in retinal locus of stimulation.

Size constancy in fishes and amphibians

My own studies with goldfish avoided the problem of a stimulus angle change during the fish's approach by using a method designed by McCleary (1960) in

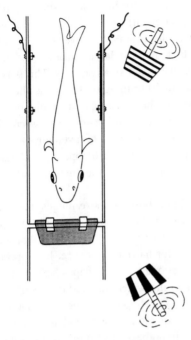

Figure 6.7. This figure taken from Ingle (1963) depicts the one-way avoidance shuttlebox, designed by McCleary for visual discrimination training. Here the discriminda and visual loci of stimuli used in the intrafield transfer paradigm are shown. The fish learn to respond to the shock-reinforced stimulus by moving forward, pushing open a swinging door, and escaping into the safe goal box within the 10-s stimulus-to-shock interval. When a second ("no go") stimulus is placed in the same location, the fish learn to inhibit the attempt at escape because the hinged door is locked from behind. After discrimination learning, transfer tests involve changing the stimulus locations, removing the door lock on all trials, and omitting shock during the critical six transfer trials. For most of the discrimination tests described in this review, stimuli are presented 10 cm from the fish's eye directly along the optic axis.

which visual stimuli are presented 4 inches away, along the optic axis, and orthogonal to the escape direction of the fish, thus holding retinal size constant. In these studies, large goldfish learned to swim forward from a start box to a goal box during the 10-s presentation of the "GO" stimulus (in order to avoid a brief shock to the tail) and then learned to withhold the escape response during a 12-s presentation of the alternative "NO GO" stimulus (Figure 6.7).

In one study, six fish were trained to avoid either a 14° high square or a circle and to withhold escape during presentation of the alternative stimulus. When each fish had reached an 18/20 learning criterion, it received a set of transfer tests using unreinforced presentations of smaller (7°) circles and squares.

However, these fish simply did not respond to the smaller shapes, apparently because smaller stimuli did not scare them sufficiently. We then retrained each fish with the small circle–small square discrimination, reversing the values for each animal. Thus a fish that had first avoided large squares (and not large circles) was taught to avoid small circles but not small squares. This was learned without apparent conflict, taking just 30–60 training trials, as had the first task. Then, following criterion performance on the new shape discrimination, all fish were tested (without reinforcement) for the retention of the original discrimination. All animals easily retained the original problem, averaging 85% correct responses over a total of 72 test trials. Thus these fish apparently classified the two discriminations as independent problems, as if the smaller square did not much resemble the large square.

My hypothesis was that stimuli within those two size ranges were naturally dissociated by function – that is, that smaller stimuli were distinguished by visual filters designed for food recognition (or preferences) and that the larger stimuli activated mechanisms designed for barrier avoidance. In support of that idea, we found that spontaneous snaps at quarter-inch shapes taped to the aquarium wall (motivated by adding sugar to the water) favored circles over squares by a 3:1 ratio and over triangles by 5:1. This hypothesis suggests that fish might show transfer of a circle–square discrimination among food-sized stimuli (e.g., between 4° and 8° sizes). By the same hypothesis, fish might transfer the circle–square task between sizes of 12° and 24°. More evidence regarding the mechanism of large circle–square discrimination is now presented.

Evidence that the food selection mechanism is size specific is obtained from more naturalistic experiments on prey selection by the European toad, *Bufo bufo* (Ewert, 1984). Ewert found that the shape of a small moving stimulus influences the rate of feeding (orienting or snapping responses) toward a moving dummy object moved horizontally around the animal with a motor-driven device. Here a wormlike object 2° high and 8° long is preferred by toads to either a 4° × 4° object or 2° × 2° square. However, that facilitation-by-elongation effect does not work for a larger stimulus: An 8° × 8° square is equal in salience to an 8° × 32° giant worm. Thus the worm shape has a special effect only when small. Note also that a vertical worm moving horizontally elicits no interest in the normal toad, whereas a vertical rectangle moving vertically is a potent prey stimulus (Ewert, 1984). Thus the worm preference does not even derive from shape per se, but rather from a specific interaction of shape and motion. It is not yet known whether an operant conditioning paradigm might teach a toad to distinguish rectangles from squares, regardless of their orientation in regard to motion direction. If that were possible, then one could do conventional tests of shape generalization after changes in size with toads, as with fish.

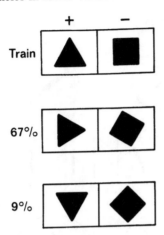

+   −

Train

67%

9%

Figure 6.8. Summary of a discrimination test by Meesters (1940) in which fish learned to approach an upright triangle for a food reward and to ignore a square of the same height (upper pair). After training, a generalization test was given with each stimulus rotated by 30° (middle pair): Fish still chose the triangle, but with a reduced frequency. When the stimuli were rotated by 45° (bottom row), they had an altogether different appearance to the fish, which now responded strongly to the diamond as "most similar" to the originally baited triangle. Meesters inferred that these fish were attending mainly to the tops of the shapes.

Rotational invariance in fish shape recognition

The pre–World War II European literature contains several studies of shape recognition by different fish species (see Herter, 1953). One typical study (Meesters, 1940) noted that fish trained for a food reward to approach a base-down triangle, but not a square, failed to generalize this learning to the same shapes rotated by 45° (Figure 6.8). In fact, they strongly avoided the upside-down triangle rather than the diamond, apparently because they had been attending to the upper vertex of the triangle and had avoided the flat upper edge of the square. In other cases reviewed by Herter (and by Ingle, 1976), fish attend to isolated features of a shape and not to the configuration gestalt. The corner of a triangle or diamond could itself be a feeding-eliciting feature; frogs do in fact approach and strike at the leading corner of a square or triangle moved horizontally before them.

Ingle (1971, 1976) examined rotational invariance in fish, using a novel three-stimulus paradigm, with the same "GO/NO-GO" avoidance method described earlier. For example, some fish learned to escape during presentation of a 14° diamond, but not in the presence of either a 14° square or a 14° circle. All six fish readily learned to stop escaping during presentation of the square but not during presentation of the circle. This consistent result indicated that the dia-

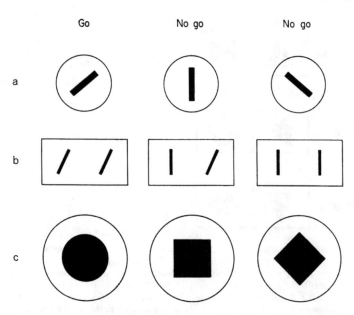

Figure 6.9. The author's original three-stimulus discrimination method designed to measure the relative discriminability of two stimuli from a third shape. Here goldfish first learned to avoid the leftmost of the stimulus set (the diamond or the parallel vertical segments) and to withhold a response in the presence of the other two members of each set. In both instances shown here, one "no go" stimulus was easily discriminated from the "go" stimulus, and the other stimulus did not inhibit escape attempts even after many days of training. We inferred that a diamond looks more like a circle than it does like a square, as would happen if the fish attended to the parallelness of the vertical sides. In the second discrimination set, we infer that "parallelness" is more distinctive to goldfish than is the absolute orientation of individual line segments. Yet, as developed in the text, we interpret this ability as a relatively low-level filter property.

mond resembled the circle more strongly than it resembled the square (its rotation). We conclude that these fish were not encoding "four corners" in order to distinguish square from circle. Rather, I hypothesized that they noticed that two sides of the square were parallel, as opposed to the lateral sides of both the diamond and the circle, each of which bows inward. This tendency to scan a shape along horizontal or vertical axes, rather than along diagonal axes, had already been suggested by Mackintosh and Sutherland (1963) to explain the failure of goldfish to easily discriminate mirror-image oblique rectangles. This is discussed by Ingle (1976) in the context of earlier studies.

I further tested the ability of goldfish to notice the "parallelness" of vertical lines set 14° apart by using another three-stimulus sequence (Figure 6.9). Fish had to avoid (1) a pair of parallel lines (both vertical or both tilted at 15°) and not to avoid (2) the opposite set of parallel lines or (3) a pair of lines in which one was vertical and one was tilted at 15° (see Figure 6.9). If the fish attended to the individual line orientations, a V-V pair would be harder to distinguish from a V-15 pair than from a 15-15 pair. However, the opposite turned out to be true for each of six fish: Parallel sets were hard to distinguish from each other but were easy to discriminate from the nonparallels.

This ability need not imply that the impression of parallelism is an abstraction, but it might reflect the sensitivity of fish to equal distances between the tops and between the bottoms of the respective line segments (see Figure 6.9). This simple width-sensitive mechanism might be similar to that used by frogs to discriminate the smallest width of apertures through which their bodies can fit (see Figure 6.3). The similarity between the goldfish's sensitivity to parallels (and hence to square vs. circle) and the frog's sensitivity to aperture width reinforced my earlier suggestion that the fish's classification of large shapes utilizes a visual filter that had evolved for discriminations of various barrier configurations. Just as aperture width estimation does not show much size invariance, the dependence on analysis of certain axes (vertical lines being salient for frogs and oblique axes being ambiguous for goldfish) also prevents these discriminations from being invariant with rotation.

The evolution of rotation invariance: A hypothesis

I propose that the ability to recognize familiar shapes after they have been rotated in the frontal plane depends on prior evolution (or perhaps coevolution) of telencephalic motor systems for dexterous control of the head. A toad (without such a mechanism) pursuing an earthworm 6 inches long switches from tongue flicks to lunging and grasping the prey with the jaws. This works well for a worm moving horizontally, yet the toad fails to rotate its head or body in order to grasp a worm moving diagonally along the ground. It is quite capable of body rotation, either while peering at a worm that had crawled into a low aperture or while turning the shoulder to protect itself against ground-level predators. Yet the toad fails to interface the retinal image of "diagonal prey" with the midbrain motor mechanism for body rotation. On the other hand, my own single-frame film analysis of an iguana lizard reaching to grasp an oriented worm shows the animal making rapid and accurate rotations of its head to match the angle of the food with the angle of the mouth.

Somewhere within the reptile's brain (probably linked to its telencephalic visual system) is a network that translates each perceived edge orientation into a central command for rotation of the head. For reptiles (and, of course, for mammals and birds), objects seen at different orientations become equivalent after the animal has rotated its head. Head rotations are also prominent in exploration of novel objects by various animals – kittens and newly hatched chicks being good examples – so that the young animal rapidly builds up experience of seeing the same object from different angles. These experiences presumably facilitate development of visuomotor skills (such as jumping, detouring, and grasping) and simultaneously provide perceptual learning useful for identification of objects following their rotation. Thus, the evolution and development of motor flexibility provides new opportunities for perceptual flexibility.

Rotational invariance in reaching for shapes: A noncognitive task?

In the evolution of cortical visual mechanisms, performance of on-line motor skills contributes to the selective value of shape invariance, as do visual recognition abilities. Here I summarize the results of a substantial, but unpublished, experiment on human subjects designed to discover whether or not shaping of the hand to pick up an object would reveal the operation of orientation invariance mechanisms. We tested 20 undergraduate students, who were asked to rapidly pick up planar shapes (one-quarter-inch thick) from a table top, starting with their hands in their laps. The shapes were either squares or triangles of various sizes (the latter were both isosceles and right triangles). Equal numbers of male and female subjects were used with both large and small hands for each sex, but all were self-proclaimed right-handers.

We filmed each trial with a super-eight camera to provide detailed single-frame analysis of the finger orientations just prior to contact with each shape. Twelve of these subjects showed consistently different finger patterns for grasping each kind of shape, regardless of the size. Squares were grasped (for these subjects) with the middle two fingers together along the top edge (and, of course, with the thumb on the parallel opposite edge). Triangles, by contrast, were grasped with the middle two fingers split. Because the other eight subjects showed variable finger patterns for the same shapes, they were not given the critical test: presentation of the three squares rotated by 45° to appear as diamonds. For the 12 discriminating subjects, nearly all trials showed that the diamonds were grasped as squares with the hand rotated.

We suspect that this unconscious arm-hand sequence is mediated by a lower-level visuomotor system (such as that of the parietal cortex) rather than by the high-level recognition mechanism of the temporal lobe. That hypothesis is supported by observations of Milner and Goodale (1990) that an agnosic patient who cannot recognize even line orientations by verbal response (although she can identify them tactually) can nevertheless rotate her hand quickly and accurately to insert a letter through a horizontal or diagonal slot. The evolutionary relationship between perceptual constancy that underlies shape recognition, and the more pragmatic but probably less articulated eye-hand constancy, remains to be explored.

Shape recognition invariant with retinal locus

The experience of transretinal equivalence is compelling. Simple geometric figures, animal outlines, or letters are readily compared to one another when presented to distant retinal loci (given adequate acuity for recognition). Perhaps the first study of intraretinal transfer of shape learning in animals was carried out by Ingle (1963) in the goldfish, using a classical conditioning paradigm devised by McCleary (1960). In this method, fish are gently wedged into a small box with a wet sponge, implanted with wires for cardiac recording, and presented with a shock-reinforced CS+ until, after 20–30 trials, a robust cardiac deceleration is conditioned. Then the CS− is alternated in a random sequence with the CS+ until little or no cardiac response is elicited by the CS−. After clear differences in response to the two stimuli are recorded for eight consecutive trials, unreinforced generalization trials are recorded in which the two conditioning stimuli are alternated in a fixed sequence (A-B-B-A-B-A) for six test trials while presented to the second (test) location. Fish are then retrained again with the same stimuli at the original locus, and a second set of generalization trials is given.

In this study, three fish were trained with CS's presented about 30° from the rostral midline along the fish's horizontal plane. They were then tested for generalization of training to loci 30° from the caudal midline, an intended disparity of 120°. However, due to occasional 30° eye saccades by the fish, the actual intrafield separation of training and test loci is 90°. Then three other fish were trained with caudal stimuli, and generalization tests were given with frontal stimuli. After first training and testing with red versus green stimuli, our critical tests were done with horizontal versus vertical striped square disks measuring about 1 inch per side. These stimuli were moved slightly in a circular path to facilitate discrimination (fish learn poorly or not at all with stationary patterns). All six fish showed a high level of transfer between these 90° disparate retinal loci: On nearly all test trials, the CS+ elicited stronger cardiac decelerations than on the CS− trials. We conclude that the distinction between horizontal and vertical stripes is represented in a neural system not constrained by the locus of retinal input.

Our tentative explanation for successful intraretinal invariance (where size and rotational invariance tests failed) is that vertical and horizontal contours have the same "motor significance" (such as "detour sideways" vs. "detour over/under"), no matter where they appear along the horizontal meridian. It remains to be seen whether fish could similarly transfer discriminations of small shapes (e.g., circle vs. square or cross vs. circle). An interesting comparison study, which might be made with toads, is to extend the observation of Ewert and Kehl (1978) that habituation of feeding toward small shapes is highly form

190

DAVID INGLE

specific. These authors found that toads habituate feeding in the presence of a particular shape moved in front of them but then dishabituate the feeding response when a new shape is presented. It is not yet known whether this kind of "pattern memory" is limited to the same area of the toad's visual field or whether it transfers widely across the retinal surface.

References

Collett, T. (1977) Stereopsis in toads. *Nature, 267*, 349–351.
Collett, T., & Harkness, L. (1982). Depth vision in animals. In D. Ingle, M. A. Goodale, R. J. W. Mansfield, *The analysis of visual behavior* (pp. 111–176). Cambridge, MA: MIT Press.
Delius, J., Hollard, V. D. (1987). Orientation invariance of shape-recognition in forebrain-lesioned pigeons. *Behavior and Brain Research, 23*, 251–259.
Ewert, J.-P. (1969). Quantitative Analyse von Reiz-Reaktions – Beziehungen bei visuellem Auslösen der Beutefang Wenderaktion der Erdkröte (*Bufo bufo* L.). *Pflügers Archiv, 308*, 225–243.
Ewert, J.-P. (1970). Neural mechanisms of prey-catching and avoidance behavior in the toad (*Bufo bufo* L.). *Brain, Behavior, and Evolution, 3*, 36–56.
Ewert, J.-P. Single unit responses of the toad's (*Bufo americanus*) caudal thalamus to visual objects. *Z. vergl. Physiol., 74*, 81–102.
Ewert, J.-P. (1984). Tectal mechanisms that underlie prey-catching and avoidance behaviors in toads. In H. Vanegas (Ed.), *Comparative neurology of the optic tectum* (pp. 247–416). New York: Plenum.
Ewert, J.-P., & Gebauer, L. (1973) Grössen Konstanzphänomene im Beutefangverhalten der Erdkröte (*Bufo bufo* L.). *Journal of Comparative Physiology, 85*, 303–315.
Ewert, J.-P., & Kehl, W. (1978). Configural prey selection by individual experience in the toad (*Bufo bufo* L.). *Journal of Comparative Physiology, 126*, 105–114.
Grobstein, P., Reyes, A., Vigzwanviger, L., & Kostyk, S. K. (1985). Prey orientation in frogs: Accounting for variations in output with stimulus distance. *Journal of Comparative Physiology, 156*, 775–785.
Herter, K. (1953). *Die Fischdressuren und ihre Sinnesphysiologischen Gründlagen.* East Berlin: Akademie Verlag.
Ingle, D. (1963). *Limits of visual transfer in goldfish.* Unpublished Ph.D. thesis, Department of Psychology, University of Chicago.
Ingle, D. (1968). Visual releasers of prey-catching behavior in frogs and toads. *Brain Behavior and Evolution*, 500–518.
Ingle, D. (1971). The experimental analysis of visual behavior. In W. S. Hoar & D. J. Randall (Eds.), *Fish physiology* (Vol. 5, pp. 9–71). New York: Academic Press.
Ingle, D. (1976). Spatial vision in anurans. In K. Fite (Ed.), *The amphibian visual system* (pp. 119–140). New York: Academic Press.
Ingle, D. (1978). Shape recognition by vertebrates. In R. Held, H. Liebowitz, & H. L. Teuber (Eds.), *Handbook of sensory physiology* (Vol. 8, pp. 267–296). Berlin: Springer.
Ingle, D. (1980). Some effects of pretectum lesions on the frog's detection of stationary objects. *Behavior and Brain Research, 1*, 139–163.
Ingle, D. (1983a). Prey-selection in frogs and toads: A neuroethological model. In E. Satinoff & P. Teitelbaum (Eds.), *Handbook of behavioral neurobiology* (Vol. 6, pp. 235–264). New York: Plenum.
Ingle, D. (1983b). Brain mechanisms of localization in frogs and toads. In J.-P. Ewert, R. Capranica, & D. Ingle (Eds.), *Advances in vertebrate neuroethology* (pp. 177–226). New York: Plenum.

Ingle, D. (1992). Spatial short-term memory: Evolutionary perspectives and discoveries from split-brain studies. *Behavior and Brain Science, 15,* 761–762.

Ingle, D. & Cook, J. (1977) The effect of viewing distance upon size-preference of frogs for prey. *Vision Research, 17,* 1009–1014.

Ingle, D. & Hoff, K. (1990). Visually-elicited evasive behavior in frogs. *Bio-Science, 40,* 284–291.

Ingle, D., Jacobson, L. S., Lassonde, M. C. & Sauerwein, H. C. (1990). Deficits in interfield memory transfer in cases of callosal agenesis. *Society for Neuroscience Abstracts, 16,* 9260

Ingle, D. & Shook B. (1984). Action-oriented approaches to visuospatial functions. In D. Ingle, M. Jeannterod, & D. Lee (Eds.), *Brain mechanisms and spatial vision* (pp. 229–258).

Lettvin, J. Y., Maturana, H. R., McCulloch, W. S., & Pitts, W. H. (1959). What the frog's eye tells the frog's brain. *Proceedings of the IRE, 47,* 1940–1951.

Lombardi, C. M. (1987). Shape oddity recognition by pigeons is independent of shape orientation. *Rev. Mex. Anal. Cond. 13,* 265–272.

Mackintosh, N. J., & Sutherland, N. S. (1963). Visual discrimination by goldfish: The orientation of rectangles. *Animal Behavior, 11,* 135–141.

McCleary, R. A. (1960). Type of response as a factor in interocular transfer in the fish. *Journal of Comparative and Physiological Psychology, 53,* 311–321.

Meesters, A. (1940). Über die Organisation des Gesichtfeldes der Fische. *Zeitschift für Tierpsychologie (Berlin), 4,* 84–149.

7   Generalizing across object orientation and size

Elisabeth Ashbridge and David I. Perrett

In this chapter we review the physiological mechanisms underlying the recognition and generalization of objects and also review the behavioral literature on mechanisms of size perception. Accounts of computational theories for orientation are to be found in chapters 4 and 5; details of human recognition is covered in chapter 3; and the neuropsychology of recognition is reviewed in chapter 8.

Single-cell studies

Orientation specificity

The majority of cells found in area V4 exhibit tuning for simple attributes of the image, including spatial frequency or stimulus width, length, and color. Some cells in V4 do show selectivity to slightly more complex features (e.g., preference for a circular but not a square shape or the angle between two contours (Figures 12 and 13 in Kobatake & Tanaka, 1994). The majority of V4 cells sensitive to simple or more complex features exhibit sensitivity to orientation (Desimone & Schein, 1987; Haenny & Schiller, 1988; Kobatake & Tanaka, 1994). Kobatake and Tanaka (1994) show an example of a V4 cell that is selective to the orientation of the optimal stimulus (a white bar presented at 315°) but generalizes across size change (two sizes were tested, short [20%] and long [100%]; see the later discussion). The main anatomical input into the inferotemporal (IT) cortex is through V4, and it is therefore perhaps not surprising that cells in the IT are also orientation sensitive (see Oram & Perrett, 1994; Perrett & Oram, 1993; Vogels & Orban, 1994). For some features that do not have an axis of elongation such as a dark spot, a circular or square shape, and radially symmetrical patterns (e.g., high-frequency Fourier Descriptors: Schwartz, Desimone, Albright, & Gross, 1983), cells with a preference for these features will automatically show tolerance of 90° or 180° rotation. In this sense, such feature detectors are orientation invariant.

This research was funded by project grants from the United Kingdom M.R.C. and the United States O.N.R.; E. Ashbridge was supported by an E.P.S.R.C. studentship.

Cells with selectivity for complex visual stimuli such as faces, hands, and other complex objects are found further down the ventral pathway in the IT cortex and superior temporal sulcus (STS) (Gross, Desimone, Albright, & Schwartz, 1985; Hasselmo et al., 1989; Perrett et al., 1984; Perrett, Rolls, & Caan, 1982; Tanaka & Fujita, 1991). In addition, it should be noted that the receptive fields of cells increase as the information is passed down the ventral stream (Desimone & Gross, 1979; Kobatake & Tanaka, 1994; Tanaka & Fujita, 1991).

To understand the role of different cortical areas in the ventral stream, Kobatake and Tanaka (1994) compared the selectivity of cell responses to object features in different areas (V2, V4, posterior inferotemporal cortex [PIT], and anterior inferotemporal cortex [AIT]). A reduction approach was used in all areas to determine the critical feature(s) for the cell's optimal response. This method starts with complex stimuli and then successively simplifies them while attempting to maintain high response rates. It was found that not only AIT cells, but also a large proportion of PIT cells (49%) and a more limited percentage of V4 cells (38%), were highly selective to complex object features (Kobatake & Tanaka, 1994).

Tanaka et al. (1991) found that cells in the AIT that respond selectively to complex objects, such as faces and features, appear to be orientation selective. Ten AIT cells responsive to faces were tested for four orientations (0°, 90°, 180°, and 270°). For these cells, the rotation of the optimal stimulus by 90° reduced the neuronal response by more than half. An additional 11 cells were reported that also exhibit orientation sensitivity but were only tested qualitatively. The optimal orientation of the face stimulus varied from cell to cell, although the upright orientation was most commonly encountered (Tanaka et al., 1991).

Orientation generalization

Physiological studies (Gross et al., 1985; Hasselmo et al., 1989; Perrett et al., 1982, 1984, 1985) have shown that cells in the IT and STS cortex of macaque monkeys are selectively responsive to faces. In an initial study by Perrett et al. (1982) of selective cells in the STS, generalization across object orientations appeared to be universal. All the face-responsive cells studied (21) did not differentiate in response magnitude between upright, horizontal, and inverted faces (Perrett et al., 1982). A closer examination of the responses indicates that cell latencies could be affected by orientation even when the response magnitude of the cells was similar for upright and inverted faces. Neural response latencies for 62% (16/26) of the cells were affected by the orientation of the image presented (Perrett et al., 1988). When the orientation of the image was changed from upright, the response latency of 10/26 cells was not affected. Fifteen of 26 cells responded with longer latencies to inverted or horizontally presented faces. Perrett et al. (1988) described this increased response latency as additional "processing time" that may parallel the increased reaction times (RTs) to identify faces or face configurations.

Hasselmo et al. (1989) tested a small group of cells that responded to a particular movement (ventral flexion of the head, head nodding). These cells continued to respond to the head movements even when the image was rotated in the picture plane, that is, upside down. This process altered the retinal or viewer-centered coordinate system but not the object-centered coordinate system because, for the latter, the positions of the relative parts of the object are related solely to the object itself (i.e., the forehead moves toward the chest) and are therefore not dependent on the view. The findings of Hasselmo et al. suggest that this small population of cells reflected the object-centered description of the movements. However, their results are limited in information about generalization of rotation in the picture plane as they apply to stimulus motion.

From these studies, it would appear that coding in the IT for simple features and more complex objects is orientation specific, whereas in the STS it is orientation general (Ashbridge, Oram, & Perrett, in prep.). We have recently been reinvestigating the extent to which cells in the STS (predominantly STPa) show orientation/size invariance (generalize across different attributes) or orientation/size specificity in their responses to heads, parts of bodies, or whole bodies. Methods and techniques have been described in detail elsewhere (Wachsmuth, Oram, & Perrett, 1994). All cells tested showed a significantly different response to the whole human body than to control stimuli and spontaneous activity (S/A). For each cell, the optimal perspective view was first defined for the upright body, and subsequently the cell was presented with that view of the whole body in different orientations and sizes. To test orientation sensitivity, the optimal body view was presented at an image size of 24.4° at a viewing distance of 4 m in eight different orientations.

Seven cells (of 25 tested) responded to all orientations at a rate significantly above S/A and control stimuli. Four of these cells responded to all orientations equally well (Figure 7.1, cell C). Three cells showed orientation tuning superimposed on the generalized response (Figure 7.1, cell B). The remaining 18 cells responded to some but not all orientations (Figure 7.1, cell A). Different cells were maximally responsive to different orientations.

All the cells displaying orientation selectivity demonstrated an approximately monotonic tuning function. The tightness of the tuning varied across cells (rotation of the stimulus away from optimal by 45° to 90° reduced most cells' responses by half). Thus, the majority of cells (21/25, 82%) were selective for orientation in the picture plane. Although the majority of tuned cells (15/21) were selective for orientations close to upright (see, e.g., Figure 7.1, cell A), some cells were selective for inverted orientations (e.g., Figure 7.1, cell B).

In summary, physiological data show that early visual areas (V1, V2, V4)

Cell Types for Orientation Coding

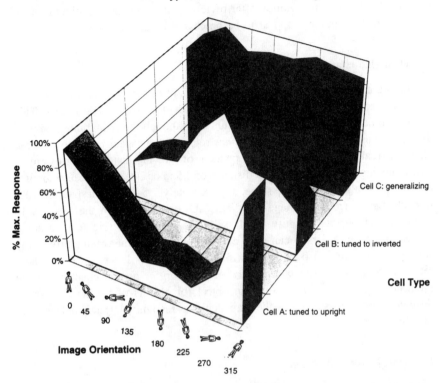

Figure 7.1. Orientation coding. The responses of three cells tested with eight different image orientations are illustrated. Orientation is defined as the angle from upright rotating anticlockwise). Responses to different stimuli are expressed as a percentage of the maximum of cell activity (where spontaneous activity = 0%). Cell A was maximally activated by orientations close to upright, whereas stimulus B was maximally activated by the sight of an inverted body. Cell C was responsive to the body presented in all orientations.

exhibit orientation-specific coding of features of objects. Cells from these areas feed into more anterior visual processing areas (PIT, AIT), where cells are selectively responsive to progressively more complex features and objects such as faces. From studies carried out so far, it appears that all IT cells exhibit orientation specificity whether the cells are selective for elementary features or more complex objects. Studies in the STS indicate the presence of cells that are selective for complex objects and that respond irrespective of the stimulus orientation. Interestingly, such cells exhibiting orientation-invariant responses to faces require extra time for the processing of unusual orientations of the stimuli. Our recent work confirms the presence of cells with orientation-invariant responses but also indicates that most coding for complex objects in the STS is orientation selective. We discuss the implications of the physiological findings for models of object recognition after reviewing the influence of stimulus size, since orientation and size appear to be processed in similar ways.

Effect of size change on object recognition

Perceiving and recognizing an object, independent of a change in distance or in physical size, does not seem a difficult task, but it is, as we will discuss. This perceptual *invariance* or *constancy* occurs even though the retinal image size of the object varies. The term *size constancy* refers to the capacity to recognize the physical (real) size of an object independent of viewing distance. For example, when viewing an adult human at a distance of 0.5 m or 200 m, one can recognize that the person's height is the same, approximately 1.5–2.0 m, despite the 400-fold change in (retinal) image size. This ability differs from the capacity to recognize an object's identity or class independent of its size (e.g., a small person and a large person can both be recognized as humans; similarly, a toy car and a real car can both be identified as cars). This latter capacity is here referred to as *size invariance* or *size generalization*. In this chapter, we are interested in how the brain codes an object (or objects of the same class) at different retinal sizes and how the brain achieves recognition that is independent of retinal size.

Behavioral studies in humans

Changing the stimulus size has been found to impair recognition in a wide variety of paradigms. Jolicoeur (1987) exposed subjects to 20 shapes, each of which was presented for 12s during the learning phase of a recognition memory task. In subsequent testing in which subjects classified the familiarity of shapes (as old or new), Jolicoeur found that recognition latencies increased when stimulus size changed between the learning and test phases. The effect of size change on recognition memory was found for meaningless shapes and for drawings of natural objects. Moreover, the greater the size change[1] (100% − 25% versus 100% − 50%), the greater the recognition impairment.

Using stimuli of different sizes (100%, 75%, 50%, 40%), Jolicoeur and Besner (1987) found that the time needed for subjects to recognize the similarity of two simultaneously presented meaningless shapes increased when stimuli were transformed in size. Similar effects have been reported by other authors (Besner, 1983; Budesen & Larsen, 1975; Larsen, 1985). Successive stimulus presentation matching paradigms produce similar results with meaningless shapes (Larsen & Bundesen, 1978) and real objects (Dickerson, 1991; Ellis, Allport, Humphries, & Collis, 1989).

Models explaining size transformations

The size transformation results just described are explainable in the context of alignment models (e.g., Ullman, 1989) that suggest that representations of objects in memory are specified in terms of size. When an object is viewed at a size that differs from the size of the stored representation, an alignment-testing process is initiated whereby feature points on the stored model are transformed in size (view and orientation) so that they align with the corresponding points on the incoming image. If an alignment is successful and multiple sets of feature points match, then the object under view is effectively recognized. Note here that alignment processes have been envisaged that match the input image to a single, stored, all-encompassing (object-centered) description (Lowe, 1987; Porrill et al., 1988; Ullman, 1989) or a single (viewer-centered) description of the object as seen in a canonical (typical) view and orientation (Palmer, Rosch, Chase, & Baddely, 1981). The idea of a single canonical representation stored in memory would explain the longer recognition times for stimuli presented in an unusual size (i.e., different from the stored representation of the object) because transformation processes, which bring stored representation and input image into alignment, presumably require time. These transformations have been referred to as *mental adjustment of size* or *size normalization* (Besner, 1983; Budesen & Larsen, 1975; Larsen 1985; Shepard & Metzler, 1971) and are thus analogous to *mental rotation*. Therefore, similar problems arise, such as the question of which is the correct size to scale to and the direction of scaling (i.e., go smaller or larger) in a complex scene.

Exceptions to the rule. Most experiments show size scaling. Biederman and Cooper (1992), on the other hand, suggested a size-invariant system of object recognition. They used a priming technique to investigate the role of size in object classification. They briefly presented subjects with two sets of 32 pictures. Objects in the second set were depicted as (1) the same exemplar, same size; (2) the same exemplar, different size; (3) a different exemplar from the same object class (e.g., a grand piano and an ordinary piano having the same name but different visual shapes), same size; or (4) a different exemplar, different size. Stimuli in the two sets could be either 6.2° (100%) or 3.5° (56%) in diameter. It was found that naming responses for second-set items were faster (i.e., "primed"). The magnitude of priming was not influenced by size change, hence Biederman and Cooper (1992) concluded that object classification was invariant across size. This finding could contradict size normalization models.

An object or shape identification system that generalizes across metric attributes (e.g., size, orientation) could operate independently of other visual systems that specify the size and orientation of objects but generalize across identity.

Several authors, including Marr and Nishihara (1978) and Biederman and Cooper (1992), note the computational advantage of an object recognition system that ignores metric variations such as size, orientation, and view. Such a system would not require separate representations of an object at different sizes, orientations, or positions. Hummel and Biederman (1992) also note that even if different object sizes are represented separately, the brain would need to employ a further size-invariant system to determine whether differently sized images represented the same object.

Other recognition experiments showed that size changes have an effect on episodic memory (memory for specific details [and context] in which an object was experienced). Subjects were asked to judge whether the target image was the same shape as the first (priming) image, ignoring the size of the images. In these experiments, a change in stimulus size affected the same–different shape judgment made by the subject (Cooper & Biederman, 1991).

In summary, earlier studies investigating effects of changes in stimulus size on recognition suggest the involvement of object image alignment and/or transformation of the incoming image to match the representation of that object stored in memory. These studies suggest that stored representations of objects include a specification of size. Biederman and Cooper's (1992) priming experiments, on the other hand, suggest some generalization across sizes.

Repetition priming for tasks involving classification of familiarity of famous people (from face images) is view or pose specific and does not generalize from face to body (Bruce & Young, 1986). Repetition priming has been interpreted as acting on visual codes (e.g., Face Recognition Units; Bruce & Young, 1986) and thus suggests that underlying visual representations of faces are view specific and body part specific. These representations may also be size and orientation specific, although the effect of size and orientation changes on repetition priming for faces have yet to be measured.

The priming tasks used by Biederman and colleagues to study object recognition are different in method from those used to study faces; Biederman and Cooper's (1992) task involved two naming responses. It is not clear that the tasks tap the level of visual representation of objects; instead, they could involve semantic or naming codes that are size and view independent. There is evidence that size change has less effect on recognition tasks that tap higher-level codes. Ellis et al. (1989) found that a small change in size (a 52% increase in area, i.e., a 7.1% increase in linear dimension) did not affect successive matching for different exemplars in the same semantic class but did affect the matching of different views of the same object.

From these findings and the findings described earlier, Biederman and Cooper (1992) concluded that the ventral pathway (the "what" pathway, leading to the IT) stores size-invariant representations of objects, whereas the dorsal pathway (the "where" pathway) stores size-dependent representations of objects. In support of their data, they suggest that only the representations stored in the ventral system mediate object-naming tasks, whereas the old–new judgment task is mediated by *both* the ventral and the dorsal representations of objects. The study of neurological patients sheds light on this suggestion.

Neuropsychological studies in humans

Neurological studies suggest that the ventral pathway is involved in processing object size. Cohen, Grey, Meyrignac, Dehaene, and Degos (1994) studied and described two hemimicropsia patients with lesions in areas 18 and 19 (posterior part of the ventral pathway). These patients perceived an apparent reduction in the object's size when the object was presented in one hemifield. Cohen et al. (1994) suggest that object size might be processed separately from other object characteristics such as color or movement. These observations could suggest that parts of the ventral stream of cortical processing are involved with the perceptual appreciation of size. These areas may encode size-specific information about visual features. That would certainly fit physiological observations of size-sensitive feature coding in the early visual cortical areas of the monkey (V2 to V4; Desimone & Schein, 1987).

The visual coding of size information in the ventral stream of processing does not preclude additional analysis of size within the dorsal stream. Patient DF (Milner et al., 1991), who suffered damage to areas 18 and 19 and the parasaggital occipitoparietal region, was able to appreciate the sizes of objects when reaching to pick them up. DF adjusted the space between her fingers appropriately to the sizes of objects during the reaching movement and before any contact with the items occurred. Yet, she showed impairment in matching the size of simultaneously presented stimuli (100% − 50%; Goodale, Milner, Jacobson, & Carey, 1991) and failed to indicate the width of objects accurately by the space between her thumb and index finger without reaching to grasp the objects.

It has been suggested that the ventral pathway from the occipital and temporal cortex is responsible for classifying shapes and recognizing objects, whereas the dorsal pathway from the occipital to the parietal cortex is responsible for visual control of actions. The dorsal stream must therefore be involved in the analysis of metric attributes of objects such as their size, orientation, view, and position (Goodale & Milner, 1992; Jeannerod, 1981, 1994; Ungerleider & Mishkin, 1982). To be able to recognize and classify an object, the orientation, size, view, and position of that object are irrelevant. By contrast, to interact physically with an object, its orientation, size, and position are critical for guiding hand and limb movements, whereas the object's identity is less relevant. Another way of characterizing the division is the idea that the dorsal pathway is responsible for the real-time motor controls and the ventral pathway is involved in representations of objects stored in memory.

DF's abilities can be interpreted as indicating (1) intact visual pathways between the visual cortex and the dorsal parietal systems involved in visual control of motor actions and (2) disrupted pathways to the ventral temporal areas that are involved in object recognition (Goodale & Milner, 1992). Thus, DF can use metric attributes of objects (i.e., stimulus orientation and size) to guide motor action using the dorsal cortical pathways, but she is impaired in recognizing the orientation, size, and shape of objects because these judgments rely on damaged ventral areas.

The dorsal stream therefore appears to be involved in processing size and orientation information (Sakata & Taira, 1994). Note that this does not exclude a role of the ventral system in processing the same stimulus dimensions for different purposes. Indeed, recognition of complex objects presumably depends on an initial analysis of the orientation and size of pattern elements.

In the intact brain, it is probable that shape information analyzed in the ventral system gains access to the parietal cortex to guide motion. It may also be the case that the parietal cortex performs some analysis of shape (apart from size and orientation) independent of inputs from the ventral stream. If so, then patients like DF may be able to demonstrate motor movements guided by further aspects of shape (in addition to size and orientation).

Neurological studies in monkeys

Weiskrantz and Saunders (1984) trained monkeys with varying lesions (to parietal cortex, prestriate cortex, PIT, AIT, and posterior STS) on a number of visually presented three-dimensional objects, each seen under constant conditions. Subsequently, the subjects were tested on transformed versions (orientation and size) of the original objects. Two transformations of size were used, one smaller and one larger than the original object. It should be noted that the size transformations were not constant across different test objects: Increases in object size ranged from 116% to 171% of the original object (100%), and decreases in object size ranged from 50% to 67%. In one experiment, parietal lesions were found to produce less impairment in size generalization compared to foveal prestriate or AIT lesions. The impairment was evident on initial transfer trials and after repeated testing.

In a second experiment, normal unimpaired monkeys had a 28% error rate on initial size transformation trials. After repeated testing with the new size-transformed target objects, the error rate improved to 12% (Weiskrantz & Saunders, 1984). Successful generalization may have been partly accomplished because of the relatively small size change during generalization and because of information from visual features (e.g., color) that are size invariant. In the second experiment, AIT and prestriate lesions produced relatively mild impairments (compared with control subjects) that were not visible on initial transfer trials (prestriate 24% and AIT 33% errors) but were evident with repeated testing (prestriate 18% and AIT 21% errors).

The interpretation of the effects of lesions on generalization across size is similar to the interpretation of orientation. Area V4 and PIT cortex may be involved in specifying size-specific (viewer-centered) information about object features, and AIT may contribute to size-independent coding of these features (object-centered representations).

In the study of Holmes and Gross (1984b), monkeys were highly trained on a simultaneously presented discrimination task (stimuli: J vs. π and P vs. T). Both stimuli were transformed on probe trials in their real size (original size 100%, transformed sizes 50% and 200%). IT-lesioned animals took longer to learn the original discriminations but generalized across size (and orientation) transformations in a way directly comparable to that of unlesioned controls.

If we are to maintain the postulate that AIT contains much of the neural apparatus for generalizing over viewing conditions, then it is necessary to allow for at least some size generalization in feature processing prior to AIT; otherwise, it would not be possible to account for the results of Holmes and Gross (1984a,b). One alternative explanation of maintained size generalization after IT lesioning in the Holmes and Gross study is that in the Wisconsin General Test Apparatus, which is typically used to train and test subjects, the distance from the subject to the stimuli varies. When the stimuli are presented, the monkey may be at the back of its transport cage before making the behavioral choice. It is therefore likely that the subject experiences the target over a range of different retinal sizes (the range of image sizes could be as large as the range during transformation testing). The monkey could learn that the range of retinal image sizes are all associated with reward and achieve generalization, particularly with the protracted testing that IT-lesioned monkeys require to reach criterion.

Single-cell studies

Size specificity and generality.   Studies of early visual areas such as the striate cortex (De Valois, Albrecht, & Thorell, 1982; Kulikowski & Bishop, 1981) have shown that cells are tuned to the size of individual elements or to the spatial frequency of repetitive patterns. Cell responses to sine wave stimuli have a bandwidth tolerance of 1.5 octaves (changing image size by a factor of 2.83 [e.g., from 100% to 35%] reduces cell responses by half). Single-cell studies in area V4 have shown that V4 cells are selectively responsive to simple or complex features. Kobatake and Tanaka (1994) compared large and small bars of the same width but differing in length $10° - 2°$ ($100\% - 20\%$). Some cells were insensitive to change in length over this range. However, size specificity for more complex shapes has not been extensively tested in area V4 to date. Size selectivity is likely to be higher in area V4 than in later areas PIT/AIT simply because receptive fields are much smaller in V4.

In subsequent stages of the ventral visual pathway (IT), cell response selectivity to complex stimuli generalizes across different spatial frequencies (Rolls, Baylis, & Hasselmo, 1987; Rolls, Baylis, & Leonard, 1985). Cells selectively responsive to the face responded well to both high- and low-pass spatial frequency-filtered images of faces where the difference between low-pass and high-pass cut-offs was on average 3.2 octaves. This shows a convergence of visual information about the same type of object (face) from different spatial scales on individual cells. Note, though, that spatial scale is not the same as size.

Shape-sensitive neurons in the IT and STS cortex respond relatively independently of stimulus position within the visual field. The cells have extremely large receptive fields (median size about $25° \times 25°$, larger in more anterior regions; (Desimone & Gross, 1979; Fujita, Tanaka, Ito, & Cheng, 1992; Gross, Rocha-Miranda, & Bender, 1972; Gross & Sergent, 1992; Tanaka, 1992).

Lueschow, Miller, and Desimone (1994) investigated IT cell sensitivity to different image sizes during performance of a delayed matching-to-sample task in macaque monkeys. On each trial, the subjects were presented a series of picture stimuli and were trained to respond when the first stimuli of the picture series reappeared. The monkeys were trained to ignore changes in size between presentations of the target picture. Two different stimuli sizes were used: the smaller typically $2°$ (50%) and the larger $4°$ (100%) wide. Lueschow et al. (1994) found that some of the visually responsive and stimulus-selective cells (56%, 21/37) showed no difference in their response to changes of stimulus size, that is, these cells were invariant to size changes. Other cells (43%, 16/37), however, did show preference to stimulus size. Of these cells, 44% (7/16) responded to *all* objects at either the larger *or* the smaller size, whereas 56% (9/16) were selective for a *particular* stimulus at a *particular* optimal size. It should be noted that cells responding independently of stimulus shape might be considered visually unselective and therefore unlikely to be sensitive to size.

Lueschow et al. (1994) suggest that object size is coded in the same way as other object features (orientation, color, shape, etc.). Information about an object's features (size, shape, and orientation) and information about the object's identity (shape selectivity with generalization over changes in size and orientation) is coded by different cell populations in the IT cortex. Depending on the type of information about an object needed for a task solution, different populations of cells would be relevant.

A more recent study of shape selectivity in the AIT confirms the existence

of cell types that generalize across size change and other cell types more specifically tuned to a particular image size (Ito, Tamura, Fujita, & Tanaka, 1995).
For each cell the optimal stimulus shape was first defined. Then this shape was
presented at different sizes, with a size change of four octaves (6.25%, 12.5%,
25%, 50%, 100%, where at 100% the stimulus size was at a distance of 57 cm
with a visual angle of 31° × 29°). The width of tuning to size varied between
cells. Of 28 cells tested, 43% (12) were size selective with size changes of more
than two octaves from optimal size eliminating responses. Of these 12 cells, 5
responded best to the largest size tested (> 25°). For the remaining cells (16/
28, 57%), size change was less influential. Twenty-one percent of the cells
tolerated a size change of at least four octaves.

   Ito et al. (1995) noted that neither the size of the optimal stimulus nor the
bandwidth of size tuning correlated with the posterior-anterior position or depth
(cortical lamina) of the recording sites within the IT cortex. Given the relatively
small number of cells sampled, the generality of this observation is limited. The
study of Ito et al. (1995) indicates that AIT processes information about an
object in both a size-dependent and a size-independent way.

   To summarize, single-cell studies of the IT cortex of the macaque monkey
have shown that the majority of cells are broadly tuned to size. From 79% to
82% of cells respond maximally to a particular size (with half of these exhibiting
narrowband size tuning and half exhibiting broadband tuning), and 18–21% of
the cells generalize across all sizes tested (Ito et al., 1995; Lueschow et al.,
1994). Obviously, the degree of generalization depends on the degree of size
change tested.

   The studies described so far have investigated size tolerance of cells sensitive
to simple shape attributes, but it appears that selectivity for more complex shapes
can be accompanied by size specificity or size tolerance. Initial qualitative studies of 14 cells selectively responsive to faces in the STS (Perrett et al., 1982)
indicated size tolerance, with cells responding to real faces at a distance of 0.2
m (subtending 70°, 100%) or 2.0 m (10%). Rolls and Baylis (1986) studied cells
selective for faces in the IT and STS cortex for their responses to different
stimuli sizes (100%[full size, 12° of visual angle at a viewing distance of 1 m],
50%, 25%, and 12.5%, and 200% where the central part of the image was
doubled in size). Some cells (6/33) showed a consistent neuronal response over
a wide range of sizes (i.e., size invariance). Other cells (13/33) showed broad
tuning (i.e., the cells responded to a wide range of sizes but showed a response
decrease with very large or very small image sizes). Fourteen of 33 cells were
tuned to a specific size (3 cells responded selectively to small images, whereas
11 cells responded to large ones).

   We have recently studied the effect of image size on 16 cell responses to the
sight of heads and bodies in area STPa (Ashbridge et al., in prep.). In these
studies, the optimal body view was first ascertained for each cell, and then this

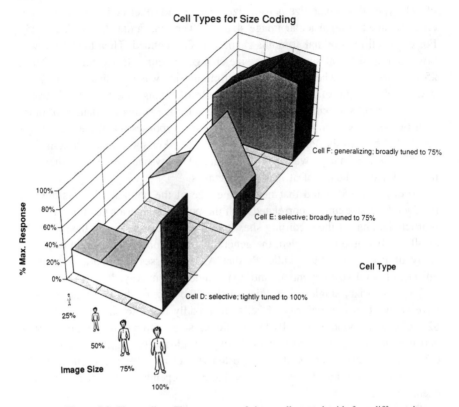

Figure 7.2. Size coding. The responses of three cells tested with four different image sizes are illustrated. Size is defined as a percentage of the maximum size (head to toe 1.73 m, visual angle 24.4°). Responses to different stimuli are expressed as a percentage of the maximum of cell activity (where spontaneous activity = 0%). Cell D was maximally activated by the largest stimulus size. Cells E and F were maximally activated by the second largest image size (75%). Tuning curves are progressively broader for cells D, E, and F.

view was presented at a range of image sizes: 100% (1.73 m, head to toe height, subtending 24.4°), 75% (18.5°), 50% (12.4°) to 25% (6.2°) at a viewing distance of 4 m. Of the 16 cells tested, two categories of responses were observed. Thirteen cells (81%) showed size specificity and were responsive to one (or more) but not all image sizes (cell E, Figure 7.2). The remaining three cells showed size generalization and responded to all image sizes at a rate greater than to the no-stimulus condition (S/A) and control objects. Of these three cells, one showed no difference in response amplitude to different image sizes (cell D, Figure 7.2), and two cells displayed some size tuning superimposed on a generalized response (e.g., cell F, Figure 7.2). Thus the majority of cells (15/16) showed sensitivity to size. Interestingly, all tuned cells were selective for the whole body at the largest (100%, e.g., cell D, Figure 7.2) or second largest (75%, e.g., cells E and F, Figure 7.2) projection size. These two sizes would correspond to images of real humans encountered at the projection distance. As for orientation, the response tuning to image size varied across cells. Some cells showed narrow tuning and responded to only one size of the body at a rate significantly different from that to control objects and S/A; other cells showed broader tuning, with the responses declining gradually as the images became smaller.

In summary, within the temporal cortex (areas IT and STS), the majority of cells appear to be size selective, whether the cells are tuned for particular simple features or for the multiple features present in a complex object. A minority (20%) of feature-sensitive cells have been found in the IT cortex that generalize over size change (from 100% to 6.25%). Furthermore, in the IT and STS cortex some 20% of cells, selective for complex objects (faces and whole bodies), generalize over large size changes (100% to 12%).

Effects of size change on memory for stimulus shape. Two types of short-term memory effects (enhancing and suppressive) are evident in the responses of IT cortex cells (Miller & Desimone, 1991; Miller, Gochin, & Gross, 1993). The enhancement mechanism is evident when the subject has to actively hold a target image in mind and compare it to subsequently presented images (Miller & De-simone, 1994). In this case, a cell's activity is increased when the target image is presented for the second time. A suppressive effect is evident during straight-forward stimulus repetition. Here the cell's activity is decreased if the same image is presented more than once in quick succession. This cell behavior occurs even when an image is repeated, regardless of whether the image is a target image or not. Thus, in the sequence ABBA, where stimulus A is the target, cell responses to B will be reduced on the second presentation.

It has been suggested that this type of suppressive mechanism may mediate automatic detection of image repetition (or registration of familiarity, Rolls, Perrett, Caan, & Wilson, 1982), whereas the enhancement mechanism may be involved in more cognitive "working memory." It is interesting to consider how change in image size effects these memory related effects. Lueschow et al. (1994) found that most cells showing suppressive effects with stimulus repetition and cells showing enhancement effects during matching-to-sample tasks exhib-ited size invariance in these effects. That is, a size change between the first and second stimulus presentations did not seem to affect the magnitude of response suppression or enhancement. Therefore the mechanism underlying both short-term memory effects must exhibit tolerance over size change.

Repetition priming tasks, in which reaction times to classify pictures are reduced when the stimuli are repeated (Biederman & Cooper, 1992), might be a psychological reflection of the short-term memory mechanisms apparent in the temporal cortex (Lueschow et al., 1994).

Conclusion

Most human and animal studies indicate that the ventral stream (V4, PIT, AIT, and STPa) is involved in the processing of information about an object's appearance, including its orientation and size. The IT cortex plays an important role in the formation of a mental representation of an object for storage in long-term memory. Ideally, for recognition purposes, a single object-centered representation that generalizes across viewing conditions is most efficient. This would allow an object to be recognized irrespective of its perceived view, orientation, size, or even part visibility (part occlusions). For behavioral interaction with an object, information about the object's location, absolute size, and orientation relative to the viewer has to be available to guide, for example, the formation of an appropriate grip size of the hand during grasping. For such visuomotor control, viewer-centered representations are essential, although information about the object's identity is less relevant. It now appears that such information about three-dimensional orientation and size is coded by cells in the parietal cortex (area LIP; H. Sakata, personal communication, 1995).

It may be more appropriate to consider orientation and size information about objects being computed separately in the dorsal and parietal systems and utilized for different visual tasks. Realizing what an object is and knowing whether it is upright (Turnbull, 1995) or how to interact with it (Goodale et al., 1991) appear to be dissociable abilities. No doubt there is considerable interplay between the dorsal and ventral streams of processing. Indeed, interactions between individuals depend on an awareness of head and body postures and orientation. Such information may well be specified by the ventral systems, including the STS, before the information is passed (through STS outputs; Harries, 1991) to dorsal systems to guide appropriate behavioral output and interactions.

Notes

1. To compare the effects of size change across different studies, we define the size of the original training or largest stimulus used in experiments as 100%; smaller sizes are expressed as a percentage of this maximum. We estimate stimulus size as a linear dimension (e.g., diameter, visual angle) rather than as an area. Thus, if a square stimulus with the sizes 10° (area 100 square degrees) is changed to a square stimulus with sides of 7.5° (area 56.25 square degrees), we refer to the stimulus sizes as 100% and 75%, respectively.

References

Besner, D. (1983). Visual pattern recognition: Size pre-processing re-examined. *Quarterly Journal of Experimental Psychology, 35* (A), 209–216.

Biederman, I., & Cooper, E. (1992). Size invariance in visual object priming. *Journal of Experimental Psychology: Human Perception and Performance, 18* (1), 121–133.

Bruce, V., & Young, A. (1986). Understanding face recognition. *British Journal of Psychology, 77,* 103–327.

Budesen, C., & Larsen, A. (1975). Visual transformation of size. *Journal of Experimental Psychology: Human Perception and Performance, 1,* 214–220.

Cohen, L., Grey, F., Meyrignac, C., Dehaene, S., & Degos, J.-D. (1994). Selective deficit of visual size perception: Two cases of hemimicropsia. *Journal of Neurology, Neurosurgery, and Psychiatry, 57,* 73–78.

Cooper, E., & Biederman, I. (1991). Evidence for size invariant representations in visual object recognition (poster abstract). *Investigative Ophthalmology and Visual Science, 32* (4), 1279.

Desimone, R., & Gross, C. G. (1979). Visual areas in the temporal cortex of the macaque. *Journal of Neuroscience, 4,* 2051–2062.

Desimone, R., & Schein, S. J. (1987). Visual properties of neurons in area V4 of the macaque – sensitivity to stimulus form. *Journal of Neurophysiology, 57*(3), 835–868.

DeValois, R. L., Albrecht, D. G., & Thorell, L. G. (1982). Spatial frequency selectivity of cells in macaque visual cortex. *Vision Research, 22,* 545–559.

Dickerson, J. A. (1991). *The recognition of transformed objects.* Ph.D. thesis, Birkbeck College, University of London.

Ellis, R., Allport, D. A., Humphreys, G. W., & Collis, J. (1989). Varieties of object constancy. *Quarterly Journal of Experimental Psychology, 41* (A), 775–796.

Fujita, I., Tanaka, K., Ito, M., & Cheng, K. (1992). Columns for visual features of objects in monkey inferotemporal cortex. *Nature, 36,* 343–346.

Goodale, M. A., & Milner, A. D. (1992). Separate visual pathways for perception and action. *Trends in Neurosciences, 15* (1), 20–25.

Goodale, M. A., Milner, A. D., Jacobson, L. S., & Carey, D. P. (1991). A neurological dissociation between perceiving objects and grasping them. *Nature, 349* (6305), 154–156.

Gross, C. G., Desimone, R., Albright, T. D., & Schwartz, E. L. (1985). Inferior temporal cortex and pattern recognition. In C. Nagass, R. Gatass, & C. G. Gross (Eds.), *Pattern recognition mechanisms* (pp. 179–201). Vatican City, Rome: Pontificae Academiae Scientiarum Scripta Varia No. 54.

Gross, C. G., Rocha-Miranda, C. E., & Bender, D. B. (1972). Visual properties of neurons in inferotemporal cortex of the macaque. *Journal of Neurophysiology, 35,* 96–111.

Gross, C. G., & Sergent, J. (1992). Face recognition. *Current Opinion in Neurobiology, 2,* 156–161.

Haenny, P. E., & Schiller, P. H. (1988). State dependent activity in monkey visual cortex: 1. Single cell-activity in V1 and V4 on visual tasks. *Experimental Brain Research, 69* (2), 225–244.

Harries, M. H., & Perrett, D. I. (1991). Visual processing of faces in the temporal cortex: Physiological evidence for a modular organization and possible anatomical correlates. *Journal of Cognitive Neuroscience, 3*(1), 9–24.

Hasselmo, M. E., Rolls, E. T., Baylis, G. C., & Nalwa, V. (1989). Object centred encoding by face-selective neurons in the cortex of the superior temporal sulcus of the monkey. *(Experimental) Brain Research, 75,* 417–429.

Holmes, E. J., & Gross, C. G. (1984a). Effects of inferior temporal lesions on discrimination of stimuli differing in orientation. *Journal of Neuroscience, 4*(12), 3063–3068.

Holmes, E. J., & Gross, C. G. (1984b). Stimulus equivalence after inferior temporal lesions in monkeys. *Behavioural Neuroscience, 98,* 898–901.

Hummel, J. E., & Biederman, I. (1992). Dynamic binding in a neural network for shape recognition. *Psychological Review, 99* (3), 480–517.

Ito, M., Tamura, H., Fujita, I., & Tanaka, K. (1995). Size and position invariance of neuronal responses in monkey inferotemporal cortex. *Journal of Neurophysiology, 73,* 218–226.

Jeannerod, M. (1981). *Attention and performance* (Vol. IX, pp. 153–168). *IX.* Hillsdale, NJ: Erlbaum.

Jeannerod, M. (1994). The representing brain: Neural correlates of motor intention and imagery. *Behavioural and Brain Sciences, 17,* 187–245.

Jolicoeur, P. (1987). A size-congruency effect in memory for visual shape. *Memory and Cognition,* *15*, 531–543.

Jolicoeur, P., & Bessner, D. (1987). Additivity and interaction between size ratio and response category in the comparison of size discrepant shapes. *Journal of Experimental Psychology— Human perception and performance, 13,* 478–487.

Kobatake, E., & Tanaka, K. (1994). Neural selectivities to complex object features in the ventral visual pathway of the macaque cerebral cortex. *Journal of Neurophysiology, 71* (3), 856–867.

Kulikowski, J. J., & Bishop, P.O. (1981). Linear analysis of the responses of simple cells in the cat visual cortex. *Experimental Brain Research, 44,* 386–400.

Larsen, A. (1985). Pattern matching: Effects of size ratio, angular difference in orientation, and familiarity. *Perception and Psychophysics, 38,* 63–68.

Larsen, A. & Bundesen, C. (1978). Size scaling in human pattern recognition. *Journal of Experimental Psychology: Human Perception and Performance, 4,* 1–20.

Lowe, D. G. (1987). Three-dimensional object recognition form single two-dimensional images. *Artificial Intelligence, 31,* 355–395.

Lueschow, A., Miller, E. K., & Desimone, R. (1994). Inferior temporal mechanisms for invariant object recognition. *Cerebral Cortex 5,* (4), 523–531.

Marr, D., & Nishihara, H. K. (1978). Representation and recognition of the spatial organization of three dimensional shapes. *Proceedings of the Royal Society of London, 200* (Series B), 269–294.

Miller, E. K., & Desimone, R. (1991) A neural mechanism for working memory and recognition memory in inferior temporal cortex. *Science, 254,* 1377–1379.

Miller, E. K., & Desimone, R. (1994). Parallel neuronal mechanisms for short-term memory. *Science, 263,* 520–522.

Miller, E. K., Gochin, P. M., & Gross, C. G. (1993). Suppression of visual responses of neurons in inferior temporal cortex of the awake macaque by addition of a second stimulus. *Brain Research, 616,* 25–29.

Milner, A. D., Perrett, D. I., Johnston, R. S., Benson, P. J., Jordan, T. R., Heeley, T. R., Bettucci, D. W., Mortara, D., Mutani, R., Terazzi, E., et al. (1991). Perception and action in visual form perception. *Brain, 114,* 405–428.

Oram, M. W., & Perrett, D. I. (1994). Modeling visual recognition from neurobiological constraints. *Neural Networks, 7*(6/7), 945–972.

Palmer, S. E., Rosch, E., Chase, P., & Baddely, D. (1981). Canonical perspective and the perception of objects. In C. Umilta & M. Moscovitch (Eds.), *Attention and performance* (pp. 135–151). Hillsdale, NJ: Erlbaum.

Perrett, D. I., Mistlin, A. J., Chitty, A. J., Smith, P. A. J., Potter, D. D., Broennimann, R., & Harries, M. H. (1988). Specialised face processing and hemispheric asymmetry in man and monkey: Evidence from single unit and reaction time studies. *Behavioural Brain Research, 29,* 245–258.

Perrett, D. I., & Oram, M. W. (1993). The neurophysiology of shape processing. *Image and Visual Computing, 11*(6), 317–333.

Perrett, D. I., Rolls, E. T., & Caan, W. (1982). Visual neurons responsive to faces in the monkey temporal cortex. *Experimental Brain Research, 47,* 329–342.

Perrett, D. I., Smith, P. A. J., Potter, D. D., Mistlin, A. J., Head, A. S., Milner, A. D. & Jeeves, M. A. (1984). Neurons responsive to faces in the temporal cortex: Studies of functional organization, sensitivity to identity and relation to perception. *Human Neurobiology, 3,* 197–208.

Perrett, D. I., Smith, P. A. J., Potter, D. D., Mistlin, A. J., Head, A. S., Milner, A. D., & Jeeves, M. A. (1985). Visual cells in the temporal cortex sensitive to face view and gaze direction. *Proceedings of the Royal Society of London B, 223,* 293–317.

Porrill, J., Pollard, S. B., Pridmore, T. P., Bowen, J. B., Mayhew, J. E. W., & Frisby, J. P. (1988). TINA: A 3D vision system for pick and place. *Image and Vision Computing, 6*(2), 91–99.

Rolls, E. T., & Baylis, G. C. (1986). Size and contrast have only small effects on the responses to faces of neurons in the cortex of the superior temporal sulcus of the monkey. *Experimental Brain Research, 65,* 38–48.

Rolls, E. T., Baylis, G. C., & Hasselmo, M. E. (1987). The responses of neurons in the cortex in the superior temporal sulcus of the monkey to band-pass spatial frequency filtered faces. *Vision Research, 27*(3), 311–326.

Rolls, E. T., Baylis, G. C., & Leonard, C. M. (1985). Role of low and high spatial frequency in the face-selective responses of neurons in the cortex in the superior temporal sulcus in the monkey. *Vision Research, 25*, 1021–1035.

Rolls, E. T., Perrett D. I., Caan, W., & Wilson F. (1982) Neuronal responses related to visual recognition. *Brain, 105*, 611–646.

Sakata, H., & Taira, M. (1994). Parietal control of hand action. *Current Opinion in Neurobiology, 4*, 847–856.

Schwartz, E. L., Desimone, R., Albright, T. D., & Gross, C. G. (1983). Shape recognition and inferior temporal neurons. *Proceedings of the National Academy of Sciences of the USA, 80*, 5776–5778.

Shepard, R. N., & Metzler, J. (1971). Mental rotation of three-dimensional objects. *Science, 171*, 701–703.

Tanaka, K. (1992). Inferotemporal cortex and higher visual functions. *Current Opinion in Neurobiology, 2*, 502–505.

Tanaka, K., & Fujita, I. (1991). Coding visual images of objects in the inferotemporal cortex of the macaque monkey. *Journal of Neurophysiology, 66*, 170–189.

Turnbull, O. H., Laws, K. R., & McCarthy, R. A. (1995). Object recognition without knowledge of object orientation. *Cortex 31*, 387–395.

Ullman, S. (1989). Aligning pictorial descriptions: An approach to object recognition. *Cognition, 32*, 193–254.

Ungerleider, L. G., & Mishkin, M. (1982). Two cortical visual systems. In *Analysis of visual behaviour* (pp. 549–585). Cambridge, MA: MIT Press.

Vogels, R., & Orban, G. A. (1994). Activity of inferior temporal neurons during orientation discrimination with successively presented gratings. *Journal of Neurophysiology, 71*(4), 1428–1451.

Wachsmuth, E., Oram, M. W., & Perrett, D. I. (1994). Recognition of objects and their component parts: Responses of single units in the temporal cortex of the macaque. *Cerebral Cortex, 4*(5), 509–522.

Weiskrantz, L., & Saunders, R. C. (1984). Impairments of visual object transforms in monkeys. *Brain, 107*, 1033–1072.

8   The neuropsychology of visual object constancy

Rebecca Lawson and Glyn W. Humphreys

1.1 Converging neurophsiological evidence concerning the achievement of visual object constancy

There is currently a diversity of theoretical accounts of the achievement of visual object constancy (see chapters 3 and 4), plus also quite sparse and often conflicting empirical data from studies with normal human subjects. Hence it becomes particularly important to seek converging evidence from other research areas, to test the range of theories that have been proposed to account for the ability to achieve object constancy. Neurophysiological evidence from single-cell recording studies provides additional evidence. Neurophysiological studies by Perrett and colleagues (Perrett et al., 1984, 1985, 1987, 1988, 1994) have provided indications of the solutions employed by the primate visual system to achieve object constancy (see Ashbridge & Perrett, this volume).

A second line of evidence comes from cognitive neuropsychological studies of neurological impairment in the achievement of object constancy, which are reviewed in detail in this chapter.

2.1 The effects of neurological damage on visual object constancy

Cognitive neuropsychological studies can be divided into two broad classes, which we will describe in separate sections. First, we review a series of large-scale studies comparing groups of patients with approximately similar lesion sites on a relatively small number of standardized tasks. Second, we review a number of detailed single case studies of patients who have been tested more extensively. Third, we consider some recent studies in which the achievement of object constancy has been used as a measure with which to investigate other types of visual processing.

This work was supported by a grant from the Human Frontier Science Program to the first author and by grants from the Medical Research Council (UK) and the European Union to the second author.

2.2 Large-scale cognitive neuropsychological studies of visual object constancy

An accumulation of evidence suggests that, relative to both normal control subjects and patients with left-hemisphere brain lesions, patients with right-hemisphere lesions are impaired at recognizing pictures that are perceptually degraded to reduce the usual redundancy present. For example, right-lesioned patients have been shown to have a specific deficit in recognizing overlapping drawings (De Renzi, Scotti, & Spinnler, 1969; De Renzi & Spinnler, 1966a), sketchily drawn scenes (Milner, 1958), and degraded silhouettes and incomplete or fragmented drawings of letters and familiar objects (De Renzi & Spinnler, 1966a; Faglioni, Scotti, & Spinnler, 1969; Kerschensteiner, Hartje, Orgass, & Poeck, 1972; Lansdell, 1968; Newcombe, 1974; Newcombe & Russell, 1969; Warrington & James 1967; Warrington & Taylor, 1973).

Warrington and Taylor (1973, 1978) noted the differential performance of right-and left-hemisphere lesioned patients on a number of visual tasks and suggested that there are two serially organized categorical stages in visual object recognition. First, the visual input is perceptually categorized – a stage of processing that may operate independently of access to semantic knowledge about the object – and subsequently the input is categorized semantically. Problems in perceptual categorization are associated with right hemisphere lesions, whereas deficits in semantic categorization are associated with left hemisphere lesions. Warrington and Taylor's stage of perceptual categorization subsumes the achievement of object constancy because it includes the ability to recognize different exemplars as belonging to the same familiar class of object (e.g., recognizing that *A* written in different fonts – a, A **A**, 𝔸 – all represent the same letter), as well as the ability to match two different views as belonging to the same object.

Evidence for Warrington and Taylor's account comes from data derived from right-hemisphere lesioned patients, who often reveal a specific deficit in matching two different depth-rotated views of the same object (generally, one view is unconventional or foreshortened and the other view is canonical; this is termed the *unusual views task*) or in recognizing unconventional or foreshortened views of objects (Layman & Greene, 1988; Warrington & James, 1986, 1991; Warrington & Taylor, 1973, 1978; however, De Renzi et al., 1969, reported that left-hemisphere lesioned patients were impaired relative to right-hemisphere lesioned patients at matching a picture of an object to a real object from the same class of exemplars). Although the studies reported by Warrington and colleagues suggest that damage to the right posterior hemisphere causes difficulties in identifying unusual views, Bulla-Hellwig, Ettlinger, Dommasch, Ebel, and Skreczeck (1992) found no difference between right- and left-hemifield lesioned patients on perceptual (and semantic) categorization tasks similar to those employed by Warrington and James (1986). However, Bulla-Hellwig et al.'s study may have been relatively insensitive to differences between damage to the right and left hemispheres because there was no discrimination between posterior and more anterior lesions (Warrington and colleagues specifically implicate the posterior right hemisphere in perceptual categorization deficits).

Right-hemisphere lesioned patients have also been reported to be impaired in recognizing objects depicted as larger or smaller than life size (Bergego, Deloche, Pradat-Diehl, Robineau, & Lauriot-Prevost, 1993; Warrington & Taylor, 1973), as well as at matching two identical prototypical views of an object, one of which was evenly lit, whereas the other was unevenly lit such that it was partly obscured by shadows (Warrington & Ackroyd, reported in Warrington, 1982). Warrington and Ackroyd found that patients with damage to the posterior right hemisphere were particularly impaired at this latter task. For such patients, changing the direction of illumination, to produce a non-prototypical image of an object, appeared to be as disruptive to picture matching as changing the angle of view in depth. Warrington and Ackroyd argued that, unlike normal subjects who effortlessly achieve object constancy, patients with right posterior lesions are impaired in their ability to compensate for any deviations from a prototypical representation. Supporting this suggestion, Benton and Van Allen (1968) reported significantly worse performance on face-matching tasks (matching across different depth-rotated views of faces and differently illuminated faces) for right-hemisphere lesioned patients compared to left-hemisphere lesioned patients and control subjects (see also De Renzi et al., 1969; Warrington & James, 1967).

Warrington and Rudge (1991) reported nine patients with tumors affecting the splenium of the corpus callosum, all of whom had deficits in visual perception. Eight of these patients were impaired at the unusual views task, and all patients tested were impaired at identifying fragmented letters. In contrast, all patients could recognize canonical views of objects and six could read well, with the remaining three being able to identify single letters. Thus, for these patients, it appeared that only atypical (unusual or fragmented) stimuli presented problems. To account for the finding that canonical views of objects were still accurately identified by these patients (see also Warrington & James, 1988), Warrington and Rudge proposed that there are two parallel routes to recognition. In one route, information from early visual sensory processing is passed directly to a semantic recognition system in the left hemisphere. This transmission route may be subcortical and intact in the patients with splenium lesions. However, early sensory information may be sufficient only to support accurate recognition of typical canonical objects. For recognition of objects seen in unusual views, a further stage of perceptual classification is required, which takes place in the posterior right hemisphere. Patients with right posterior lesions are selectively impaired with such views of objects, and patients with lesions of the splenium may be also impaired at identifying such views because lesions prevent transmission of the outputs of perceptual processing in the right hemisphere to the left hemisphere semantic recognition system.

Warrington and James (1986) extended the unusual views task to consider the recognition of three-dimensional silhouettes of familiar objects. They compared 60 control subjects and 48 right-lesioned patients on their ability to recognize the silhouettes, as indexed by the earliest point at which a subject could identify an object as it was rotated vertically or horizontally away from a foreshortened viewpoint. Unlike the unusual views task, the silhouette recognition task allowed a minimal view of an object to be nonarbitrarily selected as being the first view which most controls could recognize. Right-hemisphere lesioned patients were quantitatively impaired relative to controls in that they required a greater degree of rotation away from the foreshortened view to recognize an object. However, there were no qualitative differences relative to the controls; objects that were quickly recognized by the controls were also recognized most easily by the right-hemisphere lesioned patients, and vice versa. Warrington and James (1986) also reported that there was no evidence of a typical recognition function for different objects (there was a large variability between items) or of a constant function for a single object (performance for horizontal versus vertical rotations of a given object were very different), although it should be noted that the study employed a very small set of objects. Just six objects were used in the analysis of the results because 4 of the 10 objects tested were recognized at either floor or ceiling levels. Warrington and James argued that these results are evidence against Marr's (1982) axis-based theory of visual object recognition because recognition was not found to be uniformly related to the availability of the main axis of an object (there was no typical recognition function, either within or across objects). Instead, they suggest that object are recognized by identifying distinctive features (see also Humphreys & Riddoch, 1984).

In a similar study, Warrington and James (1991) used two-dimensional versions of the silhouettes presented in Warrington and James (1986) in an object decision task (subjects had to decide whether a given stimulus depicted a real or a nonsense object; see Riddoch & Humphreys, 1987a). The silhouette of a familiar object was presented together with three other silhouettes of nonsense shapes, which did not include any parts of real objects. In a large study involving 106 patients with unilateral lesions, patients with right posterior lesions were impaired at selecting the silhouette of the real object, and were also impaired at identifying unusual views of objects relative to patients with left posterior lesions and control subjects.

One group study that reached a slightly different interpretation of the deficit for right-hemisphere lesioned patients was reported by Layman and Greene (1988). They tested right- and left-hemisphere lesioned stroke patients and nonlesioned controls on tasks requiring the naming of canonical and unusual views of familiar objects, as well as sequential matching of photographs of familiar and novel three-dimensional objects and novel two-dimensional objects. All subjects were able to name conventional, upright views of familiar objects, in which the main axis of the object was fully revealed. All subject groups were relatively impaired at naming unconventional, upright, but foreshortened views of familiar objects. However, right-hemisphere lesioned patients were particularly disadvantaged at naming the objects seen from unusual views.

In the matching task, familiar objects were matched efficiently when two identical views or two plane-rotated views were presented; however all groups had difficulty in matching two depth-rotated views of an object. In contrast to Warrington and Taylor's (1973, 1978) results, the right-lesioned subjects were not specifically impaired at matching depth-rotated views of familiar objects relative to the left-lesioned and control subjects. However, in an equivalent matching task with novel three-dimensional Tinker Toy objects, there was a particular decrease in the performance of the right hemisphere-lesioned patients (over and above the effects found with the other subjects) when depth rotations relative to plane rotations were compared. Finally, all subjects were efficient at matching novel two-dimensional, rotated shapes.

Layman and Greene (1988) proposed that the right-hemisphere lesioned patients had a selective problem in achieving a coherent three-dimensional representation of an object, particularly when they could not call on semantic information to facilitate performance (e.g., with novel objects). As discussed later, right-lesioned patients appear to have difficulty utilizing configural information from faces in a normal manner (Dricker, Butters, Berman, Samuels, & Carey, 1978; Sergent & Villemure, 1989) and they may be forced to rely on a less efficient strategy for face and object recognition – for example, a search for individual, distinctive features. Such distinctive features may not support the derivation of three-dimensional object descriptions. In addition, Layman and Greene (1988) suggest that right-lesioned patients may have a specific impairment in depth perception (Hamsher, 1978a, 1978b; Humphreys & Riddoch, 1984), which may add additional difficulty to the problem of matching depth-rotated stimuli. To account for the accurate naming of conventional views of familiar objects by right-hemisphere lesioned patients, Layman and Greene (1988) argued that accurate depth perception is not then required, unlike the situation in which unusual, foreshortened views of objects are presented for identification. Finally, right-hemisphere lesioned patients may have particular problems in mentally rotating stimuli. For example, Ratcliff (1979) found that whereas right- and left-hemisphere lesioned patients were equally efficient in determining whether an upright front- or back-facing mannikin held a black disk in its right or left hand, right-hemisphere lesioned patients were relatively impaired at this task when the mannikin was inverted (although see Farah & Hammond, 1988; Turnbull, Laws, & McCarthy, 1995; section 2.3.4).

The essential difference between the account of Layman and Greene, and that of Warrington and collaborators, is that Layman and Greene argue for deficits in particular visual operations after brain damage (poor depth encoding, poor derivation of a three-dimensional object representation, poor mental rotation) rather than a deficit in a generic perceptual classification mechanism. There are problems with Layman and Greene's proposal, however. For example, right-lesioned patients were as accurate as left-lesioned patients and controls at matching canonical to foreshortened views of familiar objects. A deficit here might be expected (indeed, see Warrington & Taylor, 1973, 1978), unless there were sufficient distinctive features available in the foreshortened views to enable the right-hemisphere lesioned patients to identify the stimuli (particularly when paired with a typical view of the same object). Also, a feature-matching strategy should have led to successful matching of identical and plane-rotated unfamiliar objects, yet here right-hemisphere lesioned patients showed a relative deficit. However, Layman and Greene (1988) suggest that the right-lesioned patients may have adopted alternative matching strategies that resulted in errors even in conditions in which simple feature matching would have been successful.

One important new result reported by Layman and Greene is that right-hemisphere lesioned patients have a deficit in matching unfamiliar views of *novel* objects. This is evidence against Warrington and Taylor's (1978) suggestion that the problems of right-hemisphere lesioned patients in matching depth-rotated views of familiar objects result from damage to perceptual memory systems that mediate object constancy (novel objects, for which memory representations are not available, may not be matched on the basis of activation within such representations). This result does not rule out the possibility that damage has occurred to perceptual memory stores in right-hemisphere lesioned patients, but it appears probable that impaired perceptual processing, common to both familiar and novel objects, is a major cause of their deficit in achieving visual object constancy.

In an interesting extension of the visual matching tasks just described, Bottini, Cappa, and Vignolo (1991) tested right- and left-hemisphere lesioned patients and controls in a somesthetic-visual matching task. The subjects, with closed eyes, explored a stimulus for 15s and then were shown four visually presented objects, one of which matched the object they had just felt. In one condition, familiar objects were presented and the visually presented target was a different exemplar, but of the same object class as the object presented tactually. In the other condition, novel objects were presented, and the visually presented target was identical to the object presented tactually. Right-hemisphere lesioned patients were worse at matching novel objects, whereas left-hemisphere lesioned patients were more impaired at matching familiar objects. This result suggests that right hemisphere damage influences perceptual processing and the ability to achieve object constancy across visual-tactile presentations, even for meaningless stimuli, whereas left hemisphere damage affects semantic or cognitive processing.

To summarize, the group studies just reviewed indicate that right-hemisphere lesioned patients (especially those with right posterior lesions) often have particular problems in achieving object constancy. Stimuli that are atypical, that reveal fewer defining features or that are presented from an unusual perspective, are recognized inefficiently. This result has been demonstrated with both two-dimensional and three-dimensional silhouettes, unusual and foreshortened views of both familiar and novel objects, and unusually illuminated objects. However conventional, prototypical views of stimuli may be recognized with normal efficiency. Right-hemisphere lesioned patients seem to be impaired in their perceptual processing, which leads to a breakdown in their ability to achieve object constancy, rather than the breakdown being primarily a result of memory deficits (Layman & Greene, 1988), because their performance is impaired for novel as well as for familiar objects. The deficit in achieving object constancy cannot readily be accounted for by an overall worse performance at visual tasks by right-compared to left-hemisphere lesioned patients. Right-hemisphere lesioned patients are often good at recognizing complex, conventional views of objects. Furthermore, left-hemisphere lesioned patients have been shown to be impaired relative to right-lesioned patients and controls at visual function matching tasks (where, for instance, a nail has to be matched to a functionally similar item such as a hammer rather than to a visually similar item such as a golf tee) (Warrington & Taylor, 1978; but see Bulla-Hellwig et al., 1992). Importantly, although patients with right posterior lesions do seem to show specific difficulties in achieving object constancy, Warrington and James (1986) provided some evidence that these patients do not differ relative to normal controls in the strategies that they use in visual object processing. Their processing of nonprototypical views of objects simply seems to be less efficient than the visual processing of normal subjects rather than to be different in kind. This is of particular interest because it suggests that conclusions about the achievement of object constancy drawn from results of testing patients with right posterior lesions can be extrapolated to the normal population.

2.3 Single case studies of visual object constancy

Cognitive neuropsychological single case studies of patients with specific deficits in object recognition provide a further important source of evidence about how humans achieve visual object constancy. A number of detailed single case studies have now been reported of patients with the rare syndrome of visual agnosia. Such patients may have severe problems in visually recognizing even the most familiar objects. One significant advantage in studying such patients, relative to group studies with patients or normals, is that their overall efficiency of recognition is often poor, and therefore manipulations that vary the ease of recognition of an object can have profound effects on their performance. Such effects can be highly reliable even when studying single cases. In contrast, because in normal vision object constancy is achieved quickly and effortlessly, differences between experimental conditions are often relatively subtle and difficult to establish reliably.

Neuropsychological studies of agnosic patients allow us to examine their difficulties in achieving object constancy without resorting to more extreme measures (e.g., using degraded stimuli, very short stimulus presentations, very unusual views of objects). In addition, single case analyses can reveal different processing operations involved in object constancy by contrasting performance patterns across different patients; such differences may be obscured in group studies in which data from patients are pooled together (e.g., De Renzi & Spinnler, 1966a; De Renzi et al., 1969).

2.3.1 Types of agnosia and object constancy

Agnosia is defined as a disorder of recognition and identification of form that cannot be attributed to generalized intellectual deterioration, sensory impairments, disruptions of attention, or a language deficit. The agnosia is generally specific to a sensory modality, and most patients reported to date have been agnosic for visual form, although there have also been reports of auditory, tactile (Caselli, 1991a, 1991b), and color agnosia (Geschwind & Fusillo, 1966). There has been some argument about whether agnosia can be wholly explained by subtle low-level perceptual impairments, but some agnosics have no worse perceptual impairments than many non-agnosics (e.g., Newcombe & Ratcliff, 1975, Case 5: Riddoch & Humphreys, 1987a).

Lissauer (1890) distinguished between two main types of visual agnosia: apperceptive and associative. Apperceptive agnosia is characterized by difficulties in deriving an adequate visual perceptual description of the world and integrating visual information gleaned over space and time (Riddoch & Humphreys, 1987b). Patients are unable to identify objects and may not even discriminate between same and different views of an object. In at least some cases, the patients cannot copy drawings or match drawings to their names, although they can have preserved color discrimination, and moving stimuli may be recognized better than static forms (e.g., Benson & Greenberg, 1969; Campion, 1987). For this latter group of patients, the deficit in object recognition seems to affect even the encoding of two-dimensional shape information, a stage of processing even earlier than that at which object constancy occurs (Humphreys & Riddoch, 1993; Warrington, 1985). Consequently, such patients will not be discussed further here.

Associative agnosia is characterized by difficulties in making a connection between perceptual input that is processed in an apparently normal way and previously stored information, so that identification difficulties result. Teuber (1975) defined associative agnosia as a syndrome in which a normal percept has somehow been stripped of its meaning. Clinically, patients can make recognizable copies of drawings (but these are not then recognized by the patient), and they can successfully match identical views of an object (Newcombe & Ratcliff, 1975; Rubens & Benson, 1971; Taylor & Warrington, 1971). Associative agnosics have often been assumed to have a deficit in accessing semantic knowledge, or the semantic knowledge is destroyed (e.g., Warrington, 1985); as a consequence, it might be argued that their deficit lies at a level beyond which object constancy has been achieved. Again, it would follow that these patients are not relevant to the debate about object constancy.

However, recent research has suggested that the partition of agnosia into apperceptive and associative forms is too simple. A number of patients have been reported with severe problems in object recognition, yet they do not fall clearly into either category. This has led researchers to suggest a broader classification scheme in which distinctions are made between patients with a variety of problems at different visual processing stages en route to semantic access, although these problems may still be broadly classed in terms of a primarily perceptual or memorial locus of the deficit (e.g., Humphreys & Riddoch, 1993; Humphreys et al., 1994). Those patients with relatively greater impairments in identifying unusual or degraded views of objects relative to canonical views are of perhaps greatest interest for the study of visual object constancy. Such patients typically appear to have a perceptual rather than a memorial locus for their agnosia. We consider such cases in detail in the following section.

2.3.2 Perceptual agnosias

Riddoch and Humphreys (1987b; see also Humphreys & Riddoch, 1987) described a patient, HJA, who was able to copy objects that he failed to recognize visually. However, contrary to the diagnosis of an associative agnosia with intact perception, Riddoch and Humphreys showed that HJA had impaired visual-perceptual processing. For example, he was abnormally disrupted by overlapping line drawings on top of one another and by stimuli presented for relatively short durations. In addition (and in complete contrast to normal observers), he was better able to identify silhouettes than line drawings of objects. Riddoch and Humphreys suggested that HJA was impaired at integrating local information from visual forms with more global descriptions of shape; in fact, the presence of local segmentation cues in stimuli led him to parse objects incorrectly, so that his identification tended to be based on local parts and not to take account of the perceptual whole. The reliance on serial processing of the parts of objects led to his disruption by short exposure durations. Serial processing also produced problems with overlapping figures, which can be parsed in multiple ways using only local information. However, because local internal details are eliminated in silhouettes, his performance improved because there were then fewer cues to segment whole objects into disconnected parts. Similar results in another agnosic patients have been reported more recently by Butter and Trobe (1994).

Interestingly, HJA was impaired both at identifying objects presented in unusual views and in matching objects depicted from different viewing positions. The transformations that HJA found most difficult were those that reduced the saliency of the diagnostic features of the objects. This was so even when the main axis of the object was preserved in both the canonical and the unusual view (Humphreys & Riddoch, 1984). In contrast, he was relatively good at matching canonical views of objects with foreshortened views, provided that the foreshortened views preserved the diagnostic features of the objects. Humphreys and Riddoch (1984) proposed that HJA achieved object constancy by encoding the presence of distinctive local features. The descriptions of local features were coded in a nonretinotopic format, so that the feature representations could be matched even when the objects were seen from different views.

In contrast to HJA's performance on unusual-view matching tasks, Humphreys and Riddoch reported an opposite pattern of results with four patients with unilateral lesions of the posterior parts of the right hemisphere. These patients were impaired at matching canonical and foreshortened views of objects, but they remained able to match canonical views of objects with views in which the main axis of the object was preserved but its diagnostic features were obscured (*minimal-feature* views). These patients were strongly affected by transformations in depth that reduced the saliency of the main axis of the objects.

At least part of the reason for the strong effects of foreshortening observed by Humphreys and Riddoch is that the right-hemisphere lesioned patients may have been unable to recover depth information from impoverished visual cues (Layman & Greene, 1988). Consistent with this conclusion, Humphreys and Riddoch showed a significant improvement in the performance of these patients when the foreshortened objects were depicted on a background in which there were strong linear perspective depth cues (see Humphrey & Jolicoeur, 1993, for qualitatively similar facilitatory effects of depth cues with normal observers). The presence of the depth cues may have enabled the patients to encode a more accurate, object-centered representation, supporting object constancy.

In a follow-up study on the same right-hemisphere lesioned patients, Riddoch and Humphreys (1986), however, showed that, at least for three of the four patients, the problem was not just in dealing with foreshortened objects. Riddoch and Humphreys had the patients match canonical views with minimal-feature views that also varied in size. Three patients were impaired at these *size*- and *view-transformed* matches, although they were able to match objects transformed only in size or only into the minimal-feature views (Humphreys & Riddoch,

1984). For such patients, the problem seemed to be in invoking any appropriate transformation procedure when the viewpoint-dependent representations of stimuli differed greatly. Despite this problem, the patients remained relatively good at identifying objects shown in conventional views. Consistent with the larger group studies of Warrington and colleagues (e.g., Rudge & Warrington, 1991; Warrington & James, 1991), the data suggest that conventional views of objects may be recognized in a relatively direct way based on viewpoint-centered object representations. Object-centered descriptions of objects may be used only to identify objects seen from unusual views, and the ability to encode such descriptions may be selectively disrupted by lesions to the posterior right hemisphere.

Other single case studies have documented patients who were relatively good at identifying objects seen from canonical views but who were selectively impaired with unusual views (e.g., Davidoff & De Bleser, 1994; Landis, Regard, Bleistle, & Kleihues, 1988; Sergent & Signoret, 1991). In the case of Davidoff and De Bleser, this problem extended beyond unusual views of objects to include photographs and line drawings relative to real objects. The authors propose that the patient had impaired access to stored structural knowledge about objects, which led to poor performance whenever visual information was relatively impoverished (e.g., with line drawings relative to real objects). Note that such a deficit, with line drawings depicting objects in conventional views, is unlikely to be due to problems in encoding an object-centered representation if conventional views of objects can be identified directly from their familiar viewpoint (see the earlier discussion). Also, as we point out later, patients with impaired access to stored structural knowledge about objects can match objects shown in conventional and unusual views. Davidoff and De Bleser's patient was relatively poor at matching objects across viewpoint, in addition to having impaired identification of line drawings. It may be, then, that the patient had two impairments – one affecting matching across viewpoints and one affecting access to stored structural knowledge (leading to the deficit with line drawings depicting objects in conventional views). Unusually, this patient had a unilateral left posterior lesion. Apparently, the presence of an intact right hemisphere did not enable the patient to match objects in unusual views. Interestingly, Sergent and Villemure (1989) reported a patient who had had a right hemispherectomy and was densely prosopagnosic, but who had good recognition of line drawings and of unusual photographs of objects. Here the absence of a right hemisphere did not lead to impaired object constancy. Nevertheless, the patients of Landis et al. (1988) and Sergent and Signoret (1991), who were all able to recognize objects shown in conventional but not in unconventional views, had unilateral right posterior lesions. From these single case analyses, the status of right- as opposed to left-hemisphere lesions in producing deficits in object constancy remains unclear.

2.3.3 Memorial agnosias

Taylor and Warrington (1971) first reported the case of an agnosic patient with severely impaired object recognition but with the ability to match objects shown in unusual views with those shown in conventional views. The patient also appeared to have grossly impaired stored knowledge about the objects he failed to identify – for instance, even being unable to generate accurate verbal descriptions of the objects from their names. Taylor and Warrington's case was influential in persuading theorists such as Marr (1982) to argue that object constancy could be achieved in a purely data-driven way, without recourse to stored knowledge. However, in such early studies of agnosia, no distinction was drawn between the ability of patients to access different types of stored knowledge. Later studies indicate that some patients can have relatively intact access to stored knowledge about the visual form of objects but still show impaired access to stored semantic or functional knowledge (Riddoch & Humphreys, 1987a; Sheridan & Humphreys, 1993; Stewart, Parkin, & Hunkin, 1992). That being the case, it is possible that patients could match objects across viewpoint by accessing common stored structural representations for the stimuli, and yet still be impaired at visual object recognition because of a semantic problem. However, more recent studies have shown that unusual-view matching can be achieved even by patients who have poor stored knowledge of the forms of objects (such patients fail to differentiate real objects from nonobjects, show poor drawing from memory, etc.; see Forde, Francis, Riddoch, Rumiati, & Humphreys, 1997). These last results are consistent with Marr's supposition that constancy can be achieved in a data-driven manner.

2.3.4 Identifying objects rotated within the plane: Mental rotation?

In studies of the recognition and matching of stimuli presented in unusual views, the stimuli have typically been transformed in depth so that many of their main features have been obscured. Other single case studies have reported patients with problems in dealing with stimuli rotated within the picture plane. Solms, Kaplan-Solms, Saling, and Miller (1988) documented the case of a 12-year-old boy with a bilateral frontal lesion who failed to identify the orientations of individual letters or lines; he also confused letters such as p and d, and q and b (which can be mapped onto each other by a plane rotation) when the letters were presented upright and in isolation. In addition, when copying and drawing from memory the Rey figure (Rey, 1941, 1959), he often rotated the figure by 90° or 180°, and he failed to identify the right–left orientation of other people. Interestingly, this patient reported having brief episodes of upside-down vision in which he perceived his entire visual array as being inverted. Nevertheless, despite an apparently severe inability to determine the orientation of stimuli, the patient did not reveal any difficulties in object recognition. At first, this study suggests that it is not necessary to compensate (achieve constancy) for within-plane rotations for recognition to occur. However, because the patient was only tested using symbols and abstract, novel stimuli, it is not clear that the results generalized to objects.

These concerns were, to some extent, addressed by Turnbull et al. (1995), who reported another patient with difficulties in establishing the orientation of objects. This patient, LG, had a right temporo-parietal lesion. She was unable to match the orientation of a line drawing of a familiar object to the orientation of a different "model" object unless the model object was depicted as being upright. Turnbull et al. suggested that in the latter case, LG used the orientation of the upright model drawing to help her position the second drawing, but without the context of this external cue to orientation, she was unable to perform the task. This result suggests that LG still has some knowledge of the canonical orientation of objects. LG also successfully matched the orientation of pairs of simple arrow stimuli, whether the model arrow was upright or plane rotated (although she performed poorly at a line orientation matching task requiring relatively fine discrimination of orientation), indicating that the deficit was not in matching orientation per se, but rather in determining the canonical upright of familiar objects. Interestingly, LG was unable to identify reliably the upright orientation of disoriented line drawings of familiar objects that she consistently named correctly. Thus, in this case, the problem extended beyond alphabetic stimuli. Indeed, LG showed very poor identification of objects shown in unusual, depth-rotated views (cf. Warrington & Taylor, 1973), so the problem extended beyond within-plane rotations. LG's case again suggests that computation of the canonical orientation of objects is not necessary to identify objects shown in canonical views.

In a similar study, Farah and Hammond (1988) reported a patient, RT, with a large right fronto-temporo-parietal lesion and only mild problems in recognizing line drawings of objects, people, and real objects. In contrast, RT was poor at copying figures and drawing objects from memory. Most interestingly, RT achieved object constancy over plane rotation (i.e., recognized plane-rotated numbers, words, and line drawings; reinterpreted the identity of letters according to their orientation; and identified the parts of misoriented shapes) but performed poorly (and significantly worse than age-matched controls) on three different tasks designed to test mental rotation (e.g., judging whether pairs of items rotated within the plane were reflected or not with respect to one another). RT's performance on imagery tasks that did not require mental rotation appeared to be normal relative to that of controls, suggesting that RT could generate images from memory and that only the specific ability to rotate images mentally was impaired. This result demonstrates that mental rotation is not essential (although in normal subjects it may be one strategy used) to recognize disoriented objects.

Object constancy for plane rotation can be achieved without using mental rotation, at least when orientation-invariant cues are available (note that, for example, the identification of individual misoriented letters that are mirror images of each other, such as *p* and *q, b* and *d,* may well require mental rotation). Patients with the opposite pattern of impairments to RT have also been reported. For example Warrington and James (1988) and Trojano and Grossi (1992) describe agnosic patients who, despite poor object recognition, were unimpaired at spatial and mental rotation tasks. Recognition, even of disoriented objects, and mental rotation abilities appear to dissociate. Contrary to some predictions made on the basis of the literature on normal object identification, the neuropsychological data suggest that mental rotation is not necessary for object constancy.

2.3.5 Prosopagnosia and object constancy

The term *prosopagnosia* refers to patients with a specific problem in visually recognizing faces, but without necessarily having a problem in recognizing other seen objects (e.g., De Renzi, 1986). Several studies have examined the ability of prosopagnosic patients to match two different views of the same face when the face is subject to changes in illumination or in view (e.g., as when a frontal and a profile view are shown; see Benton, 1980; Benton & Van Allen, 1968; De Renzi & Spinnler, 1966b; De Renzi et al., 1969; Diamond, Valentine, Mayes, & Sandel, 1994; Sergent & Signoret, 1991; Whiteley & Warrington, 1977). Whiteley and Warrington (1977) studied three prosopagnosics, comparing their performance on matching tasks involving both unusual views of objects and different views of faces. For at least one of the cases (Case 3), there was a clear dissociation between (i) an impaired ability to match two views of the same (unfamiliar) face or to name famous faces in the presence of (ii) an intact ability to name unusual views of an object. From this result, Whiteley and Warrington suggested that face processing may involve special mechanisms distinct from those required for object processing. However, it may also be argued that the face-matching task was simply more difficult than the unusual views task, or alternatively, that face matching taps specific abilities that are also required for object processing, but usually to a lesser extent (e.g., grouping and making use of configural information). These specific processing abilities may then be selectively impaired, with the effect being more serious on face processing relative to object processing.

In an interesting extension of tests of object constancy for face stimuli, Sergent and Signoret (1991) studied three prosopagnosics with unilateral right hemisphere lesions. The patients were taught to associate names to 12 novel faces. After extensive training the patients learned to identify the faces, and when tested 1 day later, they had retained their learning. However, when the patients were asked to identify different versions of the learned faces, they performed at a chance level. Sergent and Signoret suggested that the prosopagnosic patients thus had retained some ability to learn and recognize novel face stimuli; however, they were profoundly impaired at compensating for variations in the stimulus.

These studies confirm that prosopagnosics, like agnosics, can have major problems in achieving object constancy. They also indicate that the problems can be more severe for faces than for other objects. However, the studies do not clarify whether any selective effects with faces are due to the procedures for achieving constancy being particular to faces or whether effects reflect the greater complexity of faces relative to objects.

2.3.6 Convert achievement of object constancy: Extinction

One other interesting question that neuropsychological studies of object constancy have addressed is whether the achievement of object constancy is necessarily a conscious process. That is, can constancy be achieved even without conscious awareness of the stimulus? Note that we might expect conscious processes to be necessary if some form of mental imagery is involved. This issue has been addressed using patients who show visual extinction. The term *visual extinction* refers to the situation in which patients may identify or detect single stimuli presented to the side of the space contralateral to their lesion but show impaired identification or detection of the contralateral stimulus when a second stimulus is presented simultaneously on the ipsilesional side. It has been suggested for some time that even though the contralesional stimulus appears to be "extinguished," it may still be processed to some degree. The first study showing this was reported by Volpe, Ledoux, and Gazzaniga (1979). They documented the performance of four patients with right parietal lesions who could successfully name single words or outline drawings of objects presented to the right or the left visual field, but, when stimuli were shown simultaneously and bilaterally, only the stimulus in the right visual field was accurately named. Indeed, the patients denied the presence of the contralesional stimulus on many trials with bilateral stimulus presentations. Nevertheless, even though the patients showed extinction in the identification task, Volpe et al. found that they were able to make successful same/different physical match decisions to bilateral stimuli (i.e., respond "same" when the stimuli were physically identical and otherwise respond "different"). Similar results have been reported by Karnath and colleagues (Karnath, 1988; Karnath & Hartje, 1987). The question of interest for understanding visual object constancy is whether similarly good performance can be demonstrated for extinguished stimuli when matches involve stimuli changed in viewpoint.

Berti, Allport, Driver, Dienes, Oxbury, and Oxbury (1992) reported a single patient, EM, who, after a right temporal lobectomy, showed some visual extinction. Similar to the patients reported by Volpe et al. (1979), EM could match two identical photographs of familiar objects presented simultaneously to the right and left visual fields, although under these conditions, EM was often unable to name the object presented to the left visual field. Interestingly, EM's matching performance remained accurate if two different depth-rotated views of an object were presented to the left and right visual fields, or even if two different exemplars of the same object category were presented to the right and left visual fields. This result suggests that the processes involved in visual object constancy can be computed unconsciously, so that constancy is achieved even when stimuli are subsequently "extinguished" from the conscious report.

However, there are several problems with this interpretation of the data. For instance, although EM was relatively poor at identifying contralesional stimuli under bilateral presentation conditions, some items were identified on some occasions. This might be sufficient to raise matching performance above chance levels (see Verfaillie, Milberg, McGlinchey-Berroth and Grande, in press). Also, Farah, Monheit, and Wallace (1991) have argued that identification and matching tasks are not equated for difficulty because, as typically conducted, only matching uses forced-choice procedures. The advantage for matching over identification can be reduced or even eliminated when forced-choice procedures are used for identification too (although see Verfaellie et al., in press, for a counterargument). These problems mean that, although the neuropsychological data for constancy being achieved unconsciously are intriguing, they are far from conclusive.

References

Benson, D. F., & Greenberg, J. P. (1969) Visual form agnosia. *Archives of Neurology, 20,* 82–89.

Benton, A. L. (1980). The neuropsychology of facial recognition. *American Psychologist, 35,* 176–186.

Benton, A. L., & Van Allen, M. W. (1968). Impairment in facial recognition in patients with cerebral disease. *Cortex, 4,* 344–358.

Bergego, C., Deloche, G., Pradat-Diehl, P., Robineau, F., & Lauriot-Prevost, M.-C. (1993). Visual recognition in right brain-damaged patients: Evidence from a tachistoscopic confrontation naming task. *Brain and Language, 44,* 181–190.

Berti, A., Allport, A., Driver, J., Dienes, Z. J., & Oxbury, S. (1992). Levels of processing for visual stimuli in an "extinguished" field. *Neuropsychologica, 30,* 403–416.

Bottini, G., Cappa, S. F., & Vignolo, L. A. (1991). Somesthetic-visual matching disorders in right and left hemisphere-damaged patients. *Cortex, 27,* 223–228.

Bulla-Hellwig, M., Ettlinger, G., Dommasch, D., Ebel, E., & Skreczeck, W. (1992). Impaired visual perceptual categorisation in right brain-damaged patients: Failure to replicate. *Cortex, 28,* 261–272.

Butter, C. M., & Trobe, J. D. (1994). Integrative agnosia following progressive multifocal leukoencephalopathy. *Cortex, 30,* 145–158.

Campion, J. (1987) Apperceptive agnosia: The specification and description of constructs. In G. W. Humphreys & M. J. Riddoch (Eds.), *Visual object processing: A cognitive neuropsychological approach.* (pp. 182–209). London: Erlbaum.

Davidoff, J., & De Bleser, R. (1994). Impaired picture recognition with preserved object naming and reading. *Brain and Cognition, 24,* 1–23.

De Renzi, E. (1986). Prosopagnosia in two patients with CT scan evidence of damage confined to the right hemisphere. *Neuropsychologica, 24,* 385–389.

De Renzi, E., Scotti, G., & Spinnler, H. (1969). Perceptual and associative disorders of visual recognition. *Neurology, 19,* 634–642.

De Renzi, E., & Spinnler, H. (1966a). Visual recognition in patients with unilateral cerebral disease. *Journal of Nervous and Mental Disease, 142,* 515–525.

De Renzi, E., & Spinnler, H. (1966b). Facial recognition in brain-damaged patients. *Neurology, 6,* 145–152.

Diamond, B. J., Valentine, T., Mayes, A. R., & Sandel, M. E. (1994). Evidence of covert recognition in a prosopagnosic patient. *Cortex, 30,* 377–393.

Dricker, J., Butters, N., Berman, G., Samuels, I., & Carey, S. (1978). The recognition and encoding of faces by alcoholic Korsakoff and right hemisphere patients. *Neuropsychologica, 16,* 683–695.

Faglioni, P., Scotti, G., & Spinnler, H. (1969). Impaired recognition of written letters following unilateral damage. *Cortex, 5,* 327–342.

Farah, M. J., & Hammond, K. M. (1988). Mental rotation and orientation-invariant object recognition: Dissociable processes. *Cognition, 29,* 29–46.

Farah, M. J., Monheit, M. A., & Wallace, M. A. (1991). Unconscious perception of "extinguished" visual stimuli: Reassessing the evidence. *Neuropsychologica, 29,* 949–958.

Forde, E. M. E., Francis, D., Riddoch, M. J., Rumiati, R. I., & Humphreys, G. W. (1997). Category-specific naming deficit. *Cognitive Neuropsychology, 14,* 403–458.

Hamsher, K. DeS. (1978a). Stereopsis and the perception of anomalous contours. *Neuropsychologica, 16,* 453–459.

Hamsher, K. DeS. (1978b). Stereopsis and unilateral brain disease. *Investigative Ophthalmology, 4,* 336–343.

Humphrey, G. K., & Jolicoeur, P. (1993). An examination of the effects of axis foreshortening, monocular depth cues, and visual field identification. *Quarterly Journal of Experimental Psychology, 46A,* 137–159.

Humphreys, G. W., & Riddoch, M. J. (1984). Routes to object constancy: Implications from neurological impairments of object constancy. *Quarterly Journal of Experimental Psychology, 36A,* 385–415.

Humphreys, G. W., & Riddoch, M. J. (1987). *To see but not to see: A case study of visual agnosia.* London: Erlbaum.

Humphreys, G. W., & Riddoch, M. J. (1993) The object agnosias. In C. Kennard (Ed.), *Balliere's clinical neurology: clinical neuropsychology.* London: Balliere Tindall.

Humphreys, G. W., Riddoch, M. J., Donnelly, N., Freeman, T. A. C., Boucart, M., & Müller, H. M. (1994) Intermediate visual processing and visual agnosia. In M. J. Farah & G. Ratcliff (Eds.), *The neuropsychology of high-level vision.* Hillsdale, N.J.: Erlbaum.

Karnath, H. O. (1988). Deficits of attention in acute and recovered visual hemineglect. *Neuropsychologica, 26,* 27–43.

Karnath, H. O., & Hartje, W. (1987). Residual information processing in the neglected hemifield. *Journal of Neurology, 234,* 180–184.

Kerschensteiner, M., Hartje, W., Orgass, B., & Poeck, K. (1972). The recognition of simple and complex realistic figures in patients with unilateral brain lesions. *Archiv für Psychiatrie und Nervenkrankheiten, 216,* 188–200.

Landis, T., Regard, M., Bleistle, A., & Kleihues, P. (1988). Prosopagnosia and agnosia for noncanonical views. *Brain, 111,* 1287–1297.

Lansdell, H. C. (1968). Effects of extent of temporal lobe ablations on two lateralised defects. *Physiology of Behaviour, 3,* 271–273.

Layman, S., & Greene, E. (1988). The effect of stroke on object recognition. *Brain and Cognition, 7,* 87–114.

Lissauer, H. (1890). Ein fall von seelenblindheit nebst einem Beitrage zur Theorie derselben. *Archiv für Psychiatrie und Nervenkrankheiten, 21,* 222–270.

Marr, D. (1982). *Vision.* San Francisco: W. H. Freeman.

Milner, B. (1958). Psychological deficits produced by temporal lobe excision. *Proceedings of the Association for Research in Nervous and Mental Disease, 36,* 244–257.

Newcombe, F. (1974). Selective deficits after focal cerebral injury. In S. J. Diamond & J. G. Beaumont (Eds.), *Hemisphere function in the human brain* (pp. 359–412). London: Academic Press.

Newcombe, F., & Ratcliff, G. (1975). Agnosia: A disorder of object recognition. In F. Michel & B. Schott (Eds.), *Les Syndromes des Disconnection Calleuse chez l'Homme.* Lyon.: Colluque Internationale Lyon.

Newcombe, F., & Russell, W. R. (1969). Dissociated visual, perceptual and spatial deficits in focal lesions of the right hemisphere. *Journal of Neurology, Neurosurgery and Psychiatry, 32,* 73–81.

Perrett, D. I., Mistlin, A. J., & Chitty, A. J. (1987). Visual cells responsive to faces. *Trends in Neuroscience, 10,* 358–364.

Perrett, D. I., Mistlin, A. J., Chitty, A. J., Harries, M. H., Newcombe, F., & De Haan, E. (1988). Neuronal mechanisms of face perception and their pathology. In C. Kennard & F. Clifford Rose (Eds.), *Physiological aspects of clinical neuro-ophthalmology* (pp. 98–114). London: Chapman & Hall.

Perrett, D. I., Oram, M. W., Hietanen, J. K., & Benson, P. J. (1994) Issues of representation in object vision. In M. J. Farah & G. Ratcliff (Eds.), *The neuropsychology of higher vision* (pp. 89–96). Hillsdale, NJ: Erlbaum.

Perrett, D. I., Smith, P. A., Potter, D. D., Mistlin, A. J., Head, A. S., Milner, A. D., & Jeeves, M. A. (1984). Neurones responsive to faces in the temporal cortex: Studies of functional organisation, sensitivity to identity and relation to perception. *Human Neurobiology, 3,* 197–208.

Perrett, D. I., Smith, D. D., Potter, D. D., Mistlin, A. J., Head, A. S., Milner, A. D., & Jeeves, M. A. (1985). Visual cells in the temporal cortex sensitive to face view and gaze direction. *Proceedings of the Royal Society of London B, 223,* 293–317.

Ratcliff, G. (1979). Spatial thought, mental rotation, and the right cerebral hemisphere. *Neuropsychologica, 17,* 49–54.

Rey, A. (1941). L'examen psychologique dans les cas d'encephalopathie traumatique. *Archives de Psychologie, 28,* 286–340.

Rey, A. (1959). *Le test de Copie de Figure Complexe.* Paris: Editions Centre de Psychologie Appliquee.

Riddoch, M. J., & Humphreys, G. W. (1986). Neurological impairments of visual object constancy: The effects of orientation and size disparities. *Cognitive Neuropsychology, 3,* 207–224.

Riddoch, M. J. & Humphreys, G. W. (1987a). Visual object processing in optic aphasis: A case of semantic access agnosia. *Cognitive Neuropsychology, 4,* 131–186.

Riddoch, M. J., & Humphreys, G. W. (1987b). A case of integrative visual agnosia. *Brain, 110,* 1431–1462.

Rubens, A. B., & Benson, D. (1971). Associative visual agnosia. *Archives of Neurology (Chicago), 24,* 305–316.

Rudge, P., & Warrington, E. W. (1991). Selective impairment of memory and visual perception in splenial tumours. *Brain, 114,* 349–360.

Sergent, J., & Signoret, J. L. (1991). Outstanding issues in the study of prosopagnosia. *Journal of Clinical and Experimental Neuropsychology, 13,* 34.

Sergent, J., & Villemure, J. G. (1989). Prosopagnosia in a right hemispherectomized patient. *Brain, 112,* 975–995.

Sheridan, J., & Humphreys, G. W. (1993) A verbal-semantic category-specific recognition impairment. *Cognitive Neuropsychology, 10,* 143–184.

Solms, M., Kaplan-Solms, K., Saling, M., & Miller, P. (1988). Inverted vision after frontal lobe disease. *Cortex, 24,* 499–509.

Stewart, F., Parkin, A. J., & Hunkin, N. M. (1992) Naming impairments following recovery from herpes simplex encephalitis: Category-specific? *Quarterly Journal of Experimental Psychology, 44*, 261–284.

Tarr, M. J. (1995) Rotating object to recognize them: A case study on the role of viewpoint-dependency in the recognition of three-dimensional objects. *Psychonomic Bulletin & Review, 2*, 55–82.

Taylor, A. M., & Warrington, E. K. (1971). Visual agnosia: A single case report. *Cortex, 7*, 152–161.

Teuber, H. L. (1975). Effects of brain injury on human behavior. In D. B. Tower (Ed.), *The nervous system*, Volume 2, *The Clinical Neuroscience*. New York: Raven Press.

Trojano, L., & Grossi, D. (1992). Impaired drawing from memory in a visual agnosic patient. *Brain and Cognition, 20*, 327–344.

Turnbull, O. H., Laws, K. R., & McCarthy, R. A. (1995). Object recognition without knowledge of object orientation. *Cortex, 31*, 387–395.

Verfaillie, M., Milberg, W., McGlinchey-Berroth, R., & Grande, L. (in press). Comparison of cross-field matching and forced-choice identification in hemispatial neglect. *Neuropsychology*.

Volpe, B. T., LeDoux, J. E., & Gazzaniga, M. S. (1979). Information processing of visual stimuli in an "extinguished" field. *Nature, 282*, 722–724.

Warrington, E. K. (1982). Neuropsychological studies of object recognition. *Proceedings of the Royal Society of London B, 298*, 15–33.

Warrington, E. K. (1985). Agnosia: The impairment of object recognition. In J. A. M. Frederiks (Ed.), *Handbook of clinical neurology*, Volume 1: *Clinical Neuropsychology*. Amsterdam: North Holland.

Warrington, E. K., & James, M. (1967). Disorders of visual perception in patients with localised cerebral lesions. *Neuropsychologica, 5*, 253–266.

Warrington, E. K., & James, M. (1986). Visual object recognition in patients with right hemisphere lesions: Axes or features? *Perception, 15*, 355–366.

Warrington, E. K., & James, M. (1988). Visual apperceptive agnosia: A clinico-anatomical study of three cases. *Cortex, 24*, 13–32.

Warrington, E. K., & James, M. (1991). A new test of object decision: 2-D silhouettes featuring a minimal view. *Cortex, 27*, 377–383.

Warrington, E. K., & Taylor, A. M. (1973). The contribution of the right parietal lobe to object recognition. *Cortex, 9*, 152–164.

Warrington, E. K., & Taylor, A. M. (1978). Two categorical stages of object recognition. *Perception, 7*, 695–705.

Whiteley, A. M., & Warrington, E. K. (1977). Prosopagnosia: A clinical, psychological and anatomical study of three patients. *Journal of Neurology, Neurosurgery and Psychiatry, 40*, 395–403.

9   Color constancy and color vision during infancy: Methodological and empirical issues

James L. Dannemiller

1. Introduction

The majority of objects in our environments reflect incident light to our eyes. This means that the light that reaches our eyes from an object depends on both the surface and subsurface material characteristics of the object and on the spectral distribution of the incident light. Were the incident light constant in its spectral character, there would be no problem in identifying an object based on the light that it reflects to our eyes. But as is well known, the spectral makeup of the light incident on objects in our environments is anything but constant. The light from the sun varies in its spectral distribution, depending on the time of day, weather conditions, reflection and filtering by forest canopies, and so on. This presents the visual system with a fundamental problem: A constant object does not reflect a constant spectral distribution of light to the eye. Somehow this variation in incident light must be taken into account in rendering an estimate of an object's color. This is the problem of color constancy.

The purpose of this chapter is to provide a review of what we do know about the developmental aspects of color constancy. Preliminary to understanding these studies on color vision and color constancy during infancy, a discussion of current methodologies in infant vision is presented. Brief mention is made of our current understanding of color vision and color appearance during infancy. Several empirical studies of color constancy will be discussed. Finally, the relationship between color constancy and adaptation is discussed in a developmental context.

2. Methodological preliminaries

Two primary methods are available to assess color vision and color appearance during infancy: (1) the Forced Choice Preferential Looking Technique (FPL;

The writing of this chapter was supported by a sabbatical from the University of Wisconsin—Madison and by R01 Grant HD23247 from NICHHD. I thank Dick Aslin and Marty Banks for a brief discussion of the potential relationship between chromatic discrimination and color constancy.

229

Teller, 1979) and the habituation of visual attention technique. The former is used to ask questions about basic aspects of color vision such as spectral sensitivity, chromatic discrimination, and brightness discrimination. The latter is used primarily to ask questions about the appearance of an object or pattern. My discussion is confined to behavioral techniques, although it should be noted that visually evoked potentials have also proved useful for assessing color vision in infants (Allen, Banks, & Norcia, 1993). It is useful to review these methods because most of what we know about color vision during this period is a result of studies employing these methods. The reader who is familiar with current methods of assessing visual perception in infants may skip section 2 and move to section 3.

2.1 The FPL Technique

The FPL procedure has been widely used to study color vision during infancy. This procedure combines a method of determining threshold with a technique pioneered by Fantz for assessing visual discrimination (Fantz, 1958, 1965). Fantz showed that very young infants tend to look at a patterned field if given a choice between looking at a uniform field on one side of a display and a patterned field on the other. This tendency to fixate or look longer at the patterned side of the display is sometimes referred to as a *visual preference*, hence, the name that is often attached to this technique – *preferential looking (PL)*. The term *visual preference* does not carry any connotation of aesthetics, as is often the case when one speaks of a preference: It simply implies that the infant has a tendency to fixate patterned visual stimulation rather than unpatterned visual stimulation.

As Fantz originally used this PL procedure, the amount of time that an infant spent looking at the patterned field usually was measured. This was compared to the amount of time that the infant spent looking at the uniform field. Statistical comparison across a group of infants was then used to infer the detectability of the visual pattern. If the amount of time spent looking at the pattern was significantly greater than the amount of time spent looking at the uniform field, then it was inferred that the pattern was detectable by the group as a whole. Notice that as with all statistical tests, the absence of a significant effect may not be interpreted here as a failure to detect the pattern. It is entirely possible that the infants may be able to detect the pattern but may not be motivated enough to differentially fixate it. Here we have one of the primary differences between psychophysical studies with infants and with adults. Adult subjects may be instructed to respond whenever they detect a pattern, but the experimenter can offer no such instruction to infants. Rather, the technique is limited by the strength of the natural tendency of infants to fixate the pattern in question. This makes the PL and the associated FPL procedures yield conservative estimates of what is and what is not detectable by infants. It is always possible that the infant can actually detect a stimulus with less energy, contrast, and so on than are revealed with these techniques.

Teller's adaptation of the PL technique involves adding a rigorous psychophysical procedure to measure a detection threshold for some quantity. As the name implies, the observer is required to make a forced choice on each trial. This choice usually concerns the location of the stimulus on each trial. Is the stimulus on the right or on the left? The adult who is observing the infant uses any information available from the infant to make this judgment. Orienting behaviors such as directional eye and head movements by the infant are used typically to make these judgments. Because the adult is "blind" to the location of the stimulus on each trial and because the location is randomized across trials, it follows that above-chance performance by the adult observer implies that the infant has been able to detect the stimulus. As mentioned earlier, and as noted by Teller and others, chance behavior does not imply that the stimulus was not detectable.

The structure of the data from an FPL procedure is similar to that of classical forced-choice signal detection data gathered from adult subjects, yet it is also different. It is similar because, by varying the signal strength (e.g., contrast, luminance), one can derive a psychometric function for the infant's detection of the stimulus. Just as with adults, one may use various techniques, such as maximum likelihood procedures (Maloney, 1990), to estimate a threshold from this psychometric function. It is different from adult forced-choice procedures because it is a form of double psychophysics. The forced choice by the adult observer is one step removed from the stimulus. The adult is observing the infant, who, in turn, is observing the stimulus. The psychometric function that results from this procedure, then, depends on the infant's sensitivity to the stimulus and on the adult's sensitivity to the infant's orienting signals. This latter component of the method adds a potentially "noisy" channel to the situation that is not present in the single psychophysics of classical adult forced-choice procedures (Banks & Dannemiller, 1987).

What are the practical consequences of this double psychophysics inherent in the FPL procedure? First, the addition of a potentially noisy channel to the situation can do nothing but lose information. This implies that the threshold estimated using the FPL procedure can only be regarded as a conservative estimate. Here again, we have a factor whose effect is to render conservative threshold estimates. Second, the double psychophysics of the FPL procedure may add variability to infant data that is not present in adult data. This could arise because, in addition to any individual sensitivity differences that might exist between infants, one has to consider the potential interaction between infants and the FPL observer. Some infants may be more "readable" in the cues that they emit than others. This has nothing to do with the visual sensitivity of interest, but rather with the behaviors that are indicative of detection. The ultimate result of such variability in behavioral orienting is to add group variance to threshold estimates for infants. One must keep these limitations in mind when interpreting threshold estimates and variability derived from the FPL procedure.

Fortunately, there are two arguments that makes one of these limitations less forceful. First, Banks and Dannemiller (1987) advanced an argument regarding the distinction between absolute and relative threshold values. The preceding statement that FPL results in conservative threshold estimates is certainly true as far as it goes. However, many times in the study of color vision, one is not interested in the absolute value of a threshold, but rather in its value relative to those of other thresholds collected by varying a single parameter. For example, in considering spectral sensitivity, one is interested in the relative sensitivity to light of different wavelengths. The absolute value of this threshold may be of interest in some contexts, but generally, in assessing the spectral sensitivity of infants, we are interested in how their spectral sensitivity curve compares to an adult curve collected under similar conditions or in how the shape of the curve depends on luminance level. Questions such as these, which are designed to reveal aspects of the mechanisms of color vision during infancy, are unaffected by the imposition of a double psychophysical procedure, provided that there is no interaction between the dimension of variation (e.g., wavelength) and the sensitivity of the FPL observer or the infant's orienting behavior.

Second, some of the questions that are important in studies of infant color vision are either/or questions. Can infants make Raleigh or tritan pair discriminations (Hamer, Alexander, & Teller, 1982; Varner, Cook, Schneck, McDonald, & Teller, 1985)? These questions are not about the absolute value of some threshold. Rather, the successful demonstration of a Rayleigh discrimination is sufficient to allow the inference that the infant has at least two functional cone types operating above 550 nm and the neural machinery to compare their outputs. The FPL technique, because it belongs to the class of objective signal detection procedures, is sufficient for answering such either/or questions despite its double psychophysical characteristic.

Finally, one of the reasons mentioned earlier for considering FPL thresholds to be conservative is that they are affected potentially by the motivation of the infant to orient toward the stimulus. Without some way of gauging just how strong this motivation is, one is forced to assume that the threshold might always be lower if one could somehow motivate the infant more strongly. An alternative solution to this problem is to find a behavior that is more "obligatory" in the sense that it is under more rigid stimulus control than are the typical orienting behaviors involved in FPL. An example of such a behavior is optokinetic nystagmus (OKN). Teller and Lindsey (1989) have shown that the FPL procedure may be used to make directional judgments about the tracking phase of OKN to measure sensitivity to chromatic stimuli in infants. The slopes from the psychometric functions collected with this technique are remarkably steep and typically much steeper than those collected using the standard FPL procedure. Partly this is because these psychometric functions range from 0% to 100%, in contrast to standard FPL functions, which range from 50% to 100%. That is, the observer makes a judgment about the direction of the slow phase of OKN, so these judgments range from 0% "left" to 100% "left" as the stimulus contrast is varied. But, perhaps more important, the slopes of the psychometric function in this variation of FPL may be steeper because OKN is a more strongly reflexive behavior than are the other orienting behaviors involved in standard FPL.

2.2 Habituation of visual attention

As mentioned earlier, the assessment of color constancy requires that we ask the infant how similar an object appears across an illuminant change. In adults, it is possible to use matching procedures to answer this question. It is also possible to use rating procedures in which the adult is asked to rate the similarity of appearance of the object. But these direct techniques obviously are unavailable to the experimenter who wishes to examine color constancy in infants. Instead, one may use an indirect technique – the habituation of visual attention – to ask this question. As with FPL, this technique relies on another innate tendency of infants: their tendency to respond with increased attention to novel-appearing stimuli or events.

The logic of this method is straightforward. The infant is repeatedly shown the same object, and attention to that object is monitored. Usually this is done in discrete trials, and an adult records bouts or periods of looking at the stimulus during each of these trials. As with many organisms presented with repeated stimulation, responding wanes over trials. In this case, this takes the form of less looking at the stimulus across trials. Once the average looking time has dropped to some criterion percentage of its initial level, visual attention is said to have been *habituated*. If a novel stimulus is now introduced on the next trial, and if the infant perceives this stimulus to be sufficiently different from the previously viewed stimulus, then it is expected that visual attention will recover. This takes the form of an increase in looking at the novel stimulus. In this way, one may "ask" the infant how similar the habituated and novel stimuli appear.

Several steps must be taken when this technique is used to ensure that the logic just described obtains. The habituation to the first stimulus is generally taken to imply some sort of encoding of this stimulus. The nature of this encoding is still subject to debate (Ackles & Karrer, 1991; Dannemiller & Banks, 1983b), but the important methodological issue here is that this stimulus-specific decrease in visual attention be distinguished from general fatigue. This may be accomplished in two ways. First, it is possible to assess the infant's attention to a "warm-up" stimulus prior to beginning the habituation trials. At the end of the session, this same stimulus may then be re-presented. If the infant looks at the warm-up stimulus as long at the end of the session as he or she did at the beginning of the session, then it may be inferred that the decrease in visual attention during the habituation trials was not caused by general fatigue. Another probe for the stimulus specificity of the habituation stimulus is the use of both novel and familiar intermixed test trials. If the same stimulus used during the habituation phase of the experiment is re-presented during the test phase, then any difference in visual attention between the novel and familiar test stimuli may be assumed to be due to the novelty of the test stimulus with general fatigue removed. In other words, general fatigue would be expected to affect attention to both novel and familiar stimuli equally by definition, so any difference in visual attention has this effect removed or controlled.

It is important to note the limitations of the habituation methodology for assessing the appearance of stimuli to the infant. First, failure to demonstrate significant recovery of visual attention to a novel test object does not imply that the infant cannot discriminate the habituated and novel stimuli. This is similar to the limitation in FPL that forces us to acknowledge that null results – lack of above-chance detection – do not imply lack of detection. Nonsignificant differences between two stimuli presented at test only imply that the infant finds both stimuli to be approximately equally interesting in the context of what he or she has just seen during the habituation phase of the experiment. But note also that if the same group of infants responds approximately equally to the habituated stimulus and one test stimulus, yet increases their attention to a second test stimulus, then we may rightly conclude that this second test stimulus appears different from the other two stimuli. In this sense, a within-subject demonstration of generalization to one test stimulus and lack of generalization to another stimulus at least allows us to rank order these two test stimuli in terms of how similar they both appear to the habituated stimulus. For some purposes, this may be sufficient for the experimental question being posed (see the color categorization studies in section 3).

2.3 Summary: Behavioral methodologies in infant vision and visual perception

The strengths and limitations of the FPL procedure for assessing infant color vision and the habituation of visual attention procedure for assessing the appearances of objects must be considered in interpreting the results of color vision studies with infants. Questions of color vision that allow comparison of the relative values of thresholds (e.g., spectral sensitivity) or that involve either/or aspects of color vision (e.g., Rayleigh discriminations) lend themselves well to investigation using the FPL procedure. Questions about the ordinal degree of similarity in the appearance of two or more stimuli are well suited to the habituation methodology. Questions about the absolute value of a threshold are not as easily interpreted with the FPL methodology. Despite these limitations, the research discussed in section 3 shows that we have learned much about the color vision of infants using these methods.

3. Ontogenetic aspects of color vision and color appearance

Any study of the developmental aspects of color constancy must take as its starting point our understanding of color vision in general during this period. It is also helpful to review briefly what we know about the maturity of the various anatomical structures in the visual pathway during this period. It is not my intention to provide a comprehensive review of color vision during infancy and early childhood. The reader may find such reviews in other sources (Banks & Shannon, 1993; Brown, 1987, 1990; Teller & Bornstein, 1987). Rather, I highlight the parts of what we know about the development of color vision that are relevant to the problem of color constancy. For example, it would be useful to understand the chromatic discrimination capabilities of young infants because one might argue that the problem of color constancy could actually be less severe for infants than for adults if infants' thresholds for discriminating color were substantially higher than those of adults. Subtle variations in the hue of an object under different illuminants might go unnoticed by the infant yet be readily apparent to adults. *intro - what my problem of my paper will be*

3.1. The retino-geniculo-cortical pathway

S, M, L cones

The neural substrate for color vision involves the three photoreceptor types and the postreceptoral pathways through the lateral geniculate nucleus and visual cortical areas. Hereafter, the three photoreceptor types will be referred to as the *short-, middle-* and *long-wavelength sensitive cones (SWS, MWS,* and *LWS,* respectively). Anatomical studies show that newborn human infants possess cones in their retinae (Abramov et al., 1982), but the cones near the fovea of the human newborn are morphologically distinct from those of the human adult fovea (Yuodelis & Hendrickson, 1986). This immaturity of cone morphology in the newborn's foveal area might lead one to predict that color vision at this age should be less well developed than in the adult. This is indeed the case.

Several aspects of the foveal packing structure and the morphology of the individual cones are worth noting. These anatomical aspects of the retina during this early period are reviewed in detail in Banks and Shannon (1993). First, the density of the cones near the fovea in the newborn human is much less than it is in the adult. More relevant to the question of color vision is the morphology of these individual cones. The cones in the newborn retina near the fovea are

(1) Cones - in infant S, M, L.

much shorter than their adult counterparts. In addition, the wave-guide properties of the inner segments for funneling light to the photopigment-containing outer segments are much less mature in the infant. The net effect of these morpho-logical differences in the cones of young infants is that they are much less efficient at capturing photons. The net effect of these and other immaturities in the infant retina was estimated by Banks and Shannon (1993) to be a 350:1 difference in efficiency. Such a large difference in the efficiency of capturing light is significant because all subsequent processing of color depends on the signals generated at this first stage in the visual pathway.

The anatomical data of Yuodelis and Hendrickson (1986) show that the ret-inal ganglion cells are present in humans at birth. We currently do not know how physiologically mature these ganglion cells are during this period.

The next stage in the visual pathway is the lateral geniculate nucleus (LGN). Studies by Garey (1984), de Courten and Garey (1982), and Hickey (1977) indicate that the LGN is immature at birth in humans, and that between the ages of birth and 6 months the volume of the LGN doubles to its approximate adult size. The laminar pattern so characteristic of the LGN is present at birth, indi-cating that the magnocellular and parvocellular distinction is present at least anatomically in humans at the time vision begins. There is a rapid over-proliferation of LGN synaptic connectivity over the first postnatal months, fol-lowed by a decrease to adult levels by the second year of life.

Cortical circuits are also immature at birth in humans. Conel's (Conel, 1939, 1941, 1947) elegant studies of neuronal morphology in human visual cortex show rapid development of this morphology over the first several months. As in the thalamus, there appears to be an overproduction of potential synapses in humans in the homolog of visual cortical area V1, followed by a reduction in the number of such structures to adult levels by the second year of life (Garey, 1984). Functionally, there is also evidence that the visual cortex undergoes sub-stantial postnatal maturation. Using position emission tomography, Chugani and Phelps (1986) showed striking differences in the activity of thalamic and cortical structures during the first year of life. Relative to thalamic structures, visual cortex was much less active at birth but showed continued maturation of activity over the first year of life.

Neurophysiological studies suggest that area V4 in the monkey (Zeki, 1980) and its homolog in humans (Lueck et al., 1989) are important for processing color and in the operation of color constancy (Walsh, Carden, Butler, & Kuli-kowski, 1993; although see also Heywood, Gadotti, & Cowey, 1992; Plendl et al., 1993). Unfortunately, no direct studies exist on the maturity of this cortical area early in life. We may infer from the study by Chugani and Phelps (1986) that this cortical area is probably immature at birth and shows postnatal devel-opment over the first year, like other visual cortical areas. In fact, Chugani and

Phelps suggest that structures above the midbrain are functionally quite immature at birth.

We must also consider the preretinal absorption characteristics of the lentic-
ular and macular pigments in any discussion of color vision. Longitudinal research clearly suggests that the spectral filtering properties of these structures
change over the course of the lifespan (Werner, 1982; Werner, Donnelly, &
Kliegl, 1987). In particular, less short wavelength light reaches the retina later
in life. This means that the average spectral composition of light on the retina
changes developmentally. The importance of this for color constancy is discussed later.

3.2 A brief review of color vision during infancy

I turn next to a brief review of our current understanding of the state of color
vision during early infancy. This review covers studies on basic aspects of color
vision, such as whether infants are trichromats, and studies on the appearance
of chromatic stimuli. The latter studies are included because color constancy
involves the appearance of colored surfaces under different illuminants.

3.2.1 Basic aspects of color vision during early infancy.

Infants are probably
trichromatic by the third month of life (Banks & Shannon, 1993). Of course,
this does not mean that color vision is mature by this age, but only that there
appear to be three functional cone types and the postreceptoral circuits necessary
to compare their signals. In contrast, infants 8 weeks of age and younger often
fail one or more of the chromatic discrimination tests indicative of trichromatic
vision. This conclusion is based on years of study, primarily by Teller and her
colleagues, using the FPL procedure discussed earlier (for reviews of this work,
see Banks & Shannon, 1993; Brown, 1990; Teller & Lindsey, 1993). Electrophysiological studies have contributed also to the conclusion that three functional cone types are present in the visual system, probably by 1.5 to 2 months
of age (Allen, Banks, & Norcia, 1993; Volbrecht & Werner, 1987). I will rely
on the reviews cited earlier to summarize what we know about the status of
infant color vision in the months after birth. The interested reader should consult
these sources and the original studies for details.

Consider what types of experiments are necessary to establish the existence
of trichromacy, and chromatic discrimination in particular, when the subjects
are young human infants. Classical color-matching experiments are not possible;
it is not possible to ask an infant to match a broadband light with a mixture of
three primaries. It is possible, however, to ask whether the infant is capable of
making several types of chromatic discriminations that are indicative of trichromacy. Rayleigh discriminations indicate the existence of at least two distinct

cone classes covering the long-wavelength region of the visible spectrum (over 550 nm). Normal human trichromats are dichromatic in this region because the SWS cones are too insensitive above 550 nm to provide useful signals for chromatic discrimination. So, positive evidence of discrimination of two wavelengths in this region must indicate the presence of at least two photoreceptor types and the associated neural circuits necessary to compare their signals. Tritan pair discriminations indicate the existence of functional SWS cones because the pairs of wavelengths are chosen to be indistinguishable to the LWS and MWS cones, leaving only differential activity in the SWS cones to mediate the discrimination. The successful discrimination of a tritan pair is strong evidence that the SWS cones are functional.

The numerous studies addressing these discriminations converge on the conclusion that 3-month-olds can make these two types of discriminations, most 1-month-olds fail at least one of them, and 2-month-olds are in transition. The most consistent failures involve discriminations thought to be mediated by the activity of the SWS cones. For example, Adams, Courage, and Mercer (1994) found that approximately 75% of newborn infants discriminated a broadband red (dominant wavelength 660 nm) from a neutral gray surround at all relative luminances tested. In contrast, only 14% of these same newborns discriminated a broadband blue (dominant wavelength 475 nm) from the same gray surround at all relative luminances tested. Varner et al. (1985) found that 8-week-olds could make reliable tritan pair discriminations, whereas 4-week-olds could not discriminate the wavelength pairs reliably.

Why do infants at these young ages fail to make certain chromatic discriminations that are readily made by adults with trichromatic color vision? One might be led to propose that there are specific deficits in chromatic processing mechanisms, with rapid development of these mechanisms over the first 3 months of life. But a simpler explanation for these results has been proposed (Banks & Bennett, 1988; Banks & Shannon, 1993; see also Teller & Lindsey, 1993). The poor chromatic discrimination shown by young infants is probably a manifestation of the poor efficiency of the first stage in their visual systems: the capture of photons by their photoreceptors. Recall that anatomical data indicate that the photoreceptors of the human newborn are markedly immature relative to their adult counterparts. Banks and his colleagues used ideal observer analysis (Geisler, 1989) to show that many of the discriminations failed by young infants may be explained simply on the basis of their reduced visual efficiency. Notice that this is not an explanation based on chromatic processing deficits per se, but rather one that applies to achromatic discriminations as well. The essence of the explanation is that an ideal observer who has the visual system front end (photoreceptor lattice, photoreceptor structure, and optics) of a newborn human infant would be expected to fail many of the chromatic discriminations that have been tested in previous studies.

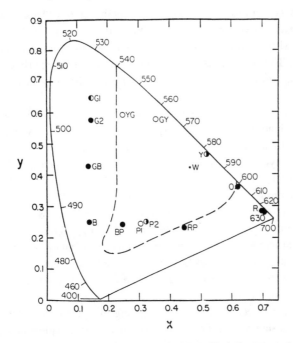

Figure 9.1. Example of calculations using an ideal observer model to predict chromatic discrimination in human infants. The dashed line shows chromaticities that should be just discriminable from white (W) for an ideal observer with the optics and photoreceptor characteristics of an 8-week-old human infant. Chromaticities inside the boundary line should not be discriminable from white; those outside the boundary line should be discriminable from white. The filled circles show chromaticities that all infants discriminated from white (W). Open circles represent consistent failures. Half-filled circles represent chromaticities that some infants discriminated from white. From Banks and Bennett (1988).

An example of such an analysis is shown in Figure 9.1, taken from Banks and Bennett (1988). Here Banks and Bennett reanalyzed the neutral point discrimination data published by Peeples and Teller (1975) and Teller, Peeples, and Sekel (1978). In these studies, 2-month-olds were tested for their ability to discriminate white light from various chromatic lights. The use of the term *neutral point test* is meant to indicate that a failure to make these discriminations in a particular region of the spectrum could indicate a form of dichromacy. Human dichromats show neutral points – regions of nondiscrimination – in particular regions of the spectrum, with the neutral point indicative of the type of dichromacy. The failures exhibited by 2-month-olds in these studies were similar, although not identical, to the failures exhibited by adult tritanopes or anomalous trichromats. The dashed curve in Figure 9.1 indicates the boundary of chromaticities that should be discriminable from white light by 2-month-olds given the stimulus conditions in the two neutral point studies. This discrimination boundary was derived by Banks and Bennett (1988) from their ideal observer analysis without any auxiliary assumptions about specific chromatic processing deficits. The predictions and the observed data match fairly closely, indicating that these chromatic discrimination failures may be explained by poor visual efficiency.

Most of the data on chromatic discriminations and the failure of infants to make those discriminations are readily explained using this poor visual efficiency hypothesis (Banks & Shannon, 1993). But not all of the data are explainable with this hypothesis. In particular, Banks and Bennett (1988) and Banks and Shannon (1993) found it necessary to invoke an additional deficit in the SWS cones or their associated postreceptoral processing pathways to explain the tritan pair discrimination failures reported by Varner et al. (1985) and other discrimination failures reported by Clavadetscher, Brown, Ankrum, and Teller (1988). The visual efficiency explanation proposed by Banks and Bennett (1988) actually predicts that 3- and 4-week-olds should be able to make many of the discriminations reported in these two studies when the data show that they fail to make these discriminations.

Finally, three other aspects of color vision during this period are relevant to the issue of color constancy. The first is the existence of chromatic opponency, the second is the operation of an achromatic channel in infants, and the third is the influence of spatial factors on infants' chromatic discriminations. Brown and Teller (1989), using a chromatic adaptation paradigm, showed that 3-month-old infants probably possess a functional red-green opponent channel. This channel computes a signal that is the difference or the ratio of the signals from the LWS and MWS cones, as has been demonstrated in adults (Ingling, 1977). It is also relevant in this regard that the achromatic or brightness channel that is thought to be the sum of the signals in the MWS and LWS cones is probably operative in very young infants. The evidence for this comes from studies by Teller and Lindsey (1989) showing that the relative luminances at which chromatic and achromatic gratings match, using a motion-nulling OKN technique, are very similar in 2-month-olds and adults using their peripheral vision. This probably indicates that the achromatic channel in young infants is similar to this channel in adults (see also Peeples & Teller, 1978).

Studies also show that chromatic discrimination by infants is heavily influenced by the size of the test field (Adams, Maurer, & Cashin, 1990; Hamer et al., 1982; Packer, Hartmann, & Teller, 1984). This is probably a manifestation of the notably coarser spatial pattern vision shown by young infants (for a review, see Banks & Dannemiller, 1987). This has implications for color constancy in the sense that objects that are quite small relative to the scale of the infant's visual system may be perceptually unstable in their chromatic appearance because of the extreme dependency of the infant's chromatic discrimination on the spatial characteristics of the stimulus.

3.2.2 Preretinal absorption effects. As noted earlier, several studies have shown changes over the lifespan in the spectral absorption characteristics of the ocular media (Werner, 1982; Werner et al., 1987). It is commonly acknowledged that such differences between adults and infants must be taken into account in trying to understand developing spectral sensitivity. Dannemiller (1989b) suggested that some computational models of color constancy would seem to imply that changes in preretinal absorption, if not taken into account, might alter the perceived color of objects. It is noteworthy in this regard that a recent study by Werner and Schefrin (1993) shows that from early adolescence through approximately 70 years of age, the locus of the achromatic point does not change significantly despite substantial prereceptoral filtering differences caused by aging. The achromatic point is the chromaticity that appears white to an observer. Werner and Schefrin noted that this invariance demands some sort of compensatory process in the visual system to preserve the constancy of "white" across the lifespan. They also noted that the type of compensation required by these developmental changes in the optic media is no different in principle from that required to compensate for changes in the spectral character of the illuminant in the course of a day. The only difference is in the time scale of these changes, although both could be considered infinitely slow given the intrinsic time constants involved in neural responses in the early visual system. They hypothesized that some of the same mechanisms involved in color constancy under different illuminants might also be involved in compensating for these developmental changes. In particular, they hypothesized that there might be some form of long-term adaptation by the photoreceptors to the chromatic locus of average daylight; the adaptation would take the form of gain changes that maintain equal outputs from the three cone types to average daylight.

3.2.3 Summary: Infant color vision. Data suggest that infants are probably trichromatic by 3 months of age. Younger infants show some failures of chromatic discrimination, especially those involving the SWS cones. There is some indication that the poor chromatic discrimination exhibited by infants under 8 to 12 weeks of age may result from a combination of poor visual efficiency and some deficit involving the SWS cones or their associated postreceptoral pathways (Banks & Shannon, 1993). Perhaps the most remarkable aspect of early color vision is its rapid development over the first 3 postnatal months (Brown, 1990). This does not imply that color vision is mature by this age; we do not currently know when color vision can be considered mature. There are clear differences between young children and adults on standard tests of color vision (e.g., Roy, Podgor, Collier, & Gunkel, 1991), although it is difficult to separate general attentional factors, especially at young ages, from true differences in color vision.

3.3 Studies of color appearance during infancy

I turn next to a review of several studies of color appearance during infancy. The most relevant studies for this purpose are those concerning hue categorization. These studies have examined evidence that infants perceptually divide the visible wavelength spectrum into the hue categories in a manner similar to adults. Other studies that have asked questions about the encoding of and short-term memory for color are also discussed.

3.3.1 Studies of infants' use of color in pattern perception.

Several studies have examined the ways in which infants encode colored forms. For example, one might wish to know whether an infant who has seen a red circle and a green square will be able to distinguish the presentation of a red square or a green circle from these two previous figures. These studies tell us something about the appearance and discriminability of chromatic patterns for young infants.

Several early studies found very little evidence that color was encoded reliably by infants during habituation. For example, Cohen, Gelber, and Lazar (1971) found that it took changes in both the color and the form of a pattern to produce reliable increases in attention following habituation. Similarly, Saayman, Ames, and Moffett (1964) found that changes in color or form alone failed to evoke differential responding, but changes on both dimensions produced reliable attentional increases in 3-month-olds. Welch (1974) also found that changes in color alone failed to evoke differential attention to a novel pattern, whereas changes in the color, shape, and arrangement of pattern elements together evoked differential attention. These studies suggest very poor encoding of color among young infants.

In contrast to these studies, Bushnell and Roder (1985) found that 4-month-olds attended more to novel combinations of color and form than they did to previously seen combinations of color and form. In other words, they encoded both the color and the form of a stimulus jointly and responded as if any change in this relationship produced a new object. This contrasts with earlier work by Cohen (1973), who found that 4-month-olds did not respond differentially to novel combinations of color and form. It is not clear why one of these studies found evidence for this type of joint encoding of color and form and the other did not. Results of these types of studies sometimes depend on the particulars of the habituation methodology used. It is clear from the Bushnell and Roder study, however, that at least under some conditions, it is possible to demonstrate that infants encode the color of an object or pattern in remembering its appearance.

Further evidence for the encoding of color by young infants comes from work by Adams and his colleagues (Adams, 1989; Adams, Courage, and Mercer, 1991; Maurer & Adams, 1987). In these studies, newborn and 1-month-old infants are habituated to an achromatic form that varies in luminance over the course of the habituation trials. In other words, the form remains achromatic over the habituation trials, but its luminance varies from trial to trial. The purpose of this luminance variation is to desensitize the infant to the absolute luminance level of the pattern. During the test phase of the experiment, a novel luminance for this achromatic stimulus is presented, as is a chromatic stimulus whose photometric luminance falls within the range previously presented during habituation. Using this procedure, Adams has been able to demonstrate that the change from an achromatic to a chromatic form produces an increase in visual attention for many chromaticities. In addition to what these results say about chromatic discrimination, they also tell us that even newborns encode the color of a form when they are repeatedly exposed to it.

Finally, several researchers have examined the specificity of color/form encoding in infants. More specifically, these investigators have asked whether multicolored objects are encoded by infants precisely enough for them to recognize changes in the spatial relationships between the colors. Dannemiller and Braun (1988) showed infants a figure of one color on a ground of another color. During habituation, the relative luminances of the figure and ground were varied over a substantial range while the colors in the figure and ground were held constant. During the test phase of the experiment, a novel relative luminance pairing for the figure and ground was presented, as was a form in which the colors of the figure and ground had been spatially switched. Five-month-old infants responded with increased attention to this reversal of the colors of the figure and ground. In other conditions, 5-month-olds also responded when the color of the figure or the ground alone was changed. These test results are shown in Figure 9.2 The infants responded most to a change in the color of either the figure or the ground alone, but they responded almost as much when the colors of the figure and ground were simply reversed. This latter result is consistent with several of the previous studies showing encoding of color by infants. Consistent with the results of Dannemiller and Braun (1988), Rovee-Collier, Schechter, Shyi, and Shields (1992) showed that 6-month-olds also encoded the chromatic figure–ground relationships in multicolored patterns.

3.3.2 Hue categorization during infancy. Color constancy involves the appearance of an object across different illuminants. Failures of color constancy in-

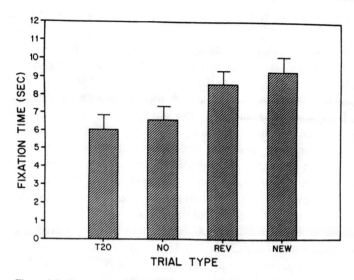

Figure 9.2. Five-month-olds' responses to a various bichromatic patterns following habituation to a similar pattern. Average fixation times on the last habituation and three test trials are shown here. T20 = last habituation trial; NO = no change in the chromatic relationship between figure and ground; REV = reversal of the colors of the figure and ground; NEW = new color substituted into either the figure or the ground. The REV and NEW trials both differ significantly from the NO trial. REV and NEW do not differ significantly from each other. During the habituation trials, the relative luminances of the figure and ground were varied over a substantial range while the two colors were held constant. From Dannemiller & Braun (1988).

volve the perception of sometimes subtle color differences when the same object is viewed under different illuminants. The most relevant studies besides those that have examined color constancy in infants directly are those that have examined hue categorization during infancy. These studies are conceptually like asking infants to make similarity judgments when shown different chromaticities. In addition to revealing the categorization of hue, they tell us something about the way in which the appearance of a form is encoded and remembered, however briefly, by the infant. Some have argued that color constancy in adults can be explained on the basis of the approximate invariance of color category (Jameson & Hurvich, 1989). In other words, human color constancy involves simply being able to compensate sufficiently for illuminant shifts to leave perception of the object in the same hue category. If this is true, then studies of infant color categorization surely are relevant to color constancy.

Bornstein and his colleagues published several studies of hue categorization in 4-month-old infants (Bornstein, 1975b; Bornstein, Kessen, & Weiskopf, 1976a, 1976b). Note that the studies reviewed earlier indicate that infants at this age probably possess trichromatic vision, so one might reasonably ask, as Bornstein did, whether or not these infants divide the visible-wavelength spectrum into color categories, as adults do. Bornstein used the habituation methodology described earlier with the following strategy for examining hue categorization. Different groups of infants were habituated to monochromatic lights of selected wavelengths. After habituating to a given light, the experimenter then tested the infant's attention to three wavelengths on separate trials. One of these was the original wavelength seen during habituation. The other two were chosen to be equidistant in nanometers but on opposite sides of the spectrum from the original habituation wavelength. One of these latter two tests was chosen to fall within the same adult hue category as the habituation wavelength, and the other was chosen to cross a hue boundary to fall into an adjacent hue category. The hue category boundaries were chosen based on published studies of adult color naming (Beare, 1963). Other groups of infants were also tested by choosing the two new wavelengths to fall within the same hue category as the habituation stimulus. These latter infants were tested to determine how similarly they perceived three wavelengths, all of which fell within the same adult hue category. All of the wavelengths were presented at the same luminance level. Whether they appeared equally bright for the infants is not possible to determine, although heterochromatic brightness matches for infants are probably similar to adult peripheral heterochromatic brightness matches to a first approximation (Teller & Lindsey, 1989).

As an example of this procedure, we may consider one of the groups tested by Bornstein et al. (1976b) and discussed in detail by them. During habituation, infants were exposed repeatedly to a 480-nm light. This wavelength appears greenish blue to adults. The two new test wavelengths were 450 nm and 510 nm. The 450-nm light appears blue to adults and falls within the same hue category for adults as the 480-nm habituation light. The 510-nm light appears bluish green and falls within a different (green) hue category from the light used during habituation. The predictions for relative responding during the test phase of the experiment are straightforward. These predictions are based on two assumptions. First, it is assumed that infants divide the wavelength range into similar categories with boundary wavelengths similar to those of adults. Second, it is assumed that infants will increase their attention most to a test wavelength that appears to them to be in a hue category different from the one they saw during habituation. Given these assumptions, it is possible to make predictions about the ordinal relationships between the responses to the various test wavelengths. The two novel wavelengths and the original wavelength used during habituation were each presented three times during the test phase after habituation. As Bornstein et al. pointed out, the re-presentation of the original wavelength probes the infant three times during the course of the test phase for his or her recognition of the original habituation wavelength.

Three hue boundaries and four hue categories were tested in this set of studies. The data conformed to the earlier predictions in almost every case. Infants tested for their responses to a change in hue across the adult blue–green boundary responded with the most attention to a wavelength that crossed this boundary. Infants tested for their responses to a change across the green–yellow adult boundary did the same. Infants tested for their responses to a change across the yellow–red boundary also conformed to predictions in one case but not in another. When infants were habituated with 600 nm and tested with this stimulus and two others – 580 nm and 620 nm – they responded most to the 620-nm light in accordance with the predictions. However, when infants were habituated to a 620-nm light and tested with 600 nm and 640 nm, the prediction is that they should have responded most to the 600-nm light because this crosses the red–yellow boundary. Instead, they actually responded most to the two wavelengths, 620 nm and 640 nm, that fell within the original adult red hue category seen during habituation, and they responded significantly less to the wavelength (600 nm) that crossed the adult hue boundary. In other words, infants in this case responded more to the familiar adult hue category than they did to the light from a novel adult hue category. Greater attention to familiar stimuli rather than to novel stimuli following habituation is sometimes observed in infants. But it is not possible to invoke procedural explanations to explain this reversal of the novelty preference because, in all the other conditions, infants responded more to the novel stimulus. It was necessary for Bornstein et al. (1976) to invoke an auxiliary assumption to explain this result. They argued that there are inherent baseline differences between wavelengths in how much attention they will evoke prior to any habituation. These baseline differences then interact with the habituation to produce the net attention during the test phase. In this case, it was necessary for Bornstein et al. to postulate that the longer wavelengths in this condition, 620 nm and 640 nm, are inherently more compelling of attention than the shorter wavelength, 600 nm. This auxiliary assumption actually has some support in data (Bornstein, 1975a). Infants at this age show increasing baseline attention levels as wavelength increases from 560 to 650 nm. So it is possible that the reversal of the normal response to novelty in this condition occurred because the longer-wavelength lights were inherently more interesting to the infants.

With the exception of this one condition, 4-month-olds in these two studies behaved as one would predict from knowing how adults divide the visible spectrum into hues. It is also relevant to note that infants who were shown three test lights falling in the same adult hue category responded approximately equally to these wavelengths. This result, in conjunction with the prior results from the infants tested with changes across adult hue boundaries, indicates that infants at this age perceive wavelengths to be similar when they fall within the same adult hue category.

Bornstein et al. (1976a, b) also provided converging evidence for this conclusion using a different technique. During the habituation phase of the experiment, they showed infants either the same wavelength on all trials or two different wavelengths alternated pseudorandomly across trials. The two wavelengths were chosen either to fall within the same adult hue category or to fall in two different adult hue categories. Again, the wavelength difference between the two alternating lights was the same in nanometers, but perceptually, adults would see the pair in one case as belonging to the same hue category and in the other case as belonging to different categories. The rate of habituation should be fastest for the group shown the single wavelength stimulus across all trials. The habituation rate should be slowest for the group shown two different wavelengths falling in different adult hue categories. The rate for the group shown two different wavelengths falling in the same adult hue category should be similar to the rate for the initial group.

The results of this procedure conformed to the predictions. The slowest habituation rate was observed in the group that saw what adults would see as two different hues randomly alternating in their presentation. The rates for the other two groups were faster and similar to one another. These results show that physically identical differences in wavelength do not produce identical rates of habituation when presented during habituation. Rather, 4-month-olds habituate more slowly when they see two wavelengths that for adults constitute different hues. By inference, then, these results converge on the conclusion that infants divide the visible spectrum in a manner similar to that of adults. This does not mean that the infant's perception of hue is the same as that of the adult, but rather that there is an approximate correspondence between the wavelength boundaries that divide the spectrum into hues for both of them (see also the discussion of related issues in Bornstein, 1985; Werner and Wooten, 1985a, 1985b).

One potential criticism of this conclusion should be addressed. It is strictly correct to speak of categorization only when the objects to be categorized are themselves discriminable. There is no direct evidence in these hue categorization studies that the different wavelengths within an adult hue category were discriminable to the infants. When infants show equal attention to two wavelengths, we are not entitled to conclude that they cannot discriminate them, any more than we are entitled to conclude that they can discriminate them but are treating them as if they fell in the same hue category. The data are simply mute on this point. We currently do not know what the wavelength discrimination capabilities of 4-month-olds are like. It is likely, however, that wavelength discrimination at this age is rather poor compared to adult wavelength discrimination (Bedford & Wyszecki, 1958) because of the poor visual efficiency of the infant's cones at this age (Banks & Shannon, 1993). Until we do have this information, then, we must treat the infant hue categorization data as analogous to the adult data but not as strictly equivalent.

These studies of hue categorization are important for our understanding of color constancy during infancy for one reason. They tell us that infants treat small differences in wavelength in a manner that depends not just on the physical magnitude of the difference, but also on the perceptual difference. Two wavelengths that are perceived as similar in hue by adults are treated also as similar by infants, whereas two wavelengths that are perceived by adults as different in basic hue are treated also as different by infants. It is possible that small residual differences in the hue of an object that accompany an illuminant change might be undetectable by the infant or ignored based on their similarity in hue if they were detectable. The type of color constancy discussed by Jameson and Hurvich (1989) as approximate invariance of color identification would then be applicable to young infants. Of course, this demands mechanisms that can compensate for the changing illuminant sufficiently to render the object in approximately the same color category.

3.3.3 Summary: Studies of color appearance in infants. The studies just discussed show that infants in the first half year of life encode the color of an object as one of its properties, and that a change in color will evoke in some circumstances an increase in attention. Infants also encode the figure–ground relationship between two colors correctly, so that a reversal in the colors of the figure and the ground also will evoke an increase in attention. Infants by 4 months of age appear to categorize hue in a manner similar to the way adults categorize it. Infants will treat small changes in wavelength in a manner that depends on whether the change crosses an adult hue boundary. A change in wavelength that leaves the stimulus within the same hue category is apparently not detected by the infant, or it is detected and treated as less interesting than a change that moves the stimulus into what would be a new hue category for adults.

4. Studies of color constancy in infants

There have been very few studies directly concerned with color constancy during the period of infancy or childhood. This is at least in part because some of the methods available for testing color constancy during adulthood (e.g., matching) are not possible with infants. Other constancies have been studied during the period of infancy, such as size constancy (McKenzie, Tootell, & Day, 1980; Slater, Mattock, & Brown, 1990) and contrast constancy (Stephens & Banks, 1985). It is difficult to test color constancy because there is one dimension that changes – the spectral character of the illuminant – but this change potentially can produce differences in three perceptual dimensions: hue, saturation, and brightness. This makes the methodological problem more difficult and makes the studies with infants only first approximations to thorough tests of color constancy.

Before reviewing two studies of color constancy during infancy, it is worth-while to examine several other reports of color constancy in developing organisms. Gogel and Hess (1951) found that newly hatched chicks exhibit color constancy, as evidenced by their consistent pecking at grain of one color independently of the illuminant spectral power distribution. Katz (1935) reported that children between the ages of 3 and 8 years exhibit adultlike whiteness constancy. This latter report was not concerned with color per se, but rather with the perception of surface lightness or perceived reflectance (albedo). We may also examine less direct evidence that suggests that color can be used as an identifying feature of objects during childhood. Johnson (1993) recently reported that 5-, 7-, and 9-year-olds named pictures of familiar objects shown in incongruent colors significantly more slowly than the same objects shown in congruent colors. For example, a picture of a blue banana was named significantly more slowly than a picture of a yellow banana. There were no differences between the ages in this tendency to name congruently colored objects more rapidly than incongruently colored objects. This result implies that color is treated as a stable property of objects at least by this age. At a minimum, this study seems to imply that some form of color constancy must be operating by this age because, if it were not, it is difficult to imagine how children would come to associate a particular color with a particular class of objects. Illumination changes would make the proximal stimulus for such an association quite variable. Color constancy would make the perceptual stimulus for this association more stable.

4.1 Empirical evidence for color constancy during infancy

Dannemiller and Hanko (1987) reported the first test of color constancy with infants. The subjects in this study were 4-month-olds. This age was chosen because the previous work on color vision and color categorization reviewed earlier indicates that infants at this age are probably trichromats, and that they categorize hue in a manner qualitatively similar to that of adults. This study used a strategy similar to those used in studies of other constancies during infancy. In these types of studies, the infant is first familiarized with or habituated to a particular distal object. Some type of transformation is then imposed. Infants are then tested for generalization both to the distally identical but proximally different object and to a new object with proximal characteristics similar to those seen during the familiarization period prior to the transformation. Prior research shows that infants at this age tend to look longer at the distally novel object. The question in the case of color constancy is, which object looks more similar perceptually to the object seen during habituation?

Fluorescent and incandescent illuminants were used in this study. It should be noted that the fluorescent illuminant is not optimal for examining color constancy because it has several sharp peaks in its spectrum. For this reason, one

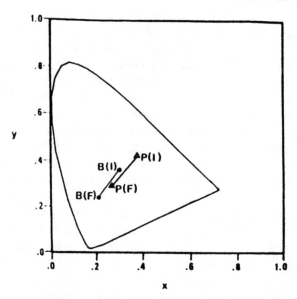

Figure 9.3. Chromaticities used to study color constancy in 4-month-old infants. P(I) = P2.5 4/8 (Munsell) under incandescent illumination: P(F) = P2.5 4/8 under fluorescent; B(I) = PB7.5 4/12 under incandescent; B(F) = PB7.5 4/12 under fluorescent. Each color was presented on a white matte background. From Dannemiller and Hanko (1987).

might also consider this to be a strong test of the operation of color constancy at this age. Two Munsell colors were chosen (P2.5 4/8 and PB7.5 4/12) based on the following considerations. The distally novel color introduced after the illuminant change should have chromaticity coordinates equal to or similar to the chromaticity coordinates of the object seen during familiarization prior to the illuminant change. It is not possible to ensure exact equivalence of this sort, but Figure 9.3 shows that the chromaticity of one of the stimuli under the incandescent illuminant PD7.5 4/12 was near the chromaticity of the other stimulus P2.5 4/8 under the fluorescent illuminant. Five 6.4° square patches of one color were displayed on white matte backgrounds.

Three basic conditions were tested in this study. These conditions may be understood by referring to Figure 9.3. In the first condition, infants were familiarized with one of the colors, and then tested with this same color and the other color without any change in the illuminant. This is not a test of color constancy, but rather a test of the infant's ability to remember the familiar color. In the second condition, infants were familiarized with either B(F) or P(I) and tested with both colors under the other illuminant. This is a test of color constancy because the infants are being tested for recognition of the familiar color after a change in illumination. In the third condition, infants were familiarized with either B(I) or P(F) and tested with both colors under the other illuminant. This is also a test of color constancy. It is perhaps the stronger of the two tests because the chromaticity of the novel reflectance after the illuminant change is close to the chromaticity of the reflectance seen before the illuminant change.

The parents of the infants were also tested by having them examine one of the stimuli under the first illuminant and asking them to remember the color of this stimulus. Next, out of their sight, the illuminant was changed and the other stimulus was added to the display. The parents were asked to choose the colored pattern that they had seen previously.

All the adults in this study correctly chose the same stimulus that they had seen prior to the illuminant change. They exhibited color constancy at least to the extent that they were not confused by a stimulus after the illuminant change that was similar in chromaticity to what they had seen prior to the illuminant change. The results with the infants were mixed. In the condition that provided the strongest test of color constancy, they showed no differential attention to the distally novel and familiar colors. In the other condition that provided a test of color constancy, however, they generalized to the distally familiar color and attended more to the distally novel color.

Can the pattern of results from this study be explained solely on the basis of the similarity of the stimuli in the adult chromaticity plane? Control conditions showed that infants responded with increased attention to a distally novel color when no illuminant change was introduced over the course of the experiment. Examine Figure 9.3 to see that this result precludes an explanation of all the results based purely on similarity in adult chromaticity space. Consider the control condition with the stimuli labeled B(I) and P(I). In this control condition, infants were familiarized with the P2.5 4/8 [P(I)] stimulus under incandescent illumination and tested with this same stimulus and with the PB7.5 4/12 [B(I)] stimulus under the same incandescent illuminant. In this condition and in its counterbalanced control, infants attended more to the distally novel stimulus. Notice the distance between P(I) and B(I) in Figure 9.3. Now compare this distance with the distance between P(I) and P(F). These latter two chromaticities are much farther apart, yet infants generalized from P(I) to P(F) after an illuminant shift from incandescent to fluorescent. This result runs counter to the argument that all of the results in this study can be explained on the basis of the similarity of the familiarization and test stimuli in chromaticity space. It suggests that some process following an illuminant change alters the generalization that these infants make to different colors from what it is when there is no illuminant change. In at least some conditions, then, these infants discriminated familiar and novel surface reflectances after an illuminant change.

Next, consider another study of color constancy that examined its status at two ages within the first 5 postnatal months using a different definition of color constancy (Dannemiller, 1989a). Craven and Foster (1992) proposed an operational definition of color constancy that differed from the standard definition, which involves precise color matching under two different illuminants. Craven and Foster suggested that one property of color constancy involves the "ability of a subject to correctly attribute changes in the colour appearance of a scene either to changes in the spectral composition of the illuminant or to changes in the reflectance properties of a scene" (p. 1360). Dannemiller (1989a) similarly asked whether 9- and 20-week-olds could distinguish between illuminant and reflectance changes when both produce changes in chromaticity.

The specific question being asked here was whether or not infants at these two ages recognize the same simulated bichromatic surface when it is displayed under two different illuminants. Pairs of natural surfaces with complementary reflectance functions illuminated with two different phases of sunlight were simulated on a color monitor. Two simulated surfaces were presented together on each trial in a Mondrian-like arrangement for the two colors. Each simulated surface occupied 50% of the available display on the monitor. Cohen's (1964) basis functions were used to compose pairs of surface reflectance functions that were complements of each other over the visible wavelength range. Figure 9.4 shows the two pairs of reflectance functions that were used. Constraining the pairs of reflectance functions in this way ensures that the average reflectance across wavelength is exactly flat and that the average chromaticity of the display is exactly that of the illuminant. Some models of color constancy (D'Zmura & Lennie, 1986) propose that color constancy is best for scenes in which the average reflectance is flat, corresponding to an average gray world (Hurlbert, 1986). Notice also that eye movements across this display coupled with a relatively long time constant of temporal integration (Fairchild & Lennie, 1992) tend to adapt the visual system to the chromaticity of the illuminant. Spectral power distributions for phases of daylight having correlated color temperatures of 4800 K and 10,000 K were synthesized from the basis functions in Judd, MacAdam, and Wyszecki (1964).

Infants were habituated to a display containing one of the pairs of reflectance functions shown in Figure 9.4. They were then exposed on different test trials to four stimuli comprising a 2 × 2 factorial manipulation of a reflectance pair and an illuminant spectral power distribution. That is, they were tested with both reflectance pairs shown in Figure 9.4 under both phases of daylight. It is important to note that between all trials in this experiment, the display assumed the average chromaticity and luminance of the pattern to be shown on the subsequent trial. This ensured a minimum intertrial preadaptation period of 10 s. Adults were also tested using a matching procedure to examine the degree of color constancy obtainable with these bichromatic displays. Four adults exhibited good color constancy under these conditions. Their matches from one illuminant to the next were quite close to what one would predict if the matches

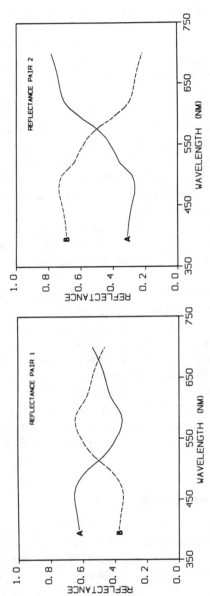

Figure 9.4. Reflectance function pairs shown in bichromatic patterns to study color constancy in 9- and 20-week-old infants. These reflectance pairings (1 and 2) were simulated on a red-green-blue monitor using two different phases of daylight on separate test trials. The patterns were displayed on the monitor using a Mondrian-like arrangement in which each reflectance in the pair (A or B) occupied 50% of the available display. The average chromaticity of a pattern in this case is exactly the chromaticity of the illuminant. From Dannemiller (1989a).

were based on simulated surface reflectances rather than on the chromaticities alone.

The final sample of infants at each age included only those infants who showed the greatest evidence of habituation during the eight familiarization trials. The 20-week-olds but not the 9-week-olds showed evidence of color constancy. The 20-week-olds responded with increased attention only to simulated changes of surface reflectance, not to simulated changes of the illuminant alone. However, 9-week-olds responded with increased attention to simulated changes either of the illuminant or of surface reflectance. In other words, 9-week-olds responded with increased attention to any change that produced chromaticities different from what they had seen during habituation. Twenty-week-olds, however, were much more selective, responding with increased attention only to a change in the pair of surface reflectances simulated on the display, and not to a change in the illuminant alone. These results are shown in Figure 9.5. Note the difference in the pattern of responding at 9 and 20 weeks of age. The data from the 20-week-olds are indicative of color constancy, whereas the data for the 9-week-olds are not.

The answer to the question posed earlier is that 20-week-olds apparently discriminate a change in illumination from a change in surface reflectances, whereas 9-week-olds do not. It is possible that the clearer results in this study compared to the previous study by Dannemiller and Hanko (1987) are the result of the use of smoother illuminant spectral power distributions. Recall that in the Dannemiller and Hanko study a fluorescent illuminant was used. Such an illuminant exhibits sharp emission peaks, unlike the smoother daylight illuminants that were simulated in the Dannemiller (1989a) study. Such smooth illuminant distributions tend to promote better color constancy because they produce less radical changes in the relative absorptions of photons reflected from the same surface.

5. Conclusions and theoretical considerations

Human infants by 5 months of age appear to have at least partial color constancy. This conclusion comes from studies in which the infant's generalization of color after an illuminant transformation was tested. Dannemiller (1989a) found that 5-month-old infants recognized the same bichromatic surface pattern after an illuminant change, but they treated a change in reflectance under the original illuminant as a novel object. In contrast, 2-month-olds treated the same surface viewed under a new illuminant as a novel surface. Five-month-olds generalized surface color after an illuminant change, whereas 2-month-olds did not. This implies development of color constancy over the first 5 months of life. These results are consistent with other data showing rapid development of color vision over the early postnatal months (Brown, 1987). Apparently, at the same

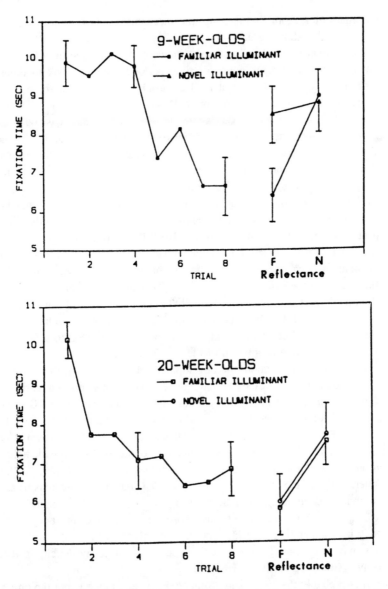

Figure 9.5. Habituation and test data from 9-and 20-week-olds for the bichromatic patterns composed of the reflectance pairings shown in Figure 9.4. The average fixation times on the eight habituation trials are shown on the left side of each figure. The responses following habituation to four test trials are shown on the right. Greater attention at this age typically indicates that infants perceived the pattern to be perceptually novel relative to what they saw during the habituation phase. Notice that 9-week-olds increase their attention to any change that produces chromaticity different from what they have seen during habituation. Twenty-week-olds, in contrast, increase their attention only when new reflectances are shown. They generalize to the same pair of reflectances seen under a new illuminant.

time that color vision is maturing, the mechanisms responsible for color constancy are also showing development.

What might be responsible for the increase in the degree of color constancy shown by human infants over this time period? We may look to theories of color constancy in adults for at least a partial answer. One of the mechanisms thought to be involved in promoting color constancy is adaptation (D'Zmura & Lennie, 1986). Von Kries adaptation involves scaling the sensitivities of the photoreceptors to the chromatic content of the scene. For example, if the illuminant tends to have relatively more long wavelength light, then the sensitivity of the LWS cones and, to a lesser extent, that of the MWS cones will be reduced to lessen what would otherwise be a large response in these cone types. Von Kries adaptation alone is insufficient to produce perfect color constancy because such a gain change on the cones cannot perfectly undo a shift in the illuminant spectral power distribution (Worthey & Brill, 1986). But perfect color constancy may not be truly indicative of adult human color vision. Changes in daylight illumination leave the rank ordering of photon catches from a natural object almost unperturbed (Dannemiller, 1993). This means that photoreceptor adaptation could still contribute substantially to color constancy. Brainard and Wandell (1992) found that the appearance of different surfaces simulated on a color monitor under different illuminants could be described well to a first approximation by assuming adaptation of the von Kries type.

What do we know about the development of adaptation of this sort? Studies of light adaptation show clearly that it develops over this period of early infancy. Slopes for increment threshold functions reach values of 0.8 to 1.0 sometimes around 3 months of age but are shallower earlier (Dannemiller, 1985; Dannemiller & Banks, 1983a; see Banks & Dannemiller, 1987, and Brown, 1990, for reviews). There are also studies showing that adaptation to chromatic fields shifts chromatic detection sensitivity during this period (Brown & Teller, 1989; Pulos, Teller, & Buck, 1980). These studies show that adaptation mechanisms are present and are developing over the early postnatal months. Development of these mechanisms could contribute to the improvement in color constancy seen in the study by Dannemiller (1989a). The lack of color constancy shown by 9-week-olds may also result from poor color encoding caused by deficits in the SWS pathways (see the earlier discussion).

It is probably the case that chromatic adaptation alone is not the only mechanism that contributes to color constancy. Brill and West (1986) have argued that chromatic adaptation and the mechanisms responsible for color constancy are not the same. One of the distinctions between the two phenomena is in their time courses. Brill and West state that chromatic adaptation is too slow to be responsible for color constancy. Chromatic adaptation *is* relatively slow. The evidence for this comes from studies that show incomplete adaptation to an illuminant shift even after long periods of time (Fairchild & Lennie, 1992).

There is also evidence from animal studies that color constancy can be disrupted by lesions of area V4 without disrupting hue discrimination (Walsh et al., 1993). Because lesions to area V4 would not impair photoreceptor adaptation, and because these lesions leave color processing intact to the extent that hue discrimination is still relatively normal, one must conclude that mechanisms beyond photoreceptor adaptation are involved in producing color constancy. It is possible that some of the improvement in color constancy observed over the first postnatal months may also occur because of maturation of these higher-order chromatic mechanisms (Krauskopf, Williams, Mandler, & Brown, 1986).

Color constancy can contribute substantially to creating a stable perceptual world for the developing human infant. Shape, size, and contrast constancy are all known to be functional during the first 6 months of life. These constancies may provide the scaffolding necessary for the infant to learn about objects, their functions, and their properties. It is difficult to imagine such learning taking place in the absence of a stable perceptual world. It is easier to imagine this learning taking place with objects that retain their size, shape, approximate surface color, and contrast across the many activities and changes in environments that tend to perturb the proximal visual correlates of these objects.

References

Abramov, I., Gordon, J., Hendrickson, A., Hainline, L., Dobson, V., & LaBossiere, E. (1982). The retina of the newborn human infant. *Science, 217*, 265–267.

Ackles, P. K., & Karrer, R. (1991). A critique of the Dannemiller and Banks (1983) neuronal fatigue (selective adaptation) hypothesis of young infant habituation. *Merrill-Palmer Quarterly, 37*, 325–334.

Adams, R. J. (1989). Newborns' discrimination among mid- and long-wavelength stimuli. *Journal of Experimental Child Psychology, 47*, 130–141.

Adams, R. J., Courage, M. L., & Mercer, M. E. (1991). Deficiencies in human neonates' color vision: Photoreceptoral and neural explanations. *Behavioural Brain Research, 43*(2), 109–114.

Adams, R. J., Courage, M. L., & Mercer, M. E. (1994). Systematic measurement of human neonatal color vision. *Vision Research, 34*, 1691–1701.

Adams, R., Maurer, D., & Cashin, H. A. (1990). The influence of stimulus size on newborns' discrimination of chromatic from achromatic stimuli. *Vision Research, 30*, 2023–2030.

Allen, D., Banks, M. S., & Norcia, A. M. (1993). Does chromatic sensitivity develop more slowly than luminance sensitivity? *Vision Research, 33*, 2553–2562.

Banks, M. S., & Bennett, P. J. (1988). Optical and photoreceptor immaturities limit the spatial and chromatic vision of human neonates. *Journal of the Optical Society of America A, 5*, 2059–2079.

Banks, M. S., & Dannemiller, J. L. (1987). Infant visual psychophysics. In P. Salaptek & L. B. Cohen (Eds.), *Handbook of infant perception.* (pp. 72–87). Orlando, FL: Academic Press.

Banks, M. S., & Shannon, E. (1993). Spatial and chromatic visual efficiency in human neonates. In K. Simons (Ed.), *Infant vision: Basic and clinical research* (in press). National Academy of Sciences Press.

Beare, A. C. (1963). Color-name as a function of wavelength. *American Journal of Psychology, 76*, 248–256.

Bedford, R. E., & Wyszecki, G. W. (1958). Wavelength discrimination for point sources. *Journal of the Optical Society of America, 48,* 129–135.

Blackwell, K. T., & Buchsbaum, G. (1988). Quantitative studies of color constancy. *Journal of the Optical Society of America A, 5,* 1772–1780.

Bornstein, M. H. (1975a). Qualities of color vision in infancy. *Journal of Experimental Child Psychology, 19,* 401–419.

Bornstein, M. (1975b). Infants' recognition memory for hue. *Developmental Psychology, 12,* 185–191.

Bornstein, M. H. (1985). Human infant color vision and color perception. *Infant Behavior and Development, 8,* 109–113.

Bornstein, M. H., Kessen, W., & Weiskopf, S. (1976a). The categories of hue in infancy. *Science, 191,* 201–202.

Bornstein, M. H., Kessen, W., & Weiskopf, S. (1976b). Color vision and hue categorization in young human infants. *Journal of Experimental Psychology: Human Perception and Performance, 2,* 115–129.

Brainard, D. H., & Wandell, B. A. (1992). Asymmetric color matching: How color appearance depends on the illuminant. *Journal of the Optical Society of America – Part A, Optics & Image Science, 9*(9), 1433–1448.

Brill, M. H., & West, G. (1986). Chromatic adaptation and color constancy: A possible dichotomy. *Color Research and Application, 11,* 196–204.

Brown, A. M. (1987). Issues in human color vision development. In J. J. Kulikowski, C. M. Dickinson, & I. J. Murray (Eds.), *Seeing contour and color* (pp. 255–262). Oxford: Pergamon Press.

Brown, A. M. (1990). Development of visual sensitivity to light and color vision in human infants: A critical review. *Vision Research, 30,* 1159–1188.

Brown, A. M., & Teller, D. Y. (1989). Chromatic opponency in 3-month-old human infants. *Vision Research, 29* (1), 37–45.

Bushnell, E. W., & Roder, B. J. (1985). Recognition of color-form compounds by 4-month-old infants. *Infant Behavior and Development, 8,* 255–268.

Chugani, H. T., & Phelps, M. E. (1986). Maturational changes in cerebral function in infants determined by 18FDG position emission tomography. *Science, 231,* 840–843.

Clavadetscher, J. E., Brown, A. M., Ankrum, C., & Teller, D. Y. (1988). Spectral sensitivity and chromatic discriminations in 3- and 7-week-old human infants. *Journal of the Optical Society of America – Part A, Optical & Image Science, 5* (12), 2093–2105.

Cohen, J. (1964). Dependency of the spectral reflectance curves of the Munsell color chips. *Psychonomic Science, 1,* 369–370.

Cohen, L. B. (1973). A two process model of infant visual attention. *Merrill-Palmer Quarterly of Behavior and Development, 19,* 157–180.

Cohen, L. B., Gelber, E. R., & Lazar, M. A. (1971). Infant habituation and generalization to differing degrees of stimulus novelty. *Journal of Experimental Child Psychology, 11,* 379–389.

Conel, J. L. (1939). *The cortex of the newborn, The postnatal development of the human cerebral cortex.* Cambridge, MA: Harvard University Press.

Conel, J. L. (1941). *The cortex of the one-month infant. The postnatal development of the human cerebral cortex.* Cambridge, MA: Harvard University Press.

Conel, J. L. (1947). *The cortex of the three-month infant. The postnatal development of the human cerebral cortex.* Cambridge, MA: Harvard University Press.

Craven, B. J., & Foster, D. H. (1992). An operational approach to colour constancy. *Vision Research, 32,* 1359–1366.

Dannemiller, J. L. (1985). The early phase of dark adaptation in human infants. *Vision Research, 25,* 207–212.

Dannemiller, J. L. (1989a). A test of color constancy in 9- and 20-week-old human infants following simulated illuminant changes. *Developmental Psychology, 25,* 171–184.

Dannemiller, J. L. (1989b). Computational approaches to color constancy: Adaptive and ontogenetic considerations. *Psychological Review, 96,* 255–266.

Dannemiller, J. L. (1993). Rank orderings of photoreceptor photon catches from natural objects are nearly illuminant-invariant. *Vision Research, 33,* 131–140.

Dannemiller, J. L., & Banks, M. S. (1983a). The development of light adaptation in the human infant. *Vision Research, 23,* 599–609.

Dannemiller, J. L., & Banks, M. S. (1983b). Can selective adaptation account for early infant habituation? *Merrill-Palmer Quarterly, 29,* 151–158.

Dannemiller, J., & Braun, A. (1988). The perception of chromatic figure/ground relationships in 5-month-olds. *Infant Behavior and Development, 11,* 31–42.

Dannemiller, J. L., & Hanko, S. A. (1987). A test of color constancy in 4-month-old human infants. *Journal of Experimental Child Psychology, 44,* 255–267.

de Courten, C., & Garey, L. J. (1982). Morphology of the neurons in the human lateral geniculate nucleus and their normal development. *Experimental Brain Research, 47,* 159–171.

D'Zmura, M., & Lennie, P. (1986). Mechanisms of color constancy. *Journal of the Optical Society of America A, 3,* 1662–1672.

Fairchild, M. D., & Lennie, P. (1992). Chromatic adaptation to natural and incandescent illuminants. *Vision Research, 32,* 2077–2085.

Fantz, R. L. (1958). Pattern vision in young infants. *Psychological Record, 8,* 43–47.

Fantz, R. L. (1965). Visual perception from birth as shown by pattern selectivity. *Annals of the New York Academy of Sciences, 118,* 793–813.

Garey, L. J. (1984). Structural development of the visual system of man. *Human Neurobiology, 3,* 75–80.

Geisler, W. S. (1989). Sequential Ideal Observer analysis of visual discriminations. *Psychological Review, 96,* 276–314.

Gogel, U., & Hess, E. (1951). A study of color constancy in the newly hatched chick by means of an innate color preference (abstract). *The American Psychologist, 6,* 282.

Hamer, R. D., Alexander, K., & Teller, D. Y. (1982). Rayleigh discriminations in human infants. *Vision Research, 22,* 575–587.

Heywood, C. A., Gadotti, A., & Cowey, A. (1992). Cortical area V4 and its role in the perception of color. *Journal of Neuroscience, 12,* (10), 4056–4065.

Hickey, T. L. (1977). Postnatal development of the human lateral geniculate nucleus: Relationship to a critical period for the visual system. *Science, 198,* 836–838.

Hurlbert, A. (1986). Formal connections between lightness algorithms. *Journal of the Optical Society of America A, 3,* 1684–1693.

Ingling, C. R. J. (1977). The spectral sensitivity of the opponent-color channels. *Vision Research, 17,* 1083–1089.

Jameson, D., & Hurvich, L. M. (1989). Essay concerning color constancy. *Annual Review of Psychology, 40,* 1–22.

Johnson, C. J. (1993, April). *Effects of color on children's identification of pictures.* Paper presented at the biennial meeting of the Society for Research in Child Development, New Orleans.

Judd, D. B., MacAdam, D. L., & Wyszecki, G. (1964). Spectral distribution of typical daylight as a function of correlated color temperature. *Journal of the Optical Society of America, 54,* 1031–1040.

Katz, D. (1935). *The world of color.* London: Kegan, Paul, Trench, Trubner.

Krauskopf, J., Williams, D. R., Mandler, M. B., & Brown, A. M. (1986). Higher order color mechanisms. *Vision Research, 26*(1), 23–32.

Lueck, C. J., Zeki, S., Friston, K. J., Deiber, M. P., Cope, P., Cunningham, V. J., Lammertsma, A. A., Kennard, C., & Frackowiak, R. S. J. (1989). The colour centre in the cerebral cortex of man. *Nature, 340,* 386–389.

Maloney, L. T. (1990). Confidence intervals for the parameters of psychometric functions. *Perception and Psychophysics, 47,* 127–134.

Maurer, D., & Adams, R. (1987). Emergence of the ability to discriminate blue from gray at one month of age. *Journal of Experimental Child Psychology, 44,* 147–156.

McKenzie, B. E., Tootell, H. E., & Day, R. H. (1980). Development of visual size constancy during the first year of human infancy. *Developmental Psychology, 16,* 163–174.

Packer, O., Hartmann, E. E., & Teller, D. Y. (1984). Infant color vision: The effect of test field size on Rayleigh discriminations. *Vision Research, 24,* 1247–1260.

Peeples, D. R., & Teller, D. Y. (1975). Color vision and brightness discrimination in two-month-old human infants. *Science, 189,* 1102–1103.

Peeples, D. R., & Teller, D. Y. (1978). White-adapted photopic spectral sensitivity in human infants. *Vision Research, 18,* 39–53.

Plendl, H., Paulus, W., Roberts, I. G., Botzel, K., Towell, A., Pitman, J. R., Scherg, M., & Halliday, A. M. (1993). The time course and location of cerebral evoked activity associated with the processing of colour stimuli in man. *Neuroscience Letters, 150* (1), 9–12.

Pulos, E., Teller, D. Y., & Buck, S. L. (1980). Infant color vision: A search for short-wavelength-sensitive mechanisms by means of chromatic adaptation. *Vision Research, 20,* 485–493.

Rovee-Collier, C., Schechter, A., Shyi, G. C. W., & Shields, P. (1992). Perceptual identification of contextual attributes and infant memory retrieval. *Developmental Psychology, 28,* 307–318.

Roy, M. S., Podgor, M. J., Collier, B., & Gunkel, R. D. (1991). Color vision and age in a normal North American population. *Graefes Archive for Clinical and Experimental Ophthalmology, 229*(2), 139–144.

Saayman, G., Ames, E. W., & Moffett, A. (1964). Response to novelty as an indicator of visual discrimination in the human infant. *Journal of Experimental Child Psychology, 1,* 189–198.

Slater, A., Mattock, A., & Brown, E. (1990). Size constancy at birth: Newborn infants' responses to retinal and real size. *Journal of Experimental Child Psychology, 49,* 314–322.

Stephens, B. R., & Banks, M. S. (1985). The development of contrast constancy. *Journal of Experimental Child Psychology, 40,* 528–547.

Teller, D. Y. (1979). The forced-choice preferential looking procedure: A psychophysical technique for use with human infants. *Infant Behavior and Development, 2,* 135–153.

Teller, D. Y. & Bornstein, M. H. (1987). Infant color vision and color perception. In P. Salapatek & L. B. Cohen (Eds.), *Handbook of infant perception* (pp. 87–94). Orlando, FL: Academic Press.

Teller, D. Y., & Lindsey, D. T. (1989). Motion nulls for white versus isochromatic gratings in infants and adults. *Journal of the Optical Society of America A, 6,* 1945–1954.

Teller, D. Y. and Lindsey, D. T. (1993). Infant color vision: okn techniques and null plane analysis. In K. Simons (Eds.), *Infant vision: basic and clinical research* (in press). National Academy of Sciences Press.

Teller, D. Y., Peeples, D. R., & Sekel, M. (1978). Discrimination of chromatic from white light by two-month-old human infants. *Vision Research, 18,* 41–48.

Varner, D., Cook, J. E., Schneck, M. E., McDonald, M. A., & Teller, D. Y. (1985). Tritan discriminations by 1- and 2-month-old human infants. *Vision Research, 25* (6), 821–831.

Volbrecht, V. J., & Werner, J. S. (1987). Isolation of short-wavelength-sensitive cone photoreceptors in 4–6-week-old human infants. *Vision Research, 27*(3), 469–478.

Walsh, V., Carden, D., Butler, S. R., & Kulikowski, J. J. (1993). The effects of V4 lesions on the visual abilities of macaques: Hue discrimination and colour constancy. *Behavioural Brain Research, 53,* 51–62.

Welch, M. J. (1974). Infants' visual attention to varying degrees of novelty. *Child Development, 45,* 344–350.

Werner, J. S. (1982). Development of scotopic sensitivity and the absorption spectrum of the human ocular media. *Journal of the Optical Society of America, 72,* 247–258.

Werner, J. S., Donnelly, S. K., & Kliegl, R. (1987). Aging and human macular pigment density. *Vision Research, 27,* 257–268.

Werner, J. S., & Schefrin, B. E. (1993). Loci of achromatic points throughout the life span. *Journal of the Optical Society of America A, 10,* 1509–1516.

Werner, J. S., & Wooten, B. R. (1985a). Two perspectives on infant color vision research. *Infant Behavior and Development, 8,* 115–116.

Werner, J. S., & Wooten, B. R. (1985b). Unsettled issues in infant color vision. *Infant Behavior and Development, 8,* 99–107.

Worthey, J. A., & Brill, M. H. (1986). Heuristic analysis of von Kries color constancy. *Journal of the Optical Society of America A, 3,* 1708–1712.

Yuodelis, C., & Hendrickson, A. (1986). A qualitative and quantitative analysis of the human fovea during development. *Vision Research, 26,* 847–855.

Zeki, S. (1980). The representation of colours in the cerebral cortex. *Nature, 284,* 412–418.

10 Empirical studies in color constancy

Jimmy M. Troost

Introduction

The type of question that is put forward when presenting the color constancy phenomenon and the selection of important issues depend on the underlying research approach. When comparing the two most popular approaches of the moment to each other, the sensory and the computational, even the description of the essence of the phenomenon differs. Following a sensory approach, color constancy is supposed to exist only to the extent that it can be observed at the receptor level, that is, can be predicted by a von Kries-like model (e.g., Lucassen, 1993; Lucassen & Walraven, 1993; Richards & Parks, 1972; Takahama, Sobagaki, & Nayatani, 1984; von Kries, 1905; Worthey & Brill, 1986). Computational approaches seem to concentrate on the question of how a trichromatic visual system (the human, preferably; see Troost & de Weert, 1991a) can be constructed that recovers the only relevant physical property of objects that is invariant under changing illuminant conditions: surface spectral reflectance (e.g., Brill & West, 1986; Buchsbaum, 1980; Dannemiller, 1989; Maloney & Wandell, 1986; Sällström, 1974; and van Trigt, 1990).

Factors like figural organization (Adelson & Pentland, 1990; Gilchrist, 1980; Gilchrist, Delman, & Jacobsen, 1982; Schirillo, Reeves, & Arend, 1990), shadows (Cavanagh & LeClerc, 1989), color categorization (Troost & de Weert, 1991b), informational cues to the illuminant (Beck, 1959, 1961), or task demands (Arend & Reeves, 1986; Troost & de Weert, 1991b) are not taken into account in the sensory and computational approaches, either because they are nonsensory or because it is not possible, or at least very difficult, to incorporate them into a mathematical description of the physical world. Nevertheless, there is enough evidence that these factors are directly or indirectly of interest and importance to the color constancy issue. So, in addition to empirical findings from the sensory and computational fields, studies of a cognitive nature will be discussed in this chapter.

The author wishes to thank Charles de Weert for thoughtful discussion and helpful comments.

Simulating object color

The current availability of color monitors and computer systems that meet the qualitative requirements for color vision research encourages the use of configurations of simulated object color on a monitor, as opposed to scenes of real objects and light sources, in color constancy experiments. Generally, the advantages of automatic stimulus presentation and response registration merely involve factors like efficiency, accuracy, and comfort of the experimenter. Obviously, this is also the case with color constancy experiments, although the colorimetric description of object color that is required for the construction of a stimulus set is by no means a trivial case.

Such a description of object color is dependent on physical factors associated with surfaces, illuminants, and observers, and, if cast shadows or ambient illumination are taken into account, other objects as well. Depending on the degree of realism that is required, more factors have to be modeled and the colorimetric description of object color becomes more complex. Fortunately, the colorimetric description can be dramatically simplified because some physical factors need not be known in much detail to obtain a certain perceptual effect. For this purpose several techniques have been developed, especially in the field of computer graphics (e.g., Borges, 1991; Rogers, 1985).

Usually the degree of realism in color constancy experiments is relatively low, a consequence of the use of Mondrian patterns, which are simple because there is homogeneous illumination and all areas in the configuration are coplanar and (nearly) equidistant to the observer's position. Furthermore, the variation that has been used most often in color constancy experiments so far is illuminant color. Usually a number of colored surfaces are presented under a few illuminants. Under each illuminant, the colorimetric description of the object color under consideration changes. Clearly, in order to construct a valid stimulus set, this change has to be specified in advance.

For stimulus configurations with a complexity similar to that of Mondrian patterns, a number of computational schemes have been developed in which only the energy of the illuminant and reflectance by the object are used (for reviews, see Brill & West, 1986; Troost & de Weert, 1992a). Depending on the amount of information that is known about objects and illuminants, one of these schemes can be followed to obtain a colorimetric description of object color. In the case of complete information – that is, when both illuminant and reflectance spectra are known – the basic colorimetric equations should be applied. Generally, however, only tristimulus values of either the illuminant or the object are known. In these cases, either a spectrum reconstruction or a tristimulus ratio model can be used (see Troost & de Weert, 1992a).

In short, the fundamental question considered by spectrum reconstruction models is how a continuous spectrum can be reconstructed if color is described by only three quantities. Even if discrete samples of the continuous spectra are taken, a relatively large number of (equally spaced) samples is required to approximate the original spectrum. So, an unsolvable set of equations is obtained because only three known quantities – that is, tristimulus values – are available to reconstruct the discrete spectrum that consists of a much larger number of unknowns. Indeed, mathematically, the number of possible spectra having the same three-parameter representations, called *metameres,* is unlimited. So, which spectrum is chosen depends on the theoretical constraint that is put on the mathematical set of possibilities.

The theoretical constraint that underlies the Sällström–Buchsbaum model (Brill & West, 1986; Buchsbaum, 1980; Sällström, 1973) is that the reflectance can be reconstructed by a linear combination of three basis vectors that are derived from all spectra in a predefined class. Often the class of Munsell colors is used because these are well documented and the reflectance spectra of Munsell papers can be described to a high degree of accuracy by a linear combination of only three basis vectors (Cohen, 1964; Parkkinen, Hallikainen, & Jaaskelainen, 1989). In another model, that of van Trigt (1990), reflectance spectra are calculated that are the smoothest according to a mathematical criterion.

Both spectra reconstruction models can be applied if illuminant spectra are known but only tristimulus values of object colors (as under a known standard illuminant) are available. Alternatively, a tristimulus ratio model can be used as well (e.g., Lucassen, 1993; Lucassen & Walraven, 1993; Troost & de Weert, 1991b). These models are based on von Kries's model for chromatic adaptation (von Kries, 1905; see also Worthey & Brill, 1986). Rather than a spectrum in tristimulus models, the illuminant invariant quantity is the tristimulus value of an object divided by the corresponding tristimulus value of the illuminant. The obtained ratios can be taken for any three-parameter representation of color.

Troost and de Weert (1992a) compared the performance of two reflectance reconstruction models, those of Sällström–Buchbaum and van Trigt, to three tristimulus ratio models based on colorimetric X,Y,Z, receptor activities L,M,S and phosphor luminances R,G,B, respectively. Although both reflectance models were considerably more accurate, the predictions of tristimulus models based on phosphor luminances (Lucassen & Walraven, 1993) are within 3 MacAdam units of color difference ($\approx$ 1 jnd) over a considerable range of illuminant shifts (see Figure 10.1).

To summarize, the results of Troost and de Weert (1992a) show that reflectance models are more accurate than tristimulus models. Their use, however, is restricted to available illuminant spectra (see, e.g., Wyszecki & Stiles, 1967). Because this restriction does not apply to tristimulus models, the choice of illuminants is unconstrained.

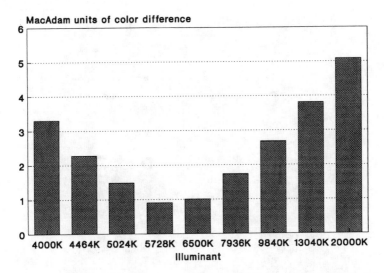

Figure 10.1. Average number of MacAdam units of color difference between the Sälls-tröm–Buchsbaum reflectance reconstruction model and the phosphor luminance tristi-mulus ratio model for a number of illuminants. Illuminant invariant quantities were calculated for more than 1,000 Munsell color specifications under CIE standard illumi-nant C. These quantities were then used to predict the color shift under the displayed illuminants for the two models. For further details, see Troost and de Weert (1992a).

Asymmetric Matching Paradigm

A typical color constancy experiment consists of an asymmetric matching task in which a subject is presented with two configurations of areas (which can be either real or simulated) that differ in color because of different illuminant con-ditions. Often Mondrian-like patterns are used that are illuminated by different light sources (e.g., Arend & Reeves, 1986; McCann, McKee, & Taylor, 1976; Valberg & Lange-Malecki, 1990), but other similar abstract configurations are used as well (e.g., Lucassen & Walraven, 1993; Tiplitz-Blackwell & Buchs-baum, 1988a, 1988b; Troost & de Weert, 1991b). Usually, the lighting condition of one configuration is kept constant during the entire experiment at an illumi-nant that strongly resembles average daylight (e.g., CIE standard source C, or D65). This configuration is called the *standard*. The illuminant condition of the other configuration, called the *test*, is varied in the experiment.

The test configuration contains a target field. The color of this field has to be matched in the matching field that is part of the standard configuration. The match is accomplished by selecting a sample from a color guide (like the *Mun-sell Book of Color*) or, in the case of simulated objects and illuminants on a color monitor, by adjusting the intensity of the *R,G,B* guns of a color monitor by means of a mouse or button box.

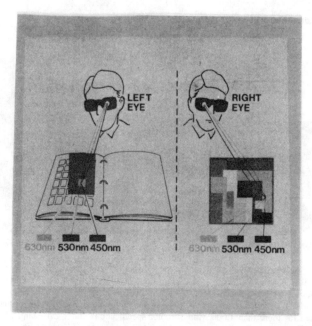

Figure 10.2. A schematic diagram of the method by which the observers selected chips in the *Munsell Book of Color* that matched the areas in the 17-area Mondrian. The observer views the *Munsell Book* with the left eye under fixed conditions, namely, the illumination is constant and a gray surround is placed over each area. The observer views the Mondrian with the right eye. The illumination on the Mondrian is varied in each of the five experiments, and the areas surrounding any particular area are arbitrary. Figure originally published by McCann et al. (1976); used by permission of Pergamon Press Ltd.

A number of empirical studies in which the asymmetric matching paradigm is utilized and that are considered to be influential by the author are now presented. The studies are interesting from both a theoretical and an empirical point of view.

Empirical test of the retinex theory

In order to quantify the predictions of the Retinex theory, McCann, McKee and Taylor (1976) conducted an experiment using the asymmetric matching paradigm. In order to keep adaptation effects as constant as possible, they presented subjects with a 17-area Mondrian stimulus to the right eye only and the *Munsell Book of Color* to the left eye only (see Figure 10.2). Each configuration was illuminated by three projectors in conjunction with narrowband interference filters with different transmissions. The settings of the three projectors illuminating the *Munsell Book of Color* were kept constant, resembling average daylight.

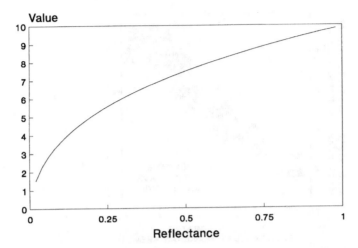

Figure 10.3. Psychophysical relation between reflectance and lightness, as expressed by the Munsell value. After Seim, Valberg (1986). *Towards a uniform color space. Colour Research and Application, 11*, 11–24.

Five different settings of the projectors were used to illuminate the 17-area Mondrian. The first illumination, the control, was identical to that falling on the *Munsell Book of Color*. The triplet of radiances that was reflected by a gray paper in the Mondrian was measured. The settings of the other four illuminants were determined by this triplet, that is, by adjusting the voltages of the three projectors so that either a red, yellow, green, or blue paper reflected the same triplet of radiances as the gray paper did under the control illuminant. Subjects had to make a color match of all 17 papers from the Mondrian with a corresponding paper from the *Munsell Book of Color*. When a successive comparison procedure was used, binocular interaction between the Mondrian and the *Munsell Book of Color* was minimized.

As was expected, McCann et al. found a relation between the reflected triplets of radiances, as integrated under the spectral sensitivity functions of the human cones, of the 17 papers in the Mondrian and all selected Munsell papers, but the linear correlation was poor. This is a typical result that demonstrates the imperfectness of human color constancy, at least in terms of quantitative color measures. Therefore a two-step transformation, following the specifications of Retinex theory, was applied to the data. First, all triplets of integrated radiances were converted to integrated reflectances by dividing them by the triplet of corresponding integrated radiances that were obtained from a reference white surface. In Retinex theory, integrated reflectance is the computational equivalent of lightness that is the biological correlate of surface reflectance. However, equal increments in reflectance do not represent equal increments in lightness sensation

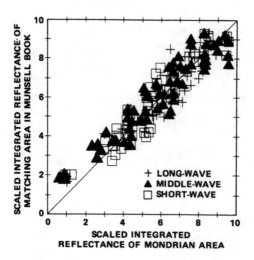

Figure 10.4. The scaled, integrated reflectance of each area in the Mondrian (horizontal axis) is plotted against the average scaled, integrated reflectance of the matching Munsell chip (vertical axis). Figure originally published by McCann et al. (1976); used by permission of Pergamon Press Ltd.

(see Figure 10.3). So, in order to obtain equal spacing, a second transformation was applied, that is, converting integrated reflectances with a psychophysical function (Glasser, McKinney, Reilly, & Schnelle, 1958) that represents the non-linear relation between lightness and reflectance. Figure 10.4 shows that the linear correlation between scaled integrated reflectances of the 17 Mondrian areas with those of the selected Munsell papers is high.

The effect of instruction

A large empirical effect on human color constancy was reported by Arend and Reeves (1986). They pointed to the ambiguity in the type of perceptual judgment that was requested from the subjects of McCann et al. Therefore, they manipulated the type of perceptual judgment by using different instructions that were found to be an important factor in the degree of color constancy that is obtained in empirical studies. They simultaneously presented two identical 32-area Mondrian configurations, one illuminated by the standard illuminant (6500K), the other by one of the test illuminants (4000K or 10000K). In fact, the configurations were simulations on a color monitor of Munsell papers as they would appear under one of the illuminants. Subjects were requested to alternate between the two configurations every second. They had to match the hue and saturation of five different target colors by means of a tablet. In the hue-match condition, subjects were instructed to match the hue and saturation of the targets as accurately as possible, whereas in the paper-match condition subjects were told that the two configurations were identical paper arrays but illuminated by different sources. They had to imagine what the target color would look like if it had been moved from the test configuration to the standard configuration and adjust the matching field accordingly. The degree of color constancy, as expressed in a Brunswik ratio, is approximately 0.4 in the hue-match condition and 0.8 in the paper-match condition. Ratios of 0.0 and 1.0 stand for no constancy and perfect constancy, respectively (see Brunswik, 1928, and Troost & de Weert, 1991b).

A psychophysical response function

Lucassen and Walraven (1993) developed a response function on the basis of an extensive set of measurements obtained from experiments with simulated papers and illuminants on a color monitor. Apart from varying the chromaticity of the test illuminant, which is common in most empirical studies, they varied the chromaticity and luminance of the standard illuminant, that is, the illuminant under which the matches had to be made. Although presenting simulations, their procedure was similar to the one used by McCann et al. (1976): Without being simultaneously visible, the test configuration was presented to one eye and the standard configuration to the other eye. Subjects were free to switch from one configuration to the other and were instructed to make an exact match in hue, saturation, and brightness. Lucassen and Walraven derived an empirical response function that contains terms for both receptor-specific contrast and stimulation. The contrast factor is similar to that of Retinex theory, and the addition of the stimulation factor explains why the predictions of Retinex theory are less successful (see Figure 10.5). An important additional finding was that a luminance difference between the standard and test configurations did not affect the hue and saturation of the matches.

Figural organization

An elegant demonstration of the relevance of a perceived spatial arrangement was given by Gilchrist (1980). He presented subjects with the stimulus shown in Figure 10.6, which is figurally organized differently by the visual system when viewed monocularly as opposed to binocularly. When viewed monocularly, the small tabs are perceived as part of the plane of their retinal surround, whereas the actual positions are perceived when the stimulus is viewed binocularly. So, the same stimulus establishes a different figural organization: Depending on whether the display is viewed monocularly or binocularly, the small tabs belong perceptually to the other large tab.

By careful manipulation of the reflectance of the tabs and the illuminance

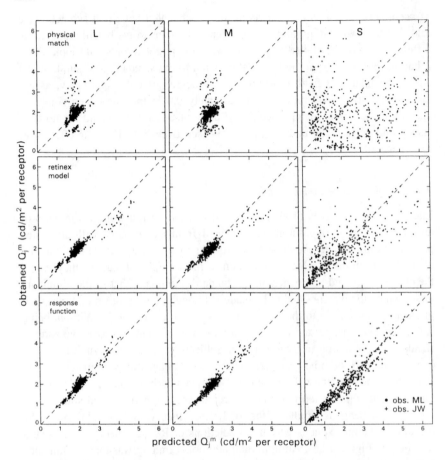

Figure 10.5. Predicted versus obtained data in terms of Qm_j, the quantity that provides a measure of the match sample (j) under the match illuminant (m). The panels are arranged in three rows, representing the predictions (for L, M, and S cones, respectively), as obtained with three different models: the physical match, retinex theory, and Lucassen and Walraven's response function. Figure originally published by Lucassen and Walraven (1993); used by permission of Pergamon Press Ltd.

conditions, the effect of figural organization on lightness perception was quantified. Gilchrist used two reflectances, low (black) and high (white), and two variations of illumination, direct and shadowed. The large tabs had different reflectances, as had the small ones. The large tabs and their coplanar small tabs had different reflectances. The intensity of the illuminant was adjusted so that the smaller tabs reflected the same absolute amount of light despite the difference in reflectance. Subjects had to match the lightness of the small tabs.

To summarize, there is a black tab and a white small tab, but when the side of the black small tab is illuminated more, it reflects as much light as does the

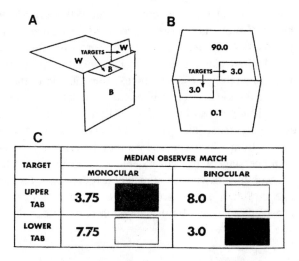

Figure 10.6. (A) Perspective view of the stimulus display used by Gilchrist (1980), showing the color (B, black; W, white) of each part. (B) Monocular retinal pattern showing luminances. (C) Average Munsell value matches for monocular and binocular viewing conditions. Figure originally published by Gilchrist (1980); used by permission of The Psychonomic Society, Inc.

white one. Consequently, the larger white tab (coplanar to the small black tab) reflects the most light and the large black tab (coplanar to the small white tab) the least (see the corresponding numbers in Figure 10.6B).

The matches in the monocular viewing condition are expected to contrast with their retinal surrounds. So, the small black tab in direct illumination is retinally surrounded by the large black tab in shadow and is perceived as lighter than the small white tab in shadow, which is retinally surrounded by the large white tab that is directly illuminated. This perceived spatial arrangement in the monocular viewing condition strongly resembles that of a classical simultaneous contrast display.

The figural organization in the binocular viewing condition is veridical; that is, because of binocular disparity, the correct spatial relations between the tabs are perceived. It is therefore expected that the observer can separate the illuminant from the object component in the light reaching the eye and, as a result, perceives the small white tab as lighter than the small black tab, although they both reflect the same absolute amount of light to the eyes. Recall that this prediction is the reverse of the one in the monocular viewing condition.

Gilchrist's results strongly confirm these expectations (see Figure 10.6C). That is, contrast matches are obtained in the monocular viewing condition and constancy matches in the binocular viewing condition, suggesting that the latter matches are caused by visual processing of binocular depth cues. Informal observations in my own lab revealed a weak confirmation of these results when a comparable stimulus configuration (i.e., real papers and light sources) was used. In a dichoptic simulation of the stimulus on a monitor, surprisingly, only contrast matches were obtained. Binocular disparity was introduced by presenting two identical patterns under a slightly different simulated orientation to the left and right eyes, respectively. Although a clear impression of depth was produced, informal observations did not reveal the spatial relations, as in the case of real papers and light sources. Of course, these informal observations do not constitute a controlled experiment from which conclusions may be drawn. They do suggest, however, that processing of binocular depth cues may not be the only explanation for the occurrence of constancy matches. It appeared, for example, that a contrast range of 900:1, which is difficult to display on a monitor, is crucial to obtain constancy matches. Further research is needed to clarify this phenomenon in more detail.

Color naming

As an alternative to the asymmetric matching paradigm, Troost and de Weert (1991b, 1992b) developed the color naming method to obtain color constancy data. Their main reason was that because colored scenes can be observed with both an analytical and a global view, experimental tasks in which responses associated with object color perception are registered should be unambiguous. The *analytical view* refers to discriminating sensory color differences up to the degree the human visual system is capable of perceiving. Professional observers, like painters or photographers, use this view in their work. Generally, they are very experienced analytical viewers because they have been extensively trained to reproduce visual scenes. This does not mean, however, that nonprofessional observers, which most people in fact are, could not adopt the analytical view. On the contrary, there are enough instances under ordinary circumstances that require an analytical view, such as dressing or choosing the colors of clothes, repainting a car, or selecting a light bulb. This view is used for any activity for which a precise comparison or judgment of color is needed. In fact, only the product of the sensory system, that is, sensory color, is inspected at the highest level of accuracy.

For most interactions with the environment, however, a categorical perception of color (see Harnad, 1987) rather than a high degree of accuracy is essential. The term *global view* is used to denote this type of color perception. If an action does not require most attentive resources to be directed to color, it is not necessary to know or be fully aware of, for example, the exact red used in a traffic light, what variety of green can be seen in a forest, whether blue the color of the shirts of teammates is exactly the same, or what shades of gray are produced on a white wall by an illuminant gradient. As long as the traffic light can be categorized as red, leaves as green, shirts as blue, and the wall as white, there are no problems in traffic participation, walking in a forest, playing football, or text editing in an office, respectively. In the global view, details in color are much less relevant.

If asymmetric matching has to be associated with one of the views described earlier, the analytical view is a more suitable candidate than the global view. Because matching takes time, observers spend time for careful inspection and comparison of two external stimuli: the color that has to be matched and the match color. Observers seem to adopt the analytical view almost automatically. Consequently, color matching under controlled conditions would be an appropriate abstraction of all tasks or interactions with the environment that require a precise examination of color. However, because color matching is time-consuming, it is not an appropriate abstraction for those actions for which an exact color specification is less relevant, that is, for which the global view is used.

If color constancy is described from a more natural perspective, its purpose should be to prevent erroneous object color perceptions due to variations in illumination, rather than to automatically eliminate the illuminant component from the light reaching the eye by peripheral mechanisms like chromatic adaptation and lateral inhibition. The contributions of the latter mechanisms to color constancy can be measured accurately with an asymmetric method but have been found to be relatively low (e.g., Arend & Reeves, 1986; Troost & de Weert, 1991b; Valberg & Lange-Malecki, 1990). Furthermore, matching takes too much time to be a valid method to investigate color constancy as an identification phenomenon under circumstances in which the global view is used, that is, when fast color categorizations have to be made. For this purpose, Troost and de Weert developed the color naming task.

Although the visual system is very sensitive to color differences, colors are perceptually grouped into discrete categories (e.g., Bornstein, 1987). A natural system of grouping colors involves labeling these categories by referring to their names (red, green, brown, etc.). Indeed, fast color judgments and useful data can be obtained if observers have to name colors (Boynton, Fargo, Olson, & Smallman, 1989; Uchikawa, Uchikawa, & Boynton, 1989a, 1989b). In Troost and de Weert's experiments, color naming responses were used to quantify color constancy. The method is very simple: Count the number of color names used for the same object when illuminated by different light sources; the lower the number of color names used, the higher the degree of color constancy. First, the names of more than 140 identically shaped but differently colored surfaces, presented against a neutral background and simulated on a color monitor as if illuminated by a standard light source (CIE illuminant D65), were registered for each subject separately. The same procedure was repeated, but now the surfaces were simulated as if they were illuminated by one of four test light sources. So, when all surfaces were presented as if illuminated by the standard and the four

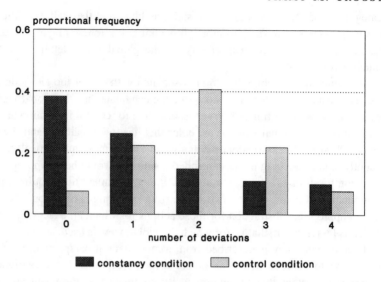

Figure 10.7. Proportional frequencies of the number of deviations that occurred in the constancy condition (darker bars) and the control condition (lighter bars) of Troost and de Weert's (1991b) color naming experiment. Color names given under the standard light source were used as targets. Under the four test light sources, the total number of deviations varied between zero and four.

test light sources were presented once to each subject, five color names for every surface and for each subject were obtained.

Next, for each subject, the four color names given under the test light sources were compared to the name given under the standard light source. Every difference from the standard name was counted as one deviation. The number of deviations from the standard name served as the constancy measure and ranged from zero to four. In Figure 10.7 (dark bars), the distribution of the number of deviations in the constancy condition is displayed. Apart from the constancy condition that was as described earlier, a control condition was added.

Recall that every target surface was presented against a neutral background and that the five illuminants induced a colorimetric shift in both target surface and background in the constancy condition. In the control condition the same surfaces and illuminants were presented, but known illuminants did not induce a colorimetric shift in the background. That is, the background was kept constant at the color of the standard illuminant. As a consequence, the state of adaptation was unchanged in the control condition and changed with the illuminants in the constancy condition. The results of the control condition are displayed in Figure 10.7 as well (light bars). They show that, on average, the five different colorimetric specifications of the target surfaces cross category boundaries more frequently in the control condition.

The difference in distributions validates the color naming method. It can be explained by the fact that in the constancy condition, compensatory mechanisms like chromatic adaptation and lateral inhibition move category boundaries consistently with the illuminant shift (see also Uchikawa et al., 1989b, for related results). Whereas different illuminations produce a shift in object color, compensatory mechanisms prevent these shifts from disturbing object identification because they remain within color category boundaries that are shifted themselves as well (Jameson & Hurvich, 1989, p. 7).

To conclude, color naming can be used as a valid method in collecting color constancy data. It is meant to obtain responses to study identification by or with color or under conditions that require a global view. As explained earlier, the analytical view is almost automatically elicited in an asymmetric matching task because two external stimuli have to be compared. The color naming task is an additional tool in color constancy research and should not be considered a competitive method for asymmetric matching.

Discussion, conclusions, and suggestions

The apparent invariance of color perceptions cannot be due solely to known automatic peripheral processes (i.e., chromatic adaptation and lateral inhibition), which suggests that to achieve color constancy, other, more intelligent processes are involved. I will try to show that, for a better comprehension of the phenomenon of color constancy, it has to be released as a special color perception phenomenon and has to be placed in the more general context of object perception. As such, it is strongly connected to the processing of figural properties in the visual image.

Katz (1911/1935) distinguished several qualities of color appearance, two of which, aperture color and surface color, are studied in color constancy research (e.g., Arend, Reeves, Schirillo, & Goldstein, 1991; Beck, 1972; Helmholtz, 1867/1962; Hering, 1874/1964; Troost & de Weert, 1991b). Whereas aperture color refers to color presented in isolation, *surface color* denotes the "belongingness" of color to an object. If chromatic color is considered as an expansion to three dimensions of achromatic color (Land, 1977, 1986a), brightness and lightness per color dimension are used as measures of the strength of sensation for aperture color and object color, respectively. Brightness is psychophysically assessed by light intensity and lightness by surface reflectance. An observation described by Hering (1874/1962, p. 10) clarifies the difference:

. . . [I]f I stand with my back to a window, hold a piece of smooth, dark-gray paper in front of me, and look with two eyes alternately at the paper and at the white-painted wall of the room behind it, then the latter appears white and the former dark gray [lightness], although the paper because of its much stronger illumination is of much stronger light intensity than the wall. Now, without changing the position of the paper or of my head in any way, let me fixate the upper edge of the paper with only one eye and try to see the colors of the paper and the wall in one plane: now indeed the wall appears darker than the paper [brightness].

In this example, the surface color mode, in which the color sensation is determined by lightness, is dominant. In order to obtain the qualitatively different brightness sensation, the observer had to force himself into the aperture mode, an impoverished viewing condition in which depth information is prevented from being processed and only the target fields are fixated (see also Gilchrist, Delman, & Jacobsen, 1982). The dependency of color sensation on the reflectance distribution when a scene is observed in its full complexity is clearly demonstrated by this kind of observation. The notion of complexity is crucial here. At the beginning of this century, *complexity* implicitly referred to the variability in the intensity distribution, due to shadow, penumbra, gradients, and three-dimensional orientation, that could be taken as informational cues of the illuminant (for reviews, see Beck, 1972; Henneman, 1935; and MacLeod, 1932). Due to concentration on the achromatic domain, in combination with the lack of a unified theoretical framework, this work still remains relatively unknown.

A more important reason for the current unfamiliarity with this work is the fact that the success of the Retinex theory (Land & McCann, 1971) in predicting color sensations based on lightness (Land, 1977; McCann et al., 1976) suggested that the surface color mode can be obtained if only a large number of differently colored fields is presented, even without those details that contain information about the illuminant distribution in a scene. In Mondrian patterns, a collage of coplanar matte papers is homogeneously illuminated by a single light source. Following this stimulus restriction, complexity is related to the number of differently colored fields in a stimulus configuration. This implies that the surface color mode can also be obtained with artificial stimuli, and consequently, that color constancy can be studied in isolation, that is, without those additional features that contribute to the object's appearance of the stimulus, like three-dimensional shape and orientation, gradients, shadows, and texture. Clearly, from the experimenter's point of view, this reduction in the number of stimulus variables is fortunate because stimulus descriptions become simpler and conditions can be controlled more easily.

Indeed, color constancy experiments have primarily been carried out with Mondrian patterns (e.g., Arend & Reeves, 1986; Land, 1977; McCann et al., 1976; Troost & de Weert, 1991b; Valberg & Lange-Malecki, 1990). For the psychophysicist who is used to working with target–surround stimuli of extreme figural simplicity, and who mainly seeks explanations that incorporate contrast ratios, every multicolored stimulus pattern is a complex one, if only because more spatial interactions are involved (e.g., Brainard & Wandell, 1986; Grossberg & Todorović, 1988; Land, 1986b; Reid & Shapley, 1988). However, compared to the complexity with which the visual system is confronted under more natural circumstances, where multiple illuminants, illuminant gradients, highlights, and shadows as well as geometric variables, specular reflectance properties, and texture of surfaces, have to be dealt with (e.g., Horn, 1986; Marr, 1982; Rogers, 1985), Mondrian patterns represent a class of visual input that puts much smaller demands on both figural and computational processing.

However, the suggestion that the visual system can be brought into the surface color mode by confronting it with a Mondrian pattern was shown to be incorrect by Arend and Reeves (1986) and Troost and de Weert (1991b). It appeared that the switch from surface color mode to aperture mode, as in Hering's observation described earlier, can in fact easily be made in the opposite direction when Mondrian-like patterns are presented to observers. If observers, being in aperture mode, are instructed to adopt the surface color mode, that is, to interpret the color differences between two stimulus patterns as the result of changed illuminant conditions, color matches are based on inferred surface characteristics rather than on the light reaching the eye. However, whereas in Hering's observation both aperture and surface color appearances emerge as direct sensations – of course, depending on the mode that is adopted – the color matches in a Mondrian environment are based on reasoning about the direct aperture color sensations, that is, "matching what one should see." In other words, the surface color mode can be adopted only when a scene is sufficiently complex in the sense that direct sensations are generated. If it is not, because important details are omitted, the observer's color sensation is automatically built up in the aperture mode.

Because the visual system has evolved under complex natural viewing conditions, the surface color mode can be taken as a default setting, giving the most reliable estimations of object color. If confronted with a much simpler scene, the visual system tries to make the best of it, and color sensations are based on spectral intensities. However, this does not mean that the latter information is eliminated or ignored in the surface color mode. On the contrary, the intensity distribution contains information concerning illuminants. Imagine a room with white walls that is illuminated by daylight through a window. The amount of light reflected from the walls decreases as a function of squared distance from the window and produces different sensations of brightness but only one lightness percept: Everywhere in the room the wall is assigned one and the same white. Although this kind of gradient can easily be solved by postulating some kind of threshold mechanism (e.g., Emerson, 1986; Grossberg & Todorović, 1988; Horn, 1974; Land, 1986a, 1986b), I prefer the type of explanation put forward by Cavanagh and Leclerc (1989) and Adelson and Pentland (1990) because it can be extended to cases that cannot be solved by merely making point-by-point comparisons of the intensity image, as in existing algorithms (see the discussion of Figure 10.8). These authors emphasize that because the origin of the light reaching the eye is an indeterminate problem, the visual system has

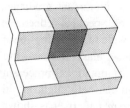 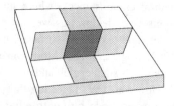

Figure 10.8. Two stimulus patterns in which the central areas (i.e., the dark quadrangle surrounded by four gray quadrangles) contain identical brightness distributions and shape relations. Figural analysis according to structural information theory predicts a preference for the step interpretation in the left pattern (A), whereas the right pattern (B) is ambiguous toward the two alternative figural interpretations. Figure created by Emmanuel Leeuwenberg.

to rely on implemented decision rules or knowledge of physical reality that restrict the number of possible solutions. For gradients, the visual system apparently tries to fix the object component while allowing variation in the illuminant component.

Adelson and Pentland (1990) used minimal-effort principles that can be taken as decision rules to elucidate the interaction between shape, illumination and reflectance. Although their model is tentative and adequate only for a limited range of stimuli, their approach looks very promising for the investigation of surface color perception within a unified framework. Figure 10.8 is an example of how the figural organization affects the lightness percept. The central areas of both Figure 10.8A and Figure 10.8B (i.e., the dark quadrangle surrounded by four gray quadrangles) contain identical brightness distributions and shape relations. A number of figural organizations of the central areas in Figures 10.8A and 10.8B are possible. I discuss two alternatives: (1) the central areas are coplanar and (2) they are arranged in a steplike shape. The crucial question is how the brightness of the central quadrangle is interpreted in either of the figural organizations. In the step interpretation, the darkness of the central quadrangle is attributed to decreased surface reflectance combined with the suggested shadow. In the coplanarity interpretation, a mosaic appears in which the darkness can only be attributed to decreased surface reflectance. If the figural properties of Figure 10.8A and Figure 10.8B are analyzed according to minimal effort principles, as used in structural information theory (see, e.g., Leeuwenberg & van der Helm, 1991), complexities are obtained for the coplanarity and step interpretations. The complexities of these different interpretations are dependent on the integration of the central areas in their corresponding contexts. If Figure 10.8A is subjected to such an analysis, a complexity of 10 units is obtained for the step interpretation and a complexity of 17 units for the the coplanarity interpretation. For Figure 10.8B, 13 complexity units are obtained for both interpretations. These results suggest a strong preference for the step interpretation for Figure 10.8A; Figure 10.8B is much more ambiguous because no preference is predicted.

Contrary to the algorithms mentioned earlier, the model of Adelson and Pentland predicts this difference. The central quadrangle in Figure 10.8A can be functionally discriminated from the one in Figure 10.8B, not because a more detailed mathematical description is used, but rather because the minimal effort principles that are incorporated for both illuminant and object components, on the one hand, and shape processing, on the other hand, generate the most likely interpretation given the constraints the visual system is assumed to put on the input data.

To conclude, Adelson and Pentland's contribution is a formal description of the interdependence of processes underlying shape and color perception that was anticipated by Koffka (1935) from a Gestalt point of view. It is based on perceptually constraining the input data by mechanisms that incorporate implemented decision rules or intuitive knowledge of physical reality. These mechanisms are probably centrally located, and as such, they can be conceived of as instances of the central factors that Helmholtz and Hering thought to be important. Although the dispute about central mechanisms still exists, it has already led to an unfavorable divergence in the literature about color constancy between those who accept the relevance of (nonsensory) processing of informational cues of illumination and/or objects (e.g., Adelson & Pentland, 1990; Beck, 1972; Cavanagh & LeClerc, 1989; Gilchrist, 1980; Rock, 1977) and those who do not (e.g., Dannemiller, 1989; Grossberg & Todorović, 1988; Land, 1977; Lucassen, 1993). Because color constancy is only partially determined by peripheral mechanisms that can be studied in isolation, that is, chromatic adaptation and lateral inhibition, the remaining variations must be resolved by central mechanisms that are also strongly involved in the processing of figural properties of the input data.

References

Adelson, E., & Pentland, A. (1990). *The perception of shading and reflectance*. Vision and Modeling Technical Report No. 140. Cambridge, MA: MIT Media Laboratory.

Arend, L., & Reeves, A. (1986). Simultaneous color constancy. *Journal of the Optical Society of America A, 3,* 1743–1751.

Arend, L., Reeves, A., Schirillo, J., & Goldstein, R. (1991). Simultaneous color constancy: Papers with diverse Munsell values. *Journal of the Optical Society of America A, 8,* 661–672.

Beck, J. (1959). Stimulus correlates for the judged illumination of a surface. *Journal of Experimental Psychology, 58,* 267–274.

Beck, J. (1961). Judgements of surface illumination and lightness. *Journal of Experimental Psychology, 61,* 368–373.

Beck, J. (1972). *Surface color perception.* Ithaca, NY: Cornell University Press.

Borges, C. (1991). Trichromatic approximation method for surface illumination. *Journal of the Optical Society of America A, 8,* 1319–1323.

Bornstein, M. (1987). Perceptual categories in vision and audition. In S. Harnad (Ed.), *Categorical perception* (pp. 287–300). New York: Cambridge University Press.

Boynton, R., Fargo, L., Olson, C., & Smallman, H. (1989). Category effects on color memory. *Color Research and Application, 14,* 229–234.

Brainard, D., & Wandell, B. (1986). Analysis of the retinex theory of color vision. *Journal of the Optical Society of America A, 3,* 1651–1661.

Brill, M., & West, G. (1986). Chromatic adaptation and color constancy. *Color Research and Application, 11,* 196–204.

Brunswik, E. (1928). Zur Entwicklung der Albedowahrnehmung. *Zeit-schrift für Psychologie, 64,* 216–227.

Buchsbaum, G. (1980). A spatial processor model for object color perception. *Journal of the Franklin Institute, 310,* 1–26.

Cavanagh, P., & Leclerc, Y. (1989). Shape from shadows. *Journal of Experimental Psychology: Human Perception and Performance, 15,* 3–27.

Cohen, J. (1964). Dependency of the spectral reflectance curves of the Munsell color chips. *Psychonomic Science, 1,* 369–370.

Dannemiller, J. (1989). Computational approaches to color constancy: Adaptive and ontogenetic considerations. *Psychological Review, 96,* 255–266.

Emerson, P. (1986). A honeycomb data array for simulating visual processes using the C programming language. *Behavior Research Methods, Instruments, and Computers, 18,* 312–320.

Gilchrist, A. (1980). When does perceived lightness depend on perceived spatial arrangement? *Perception & Psychophysics, 28,* 527–538.

Gilchrist, A., Delman, S., & Jacobsen, A. (1982). The classification and integration of edges as critical to the perception of reflectance and illumination. *Perception & Psychophysics, 33,* 425–436.

Glasser, L., McKinney A., Reilly, C., & Schnelle, P. (1958). Cube-root color coordinate system. *Journal of the Optical Society of America, 48,* 736–740.

Grossberg, S., & Todorović, D. (1988). Neural dynamics of 1-D and 2-D brightness perception: A unified model of classical and recent phenomena. *Perception & Psychophysics, 43,* 241–277.

Harnad, S. (Ed.). (1987). *Categorical perception.* New York: Cambridge University Press.

Helmholtz, H. von (1962). *Helmholtz's treatise on physiological optics* (edited and translated from the German by J. Southall). New York: Dover. (Originally published 1867).

Henneman, R. (1935). A photometric study of the perception of object color. *Archives of Psychology,* No. 179.

Hering, E. (1964). *Outlines of a theory of the light sense* (Translated from the German by L., Hurvich and D. Jameson). Cambridge, MA: Harvard University Press. (Originally published 1874.)

Horn, B. (1974). Determining lightness from an image. *Computer Graphics and Image Processing, 3,* 277–299.

Horn, B. (1986). *Robot vision.* Cambridge, MA: MIT Press.

Jameson, D., & Hurvich, L. (1989). Essay concerning color constancy. *Annual Review of Psychology, 40,* 1–22.

Katz, D. (1911/1935). *The world of color* (Translated from the German by R. MacLeod & C. Fox). London: Kegan Paul, Trench & Trubner.

Koffka, K. (1935). *Principles of Gestalt psychology.* New York: Harcourt Brace.

Land, E. (1977). The retinex theory of color vision. *Scientific American, 237,* 108–128.

Land, E. (1986a). Recent advances in retinex theory. *Vision Research, 26,* 7–21.

Land, E. (1986b). An alternative technique for the computation of the designator in retinex theory. *Proceedings of the National Academy of Science, USA, 83,* 3078–3080.

Land, E., & McCann, J. (1971). Lightness and retinex theory. *Journal of the Optical Society of America, 61,* 1–11.

Leeuwenberg, E., & van der Helm, P. (1991). Unity and variety in visual form. *Perception, 20,* 595–622.

Lucassen, M. (1993). *Quantitative studies of color studies.* Ph.D. thesis, Soesterberg, the Netherlands: Instituut voor Zintuigfysiologie TNO.

Lucassen, M., & Walraven, J. (1993). Quantifying color constancy: Evidence for nonlinear processing of cone-specific contrast. *Vision Research, 33,* 739–758.

MacLeod, R. (1932). An experimental investigation of brightness constancy. *Archives of Psychology,* No. 135.

Maloney, L., & Wandell, B. (1986). Color constancy: A method for recovering surface spectral reflectance. *Journal of the Optical Society of America A, 3,* 29–33.

Marr, D. (1982). *Vision.* San Fransisco: Freeman.

McCann, J., McKee, S., & Taylor, T. (1976). Quantitative studies in retinex theory. *Vision Research, 16,* 445–458.

Parkkinen, J., Hallikainen, J., & Jaaskelainen, T. (1989). Characteristic spectra of Munsell colors. *Journal of the Optical Society of America A, 6,* 318–322.

Reid, R., & Shapley, R. (1988). Brightness induction by local contrast and the spatial dependence of assimilation. *Vision Research, 28,* 115–132.

Richards, W., & Parks, E. (1972). Model for color conversion. *Journal of the Optical Society of America, 61,* 971–976.

Rock, I. (1977). In defense of unconscious inference. In W. Epstein (Ed.), *Stability and constancy in visual perception: Mechanisms and processes* (pp. 109–122). New York: Wiley.

Rogers, D. (1985). *Procedural elements of computer graphics.* New York: McGraw-Hill.

Sällstrom, P. (1973). *Colour and physics: Some remarks concerning the physical aspects of human color vision.* Report No. 73–09. Stockholm: Institute of Physics, University of Stockholm.

Schirillo, J., Reeves, A., & Arend, L. (1990). Perceived lightness, but not brightness, of achromatic surfaces depends on perceived depth information. *Perception & Psychophysics, 48,* 83–91.

Takahama, K., Sobagaki, H., & Nayatani, Y. (1984). Formulation of a nonlinear model of chromatic adaptation for a light-gray background. *Color Research and Application, 9,* 106–115.

Tiplitz-Blackwell, K., & Buchsbaum, G. (1988a). The effect of spatial and chromatic parameters on chromatic induction. *Color Research and Application, 13,* 166–173.

Tiplitz-Blackwell, K., & Buchsbaum, G. (1988b). Quantitative studies of color constancy. *Journal of the Optical Society of America A, 5,* 1772–1780.

Troost, J., & de Weert, Ch. (1991a). Surface reflectance and human color constancy. *Psychological Review, 98,* 143–145.

Troost, J., & de Weert, Ch. (1991b). Naming versus matching in color constancy. *Perception & Psychophysics,* 591–602.

Troost, J., & de Weert, Ch. (1992a). Techniques for simulating object color under changing illuminant conditions on electronic displays. *Color Research and Application, 17,* 316–327.

Troost, J., & de Weert, Ch. (1992b). Additional constancy data obtained with the color naming method. *Advances in Color Vision Technical Digest, 4,* 118–123.

Uchikawa, H., Uchikawa, K., & Boynton, R. (1989a). Influence of achromatic surrounds on categorical perception of surface colors. *Vision Research, 29,* 881–890.

Uchikawa, K., Uchikawa, H., & Boynton, R. (1989b). Partial color constancy of isolated surface colors examined by a color naming method. *Perception, 18,* 83–91.

Valberg, A., & Lange-Malecki, B. (1990). "Color constancy" in Mondrian patterns: A partial cancellation of physical chromaticity shifts by simultaneous contrast. *Vision Research, 30,* 371–380.

van Trigt, C. (1990). Smoothest reflectance functions. I. Definition and main results. *Journal of the Optical Society of America A, 7,* 1891–1904.

von Kries, J. (1905). Die Gesichtsempfindungen. In W. Nagel (Ed.), *Handbuch der Physiologie des Menschen* (Vol. 3, pp. 109–282). Braunschweig: Vieweg.

Worthey, J., & Brill, M. (1986). Heuristic analysis of von Kries color constancy. *Journal of the Optical Society of America A, 3,* 1708–1712.

Wyszecki, G., & Stiles, W. (1967). *Color science.* New York: Wiley.

Young, T. (1807). On the theory of light and colours. In *Lectures in natural philosophy,* Volume 2. London: Printed for J. Johnson, St. Paul's Church Yard, by W. Savage.

11   Computational models of color constancy

A. C. Hurlbert

1. Introduction

The phenomenon of color constancy has a long and rich history of study; it has been acknowledged explicitly by scientists and philosophers for at least two centuries and implicitly by poets and artists for far longer. Nor is the practice of attempting to explain color constancy new. The French scientist Monge observed in 1789 that the colors of objects viewed through colored lenses depended on the richness of the background against which they appeared (Mollon, 1985). Helmholtz (1962) concluded that the perception of color must involve an act of judgment in which the effects of the illuminant are discounted. But recently, a new approach to the study of vision, the *computational* approach, has spawned a new set of explanations. In this chapter, we review these relatively new computational models of color constancy.

1.1 The computational approach

Most computational models state the problem of color constancy thus: To recover the invariant spectral reflectance properties of object surfaces from the image irradiance, in which reflectance is entangled with surface illumination. The alleged goal of color constancy is to help determine what is in the visual world. Unlike shape, the color of an object is invariant under changes in viewpoint. If it were also entirely invariant under changes in illumination, color would be an ideal feature to use for object recognition.[1] Spectral reflectance is an invariant property of surfaces; therefore it seems plausible, if not perfectly logical, to assume that color constancy results from the attempt to recover spectral reflectance in the more general pursuit of object recognition.

Most computational models tackle the problem of color constancy for a generic visual system, one with three broadband light sensors operating in a world of flat matte surfaces illuminated by broadband lights. Most computational mod-

Research supported by the SERC/EPSRC Image Interpretation Initiative (GR/G64060), the Royal Society, and Newcastle University Research Committee. Thanks to Chris Christou and Andrew Parker of Oxford University for the use of Phos, the image generation package.

els try to attain color constancy under these limited conditions rather than to explain the limitations of human color constancy. But as with other problems in computational vision, the expectation is that the constraints needed for generic solutions might explain the particular constraints that prevent humans from attaining perfect color constancy.

1.2 Classes of computational models of color constancy

Computational models of color constancy might be considered "color appearance" or "color rendering" models because they necessarily predict the color appearance of a surface under changing illuminant. Yet they differ from such traditional *phenomenological* models, which are not reviewed here, in motivation and technique. Most "color rendering" models are designed without reference to color constancy (Hunt, 1991; Nayatani, Takahama, Sobagaki, & Hashimoto, 1990), predicting color appearance without reference to surfaces or illuminants.

Both phenomenological and computational models start with the photoreceptor activities elicited by a colored surface. Phenomenological models then apply a transformation to the receptor signals that might include parameters adjusted for the adaptational state of the eye and the color signal from the background to obtain standardized descriptors of the color appearance of the surface, as verified by color-matching experiments. Phenomenological models, then, explicitly attempt to reproduce human color matches under varying conditions. In Hunt's revised color appearance model (Hunt, 1991), for example, the equations predicting the hue and colorfulness of a color patch explicitly depend on the tristimulus values of its immediate and distant surround and of a reference white under the same illuminant.

Computational models, on the other hand, attempt to transform receptor signals into surface descriptors that represent estimates of spectral reflectance and so remain constant under changing illuminant. They are designed to achieve a presumed goal of the human visual system, rather than explicitly to predict human performance on color-matching experiments, and generally apply to more complex, less strictly defined scene configurations than do phenomenological models. Almost all varieties of computational solutions to color constancy assume that the goal of color constancy is to recover an estimate of surface reflectance.

There are two main classes of computational models of color constancy, which we may group under the headings *sensory* and *perceptual* based on their implications for human vision:

1. *Sensory*: These models require only a simple linear transformation of the initial receptor responses to produce the desired surface descriptors. They rely on a

simplified reflectance model of the world (a modified Lambertian model) and make no allowances for specular highlights, shadows, or mutual reflections. There are two subtypes:

- *Lightness algorithms:* These reduce the problem to black and white by assuming that the lightness in each of the three receptor channels may be recovered independently by the same method and that the triplet of lightnesses provides color-constant surface descriptors. Lightness algorithms generally reduce to a diagonal matrix transformation of the initial sensor responses (Finlayson, Drew, & Funt, 1993), and do not make explicit assumptions about the nature of surfaces and illuminants.
- *Linear basis algorithms:* These require that surfaces and/or illuminants be composed from a small number of fixed basis functions. Unlike lightness algorithms, these explicitly allow for nondiagonal matrix transformations that transform the initial receptor channels into new color channels in which the surface descriptors are computed.

If implemented by the human visual system, sensory algorithms could be achieved early in visual processing by adaptive scaling of the initial receptor responses, with or without combining responses to create new color channels. Thus they might take effect well before the image has been interpreted in any way – for example, before the image has been segmented into distinct surfaces or before certain image intensity changes have been classified as illumination changes such as shadows or specular highlights.

2. *Perceptual.* These models rely on more realistic reflectance models and require the presence of non-Lambertian reflection components. These *chromatic signature* algorithms analyze the variation in color of light reflected from one or more surfaces, seeking characteristic patterns in the distribution of colors in the chromaticity plane or in color three-space to find estimates of the illuminant colour or surface reflectance, using

- Specular highlights or
- Mutual reflections.

Also included in this class are

- Segmentation algorithms. These use chromatic signatures, in particular the ratio of receptor responses, explicitly to classify image intensity changes as either material boundaries or illumination shading effects. Their goal, therefore, is not to recover surface reflectance per se, but rather to mark where surface reflectance changes.

These solutions either require that image regions of specular highlights or mutual reflections be recognized as such, or may themselves drive a mechanism that identifies the physical causes of irradiance changes and therefore drives image segmentation. Thus, if implemented by the human visual system, such algorithms would necessarily occur at later stages of visual processing. Hence we may relegate these solutions to *perceptual* stages of vision.

In the human visual system, yet other solutions to color constancy may exist on even higher levels. There is some evidence from experimental studies of color constancy that familiar surfaces may act as reference surfaces to calibrate the appearance of other surfaces under changing illumination (Bramwell & Hurlbert, 1993; Fairchild, 1993). Solutions on this level may be described as *cognitive* because they require not only segmentation of the visual image into surfaces and illumination effects, but also recognition of particular objects. Computational solutions on the cognitive level might use known reference surfaces to calibrate a *sensory* or *perceptual* algorithm. This class is not discussed further here.

Most of the models described here rely on similar assumptions about the natural world and hence may be expected to fail in the same way when the assumptions are not met. Early Retinex algorithms (prototypical lightness algorithms) (Land, 1959a, 1959b) essentially assume that the brightest surface in a scene is white and therefore reflects the illuminant color; later Retinex algorithms (Land & McCann, 1971) and some linear-basis algorithms (e.g., Buchsbaum, 1980; D'Zmura & Lennie, 1986) effectively assume that the world is gray and that therefore the space-averaged light gives the illuminant color; other linear-basis algorithms assume that the number of degrees of freedom of surface reflectance is smaller than the number of receptor types sampling the light signal at each location (Maloney, 1985; Maloney & Wandell 1986). Whereas some lightness algorithms are designed to compensate for illumination that varies smoothly across space, others can compensate only for virtually uniform illumination. Yet most require a Mondrian world in which boundaries between surfaces of different reflectances are marked by step changes in image irradiance. In the following sections, we explore in more detail how particular algorithms depend on particular natural constraints.

2. Color constancy: The problem of recovering surface reflectance

The goal of most color constancy solutions is to separate and recover surface reflectance and illumination from the image irradiance equation, in which the two terms are ambiguously intertwined. The problem of separating surface reflectance from illumination itself has two parts: spatial decomposition and spectral normalization. The first is the problem of disentangling the spatial variations of the two components; the second, that of disentangling their spectral variations.

2.1 The image irradiance equation

The starting point for computational models of color vision is the image irradiance equation. This describes the relationship between the light falling on the image plane (the *image irradiance*) and the physical properties of the scene being imaged. In general, the image irradiance is proportional to the product of the light energy falling on the surface (the *surface irradiance* or *illumination*) and the proportion of incident light that the surface reflects (the *surface reflectance*).[2]

For most natural surfaces and scenes, the illumination consists of at least two distinct parts: the direct illumination from the primary light source (e.g., a desk lamp) and the indirect or mutual illumination created by light reflected from surfaces onto each other. For most natural materials, the light reflected from surfaces may also be decomposed into two parts: *body reflection* (Shafer's term) (Shafer, 1985), which emerges from the body of the material, and *interface* (Shafer, 1985), or *specular reflection*, which emerges from the air–surface interface. Paints, plastics, plants, eggshells, human skin, and many other natural materials are optically inhomogeneous, consisting of a largely transparent carrier material in which pigment particles are embedded. The body reflection, which dominates light reflected from inhomogeneous materials, emerges equally in all directions. It results from light refracted into the carrier and scattered and absorbed by pigment particles. The spectral absorbance properties of the pigment particles determine the body reflectance function, which specifies the fraction of the incident illumination that emerges at each wavelength in the body reflection. The body reflectance is the invariant surface property sought by computational models.

The interface reflection, on the other hand, is determined by the properties of the carrier material. Interface reflection arises from the air–surface interface and, for smooth surfaces, is concentrated in a single direction, the direction of perfect specular reflection. For many inhomogeneous materials, the index of refraction of the carrier is approximately constant with respect to wavelength. Thus the interface reflection emerges essentially unchanged and takes on the color of the illuminant.

For inhomogeneous materials, the full image irradiance equation is therefore

$$I(\lambda, \mathbf{x}) = [E^*(\lambda, \mathbf{n}, \mathbf{s}) + \int_s \alpha(\mathbf{x}, \mathbf{y})I(\mathbf{y}, \lambda)dS_y] \, [\rho_b(\lambda, \mathbf{x})F_b(\mathbf{v}, \mathbf{n}, \mathbf{s}) \\ + \rho_s(\lambda, \mathbf{x})F_s(\mathbf{v}, \mathbf{n}, \mathbf{s})] \tag{1}$$

where λ is wavelength; $\mathbf{x}$ is the spatial coordinate (in corresponding parts of the image and the scene)[3]; $\mathbf{n}$ is the unit vector in the direction of the surface normal at point $\mathbf{x}$; $\mathbf{v}$ is the unit vector in the direction of the viewer; and $\mathbf{s}$ is the unit vector in the direction of the light source. $E^*(\lambda, \mathbf{n}, \mathbf{s})$ is the direct illumination on point $\mathbf{x}$; $\rho_b(\lambda, \mathbf{x})F_b(\mathbf{v}, \mathbf{n}, \mathbf{s})$ and $\rho_s(\lambda, \mathbf{x})F_s(\mathbf{v}, \mathbf{n}, \mathbf{s})$ are the body and specular reflectance functions, respectively.

The full image irradiance equation therefore separates into two parts, those due to direct and indirect illumination. The second term represents the illumination created by mutual reflections between surfaces. The form factor $\alpha(\mathbf{x}, \mathbf{y})$ is defined as the fraction of the total irradiance emanating from surface $\mathbf{y}$ that falls onto point $\mathbf{x}$. It depends on the scene geometry and is symmetrical with respect to $\mathbf{x}$ and $\mathbf{y}$ for infinitesimally small areas. If, for example, points $\mathbf{x}$ and $\mathbf{y}$ lie on surfaces in the same plane, they will not reflect light onto each other, and $\alpha(\mathbf{x}, \mathbf{y})$ will be zero. The integral is taken over all points $\mathbf{y}$ in the scene (S) and so represents the sum of the light reflected from all other surfaces onto the surface at location **x**.

The equation embodies an important assumption about surface reflectance: that the spectral properties of a given material are smooth and unchanging throughout. For inhomogeneous materials, this requires that the pigment particles be uniformly distributed throughout the carrier substance and that none protrude through the surface (Shafer, 1985). This assumption of *reflectance separability* allows us to decompose each component of the surface reflectance into the product of two distinct terms, a spectral term dependent on wavelength [$\rho_b(\lambda, \mathbf{x})$] and a spatial term dependent on the imaging geometry [$F_b(\mathbf{v}, \mathbf{n}, \mathbf{s})$] (and likewise for the specular component). (The reflectance factor or *albedo* ρ_b is defined as the ratio of reflected light in a given direction to that reflected in the same direction by a perfectly reflecting diffuser identically illuminated.)

This decomposition assumes that the fraction of incident light reflected at each wavelength is not altered by the geometry of the surfaces, light source, or viewing system. It is valid for surfaces that appear equally bright from all directions. Such surfaces are said to be modified *Lambertian* surfaces.[4] For a Lambertian surface, F_b is constant with respect to **v**, **s**, and **n**; the surface reflectance function is independent of the angle at which light enters or exits the surface. That is, the surface reflectance depends solely on the material of which the surface is made and not on its orientation, shape, or position relative to the light source. ($\rho(\lambda, \mathbf{x})$ is written as a function of the spatial coordinate of the surface to illustrate that the material of which it is made may vary across space.)

Healey and Binford (1987a) have shown, using the Kubelka–Munk theory, that most inhomogeneous materials behave approximately like Lambertian surfaces in that the body reflection is roughly constant with respect to the source direction, and that therefore F_b is a function only of **v** and **n**.

The assumption that body reflectance separates into spectral and spatial components has also been experimentally validated. Lee, Breneman, and Schulte (1987) measured the spectral power distribution of reflected light from a variety of inhomogeneous materials at several viewing angles and found that for many natural materials, including plants, paints, oils, and plastics, the spectral power distribution changes in magnitude but not in shape. That is, the spectral power distribution curves are linearly related to one another at the different viewing angles, so only the brightness of the body reflection changes with viewing direction. This result indicates that for these materials, $\rho_b(\lambda)$ is indeed independent of the imaging geometry, and it is separable from F_b.

2.1.1 The neutral interface model. Some computational models further assume the *neutral interface reflection* (*NIR*) model (Lee et al., 1987). This model, common in computer graphics applications, treats surfaces as ideal optically inhomogeneous materials. It holds for materials whose refractive index is constant across the spectrum (Healey & Binford 1987b):

$$\rho_s(\lambda) = k_s. \tag{2}$$

In other words, the specular reflection is assumed neutral, constant with respect to wavelength. For materials with perfectly smooth surfaces, the geometric term F_s is a function only of the source direction **s** and the surface normal **n**, and the interface reflection is therefore concentrated in the perfect specular direction. Thus, for a smooth-surfaced, inhomogeneous material, the surface reflection will be concentrated in one direction and will take on the illuminant color. This property of most inhomogeneous materials is exploited by a class of solutions to the color constancy problem discussed in section 5.2.

The NIR model, and indeed the reflectance separability assumption that it requires, do not hold for an optically homogeneous material. These materials, such as metals or crystals, consist of a single opaque substance. The light reflected by a homogeneous material is dominated by interface reflection. The energy of the reflected light is a function both of the complex refractive index of the material, which is itself a function of wavelength, and of the imaging geometry. Thus, for homogeneous materials, the color of the interface reflection is not the same as the illuminant color, nor is it constant under changes in the illumination conditions.

Lee et al. (1987) have shown that the NIR model holds even for those materials (e.g., yellow paper) for which the spectral power distribution changes shape with viewing angle and that therefore violate the reflectance separability assumption. A plot of the chromaticities of the reflected light at different angles shows that it can everywhere be described by the sum of two lights, one with the chromaticity of the illuminant (the specular reflection), the other with the object chromaticity (the body reflection). This can occur because the chromaticities are the result of integrating the reflected light over the broad range of a sensor signal. Thus, in the integral (see section 2.3), changes in spectral power distribution with viewing angle at one wavelength may be canceled by opposite changes at another wavelength.

2.2 The Lambertian reflectance model

The full image irradiance equation (1) represents a realistic reflectance model of the world, even with its simplifying assumptions about surface reflectance. Yet all computational models of color constancy simplify the equation even further. Most rely on a spartan model of the real world, loosely based on a Lambertian reflectance model, in which surfaces are flat, matte, and engage in no mutual reflections.

2.2.1 *The single-source assumption.*   In the Lambertian world of most models, the image irradiance equation is further simplified by assuming that there is a single light source illuminating the scene. For a single direct light source, the surface irradiance E^* may be separated into the product of two terms:

$$E^*(\lambda, \mathbf{n}, \mathbf{s}) = E(\lambda)\varepsilon(\mathbf{n}, \mathbf{s}). \tag{3}$$

That is, the *single-source assumption* allows us to decompose the illumination into distinct spectral and spatial components, just as we did for surface reflectance. It implies that the illumination must vary over space in the same way for each wavelength.

The assumption is clearly violated by the presence of mutual reflections, which effectively create secondary light sources that are not in general the same color as the primary light source. Because most surfaces are not highly reflective or all-surrounding (except, of course, walls), a single surface does not usually substantially change the global illumination in an entire scene. So it is not unreasonable to assume that the sum of all mutual reflections generally creates a secondary light source that averages to the same neutral color at every location. Mutual reflections are therefore usually summed up in an additional ambient illumination term that is nondirectional and the same color everywhere. But as we shall discuss in section 5.3, mutual reflections can cause substantial local perturbations in the color of the illuminant on a surface, and these perturbations may in fact enhance, rather than degrade, color constancy (Funt, Drew, & Ho, 1991).

2.2.2 *The image irradiance equation in a Lambertian world.*   To obtain the simplified image irradiance equation used by most computational models, we start with Equation 1 and discard the terms due to specular and mutual reflections. We therefore have

$$I(\lambda, \mathbf{x}) = E^*(\lambda, \mathbf{n}, \mathbf{s}) \, [\rho_b(\lambda, \mathbf{x})F_b(\mathbf{v}, \mathbf{n}, \mathbf{s})] \tag{4}$$

Under the single-source assumption, the factors in Equation 4 may be regrouped by defining the *effective illumination* $E(\lambda)F_\varepsilon(\mathbf{x}) = E(\lambda, \mathbf{x}) = F_b(\mathbf{v}, \mathbf{n}, \mathbf{s})E(\lambda)\varepsilon(\mathbf{n}, \mathbf{s})$. All of the geometric factors have been absorbed into the single term $F_\varepsilon(\mathbf{x})$. The effective illumination is the surface illumination modified by the orientation, shape, and location of the reflecting surface and by the geometry of the imaging system. Some models that assume Lambertian reflection go further and effectively set $F_\varepsilon = 1$, so that the effective illumination is uniform across space, or $E(\lambda, \mathbf{x}) = E(\lambda)$.

The image irradiance equation then becomes

$$I(\lambda, \mathbf{x}) = E(\lambda, \mathbf{x})\rho_b(\lambda, \mathbf{x}) \tag{5}$$

and the problem of color constancy simplifies to one of disentangling the contributions of $E(\lambda)$ and $\rho_b(\lambda)$ in the image irradiance $I(\lambda)$ at each location $\mathbf{x}$ in the image.

Immediately it can be concluded that color constancy solutions based on Equation 5 can be expected to fail where the image irradiance signal is dominated by specular or mutual reflections or in a scene lit by more than one direct light source. Neither Equation 1 nor Equation 5 accurately describes light reflection from homogeneous materials, so none of the computational models described here apply to metals or other such substances.

2.3 The matrix equation

Equation 5 states a simple relationship: The image irradiance is proportional to the product of surface reflectance and illumination. But this relationship holds only for individual wavelengths, and visual systems typically do not sample the image irradiance at each wavelength of the spectrum. In biological and most artificial visual systems, the image irradiance is captured by a two-dimensional array of light sensors. The signal transmitted by a sensor is a function of the light intensity integrated over the sensor's spectral sensitivity range. In the human retina, there are three types of cone with different broadband but overlapping spectral sensitivities. The signal transmitted by a cone is a nonlinear function of the light quanta it captures and is usually approximated by a logarithm:

$$Q^v(\mathbf{x}) = \log \int a^v(\lambda)\rho(\lambda, \mathbf{x})E(\lambda, \mathbf{x})d\lambda \tag{6}$$

where v labels the type of receptor (the long-, middle-, or short-wavelength-sensitive cone), $Q^v(\mathbf{x})$ is the signal sent by the sensor, and $a^v(\lambda)$ is its spectral sensitivity function. (Because as Baylor, 1987, has shown, the cone response can be approximated as a linear function of its quantum catch within small operating ranges, we will now drop the logarithm.)

Thus, although Equation 5 serves as the starting point for several solutions to the color constancy problem, it does not adequately state the problem for biological visual systems. We may derive a more general equation that takes into account broadband sensors and that also incorporates further essential constraints on the surface reflectances and illuminants. We will show later how the various solutions to the color constancy problem each fit into the framework of this more general equation.

Many computational models make the explicit assumption that the body reflectance function $p_b(\lambda)$ of a natural material can be decomposed into the weighted sum of a small number of basis functions (Brill, 1978; Buchsbaum, 1980; D'Zmura, 1992; Forsyth, 1990a; Finlayson et al., 1993; Maloney, 1985;

Maloney & Wandell, 1986; Sallstrom, 1973).[5] The coefficients in the weighted sum then specify the surface uniquely. Several different analyses (Dannemiller, 1992; Jaaskelainen, Parkkinen & Toyooka, 1990; Maloney, 1985; Parkkinen, Hallikainen, & Jaaskelainen, 1989) have concluded that at least three degrees of freedom are necessary to represent most natural surface reflectances. Maloney (1985) showed that three basis functions could account for 99% of the variance in Krinov's (1947) set of 337 spectral reflectance functions; Dannemiller (1992) showed that an ideal observer required the same number to discriminate members of the same set of reflectances from their basis functions approximations.

The *low-dimensional, linear-basis* assumption is also generally true for natural illuminants: daylights between color temperatures 4000°K and 25000°K are well approximated by the first three principal components of all daylight distributions (Judd, MacAdam, & Wyszecki, 1964; Wyszecki & Stiles, 1982), and other broadband illuminants, such as blackbody radiators, are well described by linear combinations of the same set of basis functions (Maloney, 1985). Thus:

$$\rho_b(\lambda) \approx \rho_1 R_1(\lambda) + \rho_2 R_2(\lambda) + \rho_3 R_3(\lambda) \tag{7}$$

and

$$E(\lambda) \approx \varepsilon_1 E_1(\lambda) + \varepsilon_2 E_2(\lambda) + \varepsilon_3 E_3(\lambda) \tag{8}$$

where the $R_i(\lambda)$ are the surface reflectance basis functions and the $E_i(\lambda)$ are the illuminant basis functions. Under the linear basis model assumption, the coefficients p_i are the surface descriptions we seek to solve the color constancy problem.

So

$$Q^v(\mathbf{x}) = \int a^v(\lambda) \left[\sum_i \rho_i(\mathbf{x}) R_i(\lambda)\right] \left[\sum_j \varepsilon_j(\mathbf{x}) E_j(\lambda)\right] d\lambda \tag{9}$$

$$= \sum_i B_{vi}(\mathbf{x})\rho_i(\mathbf{x}) \tag{10}$$

where

$$B_{vi}(\mathbf{x}) = \int a^v(\lambda) R_i(\lambda) \left[\sum_j \varepsilon_j(\mathbf{x}) E_j(\lambda)\right] d\lambda \tag{11}$$

and B_{vi} is dependent on the particular illuminant $E(\lambda)$.

For a trichromatic visual system, and for surface reflectances and illuminants adequately described by 3 degrees of freedom, we may write at each location $\mathbf{x}$ in the image

$$\begin{pmatrix} B_{L1} & B_{L2} & B_{L3} \\ B_{M1} & B_{M2} & B_{M3} \\ B_{S1} & B_{S2} & B_{S3} \end{pmatrix}_{\mathbf{x}} \begin{pmatrix} \rho_1 \\ \rho_2 \\ \rho_3 \end{pmatrix}_{\mathbf{x}} = \begin{pmatrix} Q_L \\ Q_M \\ Q_S \end{pmatrix}_{\mathbf{x}} \tag{12}$$

or

$$
\begin{pmatrix} \rho_1 \\ \rho_2 \\ \rho_3 \end{pmatrix}_x = \begin{pmatrix} B_{L1} & B_{L2} & B_{L3} \\ B_{M1} & B_{M2} & B_{M3} \\ B_{S1} & B_{S2} & B_{S3} \end{pmatrix}_x^{-1} \begin{pmatrix} Q_L \\ Q_M \\ Q_S \end{pmatrix}_x \tag{13}
$$

Equation 12 may be written in vector form:

$$
\mathbf{Q(x)} = \mathbf{B}_{vi}(\mathbf{x})\rho(\mathbf{x}) \tag{14}
$$

which now resembles Equation 5 in showing explicitly that the image irradiance (as captured by the photoreceptors) is a product of illumination and surface reflectance. Here, though, the continuous-valued functions of wavelength I and ρ are replaced by their three-component vector counterparts, and E is replaced by the illuminant matrix $\mathbf{B}$. The vector $\mathbf{Q}$ represents the three samples of image irradiance taken in each of the receptor spectral channels. The vector ρ now consists of the three components of surface reflectance measured in the three spectral channels defined by the surface reflectance basis functions.

Equation 12 illustrates that to recover the set of surface descriptors ρ_i under the low-dimensional linear-basis assumption, the visual system must apply a linear transformation to the set of sensor responses Q. Because this transformation depends on the illuminant, it is obvious that the visual system must obtain some estimate of the illuminant in order to solve for constant colors. It is also obvious that the problem is underconstrained. Under the assumption that surface reflectance and illumination may each be described fully by three basis functions, there are six unknown variables at every location in the image – three components each for surface reflectance and illumination – and only three known – the three sensor signals.

The transformation in Equation 12 is exactly linear only if the low-dimensional, linear-basis assumption holds exactly. Forsyth (1990a, 1990b) writes a more exact form of Equation 13 that makes no a priori assumption about the dimensionality of surface reflectance. (Forsyth formulates the color constancy problem slightly differently: The constant descriptors recovered under the transformation are the receptor responses to the surface under a "canonical" illuminant. In other words, the transformation maps the color appearance of a surface under an unknown illuminant into its appearance under a reference illuminant.) Forsyth shows that, in general, the color-constant descriptors may be obtained by a linear transformation of the receptor responses *plus* a residual term. The residual term will be exactly zero if the dimensionality of surface reflectance equals the number of receptor types. Forsyth analyzes other conditions under which the residual term may be zero, including, for example, the case in which the unknown illuminant energy is a constant multiple of the canonical illuminant energy at each wavelength in the receptor spectral band.

Equation 13 provides a unifying framework for all solutions that assume a Lambertian world (Finlayson et al., 1993, make a similar observation). Not all solutions begin explicitly with this equation, but each can be put into this form. The solutions differ slightly in terms of (i) the constraints they place on surfaces and illuminants, (ii) the form, diagonal or nondiagonal, that they assume the matrix B_{vi}^{-1} to take, and (iii) the method used to recover B_{vi}^{-1}. Note that the assumption that the matrix is diagonal is equivalent to assuming that each sensor response need only be scaled by an illuminant-dependent factor to yield a constant surface descriptor, and that the basis functions are in the sensor channels. If a nondiagonal matrix is required for a solution, this means that each surface descriptor must be derived from a linear combination of all the sensor signals.

2.4 Natural constraints

Most models of color constancy rely on similar assumptions to solve the matrix equation (Equation 13). These take the form of constraints on the type and number of surfaces and illuminants in the scene, and on the sensors. Table 11.1 lists the natural constraints employed by color-constancy solutions, taking typical examples of each class of algorithm to illustrate the differences and similarities between them. The following sections describe the solutions, constraints, and their implications in more detail.

3. Lightness algorithms

The simplest solution to the matrix equation (13) is a form of adaptation. Each receptor response is divided by some measure of the average signal over the scene for that receptor; this is effectively the technique used by lightness algorithms (Blake, 1985; Brelstaff & Blake, 1987; Horn, 1974; Hurlbert, 1986; Land, 1959a, 1983; Land & McCann, 1971; Moore, Fox, Allman, & Goodman, 1990) pioneered by Land. In terms of Equation 13, lightness solutions find a diagonal matrix that converts the triplet of receptor responses into a triplet of constant color descriptors.

Because, as Equations 6 and 14 make clear, both the illumination and the reflectance can vary across space, lightness solutions must achieve two goals: *spatial decomposition* of the image irradiance and *spectral normalization* of the surface reflectance and the effective irradiance. Spatial decomposition requires determining which changes across space in the image irradiance arise from changes in the surface reflectance and which from illumination – for example, distinguishing between a change in surface material and a shadow. Spectral normalization requires determining the relative amounts of light in different spectral bands of the illuminant.

Table 11.1. *Natural constraints used by different classes of algorithms to solve the problem of color constancy.*

	Lightness			Linear Basis					Chromatic Signature		
	Land '59	McCann '76	Hurlbert '86	Buchsbaum '80	Maloney '85	Forsyth '90	DZmura '92	Finlayson '93	Lee '86	Healey '91	Funt '91
On surface reflectance											
Mondrian world	✓	✓	✓	✓	✓	✓	✓		✓		
Reflectance separability	✓	✓	✓	✓	✓	✓	✓	✓		✓	✓
Lambertian reflection	✓	✓	✓	✓	✓	✓	✓	✓			✓
Grey world	✓		✓	✓							
Brightest is white/ reference surface		✓				✓		✓			
Low-dimensional, linear basis				✓	✓	✓	✓	✓		✓	✓
Surface complexity	✓				✓		✓				
Specular reflection									✓	✓	
On illumination											
Single primary source		✓	✓	✓	✓	✓	✓	✓	✓	✓	✓
Spatially uniform				✓	✓		✓	✓			
Smoothly varying across space	✓	✓	✓			✓					
Low-dimensional, linear basis				✓	✓	✓	✓	✓		✓	
Mutual illumination											✓
On sensors											
Transformed spectral sensitivities								✓			
Fewer types than reflectance d.o.f.					✓						
Other											
Two views							✓				

3.1 The retinex algorithm

Land (1964) proposed that the color of an object is determined by its three lightness values in the three receptor channels: short-, middle-, and long-wavelength. (Lightness is defined by Evans, 1948, as "the visually apparent reflectance of a surface under a given set of conditions"; it is the perceptual correlate of surface reflectance.) In ingenious demonstrations, Land (1964) showed that the lightness of an object in any one channel does not vary when either the spatial or spectral properties of the illumination on the entire scene are changed. This constancy he attributed to the visual system's ability to estimate the relative amount of light an object reflects without being misled by its absolute brightness. In perhaps his best-known demonstration, Land illuminated a Mondrian with three narrowband lights. He showed that (i) changing the relative brightness of the three lights did not significantly change the colors in the Mondrian, despite changing the ratio of, say, long- to middle-wavelength light coming from any one Mondrian patch and that (ii) introducing a spatial non-uniformity (as a smooth gradient or a "mottled"ness) in one light again changed neither the lightness in that channel nor the colors in the Mondrian; two perceptibly different patches remained different even when made to reflect equal amounts of light in each channel.

Land's striking conclusions were that (i) lightness is determined independently in each receptor channel and depends only on the relative amounts of light in that channel reflected by all the surfaces in the scene; (ii) the trio of lightness values determines color; and (iii) the human visual system can establish a lightness scale that stays roughly constant for a given scene even under non-uniform illumination. Land concluded, in other words, that to perceive color the visual system compares the light intensities in one channel across space, rather than the light intensities between channels at one location in space.

Land's primary concern was to explain the "great miracle of the eye," the fact that it could "find the reflectance that lies beneath all of these variegated superficial phenomena" (Land, 1964). By "superficial phenomena," he meant chiefly those induced by spatially nonuniform illumination. Thus his goal was chiefly to demonstrate how spatial decomposition could be achieved.

Land thus reduced the problem of color constancy to one of spatial decomposition of the image irradiance in a single spectral channel – a black-and-white problem. The assumption underlying the use of his and other lightness algorithms in color computation (Blake, 1985; Horn, 1974; Hurlbert, 1986; Crick, pers. comm.) is that Equation 6 may be solved for $\rho_i(\mathbf{x})$ independently and identically for each of the three chromatic channels, and the resulting triplet of lightness values specifies color.

Formally, in terms of Equation 12, Land's assumption that lightness is computed independently in each channel means that the illuminant matrix $\mathbf{B}$ must be diagonal, and that therefore

$$B_{vv}(\mathbf{x})\rho_v(\mathbf{x}) = Q_v(\mathbf{x}) \tag{15}$$

In general, the illuminant matrix $\mathbf{B}$ will not be diagonal: for broadband illuminants and broadband sensor sensitivities, it will not.

3.1.1 The retinex algorithm: Implementations. To perform spatial decomposition, the Retinex algorithm relies on two constraints:

- *Mondrian world:* The scene is a two-dimensional Mondrian, that is, a flat surface covered with discrete patches of uniform surface reflectance. Therefore, $\rho^i(\mathbf{x})$ is uniform within patches but changes sharply at edges between patches.
- *Smoothly varying illumination:* The effective irradiance $E(\lambda, \mathbf{x})$ varies slowly and smoothly across the entire scene and is everywhere independent of the viewer's position.

(Note that although Land does not formally state these constraints as such, the key demonstrations of his retinex solution are performed on scenes that satisfy these constraints.)

One version of the retinex algorithm (performed by a hypothetical neural system involving elements of both retina and cortex) performs the step of spatial decomposition by taking the difference in log $Q_v(\mathbf{x})$ between adjacent points in many pairs along many paths radiating from $\mathbf{x}_o$, the point at which lightness is to be computed. The differences are thresholded and summed for each path, giving approximately the logarithm of the ratio between the reflectances at the start $\mathbf{x}_o$ and end points $\mathbf{w}$:

$$\begin{aligned}
\tilde{L}^v(\mathbf{x}_o, \mathbf{w}) = \sum_{i=0}^{w} T[\log Q_v(\mathbf{x}_{i+1}) - \log Q_v(\mathbf{x}_i)] &\simeq \\
\log \rho^v(\mathbf{x}_o) - \log \rho^v(\mathbf{w}) &= \\
\log[\rho^v(\mathbf{x}_o)/\rho^v(\mathbf{w})]
\end{aligned} \tag{16}$$

where T represents the thresholding operation and $\tilde{L}^v(\mathbf{x}_o, \mathbf{w})$ is the lightness at $\mathbf{x}_o$ relative to endpoint $\mathbf{w}$.

Taking thresholds of the differences along the path is essential to achieve spatial decomposition of the image irradiance if the illumination varies over the image: small changes in the image irradiance are assumed to be due to the illuminant and so are discarded. Only the abrupt changes ascribed to borders between patches of different reflectance are retained. Without thresholding, $\tilde{L}^v(\mathbf{x}_o, \mathbf{w})$ would equal $\log[(Q^v(\mathbf{x}_o)/Q^v/(\mathbf{w})]$, which, by Equation 15, reduces to $\log[(\rho^v(\mathbf{x}_o)/\rho^v(\mathbf{w})]$ only if the illumination is the same at $\mathbf{x}_o$ and $\mathbf{w}$ and therefore the illuminant factor B_{vv} cancels out in the ratio.

Spectral normalization is then achieved by averaging the relative reflectance $\tilde{L}^v(\mathbf{x}_o, \mathbf{w})$ over all N paths emanating from $\mathbf{x}_o$ to yield the lightness $L^v(\mathbf{x}_o)$:

$$L^v(\mathbf{x}_o) = \frac{\sum^N \tilde{L}^v(\mathbf{x}_o, \mathbf{w})}{N} \simeq \log \rho^v(\mathbf{x}_o) - \frac{\sum^N \log \rho^v(\mathbf{w})}{N}$$

$$= \log \rho^v(\mathbf{x}_o) - \overline{\log \rho^v(\mathbf{w})} \qquad (17)$$

where $\mathbf{w}$ labels the end point and the path. As Brainard and Wandell observe, the latter expression is equivalent to $\log[\rho^i(\mathbf{x}_o)/\hat{\rho}^i(\mathbf{w})]$, where $\hat{\rho}^i(\mathbf{w})$ is the geometric mean of surface reflectances in the scene.

In this version of the retinex algorithm, therefore, the computed lightness of a surface approximates the (logarithm of) its reflectance normalized by the geometric mean of the surrounding surface reflectances. The triplet of lightness values in the three spectral channels then defines the color of a patch. In order to recover constant colors, the algorithm must implicitly assume, then, that the average reflectance is the same in each channel and for every scene.

Thus, this version of the retinex algorithm relies on an additional constraint, the *gray-world* assumption.

> • *Gray world:* The average surface reflectance of each scene in each spectral channel is the same: gray, or the average of the lightest and darkest naturally occurring surface reflectance values.

This assumption appears in similar guise in other solutions to color constancy and has been used even longer as the basis for color reproduction algorithms. Evans was one of the first to formulate it. Hunt (1947, p. 294) quotes Evans: "The more pleasing effect is often produced in colour prints if they are so made that instead of the colour balance being correct, in which grey is printed as grey, it is so adjusted that the whole picture integrates to grey."[6]

The gray world assumption allows lightness algorithms to compensate for temporal changes in the spectral energy distribution of the illuminant on a given scene but cannot distinguish such changes from skews in surface reflectance distributions between scenes. Any multiplicative change in the receptor responses is always interpreted as a change of scale in the illuminant. Any skew in the range of surface reflectances in a scene will be incorrectly interpreted as a skew in the illuminant spectrum. Lightness algorithms that average to gray will "see" a dull red patch against a range of green patches as lighter than when seen against a range of red patches under the same illumination, and will interpret the skew toward green as a lack of red in the illuminant.

Land only implicitly used the gray world assumption. In his first demonstration of the retinex algorithm, he in fact relied instead on the *brightest-is-white* assumption by normalizing all lightness values to the signal from the brightest patch in that channel, using the "reset" operation. In the original retinex algorithm, paths are drawn across the sensor array, as earlier, and the ratio of receptor responses $Q^v(\mathbf{x})_{i+1}/Q^v(\mathbf{x})_i$ is taken at each junction in each path. Normalizing to the brightest patch is achieved by resetting to 1 each ratio that is greater than 1 before it enters the sequential product (or sum of logs). This reset operation ensures that the sequential product at sensor $\mathbf{x}_o$ for one path ending at $\mathbf{w}$, $\tilde{L}^v(\mathbf{x}_o, \mathbf{w})$ equals the ratio of the irradiance at $\mathbf{x}_o$ to the highest irradiance encountered along that path.

Under the assumptions listed earlier, this ratio is approximately equal to the ratio of surface reflectance at $\mathbf{x}_o$ to the highest reflectance along the path. The lightness at sensor $\mathbf{x}_o$, $L^v(\mathbf{x}_o)$ is then set to the geometric mean of $\tilde{L}^v(\mathbf{x}_o, \mathbf{w})$ over all paths. Assuming that, on average, the same number of paths reach the area of highest reflectance in the scene, $\tilde{L}^v(\mathbf{x}_o, \mathbf{w})$ will be a measurement of the reflectance at $\mathbf{x}_o$ normalized to the highest reflectance in the scene.

To recover constant colors, this normalization scheme relies on the assumption that the brightest patch in each spectral channel reflects all the illuminant energy in that channel:

- *Brightest is white*: The brightest patch in each spectral channel has 100% reflectance in that channel.

Note that this assumption does not require the *same* patch to have the highest reflectance in each spectral channel – that is, it does not require the presence of a pure white patch, only the presence of a patch that is "white" for each lightness channel.

This version of the retinex algorithm achieves good color constancy especially in Land's demonstrations, where the brightest patches were in fact close to white. John McCann, who continued work on the retinex after leaving Land's group, continued to use the brightest-is-white assumption implicitly and explicitly, and has done experiments concluding that a white in the field is necessary for color constancy.

3.2 Formal equivalence of lightness algorithms

Several variations on Land's retinex algorithms have been proposed (Blake, 1985; Horn, 1974; Hurlbert, 1986; Moore et al., 1990). Most are concerned with different means for achieving spatial decomposition of the image irradiance signal. Horn (1974) replaced Land's one-dimensional spatial differentiation along paths with two-dimensional spatial differentiation by the rotationally symmetric Laplacian operator ∇^2. The problem is then to recover the reflectance function whose differentiation under the Laplacian would equal the thresholded Laplacian of image irradiance:

$$\nabla^2 L(\mathbf{x}) = T[\nabla^2 Q^v(\mathbf{x})] \qquad (18)$$

This Poisson equation has known solutions under given boundary conditions. For example, Hurlbert (1986) proposed a multiple-scales algorithm that obtains the lightness in a given spectral channel by filtering the image irradiance Q through a set of difference-of-Gaussians (DOG) operators at different spatial scales and summing their thresholded outputs.

Lightness algorithms that specifically employ spatial differentiation of the image irradiance equation to decompose it into reflectance and illumination can be fit into a single formal framework, which illustrates that the distinct methods (e.g., one-dimensional differentiation along a contour or two-dimensional differentiation in a region) are equivalent. The framework also shows that each solution requires a normalizing term to achieve constant lightness across all scenes.

The optimal solution to the formal statement of the problem can then be found by applying regularization techniques, through learning with artificial neural networks, or by optimal linear estimation (Hurlbert & Poggio, 1988). The optimal operator for achieving spatial differentiation found by all of these methods is a linear filter that has in the space domain a narrow, positive peak and a broad, shallow, negative surround – that is, one that subtracts a weighted average of the (log) image irradiance values in a broad surround from the central value to obtain lightness at the center. In the spatial frequency domain, the filter is bandpass – it removes low spatial frequencies due to illumination and high spatial frequencies due to noise but retains medium-high spatial frequencies due to reflectance. The exact form of the optimal filter depends on the types of spatial variations in the illuminant that it is designed to encounter.

3.3 Lightness algorithms, von Kries adaptation, and spectral channels

The lightness algorithms just discussed assume that lightness may be recovered independently and in the same way in each spectral channel, and that the chief problem is how to remove the effect of spatial variations in the illumination. The solution is a filter that reduces sensitivity to illumination gradients – it blurs and discounts smooth shading and weak shadows. Under the gray-world assumption, lightness algorithms factor out the contribution of the illuminant by filtering out small local changes in brightness and smoothing the result over the image to obtain an average of the illuminant energy in each spectral channel. This estimate of the illuminant energy is then used to normalize the receptor response and so recover lightness. Because lightness algorithms treat each lightness channel independently, the scale of reflectance relative to the illuminant is lost for each channel.

The idea of scaling the photoreceptor responses to achieve color constancy is an old one, generally attributed to von Kries (see, e.g., Jameson & Hurvich,

1972; Worthey, 1985). In von Kries adaptation, long considered to be one of the primary mechanisms underlying color constancy, the receptor sensitivities $a^v(\lambda)$ are scaled by normalizing factors that vary with the illumination in order to keep perceived color constant. The von Kries adaptation model says that under a change in illumination from $E_1(\lambda)$ to $E_2(\lambda)$, the receptor sensitivities are scaled

$$k_1^v a^v(\lambda) \mapsto k_2^v a^v(\lambda)$$

so that

$$k_1^v \log\left[\int a^v(\lambda)\rho(\lambda, \mathbf{x})E_1(\lambda)d\lambda\right] = k_2^v \log\left[\int a^v(\lambda)\rho(\lambda, \mathbf{x})E_2(\lambda)d\lambda\right] \quad (19)$$

Lightness algorithms propose methods for computing the scaling factors k^v when the overall illumination level varies across the scene; spatial differentiation, coupled with nonlinear thresholding or reset steps, followed by integration, enables scaling factors to be recovered that approximate the mean illuminant energy in each channel. The normalizing factors therefore depend in a nonlinear (or linear, in some versions discussed earlier) way on the surround.

Although it is generally accepted that some form of spatial averaging occurs in the human visual system (see, e.g., Courtney, Finkel, & Buchsbaum, 1995), it is not known what form this averaging takes, at what level it occurs, and to what extent it accounts for human color constancy. The fact that surface colors do depend on surrounding colors, both immediately adjacent and more distant, is strong evidence for long-range normalizing effects. A deeper question links color constancy to that of color coding by the human visual system: In which spectral channels is the averaging done? If three numbers representing normalized spectral reflectance do indeed determine color appearance, in what three channels are these numbers computed?

Von Kries adaptation and Land's early retinex algorithms assume that lightness is computed in the photoreceptor spectral channels – that is, that the photoreceptor signal Q is proportional to the spectral reflectance in that channel and that those channels adequately describe surface reflectance. This is not generally true; the photoreceptor channels are not matched filters to the basis functions for spectral reflectance, and a change in illuminant energy typically does not scale the receptor responses in the same way to every surface in the scene.

Land demonstrated the retinex algorithm on Mondrians illuminated by three nonoverlapping narrowband lights, so chosen that the short- and long-wavelength lights each stimulated only one cone type (S and L, respectively), while the middle-wavelength light stimulated both the L and M cone types. The retinex computed lightness independently in each of the channels defined by the three lights. Thus, Land ensured the near-diagonality of the matrix $\mathbf{B}$: For the

S cone type, for example, the signal is simply the product of the illuminant energy and reflectance at the peak wavelength in the short-wavelength band, scaled by the S cone sensitivity at that wavelength.

The resulting lightness values approximate measurements of surface reflectance in each of the three narrowband channels defined by the light sources – and are therefore generally inadequate as a description of the full surface spectral reflectance. In general, for broadband illuminants and broadband sensors, a diagonal transformation (or adaptive scaling) of the sensor signals will not produce color-constant surface descriptors.

But, as several authors have observed, diagonal transformations can achieve color constancy even for human photoreceptors, under certain conditions, and for restricted classes of surface reflectance. West and Brill (1982) derived formulas for surface reflectances that remain color constant under von Kries adaptation. Qualitatively, these are jagged reflectances, with several peaks over the wavelength spectrum, and do not resemble the reflectance spectra of most naturally occurring surfaces.

Hurlbert (1986) illustrates that, theoretically, if the surface reflectance basis functions can be chosen so that they are equal and orthogonal with respect to integration with the a_v, then lightness values in the basis functions channels can be recovered by a diagonal matrix $\mathbf{B}$. Again, this is a strong restriction on surface reflectance that would not generally hold for naturally occurring surfaces.

This latter solution also requires that the receptor channels first undergo a linear transformation into a new set corresponding to the basis functions channels. Finlayson et al. (1993) proved that a similar transformation is necessary and sufficient to allow a second, diagonal transformation to recover color-constant descriptors, but only in the special world in which surface reflectances can be described by two basis functions and illuminants by three. This is a general proof that applies to any set of distinct sensors. The combined result of the initial linear transformation on the sensors and the diagonal transformation is, of course, a nondiagonal transformation.

Finlayson et al. (1993) propose an algorithm for finding the diagonal transformation that requires the receptor responses to two distinct surfaces, as well as the receptor responses to a reference surface (or set of surfaces) under the "canonical" illuminant. They demonstrate that for simulated collections of Munsell papers under broadband illuminants, better color constancy is achieved if a "sharpening" linear transformation is first applied to the human receptor responses, followed by a diagonal transformation, as compared with a diagonal transformation alone.

D'Zmura and Lennie (1986) suggest similarly that the three reflectance descriptors of Equation 14 can be recovered (to within a single scaling factor on the absolute brightness of the illuminant) by successively applying two transformations to the receptor signals: a diagonal transformation followed by an "adaptive linear transformation" on the scaled cone signals. Implicitly relying on the gray-world assumption, this algorithm uses space-averaged cone signals as scaling factors. The condition for achieving color constancy is that the second transformation produces sensor channels that match the basis functions for surface spectral reflectance.

D'Zmura and Lennie (1986) propose specifically that the two transformations are applied in this particular order by the primate visual system – and that therefore the output of the combined transformations is represented by the activity at the color-opponent stage. Therefore, if the primate visual system achieves color constancy, the spectral sensitivity of the color-opponent channels must match the second and third basis functions for surface reflectance. Indeed, they are similar but not identical. The shapes of the primate opponent-color channels are better predicted as the channels that achieve optimum information transmission by reducing redundancy between – or decorrelating – the cone signals (Buchsbaum & Gottschalk, 1983). The similarity in shape between the channels predicted by the analyses of color information transmission and of surface reflectance composition is nonaccidental, because each analysis performs a decomposition into principal components, which will necessarily resemble an achromatic channel and two color-opponent channels.

Another method for obtaining a diagonal matrix equation for color constancy is to introduce the integrated reflectance as the surface descriptor (see Lee et al., 1987; McCann, McKee, & Taylor, 1976; and section 5.2). This is equivalent to assuming that the scaled receptor activities will themselves serve as surface descriptors, as the early retinex algorithms do. The preceding discussion emphasizes that lightness computed in this way will not in general yield accurate and invariant estimates of surface reflectance. But lightness algorithms and other forms of von Kries adaptation (including those with nonlinear adjustments of independent cone signals) do achieve *approximate* color constancy in the natural world (e.g., Lucassen & Walraven, 1993; Moore et al., 1990). Foster and Nascimento (1994) show that for Munsell paper reflectances and daylight spectra, the ratios of cone excitations from any two surfaces within a scene (and, therefore, receptor activities scaled to "white" or "gray") do remain approximately invariant.

4. Linear Basis Algorithms

As described above, Land's retinex algorithm and other lightness algorithms may be considered a subset of solutions to the matrix equation for color constancy (Equation 13), which was derived by assuming that surface reflectances and illuminants can both be described by the linear combination of a small number of fixed-basis functions. But, as emphasized earlier, lightness algorithms do not rely explicitly on this assumption. Furthermore, they take as their chief goal that of discounting spatial variations in the illuminant to recover von Kries-type scaling factors.

In these ways, lightness algorithms differ from *linear-basis algorithms* (Brill, 1978; Buchsbaum, 1980; Maloney, 1985; Sallstrom, 1973; Yuille, 1984) that explicitly make the *low-dimensional, linear-basis* assumption. This class of algorithms is concerned with deriving a general solution to the matrix equation (Equation 13), making no assumption about the diagonality of matrix **B**. Thus, whereas in lightness algorithms the scale of reflectance relative to the illuminant for each channel cannot be recovered, in spectral basis algorithms only one normalizing factor, that of the overall illuminant intensity, is lost.

Linear-basis algorithms also differ from lightness algorithms in assuming that the illumination is uniform over the scene.

> • *Uniform illumination:* $E(\lambda, \mathbf{x})$ is uniform across space (or varies so slowly that its spatial dependence can be ignored). That is, $E(\lambda, \mathbf{x}) = E(\lambda)$ and $\varepsilon(\mathbf{x}) = \varepsilon_i$ in Equation 8.

The assumption of uniform illumination means that the illuminant matrix $B_{vi}(\mathbf{x})$ is the same at every spatial location. Linear-basis algorithms exploit the redundancy in the illuminant's contribution to the receptor signals sampled from several different surfaces in the scene and apply additional constraints to solve for the illuminant matrix.

Buchsbaum's (1980) solution relies on a form of the gray-world assumption. To achieve color constancy, Buchsbaum solves first for the illuminant vector components ε. Because Equation 9 is symmetric with respect to the components of illumination and reflectance, the photoreceptor signals can be described equally well as a linear transformation of the illuminant vector for a given surface reflectance. Buchsbaum therefore writes the matrix equation as

$$Q^v(\mathbf{x}) = \sum_j \mathbf{S}_{vj}(\mathbf{X})\varepsilon_j \tag{20}$$

where the matrix S_{vj} depends on the surface reflectance:

$$S_{vj}(\mathbf{x}) = \int a^v(\lambda)E_j(\lambda)[\sum_i \rho_i(\mathbf{x})R_i(\lambda)]d\lambda \tag{21}$$

Buchsbaum then solves for the illuminant vector ε by assuming that the illumination is uniform over the scene, and that the receptor response averaged over the scene is the same as the receptor response to a standard neutral surface.

The sensor response averaged over the scene is given by

$$\overline{Q}^v = \sum_{\mathbf{x}} b(\mathbf{x})[\sum_j \mathbf{S}_{vj}(\mathbf{x})\varepsilon_j] = \sum_j \overline{\mathbf{S}}_{vj}\varepsilon_j \tag{22}$$

where the matrix $\overline{\mathbf{S}}_{vj}$ depends explicitly on the average surface spectral reflectance of the scene:

$$\bar{S}_{vj} = \int d\lambda a^v(\lambda)E_j(\lambda)\sum_x b(\mathbf{x}) \sum_i \rho_i(\mathbf{x})R_i(\lambda) = \int d\lambda a^v(\lambda)E_j(\lambda)\bar{R}(\lambda) \tag{23}$$

where $b(\mathbf{x})$ is the weighting factor for the reflectance at $\mathbf{x}$.

The algorithm then stipulates that $\bar{S}_{vj}$ equals the response to standard neutral reflectance, R_g:

$$\bar{S}_{vj} = S_{vj}(\mathbf{g}) = \int d\lambda a^v(\lambda)E_j(\lambda)R_g(\lambda) \tag{24}$$

where $R_g(\lambda)$ is the surface spectral reflectance of a standard material, for example, a reference gray. That is, Buchsbaum assumes that the weighted average of all reflectances in a given scene is known. This is equivalent to the gray-world assumption.

Under this final constraint, the matrix $S_{vj}(\mathbf{g})$ is inverted and applied to the vector of average sensor response to recover the illuminant components ε_j. These can be substituted into Equations 11 and 13 to recover the components of surface reflectance.

Forsyth (1990b) proposes another, more general method for recovering color-constant descriptors that also relies on a prior knowledge about reference surfaces. For the conditions under which the transformation in Equation 13 is exactly linear (discussed in section 3.3), Forsyth's algorithm recovers the transformation for a set of surfaces under an unknown illuminant by (1) recording the gamut of receptor responses to a very large collection of surfaces under the canonical illuminant, (2) finding the set of feasible linear maps that transforms the receptor responses under the unknown illuminant into a subset of the canonical gamut and, (3) selecting the most likely map from the feasible set by finding the intersection of the maps for all the surfaces. In addition to requiring a record of the color appearance of a large reference set of surfaces, the algorithm requires the existence of many distinct surfaces under the unknown illuminant: a strong form of the surface complexity condition (see later).

In a world where surface reflectances and illuminant spectra each have three degrees of freedom, visual systems with only three sensors cannot recover the matrix B_{vi} (diagonal or nondiagonal) without imposing additional constraints such as the gray-world assumption. But if, for example, surface reflectances are simpler or sensor types more numerous, then there do exist direct solutions to the matrix equation. Maloney (1985) analyzes the conditions under which solutions can be obtained without imposing a priori constraints.

For example, Maloney and Wandell (1986) illustrate a solution for the case in which there is one more sensor type than there are components of surface reflectance. Let k be the number of sensors, n the degrees of freedom in surface reflectance, and m the degrees of freedom in the illuminant spectrum. Each sensor signal provides one equation of the form

$$Q^v(\mathbf{x}) = \int a^v(\lambda) \left[\sum_i^n \rho^i(\mathbf{x})\, R_i(\lambda) \right] \left[\sum_j^m \varepsilon_j^m(\mathbf{x}) E_j(\lambda) \right] d\lambda \qquad (25)$$

If $k = n + 1$, then the number of equations obtained by taking s samples of the scene for each sensor is $(n + 1)s$. Assuming that each sample is taken from an area of different surface spectral reflectance, the number of unknowns is ($sn + m$) because, under the assumption of uniform illumination, the illumination is the same at each sampled location. In principle, then, a solution can be found if the number of unknowns exceeds the number of knowns, that is, if $s > m$, or if the number of distinct surfaces sampled is greater than the number of illuminant components.

In practice, because the set of equations is nonlinear, a solution does not necessarily exist but must be demonstrated. Maloney and Wandell (1986) show that if there are only two components of surface reflectance, then the vectors of receptor responses Q^v from several samples fall in a plane, the equation of which is determined by the two columns of the illuminant matrix B_{v1} and B_{v2}, which are in turn determined by the illuminant vector ε. From the equation of the plane, the illuminant vector can be determined up to a single multiplicative constant.

It is important to note, though, that the preceding analysis shows that if there are three receptors, a unique solution can be obtained only if surface reflectance and illumination each have only 2 degrees of freedom. In every case, the *surface complexity condition* must be met: The receptor responses must be sampled from at least $(k - 1)$ surfaces. For three receptors, then, at least two distinct surfaces are required. In practice, the algorithm performs best with more than $(k - 1)$ surfaces (Maloney, 1985).[7]

The preceding equation-counting argument assumes that the task underlying color constancy is to recover constant surface descriptors from a single view of the surfaces under an unknown illuminant. D'Zmura and Iverson (D'Zmura, 1992; D'Zmura & Iverson, 1993a, 1993b) observe that the natural task of color constancy is to recover surface descriptors under changing illumination, and that multiple views under different illuminants in fact provide enough information to solve the problem.

Let v be the number of views and, hence, the number of unknown illuminants and let s be the number of surfaces sampled. Then the number of unknowns under these views is $vm + sn - 1$ (subtracting 1 for the unrecoverable overall scaling factor on the illuminant energy), and the number of knowns is kvs. In principle, then, a solution exists for three sensors and three components each of surface reflectance and illumination, provided that there are at least two views of three distinct surfaces. D'Zmura and Iverson (1993b) demonstrate that a solution does exist in this and other cases. They write an expanded version of Equation 15 in which a diagonal block matrix relates the concatenated vectors of unknown illuminants to the concatenated vector of receptor responses under the distinct views, analyze the conditions under which a solution can be obtained to this equation, and compute solutions using various sets of basis functions for surface reflectance and illumination. For example, they show that for illuminants with three components, a trichromatic visual system can recover up to eight components of surface reflectance, given three views.

4.1 Using neural networks to learn the color constancy transformation

The algorithms described earlier employ analytic techniques to determine the transformation that maps the receptor responses to a surface under unknown illuminants into color-constant descriptors under the assumption that the mapping is linear. Other techniques for finding the transformation include learning it from examples using artificial neural networks or optimal linear estimation. Hurlbert, Wen, and Poggio (1994) used artificial neural network techniques to obtain the optimal mapping and to determine whether it is indeed linear. They trained two different forms of neural network on two tasks: (1) given the color appearance of a test surface under a specific test illuminant, recover its appearance under the standard illuminant, and (2) given the color appearances of a test and a reference surface under an arbitrary test illuminant, recover the appearance of the test surface under the standard illuminant. Surfaces were Munsell papers; color appearances were specified as CIE tristimulus values; and illuminants were CIE daylights of varying temperature.

On both tasks, the networks produced good color constancy on novel papers after training on a relatively small number of samples. Interestingly, for the second task, one type of network performed more accurately when predicting color appearances for specific observers (i.e., when trained on human color constancy matching data) than when predicting perfectly constant colors.

The exact form of the transformation learned by the network on the first task was determined by recovering the equivalent polynomial of the learned mapping. As expected, the mapping is indeed approximately linear and nondiagonal, indicating that cone-opponent transformations are necessary to recover invariant surface color descriptors.

These results, together with known physiological data, suggest that the human visual system could plausibly learn and apply (via adaptive scaling) a set of linear mappings for commonly encountered illuminants.

5. Perceptual solutions

The algorithms for color constancy discussed earlier assume that the illumination is spatially and spectrally uniform, and that the world is flat and Lambertian.

But as Bajcsy, Lee, and Leonardis (1990) point out, in the real world, local variations in illumination, both spatial and spectral, are striking. Most natural materials reflect some specular light; three-dimensional objects cast shadows and colored light onto each other; many scenes are lit by multiple distinct light sources. Algorithms on the *perceptual* level exploit rather than ignore such real complications – for example, by using specular highlights to recover the illuminant color or interreflections to estimate surface reflectance. Because specular highlights and interreflections must first be identified as such, *color segmentation* algorithms may be considered necessary precursors to these algorithms because they are designed to identify shadows, shading, and other illumination effects and to distinguish them from material boundaries.

5.1 Segmentation by color

Segmentation of images into distinct objects or object parts remains a formidable problem in machine vision. Algorithms in the long tradition of black-and-white machine vision rely on detecting luminance edges as potential object boundaries. Luminance edges – suitably thresholded, enhanced, and grown – indeed suffice to segment images of matte, uniformly lit objects in uncluttered scenes. But shadows, specular highlights, and steep intensity gradients on highly curved surfaces also create luminance edges. Segmentation algorithms that use luminance edges to parse real-world scenes therefore face the problem of differentiating between spurious and real object boundaries. Color information can be crucial in solving this problem.

The main goal of *color segmentation* algorithms is to use color to identify the physical causes of image irradiance changes and thereby segment the scene into distinct materials. An ancillary objective is to assign to the distinct materials color labels that are invariant under illumination changes. Thus color segmentation algorithms differ somewhat in motivation from the algorithms explicitly designed to recover constant colors discussed earlier.

Lightness algorithms effectively label all sharp irradiance changes in the image as material boundaries. For example, lightness algorithms cannot distinguish the sharp decrease from bright to dark across a shadow edge from a reflectance change between patches of different reflectance. In large part, this is because they fail to exploit a fundamental feature of human color vision: color opponency. In contrast to lightness algorithms, segmentation algorithms allow spatially nonuniform illumination and compare signals between spectral channels at single locations to find true material boundaries.

The segmentation algorithm of Rubin and Richards (1984), for example, rules out a shadow edge if it coincides with a spectral crosspoint: that is, if the irradiance in one spectral channel decreases sharply as the irradiance in a second channel increases across the same edge. This algorithm, like most other color segmentation algorithms, makes the *single-source assumption*. Under this assumption, neither shadows nor surface orientation changes on a uniform material can produce a spectral crosspoint, although specular highlights can.

The single-source assumption also permits us to separate the illumination into the product of distinct spatial and spectral terms (see Equation 3). Spatial variations in the illumination intensity therefore cancel out in the ratio of reflected light in different spectral bands. Thus,

$$h_{\nu\mu} = \frac{Q^{\nu}}{Q^{\mu}} = \frac{E^{\nu} [\rho_b^{\nu} F_b(\mathbf{x})]}{E^{\mu} [\rho_b^{\mu} F_b(\mathbf{x})]} = \frac{E^{\nu} \rho_b^{\nu}}{E^{\mu} \rho_b^{\mu}} \tag{26}$$

where E^{ν} and ρ_b^{ν} are the components of illuminant and reflectance in the νth spectral band, respectively.

The band ratio $h_{\nu\mu}$, or *hue*, as we may loosely call it (Hurlbert, 1992), will change only when surface reflectance changes and so may be used to mark changes in surface material. This simple idea underlies several segmentation and recognition algorithms (Funt & Finlayson, 1991; Gershon, Jepson, & Tsotsos, 1986; Healey & Binford, 1987a; Hurlbert, 1992; Sung, 1992). Rubin and Richards (1984), for example, use *ordinality* to characterize regions marked by edges that produce spectral crosspoints, where ordinality is defined by the signs of the color-opponent ratios:

$$\frac{Q^{\nu} - Q^{\mu}}{Q^{\mu} + Q^{\nu}} \tag{27}$$

Ordinality gives a crude spectral characterization of a material marked by the preceding segmentation step.

These algorithms act primarily but not perfectly to distinguish material boundaries from shadows or shading due to surface orientation changes. Neither spectral crosspoints nor hue changes are sufficient to identify material boundaries in the absence of the single-source assumption or in the presence of specular highlights. For example, if two spatially and spectrally distinct light sources illuminate a uniform surface, their energies can be adjusted to produce a spectral crosspoint at an edge. Similarly, a strong specular highlight produced by a spectrally biased light source can give rise to both a spectral crosspoint and a change in hue.

Strictly speaking, the existence of a visible shadow implies the existence of more than one light source. That is, if an object is illuminated by a single, localized light source, the shadow it casts will be totally dark unless the shadowed area is illuminated by a second source not occluded by the object. But the single-source assumption may still hold, and therefore segmentation algorithms may still work, if the gray-world assumption holds and the secondary light source consists only of indirect illumination from other surfaces. In a gray world, the diffuse interreflections between object surfaces average to the color of the light source, and the "shadow" source therefore has the same color as the primary light source. Gershon et al. (1986) relax the single-source assumption by allowing ambient illumination to be colored differently from the primary illuminant.

Such segmentation algorithms work reasonably well in a Lambertian world but are flummoxed by specular reflections, which effectively violate the constraint that a uniform surface must have a uniform reflectance. But these algorithms may therefore help mark regions where specular highlights occur (e.g., where the hue ratio changes in conjunction with a large brightness increase), and highlights can provide other benefits. Under the NIR model (valid for inhomogeneous materials like plastics, paint, and skin), specular reflections take on the illuminant color. The color of light reflected from a glossy object will be a mixture of the invariant object color ("body" color, as Shafer, 1985, calls it) and the illuminant color. Several authors use this fact in different implementations toward different goals.

5.2 Using specular highlights to find the illuminant color

According to the full image irradiance equation (but neglecting mutual reflections for the moment), the light reflected from an inhomogeneous material is the sum of two components: specular reflection from its surface and diffuse reflection from the pigment particles embedded in the material. The law of color additivity ensures that the color of the reflected light is the sum of the colors of these components. Because the contributions of the body and specular reflections vary across the surface, depending on the geometric factors F_b and F_s, the weights in the color mixture also vary across the surface. For example, in regions of strong specular reflection, the color of the reflected light will be dominated by the illuminant color. Where the specular reflection is weak, the light will have the color of the body reflection. Elsewhere the color must be a linear combination of the two. Hence, the colors of light reflected from a single surface form a regular pattern in color space. Several authors (D'Zmura & Lennie, 1986; Healey, 1991; Klinker, Shafer, & Kanade, 1988; Lee, 1986) have made this observation and have proposed algorithms that analyze the chromatic signature of specular objects to segment scenes or recover the illuminant color. One such algorithm (Lee, 1986) is based on the following analysis:

The receptor response to a non-Lambertian material is given by

$$Q^v(\mathbf{x}) = \int d\lambda a^v (\lambda)E(\lambda)[\rho_b(\lambda)F_b(\mathbf{x}) + \rho_s F_s(\mathbf{x})] \tag{28}$$

or (approximately)

$$Q^v(\mathbf{x}) = E^v[\rho_b^v F_b(\mathbf{x}) + \rho_s F_s(\mathbf{x})] \tag{29}$$

where E^v and ρ_b^v are the components of illuminant and reflectance in the vth spectral band, respectively.[8]

Using the spectral band ratios introduced above as our chromaticity coordinates, we obtain:

$$\frac{Q^v}{Q^\mu} = \frac{E^v[\rho_b^v F_b(\mathbf{x}) + \rho_s F_s(\mathbf{x})]}{E^\mu[\rho_b^\mu F_b(\mathbf{x}) + \rho_s F_s(\mathbf{x})]}$$

$$= \frac{E^v\,[\rho_b^v\left(\dfrac{F_b(\mathbf{x})}{F_s(\mathbf{x})}\right) + \rho_s]}{E^\mu\,[\rho_b^\mu\left(\dfrac{F_b(\mathbf{x})}{F_s(\mathbf{x})}\right) + \rho_s]}$$

$$(30)$$

Where $F_b(\mathbf{x})$ is small compared to $F_s(\mathbf{x})$, the contribution of the body reflectance term becomes negligible and the ratio tends toward the light source color, that is,

$$\frac{Q^v}{Q^\mu} \longmapsto \frac{E^v}{E^\mu} \tag{31}$$

For large $F_b(\mathbf{x})/F_s(\mathbf{x})$, the ratio tends toward the color of the body-reflected light:

$$\frac{Q^v}{Q^\mu} \longmapsto \frac{E^v \rho^v}{E^\mu \rho^\mu} \tag{32}$$

At every point $\mathbf{x}$ pairs of ratios satisfy the linear relationship

$$\frac{Q^w}{Q^\mu} = a\frac{Q^v}{Q^\mu} + c \tag{33}$$

where $a = \dfrac{E^w\,(\rho^w - \rho^\mu)}{E^v\,(\rho^v - \rho^\mu)}$ and $c = \dfrac{E^w\,(\rho^v - \rho^w)}{E^\mu\,(\rho^v - \rho^\mu)}$.

Therefore, the chromaticities of light reflected from different regions on a glossy surface, respectively dominated by specular and diffuse reflections, will fall on a line connecting the coordinates of the illuminant color and the body-reflected color (see Figure 11.1). (The effect of the specular highlight is to move the color of the reflected light away from the body-reflected color and toward the reference "white" of the light source, or in other words, to "desaturate" it.)

Lines corresponding to several surfaces in the same scene will intersect at the illuminant chromaticity (see Figure 11.1). One solution to the problem of color constancy is to find this intersection. The *chromaticity convergence* algorithm (Lee, 1986) begins by detecting color edges – that is, marking points where the ratio Q^v/Q^μ changes, as in the color segmentation algorithms described

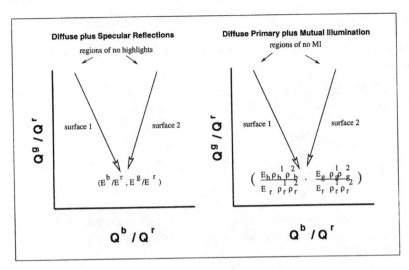

Figure 11.1.(a) Chromaticities from two inhomogeneous materials illuminated by the same source fall on two lines that intersect in the color of the light source. The upper parts of the lines represent chromaticities from regions with weak or no specular highlights. (b) Chromaticities from two surfaces engaging in mutual illumination, under the same primary illuminant, fall on lines that intersect in the color of the mutually reflected light.

earlier. The algorithm selects color edges that arise from specular highlights by collecting ratios along directions in which the image irradiance changes most steeply (on the principle that specular highlights generate maximal changes in image brightness) and accepts those data sets that are well fit by lines. The intersection of the best-fitting lines from several surfaces yields the illuminant color.

Klinker et al. (1988) make the equivalent observation that in color three-space, the color of the light reflected from a single inhomogeneous material is the vector sum of the illuminant color and the body color (the *Dichromatic Reflection Model*). Colors from different regions of the material fall in a planar cluster shaped like a "skewed T" in color three-space. To segment a scene into objects, Shafer, Kanade, Klinker, and Novak (1990) plot the color triplets from all image locations and carve the resulting three-dimensional histogram into a series of planes, each of which contains a color distribution consistent with reflection from a single object. To identify the illuminant color, they search for the intersection line of several object planes, as do Tominaga and Wandell (1990).

Healey (1991) uses the same idea, that for many materials the reflected light color is the sum of the body and illuminant colors, to recover the full surface reflectance spectrum. His algorithm requires a single surface, on which it identifies a region of pure body reflection and a region dominated by specular reflection. In each of several wavelength channels, the algorithm computes the difference in intensity between the two regions, which must correspond to the pure specular reflection, and by the NIR model, to the source intensity in that wavelength channel. The contribution of the illuminant to the body reflection is then factored out, leaving the invariant surface reflectance in that channel. The algorithm then uses the low-dimensional, linear basis assumption to reconstruct the full surface spectral reflectance function.

Brill (1990) unifies these approaches in a general framework for segmentation of scenes with specular or matte surfaces under one or more illuminants, translating and elaborating on the work of the Russian Nikolaev.

These algorithms have been devised chiefly for use by an artificial visual system or as theoretical solutions to the color-constancy problem, rather than as models of mechanisms used by the human visual system. There are obvious arguments against the proposal that the human visual system relies on such mechanisms. Even in ideal form, implemented by an ideally efficient visual system, the solutions impose strict requirements: the single-source assumption (the illuminant color must be the same for all objects in the scene, so that it may be identified as the common component to all reflected light); reflectance separability; and, of course, the presence of significant specular reflections. Even where they do not require identification of regions of pure body reflection or prior segmentation of the scene into distinct surfaces, they are greatly aided by such preprocessing.

Where the single-source assumption is met, the materials perfectly satisfy the NIR model, and the sensors reliably record the image irradiance, the chromatic signature fits the prediction. But for real images, the signature is much harder to decipher: Color values deviate from the predicted patterns due to internal noise in the sensors, the existence of multiple light sources (including interreflections), variations in surface reflectance across a supposedly uniform material, and deviations from the NIR model. Noise due to these causes is amplified by taking ratios in converting sensor signals to chromaticity coordinates.

5.3 Using mutual reflections to find the body color

Although specular highlights violate the assumption of Lambertian reflection on which many solutions to color constancy depend, their chromatic signature actually reveals the illuminant color and thereby provides a distinct route to constant colors. Mutual reflections violate another critical assumption, that of a single light source, but their chromatic signature also can be interpreted to yield information about the invariant reflectance properties of surfaces.

Temporarily ignoring specular reflections (which we will justify later), we may rewrite the image irradiance equation as

$$I_i(\lambda,\mathbf{x}) = \left[E_i^*(\lambda,\mathbf{x}) + \sum_j \alpha_{ij}(\mathbf{x})I_j(\lambda, \mathbf{x}) \right] [\rho_i(\lambda)F_i(\mathbf{x})] \tag{34}$$

where the integral over space has been converted into a discrete sum, α_{ij} is the geometric form factor between surface i and j at point $\mathbf{x}$ on surface i,[9] ρ_i is the invariant body reflectance factor of surface i, and F_i is its geometric component. The discrete sum therefore represents the contribution of all other surfaces to the indirect illumination at $\mathbf{x}$ on surface i. As the spectrum of light reflected from surface j onto i depends in turn on the spectrum reflected from i onto j, Equation 34 generates a set of simultaneous equations that can be solved exactly for each wavelength λ. We can simplify the equations by considering the case of only two surfaces and assuming that light bounces only once between them (following Funt et al., 1991). Then the signal in the νth receptor channel for surface 1 is

$$Q_1^\nu(\mathbf{x}) = kE^\nu \rho_1^\nu[F_1(\mathbf{x}) + \alpha_{12}(\mathbf{x})\rho_2^\nu] \tag{35}$$

or, equivalently,

$$Q_1^\nu(\mathbf{x}) = kE^\nu \rho_1^\nu\alpha_{12}(\mathbf{x}) \left[\frac{F_1(\mathbf{x})}{\alpha_{12}(\mathbf{x})} + \rho_2^\nu \right] \tag{36}$$

where ρ_2^ν is the integrated reflectance of the second surface in the νth channel. This equation now has exactly the same form as Equation 29 for the sum of diffuse and specular reflections. It illustrates that the color of the light reflected from a surface participating in mutual reflections with one other surface is a mixture of the colors of the primary reflected light and the mutually reflected light. Colors from different regions of one surface will fall on a line in chromaticity space (or in a plane in color three-space) whose equation is given by

$$\frac{Q_1^w}{Q_1^\nu} = a\frac{Q_1^\mu}{Q_1^\nu} + c \tag{37}$$

where $a = \dfrac{E^w\rho_1^w (\rho_2^w - \rho_2^\nu)}{E^\mu\rho_1^\mu(\rho_2^\mu - \rho_2^\nu)}$ and $c = \dfrac{E^w\rho_1^w (\rho_2^\mu - \rho_2^w)}{E^\nu \rho_1^\nu(\rho_2^\mu - \rho_2^\nu)}$.

Where the factor α is small compared to the body reflectance factor F, the light from surface 1 will be dominated by primary reflections, and the receptor response ratios will be the same as for a Lambertian surface under a single light source. One endpoint of the line in chromaticity space therefore approaches the color of the body reflected light:

$$\frac{Q_1^\mu}{Q_1^\nu} \longmapsto \frac{E_1^\mu\rho_1^\mu}{E_1^\nu\rho_1^\nu} \tag{38}$$

The other endpoints to the color of the mutually reflected light, which in the first-order approximation here is the color of the primary light source modified by one reflection each from the two surfaces:

$$\frac{Q_1^\mu}{Q_1^\nu} \mapsto \frac{E_1^\mu \rho_1^\mu \rho_2^\mu}{E_1^\nu \rho_1^\nu \rho_2^\nu} \tag{39}$$

Lines from the two surfaces will intersect at the secondary light source color. In theory, then, the ratio of the two endpoints of the line for one surface yields a measure of the reflectance of the second surface:

$$\frac{\dfrac{Q_1^\mu}{Q_1^\nu}_{\text{secondary}}}{\dfrac{Q_1^\mu}{Q_1^\nu}_{\text{primary}}} = \frac{\dfrac{E_1^\mu \rho_1^\mu \rho_2^\mu}{E_1^\nu \rho_1^\nu \rho_2^\nu}}{\dfrac{E_1^\mu \rho_1^\mu}{E_1^\nu \rho_1^\nu}} = \frac{\rho_2^\mu}{\rho_2^\nu} \tag{40}$$

In practice, the procedures of finding endpoints and taking ratios are highly vulnerable to deviations from the ideal in real images and to noise inherent in any biological or artificial imaging system. Figure 11.2 illustrates that the first-order approximation holds adequately when the light is allowed to bounce infinitely many times between the surfaces. Figure 11.2 depicts two planar surfaces (of finite dimension) inclined at an opening angle of 40°, simulated with a global radiosity package[10] that solves exactly the set of simultaneous equations represented in Equation 34 for the full visible spectrum, sampled at 10-nm intervals. In the simulation, the surfaces are "coated" with spectral reflectances corresponding to two Munsell papers, an orange (YR 8/4) and a lavender (RP 8/4), and viewed under daylight. The chromatic signature of the light reflected from the two planes fits the theory: The fitted lines from the two surfaces intersect in a color that closely approximates the color of the mutually reflected light predicted by the one-bounce model. (Note that the intersection of the lines fitted to the data actually gives a better approximation to the color of the mutually reflected light, both because it is from a realistic simulation and because the one-bounce estimate relies on somewhat inaccurate estimates of the true spectral reflectances of the papers.)

When the illuminant is changed on the surfaces, from (reddish) D42 to (bluish) D100, the signature shifts in color space, but the invariant body colors predicted for the two surfaces (from the ratios of endpoints) remain roughly constant. Thus the theory predicts that two surfaces should remain more constant in color under changes in illumination when they engage in mutual illumination than when they do not.

Chromatic signatures from objects in the real world also comply with the theory: In Figure 11.3, a blue clay cone sits in front of a folded card that is lavender on one side and orange on the other, illuminated by tungsten light.

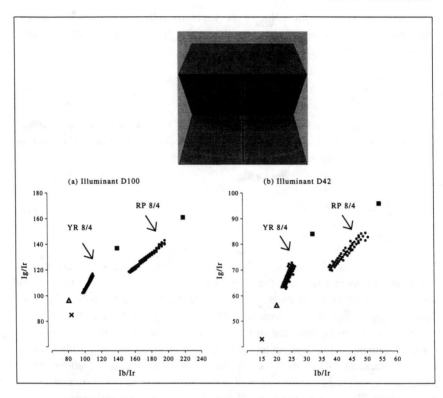

Figure 11.2. Scatter diagram of chromaticities from the vertical slice shown (filled circles) across the join between two cards (Munsell papers YR 8/4 and RP 8/4) inclined at an opening angle of 40° under (a) daylight of temperature 10,000°K and (b) daylight of temperature 4200°K, simulated with a full radiosity package. Chromaticities are given as ratios of CRT phosphor RGB intensities, obtained by conversion from the CIE tristimulus values of the simulation. Filled squares mark the chromaticities from an otherwise identical image simulated with no mutual illumination. Crosses mark the intersection of the lines fitted to the chromaticity clusters. Open triangles mark the chromaticity of the mutually reflected light predicted by a one-bounce model of mutual reflection $\left(\dfrac{E_1^B \rho_1^B \rho_2^B}{E_1^R \rho_1^R \rho_2^R}, \dfrac{E_1^G \rho_1^G \rho_2^G}{E_1^R \rho_1^R \rho_2^R} \right)$, using estimates of ρ^R, ρ^G, and so on obtained from the chromaticities of the papers simulated under illuminant D65. The ratios of the coordinates of the endpoints of one line give the body color of the other surface, according to the theory described in the text. The coordinates calculated in this way do remain roughly invariant under the illumination shift and close to the coordinates of the papers under D65: for paper YR 8/4, about (0.36, 0.54), and for RP 8/4, about (0.67, 0.65) (scaled values).

Chromaticities from the region of the cone illuminated by reflections from the card, as well as by the primary light source, fall on a line, as predicted. One end of the line points to the cluster of chromaticities that arise from the same region of the cone when it is identically illuminated against a white background and therefore unperturbed by mutual reflections from the orange card – this

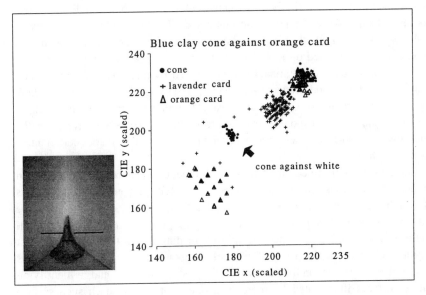

Figure 11.3 Scatter diagram of chromaticities from the regions marked by thick black lines in an image of a blue cone against a folded card painted orange on the left, lavender on the right (shown here as its luminance image). The full-color image was obtained with a charge coupled device (CCD) camera fitted with four sets of filters, closely approximating the spectral sensitivities of the CIE $\bar{x}$ (two additive parts), $\bar{y}$, and $\bar{z}$ color-matching curves. The chromaticity coordinates given are scaled approximations to the true CIE coordinates. The small cluster of dots (*arrow*) show the chromaticities from the cone when identically illuminated but imaged against a flat white background. The upper cluster of dots therefore represents the chromatic perturbations caused by indirect illumination from the colored cards. The lowest cluster of overlapping chromaticities from the orange and lavender cards gives the color of the mutually reflected light between them. The cone does not shed significant indirect illumination on the cards in the regions marked.

cluster gives the color of the primary reflected light. The signatures from the two cards form two lines that intersect in the color of their mutually reflected light.

The noisiness of the chromaticity clusters (even from the small regions used) suggests that methods for fitting lines and finding intersections for real-world data will be inherently fragile. Funt and Drew (1991) describe a more extended analysis in color three-space that is still subject to numerical instabilities. The algorithm, designed for machine vision, starts with a histogram of color values plotted in the RGB space of sensor responses and uses a technique similar to that of Tominaga and Wandell (1990) to identify planar clusters arising from individual surfaces. The intersection of two planes corresponding to two surfaces participating in mutual reflection gives the vector defining the color of the mutually reflected light. For each plane, the algorithm finds the (roughly) orthogonal vector that defines the body-reflected color of the corresponding surface. As such, it stops short of finding constant colors: The body color that it recovers is uncorrupted by mutual reflections but changes with changing illuminant. (In another algorithm based on Equation 35, Funt et al., 1991, assume that both the surface reflectance and illuminant can be defined by three basis functions, and that regions of pure body reflection on each of the two surfaces can be identified, together with a region of strong mutual reflection on one surface. The algorithm then uses the sensor responses from these regions to solve iteratively for the three invariant surface reflectance coefficients and two illuminant coefficients – fixing the third.)

The appeal of the method of finding chromatic signatures is that it has an immediately obvious interpretation in terms of color-opponent cells, the outputs of which are essentially the ratios of cone activities and therefore provide the axes of a chromaticity plane. The outputs of two types of color-opponent cell could be compared across space simply by feeding into a third-order cell that registers changes in the ratio of the color-opponent cell outputs. Such cells would also aid in segmenting the scene into distinct surfaces and in identifying single surfaces illuminated by more than one light source; each such surface would produce a distinctive chromatic signature. Alternatively, the visual system might use chromatic signatures merely to identify regions of specular highlights and mutual reflections, even if it then discards the potential cues to color constancy they contain.

This analysis of chromatic signatures also has appeal because it involves the same procedure for regions of specular highlights and mutual reflections. Because regions of strong specular reflections (in the direction of the viewer) tend not to occur in regions of strong mutual reflections, the local signature of one type of reflection is rarely corrupted by the other. (That is, where there is a highlight from the direct light on the surface, as seen by the viewer, there will tend not to be strong mutual reflections from other surfaces. The requirements that both surfaces be visible to the light source and to each other, and that the viewing angle lie in the direction of specular reflection, tend to be mutually exclusive.)

This is not to say that specular reflections cannot contribute to the light reflected from one surface onto another. In fact, as Bajcsy et al. (1990) observe, the mutual reflections caused by specular light from one surface onto the body reflectance of another (specular-body reflections) are stronger than body-body reflections. But the latter more greatly perturb the color of light reflected from a surface. Because specular light tends to take on the color of the primary illuminant (for inhomogeneous materials) specular-body mutual reflections tend not to disrupt the chromatic signature of a surface.

Bajcsy et al. (1990) show that where mutual reflections are small and are due primarily to specular light reflected from one object onto another, the color signals from a single glossy material still fall on a plane in three-space, the interreflection colors forming a small deviation from the skewed T distribution formed by the illuminant and body color vectors. As Klinker et al. (1988) do for highlights, Bajcsy et al. pare away the deviant color values to generate matte images devoid of mutual reflections, which can then be fed to traditional machine vision algorithms designed for a Lambertian world.

These algorithms demonstrate how to exploit information in a complicated, realistic image irradiance equation. The ostensibly simplifying assumptions underlying lightness algorithms, for example, might actually make the problem harder. It might be easier for our visual system to recover the illuminant color given shading, three-dimensional curvature, and specularities. Beck's (1972) observation that "The fact that colour often appears to be more constant in everyday conditions than in laboratory experiments suggests that the factors affecting constancy depend on the perceptual setting" (p. 56) supports the notion that these real-world imaging complications might in fact aid color constancy.

Notes

1. Color is rarely an exclusive property of an object, at least on a coarse scale. Bananas and lemons are both yellow. Particularly for category-level recognition, color might not be sufficient to trigger unique recognition. On a finer scale, though, color and associated surface properties may indeed be exclusive: The glossy, finely pocked yellow of a lemon is very different from the buttery pale yellow of a just-ripe banana.

2. Image irradiance (the light falling *on* the image) is proportional to surface radiance (the light exiting *from* the surface) by factors dependent on the imaging geometry – e.g., the focal length, diameter of the entrance pupil, and the off-axis angle, the last of which varies with position in the image. Irradiance is specified in units of Watts per meter squared (W/m^2). Radiance is specified in units of Watts per steradian per meter squared.

3. The right-hand side of Equation 1 specifies the scene – the light intensity emerging from the scene at point x_s. The image irradiance at the point x_i to which x_s projects is proportional to the scene radiance. Hence we may (loosely) write that the image irradiance at x equals the right-hand term.

4. Lambertian surfaces have constant luminance, i.e., the luminous intensity emitted per unit surface area – or received per unit surface area of observer – is constant. This means that the luminous intensity in a given direction varies as the cosine of the angle between that direction and the surface normal. Ideal Lambertian reflection is not only diffuse but also white.

5. The idea of exploiting the low dimensionality of surface reflectance to recover constant colors is generally attributed to Sallstrom (1973); see Maloney (1985) for a discussion of the origins of the idea.

6. Quote attributed to R. M. Evans, U.S. Patent 2571697, 1946.

7. The algorithm can also be modified to accommodate spatially varying illumination (Maloney, 1985), but because this requires that the illuminant be constant over sampled subregions of the image – each of which must satisfy the surface complexity condition – it still essentially requires the assumption of uniform illumination.

8. Lee et al. (1987) show how Equation 29 follows exactly from Equation 28 if we define $E^y =$

$\int d\lambda\ a^v(\lambda)E(\lambda)$ and ρ^v_b, the integrated diffuse reflectance factor in the vth receptor spectral chan-

$$\text{nel, as } \frac{\int d\lambda\ a^v(\lambda)\ \rho_b\ (\lambda)E(\lambda)}{\int d\lambda\ a^v(\lambda)E(\lambda)}.$$

9. The equation effectively assumes that the surfaces j have been tessellated into pieces of unit area.
10. The radiosity package was modified from one developed by C. G. Christou, A. J. Parker, B. G. Cumming, and A. Zisserman at Oxford University.

References

Bajcsy, R., Lee, S., & Leonardis, A. (1990). Color image segmentation with detection of highlights and local illumination induced by inter-reflections. In *Proceedings of the International Conference on Pattern Recognition*, pp. 785–790.

Blake, A. (1985). On lightness computation in Mondrian world. In T. Ottoson & S. Zeki (Eds.), *Central and peripheral mechanisms of colour vision* (pp. 45–49). New York: Macmillan.

Bramwell, D. I., & Hurlbert, A. C (1993). The role of object recognition in colour constancy. *Perception, 22*, S62.

Brelstaff, G., & Blake, A. (1987). Computing lightness. *Pattern Recognition Letters, 5*, 129–138.

Brill, M. (1978). A device performing illuminant-invariant assessment of chromatic relations. *Journal of Theoretical Biology, 71*, 473–478.

Brill, M. (1990). Image segmentation by object color: A unifying framework and connection to color constancy. *Journal of the Optical Society of America A, 7*(10), 2041–2047.

Buchsbaum, G. (1980). A spatial processor model for object color perception. *Journal of the Franklin Institute, 310*, 1–26.

Buchsbaum, G., & Gottschalk, A. (1983). Trichromacy, opponent colours coding and optimum colour information transmission in the retina. *Proceedings of the Royal Society London B, 220*, 89–113.

Courtney, S., Finkel, L., & Buchsbaum, G. (1995). Network simulations of retinal and cortical contributions to color constancy. *Vision Research, 35*(3), 413–434.

Dannemiller, J. (1992). Spectral reflectance of natural objects: How many basis functions are necessary? *Journal of the Optical Society of America A, 9*, 507–515.

D'Zmura, M. (1992). Color constancy: Surface color from changing illumination. *Journal of the Optical Society of America A, 9*(3), 490–493.

D'Zmura, M., & Iverson, G. (1993a). Color constancy. I. Basic theory of two-stage linear recovery of spectral descriptions for lights and surfaces. *Journal of the Optical Society of America A, 10*(10), 2148–2165.

D'Zmura, M., & Iverson, G. (1993b). Color constancy. II. Results for two-stage linear recovery of spectral descriptions for lights and surfaces. *Journal of the Optical Society of America A, 10*(10), 2166–2180.

D'Zmura, M., & Lennie, P. (1986). Mechanisms of color constancy. *Journal of the Optical Society of America, 3*, 1662–1672.

Evans, R. M. (1948). *An introduction to color*. New York: Wiley.

Fairchild, M. (1993). Chromatic adaptation in hard-copy/soft-copy comparisons. *SPIE Proceedings: Color Hard Copy and Graphic Arts II, 1912*, 47–61.

Finlayson, G., Drew, M., & Funt, B. V. (1993). *Color constancy: Diagonal transforms suffice*. CSS/LCCR TR93-02. SFU, Burnaby, B. C., Canada: Centre for Systems Science.

Forsyth, D. (1990a). A novel algorithm for color constancy. *International Journal of Computer Vision, 5*, 5–36.

Forsyth, D. A. (1990b). Colour constancy. In A. Blake & T. Troscianko (Eds.), *AI and the eye* (pp. 201–227). Chichester, U.K.: Wiley.

Foster, D. H., & Nascimento, S. M. C. (1994). Relational colour constancy from invariant cone-excitations ratios. *Proceedings of the Royal Society of London B, 257*, 115–121.

Funt, B. V. & Drew, M. (1991). *Color space analysis of mutual illumination.* CSS/LCCR TR91–03, SFU. Burnaby, B.C., Canada: Centre for Systems Science.

Funt, B. V., Drew, M., & Ho, J. (1991). Color constancy from mutual reflection. *International Journal of Computer Vision, 6*, 5–24.

Funt, B. S., & Finlayson, G. D. (1991). *Color constant color indexing.* CSS/LCCR TR91–09. Centre for Systems Science, Simon Fraser University.

Gershon, R., Jepson, A. D., & Tsotsos, J. K. (1986). Ambient illumination and the determination of material changes. *Journal of the Optical Society of America, 3*(10), 1700–1707.

Healey, G. (1991). Estimating spectral reflectance using highlights. *Image and Vision Computing, 9*(5), 333–337.

Healey, G., & Binford, T. O. (1987b). *The role and use of color in a general vision system.* Technical Report. Stanford, CA: Artificial Intelligence Laboratory, Stanford University.

Healey, G., & Binford, T. O. (1987a). Color algorithms for a general vision system. In *Proceedings of the 10th International Joint Conference on Artificial Intelligence* (pp. 759–762).

Helmholtz. H., von. (1962). *Treatise on physiological optics.* New York: Dover. (Originally published 1866).

Horn, B. K. P. (1974). Determining lightness from an image. *Computer Graphics and Image Processing, 3*, 277–299.

Hunt, R. (1991). Revised colour-appearance model for related and unrelated colours. *Color Research and Applications, 16*(3), 146–165.

Hurlbert, A. C. (1986). Formal connections between lightness algorithms. *Journal of the Optical Society of America A, 3*, 1684–1693.

Hurlbert, A. C. (1992). Neural network approaches to color vision. In H. Wechsler (Ed.), *Neural networks for perception.* Vol. 1, Academic Press.

Hurlbert, A. C., & Poggio, T. A. (1988). Synthesizing a color algorithm from examples. *Science, 239*, 482–485.

Hurlbert, A. C., Wen, W., & Poggio, T. (1994). Learning colour constancy. *Journal of Photographic Science, 42*, 89–90.

Jaaskelainen, T.,Parkkinen, J., & Toyooka, S. (1990). Vector-subspace model for color representation. *Journal of the Optical Society of America A, 7*, 725–730.

Jameson, D., & Hurvich, L. (1972). Color adaptation: Sensitivity, contrast, after-images. In D. Jameson & L. Hurvich (Eds.), *Handbook of sensory physiology, Volume*II/4, *Visual psychophysics* (chap. 22, pp. 568). New York: Springer-Verlag.

Judd, D., MacAdam, D. L., & Wyszecki, G. W. (1964). Spectral distribution of typical daylight as a function of correlated color temperature. *Journal of the Optical Society of America, 54*, 1031.

Klinker, G. J., Shafer, S. A., & Kanade, T. (1988). The measurement of highlights in color images. *International Journal of Computer Vision, 2*, 7–32.

Krinov, E. (1947). Spectral'naye otrazhatel'naya sposobnost'prirodnykh obrazovanii. Technical report, Izd. Akad. Nauk USSR (Proc. Acad. Sci. USSR) (Trans. by G. Belkov, "Spectral reflectance properties of natural formations," Technical Translation TT-439). (Ottawa: National Research Council of Canada, 1953).

Land, E. H. (1959a). Color vision and the natural image. *Proceedings of the National Academy of Science, 45*, 115–129.

Land, E. H. (1959b). Experiments in color vision. *Scientific American, 201*, 223.

Land, E. H. (1964). The retinex. *American Scientist, 52*, 247–264.

Land, E. H. (1983). Recent advances in retinex theory and some implications for cortical computations: Colour vision and the natural image. *Proceedings of the National Academy of Science, 80*, 5163–5169.

Land, E. H., & McCann, J. J. (1971). Lightness and retinex theory. *Journal of the Optical Society of America, 61,* 1–11.

Lee, H. -C. (1986). Method for computing the scene-illuminant chromaticity from specular highlights. *Journal of the Optical Society of America, 3,* 1694–1699.

Lee, H.-C., Breneman, E. J., & Schulte, C. P. (1987). *Modeling light reflection for computer color vision.* Technical Report. Eastman Kodak.

Lucassen, M., & Walraven, J. (1993). Quantifying color constancy – evidence for nonlinear processing of cone-specific contrast. *Vision Research, 33*(5–6), 739–757.

Maloney, L. T. (1985). *Computational approaches to color constancy.* Technical Report 1985–01. Stanford CA: Stanford University.

Maloney, L. T., & Wandell, B. (1986). Color constancy: A method for recovering surface spectral reflectance. *Journal of the Optical Society of America 3,* 29–33.

McCann, J. J., McKee, S., & Taylor, T. H. (1976). Quantitative studies in retinex theory – a comparison between theoretical predictions and observer responses to the colour Mondrian experiments. *Vision Research, 16,* 445–458.

Mollon, J. (1985). Studies in scarlet. *The Listener,* 6–7.

Moore, A., Fox, G., Allman, J., & Goodman, R. (1990). A VLSI neural network for color constancy. *Advances in Neural Information Processing Systems, 3.*

Nayatani, Y., Takahama, H., Sobagaki, H., & Hashimoto, K. (1990). Colour-appearance model and chromatic-adaptation transform. *Color Research and Applications, 15,* 210–221.

Parkkinen, J., Hallikainen, J., & Jaaskelainen, T. (1989). Characteristic spectra of Munsell colors. *Journal of the Optical Society of America A, 6,* 318–322.

Rubin, J., & Richards, W. (1984). *Colour vision: Representing material categories.* Memo 764. Cambridge, MA: Artificial Intelligence Laboratory, Massachusetts Institute of Technology.

Sallstrom, P. (1973). *Colour and physics: Some remarks concerning the physical aspects of human colour vision.* Report No. 73–09. Stockholm. Institute of Physics, University of Stockholm.

Shafer, S. A. (1985). Using color to separate reflection components. *Color Research and Applications, 10*(4), 210–218.

Shafer, S. A., Kanade, T., Klinker, G. J., & Novak, C. L. (1990). Physics-based models for early vision by machine. In *Proceedings of the SPIE, Volume 1250: Perceiving, measuring, and Using Color* (pp. 222–235). Santa Clara, CA:

Sung, K. -K. (1992). *A vector signal processing approach to color.* Technical Report 1349. Cambridge, MA: Artificial Intelligence Laboratory, Massachusetts Institute of Technology.

Tominaga, S., & Wandell, B. (1990). Component estimation of surface spectral reflectance. *Journal of the Optical Society of America, 7,* 312–317.

West, G., & Brill, M. H. (1982). Necessary and sufficient conditions for von Kries chromatic adaptation to give color constancy. *Journal of Mathematical Biology, 15,* 249–258.

Worthey, J. A. (1985). Limitations of color constancy. *Journal of the Optical Society of America, 2,* 1014–1026.

Wyszecki, G., & Stiles, W. (1982). *Color science.* New York: Wiley.

Yuille, A. L. (1984). A method for computing spectral reflectance. Memo 752. Cambridge, MA: Artificial Intelligence Laboratory, Massachusetts Institute of Technology.

12   Comparative aspects of color constancy

Christa Neumeyer

Introduction

The colors that are biologically relevant are the colors of objects. The light reflected by objects is determined by the absorption characteristics of their surfaces and by the spectral composition of the incident light. If the task of the color vision system of an animal is to improve discrimination and recognition of objects in its visual world, it is self-evident that a mechanism is required to compensate for the spectral changes of natural daylight. It is reasonable to assume that the ability to keep the effect of illumination constant has been developed during evolution together with color vision itself. To go a step further, one may even assume that the necessity to compensate for the spectral changes of natural daylight was the cause for the evolution of color vision. This interesting idea was stated by von Campenhausen (1986). The consideration proceeds from a monochromat, an animal that has only one type of photoreceptor. All objects seen by this animal will differ only in brightness (or lightness if we refer only to surfaces). Under a natural skylight that varies in its spectral composition, the light reflected by an object will vary too, and lightness will change accordingly. The problem for a monochromat under natural daylight consists in the fact that the lightness of an object does not change in the same way as the lightness of its surroundings, so that the lightness ratio between object and surround changes and may even be reversed. For example, a ripe red fruit found by the animal under an evening sky in which long-wavelength light is predominant will appear lighter than the surrounding green leaves. At noon under a blue sky, the same fruit will appear darker than the surrounding leaves, and it is possible that an unripe green fruit will appear in the same lightness as the ripe one under the evening sky of the day before.

That a monochromatic visual system indeed judges the lightness of different

I am most grateful to Vadim V. Maximov in Moscow for sending me all his papers dealing with color constancy in animals and to O. Belovsky, who was so kind as to translate them. Saskia Dörr was of great help in finding literature and calculated the color loci shown in Figure 12.7. I would also like to thank A. R. Kezeli in Tbilisi for sending me an English summary of his cat experiments; C. von Campenhausen, M. Tritsch, and S. Dörr for critically reading the text; and Neil Beckhaus for correcting the English.

colored surfaces differently under a changing spectral composition of illumination was shown by human observers wearing goggles of low transmittance that caused them to see with the rods only (von Campenhausen, 1986). Thus, a monochromatic animal cannot rely on lightness to recognize an object under natural daylight if it does not have a mechanism to compensate for the spectral changes. A compensating system, however, requires the ability to determine differences in the spectral distribution of daylight, and for this task at least two photoreceptors with different spectral sensitivities are necessary. The existence of two photoreceptor types, however, is also the prerequisite for color vision. Von Campenhausen thought that there might exist "living fossils," animals that possess two or more photoreceptor types that are not used for color vision but only to provide lightness constancy. The cat was assumed to be a possible candidate for such a "color-blind but lightness-constant" animal (see section 5).

Our knowledge of color vision in animals is obtained from behavioral experiments. Only in a few species have various aspects of color vision been so thoroughly investigated that a detailed comparison with human color vision is possible. Apart from Old World monkeys, which have a color vision very similar to that of humans, the most thoroughly investigated species are the honeybee and cyprinid fishes. Because one can assume that the highly effective color vision in these three animal groups has developed independently of each other during evolution, a comparison of these color vision systems should be informative. The question of whether animals are equipped with color constancy, and how they solve this task, has so far been posed only in a few species. In most cases, color constancy has been shown only qualitatively. In some animals, the phenomena of simultaneous and successive color contrast have been investigated; these phenomena can be regarded as side effects of the mechanisms providing color constancy. In the following sections the experiments performed to show color constancy (and, in some cases, color contrast) in animals will be described.

Experimental evidence for color constancy in animals

1. The honeybee

The honeybee is an ideal animal in which to study color vision and other sensory capacities. Single worker bees can easily be trained on color and other stimuli by giving food rewards (drops of sugar water), which they deliver in the hive. As honeybees never become satiated, they cooperate continuously for many hours per day for up to 4 weeks. Honeybees possess a highly efficient trichromatic color vision, shown for the first time in the early training experiments by Karl von Frisch (1914) and further investigated by Kühn (1927), Daumer (1956),

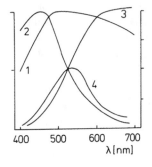

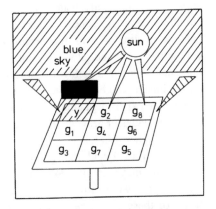

Figure 12.1. Experiment to show color constancy in the honeybee. Left: Spectral radiant flux of direct sunlight (1) and light of the blue sky (2), and spectral reflectance of the colored papers: (3) yellow, and (4) green. (Ordinate: arbitrary scale; abscissa: wavelength.) After Mazokhin-Porshnjakov (1966; Figure 1). Right: Rotating table with nine colored papers: one yellow (y), and eight different shades of green (g1–g8). The bees were trained on the yellow paper under direct sunlight. In the test, the yellow paper was shaded by a screen (black rectangle), so that it was illuminated by the blue sky only. After Mazokhin-Porshnjakov (1966, Figure 2).

von Helversen (1972), and Menzel and his coworkers (for a review, see Menzel and Backhaus, 1989, 1991). The three retinula cell types that are the basis of color vision are maximally sensitive in the ultraviolet (350 nm), in the short wavelength range (450 nm), and in the mid-wavelength range (530 nm) (Autrum & von Zwehl, 1964; Menzel & Blakers, 1976; Menzel, Ventura, Hertel, de Souza, & Greggers, 1986). Wavelength discrimination was found to be optimal around 400 nm and around 500 nm (von Helversen, 1972).

The first experiment showing that honeybees possess color constancy was performed by Mazokhin-Porshnjakov (1966). The initial question was the following: Are bees able to recognize a yellow flower, for example a dandelion (*Taraxacum officinale*) by its color under different conditions of illumination, in the shade and in sunshine? In the shade, the dandelion will reflect mainly the blue light of the sky, in sunlight mainly the direct light of the sun, containing relatively more long wavelength radiation (Figure 12.1, left). Thus, in the shade, the yellow flower will reflect light in a spectral distribution similar to that reflected by a "green" object, whereas in sunlight the spectral distribution resembles the reflection of a "yellow" object. In the experiment, which was performed under the open sky, nine square pieces of colored paper (eight green ones of different brightness and one yellow one) were shown on a rotating table (Figure 12.1, right). The bees were trained to land on the yellow paper, where they found sugar water in a small glass dish, whereas the dishes on the green papers contained only water. The training was performed in the sunshine on cloudless days. At about noon, after the bees had reliably found the yellow color, a quadrangular vertical screen was introduced that threw a shadow on the yellow piece of paper alone. Despite the fact that the light reflected by this paper must have been less yellow or more greenish (because the incident skylight was more blueish), the bees found and landed on the yellow paper without hesitation. In another experiment, the bees were able to distinguish a yellow paper from different shades of gray and from a gray paper on which yellow light was thrown through a glass filter.

Between 1971 and 1979, a series of experiments was performed in which color constancy, simultaneous color contrast, and successive color contrast in the honeybee were shown and quantitatively described (Neumeyer, 1980, 1981). In all of these experiments, the bees made choices between nine small pieces (10 × 10 mm) of differently colored paper (*test fields*) that built up (for a human observer) a series of colors ranging from a yellow of medium saturation over two steps of less saturated yellow and gray to five steps of increasingly saturated blue. For the honeybee, the test field colors represented different shades of blue-green, as inferred from the location of the test field loci in comparison to the loci of the spectral colors in the color triangle of the honeybee (Figure 12.2).

Individual bees were trained on one medium blue test field (test field 6), while this and the other eight test fields were shown on a gray background. Because of the bees' excellent color memory, it can be expected that the bee will always select the test field that appears in the same hue as test field 6 in the training situation. Thus, a constant choice behavior indicates a constant perceived hue, whereas changes in the color preference imply shifts in perceived hue (the method was introduced by Otto von Helversen for the investigation of simultaneous color contrast).

To study color constancy, the nine yellowish and blueish test fields were irregularly distributed on a large gray background (50 cm in diameter) that covered the surface of a rotating table. The bees were trained on test field 6 while the entire rotating table, and most of the experimental room, were illuminated from above by the white light of two slide projectors. In the test situation, the spectral composition of the illumination was changed by inserting yellow or blue filters into one of the two projectors and by attenuating the white light in the second projector with neutral density filters. Figure 12.3 shows the results. Under the two colored illuminations Y1 and B1, the choice behavior of the honeybees was exactly the same as under the white training illumination: Test field 6 was chosen just as often. Test field 6 was also clearly preferred under the stronger yellow and blue illuminations Y2, Y3, and B2 but less so under B3. It was only under Y4 that the bees could not recognize the training color, and selected the brightest or darkest test fields in the series. Thus, under

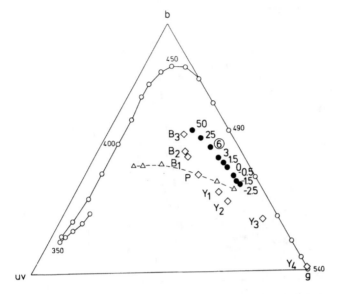

Figure 12.2. Characterization of the test field and illumination colors in the color triangle of the honeybee. The color triangle was calculated on the basis of the spectral sensitivity functions of the retinula cells types weighted by 5.6 : 2.6 : 1 (uv: b: g) (from Neumeyer, 1980, Figure 4). uv, b, g: corners of the triangle indicating exclusive excitation of the uv-, blue- and green-retinula cell type. 300–540 nm: loci of the spectral colors. 50 – −2.5: loci of the nine test fields (dark symbols) illuminated with the white projector light P. 6: training test field. Open symbols: loci of the yellow (Y1–Y4) and blue (B1–B3) illuminations. Triangles: loci of spectral distributions of daylight between 30,000 and 2,600°K (from Neumeyer, 1981, Figure 5).

all illuminations except Y4, the bees were clearly able to recognize training test field 6.

To understand this result, the color loci of the nine test fields illuminated with the colored light were calculated, and are shown together with the loci calculated for white illumination P in the color triangle in Figure 12.4. In Figure 12.4a, the loci are shown for the yellow illumination Y1 and for the blue illumination B1, that is, for conditions in which the bees showed perfect color constancy. Under illumination Y1, the loci of all test field colors (squares) are shifted toward the "g" corner of the color triangle, indicating a stronger stimulation of the "green" retinula cells than under the white illumination P; under illumination B1, the loci are shifted toward the "b" corner, indicating a relatively stronger excitation of the "blue" retinula cell type.

Under Y1, test field 50 is located next to training test field 6 under white light P. Thus, if color recognition were determined by the excitation ratio of the retinula cells, the bees should have selected test field 50 under illumination Y1,

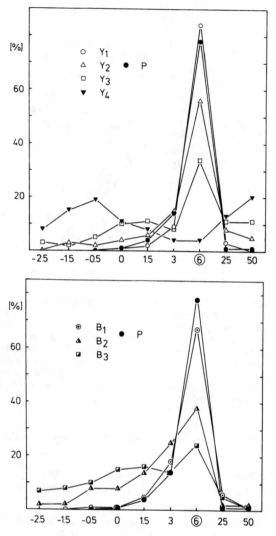

Figure 12.3. Color constancy in the honeybee: choice behavior in the presence of differently colored illuminations. The bees were trained on test field 6 under illumination P. Tests were performed under yellow illuminations Y1–Y4 (top), and under blue illuminations B1–B3 (bottom). Abscissa: test field colors. Ordinate: Percentage of relative choice frequency. (Reprinted with permission.)

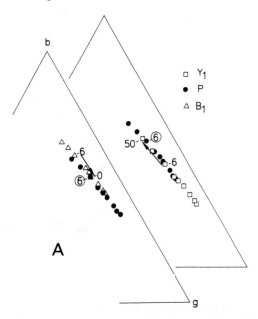

Figure 12.4a. Test field loci calculated for different illuminations to demonstrate the color constancy effect. Dark symbols: test field loci under "white" training illumination P. 6: training test field under white illumination. Right triangle: Under yellow illumination Y1 the test field loci (squares) are shifted toward the "green" corner of the triangle indicating stronger excitation of the "green" retinula cell type. Test field 50 is now located next to training test field 6 under illumination P, indicating a very similar excitation ratio of the retinula cells under the two illuminations. Despite this fact, bees chose test field 6 under Y1. Thus, the compensating effect of the color constancy mechanism can be demonstrated by an arrow connecting test field 6 under illumination Y1 with test field 6 under training illumination P. Left color triangle: test field loci under illumination B1 (triangles). Now test field 0 coincides with the locus of test field 6 under the training illumination P. The color constancy effect can be read from the arrow connecting the loci of test field 6 under blue and white illumination.

which was not the case. The fact that the bees chose test field 6 under Y1 as often as in the training situation P indicates that there is a color constancy mechanism that must have compensated for the effect of the colored illumination in such a way that all test fields appeared in the same hue as under white illumination. Under the blueish light B1, test field 0 is located at the same position in the color triangle as training test field 6 under white illumination P. This means that test field 0 objectively reflected the same light as training color 6 under white illumination. The fact that the bees did *not* choose test field 0, but instead training test field 6, indicates again the compensating effect of the color constancy mechanism. The strength of the compensating effect can be depicted by arrows connecting the loci of test field 6 calculated for the yellowish

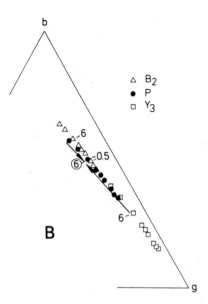

Figure 12.4b. Test field loci under the extreme conditions of illuminations B2 and Y3 where color constancy was still possible. Whereas the location of the test field loci for illumination B2 was not very different from those under B1, illumination Y3 shifted the loci so far toward the "g" corner of the triangle that the excitation of test field 6 did not resemble that of any test field under P. Despite this, the bees still preferred test field 6. (Data from Neumeyer, 1981.)

and blueish illumination with the locus of test field 6 under white illumination P.

In Figure 12.4b, the test field loci are shown for the more extreme cases under illuminations B2 and Y3, in which color constancy was less perfect than under Y1 and B1 but still possible, as indicated by the preference for training test field 6.

One might argue that the constant choice behavior of the honeybee is not due to color constancy but to a "relative" color memory that allows the bee to select a hue after a comparison with all the other colors shown. That this is not the case was demonstrated when simultaneous color contrast and successive color contrast were tested with the same nine test fields. Here, the bees did *not* prefer training test field 6 but rather other test fields, indicating a change in perceived hue (see later).

In a more recent experiment, Annette Werner investigated color constancy in honeybees with a different method (Werner, 1990; Werner, Menzel, & Wehrhahn, 1988) that is reminiscent of the Mondrian configuration in the experiments by Edwin Land. However, the color stimuli used were not reflecting surfaces but colored glass filters (5 × 5 cm) illuminated from behind. The 13 filters were presented in a checkerboard pattern consisting of 5×5 square fields so that a colored field was always located next to a black one. The checkerboard was shown to the bees surrounded by black velvet in a dark room. The glass filters were illuminated from behind by a mixture of three colored lights with spectral distributions similar to the spectral sensitivity of the three retinula cell types. The bees were trained on one of the 13 colors when all filters were illuminated with a certain mixture of the three colored lights. Tests were performed under a different illumination (a mixture with differently weighted components) that was chosen in such a way that now another filter transmitted the same amount of ultraviolet, blue and green light as the training filter with the previous training illumination. However, the relative frequency with which the training filter and the matched filter were chosen by the bees did not change significantly: The bees still preferred the training filter. Thus, color constancy was shown even under impeded conditions in which the visual system could have inferred the color of illumination from the sample of differently colored fields but not from a background as well.

2. Cyprinid fishes

In his early training experiments, Karl von Frisch (1913) showed that a cyprinid fish, the minnow (*Phoxinus leavis*), has a color vision similar to that of humans, with the ability to discriminate blue, green, yellow, and red from shades of gray. In the first, more detailed studies using monochromatic light, it was demonstrated that minnows are also able to see and to discriminate ultraviolet light (Schiemenz, 1924; Wolff, 1925), a fact neglected for a long time. That the goldfish possesses an ultraviolet-sensitive cone type in addition to three other cone types was shown first in behavioral experiments (Hawryshyn & Beauchamp, 1985; Neumeyer, 1985) and more recently by microspectrophotometry (Bowmaker, Thorpe, & Douglas, 1991). Color vision in goldfish (and probably in other cyprinid fishes as well) is tetrachromatic (Neumeyer, 1992; for a review, see Bowmaker, 1990; Douglas & Hawryshyn, 1990).

The problem that a fish with a highly developed color vision must also be able to provide color constancy was already stated by Burkamp (1923). He trained cyprinid fishes of different species kept together in the same tank (*Phoxinus laevis, Rhodeus amarus, Idus melanotus, Tinca vulgaris*) to take food (minced meat) from 1 of 24 small, colored boxes made of zinc. The boxes were painted in the colors red, yellow, green, blue, and gray. The colored paints were used pure and also mixed with white or black, so that from each color five different lightness steps were obtained. The fish were trained on one color, which was shown together with the different lightness steps of the same color, 17 different shades of gray, and medium-lightness steps of the other colors. The room was illuminated by natural daylight through a window facing north. During the tests, the window was covered with colored gelatine sheets. In the first experiments, fish trained on yellow or red were tested under a reduced intensity of natural daylight. In all tested cases, the fish preferred the lightness step of the color on which they had been trained rather than the lighter colors or even the gray steps. From this result, the existence of lightness constancy was concluded. In the tests under colored illumination, the fish still preferred the training color, but they were less certain, choosing other colors and gray steps more frequently. The illumination color used was either the same color as that on which the fish were trained or its complementary color. Assuming that the choices of the fish are determined by the retinal stimulus only, the fish trained on red, for example, should choose white or gray colors under red illumination, and under green illumination they should not recognize the training color at all. Neither was the case: The fish always found the training color, although the preference was not as strong as under the training illumination. Burkamp explained the results by assuming the action of a regulation system that transforms the retinal stimulation such that object colors can be recognized in the presence of all illumination colors.

Because of the limited ability to measure the spectral distribution of illumination and remission at Burkamp's time, the color constancy effect could not be quantified. To overcome the disadvantage of the early experiments, Vadim V. Maximov and his colleagues in Moscow performed an experiment with the carp (*Cyprinus carpio*) (Dimentman, Karas, Maximov, & Orlov, 1972). One-year-old carp (8–12 cm long) were trained using a classical conditioning method similar to that of McCleary and Bernstein (1959): Colored paper (3 × 2 cm) on a white background (8 × 10 cm) was presented at a distance of 20 cm to the restricted fish. The positive stimulus was accompanied by a weak electric shock. As a response, a reduction in heartbeat rate was observed, which was used in the tests as an indicator for recognition. The training color was always red (r1, r2, and r3), presented on a white background. Different shades of gray (gr), black (b), and green (g1 and g2) were shown on a white background without punishment. In Figure 12.5 the spectral reflection of all papers used, the spectral emission of the illuminating lamp, and the spectral transmission of the colored filters are shown.

Fish 27 was trained on the red papers r1, r2, and r3 under blue illumination (filters BG 13 × BG 26). As shown in Figure 12.6A, the reduction in heartbeat rate was highest when these colors (open circles) were shown under the blue training illumination. The rate was unaffected by the gray or green papers (dark symbols). When Fish 27 was tested under white illumination, the effect of the red papers was still strongest; this was the case even under the green illumination GG 16. A further test under white illumination yielded weaker responses, which was explained by habituation. Figure 12.6B shows the results obtained with fish 31, which was trained under the white light. In the test under blue illumination,

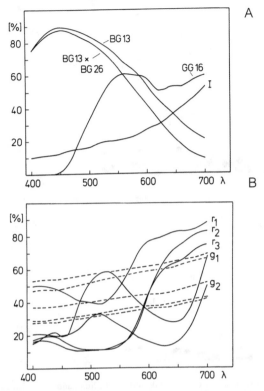

Figure 12.5. Papers and illuminations used to show color constancy in the carp. Above: relative spectral transmission of the filters (GG 16, BG 13, BG13, × BG 26); I: spectral emission of the tungsten lamp. Below: relative spectral reflectance of the different red, green, and gray papers used. rl–3: red; g1,2: green; broken lines: gray papers. (After Dimentman et al., 1972, Figure 1.)

the responses elicited by the red papers were still stronger than those on the other gray and green papers. Corresponding results were obtained with two other fish trained under blue illumination (as with fish 27).

To quantify the color constancy effect, Maximov and his colleagues calculated the color loci of the used papers under the different illumination colors and presented them in color space (based on the absorption spectra of the goldfish cones measured by Marks, 1965). In Figure 12.7, the loci are shown in the b,g,r plane of the color tetrahedron of the goldfish recalculated by using the most recent absorption spectra measured by Bowmaker et al. (1991). The color loci of the red papers r2 and r3 illuminated by the blue light (dark symbols) are located next to the loci of the gray papers illuminated by the green light GG 16 (open triangles). Thus, the gray papers illuminated with the greenish light and the red papers illuminated by blue light excite the cone types in equal ratios.

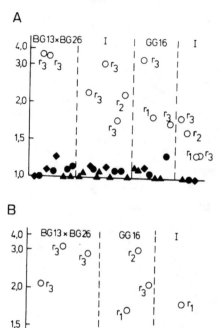

Figure 12.6. Response behavior of carp under different illuminations. A: fish 27 trained under illumination BG 13 × BG 26 on the red papers r1–3. B: fish 31 trained under white illumination I. Abscissa: temporal sequence of the trials; ordinate: response in relative units indicating the deceleration of the heartbeat rate. Open symbols: responses on the red training colors; closed symbols: responses on green, gray, and black. I: tests under the tungsten light; GG 16: tests under green illumination. (After Dimentman et al., 1972, Figure 3.)

The fact that the carp did not respond to these papers, but only to the red ones (which excite the cone types in an entirely different excitation ratio), indicates the existence of color constancy.

In his article "The goldfish as a retinex animal," David J. Ingle (1985) showed color constancy in the goldfish by using a colored Mondrian pattern comparable to that used in human color vision by Edwin Land. Figure 12.8 shows the experimental setup, consisting of colored papers illuminated by an additive mixture of blue, green, and red light. In the pretraining situation, the goldfish learned to approach a yellow paper (two fish; one other fish was trained on green, with corresponding results) by giving a food reward (a little piece of liver from a pipette) and to ignore a yellow-green paper and an orange paper shown for comparison. All papers were shown on a white background and il-

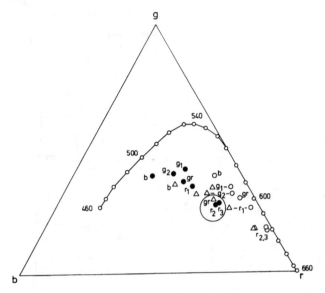

Figure 12.7. Color loci of the papers under different illuminations calculated on the basis of the cone sensitivity functions of the goldfish (using the absorption spectra measured by Bowmaker et al., 1991). The triangle represents the basis of the color tetrahedron shown in Neumeyer (1992). 460–660: loci of the spectral colors. Dark symbols: red (r) green (g), gray (gr), and black papers under the BG 13 × BG 26 training illumination. Open triangles: loci under the green illumination (GG 16); open circles: loci under the tungsten light I. Encircled area: under the green illumination, the loci of the grey test fields are located next to the loci of the red test fields under the training illumination.

luminated by white light. In the next training step, the three colors were presented on a background consisting of a Mondrian pattern (the pattern inside the tank in Figure 12.8), and again choices of the yellow paper were rewarded. Finally, the colors were part of the Mondrian itself. In the training situation with the "flat" Mondrian, the illumination was adjusted in such a way that a medium gray paper reflected equal intensities of red, green, and blue light when measured with a telephotometer. In the first critical test, the illumination of the Mondrian was changed in such a way that the light reflected by the training paper now contained equal intensities of red, green, and blue light, thus giving the same stimulus as the gray paper under the training illumination. Despite this, the goldfish continued to select the yellow paper almost exclusively (with the same high rate of 90–100% as in the training situation). In the second critical test, the yellow paper reflected the same light as the green paper in the training condition. In this case also, the fish continued to choose the training paper irrespective of the different spectral composition of the reflected light.

Thus, Ingle's experiment showed that the goldfish preferred the training color despite the fact that the light reflected from this paper was not the same as in

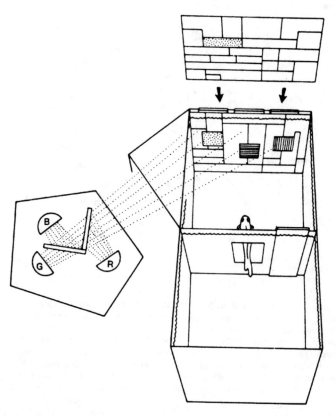

Figure 12.8. Experimental set-up to show color constancy in goldfish in the experiment by Ingle (1985). A Mondrian pattern presented at one wall of the tank was illuminated by a mixture of blue, green, and red light through a water-filled prism shown at the left. During the training phase, the fish saw the training color together with two other colors through apertures of the Mondrian (shown inside the tank). In the final tests, these colors were part of the Mondrian itself (shown above the tank). (From Ingle, 1985; reprinted with permission. Copyright 1985 by AAAS.)

the training situation. An even better indication of color constancy would have been if the fish had been given the opportunity to choose a color objectively identical to the training color under white illumination and did *not* select it under changed illumination. It cannot be excluded that the color chosen was most similar to the training color among all other colors shown but not identical in hue. This problem arises because the colors were not specified on the basis of goldfish cone excitation, but rather on the basis of photometric measurements adjusted to the spectral sensitivity of the human visual system (see also Young, 1987).

3. Amphibia

Frogs, toads, and salamanders possess two spectral types of rods, of which the "green" rods are sensitive in the short-wavelength range (λ maximum around 432 nm), and two types of cones with maximal absorption of the photopigments at about 500 nm and at 570 nm. Frogs and toads are also sensitive to ultraviolet light (Zipse, 1935), which is, however, at least in *Salamandra salamandra*, not due to a separate ultraviolet photoreceptor. The dimensionality of color vision in frogs and toads is still unclear. The European tiger salamander (*S. salamandra*) seems to have trichromatic color vision (Przyrembel, Keller, & Neumeyer, 1995).

Color constancy in amphibia seems to have been investigated in one experiment only, performed by Gnyubkin, Kondrashov, and Orlov (1975). They tested mating toads for their spontaneous color preferences. Male *Bufo bufo* were removed from their females and put separately into a tank in which differently colored ping-pong balls were shown against a white background. To get the toads interested in the stationary balls at the bottom of the tank (at a depth of 30–40 cm), a black cork on a nylon string was moved up and down until the toad came closer. Then the cork was removed, and the toad selected one of the balls by climbing on it and trying to hold it with his forelegs. The toads spontaneously preferred blue or light blue balls, but refused red and green ones. When colored balls were presented together with gray balls of different lightness, they always preferred blue, indicating that they possess color vision. Very similar preferences were found under sunlight, as well as under a tungsten lamp. Spectral remission of the colors used was measured, and the color loci of the reflected light were calculated on the basis of the absorption spectra of the frog photopigments (Liebman & Entine, 1968). The calculation showed that the blue ball under the tungsten lamps stimulates the receptor types in a way similar to that of the green ball under sunlight. Despite this fact, the toads clearly preferred the blue ball but never selected the green one. This result indicates that *B. bufo* possesses color constancy. Even color contrast could be shown with this method: Gray balls presented in front of a red background were chosen, which was never the case when they were shown against a white background.

4. Birds

One of the first experiments in color constancy was performed by Wolfgang Köhler (1915) with chimpanzees (see later) and with hens. The birds were used in these experiments to determine whether the constancy found in the chimpanzee should be regarded as an ability that is similar to that of humans because of the close relationship of the two species, or whether constancy is a more general property of animals with a highly evolved visual system. Because the changes between direct sunlight and shade appeared to Köhler to be more prominent and important under natural conditions than changes in spectral composition, he used only white and black papers presented outdoors in the sun or in the shade. Two hens were trained to peck wheat grains from a white paper but not from a black one, from which they were chased away; two hens were trained on the black paper. Both papers were presented under direct sunlight in the training situation. During the tests the white paper was shaded and the black one was directly illuminated. In 24 of 25 critical tests, the hens preferred the training paper despite the fact that the directly illuminated black paper reflected 1.3 to 4.1 times more light (measured with a photometer) than the white paper. Köhler drew the conclusion that vision of surface colors is independent of illumination and that this ability is not restricted to anthropoid primates.

In the article "Experimental Studies in Comparative Psychology," Katz and Révész (1921) extended Köhler's experiment by using white and strongly colored rice grains. The hens were trained to peck only the white ones. If the white grains were illuminated by colored light so that the reflected light was about the same as the colored grains in the earlier training situation, the hen took the (actually white) grains without hesitation. Katz and Révész, as well as Köhler, also discuss their findings in the context of Helmholtz's hypothesis that experience might determine constancy. They state that in the case of the hens they had been testing, this possibility can probably be ruled out.

The only more recent experiments seem to be investigations with hollow-dwelling song birds, unfortunately only briefly reported in Maximov (1989). Breeding pairs of birds (probably *Muscicapa hypoleuca, Parus major*, and *Passer montanus*) were studied in the wild, where they had to find the entrance of their nest box by choosing between two nest boxes marked with colored stimuli and illuminated with white or colored light. Obviously, the birds showed color constancy under these conditions. However, it seems that there were differences in comparison to other animals investigated by Maximov and his colleagues, which Maximov attributes to the fact that birds have a tetrachromatic color vision.

5. The cat

Mammals, with the exception of primates, seem to have the poorest color vision of all vertebrates: All of the more recently investigated species (e.g., squirrels, dogs, pigs, tupaias) have turned out to have dichromatic color vision with two cone types, one with maximal sensitivity at around 450 nm and a second one in the mid- or long-wavelength range (for reviews, see Jacobs, 1981; Jacobs, Deegan, Crognale, & Fenwick 1993; Neumeyer, 1991). Rats even seemed to be monochromats until it was shown that they are highly sensitive in the ultraviolet range, which is possibly due to a special receptor type (Jacobs, 1992; Jacobs, Neitz, & Deegan, 1991). The dimensionality of color vision in cats is still not clear. It was reported to be extremely difficult to train cats to discriminate colored stimuli, especially when colored light was used. Using surface colors seems to make it easier, but even then hundreds of trials are necessary for success. In an investigation using playing behavior with a dummy mouse, Buchholz (1953) showed that the cat is able to discriminate red and violet from various shades of gray, as well as red, yellow, orange, green, and violet from each other. Electrophysiological investigations indicated that the cat may have the precondition for trichromatic color vision, as the responses of ganglion cells revealed the existence of three cone types (Crocker, Ringo, Wolbarsht, & Wagner, 1980). A behavioral training experiment tested whether cats are able to discriminate between purple and green (Kezeli, Maximov, Domashvili, Homeriki, & Tschvediani, 1987). The colored papers (12 different purples and 12 greens) were selected in such a way that there would be difficulties in discrimination under the assumption that the cat has dichromatic color vision with a short-wavelength (450 nm) and a long-wavelength (555 nm) cone type, but that discrimination should be easy if there is a green cone type (500 nm) in addition. The cats trained on purple were clearly able to discriminate this color from green. Thus, it seems possible that color vision in cats is trichromatic.

In a further experiment, Kezeli, Maximov, Homeriki, Anjaparidze, and Tschvediani (1991) investigated color constancy in the cat. Three sets of color stimuli were used – blue, purple, and yellow – which were always presented in pairs (15 × 15 cm each). Three adult cats were trained to get a food reward after approaching the purple field, the entire scene being illuminated with an incandescent bulb. The spectral reflection of the colored papers was determined, and the color loci were calculated on the basis of the three cone sensitivity spectra presumably underlying cat color vision (Figure 12.9). In the tests, the illumination was changed and appeared blue or orange, respectively. The blue illumination was chosen in such a way that the yellow papers stimulated the cone types in a way similar to that of the purple ones under the white light (and the purple ones in the same way as the blue ones under the white light). Under the orange illumination, the light reflected from the blue papers stimulated the cone types in a way similar to that of the purple ones under the white illumination (and the purple ones similarly to the yellow ones under the white light) (Figure 12.9). Table 12.1 shows the results: The cats preferred the purple colors at the same high rate under blue and orange illumination as under the white training illumination. If, however, not the entire scene but only the colored papers were illuminated by the colored light, the cats responded according to the actual reflection, choosing the yellow papers under blue illumination and the blue papers under orange illumination, as predicted (Table 12.2).

Another type of experiment was performed by Mark Tritsch (1993). As men-

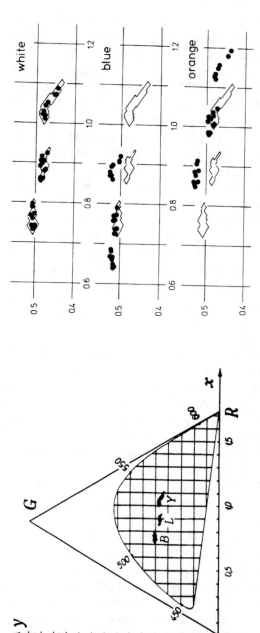

Figure 12.9 Left: color loci of the blue (B), purple (L), and yellow (Y) papers in the color triangle of the cat, calculated under the assumption that the cat possesses trichromatic color vision (from Kezeli et al., 1991) on the basis of cone sensitivity spectra with maximal sensitivity at 450 nm, 500 nm, and 550 nm. Right: middle part of the triangle with color loci (dots) representing single papers. Upper row: loci calculated for white illumination (CIE standard source "A"); middle row: loci calculated for blue illumination; lower row: orange illumination. The illuminations were selected in such a way that, under the blue illumination, the purple papers stimulated the receptors in the same way as the blue papers under the white training illumination, and under the orange illumination in the same way as the yellow papers under the white illumination. (After Kezeli, personal communication.)

Table 12.1. *Choice behavior of the cats in a two-choice situation in which test fields, background, and the walls of the cage were illuminated by white, blue, or orange light, respectively.* N = *absolute number of choices.*

| | Test fields | | | | | | |
	Purple	:	Blue	*N*	Purple	:	Yellow	*N*
Illumination								
White "A"	92%		8%	326	100%		0%	416
Blue	100%		0%	56	99%		1%	89
Orange	98%		2%	95	97%		3%	65

Source: From Kezeli (personal communication).

Table 12.2. *Choice behavior of the cats in a control situation in which only the test fields were illuminated by colored light.*

| | Test fields | | | | | | |
	Purple	:	Blue	*N*	Purple	:	Yellow	*N*
Illumination								
White "A"	99%		1%	29	100%		0%	16
Blue	92%		8%	32	22%		78%	42
Orange	35%		65%	36	9%		91%	32

tioned in the Introduction, it was the hypothesis of von Campenhausen (1986) that a correction for the changes in the spectral composition of natural daylight is necessary to obtain lightness constancy, and that some animals might use the two or more cone types necessary for this task not for color vision but only to keep the lightness ratios constant. The cat, which does not seem to be very interested in color according to its poor performance in most experiments, seemed to be a likely candidate for such a color-blind and lightness-constant animal. To test this hypothesis, Tritsch trained four cats to approach a blue paper while an orange paper was shown for comparison. For illumination, he used blue and yellow fluorescent tubes with independently variable intensities. Ten different mixture ratios between blue and yellow light were used, which were adjusted to a constant mean brightness for the cat. The training started under the stronger blue illumination (9/1: blue/yellow), and the cats chose the blue paper in about 95% of all trials after 4–5 days. Then the cats were tested under the yellow illumination (1/9: blue/yellow). In this case, the cats clearly preferred the orange paper (77–100%). This means that the cats chose the paper that reflected more light, as in the training situation. If the cats discriminated only on the basis of lightness, there should be an illumination ratio in which the blue and orange papers appear equal to the cat. To find this point, the ratios were changed stepwise from blue to yellow illumination in successive training sessions (reward was given at the blue paper). The result was surprising: Three of the four cats tested continued to choose the blue paper even at step 3/7 of the mixture, in which both papers were calculated to be equal in lightness. The fourth cat made choices in a 50:50 ratio at the equal-lightness point and preferred the orange paper under the stronger yellow illumination. Only after 18 more days of training did this cat also prefer the blue paper. The results indicate that at the beginning of the training, the cats discriminated between the two papers on the basis of lightness only. After the illumination color was changed moderately, they discriminated on the basis of hue. After this switch in discrimination criterion, the cats also showed a remarkable color constancy. Thus, the hypothetical color-blind and lightness-constant animal has not yet been found. The cat seems to use the constancy mechanism in the context of color vision.

6. Monkeys

Wolfgang Köhler (1915) trained two chimpanzees to find food in a white box but not in a black one. In the test, the black box was exposed to direct sunlight, and the white one was in a shadow cast by an overhead plank. The reflected light was measured by a photometer. Although the black box in the sun reflected about seven times as much light as the white box in the shade, the chimpanzee selected the white one, making only two errors in 14 tests. The second subject made three errors in 30 tests when the black box reflected about five times as much light as the white box in direct sunlight.

The experiment performed with four rhesus monkeys (*Macaca mulatta*) by Locke (1935) can be regarded as an extension of Köhler's experiment, but it provided better-controlled illumination conditions. Also, in this experiment, mainly lightness constancy was studied, but not color constancy in its strict sense. The monkeys were trained to respond to a white but not to a black field that could be seen through two small windows. The two fields were presented in two compartments of the cage, separated by a wall (covered with white paper next to the white field and with black paper next to the black field), so that the black and white fields could be illuminated independently of each other. Correct choices of the monkeys were rewarded with a raisin. In the first part of the experiment, the monkeys were trained under various intensities of room illumination on the white field, which was always in the shade. Under this condition, the monkeys chose the white field, although the black one reflected a higher intensity of light. Then the black field was illuminated separately by a projector at increasingly higher levels. At a certain intensity level the monkeys became uncertain, looking repeatedly at the white and black fields before they chose the white one; finally, at even higher intensity levels, they chose the black field. Furthermore, the stimulus situation was complicated by introducing discs that cast shadows. Under these more complex stimulus conditions, the animals showed a higher constancy than in the case of the homogeneous fields. Under the same stimulus conditions, the monkeys performed better than humans.

Two rhesus monkeys (*M. mulatta* and *M. nemestrina*) were trained more recently by Dzhafarli, Maximov, Kezeli, and Antelidze (1991). As in the cat experiment by Kezeli et al. (1991), pairs of colored papers were shown that belonged to three groups: green, blue, and orange. In each group there were six papers differing slightly in color and brightness. Training was performed under natural daylight, estimated to be equal to 6500°K; in the test situation, an incandescent lamp equal to standard illumination A was used. The monkeys were trained to respond to the green papers. In the test, the monkeys still clearly preferred the green papers, despite the fact that the light reflected by the blue papers now stimulated the cone types in the same ratios as the green papers under natural daylight.

Experimental evidence for simultaneous and successive color contrast in animals

Color constancy and color contrast phenomena may be regarded as two sides of the same coin. More specifically, color contrast may be seen as a side effect of the mechanisms providing color constancy. *Simultaneous color contrast* in human color vision means that a small gray test field surrounded by a larger colored field will not be perceived as gray but rather as a hue complementary to the hue of the surround. As it is observed under strict fixation and very short exposure times, the mechanism must consist in neuronal interactions between adjacent elements in the retina or at higher levels. Lateral inhibitory interactions between photoreceptor channels of the same spectral type would explain qualitatively the effect of simultaneous color contrast (Cornsweet 1970, 380ff.). *Successive color contrast* is a special case of colored afterimages and is observed after prolonged stimulation by a color stimulus. The "contrast" consists in perceiving the complementary hue of the previous stimulus in the area stimulated earlier by the colored field. The entire visual field can be tinged with the complementary hue if the observer was exposed to colored illumination. The effect can be described as an aftereffect of chromatic adaptation.

If color contrast phenomena are side effects of the mechanisms responsible for color constancy, they should also be found in animals. Furthermore, a detailed investigation of these phenomena can give insight into the mechanisms underlying color constancy.

In the honeybee, simultaneous color contrast was shown for the first time by

Alfred Kühn (1927): Bees trained to find sugar water on a yellow ring on a gray background selected in the test a gray ring on a blue background, which was never chosen when presented on a gray background. To analyze simultaneous color contrast in the honeybee quantitatively (Neumeyer, 1980), the same test fields were used as for the investigation of color constancy (see earlier). Bees were trained on test field 6 while this and the other eight test fields were shown on a large gray background. In the tests, the same test fields were presented on a yellow or a blue background. In this situation the choice behavior of the bees changed: Instead of choosing test field 6, the bees preferred the more yellow/greenish test field − 0.5 on the yellow background and the more blueish test field 25 on the blue background (Neumeyer, 1980; Figure 3).

The same changes in choice behavior, and thus the same shifts in perceived hue, were observed when the test fields (10 mm in diameter) were surrounded by narrow yellow or blue rings 5–10 mm wide, respectively. This and additional experiments with black rings separating the test fields from small and large surrounds, and with variations in the size of the test fields, indicated that lateral neuronal interactions between adjacent regions in the eye of the honeybee are, at least in part, responsible for the simultaneous color contrast effect.

Successive color contrast, that is, the temporal aftereffect of presenting a colored field, could also be demonstrated in the honeybee (Neumeyer, 1981). Here bees were trained again on test field 6 on a large gray background. Choice behavior was tested on all nine test fields on the same gray background *after* the bees were exposed for 1, 2, or 5 min to a large yellow or blue field (the same colors used in the simultaneous color contrast experiment as surround). The time course of the choices showed that the bees selected within the first 30 s test field 6, but also to a high degree the less blue test fields 3, 1.5, 0, and even 0.5, −1.5, and −2.5 after adaptation to the yellow field. The aftereffect was observable up to about 3 min and was strongest for the longest exposure time of 5 min. Successive color contrast elicited by the blue field was less pronounced.

Successive color contrast could also be measured in the color constancy experiment after the colored illumination was replaced by the white illumination P (Neumeyer, 1981, Figure 7).

As far as I know, there is only one other experiment in which successive color contrast could be shown: The aphid (*Myzodes persicae* Sulz.), which spontaneously tries to pierce yellow surfaces (but never gray or differently colored ones), showed this behavior after preexposure to a blue background, also on gray surfaces (Moericke, 1950).

In various species of fish, simultaneous color contrast was shown by Herter (1950) qualitatively. To analyze simultaneous color contrast in more detail, Saskia Dörr trained goldfish to approach one colored test field out of a group of 9 of 11 differently colored test fields between red and green when presented on a gray background. In the tests, the same test fields were shown on yellow-green or red backgrounds, respectively. As in the honeybee experiments, the goldfish did not choose the training test field but preferred other test fields, indicating a shift in perceived hue (Dörr & Neumeyer, 1997). To obtain maximal contrast effects, small colored annuli were sufficient, as long as the ratio between surround width and test field radius was about 1:1.

Simultaneous color contrast was also shown in chimpanzees by Grether (1941). Trained to discriminate between two test fields illuminated with unsaturated red and green light in a gray surround, the chimpanzees had to choose between two white fields in a red and green surround in the test situation. Here the animals trained on the reddish test field pointed to the white field in a green surround (after having touched in the very first trials the red surround).

Conclusions from behavioral experiments in the honeybee

In the case of the honeybee, as the most thoroughly investigated animal, we concluded that the same mechanisms that may account for simultaneous and successive color contrast are also responsible for color constancy. The interpretation of the simultaneous color contrast effect was as follows: The yellow background shifted the perceived hue of all test fields toward blue. Thus, training test field 6 was not chosen because it appeared to be a much stronger blue to the bee than in the training situation. Test field -0.5, which was chosen instead and which appeared to humans to be yellowish (!), was selected by the bees on the yellow background because it resembled training test field 6 on a gray background. Accordingly, the blue background shifted the perceived hue of all test fields toward yellow/green; therefore, an objectively stronger blue test field (25) was preferred by the bees instead of training test field 6. As shown in Figure 12.10, the direction of the hue shift for the yellow surround was the same as the compensatory shift of color constancy under yellow illumination (Figure 12.4); the same holds for blue surround and blue illumination.

As an underlying mechanism for simultaneous color contrast, we assumed lateral inhibitory interactions, specified in the sense that inhibition between photoreceptors (or interneurons driven by them) of the *same* spectral type is *stronger* than inhibition between different spectral types (proposed by Cornsweet, 1970, pp. 380ff., for a qualitative explanation of simultaneous color contrast in human color vision). An inhibitory network of this type would have a twofold effect: It would provide (1) a hue shift of test fields surrounded by colored fields (color contrast) and (2) a hue shift of test fields *and* surround when light reflected by both of them is altered by colored illumination (color constancy).

A hue shift similar to that found in simultaneous color contrast was found when successive color contrast was tested. The latter, which could be observed for up to 3 min, was interpreted as an aftereffect of selective chromatic adap-

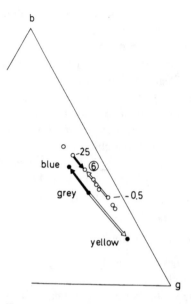

Figure 12.10. Effect of simultaneous color contrast in the honeybee represented in the color triangle (see also Figure 12.2). Open symbols: loci of the test field colors. Gray, yellow, blue: loci of the surround colors. "25": test field chosen in the presence of blue surround; "−0.5": test field chosen in the presence of yellow surround. The dark arrow represents the shift of the test field hues in the presence of blue surround for test field 25 as an example; the open arrow shows the corresponding hue shift for test field −0.5 for the yellow surround. (After Figure 4, in Neumeyer, 1980.)

tation. The changes in perceived hue observed in simultaneous and successive color contrast could be explained by assuming a selective sensitivity reduction of the green and blue retinula cell types, respectively. That there is indeed such a reduction in sensitivity was measured (Neumeyer, 1980): Two screens (5 cm in diameter) illuminated by monochromatic light were surrounded by large colored fields (the same papers used in the color contrast experiments). Bees were trained on the unilluminated screen, and the comparison screen was illuminated with monochromatic light of variable intensity. In the presence of the yellow field, sensitivity for wavelength 535 nm was selectively reduced by a factor of 0.32 (in relation to the value found with the gray surround), and in the presence of the blue field, sensitivity for wavelength 431 nm was reduced by a factor of 0.77. Test field loci calculated on the basis of retinula cell sensitivity functions weighted by these factors gave shifts in the same direction found in the color contrast and color constancy experiments. The strength of the effect for the blue field was exactly the same as that found in simultaneous color contrast with the blue surround. In the case of the yellow field, the calculated effect was stronger (Neumeyer, 1980; Figure 6).

Thus, the overall effect of color constancy and color contrast can be explained by assuming selective chromatic adaptation, that is, a mechanism assumed by von Kries to explain similar effects in human color vision (Wyszecki & Stiles, 1982, p. 431). The physiological mechanisms underlying a selective reduction of sensitivity, however, may be manifold: (1) fast neuronal inhibitory interactions; (2) relatively slow mechanisms of receptor adaptation (pupil mechanisms in retinula cells, shifts in the equilibrium between the concentration of rhodopsin and metarhodopsin, changes in the amplifying mechanisms within photoreceptors); and (3) central *Umstimmungs* – processes that adjust a "zero" or "neutral" point of color perception.

Electrophysiological investigations in the honeybee so far have not provided insight into the neural mechanisms responsible for color constancy. The color opponent cells found by Kien and Menzel (1977), Hertel (1980), and Riehle (1981) do not explain simultaneous color contrast (see the discussion in Menzel & Backhaus, 1989, p. 292).

Concluding remarks

In all animals investigated so far, color constancy was found. Even animals with color vision systems probably developed during evolution independently of each other, such as the honeybee, the goldfish, and the rhesus monkey, show this property. This indicates that color constancy, that is, the compensation for changes in the spectral composition of natural daylight, is indeed essential for color vision. To estimate the selective pressures acting on color vision, it will be necessary to measure the spectral irradiances in the natural habitat of the animal in question. That there might be tremendous changes in the spectral composition of daylight was shown by Endler (1993) for the situation in forests. Even more complicated should be the light situation for water-living animals, as the absorption conditions of water have also to be taken into account (Kirk, 1983). So far, no color vision system has been investigated well enough to allow statements about how closely color constancy is adapted to the specific changes in natural light conditions. In the honeybee, we had the impression that the ability to compensate for blue light is weaker than the ability to compensate for yellow light. This finding would be in line with the fact (indicated by the triangles and the broken line in Figure 12.2) that the changes in the relative excitation of the blue retinula cells are smaller than the changes in the yellow/green retinula cells when natural daylight is changing.

Color constancy in animals has also not been investigated well enough to allow predictions about the underlying neural mechanisms. Specific stimulus conditions have to be designed to find out whether a von Kries type of mechanism, in which single photoreceptor channels are modulated independently of each other, is sufficient to explain all cases, or whether an active internal increase in the "complementary" excitation compensates for the effect of colored illumination.

Following a consideration of Erich von Holst (1957), the necessity to achieve color constancy seems to determine the properties of color vision more generally. As explained for human color vision, the circular arrangement of hues, the existence of white and complementary colors, color contrast, and colored afterimages can be understood in the context of color constancy. A central point here is that the visual system tends to perceive the color of illumination as neutral or white. The color of illumination is determined from the object colors in the visual field by making the hypothesis that the illumination color is equal to the color predominant in the visual field (as it is highly unlikely that all objects have the same color). To achieve color constancy, this predominant color is defined as the neutral point, which is made "colorless" by internally adding the complementary color. These considerations by von Holst can be applied to the color vision of animals and give an explanation for the striking similarities with human color vision. At least in the honeybee and goldfish, color contrast, color constancy, complementary colors, and purple colors were indeed found. Whether or not an animal perceives the color of "white light" as neutral, however, this central point of the consideration is very difficult to prove. It was probably shown in the honeybee (Menzel, 1981) but in no other animal so far.

Note added in proof: In goldfish, color constancy is now investigated quantitatively in detail (see Dörr, 1996; Dörr & Neumeyer, 1996).

References

Autrum, H. J., von Zwehl, V. (1964). Die spektrale Empfindlichkeit einzelner Sehzellen im Bienenauge. *Zeitschrift für vergleichende Physiologie, 48*, 357–384.

Bowmaker, J. K. (1990). Visual pigments of fishes. In R. H. Douglas & M. B. A. Djamgoz (Eds.), *The visual system of fish*. London: Chapman and Hall.

Bowmaker, J. K., Thorpe, A., & Douglas, R. H. (1991). Ultraviolet-sensitive cones in the goldfish. *Vision Research, 31*, 349–352.

Buchholz, C. (1953). Untersuchungen über das Farbensehen der Hauskatze (*Felis domestica* L.). *Zeitschrift für Tierpsychologie, 9*, 462–470.

Burkamp, W. (1923). Versuche über das Farbenwiedererkennen der Fische. *Zeitschrift für Sinnesphysiologie, 5*, 133–170.

Campenhausen, C. von (1986). Photoreceptors, lightness constancy and color vision. *Naturwissenschaften, 73*, 674–675.

Cornsweet, T. N. (1970). *Visual perception*. New York: Academic Press.

Crocker, R. A., Ringo, J., Wolbarsht, M. L., & Wagner, H. G. (1980). Cone contributions to retinal ganglion cell receptive fields. *Journal of General Physiology, 76*, 763–785.

Daumer K. (1956). Reizmetrische Untersuchung des Farbensehens der Bienen. *Zeitschrift für vergleichende Physiologie, 38*, 413–478.

Dimentman, A. M., Karas, A. Y., Maximov, V. V., & Orlov, O. Y. (1972). Constancy of object color perception in the carp (*Cyprinus carpio*). *Pavlov Journal of Higher Nervous Activity, 22*, 4, 772–779 (in Russian).

Dörr, S. (1996). *Quantitative Untersuchungen zur Farbkonstanz beim Goldfisch.* Thesis, Mainz.

Dörr, S., & Neumeyer, C. (1996). The goldfish – a colour-constant animal. *Perception, 25,* 243–250.

Dörr, S., & Neumeyer, C. (1997). Simultaneous color contrast in goldfish. *Vision Research, 37,* 1581–1593.

Douglas, R. H., & Hawryshyn, C. W. (1990). Behavioural studies of fish vision: An analysis of visual capabilities. In R. H., Douglas & M. B. A. Djamgoz (Eds.), *The visual system of fish.* London: Chapman and Hall.

Dzhafarli, M. T., Maximov, V. V., Kezeli, A. R., & Antelidze, N. B. (1991). Color constancy in monkeys. *Sensory systems, 5/3,* 41–46 (in Russian); translated into English and published by Plenum Press (1992).

Endler, J. A. (1993). The color of light in forests and its implications. *Ecological Monographs, 63,* 1–27.

Frisch, K. von (1913). Weitere Untersuchungen über den Farbensinn der Fische. *Zoologisches Jahrbuch, Abteilung für Allgemeine Zoologie und Physiologie, 34,* 43–68.

Frisch, K. von (1914). Der Farbensinn und Formensinn der Biene. *Zoologisches Jahrbuch, Abteilung für Allgemeine Zoologie und Physiologie, 35,* 1–182.

Gnyubkin, V. F., Kondrashov, S. L., & Orlov, O. Y. (1975). Colour constancy in the toad (*Bufo bufo L.*). *Pavlov Journal of Higher Nervous Activity, 25,* 5, 1083–1089 (in Russian).

Gnyubkin, V. F., Kondrashov, S. L., & Orlov, O. Y. (1975). Constancy of colour perception in the grey toad. *Biophysics, 20,* 737–743.

Grether, W. F. (1941). The magnitude of simultaneous color contrast and simultaneous brightness contrast for chimpanzee and man. *Journal of Experimental Psychology, 30,* 69–83.

Hawryshyn, C. W., & Beauchamp, R. (1985). Ultraviolet photosensitivity in goldfish: An independent u.v. retinal mechanism. *Vision Research, 25,* 11–20.

Helversen, O. von (1972). Zur spektralen Unterschiedsempfind-lichkeit der Honigbiene. *Journal of Comparative Physiology, 80,* 439–472.

Hertel, H. (1980). Chromatic properties of identified interneurons in the optic lobes of the bee. *Journal of Comparative Physiology, 137,* 215–231.

Herter, K. (1950). Über simultanen Farbkontrast bei Fischen. *Biologisches Zentralblatt, 69,* 283–300.

Holst, E. von (1957). Aktive Leistungen der menschlichen Gesichtswahrnehmung. *Studium Generale 10,* 231–243.

Ingle, D. J. (1985). The goldfish as a retinex animal. *Science, 227,* 651–654.

Jacobs, G. H. (1981). *Comparative color vision.* New York: Academic Press.

Jacobs, G. H. (1992). Ultraviolet vision in vertebrates. *American Zoologist, 32,* 544–554.

Jacobs, G. H., Neitz, J., & Deegan, J. F. II (1991). Retinal receptors in rodents maximally sensitive to ultraviolet light. *Nature, 353,* 655–656.

Jacobs, G. H., Deegan, J. F., Crognale, M. A., & Fenwick, J. A. (1993). Photopigments of dogs and foxes and their implications for canid vision. *Visual Neuroscience, 10,* 173–180.

Katz, D., & Révész, G. (1921). Experimentelle Studien zur vergleichenden Psychologie (Versuch mit Hühnern). *Zeitschrift für angewandte Psychologie, 18,* 307–320.

Kezeli, A. R., Maximov, V. V., Lomashvili, N. I., Homeriki, M. S., & Tschvediani, N. G. (1987). Participation of the green-sensitive receptor in the cat retina in light discrimination. NIH-87-386, Fiziol. Zh SSSR im I. M., *Sechenova, 63,* 883–887 (NIH Library Translation).

Kezeli, A. R., Maximov, V. V., Homeriki, M. S., Anjaparidze, S. & Tschvediani, N. G. (1991). Colour constancy and lightness constancy in cats. *Perception, 20,* 132.

Kien, J., & Menzel, R. (1977). Chromatic properties of interneurons in the optic lobes of the bee. II. Narrow band and colour opponent neurons. *Journal of Comparative Physiology, 113,* 35–53.

Kirk, J. T. O. (1983). *Light and photosynthesis in aquatic ecosystems.* Cambridge: Cambridge University Press.

Köhler, W. (1915). Aus der Anthropoidenstation auf Teneriffa II. Optische Untersuchungen am Schimpansen und am Haushuhn, Abhandlungen der Königlich Preussischen Akademie der Wissenschaften (1915/3).

Kühn, A. (1927). Über den Farbensinn der Bienen. *Zeitschrift für vergleichende Physiologie, 5*, 762–800.

Liebman, P. A., & Entine, G. (1968). Visual pigments of frog and tadpole (*Rana pipiens*). *Vision Research, 8*, 761–775.

Locke, N. M. (1935). Color constancy in the rhesus monkey and in man. *Archives of Psychology, 193*, 1–38.

Marks, W. B. (1965). Visual pigments of single goldfish cones. *Journal of Physiology* (London), *178*, 14–32.

Maximov, V. V (1989). Colour constancy in animals. In J. Erber, R. Menzel, H. J. Pflüger, & E. Todt (Eds.), *Neural mechanisms of behavior* p. 183). Proceedings of the 2nd International Congress of Neuroethology, September 10–16, 1989. Stuttgart: Thieme.

Maximov, V. V., Orlov, O. Y., & Reuter, T. (1985). Chromatic properties of retinal afferents in the thalamus and the tectum of the frog (*Rana temporaria*). *Vision Research, 25*, 1037–1049.

Maximova, E. M., Dimentman, A. M., Maximov, V. V., Nikolaev, P. P., & Orlov, O. Y. (1975). Physiological mechanims of colour constancy. *Neurophysiology, 7*, 21–26.

Mazokhin-Porshnjakov, G. A. (1966). Recognition of colored objects by insects. In C. G. Bernhard (Ed.), *The functional organization of the compound eye*. Oxford: Pergamon Press.

McCleary, R. A., & Bernstein, J. J. (1959). A unique method for control of brightness cues in study of color vision in fish. *Physiological Zoology, 32*, 284–292.

Menzel, R. (1981). Achromatic vision in the honeybee at low light intensities. *Journal of Comparative Physiology, 141*, 389–393.

Menzel, R., & Blakers, M. (1976). Colour receptors in the bee eye – morphology and spectral sensitivity. *Journal of Comparative Physiology A, 108*, 11–33.

Menzel, R., Ventura, D. F., Hertel, H., de Souza, J., & Greggers, U. (1986). Spectral sensitivity of photoreceptors in insect compound eyes: Comparison of species and methods. *Journal of Comparative Physiology A, 158*, 165–177.

Menzel, R., & Backhaus, W. (1989). Color vision in honey bees: Phenomena and physiological mechanisms. In D. G. Stavenga, & R. C. Hardie, (Eds.), *Facets of vision* (pp. 281–297). Berlin Heidelberg: Springer.

Menzel, R., & Backhaus, W. (1991). Colour vision in insects. In P. Gouras (Ed.), *Vision and visual dysfunction, volume 6: The perception of colour* (pp. 262–293). Houndsmills, England: Mac-Millan Press.

Moericke, V. (1950). Über das Farbensehen der Pfirsichblattlaus (*Myzodes persicae* Sulz.). *Zeitschrift für Tierpsychologie, 7*, 265–274.

Neumeyer, C. (1980). Simultaneous color contrast in the honeybee. *Journal of Comparative Physiology, 139*, 165–176.

Neumeyer, C. (1981). Chromatic adaptation in the honeybee: Successive color contrast and color constancy. *Journal of Comparative Physiology, 144*, 543–553.

Neumeyer, C. (1985). An ultra-violet receptor as a fourth receptor type in goldfish color vision. *Naturwissenschaften, 72*, 162–163.

Neumeyer, C. (1991). Evolution of colour vision. In J. Cronly-Dillon (Ed.), *Vision and visual dysfunction* (Vol. 2, pp. 284–305). Houndsmills, England: Macmillan.

Neumeyer, C. (1992). Tetrachromatic color vision in goldfish: Evidence by color mixture experiments. *Journal of Comparative Physiology A, 171*, 639–649.

Przyrembel, C., Keller, B., & Neumeyer, C. (1995). Trichromatic color vision in the tiger salamander (*Salamandra salamandra*). *Journal of Comparative Physiology A, 176*, 575–586.

Riehle, A. (1981). Color opponent neurons of the honey bee in a heterochromatic flicker test. *Journal of Comparative Physiology 142*, 81–88.

Schiemenz, F. (1924). Über den Farbensinn der Fische. *Zeitschrift für vergleichende Physiologie, 1*, 175–220.

Tritsch M. (1993). Color choice behavior in cats and the effect of changes in the color of the illuminant. *Naturwissenschaften, 80*, 287–288.

Werner, A. (1990). *Farbkonstanz bei der Honigbiene Apis mellifera.* Dissertation, Fachbereich Biologie, Freie Universität, Berlin.

Werner, A., Menzel, R., & Wehrhahn, C. (1988). Color constancy in the honeybee. *Journal of Neuroscience, 8*, 156–159.

Wyszecki, G., & Stiles, W. S. (1982). *Color science, 2nd ed.* New York: Wiley.

Wolff, H. (1925). Das Farbunterscheidungsvermögen der Ellritze. *Zeitschrift für vergleichende Physiologie, 3*, 279–329.

Young, R. A. (1987). Color vision and retinex theory. *Science, 238*, 1731–1732.

Zipse, W. (1935). Können unsere einheimischen Frösche und echten Kröten ultraviolettes Licht sehen? *Zoologisches Jahrbuch, 55*, 487–524.

13   The physiological substrates of color constancy

Hidehiko Komatsu

Introduction

In this chapter, physiological mechanisms of color processing in the visual system are outlined and discussed in the context of their possible contribution to the mechanisms underlying color constancy. Figure 13.1 shows the visual pathway related to color processing and areas in the cerebral cortex that are involved in this pathway. Many physiological experiments describe the relation between void color and the responses in the nervous system, particularly in lower stages of processing. However, the relationships between neural responses and surface color perception are more informative for understanding how we see color and it is these with which this chapter is concerned.

An important feature of color constancy to be discussed is its approximate nature – colour constancy is not perfect (Chapter 10, this volume). Rather, as stated by Judd (1960), "Colour constancy, like colour memory, is an approximate process in which coloured surfaces retain their membership of a color category" (p. 263). Color perception does appear to be organized categorically, and the perceptual categories are thought to have biological foundations (e.g., Bornstein, 1987; Matuzawa, 1985; Sandell, Gross, & Bornstein, 1979; Chapter 9, this volume). At higher stages of processing, specifically in cortical area V4, several studies have directly examined neural mechanisms of color constancy, and these are examined in detail. In the final section, the two classes of mechanisms related to the occurrence of color constancy, namely, chromatic adaptation and simultaneous mechanisms, are explored and possible sites considered. Most of the physiological studies described in this chapter were done using macaque monkeys, which are known to have cone sensitivities, behavioral spectral sensitivity, and wavelength discrimination functions similar to those of humans, as well as similar suprathreshold color categorization (Baylor, Nunn, & Schnapf, 1987; Bowmaker & Dartnall, 1980; Bowmaker, Dartnall & Mollon, 1980; De Valois, Morgan, Polson, Mead & Hull, 1974; Marks, Dobelle, & MacNichol, 1964; Oyama, Furusaka & Kito, 1979; Schnapf, Kraft, & Baylor, 1987; Sandell et al., 1979).

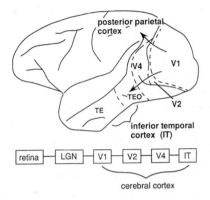

Figure 13.1. Bottom diagram: Visual pathway related to the processing of color information. LGN, lateral geniculate nucleus; V1, the primary visual cortex; V2, V4, TEO, TE, IT, inferior temporal cortex. Top diagram: Major areas in the cerebral cortex that are involved in the color processing are shown on the lateral surface of the cerebral cortex of the macaque monkey. Two curved lines with an arrowhead indicate two major cortical visual streams; one connects V1 and the posterior parietal cortex, and the other connects V1 and the inferior temporal cortex.

2. Cortical chromatic processing

2.1 General organization of the cortical stage

Most of the projections from the lateral geniculate nucleus (LGN) to the cerebral cortex terminate at area V1 in the macaque monkey. Neurons in the parvocellular and magnocellular systems project to different layers of V1; the former projects mainly to layer 4Cb and the latter mainly to layer 4Ca (Lund, 1988; Merigan & Maunsell, 1993).

Cytochrome oxidase (CO) staining of area V1 reveals that densely stained spots are distributed in a patchlike fashion mainly in the superficial layers. These spotlike areas, called blobs, are distinguished from interblob regions. As will be described later, there are differences in the physiological properties of neurons between blob and interblob regions. In addition to these regions, layer 4B is often regarded as a third compartment of area V1. This layer receives projections from layer 4Ca and sends fibers to other extrastriate areas such as area (Shipp & Zeki, 1989). On the other hand, blob and interblob regions receive inputs from the parvocellular system through direct and indirect inputs from layer 4Cb. In addition, these regions receive inputs from the magnocellular system through direct and indirect inputs from layer 4Ca. It is likely, therefore, that some integration of signals from the parvocellular and magnocellular systems takes place in area V1 (Merigan & Maunsell, 1993).

Visual information is transferred from area V1 to the extrastriate cortical areas (Felleman & Van Essen, 1991; Maunsell & Newsome, 1987; Van Essen, 1985; Zeki & Shipp, 1988). Two major streams of information flow are distinguished in this stage (Figure 13.1), one of which connects area V1 to the posterior parietal cortex; this pathway is thought to subserve the processing of space and motion (Maunsell & Newsome, 1987; Ungerleider & Mishkin, 1982). Another stream connects area V1 to the inferior temporal cortex; this pathway is thought to be involved in color perception. This pathway includes areas V2, V4, and the inferior temporal cortex, as well as area V1. In V2, three subregions are distinguished by CO staining (Livingstone & Hubel, 1982, 1984; Tootell, Silverman, De Valois, & Jacobs, 1983). Densely stained regions called *stripes* are interleaved with less densely stained regions called *interstripes* or *pale stripes*. Stripes are further subdivided into *thin stripes* and *thick stripes*, which alternate with each other. These three subregions in V2, namely, thin stripes, thick stripes, and interstripes, have neurons with different physiological properties and have connections with different subregions in V1; neurons in blobs in V1 send fibers to thin stripes in V2; those in interblobs in V1 send fibers to interstripes in V2; and those in layer 4B in V1 send fibers to thick stripes in V2 (Livingstone & Hubel, 1983, 1984, 1987). Neurons in thin stripes and interstripes project to V4 (DeYoe & Van Essen, 1985; Shipp & Zeki, 1985; Van Essen, Felleman, DeYoe, Olavarria, & Knierim, 1990). It has been shown that V4 receives inputs from both parvocellular and magnocellular systems in experiments that selectively block the activities of the parvocellular or magnocellular layers in the LGN (Ferrera, Nealy, & Maunsell, 1992). Thus the integration that begins as early as V1 continues throughout the higher visual cortical areas.

2.2 Cortical visual area V1

With regard to the processing of color in area V1, we can find several properties that are not observed in the opponency stages of the retinal ganglion cells and the LGN. The most salient spatial feature of V1 neurons is the emergence of orientation selectivity; some of these cells also have wavelength selectivity. Figure 13.2 shows the range of spectro-spatial antagonisms of the receptive fields in V1 (Dow & Gouras, 1973; Hubel & Wiesel, 1968; Poggio, Baker, Mansfield, Sillito, & Grigg, 1975). Other neurons with color as well as orientation selectivity receive inputs from different classes of cones in the same region, thus showing only color opponency (Fig. 13.2A) (Gouras, 1974; Poggio, et al., 1975). From a purely chromatic viewpoint, the most interesting class of neurons to emerge in V1 are the *double opponent* neurons shown in Figure 13.2D (Livingstone & Hubel, 1984; Michael, 1978b), which receive antagonistic inputs to the center of the receptive field and antagonistic inputs of opposite polarity to the receptive field surround. For example, the center of the receptive field may be excited by long-wavelength ("red") light and inhibited by

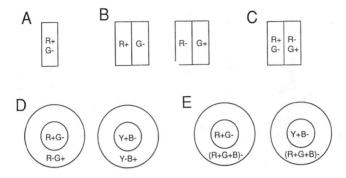

Figure 13.2. Various types of color-selective neurons reported in area V1 that are not observed in the preceding stages. The symbols R, G, and B are used here rather than L, M, and S because some of the studies of double opponency analyzed the neural responses with respect to spectral colors rather than cone inputs.

middle-wavelength ("green") light, whereas the surround region is excited by green and inhibited by red. Some of the early studies of double opponency did not analyze the cone inputs to the center and surround regions; rather, they classified neurons according to the responses to colors in different regions of the spectrum. Some of the double opponent neurons have also been shown to have orientation selectivity (Fig. 13.2C) (Michael, 1978b). The double opponent neurons also respond to achromatic gratings of a preferred spatial frequency (Lennie, Krauskopf, & Sclar, 1990; Thorell, De Valois, & Albrecht, 1984); this raised questions about the existence of purely spectral double opponent neurons in area V1 (Lennie & D'Zmura, 1988). The answer may lie in the findings of Ts'o and Gilbert (1988), who recorded from the blob regions in laminae 2 and 3 of area V1. They confirmed Hubel and Livingstone's finding that cells in the blobs were not orientation selective, but they found little evidence of double opponency. They did, however, observe cells that had antagonistic centers and broadband surrounds, cells that are now known as *modified type II cells* (Fig. 13.2E).

Receptive field organization similar to that observed in the opponent stage is also seen in area V1. Some of the V1 neurons are excited by a stimulus in one region of the spectrum that is presented at the center of the receptive field and are inhibited by a stimulus in the other region of the spectrum that is presented at the surround (color-opponent, center-surround type such as the R^+/G^- type). Two subregions in V1 draw special attention with respect to the processing of color. One of these regions is layer 4Cb, where the axons from the parvocellular layers in the LGN terminate. In contrast to other layers in V1, there are no orientation-selective neurons in this layer. In this layer, neurons have concentric receptive fields, and they are either color-opponent or broadband-type neurons.

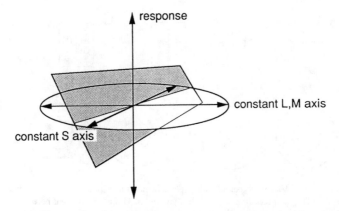

Figure 13.3. Color selectivity of neurons in the parvocellular system can be well described within a simple color space. This space aims to represent responses of a neuron in this system to isoluminant stimuli of various chromaticities that cover the entire receptive field when the neuron is adapted to a gray field. This three-dimensional space consists of a plane that represents isoluminant colors (isoluminant plane) and an axis perpendicular to the isoluminant plane that represents the responses of the neuron. The isoluminant plane is characterized by two axes. One axis represents the area where the signal from cone S is constant and the signals from cones L and M can vary in a balanced opposition (constant S axis). The other axis represents the area where the signals from cones L and M are constant and the signal from cone S varies (constant L, M axis), that is, the tritanopic confusion line. Because responses of neurons in the parvocellular system are linear summations of signals of different classes of cones, responses to various isoluminant colors can be represented by a plane in this space. Responses of L/M-type neurons maximally change their activities when the color varies along the constant S axis; thus, these neurons are represented as planes with the direction of tilt along the constant S axis. By contrast, responses of S/L+M-type neurons maximally change their activities when the color varies along the constant L,M axis; thus these neurons are represented as planes with the direction of tilt along the constant L,M axis.

There is some disagreement about the properties of color opponency and spatial organization of the receptive fields. Livingstone and Hubel (1984) reported that many neurons in this layer are of the color-opponent, center-surround type and that there are no double opponent neurons. However, Michael (1978a) reported that many double opponent neurons exist in this layer. Furthermore, Gouras (1974) reported that some of the neurons receive spatially overlapping inputs from different classes of cones with the opposite polarities (color-opponent, center-only or Type II neurons).

Another feature in area V1 that is given special attention with respect to color processing is the blobs which exist mainly in layers 2 and 3. Livingstone and Hubel (1984) found that many neurons in the blob regions are not orientation selective and are either color-opponent or broadband neurons. They also reported that most of the color-opponent neurons in the blobs are double-opponent neurons because they do not respond to any large stimuli covering the entire receptive field, regardless of chromatic or achromatic content. Ts'o and Gilbert (1988) confirmed the finding that many neurons in the blobs are not orientation selective, but they claimed that there are very few double-opponent neurons in the blobs and that many neurons with color opponency in the receptive field center have antagonistic broadband surround (Fig. 13.2E). We can expect that neurons with such receptive field organization will not respond to any homogeneous stimuli covering the entire receptive field, and that they will respond to an achromatic grating with an adequate spatial frequency. Therefore, it seems that such neurons can explain at least part of the discrepancy concerning the double-opponent neurons in area VI of the macaque.

There is a different kind of discrepancy about the types of color selectivity of neurons in the blobs. Livingstone and Hubel (1984) reported that all R/G, B/Y, and broadband types coexist in a single blob, but Ts'o and Gilbert (1988) claimed that R/G and B/Y types of neurons are segregated in different blobs. On the other hand, Yoshioka found that neurons selective to endspectral colors (R or B) exist in the blob regions, and that those selective to midspectral colors (G or Y) exist in the interblob regions (Yoshioka, 1989; Yoshioka, Dow, & Vautin, 1988). In his report, endspectral color-selective cells in the blobs are not orientation selective, and midspectral color-selective cells in the interblobs are mainly orientation selective. Tootell, Silverman, Hamilton, De Valois, and Switkes (1988) also reported that the blob regions are activated by grating stimuli containing endspectral colors in their 14C-2-deoxy-d-glucose (2DG) experiments.

The most quantitative study of the cone inputs to color-selective neurons in area V1 was done by Lennie and colleagues (1990) using a method similar to that employed to characterize the chromatic properties of the LGN neurons by Krauskopf, Lennie, and Derrington, (1984). They examined neural responses using visual stimuli whose chromaticity and luminance were temporally modulated along certain directions in the color space around a white point. Neurons that respond to stimuli modulated on the isoluminant plane are often found in layer 4Cb and, for most of them, responses are expressed as linear combinations of cone signals. In contrast to the LGN, where the combinations of cone signals are limited in a small number of ways, the combinations and weights of signals from different types of cones vary from one neuron to the other in area V1. If color selectivity of these neurons in area V1 is represented in the space as shown in Figure 13.3 responses to various isoluminant colors consist of a plane because responses of these V1 neurons, like those in the parvocellular system, are a linear summation of cone signals. However, in contrast to neurons in the parvocellular system, the direction of the tilt of such planes is not restricted to the directions of cardinal axes, such as the constant S axis or the constant L,M axis; instead, they can be in any direction in the isoluminant plane.

As the direction of tilt of the plane represents the preferred color for a given neuron, various directions of the tilt of the plane among a population of neurons indicate the preferred color difference from neuron to neuron. With respect to the categorization of color, it is conceivable that area V1 is related to color categorization that is more complicated than that for the four basic color categories. For example, purple is not included in the four basic color categories but is included in the eight basic color names (red, orange, yellow, green, blue, purple, pink, and brown). These eight basic color categories are commonly observed in different human races (Berlin & Kay, 1969; Boynton & Olson, 1987; Uchikawa & Boynton, 1987), as well as in chimpanzees (Matuzawa, 1985), and are thought to have biological foundations (Bornstein, 1987). Vautin and Dow (1985) found neurons in V1 that have two peaks at both ends of the spectrum, red and blue, and respond to purple preferentially. However, in contrast to the rough correspondence between the categorization into four basic colors and neural representation of color at the opponent stage (though not perfect, as described earlier), there is no clear evidence of the existence of separate classes of neurons in V1 or in the later stages that correspond to the color category consisting of the eight basic colors.

Of these basic color names, orange and brown are particularly interesting with respect to the perception of surface color. The other six basic colors do not depend on the luminance contrast with the surrounding field, but orange and brown do. Even if the spectral composition of the light from a given area is the same, the color of the light is perceived as orange when the background is darker than the stimulus, but it is perceived as brown when the background has the opposite contrast. When a given area in the visual field has luminance lower than that of the background, the area appears to have color attached to a surface of an object (*surface color* mode); thus, brown is perceived only in the surface color mode. Yoshioka and colleagues reported that some color-selective neurons in area V1 respond only to stimuli lighter than the background; some other neurons respond irrespective of the luminance contrast; and the remaining neurons respond only to stimuli darker than the background (Yoshioka, 1989; Yoshioka et al., 1988). These color-selective neurons that prefer darker stimuli tend to have broad color tuning, but some of them have a preference for brown or maroon. Yoshioka et al. also reported that similar types of dark, color-sensitive neurons were found in areas V2 and V4 as well.

2.2.1 Area V2.   Area V2 is less well studied than area V1 concerning the representation of color. Of the subregions in V2, the thin stripes that can be identified by CO staining draw special attention because blob regions in V1 send fibers to thin stripes. It is reported that color-selective neurons are more frequently observed in thin stripes than in other subdivisions in V2 (Hubel & Livingstone, 1987). Neurons in thin stripes do not have orientation selectivity, and they are either broadband, double opponent, or color-opponent center-only type neurons (Hubel & Livingstone, 1987). Different reports disagree about the color selectivity of neurons in thin stripes as they do about the blobs in area V1. Ts'o, Gilbert, and Wiesel (1990) reported that R/G-type neurons and B/Y-type neurons are segregated in different thin stripes. On the other hand, Yoshioka found that neurons selective to endspectral colors exist in thin stripes and that those selective to midspectral colors exist in the interstripe regions (Yoshioka, 1989; Yoshioka et al., 1988). He also reported that color-selective neurons that prefer stimuli darker than the background exist in the thick stripes.

2.2.2. Area V4. Area V4 extends from the anterior bank of the lunate sulcus (LS) to the posterior bank of the superior temporal sulcus (STS) and covers the entire prelunate gyrus. The size of the receptive field is on average about 30 times larger than that in area V1. This area seems to be organized in a retinotopic fashion and represents the contralateral visual field, although this is much less obvious than in area V1. Many neurons in V4 have color selectivity, but the proportion of such neurons varies in different reports (Schein & Desimone, 1990; Schein, Marrocco, & de Monasterio, 1982; Zeki, 1973, 1977). This may be due to the use of different criteria for the classification of neurons as color selective or not (Schein & Desimone, 1990), but it may also be due to the existence of distinct subregions in V4. For example, Zeki (1977) suggested that color-selective neurons are observed more frequently in the anterior bank of the LS and in the posterior bank of the STS than in the prelunate gyrus. It is suggested that there is modularity on a smaller scale in V4 as well because terminals of the projections from thin stripes in V2 and those from interstripes are segregated in V4 (Van Essen et al., 1990).

Many neurons in V4 are selective to spatial features such as orientation, length, width, or spatial frequency of the stimuli (Desimone & Schein, 1987), but the relationships between the selectivities to color and these spatial features have not been studied in detail. Schein and Desimone (1990) suggested that selectivities to color and orientation are independent properties of V4 neurons. In areas V1 and V2, it seems that spatial and chromatic properties of the neurons are closely correlated because many neurons with clear color selectivity are not orientation selective. On the contrary, in later stages, it seems that the relationships between the selectivities to form and color differ from one neuron to the other, and independence of the selectivities to chromatic and spatial parameters is reported in V3 (Burkhalter & Van Essen, 1986), V4, and the inferior temporal cortex (Komatsu & Ideura, 1993).

There is controversy about the basic color-selective properties of V4 neurons. Zeki (1980) suggested that V4 neurons are more narrowly tuned to wavelength than those at prior stages. However, other studies reported that the bandwidths of the spectral response curves of V4 neurons are similar to those at prior stages (de Monasterio & Schein, 1982; Schein & Desimone, 1990). It is also reported that many color-selective neurons respond to white light, at least to some degree, and do not show overt color opponency (Schein & Desimone, 1990). Desimone, Schein, Moran, and Ungerleider (1985) suggested that these properties are similar to broadband color filters such as a piece of colored glass.

A distinct property of V4 neurons is that many of them have a large, silent, suppressive surround around the receptive field (Desimone & Schein, 1987; Desimone et al., 1985; Schein & Desimone, 1990). For such neurons, stimulation of the surround by itself does not generate any response, but it can suppress the response to the stimuli presented within the (classical) receptive field. This suppression is most obvious when the stimuli presented within the receptive field and its surround have the same parameters, such as color or spatial frequency. We can assume that these suppressive surrounds are useful for figure–ground segregation and in detecting stimuli that are different from the background. These neurons may also be useful to the computation required for color constancy, as will be explained in the last section.

Zeki (1980, 1983a, 1983b) conducted a series of very important experiments and suggested that V4 neurons respond to the "perceived color" rather than the wavelength composition of the stimulus. He used Mondrian stimuli and examined whether neurons in V1 and V4 respond to the perceived color or the wavelength composition of the stimulus. In these experiments, a pattern was made by juxtaposing variously colored patches. This pattern was illuminated by three projectors, each of which projects long-wavelength, middle-wavelength, or short-wavelength light. When the amount of light coming from each projector was adjusted, it was possible to make the light coming from an area in the Mondrian, say a red patch, under one illumination condition identical to the light coming from another area, say a white patch, under a different illumination condition. However, the white patch appeared to be white under either illumination; a manifestation of color constancy. Color selectivities of neurons in areas V1 and V4 were then examined when their receptive fields were situated within one of these patches. Zeki found that V1 neurons respond to the wavelength composition of the light, but he found that there are neurons in V4 whose responses parallel the perceived color, suggesting that color constancy occurs at or before V4. However, with regard to the results indicating that V1 neurons lack mechanisms needed for color constancy, it has been pointed out that responses of V1 and V4 neurons were tested using patches of the same size (Maunsell & Newsome, 1987). So it might be possible that such mechanisms were overlooked in V1 because stimulus dimensions exceeded the critical size at which such possible mechanisms effectively work.

Several experiments have tested the effects of V4 lesions on the color discrimination ability of monkeys. Heywood and Cowey (1987) found that the thresholds for the discrimination of hue and saturation rose after V4 lesions. On the other hand, Dean (1979) and Walsh, Carden, Butler, and Kulikowski (1993) found no change in the threshold for discrimination, although their animals with V4 lesions required a longer time for relearning than the control animals. Wild, Butler, Carden, and Kulikowski, (1985) also found no significant difference in the ability for hue discrimination between V4-lesioned and control animals. Heywood and colleagues more recently repeated a similar test for the ability of hue discrimination in monkeys with V4 lesions using color stimuli presented on a CRT display, but they found no deficit in hue discrimination (Heywood, Gadotti, & Cowey, 1992). They argued that a plausible reason for such a discrepancy is that the hue steps used in the earlier experiments were smaller than those used in the later experiments. But they also suggested another possibility: that the deficit observed in the earlier study using Wisconsin General Testing Apparatus (WGTA) may be a deficit in color constancy rather than a deficit in hue discrimination because, in WGTA, chromaticity of the stimulus may change, depending on the location in the cage from which the animal views the stimulus. Walsh and colleagues (1993) found that animals with V4 lesions tend to have difficulty maintaining good scores, although they can discriminate the stimulus well. Because the criterion of the discrimination differs among these studies, the instability of the behavioral performance after V4 lesioning may also be responsible for the discrepancy among different studies. Recently, Schiller (1993) systematically tested the effects of partial V4 ablation on the discrimination abilities for various visual attributes using head-restrained monkeys that respond to stimuli by saccadic eye movements. In these experiments, the ablation of V4 affected only part of the visual field. Schiller quantitatively compared the abilities of color discrimination measured in the normal visual field and those measured in the affected field using visual stimuli presented on a CRT display and varying the parameters of the stimuli systematically. He found clear evidence that the ability to discriminate hue and saturation deteriorates when the differences between discriminating stimuli are relatively small with respect to these parameters. To summarize, ablation of V4 seems to cause a mild deficit in the discrimination of hue and saturation, but even after a total V4 lesion, abilities for color discrimination are preserved fairly well.

Effects of V4 lesions on the ability to achieve color constancy were examined by Wild et al. (1985) and Walsh et al. (1993). In the experiments conducted by Wild and colleagues, two checkerboard patterns were presented to the animal in each trial. Each pattern consisted of many orange patches, but only one of them contained a green patch. The animal was required to choose the checkerboard pattern containing a green patch. Checkerboard patterns were illuminated by two projectors, each of which projected either red or green monochromatic light; the relative amounts of light from each projector were varied. If these patterns were illuminated by only one of the monochromatic lights, the patterns appeared to be monochromatic, consisting of many patches with different lightness. If only a small amount of light is added from the other projector, the pattern containing the green patch can be easily chosen by normal humans and monkeys. But the animals with partial V4 lesions failed to discriminate these two patterns, and their scores were much worse than those of the controls for any relative amounts of lights except when the amounts of light from two projectors were the same or when only one of the projectors was lit.

In the experiments by Walsh and colleagues, monkeys were trained to discriminate Munsell colors surrounded by a Mondrian pattern and to choose a color chip (positive stimulus) from among other colors (negative stimulus). The training of this task was conducted under white illumination. Then the illumination was changed so that either the wavelength composition of the positive stimulus was now the same as that of the negative stimulus in the original condition or the wavelength composition of the negative stimulus was now the same as that of the positive stimulus in the original condition. The performance of the animals with V4 lesions was significantly degraded compared with that of the normal animals, and it was concluded that ablation of V4 causes deficits in color constancy. The authors argued that the deficits in color discrimination tasks observed in some of the experiments were so mild that they cannot explain the deficits observed in the tasks designed to test the ability of color constancy. In a different experiment, Walsh, Kulikowski, Butler, and Carden (1992) examined how V4 lesions affect the categorization of color into four basic color categories (R, Y, G, B). Monkeys were taught a color discrimination task using Munsell colors, and two negative stimuli were prepared for each of the positive stimuli. These two negative stimuli were the same distance from the positive stimuli with respect to their dominant wavelengths; one of them belonged to the same color category as the positive stimulus, but the other did not. It was often assumed that the ventral pathway, particularly the inferior temporal cortex, is involved in the categorization of visual stimuli. However, Walsh et al. were the first to deal explicitly with categories as a variable in the effect of lesions in this pathway on the categorization of color stimuli. They found that the overall performance of V4-lesioned animals was worse than that of the control animals, but both V4-lesioned and control animals exhibited poorer performance when the positive and negative stimuli belonged to the same category. This suggests that animals with V4 lesions use the same color categories as normal monkeys and that the boundaries between categories are not shifted by the lesion. This seems reasonable because the basic four color categories are likely to be formed at the opponent stage or early cortical stage.

2.2.3 Inferior temporal cortex.   The inferior temporal (IT) cortex is believed to play an important role in the recognition and memory of visual stimuli (Gross, 1973; Mishkin, 1982; Miyashita & Chang, 1988; Ungerleider & Mishkin, 1982). The posterior one-third of the IT cortex (area TEO; von Bonin & Bailey, 1947) can be distinguished from the remaining part (area TE) physiologically and anatomically. Fibers from V4 neurons terminate in area TEO and in the posterior part of area TE, and the anterior part of TE receives direct inputs from area TEO and the posterior part of TE. In area TEO, the size of the receptive field enlarges two to four times compared to that of V4, and this area still seems to have crude retinotopic organization. In area TE, the receptive fields of neurons further enlarge, not only in the contralateral visual field but also in the ipsilateral visual field; usually they include the center of the visual field. Receptive field sizes become more than 100 times larger than in V1, and there seems to be no retinotopic organization in area TE. Many neurons in the IT cortex, like those in the preceding stages, respond to simple visual stimuli, such as slits or spots, and exhibit selectivity to various parameters, such as color or orientation of these stimuli. Several studies have shown that there are neurons in the IT cortex, particularly in TE, that preferentially respond to certain complicated shapes or patterns or to a particular combination of these and colors (Gross, 1973; Desimone, Albright, Gross, & Bruce, 1984; Gross, Rocha-Miranda, & Bender, 1972; Komatsu & Ideura, 1993; Perrett, Rolls, & Caan, 1982; Richmond, Optican, Podell, & Spitzer, 1987; Sato, Kawamura, & Iwai, 1980; Schwartz, Desimone, & Albright, 1983; Tanaka, Saito, Fukada, & Moriya, 1991; Yamane, Kaji, & Kawano, 1988).

Komatsu and colleagues studied the color selectivity of IT neurons by examining how the magnitudes of responses of each neuron are distributed on the CIE (Commission Internationale de l'Eclariage) xy-chromaticity diagram (Komatsu, Ideura, Kaji, & Yamane, 1992). They found that many IT neurons respond selectively to hue and saturation, and that each of these neurons represents only a small part of the chromaticity diagram. The population of these color-selective neurons as a whole represents the entire region of the diagram examined, although the representation around the white point is rather weak. Informal observation suggests that the regions in the color diagram where highly color-selective neurons respond (Figure 10 of Komatsu et al., 1992) are similar in shape and size to the regions where different color names are assigned in the experiments studying the finer color categorization using the eight basic color names (Shinoda, Uchikawa, & Ikeda, in press; Uchikawa, Kuriki, & Shinoda, 1993). However, the boundaries of these regions shown in physiological and psychophysical experiments do not necessarily coincide.

Komatsu suggested that many color-selective IT neurons receive inputs that are nonlinear summations of cone signals (Komatsu, in press). This suggestion is made because the contour lines of these neurons in the color diagram representing response magnitudes are clearly curved. Because a space representing cone signals and a CIE color space are related by a linear transformation, it is expected that iso-response contour lines are straight in the CIE chromaticity diagram if a neuron receives inputs that are a linear summation of cone signals.

As it is indicated that the responses of most of the color-selective neurons in V1 are linear summations of cone signals, nonlinear combinations of these signals probably occur somewhere between area V1 and the IT cortex. Komatsu also suggested that as a result of such transformation, it is possible that a given neuron responds selectively to any particular range of hue and saturation. Many color-selective IT neurons have specificity to the size of the stimuli (Komatsu et al., 1992). Some of them prefer a large stimulus (exceeding 10° or more). This preference for a large stimulus is not observed in the preceding stages. As described earlier, many V4 neurons have a silent, suppressive surround. It is reported that such surrounds have specificity to color. One possible mechanism of generating such a surround in V4 is due to the feedback connections from the IT cortex.

3. Mechanisms related to color constancy

Color constancy is a process in which effects of illumination are discounted from the light reflected from a surface. Chromatic adaptation and some simultaneous mechanisms are thought to be involved in color constancy. In this section several examples of these mechanisms are described, even though most of them are still hypothetical, and the implication of these mechanisms in color constancy will be considered.

3.1 Chromatic adaptation

After the eye is exposed to certain types of chromatic stimulation, the state of the visual system is altered, so that neural responses to a color stimulus change even though the physical contents of the stimulus are the same. This phenomenon is referred to as *chromatic adaptation*. It is thought to occur at several different stages in the visual system.

3.1.1 Chromatic adaptation at the receptor level. First, let's consider a system consisting of only one type of photoreceptor. Changes in the intensity of light falling on a certain point on the retina occur when lights reflected from different surfaces in the scene reach this point as a result of eye movements or when illumination changes occur. The time course of the latter process is usually much slower than that of the former process, but the change in light intensity can be much larger for the latter than for the former. At any one time, the intensity of light reflected from various surfaces in the scene lies within a small range (<10: 1), but the range of illumination to which we can be exposed under daily conditions is much larger (about 1010:1) (Lennie & D'Zmura, 1988). Therefore, to encode the various lightnesses of different surfaces efficiently, it is reasonable to change the sensitivity of visual neurons, depending on the illumination level (light adaptation). Such a change in the sensitivity of the visual system is revealed psychophysically as the change in the threshold for the detection of a test light on a uniform background under different illumination of the background. Even when the light intensities from various surfaces in a scene change due to the change in illumination, the ratio of the light intensities from one surface compared to another surface does not change. Thus the relative light intensity, namely, contrast, provides very useful information about the surface lightness that is a property invariant to the illumination. If the visual system generates the same signal to the same amount of contrast, the threshold for the detection of a test light will change in proportion to the illumination of the background. This relation between the detection threshold and illumination is known to hold under limited conditions of stimulation such as long duration and large area stimuli. Let's consider the system for color that has more than one class of receptors (cones). If each of the three classes of cones changes its sensitivity in the same way described earlier, the color system can signal three sets of relative reflectance values that are inherent in each surface and invariant to the illumination; this will result in perfect color constancy. A hypothetical mechanism like this, in which the gains in the three cone systems are independently adjusted in proportion to the light intensity, is known as *von Kries's proportionality rule*. Although Valeton and van Norren (1993) confirmed that chromatic adaptation starts to occur at the level of cones by extracellular recordings from monkey cones, the processes of chromatic adaptation of different classes of cones are not completely independent as shown by psychophysical experiments (Lennie & D'Zmura, 1988). It has also been shown that not only multiplicative mechanisms work for chromatic adaptation at the level of cones, as assumed in the von Kries rule; different kinds of mechanisms work as well (Valeton & van Norren, 1983).

3.1.2 Chromatic adaptation at the opponent stage. In classical psychophysical experiments of chromatic adaptation, chromaticity and/or luminance of the stimulation field changes in time, causing chromatic adaptation. In contrast, Williams, and Heeley (1982) employed a different paradigm to produce chromatic adaptation in which chromaticity and/or luminance is modulated sinusoidally in time along certain axes in the color space for a certain period of time. In this paradigm, average chromaticity and/or luminance of the stimulation field is constant across time, so no adaptation will occur at the receptor stage. However, if there is a neural mechanism that represents a certain axis in color space in a later stage, such a mechanism will be selectively adapted if the stimulus modulation occurs along this axis. As a measure of adaptation, Krauskopf et al. examined the rise in chromatic detection threshold. They found that the constant blue axis and the constant L,M axis consist of cardinal axes in the color space in the sense that modulation of color along one of these axes influences the chromatic detection threshold only on that axis. This is coincident with the fact that there are two classes of color-selective neurons in the opponent stage that represent either the constant blue axis or the constant L,M axis. Chromatic adaptation, as indicated by Krauskopf and colleagues, likely results from the selective activation of these classes of neurons.

3.1.3 Chromatic adaptation at the cortical stage. Webster and Mollon (1991) tested suprathreshold color appearance, using the matching method instead of the chromatic detection threshold when chromatic adaptation was produced by the method used by Krauskopf and colleagues. They found that color appearance is distorted away from the direction in color space to which the observer has adapted irrespective of whether the direction is along the cardinal axes in the opponent stage or not. This suggests that color appearance is represented by multiple channels tuned to different directions in color space. The site of this type of chromatic adaptation is presumably cortical, and the results obtained in area V1 by Lennie and colleagues (1990) seem to be consistent with such a model.

As described earlier, chromatic adaptation is likely to occur at several different stages in the visual system. All these mechanisms are effective in discounting the effects of illumination and thus are able to contribute to color constancy. However, in natural conditions, it is very likely that chromaticity and luminance of the stimulation field change in time as a result of the change in illumination. Therefore, chromatic adaptation occurring before the opponent stage is likely to play a dominant role.

3.2 Simultaneous mechanisms

In this last section, several models based on physiologically identified neurons as parts of the possible neural substrates for the simultaneous mechanisms for color constancy will be described.

Involvement of simultaneous mechanisms in color constancy has been one of the central problems in the mechanisms of color constancy since the time of the experiments conducted by Land and colleagues using Mondrian stimuli (Land, 1977, 1983; Land & MaCann, 1971). In these experiments, an observer viewed a two-dimensional pattern consisting of juxtaposed, variously colored patches, and the color appearance of each patch was examined under varying illumination. These experiments indicated the importance of sampling color signals from a wide region in the visual field to obtain the surface reflectance of a given patch in the Mondrian stimulus by discounting the effect of illumination. Land then proposed several computational algorithms for such a process (see chapters 10 and 11).

If Land-like computations occur, then neurons need to exist that receive signals from each cone in a spatially antagonistic fashion, such as the L^+ center/

L⁻ surround type, to detect contrast in each cone mechanism. Such neurons have not been found. However, an equivalent computation, as Land proposed, can be made with neurons in which a linear combination of cone signals is fed into the center and surround of the receptive field in an opponent fashion (Horn, 1974). Livingstone and Hubel (1984) suggested that double opponent neurons can be utilized for such computation and for detecting contrast for a given chromatic opponent channel.

More recently, Land (1986) proposed a more biologically plausible algorithm for calculating the surface reflectance of a target patch in a Mondrian pattern that is scaled to the average of the reflectances in the region surrounding the target patch. In this algorithm, for each color channel, signals from that channel are sampled from the region surrounding the target patch in such a way that signals from patches close to the target are more densely sampled and those from distant patches are less densely sampled. Signals from the target patch are then scaled to the average signals from the surround region that is obtained as described to calculate the surface reflectance or color of the target patch. The range for sampling and the weight for scaling signals according to the distance from the target were empirically determined, and this alternative algorithm yielded a good estimate of the surface reflectance of the target patch.

Area V4 neurons seem to have properties particularly well suited for such a computation. Many of them have large suppressive surrounds with wavelength selectivity similar to that within the classical receptive field (Schein & Desimone, 1990) so that they can work to discount the color of the large surrounding region. Hurlbert and Poggio (1988) induced an optimal operator from many examples of images that can estimate surface reflectance using image irradiance for a single color channel. They found that their operator has a spatial structure similar to that of the operator employed in Land's modified algorithm, as well as the receptive field of neurons that Schein and Desimone found in V4.

Although each V4 neuron can detect color in a very limited region in the visual field, the silent suppressive surround of these neurons carries information about the color of a large region in the visual field. One possible way to obtain such color information of a wide field is by means of local connections within V4, as suggested by Schein and Desimone. Another possible way is by means of the feedback connections from IT cortex. It is reported that there are neurons in IT that respond selectively to the color spreading across a wide region in the visual field (Komatsu et al., 1992).

In Land's algorithms described earlier, patches surrounding the target point are randomly sampled, without regard to the color of the patches, and the lights from them are averaged. If the surrounding region has on average a flat surface reflectance (in other words, gray), the average of the lights reflected from the surrounding region provides a good estimate of the wavelength composition of illumination, so the surface reflectance of the target patch can be computed by discounting the average light of the surrounding region from the light reflected from the target patch. If, however, the surrounding region has, on average, non-flat surface reflectance, the average of the lights reflected from that region no longer provides a good estimate of the illumination. This happens, for example, when the scene consists of objects with similar surface materials, such as a forest in which the green color of leaves predominates in the scene. In such a case, the green color will be discounted too much from the lights reflected from the target objects in the forest if the mere average of the lights from the scene is used for scaling.

Rubin and Richards (1982, 1988) theoretically analyzed natural constraints about the color and luminance contrasts at various types of edges in the natural image. They found regular relationships about these contrasts at the edges where two regions with different surface materials adjoin (1988). In order to estimate the wavelength composition of the illumination, they proposed that instead of randomly sampling the surrounding regions, as Land did, sampling only adjoining pairs of regions where surface materials are different. They also suggested that detection of edges where different surface materials adjoin can be done using an operator with an organization similar to that of the receptive field of the double-opponent simple cells found in area V1 by Michael (Michael, 1978b).

References

Baylor, D. A., Nunn, B. J., & Schnapf, J. L. (1987). Spectral sensitivity of cones of the monkey *Macaca fascicularis. Journal of Physiology, 390*, 145.

Berlin, B. & Kay, P. (1969). *Basic color terms.* Berkeley: University of California Press.

Bornstein, M. H. (1987). Perceptual categories in vision and audition. In S. Harnad (Ed.), *Categorical perception* (pp. 287–300). Cambridge: Cambridge University Press.

Bowmaker, J. K., & Dartnall, H. J. A. (1980). Visual pigments of rods and cones in a human retina. *Journal of Physiology, 298*, 501–511.

Bowmaker, J. K., Dartnall, H. J. A., & Mollon, J. D. (1980). Microspectrophotometric demonstration of four classes of photoreceptor in an old world primate, *Macaca fascicularis. Journal of Physiology, 298*, 131–143.

Boynton, R. M., & Olson, C. X. (1987). Locating basic colors in the OSA space. *Color Research and Application, 12*, 94–105.

Burkhalter, A., & Van Essen, D. C. (1986). Processing of color, form and disparity information in visual areas VP and V2 of ventral extrastriate cortex in the macaque monkey. *Journal of Neuroscience, 6*, 2327–2351.

de Monasterio, F. M., & Schein, S. J. (1982). Spectral bandwidths of color-opponent cells of geniculocortical pathway of macaque monkeys. *Journal of Neurophysiology, 47*, 214–224.

De Valois, R. L. (1973). Central mechanisms of color vision. In R. Jung, (Ed.), *Handbook of sensory physiology* (pp. 119–143). New York: Springer-Verlag.

De Valois, R. L., Morgan, H. C., Polson, M. C., Mead, W. R., & Hull, E. M. (1974). Psychophysical studies of monkey vision. I. Macaque luminosity and color vision tests. *Vision Research, 14*, 53–67.

Dean, P. (1979). Visual cortex ablation and thresholds for successively presented stimuli in rhesus monkeys: II. Hue. *Experimental Brain Research, 35*, 69–83.

Derrington, A. M., Krauskopf, J., & Lennie, P. (1984). Chromatic mechanisms in lateral geniculate nucleus of macaque. *Journal of Physiology, 357,* 241–265.

Desimone, R., Albright, T. D., Gross, C. G., & Bruce, C. (1984). Stimulus-selective properties of inferior temporal neurons in the macaque. *Journal of Neuroscience, 4,* 2051–2062.

Desimone, R., Schein, S. J., Moran, J., & Ungerleider, L. G. (1985). Contour, color and shape analysis beyond the striate cortex. *Vision Research 25,* 441–452.

DeYoe, E. A., & Van Essen, D. C. (1985). Segregation of efferent connections and receptive field properties in visual area V2 of the macaque. *Nature, 317,* 58–61.

Dow, B. M., & Gouras, P. (1973). Color and spatial specificity of single units in rhesus monkey foveal striate cortex. *Journal of Neurophysiology, 36,* 79–100.

Felleman, D. J., & Van Essen, D. C. (1991). Distributed hierarchical processing in the primate cerebral cortex. *Cerebral Cortex, 1,* 1–47.

Ferrera, V. P., Nealy, T. A., & Maunsell, J. H. R. (1992). Mixed parvocellular and magnocellular geniculate signals in visual area V4. *Nature, 358,* 756–758.

Gouras, P. (1974). Opponent-colour cells in different layers of foveal striate cortex. *Journal of Physiology, 238,* 583–602.

Gross, C. G. (1973). Visual functions of inferotemporal cortex. In R. Jung, (Ed.), *Handbook of sensory physiology* (Vol. 7, pp. 451–482). Berlin: Springer.

Gross, C. G., Rocha-Miranda, C. E., & Bender, D. B. (1972). Visual properties of neurons in inferotemporal cortex of the macaque. *Journal of Neurophysiology, 35,* 96–111.

Heywood, C. A., & Cowey, A. (1987). On the role of cortical area V4 in the discrimination of hue and pattern in macaque monkey. *Journal of Neuroscience, 7,* 2601–2617.

Heywood, C. A., Gadotti, A., & Cowey, A. (1992). Cortical area V4 and its role in the perception of color. *Journal of Neuroscience, 12,* 4056–4065.

Heywood, C. A., Shields, C., & Cowey, A. (1988). The involvement of the temporal lobes in colour discrimination. *Experimental Brain Research, 71,* 437–441.

Horn, B. K. P. (1974). Determining lightnesses from an image. *Computer Graphics and Image Processing, 3,* 277–299.

Hubel, D. H., & Wiesel, T. N. (1968). Receptive fields and functional architecture of monkey striate cortex. *Journal of Physiology, 195,* 215–243.

Hurlbert, A. C., & Poggio, T. A. (1988). Synthesizing a color algorithm from examples. *Science, 239,* 482–485.

Judd, D. B. (1960). Appraisal of Land's work on two-primary color projections. *Journal of the Optical Society of America, 50,* 254–268.

Komatsu, H. (in press). Neural coding of color and form in the inferior temporal cortex of the monkey. *Biomedical Research.*

Komatsu, H., & Ideura, Y. (1993). Relationships between color, shape, and pattern selectivities of neurons in the inferior temporal cortex of the monkey. *Journal of Neurophysiology, 70,* 677–694.

Komatsu, H., Ideura, Y., Kaji, S., & Yamane, S. (1992). Color selectivity of neurons in the inferior temporal cortex of the awake macaque monkey. *Journal of Neuroscience, 12,* 408–424.

Krauskopf, J., Williams, D. R., & Heeley, W. (1982). Cardinal directions of color space. *Vision Research, 22,* 1123–1131.

Land, E. H. (1977). The retinex theory of color vision. *Scientific American, 237,* 108–128.

Land, E. H. (1983). Recent advances in retinex theory and some implications for cortical computations: Color vision and the natural image. *Proceedings of the National Academy of Science of the USA, 80,* 5163–5169.

Land, E. H. (1986). An alternative technique for the computation of the designator in the retinex theory of color vision. *Proceedings of the National Academy of Sciences of the USA, 83,* 3078–3080.

Land, E. H., & MaCann, J. J. (1971). Lightness and retinex theory. *Journal of the Optical Society of America, 61,* 1–11.

Lennie, P., & D'Zmura, M. (1988). Mechanisms of color vision. *CRC Critical Reviews in Neurobiology, 3,* 333–399.

Lennie, P., Krauskopf, J., & Sclar, G. (1990). Chromatic mechanisms in striate cortex of macaque. *Journal of Neuroscience, 10,* 649–669.

Livingstone, M. S., & Hubel, D. H. (1982). Thalamic inputs to cytochrome oxidase-rich regions in monkey visual cortex. *Proceedings of the National Academy of Sciences of the USA, 79,* 6098–6101.

Livingstone, M. S., & Hubel, D. H. (1983). Specificity of cortico-cortical connections in monkey visual cortex. *Nature, 304,* 531–534.

Livingstone, M. S., & Hubel, D. H. (1984). Anatomy and physiology of a color system in the primate visual cortex. *Journal of Neuroscience, 4,* 309–356.

Livingstone, M. S., & Hubel, D. H. (1987). Connections between layer 4B of area 17 and the thick cytochrome oxidase stripes of area 18 in the squirrel monkey. *Journal of Neuroscience, 7,* 3371–3377.

Lund, J. S. (1988). Anatomical organization of macaque monkey striate visual cortex. *Annual Review of Neuroscience, 11,* 253–288.

Marks, W. B., Dobelle, W. H., & MacNichol, E. F. (1964). Visual pigments of single primate cones. *Science, 143,* 1181–1183.

Matuzawa, T. (1985). Colour naming and classification in a chimpanzee. *Journal of Human Evolution, 14,* 283–291.

Maunsell, J. H. R., & Newsome, W. T. (1987). Visual processing in monkey extrastriate cortex. *Annual Review of Neuroscience, 10,* 363–401.

Merigan, W. H., & Maunsell, J. H. R. (1993). How parallel are the primate visual pathways? *Annual Review of Neuroscience, 16,* 369–402.

Michael, C. (1978a). Color vision mechanisms in monkey striate cortex: Dual-opponent cells with concentric receptive fields. *Journal of Neurophysiology, 41,* 572–588.

Michael, C. (1978b). Color vision mechanisms in monkey striate cortex: Simple cells with dual opponent-color receptive fields. *Journal of Neurophysiology, 41,* 1233–1249.

Mishkin, M. (1982). A memory system in monkey. *Philosophical Transactions of the Royal Society of London B Biological Science, 298,* 85–95.

Miyashita, Y., & Chang, H. S. (1988). Neuronal correlate of pictorial shortterm memory in the primate temporal cortex. *Nature, 331,* 68–70.

Oyama, T., Furusaka, T., & Kito, T. (1979). Color vision tests of Japanese and rhesus monkeys. In D. M. Taub, & F. A. King (Eds.), *Current perspectives in primate biology* (pp. 253–269). New York: Van Nostrand Reinhold.

Perrett, D. I., Rolls, E. T., & Caan, W. (1982). Visual neurons responsive to faces in the monkey temporal cortex. *Experimental Brain Research, 47,* 329–342.

Poggio, G. F., Baker, F. H., Mansfield, R. J. W., Sillito, A., & Grigg, P. (1975). Spatial and chromatic properties of neurons subserving foveal and parafoveal vision in rhesus monkey. *Brain Research, 100,* 25–59.

Richmond, B. J., Optican, L. M., Podell, M., & Spitzer, H. (1987). Temporal encoding of two-dimensional patterns by single units in primate inferior temporal cortex. I. Response characteristics. *Journal of Neurophysiology, 57,* 132–146.

Rubin, J. M., & Richards, W. A. (1982). Color vision and image intensities: when are changes material? *Biological Cybernetics, 45,* 215–226.

Rubin, J. M., & Richards, W. A. (1988). Color vision: Representing material categories. In W. Richards (Ed.), *Natural computation* (pp. 194–213). Cambridge, MA: MIT Press.

Sandell, J. H., Gross, C. G., & Bornstein, M. H. (1979). Color categories in macaques. *Journal of Comparative Physiology and Psychology, 93,* 626–635.

Sato, T., Kawamura, T., & Iwai, E. (1980). Responsiveness of inferotemporal single units to visual pattern stimuli in monkeys performing discrimination. *Experimental Brain Research, 38,* 313–319.

Schein, S. J., & Desimone, R. (1990). Spectral properties of V4 neurons in the macaque. *Journal of Neuroscience, 10,* 3369–3389.

Schein, S. J., Marrocco, R. T., & de Monasterio, F. M. (1982). Is there a high concentration of color-selective cells in area V4 of monkey visual cortex? *Journal of Neurophysiology, 47,* 193–213.

Schiller, P. H. (1993). The effects of V4 and middle temporal (MT) area lesions on visual performance in the rhesus monkey. *Visual Neuroscience, 10,* 717–746.

Schnapf, J. L., Kraft, T. W., & Baylor, D. A. (1987). Spectral sensitivity of human cone photoreceptor. *Nature, 325,* 439–441.

Schwartz, E. L., Desimone, R., & Albright, T. D. (1983). Shape recognition and inferior temporal neurons. *Proceedings of the National Academy of Sciences of the USA, 80,* 5776–5778.

Shinoda, H., Uchikawa, K., & Ikeda, M. (in press). Categorical color space on CRT in the aperture and the surface color mode. *Color Research Applications.*

Shipp, S., & Zeki, S. (1985). Segregation of pathways leading from area V2 to areas V4 and V5 of macaque monkey visual cortex. *Nature, 315,* 322–325.

Shipp, S., & Zeki, S. M. (1989). The organisation of connections between areas V5 and V1: Macaque monkey visual cortex *European Journal of Neuroscience, 1,* 309–332.

Tanaka, K., Saito, H., Fukada, Y., & Moriya, M. (1991). Coding visual images of objects in the inferotemporal cortex of the macaque monkey. *Journal of Neurophysiology, 66,* 170–189.

Thorell, L. G., De Valois, R. L., & Albrecht, D. G. (1984). Spatial mapping of monkey V1 cells with pure color and luminance stimuli. *Vision Research, 24,* 751–769.

Tootell, R. B. H., Silverman, M. S., De Valois, R. L., & Jacobs, G. H. (1983). Functional organization of the second cortical visual area in primates. *Science, 220,* 737–739.

Tootell, R. B. H., Silverman, M. S., Hamilton, S. L., De Valois, R. L., & Switkes, E. (1988). Functional anatomy of macaque striate cortex III: Color. *Journal of Neuroscience, 8,* 1569–1593.

Ts'o, D. Y., & Gilbert, C. D. (1988). The organization of chromatic and spatial interactions in the primate striate cortex. *Journal of Neuroscience, 8,* 1712–1727.

Ts'o, D. Y., Gilbert, C. D., & Wiesel, T. N. (1990). Functional architecture of color and disparity in visual area 2 of macaque monkey. *Society for Neuroscience Abstracts, 16,* 203.

Uchikawa, K., & Boynton, R. M. (1987). Categorical color perception of Japanese observers: Comparison with that of Americans. *Vision Research, 27,* 1825–1833.

Uchikawa, K., Kuriki, I., & Shinoda, H. (1993). Categorical color-name regions of a color space in aperture and surface color modes. *Journal of the Illuminating Engineering Institute of Japan, 77,* 346–354.

Ungerleider, L. G., & Mishkin, M. (1982). Two cortical systems. In D. J. Ingle, M. A. Goodale, & R. J. W. Mansfield (Eds.), *Analysis of visual behavior* (pp. 549–580). Cambridge, MA: MIT Press.

Valeton, J. M., & van Norren, D. (1983). Light adaptation of primate cones: An analysis based on extracellular data. *Vision Research, 23,* 1539–1547.

Van Essen, D. C. (1985). Functional organization of primate visual cortex. In E. G. Jones, & A. Peters (Eds.), *Cerebral cortex* (Vol. 3, pp. 259–329). New York: Plenum.

Van Essen, D. C., Felleman, D. J., DeYoe, E. A., Olavarria, J., & Knierim, J. (1990). Modular and hierarchical organization of extrastriate visual cortex in the macaque monkey. *Cold Spring Harbor Symposia on Quantitative Biology, 55,* 679–696.

Vautin, R. G., & Dow, B. M. (1985). Color cell groups in foveal striate cortex of the behaving macaque. *Journal of Neurophysiology, 54,* 273–292.

von Bonin, G., & Bailey, Y. (1947). *The neocortex of Macaca mulatta.* Urbana: University of Illinois Press.

Walsh, V., Carden, D., Butler, S. R., & Kulikowski, J. J. (1993). The effects of lesions of area V4 on the visual abilities of macaques: Hue discrimination and colour constancy. *Behavior and Brain Research, 53,* 51–62.

Walsh, V., Kulikowski, J. J., Butler, S. R., & Carden, D. (1992). The effects of lesions of area V4 on the visual abilities of macaques: Colour categorization. *Behavior and Brain Research 52*, 81–89.

Webster, M. A. & Mollon, J. D. (1991). Changes in colour appearance following post-receptoral adaptation. *Nature, 349*, 235–238.

Wild, H. M., Butler, S. R., Carden, D., & Kulikowski, J. J. (1985). Primate cortical area V4 important for colour constancy but not wavelength discrimination. *Nature, 313*, 133–135.

Yamane, S., Kaji, S., & Kawano, K. (1988). What visual features activate face neurons in the inferotemporal cortex of the monkey? *Experimental Brain Research, 73*, 209–214.

Yoshioka, T. (1989). Color and luminance organization in visual cortical areas V1, V2 and V4 of the macaque monkey. *Experimental Brain Research*.

Yoshioka, T., Dow, B. M., & Vautin, R. G. (1988). Close correlation of color, orientation and luminance processing in V1, V2, and V4 of the behaving macaque monkey. *Society for Neuroscience Abstracts, 14*, 457.

Zeki, S. M. (1973), Colour coding in rhesus monkey prestriate cortex. *Brain Research, 53*, 422–427.

Zeki, S. M. (1977). Colour coding in the superior temporal sulcus of rhesus monkey visual cortex. *Proceedings of the Royal Society of London B, 197*, 195–223.

Zeki, S. M. (1980). The representation of colours in the cerebral cortex. *Nature, 284*, 412–418.

Zeki, S. M. (1983a). Colour coding in the cerebral cortex: The reaction of cells in monkey visual cortex to wavelengths and colours. *Neuroscience, 9*, 741–765.

Zeki, S. M. (1983b). Colour coding in the cerebral cortex: The responses of wavelength-selective and colour-coded cells in monkey visual cortex to changes in wavelength composition. *Neuroscience, 9*, 767–781.

Zeki, S. M., & Shipp, S. (1988). The functional logic of cortical connections. *Nature, 335*, 311–317.

14   Size and speed constancy

Suzanne P. McKee and Harvey S. Smallman

In his 1963 *Nature* paper, Richard Gregory defined size constancy as "the tendency for objects to appear much the same size over a wide range of distances in spite of the changes of the retinal images associated with distance of the object." As this definition makes clear, size constancy is about the appearance of objects, about what things look like. Strictly speaking, size constancy denotes only that the apparent size of an object is nearly invariant with changes in distance, not that the observer perceives the true physical size of an object. This invariance implies, however, that some process corrects the angle subtended on the retina by some measure of relative distance, and thus that observers have good information about the *relative* physical size of the objects surrounding them. If the body is used to provide a "metric" for both size and distance, such as a hand viewed at arm's length, then, in principle, true physical size could be estimated with some degree of accuracy (Morgan, 1989). In this chapter, we will examine how well observers estimate objective size.[1] Because speed constancy is often treated as an extension of size constancy, we will also look at the human ability to estimate objective speed.

Size constancy

Stripped of phenomenology, size constancy seems to be a fairly simple problem in visual processing. The human visual system measures the angle subtended by an object on the retina, estimates the object's relative distance, and scales the measured retinal subtense by the estimated distance to obtain an estimate of objective size (Andrews, 1964; Boring, 1946; Epstein, 1973). In a computational context that stresses measurement and scaling, the argument between the Structuralist and Gestalt schools becomes a question of information access. Does the observer have direct access to information about retinal subtense, as the Structuralists might claim (left side of Figure 14.1)? Or is the information about

This chapter was supported by AFOSR Grant F49620-95-1-0265, NEI Grant RO1-EY06644, and NEI Core Grant EY06883. The views and conclusions contained herein are those of the authors and should not be interpreted as necessarily representing the official policies or endorsements, either expressed or implied, of the Air Force Office of Scientific Research, the National Eye Institute, or the U.S. government.

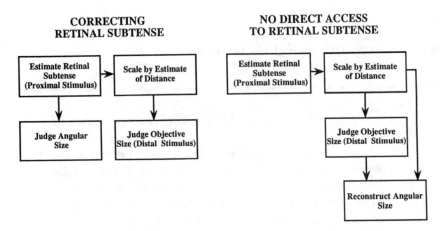

Figure 14.1. Flow charts showing two different conceptual frameworks for size constancy.

retinal subtense lost in the scaling process, so that the observer must compensate for constancy scaling in order to estimate angular size indirectly, as the Gestaltists would claim (right side of Figure 14.1)?

Although the flow charts convert a philosophical controversy into an explicit computational formulation, the representation of size processing in these diagrams is simplistic. For one thing, it is unlikely that normal observers have direct access to information about *retinal* subtense per se. Obviously, all human judgments involve cortical processing, but some types of processing can alter the retinal geometry, converting it into a form that is no longer isomorphic with the angles subtended on the retinae. An example of this type of conversion is the lateral separation between two features at different viewing distances, for example, telephone poles at different distances from the head. The apparent separation between them does not correspond to the lateral separation on either of the two retinae because the visual direction of the feature lying off the fixation plane is roughly halfway between the disparate locations on the two retinae. Does this fact about binocular processing imply that the Gestalt sequence shown on the right of Figure 14.1 is correct? Not necessarily. Angular information is exceptionally useful, so it is difficult to believe that all information about angular subtense is lost or discarded in the processing of size and is recalculated only in response to the artificial demands of a psychophysical experiment. For example, a systematic change in the angles subtended by the elements of a regular pattern (*texture gradient*) is interpreted as a change in relative depth, indicating that angular measurements are accessible at cortical levels responsible for the processing of depth and shape. Moreover, we are certainly aware of these texture gradients, despite perceptual evidence that the receding pattern is composed of elements of the same size. Is this angular information known directly (left side of Figure 14.1) or indirectly (right side of Figure 14.1)? How can we tell?

The most serious problem with the sequences shown in Figure 14.1 is that no experimental test would decide between them. Both sequences could produce veridical estimates of objective and angular size, provided that the initial estimates of retinal subtense and distance to the object were correct and the observer interpreted the experimental instructions appropriately. It might seem that the indirect estimate of angular size (Figure 14.1, right) would be less exact than the direct estimate (Figure 14.1, left) because it involves additional operations, but that is true only if the additional operations introduce additional uncertainty or noise into the judgment. What is missing from the sequences in Figure 14.1 are the pervasive sources of biological noise that limit all human judgments. Even the most attentive observer will make mistakes in judging objective size because of noise in the sensory processes that encode the relevant dimensions. These errors in discriminating between stimuli, or in matching one stimulus to another, provide clues about the coding sequence that underlies human size judgments. Rather than concentrating on what is perceived, we examine how well human observers can judge objective size, no matter what their percepts are. What kinds of errors do they make in judging either angular or objective size? We use the results from numerous perceptual and psychophysical studies to construct a better diagram of how the human brain processes both angular and objective size.

Accuracy and precision

Although the terms *accuracy* and *precision* are often used interchangeably, they refer to different types of measurement errors (Bevington, 1969). Accuracy indicates how close a given measurement comes to the true value, whereas precision shows the reliability (or variance) of the measurement. These two indices of error are independent. Random noise affects the precision of human judgments but not their accuracy. A measurement can be accurate but very imprecise, as when the mean of a set of judgments equals the true value but has a large standard error. A measurement can also be precisely wrong (inaccurate), as in the case of a systematic bias with a small standard error.

Accuracy and precision are easily distinguished in psychophysical studies. For example, in size discrimination experiments, observers are asked to judge whether the test stimulus is larger or smaller than the standard. The percentage of trials on which the test is judged larger is plotted as a function of its physical size, and the resulting psychometric function can be fitted with a cumulative normal curve. The cumulative normal curve has two independent parameters: the mean, which defines the location of the curve along the stimulus axis, and the standard deviation, which defines the steepness of the curve. The mean of the fitted function corresponds to the *point of subjective equality (PSE)*, which refers to the value of the test stimulus that the observer sees as equal to the standard. The slope of the function determines the precision of the increment threshold; one common definition of threshold is the incremental change in the stimulus that produces one standard deviation change in response ($d' = 1.0$). The most useful estimate of precision is the dimensionless Weber fraction (threshold/mean) because it allows comparison of the biological errors associated with different dimensions, such as size errors with disparity errors.

For the most part, studies of constancy have focused only on accuracy – on how well observers reproduce (*match*) the objective size of the test object. Usually, judgments from all observers are lumped together to estimate a common mean and a standard deviation. This approach necessarily confounds the diversity of the sample with the variability of individual performance. For example, observers tend to overestimate an object's size with increasing distance, a phenomenon known as *overconstancy* (Carlson, 1960; Gilinsky, 1955; Sedgwick, 1986). However, the standard deviation of the pooled judgments from many observers often overlaps the correct physical size of the test object. Does this result mean that all observers see the test object as larger than its true size, but that there is considerable variability in their judgments? Or does it mean that some observers consistently see the test object as larger, whereas a smaller number consistently encode the correct size of the test object? Ideally, constancy studies should examine human diversity (many observers), as well as assess individual precision (repeated measurements on the same observer).

Few studies have made direct measurements of the Weber fractions for objective size, but precision can be estimated indirectly by dividing the average error or standard deviation of an individual's judgments by his or her mean. The flow charts in Figure 14.1 suggest that there are at least two sources of potential noise in any objective size calculation: (1) the noise in the estimate of the angle subtended on the retina and (2) the noise in the estimate of the object's distance. The noise in angular subtense is best inferred from the increment threshold for lateral separation between targets presented in the fixation plane, where there is no uncertainty about distance. In this type of measurement, the observer judges whether the distance separating a pair of lines or points is greater or smaller than the standard separation – a simple size judgment for targets presented at a fixed viewing distance. The Weber fraction for lateral separation is 2–4% (Burbeck, 1987a; Klein & Levi, 1987; McKee, Welch, Taylor, & Bowne, 1990). Therefore, we might expect the Weber fraction for objective size judgments, involving comparisons at different distances, to be greater than 2–4% because of additional noise from the distance estimates. That is true only if the noise in the distance estimates is comparable to or larger than the noise in the estimates of retinal subtense. As we describe next, distance estimates are quite imprecise.

Estimating distance

Every introductory psychology book lists a large number of cues to distance. These include binocular parallax, accommodation, motion parallax, interposition (occlusion), familiar size cues, aerial and linear perspective, and texture gradients.[2] We will not attempt to describe in detail how each is used to estimate depth or how they are used in combination (see Chapter 15, this volume; see also Landy, Maloney, Johnston, & Young, 1995; Yuille & Bülthoff, 1993). Instead, we are concerned with the range, accuracy, and precision of each cue because these limitations affect size constancy. Certainly, not all cues are equally useful in estimating distance. Interposition specifies only which object is in front of the other, not the distances separating them. Familiar size relies on exact knowledge of the dimensions of a recognized object to provide a distance scale. Accommodation works only at short distances because it is driven by the defocus produced by objects lying outside the focal plane. Human sensitivity for defocus is roughly 0.2–0.4 diopter under optimum conditions (Campbell, 1957; Legge, Mullen, Woo, & Campbell, 1987), so accommodative information about distance is constrained to 2 m or less.[3]

Binocular parallax,[4] sometimes called *convergence angle*, is potentially the most powerful cue to object distance. Information about binocular parallax can be obtained either indirectly, from the neural signal transmitted to the convergence system to minimize disparity, or directly from the sensed position of the eyes. Foley (1980) estimated the precision of parallax judgments as about 5 arcmin at 4 m, or roughly 10% of the parallax angle. At larger distances, 5 arcmin of disparity translates into a very large uncertainty about linear distance, so binocular parallax is not very useful at distances much beyond 8 m. Distance information derived from binocular parallax is known to be *inaccurate*. When based on parallax alone, the perceived distance of a near object exceeds its physical distance, whereas the distance of a far object is seen as less than its physical distance (Foley, 1980).

Relative disparity, that is, the difference in the disparity of two features, can be used to judge the distance separating objects. However, the interpretation of a given disparity difference depends on the estimated viewing distance; 10 min of disparity at a viewing distance of 1 m corresponds to a much smaller objective distance than 10 min of disparity at a viewing distance of 5 m. Inaccuracies in estimating distance from binocular parallax will therefore affect the accuracy of relative disparity judgments as well (Foley, 1980; Norman, Todd, Perotti, & Tittle, 1996; chapter 15, this volume). As one example, Johnston (1991) reported that a three-dimensional shape defined only by disparity appeared thicker or thinner (its dimension along the *z*-axis) at different viewing distances. Relative disparity judgments, even those made at a fixed viewing distance, are also not very *precise*. Under the best circumstances, the Weber fraction for relative disparity is 5–6%, and it is often found to be much higher (McKee, Levi, & Bowne, 1990; Norman et al., 1996).

When the head translates, objects at different distances move at different speeds on the retina – motion parallax. If the motion is self-generated, so that the observer has some way of calibrating relative speed, motion parallax can be a robust cue to distance. Available evidence indicates that, by itself, motion parallax produces fairly accurate estimates of relative distance (Huber & Davies, 1995; Landy et al., 1995; Rogers & Collett, 1989; Rogers & Graham, 1979). The precision of distance information derived from motion parallax depends on speed discrimination. The Weber fraction for moderately fast angular speeds (>3 deg/sec) is 5–8%. Because normal head movements are not very fast, distant objects may move at speeds considerably slower than 3 deg/sec where the Weber fraction for speeds is much higher, meaning that estimates of distance based on motion parallax would be less precise.

The texture elements that define a surface gradually decrease in angular subtense with increasing distance. As noted earlier, this texture gradient can be used to judge relative distance. Linear perspective depends on a similar decrease in the angle between straight contours extending toward the horizon. Given a scaling factor that specifies the distance associated with a particular angular subtense, the observer could, in principle, judge the physical distance to any object sitting on a flat, regularly textured surface. Unfortunately, changes in angular subtense produced by surface tilt or by large-scale physical irregularities, such as a change from pebbles to boulders, are necessarily confounded with the angular changes produced by distance. These confounds, as well as the possible inaccuracy of the scaling factor, compromise the accuracy of texture cues to distance in natural environments. Texture and perspective cues do, however, supply the most precise information about distance because they are based on the same precise information used for angular judgments of lateral separation. As noted earlier, the precision of angular judgments is roughly 2–4%.

In reduced viewing conditions, inaccuracies in estimating distance should necessarily lead to systematic biases in size constancy. Such biases may be less likely in natural environments where distance information from one source could be used to correct distance information from another source (Landy et al., 1995). Improving the precision of distance estimates is more problematic because there is no way to reduce the inherent noise associated with these estimates. In circumstances where many cues to depth are available (short distances and natural surroundings), probability summation among independent estimates of distance could improve precision. However, experimental measurements show that depth judgments in multi-cue conditions are not generally more precise than single-cue depth judgments (Norman et al., 1996).

If we assume that the estimate of the angular subtense (the proximal stimulus) and the distance estimate are independent, we can use a simple propagation of error approach[5] to predict the precision of size constancy. For example, the predicted precision of size constancy is about 5.4% based on the most precise Weber fractions for angular subtense (2%) and motion parallax (5%). Using Foley's estimate of the precision of binocular parallax (10%) produces a corresponding increase in the predicted threshold to slightly over 10%. On the other hand, if the observer can utilize texture information to estimate distance (2%), size constancy could achieve a precision of less than 3%. The precision of size constancy judgments can thus reveal much about how distance information is integrated into the size estimate.

The accuracy and precision of objective size judgments

The first experimental measurements of size constancy were made in the late nineteenth century by Martius in Wundt's laboratory (Boring, 1942). Martius reported perfect size constancy, but subsequent measurements by Thouless (1931) indicated that perceived size was a compromise between angular subtense and physical size. In an excellent and often cited study, Holway and Boring (1941) examined how various sources of depth information influenced perceived size. Five observers made repeated matches of a circular test target presented at distances ranging from 10 to 120 ft. The test, actually a circular patch of light projected on a screen, subtended 1 degree at all viewing distances. The observer sat at the intersection of two dimly lit corridors and adjusted the comparison target, 10 ft away in one corridor, until it matched the test target in the other corridor (graduate students take note: all measurements were made after midnight!). Available depth information was successively reduced from a ''full-cue'' binocular condition to a condition that employed monocular viewing, then monocular viewing through an artificial pupil, and finally monocular viewing, an artificial pupil, and a long reduction tunnel made of heavy black cloth. The use of an artificial pupil (1.8 mm) to reduce distance cues is rather curious because, although it would minimize accommodation cues, accommodation would not be much use for the large distances employed in this study. More likely, the artificial pupil made it difficult for the observers to estimate relative size and texture cues in the low illumination, the cues that the reduction tunnel was expected to eliminate.

As Figure 14.2 shows, size constancy was accurate when adequate information about depth was available. Predictably at these large viewing distances, binocular parallax did not confer any benefit over good monocular depth information. In fact, when the test target was viewed binocularly, its objective size was slightly overestimated, although this pattern was not universal (note the differences between the observers in the small graphs at the bottom of Figure 14.2). Some observers, relying on binocular parallax at only the short distances

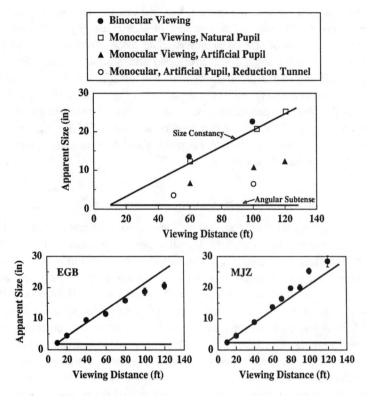

Figure 14.2. Results from the classic size constancy study by Holway and Boring (1941). Observers matched the size of a comparison disc viewed at a fixed distance to the objective size of a test disc viewed at various distances. The upper graph shows pooled results for the various experimental conditions listed in the top box. The lower graphs show individual results from two observers in the binocular condition.

where it is useful, may have underestimated the 10-ft distance to the comparison target and so systematically increased the size of their matches. Contrary to the expectations of the experimenters, observers never adjusted the comparison target to match the angular subtense of the test target, even in the most reduced condition. Fragmentary information about linear perspective and texture from the dimly illuminated reduction tunnel was sufficient to promote some tendency toward constancy. Subsequent studies managed to eliminate the residual light reflected from the surroundings and obtained perfect angular matches (Lichten & Lurie, 1950; Over, 1960).

Judgments of objective size at great distances are surprisingly accurate. Gibson (1950) asked observers to choose which of a set of nearby wooden posts matched a similar barely visible post located more than 2,000 ft away. The judgments were made in a barren open field and, at 2,000 ft, the test post

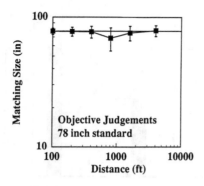

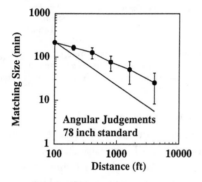

Figure 14.3. Results from the Gilinsky (1955) study showing observers' ability to match either the objective size of a test target (upper graph) or the angular subtense of a test object, depending on instructions from the experimenter. Data pooled from all observers.

subtended only about 8 arc minutes. Despite the difficulty of the judgment, observers chose the correct post. Gilinsky (1955) extended the range to an even greater distance (4,000 ft) and again found remarkable accuracy. In addition, Gilinsky asked her observers to match the angles subtended by the distant test objects; these matches were much less accurate than the objective matches (see Figure 14.3). Generally, her observers overestimated angular subtense, a result confirmed in a later study by Leibowitz and Harvey (1967).

The constancy judgments in the Holway–Boring study were also quite *precise*. In Figure 14.4, we have plotted "pseudo-Weber" fractions (mean variation/mean) for the two observers who participated in all experimental conditions. These values are averaged over all test distances; individual fractions for particular distances were even better. In fact, the best pseudo-Weber fractions for size constancy were about 2%, equal to the best Weber fractions for lateral separation measured in a single plane. In a later study, Burbeck (1987b) confirmed this Holway–Boring result. Using a standard increment threshold para-

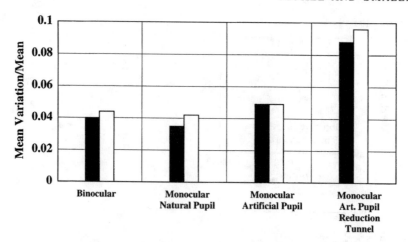

Figure 14.4. Precision measures for size constancy derived from data presented in Holway and Boring (1941). Mean variation is divided by the mean stimulus value for the
two observers (represented by black and white bars) who participated in all conditions.

digm and the contemporary stimulus of choice, a sinusoidal grating, Burbeck
measured spatial frequency discrimination for gratings presented at the same
distance on two adjacent cathode ray tube (CRT) screens. The spatial frequency
in cycles per degree of the gratings differed only by a small amount – the tested
increment. Guided by feedback, Burbeck's observers judged which grating had
the higher spatial frequency. She then moved one of the screens to twice the
distance of the other and repeated the threshold measurements. Although the
basic spatial frequency of the gratings in angular units (cycles/degree) now differed by a factor of 2, the thresholds were nearly identical to those measured
when the screens were at the same distance. In short, the Weber fraction for
objective spatial frequency (cycles/cm) was about 3%, comparable to the best
judgments of lateral separation made in the fixation plane.

Burbeck also asked her observers to judge small differences in the angular
spatial frequency (cyc/deg) of the targets presented at two different distances.
Initially, observers found the angular judgments almost impossible, but with
feedback and considerable practice, they were able to perform with a precision
about equal to that of their objective judgments. Burbeck argued that the angular
frequency was indirectly estimated from objective frequency information. She
concluded that observers have no direct access to spatial frequency, or to any
other kind of spatial information, expressed in angular units. This provocative
conclusion is consistent with the Gilinsky results shown in Figure 14.3, but
it is difficult to reconcile with the imprecision of distance judgments. If the
observer has access only to size information that is automatically scaled for
viewing distance, why are size judgments so precise when distance judg-

Size Constancy from Relative Size

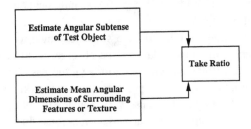

Figure 14.5. Flow chart showing the operations used to estimate objective size from angular relationships.

ments are so much noisier? A texture cue might account for the precision of Burbeck's results. Do her results imply that all size information is automatically scaled by depth calculated from texture gradients? Even if the texture-gradient cue to depth accounts for the precision of size constancy, it is unlikely that texture gradients can provide depth information of sufficient *accuracy* to explain the accuracy of size constancy at great distances, for example, the Gilinsky results.

The accuracy and precision of size constancy judgments force a different conclusion. In natural circumstances, observers do not use depth estimates to calculate objective size. Instead, they rely on the relational determination of size, a cue that can supply accurate, precise information about relative size without requiring an independent estimate of distance (Gibson, 1950; Hochberg, 1972; Rock, 1977; Rock & Ebenholtz, 1959; Sedgwick, 1986).

Relative size

The mean angular dimensions of our surroundings decrease with increasing distance, so the ratio of the angle subtended by an object to the mean of the angles subtended by its surroundings is fairly invariant with viewing distance. The observer can equate the objective size of two objects, as required in size constancy experiments, by simply equating the ratio of the test and comparison objects to their respective surroundings (Figure 14.5). When the surroundings contain a regularly textured surface, such as a floor covered with tiles, the texture supplies a local metric that is automatically scaled with distance; the dimension of an object sitting on the textured surface can be measured in the number of contiguous texture elements and thus equated to other objects at other positions on the surface (Gibson, 1950; Nakayama, 1994). Note that, in this case, texture is *not* being used to estimate distance; instead, it is serving as a local ruler for size estimates.

Relational effects have a measurable influence on size judgments, even with binocular viewing at small distances. Rock and Ebenholtz (1959) asked observers to match the length of a line surrounded by a small rectangle to a similar line surrounded by a rectangle three times larger. The observer had to turn 180 degrees to view each of the rectangular configurations in succession; the two configurations were self-luminous and were presented in total darkness at the same fixed distance of 5 ft. Although a few observers matched the physical size of the lines, about half of the group made near-perfect relational matches, that is, the line in the smaller rectangle was shortened so that it was proportionally the same length as the line in the larger rectangle. Is this result due to individual differences in the interpretation of the experimental instructions? Maybe. When Wenderoth (1976) replicated the Rock–Ebenholtz study with instructions that stressed a match based on physical equality, none of the observers made perfect relational matches. Nevertheless, despite instructions to the contrary, Wenderoth's observers still reported that the lines were equal when the line in the smaller rectangle was, on average, 15% shorter than a true physical match. In both studies, observers recognized that the two configurations were at the same distance, but their size judgments were influenced by relational effects nonetheless.

The effect found in Wenderoth's study is about the same magnitude as the size misjudgments found in many geometric illusions. For example, in the Ponzo illusion (Figure 14.6A), the upper line looks longer than the lower line, although the two lines are actually the same physical length. Gillam (1973) found that observers equated the two line lengths in the Ponzo illusion when the physical length of the lower line was about 14% more than that of the upper line, a value very close to Wenderoth's result. Gregory (1963, 1973) argued that geometric illusions of this type are examples of inappropriate constancy scaling. Although observers know that the two short horizontal lines are on a frontoparallel surface at the same distance, the linear perspective cues associated with the two converging lines trigger an automatic rescaling of size.

Humphrey and Morgan (1965) challenged Gregory's idea by inventing a clever variant of the Ponzo illusion in which the horizontal lines were simply rotated 90 degrees (Figure 14.6B). The two vertical lines now appeared to be the same length, despite the presence of the perspective cues. If the observer had calculated depth from the perspective cues and then rescaled all other features, the vertical lines should have been affected in the same way as the horizontal lines. However, as noted earlier, relational size effects do not require the observer to estimate or calculate depth. Instead, the effects depend only on the ratio of local angular measurements – in this case, the ratio of the horizontal line length to the local separation between the converging lines. As Gillam

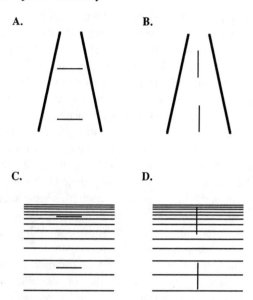

Figure 14.6. (A) The Ponzo illusion; horizontal bars are the same length. (B) Humphrey –Morgan variant, with vertical bars of the same length that appear the same length. (C,D) Illustrations based on Gillam (1973) showing that foreshortening affects the apparent length of vertical bars (D) but not of horizontal bars.

(1973) has reasoned, in perspective processing the lateral distances between the converging lines represent equal horizontal distances, so in the Ponzo illusion only the size of horizontal dimensions should be affected. On the other hand, as Gillam has also shown, texture foreshortening of the type shown in the lower half of Figure 14.6 differentially affects vertical dimensions because the observer interprets the spaces between each pair of long horizontal lines as representing an equal vertical distance. In this case, the illusion works for the orthogonal direction; the upper *vertical* line appears longer than the lower *vertical* line, although once again, the vertical lines are of equivalent physical length. When the lines are rotated 90 degrees, the illusion disappears (compare Figures 14.6C and 14.6D).

Geometric illusions may be based on processes that are unrelated to size constancy. Still, several observations make Gregory's hypothesis at least plausible. First, if an elaborate pictorial representation of depth is added around the converging lines in the Ponzo illusion, the perceived illusion is even greater (Coren & Girgus, 1978; Sedgwick & Nicholls, 1993). Second, the accuracy and precision of size constancy at long distances are most easily explained by assuming that the observer uses relational cues, and because this relational process is largely automatic, it could be misapplied. Finally, Gillam (1973) noted that foreshortening has a different dependence on distance than does linear perspective. She found that the magnitude of the illusion in the foreshortening configuration (Figure 14.6D) was correspondingly smaller than that found in the perspective configuration (Figure 14.6C), as predicted from the differential effects of these two pictorial cues. Gillam's results suggest that visual processing of relative size is remarkably subtle and is tightly bound to an implicit understanding of how texture and perspective change with distance. So, although relational effects do not depend on a distance calculation, their power in affecting perceived size probably derives from their association with distance.

The precision of size constancy in the Burbeck (1987b) study (Weber fractions of 2–4%) suggests that her observers were basing their judgments on the relative size cue – the relative width of the grating bars to the angle subtended by the monitor screen – a cue that was not available for the angular judgments in her study. Still, this conclusion raises a puzzling question: Why were her observers able to use angular relationships, that is, the angular ratio of bars to screen, to judge objective size, but found it difficult to compare the angular spatial frequency of the sinusoid on one screen to that on the other screen? Presumably, the relational effects must interfere with direct encoding of angular subtense (as in the Ponzo illusion), with the result that judgments of angular subtense in natural contexts are often inaccurate. This interference is not inescapable because, with feedback, observers can learn to make precise judgments of angular size despite their percepts.

Does the observer rely exclusively on relational size information when judging the objective size of visual features? Obviously not. By itself, relative size produces only small changes in perceived size. Consistency with other depth information is required to generate true size constancy, that is, the percept that two identical objects at different distances are the same size. Consider the Ponzo illusion once again. The horizontal lines in Figure 14.7A do not appear equally long, but neither do the lines in Figure 14.7B, which are matched in terms of relative size (same proportion of the lateral separation between the tilted lines). In this situation, where all the other depth information asserts that the pictured lines are on a frontoparallel surface, the relational effects are minimal. In Figure 14.7C, the lower line has been increased in length by only 15% and now looks about equal to the upper line. Even if the converging lines in Figure 14.7B were the baseboards of a real hallway, and the horizontal lines were identical decorative markings on widely separated floor tiles, they might not *appear* exactly identical. Still, the depth information would likely induce a percept of near equality. If an observer were asked to draw a matching line, equal to one down the hall, the relational information supplied by the converging diagonals would improve both the accuracy and the precision of the match. You can check your own ability to judge relative size. Is the lower line of Figure 14.7D the same

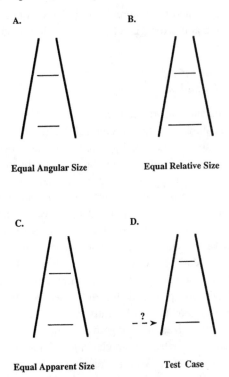

A. Equal Angular Size

B. Equal Relative Size

C. Equal Apparent Size

D. Test Case

Figure 14.7. (A) Ponzo illusion with bars of the same angular subtense. (B) Horizontal bars are of the same proportional length in relation to the lateral separation between tilted lines, yet they do not appear equally long. (C) The lower horizontal bar is 15% longer than the upper bar and now appears to be the same length. (D) Do the horizontal bars have the same proportional length (as in B)?

relative length as the upper line? If not, is it too large or too small? Try drawing a line in the correct relationship if you think the lower line is in error.[6] Now judge the relative depth of these two horizontal lines using the information from the linear perspective cues. You will probably find that the depth judgment is more difficult than the relative size judgment. Using texture gradients to judge relative distance, that is, whether one object is three times as far away as another, is undoubtedly more difficult than judging the equivalence of local ratios for each object. Therefore, size constancy can be extremely precise under circumstances where the depth information is too noisy or inaccurate to supply a scaling factor of the requisite precision. Two predictions follow from this argument. First, an observer's depth and size estimates will not always be strongly correlated – a result often observed in studies of size constancy (see chapter 18, this volume; Epstein, Park, & Casey, 1961; Sedgwick, 1986). Second, if the texture

or frame surrounding the test object and the comparison object are quite different, observers should make systematic errors, an effect evident in the study by
Norman et al. (1995).

Size constancy from distance information

In natural full-cue conditions, distance information appears to play a "supporting role" in size constancy. Size judgments are based on the ratio of the angles
subtended by objects with respect to their surroundings, and distance information
supplies a kind of consistency check. However, in the absence of adequate
relational information, distance cues are sufficient to promote size constancy.

Almost any isolated cue to distance is somewhat effective in laboratory settings. When accommodation and convergence supplied the only depth information, Harvey and Leibowitz (1967) found that observers were moderately
accurate in matching the objective size of rods viewed at a distance of less than
1 m. Hell (1978) found that monocularly viewed rods, presented with their ends
obscured in an otherwise empty visual field at different distances, were matched
on the basis of their angular subtense, provided that the observer's head was
stationary. However, when the head was moved laterally, the matches fell halfway between angular and objective sizes, showing that motion parallax can
produce some degree of size constancy. Binocular viewing is unnecessary for
constancy in natural settings, but relative disparity alone can produce fairly
accurate and precise estimates of objective size, provided that the viewing distance is fixed (McKee & Welch, 1992).

Other minor cues can also influence size constancy. For example, Gregory,
Wallace, and Campbell (1959) showed that knowledge of our own movements
affects perceived size. The apparent size of an afterimage is usually determined
by its angular subtense relative to the apparent distance of the surface on which
it is "projected." When projected on a nearby surface, it appears much smaller
than when projected on a more distant one, despite its fixed angular subtense.
This effect is known as *Emmert's law* (Gregory, 1987). Gregory et al. (1959)
noticed that afterimages viewed in total darkness appeared to change size when
the head was moved forward and back. Thus, information about changes in
distance associated with voluntary movements can be used to scale size, at least
when no other information about distance or relative size is available. Knowledge about the size of a familiar object affects judgments when the object is
viewed monocularly in total darkness. For example, enlarged versions of common coins are underestimated in these circumstances (Epstein, 1967).

We argued earlier that relational effects interfered with the accuracy and
precision of angular size judgments. What happens to angular judgments in the
absence of any information about relative size? In their study of size constancy
based on disparity alone, McKee and Welch (1992) compared objective and

angular size thresholds. Observers were asked to discriminate small changes in the vertical distance separating a pair of horizontal lines. From trial to trial, the target was presented at random at one of nine disparities spanning a range of ± 40 arcmin centered on the fixation plane. The lines were actually displayed at a fixed distance in a stereoscope, but the changes in disparity created compelling changes in apparent depth. For the objective size judgments, the vertical separation between the lines in angular units was scaled, based on calculations from relative disparity, as though the physical distance to the target were really changing. Guided by error feedback, observers were required to judge the vertical separation in physical units (height in centimeters). For the angular judgments, the mean angular subtense was fixed with changes in disparity, and observers used feedback to judge incremental changes in the angle separating the lines. As shown in Figure 14.8, angular thresholds were somewhat better than objective thresholds, although this difference was not significant at large separations. This result argues that angular size is *not* calculated indirectly from objective size.

Discrimination thresholds for targets presented only in the fixation plane (zero disparity) were also included in this study. These fixation plane thresholds were consistently better than the angular thresholds, providing additional evidence that observers do not have access to the "angle on the retina," or else the angular and fixation plane thresholds would be identical. Individuals with normal stereopsis only have a representation of size or location that is mediated by their binocular system – by the fusion of the signals from both eyes' retinae. The data in Figure 14.8 were obtained for a duration too brief to permit a change in convergence (150 msec). Therefore, separation judgments for targets presented off the fixation plane were mediated by disparity mechanisms responsive to nonzero disparities. These mechanisms are less sensitive to size than mechanisms that respond only to targets in the fixation plane, accounting for part of the loss in the precision of the angular judgments. However, even when the targets were presented for a longer duration (1500 msec) and observers were encouraged to converge to the targets presented at different depths, angular size thresholds remained slightly higher than thresholds for targets presented only in a single plane. McKee and Welch speculated that interference from size constancy scaling might have produced the small decrement in performance.

The surprising result is that the objective size thresholds were so precise (~6.5%). Disparity increment thresholds are known to be 10% or greater for durations as short as 150 msec (McKee, Levi, & Bowne, 1990). Thus, if objective size were calculated by combining the disparity estimate with the angular size estimate, the thresholds should be much higher. The explanation may be that the observers were not making an exact estimate of disparity. Instead, they could have used the widely separated depth planes as a code to rescale the angular estimate; for example, the second plane from the front requires the

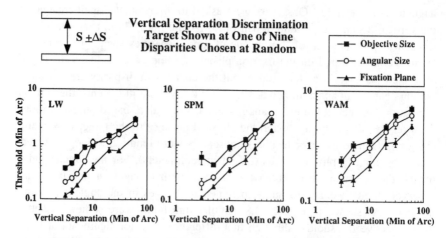

Figure 14.8. Data from McKee and Welch (1992). Increment thresholds for judging vertical separation between lines diagrammed at the top of figure for three observers. Squares show objective size thresholds measured when angular separation was scaled by disparity as though the physical distance to the target was changing; targets were presented at random at one of nine different disparities from trial to trial (see text). Open circles show angular size thresholds for unscaled targets presented in the same random disparity condition. Triangles show size thresholds for targets presented in the fixation plane only.

second largest scale. With feedback, observers are very good at using multiple implicit "standards." Morgan (1992) asked observers to judge relative width for targets presented randomly at different orientations from trial to trial. Each orientation had a different implicit standard: for example, for vertical, 10 arcmin ± Δ; for oblique, 11 arcmin ± Δ; for horizontal, 12 arcmin ± Δ. The observers were never shown the standard width for any of the orientations; instead, they learned a different internalized standard for each orientation. These multiple-standard width judgments were nearly as good as judgments made with a single standard width. In an earlier study on velocity constancy, McKee and Welch (1989) asked observers to label 10 widely separated depth planes with a number from 0 to 9. After a small amount of practice, observers accurately labeled each depth plane on about one-third of the trials, and they were seldom off by more than one adjacent plane when they mislabeled the planes. This pattern of errors should increase the single-plane threshold by about a factor of 1.5, according to calculations. In the McKee–Welch study of size constancy, the observed increase from the single-plane threshold (~3.5%) to the objective-size threshold (~6.5%) is close to this prediction. Thus, it is certainly possible that the precision of the objective size thresholds was based on a learned code for rescaling.

Is this result merely a laboratory curiosity? Perhaps, but in familiar settings (office, laboratory, kitchen, playing field), a learned code for rescaling might prove useful, given the imprecision or inaccuracy of extant depth estimates. We next consider an unusual example of recoding size judgments.

Learning constancy

Although we have a number of "hard-wired" neural systems for estimating relative depth (disparity detectors, motion detectors, and the like), size constancy is undoubtedly based on our long experience with real objects and surfaces – on a learned calibration. Depth judgments are affected by ongoing changes in the reliability of different sources of information (Young, Landy, & Maloney, 1993), so active recalibration of size may also occur. Can observers learn to make accurate size judgments based on orderly but *unnatural* information?

In the McKee–Welch study described earlier, separate psychometric functions were generated for each of the nine tested disparities; the point of subjective equality (the stimulus value corresponding to the 50th percentile on each psychometric function) was taken as a measure of perceived size. As shown by the open symbols in the upper graphs in Figure 14.9, the two observers were reasonably accurate in judging objective size. McKee and Welch next exactly inverted the natural relationship so that the angular separation *decreased* as the target appeared closer in depth and *increased* as the target appeared farther away; the angular separation for +40 arcmin of disparity in their "anti-constancy" experiment was set equal to the separation used for −40 arcmin in their constancy experiment. In brief experimental sessions taken over a couple of days (600 trials total), observers practiced judging objective size, using error feedback to recalibrate their size judgments in this unnatural condition. Then they made the measurements shown in Figure 14.9 (filled symbols in upper graphs). Surprisingly, the anti-constancy condition produced results that were just as accurate as those in the constancy condition. The anti-constancy judgments were less precise (lower graph in Figure 14.9), but, with more than 2 days of practice, the errors might have reached the same level as the constancy measurements.

Did the target seem to be the same size in the anti-constancy condition? No. The inverted relationship was, in fact, exaggerated by natural size constancy, so that the distant target looked enormous compared to the puny distance separating the lines at the nearest disparity. Even weeks of practice could not have overcome continuous natural feedback about the real relationship between relative disparity and angular subtense. Nevertheless, these results suggest that there is a flexible calibration mechanism involved in size constancy. If observers had been immersed in a virtual reality domain where the natural relationship between depth and angular subtense was universally inverted, the recalibration might have become sufficiently automatic to foster an *appearance* of constant size.

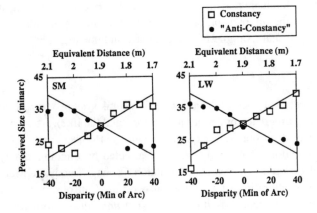

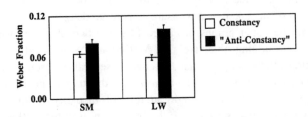

Figure 14.9. Data from McKee and Welch (1992). Upper graphs show PSEs for two subjects for the constancy and anti-constancy conditions. Open squares are based on the condition in which angular separation was scaled by disparity as though the physical distance to the target was changing; filled circles are based on the condition in which the constancy relationship was inverted so that angular subtense increased with increasing distance (see text). The lower graphs show precision measures (Weber fractions) for the same conditions. Target separation in the fixation plane was 30 arcmin.

Indeed, work from the Ross laboratory on the size adaptation experienced by scuba divers indicates that as little as 20 min of altered underwater optics can affect apparent size in normal viewing conditions for a few minutes after leaving the water (Franklin, Ross, & Weltman, 1970; Ross, Franklin, Weltman, & Lennie, 1970).

Dual calculations?

Certain kinds of information are lost in the course of visual processing. We can discriminate between wavelengths, but we have no knowledge of the separate signals in the three types of cones. We can see changes in disparity, but we cannot identify the contribution of each eye to the fused image (Templeton &

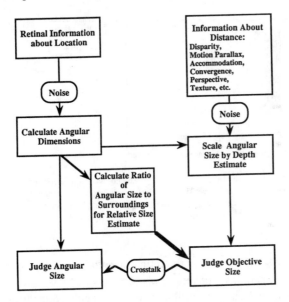

Figure 14.10. Flow chart showing dual calculations of angular and objective size, as described in text.

Green, 1968). Is size constancy like that? Have we lost information about angular subtense in the process of constructing a representation of true size? The results from the McKee–Welch study indicate that "angle on the retina" is not a given. Like all other information about the physical world, it must be translated from the light distribution on the retina into a neural representation of relative positions and lateral distances. This neural calculation could automatically include the scaling required for size constancy, such that subsequent stages would have no access to angular information. Apparently, it does not. There are far too many indications that we also have access to good information about angular size.

Rather than the simple dichotomy diagrammed in Figure 14.1, the human brain must be simultaneously calculating both the angular and objective dimensions of the whole visual scene (Rock, 1977). The flow chart in Figure 14.10 summarizes our view of these dual calculations. Size constancy depends on two separate processes: (1) angular size scaled by depth and (2) relative size calculated from the ratio of local angular measurements (Hochberg, 1972). The relative size calculation provides the most precise information, but in the absence of depth signals from the other processing stream, relative size is not sufficient to promote accurate judgments of objective size. As one would expect, size constancy is promoted or enhanced by the concurrence of many cues to depth.

The noise sources, indicated by the oval shapes in Figure 14.10, are primarily

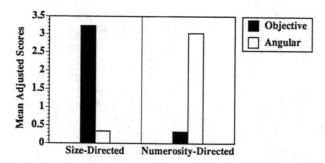

Figure 14.11. Data from Epstein and Broota (1986) showing the effect of attention on whether observers make objective size matches (dark bars) or angular size matches. When attention is directed to the size of the square, they make objective size matches. When attention is directed to the number of dots on the square, they make angular size matches of the square.

associated with the low-level detectors for retinal location (local sign) and distance (disparity, motion parallax, convergence, accommodation, texture coding). We suspect that the neural calculation that translates angular dimensions into objective dimensions is very efficient. For example, in Figure 14.8, objective thresholds are slightly higher than angular thresholds, a difference that is exaggerated at small separations; this pattern is consistent with an additive source of noise. The calculation of objective size from angular dimensions at various disparities adds about 20 arcsec of uncertainty to the objective thresholds. We also concede that the automatic scaling of size with distance does interfere slightly with the calculation of angular size in natural surroundings, a noise source we have labeled "crosstalk" in the flow chart.

What determines which of the dual calculations dominates size perception? To some extent, it depends on where the observer's attention is directed. Epstein and Broota (1986) used different tasks to direct attention either to the size of an object or to the markings on it. They presented observers with posterboard squares of various sizes, each covered with a variable array of randomly positioned dots. In one condition, observers were asked to judge the size of the squares presented briefly at various distances. After each square had disappeared, observers marked a test sheet that pictured potential choices for a match; the choices included the objective size of the square, the angular subtense, and some intermediary sizes. In the other condition, the observers were asked to judge, as quickly as possible, whether the number of dots on the square was odd or even. After they had made several numerosity judgments, they were asked to judge the size of the square seen on the last trial. Epstein and Broota compared the matches chosen in the last trial for the two conditions. When attention was directed to the size of the square, observers matched the square on the basis of objective size, but when their attention was directed to the dots, they chose a

Indirect Calculation of Angular Speed **Direct Calculation of Angular Speed**
from Distance and Time Estimates **from Signals in Motion Detectors**

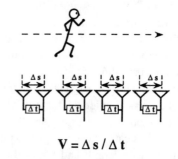

$$V = \frac{\text{Distance Traversed (S)}}{\text{Time Taken for Traverse (T)}}$$

$$V = \Delta s / \Delta t$$

Use size constancy scaling to convert distance
traversed from angular units (deg) into
objective units (m)

Local motion detectors encode the time
taken to cross the distance separating
pair of receivers. Angular speed
(deg/sec) could be converted directly
into objective speed (m/sec).

Figure 14.12. Two procedures for calculating speed. In the left half of the figure, speed
is calculated from the distance traversed by the target and the time taken for traverse.
In the right half of the figure, speed is calculated from motion detectors that perform the
calculation for distances smaller than the whole traverse (see text). Speed constancy could
be based on rescaling information from either procedure.

match on the basis of angular subtense (see Figure 14.11). This result makes
sense if we consider that angular information is used to specify the "background" of our surroundings, that is, to specify the texture and perspective cues
that provide information about relative depth. An object of interest is the "figure" on this "background," and generally, we want to know its true physical
size in order to decide the appropriate behavioral response. Is the beast before
us a cat or a tiger? Thus, these parallel calculations serve different functions in
guiding human action, and apparently, we need some awareness of both for our
own well-being.

Speed constancy

As you walk away from a moving object, the retinal speed of the object decreases, but it does not appear to slow down. *Speed constancy* refers to the
human ability to compensate for the changes in angular velocity associated with
changes in viewing distance and thereby to maintain an invariant estimate of
objective speed. It is usually treated as an extension of size constancy because
of an assumption about how angular speed is encoded by the human visual
system. As shown on the left side of Figure 14.12, speed could be calculated
from separate measurements of the distance traversed by the moving target and

of the time taken to cover that distance. If the distance measurement were scaled by the same neural calculation used for size constancy, perceived speed would be invariant with viewing distance. In fact, this formulation of speed constancy is nearly correct. What is incorrect is the scheme for encoding angular speed.

When you take a motor trip, you don't have to wait until you've completed your journey to know how fast your car was moving. Instead, you read the car's speedometer. Similarly, the motion system can estimate speed from the signals generated while the target is in transit. There is abundant physiological and psychophysical evidence for specialized motion mechanisms that measure space and time on a small scale (see the right side of Figure 14.12). There are also psychophysical data that argue explicitly against an indirect estimate of speed from traverse length and target duration. McKee (1981) measured speed discrimination for targets that moved across a fixed aperture. Because the length of the traverse was fixed, the time the target spent crossing the aperture necessarily varied with target speed, so observers could have judged speed on the basis of duration. However, McKee showed that the speed judgments for the moving targets were more precise than comparable duration judgments for static targets (a result confirmed by Orban, de Wolf, & Maes, 1984). In short, speed discrimination is based on a temporal signal that is more precise than the time estimate associated with the whole traverse.

In contrast to these findings, Mandriota, Mintz, and Notterman (1962) had earlier shown that random variations in the distance traversed by the target elevated speed discrimination thresholds dramatically. McKee noted similar difficulties initially when she randomized the length of the traverse from trial to trial, but with considerable practice and feedback, her observers learned to ignore these random variations and to respond as precisely as when the target traverse was fixed. Apparently, when naive observers are asked to judge how fast something is moving, they tend to pay attention to traverse length and other spatial attributes of the target; they estimate speed indirectly from lateral distance (a *static*, position-based signal) and duration (left side of Figure 14.12). We will call this speed estimate *indirect* because it is not based on *motion* signals. The indirect approach to calculating speed seems to interfere with optimal use of the motion-based signal until observers learn from feedback to respond only on the basis of this more precise signal – another case of dual calculations! We will argue that this precise motion-based signal is encoded only in angular units (deg/sec). Speed constancy, on the other hand, is based on the indirect estimate of speed.

Speed constancy and spatial scaling

In 1931, J. F. Brown published the first important study of speed constancy. As in other studies of size constancy, his observers were shown the moving test target presented at various distances and were asked to adjust the speed of a comparison target, presented always at 1 m, until it equaled the test speed. Both targets consisted of small black squares pasted on rolls of white paper that ran between two revolving drums driven by an electric motor, all mounted within light-tight boxes. The squares were spaced such that a single square was seen at any given time moving past a fixed aperture at the front of the apparatus. Illumination from within the boxes ensured that only the moving square and its white background were visible through the apertures; otherwise, the room was darkened. Brown reported excellent speed constancy at distances ranging from 3 to 10 m and only a small deviation from an objective match (in cm/sec) at 20 m; none of the matches were based on the angular speed (deg/sec) of the test.

Because viewing was monocular in a totally dark room, it was clear that some type of relational information must account for the objective matches. Rather than assuming that speed constancy was a straightforward extension of size constancy, Brown proposed that perceived speed depended on context effects, that is, on the spatial dimensions of the moving target relative to the surroundings, particularly the framing aperture. To confirm his hypothesis, he increased all the spatial dimensions of the test display (the black squares and the aperture) by a factor of 2 and showed that the matching speed, in centimeters per second, doubled. Further increases in the spatial dimensions produced corresponding increases in matching speed. Proportionality was not perfect – scaling the dimensions by a factor of 10 increased perceived speed by only a factor of 8 – but the effects were generally consistent with Brown's hypothesis.

Brown called this phenomenon *velocity transposition* because the spatial scaling effects had induced observers to accept matches between speeds that were physically quite different, contrary to the common conception of constancy. In an essay published some 8 years later, Wallach (1939) argued forcefully that Brown had actually identified the mechanism of speed constancy. What Wallach noted was that observers accepted matches between test and comparison speeds when the ratios of the *angular* speeds to the *angles* subtended by the surrounding apertures were equal. Clearly, this condition was satisfied in Brown's constancy study because the whole test apparatus was moved to different distances, so the angular dimensions of speed and surroundings were naturally scaled together. Wallach maintained that the transposition study had triggered constancy scaling by increasing all the visible dimensions of the target, as though the test display had moved closer to the observer. Wallach found one of Brown's results particularly interesting. Brown had repeated his transposition study with *binocular* viewing and found roughly the same speed matches as for monocular viewing. Unlike relative size effects, the relative speed effects were strong enough to override contrary binocular depth information completely. Wallach concluded that, in contrast to size constancy, angular speed was not scaled by measures of depth to achieve constancy. Speed constancy depended only on relational effects – the ratio of the angular speed to the angles subtended by the surroundings.

There have been two challenges to Wallach's conception. First, Smith and Sherlock (1957) suggested that Brown's observers were actually matching the rate at which the moving dots were passing the edge of the aperture, not the speed. In contemporary jargon, they were matching the temporal frequencies of the targets. Clearly, if all spatial dimensions were increased by a factor of 2, the speed would also have to be doubled to produce the same rate past some fixed position. Smith and Sherlock (1957) demonstrated that observers could make frequency matches when the physical velocities differed considerably, a result that lent plausibility to their conjecture. Subsequent work (Diener, Wist, Dichgans, & Brandt, 1976) has shown that temporal frequency does indeed affect perceived speed. However, practiced observers can discriminate fine differences in speed despite random variations in temporal frequency (Chen, Bedell, & Frishman, 1995; McKee, Silverman, & Nakayama, 1986; Smith & Edgar, 1991); they are undoubtedly basing their judgments on the precise motion-based signal described earlier (right side of Figure 14.12) rather than the confounding dimensions that usually covary with speed changes, such as temporal frequency, distance traversed, target duration.

The second challenge came from Rock, Hill, and Fineman (1968; see also Epstein, 1978), who questioned Wallach's assertion that depth scaling played no significant role in speed constancy. With heroic experimental efforts, they managed to demonstrate some degree of speed constancy from depth alone. This study is interesting from the contrary viewpoint as well; even a hint of relational information tended to override the depth information. Indeed, subsequent work has tended to support Wallach's position. Zohary and Sittig (1993) measured speed constancy with a sparse pattern of randomly positioned dots displayed on two CRT screens. The drifting dots were viewed binocularly at two distances (1 and 2 m) but behind apertures of the same angular subtense. Observers adjusted the speed of the nearer target to match the more distant target. They easily matched the physical speeds of the dots, exhibiting good speed constancy. When Zohary and Sittig scaled the size and spacing of the dots on the near screen so that they subtended the same visual angles as the dots on the far screen, speed constancy disappeared. Observers made the matches on the basis of angular speeds despite the obvious difference in the depth of the targets. Because there was no difference in aperture size, the speed constancy found with the unscaled dots must have been based on texture scaling – on the ratio of the angular speed to the angles subtended by the moving texture. By matching the angular size of the textures, Zohary and Sittig had produced a modern variant of velocity transposition. Or was this result another case of temporal frequency matching?

The stimuli in the Zohary–Sittig study were limited-lifetime dots, appearing and then disappearing at random locations across the screen, so it was impossible to assign a frequency rate to any one location. Nevertheless, on average, the spatial frequency[7] spectrum of the dots on the near screen was about half that of the unscaled dots on the far screen. In angular units, velocity (degrees per second) equals temporal frequency (cycles per second) divided by spatial frequency (cycles per degree), so temporal frequency equals velocity multiplied by spatial frequency. To match the temporal frequency of the farther dots, the angular velocity of the near target had to be doubled, exactly the compensation for distance needed to equate the physical speeds (centimeters per second) of the two displays. By scaling the size of the dots on the near screen, Zohary and Sittig had equated the spatial frequency content of the two displays; thus, the temporal frequencies were matched when the angular speeds were matched, so speed constancy disappeared. However, Zohary and Sittig also manipulated the size of the dots and their spacing separately. For some observers, speed constancy was unaffected by a change in dot spacing but diminished greatly with a change in dot size, consistent with temporal frequency coding. For others, changing either size or spacing produced matches halfway between the angular and objective speeds – less secure evidence for temporal frequency coding. One thing was clear from the Zohary–Sittig study: Depth alone was not sufficient to promote speed constancy.

McKee and Welch (1989) confirmed this result in an earlier study. They asked observers to discriminate small changes in speed while they randomly varied the target disparity. The distance traversed and the target duration were also randomly varied to encourage observers to respond on the basis of speed per se. As in their study of size constancy, they assumed that the PSEs from the psychometric functions were a measure of perceived speed. In Figure 14.13, the ratio of the PSE (angular units) to the mean speed is plotted as a function of target disparity. The oblique line shows the predicted ratios for speed constancy. In the absence of feedback or instructions, the observers spontaneously judged the speed on the basis of angular speed, not objective speed. The disparity variations had no effect on either the accuracy or the precision of their angular speed judgments.

Incorporating feedback into their experimental procedure, McKee and Welch next asked observers to discriminate small changes in objective speed (cm/sec). With feedback and practice, observers did learn to scale speed by perceived depth. However, their objective speed judgments were much less precise than angular speed judgments made with the same random variations in disparity (see the top graph in Figure 14.14). To account for the imprecision of the objective thresholds, McKee and Welch speculated that observers were estimating speed indirectly from target duration and from the objective distance (cm) traversed on every trial. They made concurrent measurements of the precision in judging the objective distance (in cm) traversed by the target–size constancy for trav-

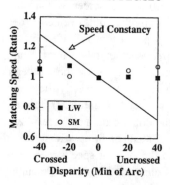

Figure 14.13. Data from McKee and Welch (1989). Ratio of matching speed to mean speed (10 deg/sec) as a function of disparity. From trial to trial, the target was presented at one of five disparities chosen at random. Observers judged whether the target was faster or slower than the mean value (method of single stimuli). No feedback was given. The tilted line shows the prediction for speed constancy scaling based on disparity.

erse length. From the precision of these measurements and the known precision of duration judgments, they were able to predict the objective speed thresholds, confirming the plausibility of their speculation. So, it is possible for human observers to use depth information for speed constancy, but they are not particularly proficient in its use.

Scaling angular speed or angular distance traversed?

Although Wallach (1939) stressed relational scaling of the angular *speed*, the calculation just described shows that relational scaling of the distance traversed would work as well. In the absence of any visible surroundings, Epstein and Cody (1980) found that the angle subtended by the traverse length alone was sufficient to promote changes in perceived speed. In this study, the test and comparison targets were single points that moved back and forth across their specified traverse distances. When the distance traversed by the test target was smaller than the distance traversed by the comparison target, observers increased the matching speed of the comparison. Epstein and Cody suggested that the distance traversed defined a relational spatial scale. Obviously, the two targets moving at the same angular speed moved the same angular distance in the same time, but the proportion of their total traverse was different. If the test target crossed the whole traverse in the time it took for the comparison target to cross half of its longer traverse, observers perceived the test to be moving faster than the comparison target, so the comparison speed was increased. Because the targets moved repetitively over the same distance (''wrap-around''), the observ-

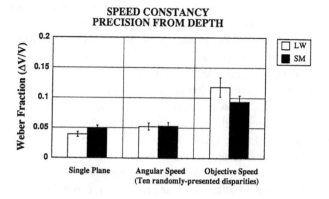

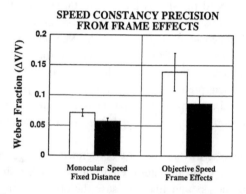

Figure 14.14. Data from McKee and Welch (1989). Upper graph: Weber fractions for speed discrimination for fixation plane targets (labeled "Single Plane"), for angular speed discrimination with random variations in disparity from trial to trial, and for objective speed discrimination with the same random variations in disparity. Feedback was given. Lower graph, left side: monocular speed discrimination averaged from two *fixed* viewing distances – the control condition for frame effect study. Right side: monocular speed discrimination when observers rocked back and forth from one distance to the other on alternate trials, showing frame effects on precision of speed constancy. Feedback was given.

ers might have made their matches on the basis of repetition *rate*. If so, they were not very good at it because the ratios of the angular speed to the angle subtended by the traverse were far from equal. When Epstein and Cody added frames scaled to the size of the traverse, the ratios were somewhat nearer to the transposition prediction but still not perfect, particularly for faster speeds. Because the frames did not change the repetition rate, perceived speed was not entirely determined by target temporal frequency. Of more importance in this context, this study shows that observers generally rely on traverse length, scaled by implicit or explicit surroundings, when asked to equate perceived speeds.

McKee and Welch (1989) also measured frame effects on speed discrimination. The observer viewed the moving target monocularly on a standard CRT screen (the "frame") and, in the intervals between trials, rocked forward or back so that the viewing distance changed from 28 cm to 57 cm on alternate trials. Because angular speed was changing by about a factor of 2 from trial to trial, observers had to rely on scaled changes in their surroundings to compensate for the changes in viewing distance. In short, they were being asked to judge objective speed using the transposition scaling first identified by Brown. Despite the guidance provided by feedback, their Weber fractions for transposed speed were considerably less precise than their monocular judgments[8] of angular speed (see the bottom graph in Figure 14.14). Frame effects were not much better than disparity in producing precise judgments of objective speed.

These results argue that speed constancy depends on scaling the distance traversed rather than direct scaling of the angular speed. Otherwise, it is difficult to explain why objective speed thresholds are two to three times the angular thresholds. Based on a propagation-of-error calculation in which different sources of error were assumed to be independent, McKee and Welch (1989) predicted objective speed thresholds from the measured errors in the angular speed and in the depth judgments; the measured objective speed thresholds were significantly higher than their predictions. In contrast, similar predictions for size constancy were in good agreement with the measured thresholds. We thus attribute the loss of precision in objective speed thresholds to the indirect calculation of speed.

In laboratory situations, the traverse has a well-defined, if arbitrary, length. How can speed constancy operate in natural environments where the traverse length for an object in motion is undefined because the object is still moving? Does the observer have to wait until the object disappears before judging its speed? Objects usually have a static background that can be used to scale the distance moved per unit time. Because both the average angle subtended by the background texture and the angular velocity are scaled with viewing distance, the "proportion" of background moved per unit time remains constant as the viewing distance increases – the transposition effect again. Temporal frequency coding, the alternative to the indirect calculation of speed, may underlie speed constancy in some conditions. The temporal frequency spectrum of any transient signal is invariant with distance because the decrease in the angular velocity and the increase in the spatial frequency spectrum cancel. Temporal frequency judgments are somewhat less precise than speed judgments (McKee et al., 1986; Pasternak, 1987; Smith & Edgar, 1991), which would account for the imprecision of speed constancy.

Three procedures for calculating speed

In summary, angular speed can be calculated with high precision from the signals generated by primary motion units (Grzywacz & Yuille; 1990; Heeger,

Wide Receiver is moving 12 miles/hour

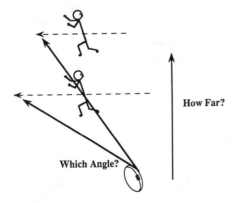

Figure 14.15. Example showing that angular speed information is needed to guide eye and body movements. A quarterback in American football needs information about *angular* speed in order to determine the angle at which the football needs to be thrown to reach the receiver. This angular information is lost in objective speed calculation.

1987). Objective speed, on the contrary, depends on two less precise calculations: (1) temporal frequency coding and (2) the indirect calculation of speed from duration and a scaled representation of distance traversed.

It is nevertheless puzzling that the visual system does not transform the angular speed signal directly into some representation of objective speed. One answer comes from a consideration of the uses of angular speed information. Like angular sizes, angular speeds define the "background" of the visual world; they are the raw data of optic flow, providing information about object boundaries and relative depth. Angular speed also guides the human motor system; it is the primary input to pursuit eye movements and other kinds of movement that involve rapid adjustment in the pursuit of a moving object. In American football, the best quarterbacks[9] adjust their passes so that the ball will arrive a second or two later at the predicted location of a receiver running across the football field. Knowing that the wide receiver is running at a rate of 12 miles an hour is not helpful because objective speed carries no information about the angle required for the ball to reach its target (see Figure 14.15). The quarterback needs separate, independent information about both the receiver's distance and the receiver's *angular* speed so that he can adjust the angle of his arm and hand in a throwing motion that will deliver the ball to the appropriate location. Of course, the quarterback can reconstruct angular speed indirectly from objective speed and the estimated depth of the receiver, but this reconstruction would necessarily have more error than the direct estimate of angular speed because it would include noise from the depth signal. It is a much better strategy to use the angular speed signal, uncontaminated by depth noise, as the basis of fine motor control.

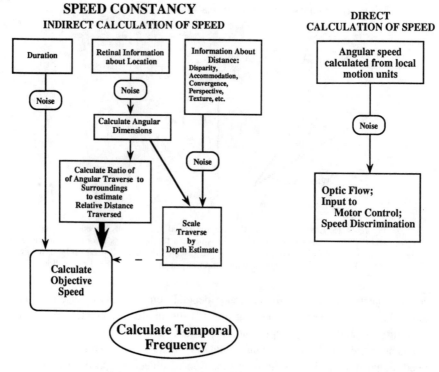

Figure 14.16. Flow charts showing dual calculation of objective and angular speed information. Objective speed can be calculated from temporal frequency information; it can also be calculated indirectly from target duration and from the distance traversed, where traverse is scaled by the same procedures as in size constancy. Angular speed information is based on calculation from signals generated by motion detectors.

Objective speed information is chiefly useful in maintaining an object's identity; the apparent speed of an object moving across our visual field should not change as we change our viewing distance. Whereas body movements require high precision, object identity does not, so there is no functional demand for a highly precise representation of objective speed. In psychophysical experiments, learning fine speed discrimination is quite difficult, which suggests that we are largely unaware of the precise background signal that guides our movements and defines our visual world. When we *attend* to a target, we see its scaled objective speed.

An overview of speed constancy processing is shown in Figure 14.16. As in the case of size constancy, we are proposing a dual calculation of the objective and angular speeds. Wallach contended that speed constancy could not be an extension of size constancy because it did follow the same rules that governed size constancy. Speed constancy does indeed depend on a different algorithm from the one that governs size constancy, but many of the components are similar. The "distance traversed" is scaled by the same information as size, but relational scaling (large solid arrow) is weighted so heavily that it generally overwhelms depth scaling (small dotted arrow). In addition, the calculation of temporal frequency provides a strong alternative to scaling the distance traversed. There is no evidence indicating how these two alternative procedures for speed constancy are combined, so we have left them separate in the diagram.

Notes

1. In all experimental measurements of size constancy, observers judge the *relative* size of one object with respect to another. It is difficult to determine if observers also have correct information about the true physical size of the objects (the *absolute* size). Thus, we generally will not distinguish between relative and absolute judgments of objective size.
2. Sedgwick (1986) contains a superb summary on the use of perspective and texture information to estimate distance.
3. Diopter is a measure of lens power and equals the reciprocal of the focal length in meters.
4. The angle subtended at a point by straight lines from the rotation centers of the eyes.
5. Predicted error $= \sqrt{(\text{error}_x{}^2 + \text{error}_y{}^2)}$.
6. The lower line is about 20% too short.
7. Spatial frequency varies inversely with angular dot size. Viewing the dots at half the distance would double their angular subtense and roughly halve the peak of the spatial frequency spectrum. Changes in the spacing of randomly positioned dots should not affect the content of the spectrum.
8. For the monocular control, observers discriminated small differences in angular speed at each of the two distances (28 cm and 57 cm) while remaining stationary; their Weber fractions for these two fixed distances were averaged.
9. The quarterback is the player who throws the football forward to the receivers after it is handed to him by the player in the center of the forward line.

References

Andrews, D. P. (1964). Error-correcting perceptual mechanisms. *Quarterly Journal of Experimental Psychology, 16*, 105–115.

Bevington, P. R. (1969). *Data reduction and error analysis for the physical sciences*. New York: McGraw-Hill.

Boring, E. G. (1942). *Sensation and perception in the history of experimental psychology*, (pp. 288–299). New York: D. Appleton-Century.

Boring, E. G. (1946). The perception of objects. *American Journal of Physics, 14*, 99–107.

Brown, J. F. (1931). The visual perception of velocity. *Psychologische Forschung, 14*, 199–232.

Burbeck, C. A. (1987a). Position and spatial frequency in large-scale localization judgments. *Vision Research, 27*, 417–427.

Burbeck, C. A. (1987b). On the locus of spatial frequency discrimination. *Journal of the Optical Society of America A, 4*, 1807–1813.

Campbell, F. W. (1957). The depth of field of the human eye. *Optica Acta, 4*, 157–164.

Carlson, V. R. (1960). Overestimation in size-constancy judgments. *American Journal of Psychology, 73,* 199–213.

Chen, Y., Bedell, H. E., and Frishman, L. J. (1995). Velocity discrimination between stimuli of different spatial frequencies. *Investigative Ophthalmology and Visual Science (Supplement), 36,* S54.

Coren, S., & Girgus, J. S. (1978). *Seeing is deceiving: The psychology of visual illusions.* Hillsdale, NJ: Erlbaum.

Diener, H. C., Wist, E. R., Dichgans, J., & Brandt, Th. (1976). The spatial frequency effect on perceived velocity. *Vision Research, 16,* 169–176.

Epstein, W. (1967) The assumptive context: I. The perception of size and distance. In *Varieties of perceptual learning* (pp. 21–53). New York: McGraw-Hill.

Epstein, W. (1973). The process of 'taking-into-account' in visual perception. *Perception, 2,* 267–285.

Epstein, W. (1978). Two factors in the perception of velocity at a distance. *Perception & Psychophysics, 24,* 105–114.

Epstein, W., & Broota, K. D. (1986). Automatic and attentional components in perception of size-at-a-distance. *Perception & Psychophysics, 40,* 256–262.

Epstein, W., & Cody, W. J. (1980). Perception of relative velocity: A revision of the hypothesis of relational determination. *Perception, 9,* 47–60.

Epstein, W., Park, J., & Casey, A. (1961). The current status of the size-distance hypothesis. *Psychological Bulletin, 58,* 491–514.

Foley, J. M. (1980). Binocular distance perception. *Psychological Review, 87,* 411–434.

Franklin, S. S., Ross, H. E., & Weltman, G. (1970). Size-distance adaptation invariance in perceptual adaptation. *Psychonomic Science, 21,* 229–231.

Gibson, J. J. (1950). *The perception of the visual world.* Boston: Houghton Mifflin.

Gilinsky, A. S. (1955). The effect of attitude upon the perception of size. *American Journal of Psychology, 68,* 173–192.

Gillam, B. (1973). The nature of size scaling in the Ponzo and related illusions. *Perception & Psychophysics, 14,* 353–357.

Gregory, R. L. (1963). Distortion of visual space as inappropriate constancy scaling. *Nature* (London), *199,* 678–680.

Gregory, R. L. (1973). The confounded eye. In R. L. Gregory & E. H. Gombrich (Eds.), *Illusion in nature and art* (pp. 12–41). New York: Scribner's.

Gregory, R. L. (1987). Emmert's law. In R. L. Gregory (Ed.), *The Oxford companion to the mind* (pp. 218–219). Oxford: Oxford University Press.

Gregory, R. L., Wallace, J. G., & Campbell, F. W. (1959). Changes in the size and shape of visual after-images observed in complete darkness during changes of position in space. *Quarterly Journal of Experimental Psychology, 11,* 54–56.

Grzywacz, N. M., & Yuille, A. L. (1990). A model of the estimate of local image velocity by cells in the visual cortex. *Proceedings of the Royal Society London B, 239,* 129–161.

Harvey, L. O., & Leibowitz, H. W. (1967) Effects of exposure duration, cue reduction, and temporary monocularity on size matching at short distances. *Journal of the Optical Society of America, 57,* 249–253.

Heeger, D. J. (1987). A model for the extraction of image flow. *Journal of the Optical Society of America A, 4,* 1455–1471.

Hell, W. (1978). Movement parallax: An asymptotic function of amplitude and velocity of head motion. *Vision Research, 18,* 629–635.

Hochberg, J. (1972). Perception II. Space and movement. In J. W. Kling & L. A. Riggs (Eds.), *Woodworth & Schlosberg's experimental psychology* (3rd ed., pp. 475–550). New York: Holt, Rinehart & Winston.

Holway, A. H., & Boring, E. G. (1941). Determinants of apparent visual size with distance variant. *American Journal of Psychology, 54,* 21–37.

Huber, J., & Davies, I. (1995). Motion parallax: A weak cue for depth in telepresence systems. *Perception (Supplement), 24,* 106.

Humphrey, N. K., & Morgan, M. J. (1965). Constancy and the geometric illusions. *Nature, 206,* 744–745.

Johnston, E. B. (1991). Systematic distortions of shape from stereopsis. *Vision Research, 31,* 1351–1360.

Klein, S. A., & Levi, D. M. (1987). Position sense of the peripheral retina. *Journal of the Optical Society of America A, 4,* 1543–1553.

Landy, M. S., Maloney, L. T., Johnston, E. B., & Young, M. (1995). Measurement and modeling of depth cue combination: In defense of weak fusion. *Vision Research, 35,* 389–412.

Legge, G. E., Mullen, K. T., Woo, G. C., & Campbell, F. (1987). Tolerance to visual defocus. *Journal of the Optical Society of America A, 4,* 851–863.

Leibowitz, H. W., & Harvey, L. O., Jr. (1967). Size matching as a function of instructions in a naturalistic environment. *Journal of Experimental Psychology, 74,* 378–382.

Lichten, W., & Lurie, S. (1950). A new technique for the study of perceived size. *American Journal of Psychology, 63,* 280–282.

Mandriota, F. J., Mintz, D. E., & Notterman, J. M. (1962). Visual velocity discrimination: Effects of spatial and temporal cues. *Science, 138,* 437–438.

McKee, S. P. (1981). A local mechanism for differential velocity detection. *Vision Research, 21,* 491–500.

McKee, S. P., Levi, D. M., & Bowne, S. F. (1990). The imprecision of stereopsis. *Vision Research, 30,* 1763–1779.

McKee, S. P., Silverman, G. S., & Nakayama, K. (1986). Precise velocity discrimination despite random variations in temporal frequency and contrast. *Vision Research, 26,* 609–620.

McKee, S. P., & Welch, L. (1989). Is there a constancy for velocity? *Vision Research, 29,* 553–561.

McKee, S. P., & Welch, L. (1992). The precision of size constancy. *Vision Research, 32,* 1447–1460.

McKee, S. P., Welch, L., Taylor, D. G., & Bowne, S. F. (1990). Finding the common bond: Stereoacuity and the other hyperacuities. *Vision Research, 30,* 879–891.

Morgan, M. J. (1989). Vision of solid objects. *Nature, 339,* 101–103.

Morgan, M. J. (1992). On the scaling of size judgments by orientational cues. *Vision Research, 32,* 1433–1445.

Nakayama, K. (1994). James J. Gibson – an appreciation. *Psychological Review, 101,* 329–335.

Norman, J. F., Todd, J. T, Perotti, V. J., & Tittle, J. S. (1996). The visual perception of 3-D length. *Journal of Experimental Psychology: Human Perception and Performance, 22,* 173–186.

Orban, G. A., de Wolf, J., & Maes, H. (1984). Factors influencing velocity coding in the human visual system. *Vision Research 24,* 33–39.

Over, R. (1960). The effect of instructions on size-judgments under reduction conditions. *American Journal of Psychology, 73,* 599–602.

Pasternak, T. (1987). Discrimination of differences in speed and flicker rate depends on directionally-selective mechanisms. *Vision Research, 27,* 1881–1890.

Rock, I. (1977). In defense of unconscious inference. In W. Epstein (Ed.), *Stability and constancy in visual perception: Mechanisms and processes* (pp. 95–125). New York: Wiley.

Rock, I., & Ebenholtz, S. (1959). The relational determination of perceived size. *Psychological Review, 66,* 387–401.

Rock, I., Hill, A. L., & Fineman, M. (1968). Speed constancy as a function of size constancy. *Perception & Psychophysics, 4,* 37–40.

Rogers, B. J., & Collett, T. S. (1989). The appearance of surfaces specified by motion parallax and binocular disparity. *Quarterly Journal of Experimental Psychology, 41A,* 697–717.

Rogers, B. J., & Graham, M. (1979). Motion parallax as an independent cue for depth perception. *Perception, 8,* 125–134.

Ross, H. E., Franklin, S. S., Weltman, G., & Lennie, P. (1970). Adaptation of divers to size distortion under water. *British Journal of Psychology, 61*, 365–373.

Sedgwick, H. A. (186). Space perception. In K. R. Boff, L. Kaufman, & J. P. Thomas (Eds.), *Handbook of perception and human performance* (Vol. I, pp. 21–57). New York: Wiley.

Sedgwick, H. A., & Nicholls, A. L. (1993). Interaction between surface and depth in the Ponzo illusion. *Investigative Ophthalmology and Visual Science Supplement, 34*, 1184.

Smith, A. T., & Edgar, G. K. (1991). The separability of temporal frequency and velocity. *Vision Research, 31*, 321–326.

Smith, O. W., & Sherlock, L. (1957). A new explanation of the velocity-transposition phenomenon. *American Journal of Psychology, 70*, 102–105.

Templeton, W. B., & Green, F. A. (1968). Chance results in utrocular discrimination. *Quarterly Journal of Experimental Psychology, 20*, 200–203.

Thouless, R. H. (1931). Phenomenal regression to the real object. *British Journal of Psychology, 21*, 335–359.

Wallach, H. (1939). On constancy of visual speed. *Psychological Review, 46*, 541–552.

Wenderoth, P. (1976). The contribution of relational factors to line-length matches. *Perception, 5*, 265–278.

Young, M. J., Landy, M. S., & Maloney, L. T. (1993). A perturbation analysis of depth perception from combinations of texture and motion cues. *Vision Research, 33*, 2685–2696.

Yuille, A. L., & Bülthoff, H. H. (1993). *Bayesian decision theory and psychophysics*. CogSci Memo No. 20. Tübingen: Max-Planck-Institut für biologische Kybernetik, Arbeitsgruppe Bülthoff.

Zohary, E., & Sittig, A. C. (1993). Mechanisms of velocity constancy. *Vision Research, 33*, 2467–2478.

15   Depth constancy

Thomas S. Collett and Andrew J. Parker

Three distinct processes are generally held to contribute to depth, size, and shape constancy. The first is *distance scaling*: the notion that the interpretation of the angular sizes (or the binocular disparities or the relative motion of surfaces) within the retinal image varies with an observer's judgment of his or her distance from the surface (von Helmholtz, 1910/1962, p. 318; von Kries, 1910/1962, pp. 383ff). The term *distance scaling* is somewhat unfortunate because it encourages the thought that a single distance-related signal acts to adjust an observer's estimate of size or depth. In reality, there is unlikely to be such a unitary signal. More likely, there are several different signals acting in a variety of places within the nervous system that differ in their accuracy and range and in the type of information that they supply. The essence of distance scaling is that information from sources such as eye position, accommodation, or the global pattern of vertical stereo disparities in the scene modulates the interpretation of local visual information derived from the object itself.

In contrast, the second type of information that influences the perceived three-dimensional shape of an object is entirely *intrinsic* to the image of the viewed object. For example, gradients of motion in the retinal image depend (among other things) on the underlying shape of the surface. In principle, shape can be recovered by integrating image gradients over space (Longuet-Higgins & Prazdny, 1981; Ullman, 1979), without any knowledge of viewing distance. In practice, there is often interaction between such processes: Information about three-dimensional shape may influence estimates of depth and size, and vice versa, so that the perceptions of size, shape, and depth are not independent.

The third contribution to these constancies is the most uncertain. It comes from diverse *higher-level* factors that depend on knowledge of the visual world and affect perceived depth, size, or shape. Examples include an appreciation of the absolute size of individual familiar objects, such as a human head or a dollar bill (a particular favorite of psychologists), as well as more general information

We thank our collaborators, Elizabeth Johnston, Bruce Cumming, Urs Schwarz, and Erik Sobel, for many enlightening discussions of the problems raised in this review. This chapter is an editor's shortened version of our original submitted in 1995. Work in AJP's laboratory is sponsored by the SERC, MRC, The Wellcome Trust, the Oxford McDonnell–Pew Centre in Cognitive Neuroscience, and the JCI on Human–Computer Interaction (MRC, ESRC, SERC).

about the spatial layout of visual scenes that comes from an implicit understanding of the laws of linear perspective. Visual knowledge of this kind may turn out to be embedded in the neural systems concerned with lower-level visual processing. Stereo vision, for instance, incorporates an understanding of what happens when a front surface partially occludes a rear one so that a region of the rear surface is seen by only one eye. The depth of such an "ecologically valid" unpaired region of a stereogram is seen stably, without binocular rivalry, as belonging to the rear surface (Nakayama & Shimojo, 1990; Shimojo & Nakayama, 1990). In other words, the perceived appearance of the stereogram corresponds to the most common real-world configuration that is capable of generating that image (Nakayama & Shimojo, 1992).

In this chapter we are concerned primarily with depth scaling. However, one of the most interesting features of three-dimensional vision is that it relies on many sources of information. Data from different cues must be merged coherently and flexibly. In the concluding sections, we discuss interactions between depth cues and the contributions that their study brings to an understanding of data fusion in the visual system.

1. Estimates of distance and depth

1.1 Multiple cues to distance and the precision of distance and depth estimates, as revealed in motor tasks

In an impoverished scene, the accuracy of our distance judgments is low: We are very bad at locating isolated points of light. But, given a rich visual environment, we can measure distances accurately over many meters (Figure 15.1). If subjects are asked first to look at a target in normal surroundings, then to close their eyes and walk toward it without any visual feedback, they do so with very little error (Loomis, Da Silva Fujita, & Fukusima, 1992; Thomson, 1983). Subjects do badly when performing the same task with reduced cues – a small, illuminated target seen at eye level in an otherwise darkened laboratory. Their performance is equally bad whether they give a verbal report of the target's distance or walk toward it (Philbeck & Loomis, in press).

Precise estimates of viewing distance are likely to depend on many cues, with different cues contributing over different ranges. Oculomotor cues, that is, information derived from vergence and accommodation, are typically described as short-range, operating at most over 1 or 2 m. Longer-range cues, such as texture or perspective, have been more difficult to investigate. Philbeck and Loomis (1997) asked what cues support accurate distance judgments over the range 1 to 5 m. They found that when illuminated targets in an otherwise darkened room were set on the ground instead of at eye level, perceived distance

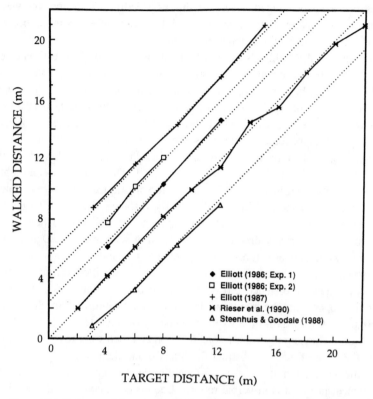

Figure 15.1. Summary of five experiments by different authors in which subjects walked to a previously viewed target with their eyes closed. Walked distance is plotted against target distance. Data are shifted vertically for clarity. Dotted lines have a slope of unity and an intercept of zero (Loomis et al., 1992).

correlated strongly with target distance. In this case, subjects relied on angular elevation within the visual field as a useful cue to distance (see also Warren & Whang, 1987). As expected, vergence and accommodation contributed weakly to estimates of egocentric distance from 2 to 5 m, although they were more helpful at shorter distances. Observer motion (motion parallax) also turned out to be of little use in measuring absolute distance. This is somewhat surprising if we suppose that human observers, like gerbils (Goodale, Ellard, & Booth, 1990) and locusts (Sobel, 1990), can use the magnitude or speed of their displacement to calibrate visual motion parallax.

The same pattern of results was found whether perceived distance was expressed through "blind" walking or reported verbally. Thus, although walking is a convenient and accurate measure of the egocentric distance of a target, it does not have privileged access to this knowledge. The same knowledge of location controls a variety of actions, with the occurrence of similar errors when information is missing (Philbeck & Loomis, 1997).

Loomis et al. (1992) also used blind walking to study how estimates of size and depth intervals change with distance over the range 4 m to 12 m. Two steel rods, 16 cm high, were stuck into a field to define either an interval in depth or one in a frontal plane. Subjects viewed this interval binocularly over a range of distances. When they had finished viewing the scene, they closed their eyes and the experimenters removed the rods. The subjects then walked to where they thought the first target to be and, after a brief pause, walked, with their eyes still closed, to the position of the second target. The subjects' remarkable performance is shown in Figure 15.2. The intervals are usually overestimated, but this error is constant and independent of the distance of the first target.

These results contrast strongly with subjects' performance when they stand still and report verbally on the width or depth of such intervals. Depth estimates are then systematically foreshortened relative to width estimates. A square on the ground is perceived as a rectangle that becomes increasingly squashed in depth as viewing distance grows. Loomis, Da Silva, Philbeck, and Fukusima (1996) suppose that the two tasks draw on different information. Subjects in the walking task may avoid the explicit encoding of the intervals between the two steel rods. They simply walk to one location and then walk to the other location. Had they been forced to abstract the interval and then to express it by walking an equivalent depth at the viewing location, the distance walked would be foreshortened, just as it is in verbal reports. Loomis et al. conclude that subjects can perceive and store accurately the egocentric distances and directions of several locations in space without necessarily having a precise sense of the distance between those locations.

At a closer range, observers have been asked to reach to different locations on a virtual surface without being able to see their hands (Figure 15.3). The distribution of the endpoints of the movements shows that the slant and shape of the surface are accurately encoded (Cook & Griffiths, 1991). Systematic errors occur in individual endpoints, but these are constant over the whole surface. There is also some compression of the indicated curvature that results from the subjects' tendency to underreach as the distance of the surface increases from 25 to 50 cm. However, it is again uncertain whether these results are best interpreted in terms of the perception of a surface's shape or in terms of independent estimates of the egocentric distances to different points on the surface.

The use of multiple cues to distance has recently been explored in a study of stabilizing eye movements (Schwartz & Miles, 1991). In order to maintain fixation on a target while the head moves from side to side, we must make compensatory eye movements in the opposite direction. The closer the target, the larger the required compensatory movements. These eye movements are

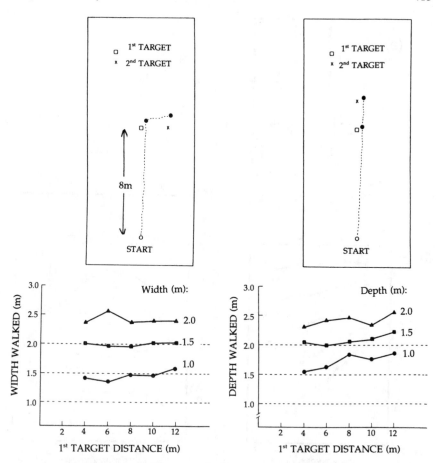

Figure 15.2. (a) Trajectories of subjects asked to walk through previously viewed depth and width intervals. (b) Average responses for different widths and depths viewed at different distances (Loomis et al., 1992).

driven primarily by signals from the vestibular system, so that the amplitude of the controlling signals needs to be modulated according to target distance. Schwartz and Miles established first that the amplitude of this translational vestibulo-ocular reflex scales proportionately with the inverse of the target distance, although often with an inadequate gain. Monkeys sat on a sled and fixated a light. To exclude any visual feedback, the fixation light was extinguished just before and during the time that the sled was moved to elicit the reflex. To investigate the cues employed in distance scaling, vergence and accommodative state were manipulated before the light was switched off. Measurements of oculomotor state and of the magnitude of the reflex revealed that both vergence

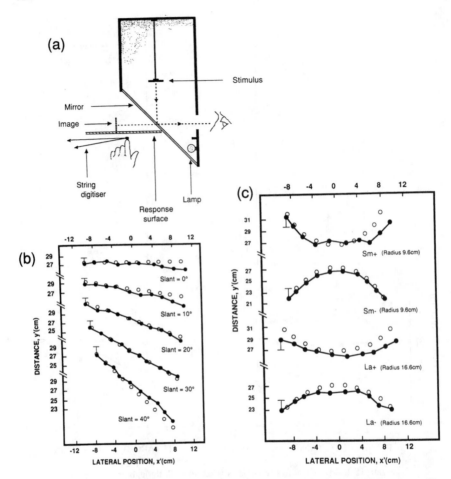

Figure 15.3. Reaching at a virtual surface without a view of the hand. (a) Apparatus. (b) Reaching at different points on slanted or curved surfaces. Open circles show the position on the surface; closed circles give the mean of the terminal position. Error bars show standard deviations (Cook and Griffiths, 1991).

and accommodation contribute to scaling; however, on their own, they do not completely account for the scaling found. Other, more elusive distance cues participate in modulating what one might have imagined to be a rather low-level, machine-like reflex, suggesting that these cues might be less "cognitive" (and perhaps therefore more tractable) than is often supposed.

In this section we have seen that estimates of distance, as revealed in the performance of motor tasks, can be impressively accurate over a long range (Fig. 15.1). This capacity raises many interesting and unanswered questions about the way in which long range pictorial and perspective cues are calibrated, how quantitative information might be derived from them and merged with estimates from oculomotor cues.

1.2 Perceptual measures of depth intervals

Analysis of the way in which distance signals influence eye, hand, or whole body movements is relatively straightforward, for it is obvious that something can be measured and, with current techniques, the measurements can be made precisely. On the other hand, psychologists have long grappled with the problem of measuring conscious percepts without reaching a consensus about the best way of doing it. Theoretical objections have been leveled against almost every psychophysical technique that has been employed to investigate depth constancy.

One common method is a matching task in which an observer adjusts a matching or probe target to generate a depth interval that is similar to one produced by some experimental configuration. Subjects might, for instance, be asked to match a perceived depth interval to an interval on a scale that is viewed at a fixed distance in a frontal plane. There is always some uncertainty about how the matching target itself is perceived, and consequently there is no guarantee of a linear relation between the perceived depth interval and the measurement scale.

A rather different method is for observers to generate their own internal standard and to compare stimuli with it (Heine, 1900, cited by von Kries, 1962/1910). For instance, Johnston (1991) asked subjects to compare a simulated three-dimensional shape with an internal standard. Subjects at different viewing distances are shown a simulated horizontal tube with one of a family of cross sections, varying from a flattened semiellipse, through a semicircle, to an elongated semiellipse. The subjects must state whether the tube has a flattened or an elongated elliptical cross section. They quickly develop a clear internal notion of a standard tube of circular cross section. The uncertainties here are as follows: Can the subject generate a perfect internal standard, as specified by the experimenter? (Any discrepancies will lead to apparent perceptual errors.) Is the internal standard indeed a fixed entity that does not vary systematically when different external stimuli are presented? How should distortions of perceived shape be partitioned among possible inaccuracies of perceived size and of perceived depth or a combination of both?

Such theoretical difficulties plague attempts to examine the precision of perceived depth from binocular disparity. But it is encouraging that in practice different groups using very different psychophysical techniques have arrived at quite similar conclusions. Thus, older estimates of the scaling of stereo-induced depth reviewed by Foley (1980, 1985) agree roughly with those from more recent studies in which the depth between simulated abutting flat surfaces was judged by a matching technique (Collett, Schwarz, & Sobel, 1991) or in which the shape of a hemi-cylinder was compared with an internal standard (Cumming, Johnston, & Parker, 1991; Johnston, 1991). The studies cited by Foley used point or line targets, which provided sparse stereo information, whereas the more recent experiments presented computer-generated simulations of densely textured surfaces. In all cases, the depth associated with a given horizontal disparity increased with viewing distance, but the scaling was inadequate to give full constancy (see below).

1.3 Strategies for comparing depths

Some experimental tasks can be performed using strategies that bypass the need for accurate distance scaling. Such "shortcuts" are interesting because they may account in part for the accurate depths reported under natural conditions. One example is a matching task in which observers compare the perceived depth between two stereoscopic stimuli presented at different distances. Good performance is possible without knowing the absolute distance of either stimulus. Depth comparisons can be made using only the ratio of the two viewing distances – a much easier measurement when the ground is textured, for instance, or when objects of the same physical size are present at the two viewing distances.

This can be turned to good account in a natural environment, where an observer can gauge the depth of an unknown object by comparing it with a familiar object at some other distance. In one careful study, Cook (1978) had subjects mark off a series of equal intervals on a richly textured horizontal surface that extended into the distance. The intervals varied from 25 to 175 cm. All the data from a single subject, irrespective of interval size, could be fitted by a function of the form $D' = kD^\beta$, where D' is judged depth and D actual depth (Figure 15.4). Here k is a dimensionless constant with a value that cannot be determined by matching tests (see the previous paragraph). The exponent, β, that fitted the data of a given individual remained constant over several weeks. For a group of 40 observers, β ranged between 0.776 and 1.29, with a mean value that, taken over all experiments, was slightly less than 1 (.947). The closeness of the overall results to the predictions of perfect depth scaling is likely to be a consequence of the nature of the comparison task in which subjects compare depths across a plane with a well-defined, regular surface texture.

Spuriously good depth constancy is found when observers report on a perceived depth interval by moving a probe in depth at the same viewing distance as the interval to be judged or by superimposing depth probes on a natural scene. In either case, the task can be solved by direct "disparity matching." This may explain why distance scaling of stereo depth stimuli generated on a display monitor seems to improve markedly if the monitor is viewed in a brightly lit

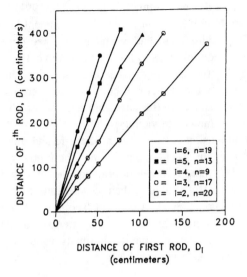

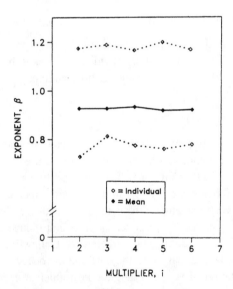

Figure 15.4. Perceived distance with many cues present. Top: Observers' mean judgments of equal-distance steps for five different step sizes. Observers instructed the experimenter where to position horizontal rods of irregular lengths so that the rods marked off a series of equidistant steps on a textured surface. Bottom: Mean and individual values of the exponent, β. See text. (Cook, 1978.)

and familiar lab rather than in a darkened tunnel (Collett et al., 1991). Indeed, the improvement in constancy bestowed by an enriched environment lasts for a short while after the viewing environment has been impoverished once more (Glennerster et al., 1996). One possible reason for the improvement is that the subject's estimate of the viewing (or scaling) distance is enhanced by the richer environment, with many perspective and pictorial cues. But another possibility is that disparities at the viewing distance of the screen are calibrated with respect to known depth intervals in the immediate vicinity.

There is a kind of creative tension between the naturalistic and more laboratory-based studies surveyed in this section. The former show how good we can be at performing tasks when there is ample information and an opportunity to employ a variety of strategies. But it is hard then to determine exactly how this high level of performance is achieved. Analytical laboratory experiments can more easily explore what cues are used and how they are exploited, but by restricting an observer's access to the information normally available in the world, the system may no longer perform at its best.

2. Distance cues involved in scaling depth

This section considers the individual distance cues that have been proposed to play a role in scaling depth. Most of the available evidence relates to binocular stereo disparities, but there are a few studies using motion parallax.

2.1 Convergence and accommodation

The vergence angle between the two eyes decreases with fixation distance so that a signal related to this angle could, in principle, supply a measure of viewing distance for scaling disparity. Whether this in fact occurs was fiercely debated for a remarkably long time. Wheatstone (1852), in his second paper on stereopsis, had already stated that vergence angle affects the perceived size, distance, and depth of an object but that changes in vergence angle do not induce a sense of motion in depth – exactly the modern view (Erkelens & Collewijn, 1985). The current consensus, due in large measure to the data and advocacy of Foley (1980, 1985), is that manipulation of vergence angle does influence depth perception, at least over distances of a few meters. A three-dimensional stimulus of fixed angular size and disparity will appear both larger and deeper as the inclination between the optic axes decreases. But these changes are smaller than the geometry of the situation predicts, even when vergence and accommodation are changed in a naturally consistent manner.

The effect of vergence on depth or on three-dimensional shape judgments can be quantified in terms of a "scaling distance." To compute this scaling distance, one assumes that the stereoscopic system scales disparities correctly

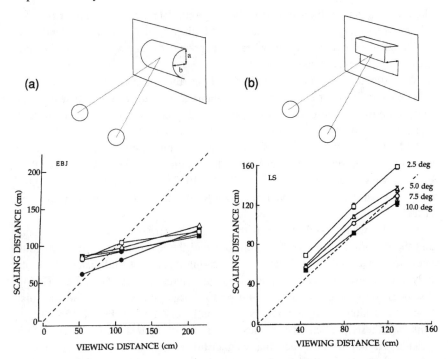

Figure 15.5. Scaling distance plotted against viewing distance for two different tasks. (a) Judging the shape of a simulated hemicylinder at different simulated viewing distances. Error bars show 95% confidence limits (Johnston, (1991). (b) Judging the simulated depth between two abutting planes for targets of different angular sizes viewed at different real distances within a light-tight tunnel with only the stereo images visible. Error bars represent standard errors of the mean. Note that gain is steeper with smaller targets than with larger targets (Collett et al., 1991).

according to the distance information it receives, but that it is not necessarily supplied with accurate estimates (von Helmholtz, 1910/1962). Given a depth value generated by a particular disparity, one can then ask: What distance estimate does the stereoscopic system use for its computations? Several studies find that the scaling distance defined in this way increases linearly with viewing distance, but that the slope of the function relating the two variables is significantly less than unity (Figure 15.5).

In their review of depth constancy, Ono and Comerford (1977) suggested that full stereoscopic depth constancy may occur for viewing distances up to about 200 cm but that it breaks down at greater distances. The evidence now available suggests that, with vergence as the major cue to distance, veridical stereo depth occurs at only one viewing distance. In other words, there is only one point at which scaling distance equals viewing distance (Foley, 1980, 1985). The mean value of this equality for the subjects studied by Johnston (1991) was about 80 cm, and in the study of Collett et al. (1991) the mean value was about 60 cm when images were 9.5° wide by 6° high. At smaller distances depth will be increasingly overestimated, whereas at greater distances depth will be progressively underestimated.

Why should this gain be less than 1? Does the vergence system really give a systematically incorrect estimate of distance? One suggestion is that the estimate supplied by the oculomotor system is correct but that other cues intrude and influence depth judgments, despite an experimenter's strenuous efforts to exclude them. In the absence of visual information to support it, a cue that is normally present in natural scenes may be assigned a default value rather then given a weight of zero. Gogel and Tietz (1973), for instance, describe how people, when they are deprived of all useful distance cues, judge targets to be at about 200 cm.

Consider what would happen if the weights accorded to the vergence signal and the remaining cues were to sum to 1 and the estimate from the remaining cues were independent of distance. The scaling distance would then be accurate only at the viewing distance signaled by the remaining cues. At shorter viewing distances the scaling distance would be too large, and at longer viewing distances the scaling distance would be too small, very much as Figure 15.5 shows. This hypothesis predicts that the scaling of stereo depth should be perfect with a richer array of distance cues, but whether this is so is unknown. Unfortunately, this is a difficult question to answer experimentally, with many methodological problems (see sections 1.3 and 2.3).

Another, less convincing possibility is that oculomotor adjustments are inadequate in the dimly lit environments in which many psychophysical experiments are performed and that errors tend systematically towards the 1.16-m average fixation distance that is seen in the dark (Owens & Leibowitz, 1976, 1980). This effect is unlikely to account for the general pattern of results. Equally inadequate vergence scaling is also found in experiments with bright stimuli that are 70° across (Bradshaw, Glennerster, & Rogers, 1996).

Lastly, it may be that whatever the available cues to distance, *stereo* depth is only perceived veridically at about 70 cm, a distance at which objects are often held and manipulated. This kind of explanation is emphasized by the neural network model of Pouget and Sejnowski (1994), in which signals related to scaling distance (either vergence or vertical disparity) are combined with binocular disparity signals. Although the network exhibits a form of depth constancy, no single element signals depth directly: The signals relating to depth are distributed across the network and are chiefly manifest in a distance-dependent modulation of the binocular disparity signals.

Pouget and Sejnowski (1994) show that if the depth-related signals are extracted from the elements of the network by means of a biased statistical estimator, then the visual system as a whole could have an improved sensitivity to *relative* depth. However, the penalty for using a biased estimator is that the absolute depth signaled by the network is not veridical. The effect of using a biased estimator is rather like that of inspecting a photograph with a lens that both magnifies and distorts parts of the image selectively. The magnification gives enhanced sensitivity to detail (relative depth), but the distortion means that the magnified image no longer accurately resembles the original.

Pouget and Sejnowski apply this line of reasoning to two distinct phenomena: (i) the distortions of depth scaling signals inferred from psychophysical measurements and (ii) the nonlinear relationship between perceived depth and binocular disparity found when targets are viewed at a fixed distance (Richards, 1971). Bearing in mind that the elements in the simulated network carry signals relating to both absolute depth and binocular disparity, the model predicts that there should be an overrepresentation of neurons wherever discrimination of either physical depth or binocular disparity is good. It is certainly plausible to suggest that the neurons sensitive to absolute depth should be clustered around the natural distance for grasping. Overall, the model captures the important point that human stereo vision is remarkably sensitive to relative depth, as well as giving an elegant explanation of why distance scaling should not have a gain of 1.

There are obvious limits to the range of viewing distances over which vergence can contribute usefully to the scaling of disparity. The vergence angle measured during fixation is quite noisy, fluctuating as much as 1°, especially when objects are nearby (Collewijn, Steinman, Erkelens, & Regan, 1991). A vergence angle of 1° corresponds to a viewing distance of about 3.5 m and, given this uncertainty, we might expect the relative weighting accorded to vergence to fall and for other cues to become increasingly dominant as this distance is approached. There is some evidence that this happens. Leibowitz and Moore (1966) find that the effect of convergence and of accommodation on perceived size becomes very small for simulated distances that are greater than 1 m.

Correspondingly, the importance of other distance cues increases. Image size is used as a distance cue and provides one example. Unfamiliar stimuli of different sizes viewed monocularly at a constant distance look closer when they are of larger angular size (for a review, see Sedgwick, 1986). The same holds for binocularly viewed targets. In this case, the influence of image size on perceived distance, size, and stereoscopic depth increases with viewing distance over the range of 45 to 135 cm, suggesting that oculomotor cues are gradually supplanted by alternative ones (Collett et al., 1991).

Neural signals related to vergence angle have been recorded in a variety of sites in the primate brain (Gnadt & Mays, 1991; Judge & Cumming, 1986; Mays, 1984; Zhang, Mays, & Gamlin, 1992). However, it is unknown how vergence related signals influence visual neurons involved in disparity processing and whether neurons that are concerned with the appreciation of size or of structure from motion are modulated by changes in vergence state.

A related psychophysical question is whether vergence scales the perception of size or of monocularly perceived depth intervals. Vergence angle is well known to influence the perceived size of a target of constant angular size (Heineman, Tulving, & Nachmias, 1959; McKee & Smallman, this volume), although, as with stereo depth, scaling through vergence is inadequate for full constancy (Collett et al., 1991; Cumming et al 1991). To test whether depth generated through motion parallax is scaled by vergence, Rivest, Ono, and Saida (1989) simulated a corrugated surface by generating the appropriate relative motion across a field of random dots in synchrony with an observer's lateral head motion (Rogers & Graham, 1979). Polarization filters over each eye and over the display ensured that only one eye saw the surface. Convergence was changed by altering the separation of two fixation points, one viewed by each eye. Vergence angle did not influence the perceived depth of the corrugations. One critical complication with this experiment is that there were many additional monocular cues to the distance of the surface. As a result, the binocularly fused fixation point and the monocularly viewed sinusoidal surface may not necessarily have appeared in the same depth plane.

2.2 Binocular vertical disparities

Binocular disparity can be conceived as a vector quantity that specifies the spatial transformation between the images in the left and right eyes (e.g., Figure 15.6). This vector can easily be decomposed into horizontal and vertical components. This decomposition is more than a mathematical convenience, for the two components play rather different roles in stereo vision (Mayhew & Longuet-Higgins, 1982; Porrill Mayhew, & Frisby, 1987). The horizontal component carries primarily information about local depth, whereas the vertical component depends largely on viewing geometry and not on the distance in object space between a feature and the fixation plane. Mayhew and Longuet-Higgins (1982) proved that, in principle, eye position could be recovered from the pattern of vertical disparities and that, consequently, this purely visual information could supply a scaling factor for horizontal disparities equivalent to the signal that can be derived from a motor estimate of vergence angle. The spatial array of vertical disparities in the visual field has a value of zero in the vertical and horizontal meridians (Figure 15.6). Away from the horizontal meridian, the viewing distance is related to the gradient of the vertical disparities. It would be feasible to compute a calibration signal for conventional horizontal disparities from this gradient alone; extraretinal information would not be required.

In reality, the human visual system seems not to exploit vertical disparities in exactly this way. One can simulate the changes in vertical disparity that occur when an object is viewed at different distances while holding horizontal disparities constant. Such manipulations have little or no effect on the perceived

(a)

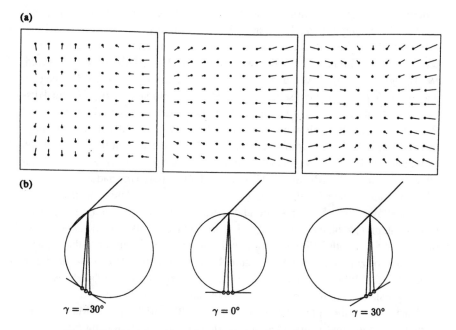

(b)

$\gamma = -30°$ $\gamma = 0°$ $\gamma = 30°$

Figure 15.6. (a) A two-dimensional depiction of the disparity field that arises when an observer views the center of a slanted planar surface with different angles of gaze. Each vector represents the left (dot) and right (tip) image positions of some point on the surface. Note that the magnitude of the horizontal component of the disparities varies with the angle of gaze and the vertical disparities are zero along the horizontal meridian. The vertical disparities are also zero in the vertical meridian when the gaze angle is zero and the slope of the vertical disparity field as a function of horizontal position is linked to the absolute distance of the surface from the observer. The first relationship can be exploited to recover gaze angle, and the second can be used to recover vergence angle. Recent psychophysical evidence suggests that the first but not the second of these relationships is exploited by the human visual system. (b) Cross section of viewing geometry used to generate disparity fields. Drawing shows left, right, and cyclopean eyes, as well as the Vieth–Müller circle. The sloping line at the top indicates a planar surface. Fixation distance is 50 cm, interocular distance is 6.5 cm, and the planar surface is slanted at 45° around a vertical axis relative to the cyclopean visual axis (Gårding et al., 1995).

depth of simulated three-dimensional shapes or on the perceived depth between two surfaces using images that are 10° to 25° across (Cumming et al., 1991; Rogers & Bradshaw, 1993; Sobel & Collett, 1991). When images are much larger (about 70° across), the same manipulation of vertical disparity does have a small but significant influence on perceived depth (Rogers & Bradshaw 1993). But the magnitude of this effect falls far short of what one would expect on geometric grounds. These psychophysical observations indicate that the vertical component of the disparity field is not strongly involved in depth scaling of binocular disparity, either on its own or in supplementing the information from oculomotor cues. With 70° displays, Bradshaw et al. (1996) found that the percentage constancy for vertical disparity alone, or vergence alone, or the two combined was about 15%, 19%, and 37%, respectively.

Nonetheless, the vertical component does play an important role in stereoscopic vision (Gillam, Chambers, & Lawergren, 1988; Gillam & Lawergren, 1983). Ogle (1950) discovered this long ago by magnifying vertically the image in one eye. One perceptual consequence of adding this global pattern of vertical disparities is to make a fronto-parallel plane appear slanted. Similarly, Rogers and Bradshaw (1995) have shown that vertical disparity powerfully influences judgments of the flatness of a simulated fronto-parallel plane, a point first made by von Helmholtz (1910/1962). Vertical disparities across the plane were adjusted to simulate different viewing distances. This manipulation altered the pattern of horizontal disparities needed for the plane to appear flat. At simulated far distances, a much shallower gradient of horizontal disparities was required for a surface to appear flat than was the case at simulated near distances. This is as the geometry of the situation demands. With vergence held constant, the magnitude of the required change in horizontal disparities to ensure flatness was about 60% of that predicted geometrically. When vergence and vertical disparity both simulated the same viewing distance, the required changes were exactly as predicted.

What then is the role of vertical disparity? The proposal by Mayhew and Longuet-Higgins that it provides information about global viewing geometry is supported by the finding that vertical disparities must be manipulated over large areas to induce significant perceptual effects. Gårding, Porrill, Mayhew, and Frisby (1995) made a similar point in a slightly different way. Horizontal disparities have, of course, a local effect: If a small patch within a surface is given a different set of *horizontal* disparities from its surroundings, the patch will be seen to stick out or to recede. But changes to the *vertical* disparities within a local patch have no effect on the depth of the patch relative to the surrounding surface. (In more complex scenes, vertical image differences may have a more local role. Anderson [1994] has recently pointed out that they are created when one object occludes another and can help indicate occlusion boundaries.)

Gårding et al. (1995) account for these various results within an appealing theoretical framework. They suggest that the stereo system computes the relative rather than the absolute depth within a scene; that is, depth order, collinearity, and coplanarity are recovered from the binocular disparity field, but metric depth (depth constancy) is not. Gårding et al. emphasize that horizontal disparities alone cannot even specify relative depth because the relation between horizontal disparity and relative depth varies with viewing angle (Figure 15.6). They show that the vertical component of the disparity field could be used to correct for changes in viewing angle and so normalize the relation between disparity and relative depth. The same normalizing process will also account for the effect of vertical disparities on the flatness of a fronto-parallel plane and lead to a small amount of depth scaling.

2.3 Retinal elevation and other perspective cues

For an observer looking at a flat object on a horizontal ground surface, the object seems closer when it is lower in the visual field. Observers exploit this geometry and judge point sources of light to be more distant when they are higher in the visual field. These effects are strongest when the lights are seen on a featured ground plane (Philbeck & Loomis, in press; Sedgwick, 1986). The apparent size of stimuli also increases with height in the visual field (Sedgwick, 1986; Warren & Whang, 1987). So far, it is unknown whether this distance cue influences the scaling of stereoscopic depth.

O'Leary and Wallach (1980) performed a simple experiment to test whether perspective cues might help to scale perceived depth. Subjects judged the slant of the plane between two vertical metal rods that were separated horizontally and in depth. The perceived distance of the rods was manipulated by equipping subjects with spectacles fitted with lenses and prisms to induce compatible changes in vergence and accommodation. This manipulation distorted estimates of slant, but the distortion was less marked when the rods were viewed on a table with a checkered cloth than when they were seen in isolation. O'Leary and Wallach supposed that the strong perspective of the checkered cloth reduced the influence of oculomotor cues. But it is unclear whether the checkered surface exerted its effect through distance scaling or whether it acted more locally by an immediate influence of the square pattern below the rods on the slant of the plane between them. More recent investigations suggest that texture has only a weak effect on the distance scaling of stereo depth (Frisby et al., 1995).

2.4 Conclusions

There is clear evidence for the contribution of nonvisual cues, such as vergence angle, to distance scaling. Nonetheless, the size of the contribution, as measured in the laboratory, falls well below that required for full depth constancy. A number of other cues, both visual and nonvisual, could contribute to the scaling signal in natural viewing conditions, but hard evidence is scant. The theoretical possibility that the binocular stereo system achieves depth constancy solely from the pattern of vertical and horizontal disparities does not seem to be realized. Indeed, it is still uncertain whether there exists a range of viewing distances over which *stereo* depth is properly scaled by distance cues. Full depth constancy can be found at close range in natural rich environments, but it is difficult to establish unequivocally that this is achieved through distance scaling alone without the aid of some other mechanism.

3. Combining depth cues

In previous sections, we have considered some of the problems of deriving accurate shape or depth information from single cues, and we have raised the possibility that some of these difficulties can be overcome by combining information from several cues. Here we discuss cue combination more fully. Psychophysical evidence points toward two rather separate interactions between depth cues: one in which information from different cues is simply pooled in order to improve the precision of an overall depth estimate and another in which qualitatively different kinds of information are combined to overcome the ambiguities or to supply information that is missing when percepts are based on a single cue (Bülthoff & Mallot, 1988; Clark & Yuille, 1990; Maloney & Landy, 1989). For example, the static occlusion of one surface by another can only reveal the ordering of these surfaces (which surface lies in front of which), whereas motion parallax tells how depth varies across a surface, but often with intaglio-relief ambiguity. Braunstein, Anderson, and Riefer (1982) showed that occlusion disambiguates the parallax information and that together the two cues yield an accurate and stable impression of three-dimensional shape.

Over the past 10 years, research on cue combination (sometimes called *data fusion*) has been influenced by two related strands of research, one conceptual and one experimental. Marr (1976) introduced the engineering principle of modular design to the study of visual information processing. At around the same time, physiologists started to explore the properties of neurons in various extrastriate visual areas, finding that some of these properties appeared to map nicely onto specific subtasks (a view put forward most strongly by Zeki, 1993). Both ideas encouraged psychophysicists to think in terms of a set of separate visual modules, each responsible for an operation such as "depth from motion," "depth from stereo," or "depth from texture."

More recently, attempts have been made to discover the ways in which these hypothetical modules might communicate with each other, so that, for instance, a module devoted to one depth cue could provide another module with missing information that is necessary to complete its computation of a depth estimate. Although it has been possible to show empirically that ambiguities or uncertainties can be reduced by supplying extra information, it is hugely difficult, on the basis of psychophysical experiments, to reach unassailable conclusions about exactly how modular the system is and where in the stream of processing any interactions might occur. Direct physiological evidence can sometimes give more insight. For instance, a powerful demonstration of the functional interaction of motion information and stereo is the discovery (Roy, Komatsu, & Wurtz, 1992; Roy & Wurtz, 1990) that some neurons in area MST of the medial temporal lobe respond best to motion in one horizontal direction when binocular stereo disparities are crossed and to motion in the opposite direction when disparities are uncrossed.

Nonetheless, the idea of separate modules has been an important conceptual tool for interpreting a number of recent psychophysical experiments. The next two sections discuss the two forms of interaction just identified. In the first case, each module is thought to contribute a depth signal, and the interaction between depth cues is simply a weighted mixture of the signal emerging from each module. In the second case, the interaction is more complex. For example, information from one module may calibrate the output of another module or may provide information that is essential for the module to generate an unambiguous estimate of depth.

3.1 Weighted averaging (linear combination)

Conceptually, the simplest form of interaction is that the depth signaled by each cue contributes to a statistical estimate. The depth value used by the visual system is then a weighted average of the depths signaled by each independent depth module, with the weights selected according to the statistical reliability of the cues involved. This is a useful strategy for increasing the precision of perceived depth, provided that each module does give a statistically independent estimate of the depth of the scene and that local patches of the scene can be described as possessing a single depth value.

However, some of the assumptions made in this scheme are not always valid. The pooling of several local depth signals to give a single estimate of depth is an inappropriate strategy for objects such as natural vegetation viewed close up, where stereo may resolve differences that are invisible to texture processing. The assumption of independence is also sometimes questionable, as noise early in the visual pathway may be distributed equally in signals to several modules.

Nonetheless, linear pooling of depth information provides a reasonable description of human performance for some combinations of cues (Dosher, Sperling, & Wurst, 1986). Bülthoff and Mallot (1988), for instance, explored the human perception of three-dimensional shapes depicted with stereo, texture, and shading cues. The shape of the surface was gauged from the setting of a local depth probe. The addition and removal of cues caused changes in perceived shape that can be described by a linear model (provided that the vetoing of one cue by another is understood to be the allocation of a weight of zero to the vetoed cue). Linearity can be tested more rigorously if the depth signaled by each cue can be varied quantitatively and independently. Johnston, Cumming, and Parker (1993) used conditions in which this was feasible and found that perception of the depth signaled by combinations of texture and binocular disparity could be fitted precisely by a simple additive model.

The linear combination of binocular disparity and texture is relatively straightforward if, as is often supposed, both cues supply information directly about the gradient of depth across a surface. More elaborate processing is needed when two cues deliver depth information in different formats, one supplying absolute depth and the other the gradient of depth, for example. A linear model need not be abandoned in such cases, but different procedures will be needed for pooling information, and there will also be changes in the predictions of linear statistical estimators.

One interesting question about linear pooling is how the visual system assigns weighting factors to individual depth cues. If pooling is conducted in order to optimize an overall estimate, then the weights are likely to be determined by the quality (statistical reliability, precision) of the information that is available from each cue. Such problems have been explored in machine vision (Clark & Yuille, 1990) but have been little treated in the human literature (but see Blake, Bülthoff, & Sheinberg, 1993).

It is already clear that weights attached to different cues are not fixed but are situationally dependent. Their values may vary with the particular set of depth cues that are available. Stereo is presumably downgraded when one eye is closed, whereas depth from motion may be given a low weighting in a stationary scene with a stationary observer. There is also the problem of dealing with large discrepancies between cues when simple averaging is not the best strategy. One possibility is to discard outlying estimates or those known to come from less reliable sources. For instance, Bülthoff and Mallot (1988) found that shading on its own specified the curvature of a surface rather weakly, but in the presence of conflicting stereo information, shading ceased entirely to influence perceived shape. In their terminology, it was vetoed or, in other words, assigned a weight of zero. Norman and Todd (1995) presented displays with two cues that provided conflicting information. Stereo specified a surface with horizontal corrugations and motion vertical corrugations or vice versa. Horizontal corrugations were seen and vertical corrugations were suppressed over a wide range of amplitudes, whether the horizontal corrugations were signaled by motion or by stereo.

Weights also change with viewing distance. Johnston et al. (1993) explored the relative weighting of stereo and texture cues at two different viewing distances. At the nearer distance, texture was assigned a small weight. But at the farther distance, where the same depth induces smaller disparities that are more prone to noise, human observers decreased the weight given to stereo in relation to that given to texture. For a similar reason, the weighting accorded to vergence drops with viewing distance (see section 2.1). However, it is not yet clear whether such weight changes should be considered in terms of active adjustments to a gain ''knob'' controlling a module's output signal or whether the small amplitude of the stereo signal at large viewing distances automatically reduces its significance relative to strong signals from other sources. For instance, when shape has to be extracted from motion and texture cues, a smaller weight was accorded to motion when the reliability of motion was reduced (Young, Landy, & Maloney, 1993).

The derivation of appropriate values for weighting factors is essentially a problem of perceptual learning, and it might be fruitful to examine interactions between cues from this point of view. For example, it would be good to know how accurately human observers can monitor the longer-term nature of the statistics of the perceptual input and whether they are prepared to reduce the weighting factors of cues that become unreliable (see, e.g., Morgan, 1992).

Under some conditions, perceptual learning does more than change weights. When an animal becomes accustomed to a particular situation, entirely new distance cues may be brought into play. An excellent example is a study on gerbils (Goodale et al., 1990) that were trained to jump across a gap to pick up sunflower seeds placed on a platform situated at a variable distance from them. The animals adjusted the size of their leaps to match the width of the gap. Initially, distance was gauged through motion parallax: The gerbils bobbed their heads up and down before jumping, and the amount of head bobbing increased with the gap's width. When the animals had become familiar with the platform, head bobbing decreased and the apparent size of the platform became an index of its distance. This was demonstrated by introducing probe trials with platforms of different sizes. A narrower platform caused the gerbil to increase the distance it jumped, whereas a wider platform elicited shorter jumps.

3.2 Cooperation and supplementation

More interesting interactions between depth cues occur when one cue supplies depth or distance information that cannot be obtained from another. This will often happen when the two cues deliver different forms of geometric information. The distinct contributions of binocular disparity and motion parallax to the perception of three-dimensional shape provide a telling example of the complex interactions that can occur. As discussed in sections 3.1 and 3.2, shape from the binocular disparity field is only perceived veridically if disparities are properly scaled by an accurate measure of viewing distance, whereas shape derived from image motion is not subject to distortions from inaccurate scaling but may suffer from intaglio-relief ambiguity.

Johnston, Cummings, and Landy (1994) examined the interactions of stereo and motion in the three-dimensional shape judgment task described earlier, in which observers are asked to judge whether the depth of a cylindrical tube of elliptical cross section is equal to its half-height. They first confirmed that shape is correctly judged at both near and far viewing distances from motion cues alone. With stereo alone at a 2-m viewing distance, a correctly simulated cylinder appeared noticeably flattened; its cross section needed to be elongated in depth to be seen as circular (cf. Johnston, 1991). However, when stereo and motion information were both available, observers judged the shape of the cylinder veridically. This result might suggest that stereo information is simply vetoed. However, this is not the case (Figure 15.7). For when incongruent stereo and parallax signals were provided, it emerged that the depth/height ratio signaled by stereo influenced the depth/height ratio that had to be signaled by motion in order for the tube to appear cylindrical. Had stereo been vetoed, the plots would have been flat. Instead, the two cues can be seen to be weighted roughly equally. The important implication of this result is that inaccuracies of three-dimensional shape due to stereo are in some way corrected by congruent motion information (see also Tittle & Braunstein, 1993) and that this pooling is a non-linear interaction.

Additional evidence for what have been called *strong* interactions between motion and stereo come from experiments with two-frame apparent motion. When motion information is limited to two *perspective* views of a rigid object presented in alternate frames, shape can be recovered in principle, provided that the visual system can use very fine-grained differences in the motion field. In practice, the system is likely to be too noisy for this to be feasible (Ullman, 1979). Richards (1985) pointed out that shape could be extracted more easily from two views if motion parallax and binocular disparity were available simultaneously. Johnston et al. (1994) explored this situation psychophysically. When the cylinder was displayed with two-frame apparent motion at different viewing distances, human observers could not correctly form a judgment of the three-dimensional shape of the cylinder. The same happened with stereo alone. But when binocular stereo was added to two-frame motion, shape was accurately recovered. Interaction between motion and stereo can thus ensure veridical shape perception without any need for distance scaling.

Supplementation of a different kind occurs when one set of cues provides coarse distance information and sets the operating point of another high-resolution system with a more limited range. For instance, vergence eye movements allow the high-resolution disparity system, which can measure only a few degrees of disparity, to be placed at selected points within a scene. Frogs, without the ability to converge their eyes, may use retinal elevation for a similar purpose. These animals estimate roughly the distance of prey on the ground from the prey's retinal elevation. Because the ground is often bumpy and frogs do not have a veridical knowledge of eye height, elevation cannot give precise distance information. Under normal circumstances, the estimate from elevation is fine-tuned by other distance cues, most probably stereo and accommodation that, as a consequence, need only work over a limited range extending on either side of the assumed ground plane (Collett & Udin, 1988).

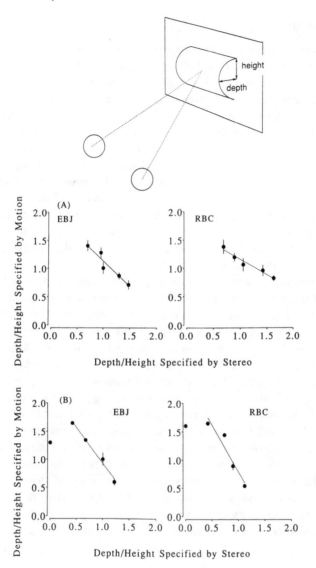

Figure 15.7. Data showing that both stereo and motion contribute to the perceived shape of a simulated hemicylinder when depth is simulated by congruent or incongruent stereo and motion. Data points give the combination of stereo and motion needed for the cross section of the hemicylinder to appear circular, that is, for apparent depth to equal apparent height. Stereo and motion are specified in terms of the ratio of simulated depth to height. (A) Viewing distance 200 cm. (B) Viewing distance 50 cm (Johnston et al., 1994).

3.3 Disambiguation

Another form of interaction between cues occurs when one cue supplies information that disambiguates another (Bülthoff & Mallot, 1988). The most familiar examples come from motion parallax, where the percept induced by motion on its own is often ambiguous. If relative motion specifies a sinusoidal surface, like a rigid sheet of corrugated iron that is rocking backward and forward, then the phase of the corrugations in depth is uncertain and periodically flips through 180°, so that peaks become troughs and vice versa. The true depth relationships can be specified by a variety of additional information. The bounding contour of the shape has a strong influence in resolving ambiguities. If the sinusoidal sheet is viewed on a computer screen through an occluding window that hides the sinusoidal contours at the edge of the sheet, then the sign of the depth from motion is much more uncertain than if observers are allowed to see the motion transformations of the contours at the edge of the sinusoidal sheet (Parker, Cummings, Johnston, & Hurlbert, 1994).

However, the single cue that most powerfully eliminates perceptual ambiguity in patterns of this kind is binocular stereo. For instance, a very small disparity difference between peaks and troughs is enough to determine convex/concave judgments and so resolve the whole figure (Rogers & Collett, 1989). One way of characterizing the interaction between stereo and motion, considered in the last two sections, is to say that the motion information in the display is compatible with a single shape, which, depending on absolute size, may be feasibly placed at a range of different viewing distances and may suffer a intaglio-relief ambiguity. On the other hand, stereo is consistent with a family of objects, whose exact shape will depend on the interpretation of stereo in combination with a measure of viewing distance. The motion and stereo are conjointly compatible with one shape and viewing distance, possibly providing complete depth constancy without recourse to visuomotor cues. This, however, somewhat overstates the case as it stands at present. Although it is now clear that the joint operation of these cues is enough to give shape constancy, it remains to be seen whether they also yield metrically accurate size and depth constancy.

References

Anderson, B. L. (1994). The role of partial occlusion in stereopsis. *Nature, 367*, 365–367.

Blake, A., Bülthoff, H. H., & Sheinberg, D. (1993). Shape from texture: Ideal observers and human psychophysics. *Vision Research*, 33(12), 1723–1737.

Bradshaw, M. F., Glennerster, A., & Rogers. B. J. (1996). The effect of display size on disparity scaling from differential perspective and vergence cues. *Vision Research 36*, 1255–1264.

Braunstein, M. L. (1976). *Depth perception through motion*. New York: Academic Press.

Braunstein, M. L., Andersen, G. J., & Riefer, D. M. (1982). The use of occlusion to resolve ambiguity in parallel projections. *Perception & Psychophysics, 31*, 261–2567.

Bülthoff, H. H., & Mallot, H. A. (1988). Integration of depth modules: Stereo and shading. *Journal of the Optical Society of America A, 5*(10), 1749–1758.

Clark, J. J., & Yuille, A. L. (1990). *Data fusion for sensory information processing.* Boston: Kluwer.

Collett, T. S., Schwarz, U., & Sobel, E. C. (1991). The interaction of oculomotor cues and stimulus size in stereoscopic depth constancy. *Perception, 20,* 733–754.

Collett, T. S., & Udin, S. B. (1988). Frogs use retinal elevation as a cue to distance. *Journal of Comparative Physiology A, 163,* 677–683.

Collewijn, H., Steinman, R. M, Erkelens, C. J., & Regan, D. (1991). Binocular fusion, stereopsis and stereoacuity with a moving head. In D. Regan (Ed.), *Binocular vision,* Volume 9, *Vision and visual dysfunction* (pp. 96–111). London: Macmillan.

Cook, M. (1978). The judgement of distance on a plane surface. *Perception & Psychophysiology, 23,* 85–90.

Cook, M., & Griffiths, K. (1991). Representation of spatial structure in reaching to a visual target. *Journal of Experimental Psychology: Human Perception and Performance 17,* 1041–1056.

Cumming, B. G., Johnston, E. B., & Parker, A. J. (1991). Vertical disparities and the perception of three-dimensional shape. *Nature, 349*(6308), 411–413.

Dosher, B. A., Sperling, G., & Wurst, S. A. (1986). Tradeoffs between stereopsis and proximity luminance covariance as determinants of perceived 3-D structure. *Vision Research, 26*(6), 973–990.

Erkelens, C. J., & Collewijn, H. (1985). Motion perception during dichoptic viewing of moving random-dot stereograms. *Vision Research, 25,* 583–588.

Foley, J. M. (1980) Binocular distance perception. *Psychology Reviews, 87,* 411–434.

Foley, J. M. (1985) Binocular distance perception:egocentric tasks. *Journal of Experimental Psychology: Human Perception and Performance, 11,* 133–149.

Frisby, J. P, Buckley, D., Wishart, K. A., Porrill, J., G°arding, J., & Mayhew, J. E. W. (1995). Interaction of stereo and texture cues in the perception of three-dimensional steps. *Vision Research, 35,* 1463–1472

Gårding, J., Porrill, J., Mayhew, J. E. W., & Frisby, J. P. (1995). Stereopsis, vertical disparity and relief transformations. *Vision Research, 35,* 703–722.

Gillam, B., Chambers, D., & Lawergren, B. (1988). The role of vertical disparity in the scaling of stereoscopic depth perception: An empirical and theoretical study. *Perception & Psychophysics, 44,* 473–483.

Gillam, B., & Lawergren, B. (1983) The induced effect, vertical disparity and stereoscopic theory. *Perception & Psychophysics, 34,* 121–130.

Glennerster, A., Rogers, B. J., & Bradshaw, M. F. (1996). Stereoscopic depth constancy depends on the subject's task. *Vision Research, 36,* 3441–3456.

Gnadt, J. W., & Mays, L. E. (1991). Depth tuning in area LIP by disparity and accommodative cues. *Society for Neuroscience Abstracts, 17,* 1113.

Gogel, W. C., & Tietz, J. D. (1973). Absolute motion parallax and the specific distance tendency. *Perception & Psychophysics, 13,* 284–292.

Goodale, M. A., Ellard, C. G., & Booth, L. (1990). The role of image size and retinal motion in the computation of absolute distance by the mongolian gerbil (*Meriones unguiculatus*). *Vision Research, 30,* 399–413.

Heinemann, E. G., Tulving, E., & Nachmias, J. (1959). The effect of oculomotor adjustment on apparent size. *American Journal of Psychology, 72,* 32–45.

von Helmholtz, H. (1910/1962). *Handbook of physiological optics,* Volume III (Trans. 1925 by J. P. C. Southall). New York: Dover.

Johnston, E. B. (1991). Systematic distortions of shape from stereopsis. *Vision Research, 31,* 1351–1360.

Johnson, E. B., Cumming, B. G., & Landy, M. S. (1994). Integration of stereopsis and motion shape cues. *Vision Research, 34*(17), 2259–2276.

Johnston, E. B., Cumming, B. G., & Parker, A. J. (1993). Integration of depth modules: Stereopsis and texture. *Vision Research, 33,* 813–826.

Judge, S. J., & Cumming, B. G. (1986). Neurons in the monkey mid-brain with activity related to vergence eye movement and accommodation. *Journal of Neurophysiology, 55,* 915–930.

von Kries, C. (1910/1962). Notes. In H. von Helmholtz, *Handbook of physiological Optics,* Volume III (Trans. 1925 by J. P. C. Southall). New York: Dover.

Leibowitz, H., & Moore, D. (1966). Role of changes in accommodation and vergence in the perception of size. *Journal of the Optical Society of America, 56,* 1120–1123.

Longuet-Higgins, H. C., & Prazdny, K. (1981). The interpretation of moving retinal images. *Proceedings of the Royal Society of London B, 208,* 385–397.

Loomis, J. M., Da Silva, J. A., Fujita, N., & Fukusima, S. S. (1992). Visual space perception and visually directed action. *Journal of Experimental Psychology: Human Perception and Performance, 18,* 906–921.

Loomis, J. M., Da Silva, J., Philbeck, J. W., & Fukusima, S. S. (1996). Visual perception of location and distance. *Current Directions in Psychological Science, 5,* 72–77.

Maloney, L. T., and Landy, M. S. (1989). A statistical framework for robust fusion of depth information. In W. A. Pearlman (Ed.), *Visual communications and image processing IV: Proceedings of the SPIE, 1199,* 1154–1163.

Marr, D. (1976). Early processing of visual information. *Philosophical Transactions of the Royal Society of London B, 275,* 483–519.

Marr, D. (1982) *Vision.* San Francisco: W. H. Freeman.

Mayhew, J. E. W., & Longuet-Higgins, H. C. (1982). A computational model of binocular depth perception. *Nature, 297,* 377–378.

Mays, L. E. (1984). Neural control of vergence eye-movements: Convergence and divergence neurons in midbrain. *Journal of Neurophysiology, 51,* 1091–1108.

Morgan, M. J. (1992). On the scaling of size judgments by angular cues. *Vision Research, 32,* 1433–1455.

Nakayama, K., & Shimojo, S. (1990). Da Vinci stereopsis: Depth and subjective occluding contours from unpaired image points. *Vision Research, 30,* 1811–1825.

Nakayama, K., & Shimojo, S. (1992). Experiencing and perceiving visual surfaces. *Science, 257,* 1357–1363.

Norman, J. F., & Todd, J. T. (1995). The perception of 3-D structure from contradictory patterns. *Perception & Psychophysics, 57,* 826–834.

Ogle, K. N. (1950). *Researches in binocular vision.* Philadelphia: W. B. Saunders.

O'Leary, A., & Wallach, H. (1980). Familiar size and linear perspective as distance cues in stereoscopic depth constancy. *Perception & Psychophysics, 27,* 131–135.

Ono, H., & Comerford, J. (1977). Stereoscopic depth constancy. In W. Epstein, *Stability and constancy in visual perception: Mechanisms and processes* (pp. 17–39). New York: Wiley.

Owens, D. A., Leibowitz, H. W. (1976). Oculomotor adjustments in darkness and the specific distance tendency. *Perception & Psychophysics, 20,* 2–9.

Owens, D. A., & Leibowitz, H. W. (1980). Accommodation, convergence and distance perception in low illumination. *American Journal of Optometry and Physiological Optics, 57,* 540–550.

Parker, A. J., Cumming, B. G., Johnston, E. B., & Hurlbert, A. C. (1994). Multiple cues for three-dimensional shape. In M. Gazzaniga (Ed.), *The cognitive neurosciences: A handbook for the field* (pp. 376–395). Cambridge, MA: MIT Press.

Philbeck, J. W., & Loomis, J. M. (1997). A comparison of two indicators of perceived egocentric distance under full-cue and reduced-cue conditions. *Journal of Experimental Psychology: Human Perception and Performance, 23,* 72–85.

Porrill, J., Mayhew, J. E. W., & Frisby, J. P. (1987). Cyclotorsion, conformal invariance and induced effects in stereoscopic vision. In *Frontiers of visual science: Proceedings of the 1985 symposium* (pp. 90–108). Washington, DC: National Academy Press.

Pouget, A., & Sejnowski, T. J. (1994). A neural model of the cortical representation of egocentric distance. *Cerebral Cortex, 4,* 314–329.

Richards, W. (1971). Anomalous stereoscopic depth perception. *Journal of the Optical Society of America, 61*, 410–414.

Richards, W. (1985). Structure from stereo and motion. *Journal of the Optical Society of America A, 2*, 343–349.

Rivest, J., Ono, H., & Saida, S. (1989). The roles of convergence and apparent distance in depth constancy with motion parallax. *Perception & Psychophysics, 46*, 401–408.

Rogers, B. J., & Bradshaw, M. (1993). Vertical disparities, differential perspective and binocular stereopsis. *Nature, 361*, 253–255.

Rogers, B. J., & Bradshaw, M. F. (1995). Disparity scaling and the perception of frontoparallel surfaces. *Perception, 24*, 155–179.

Rogers, B. J., Collett, T. S. (1989). The appearances of surfaces specified by stereo and motion. *Quarterly Journal of Experimental Psychology, 41A*, 697–717.

Rogers, B. J., & Graham, M. E. (1979). Motion parallax as an independent cue for depth perception. *Perception,9*, 125–134.

Roy, J.-P., Komatsu, H., & Wurtz, R. H. (1992). Disparity sensitivity of neurons in monkey extrastiate area MST. *Journal of Neuroscience, 12*, 2478–2492.

Roy, J.-P., & Wurtz, R. H. (1990). The role of disparity-sensitive cortical neurons in signalling the direction of self motion. *Nature, 348*, 160–162.

Schwarz, U., & Miles, F. A. (1991). Ocular responses to translation and their dependence on viewing distance. 1. Motion of the observer. *Journal of Neurophysiology, 66*, 851–864.

Sedgwick, H. A. (1986). Space perception. In K. R. Boff, L. Kaufman, & J. P. Thomas (Eds.), *Handbook of perception and human performance*, Volume 1, *Sensory processes and perception*. New York: Wiley.

Shimojo, S., & Nakayama, K. (1990). Real world occlusion constraints and binocular rivalry. *Vision Research, 30*, 69–80.

Sobel, E. C. (1990). The locust's use of motion parallax to measure distance. *Journal of Comparative Physiology A, 177*, 579–588.

Sobel, E. C., & Collett, T. S. (1991). Does vertical disparity scale the perception of stereoscopic depth? *Proceedings of the Royal Society of London B, 244*, 87–90.

Thomson, J. A. (1983). Is continuous visual monitoring necessary in visually guided locomotion? *Journal of Experimental Psychology: Human Perception and Performance, 9*, 427–443.

Tittle, J. S., & Braunstein, M. L. (1993). Recovery of 3-D shape from binocular disparity and structure from motion. *Perception & Psychophysics, 54*, 157–169.

Ullman, S. (1979) The *interpretation of visual motion*. Cambridge, MA: MIT Press.

Wallach, H., & Zuckerman, C. (1962). The constancy of stereoscopic depth. *American Journal of Psychology, 76*, 404–412.

Warren, W. H., & Whang, S. (1987). Visual guidance of walking through apertures: Body scaled information for affordances. *Journal of Experimental Psychology: Human Perception and Performance, 13*, 371–383.

Wheatstone, C. (1852) Contributions to the physiology of vision – part the second. On some remarkable, and hitherto unobserved, phenomena of binocular vision (continued). *Philosophical Transactions of the Royal Society of London, 142*, 1–17.

Young, M. J., Landy, M. S., & Maloney, L. T. (1993). A perturbation analysis of depth perception from combinations of texture and motion cues. *Vision Research, 33*, 2685–2696.

Zeki, S. (1993) *A vision of the brain*. Oxford: Blackwell.

Zhang, Y., Mays, L. E., & Gamlin, P. D. R. (1992). Characteristics of near response cells projecting to the oculomotor nucleus. *Journal of Neurophysiology, 67*, 944–960.

16   The perception of dynamical constancies

Mary K. Kaiser

Perception of dynamics

The idea that one can actually perceive the dynamics of an event in which one is neither the agent nor the object is not obvious. After all, dynamics describe the motion of objects in relation to the forces acting on them. Forces require the definition of mass, and mass (as anyone can tell you) cannot be perceived directly. When Michotte presented his studies on the perception of causality (Michotte, 1947/1963), the common assumption was that perceived causality resulted from the observer's attributing causal relations to object motions, much as Heider and Simmel's (1944) films of moving geometric forms produced attributions of aggression and fear. In fact, whereas many of Michotte's stimuli were described in physically causal terms (e.g., ball A "launched" ball B), some evoked far more anthropomorphic descriptions (e.g., ball A "chased" ball B). Were observers actually "seeing" causal relations in Michotte's stimuli, or were they merely attributing causality based on some broad Humeian notions of temporal and spatial proximities of motion?

In fact, Michotte's stimuli provide a very poor test case for the idea that dynamics might be directly perceived. Although highly sophisticated when compared to most motion stimuli of the time (the work was conducted in the mid-1940s), Michotte's objects did not demonstrate veridical dynamics; collisions showed no damping, temporal lags could occur at the collision point, and the aperture/disk apparatus produced poor motion quality. It is little wonder that Michotte's observer engaged in animistic responses; virtually all the events he showed would require the forms to have an internal energy source.

Michotte's work was not well integrated into perceptual psychology at the time he first presented it. It remained somewhat of an intellectual curiosity, a fascinating Gestaltist demonstration, until researchers building on the event psychology of Gibson and Johansson revisited the question of perceiving dynamics. The ecological approach to visual perception, led in the United States by James J. Gibson (1950, 1966, 1979), and the visual event psychology movement in Europe, led by Gunnar Johansson (1950), both revitalized and redefined psychology's approach to higher-order motion perception. Rather than viewing motion as a complication of static form perception, both schools recognized and

436

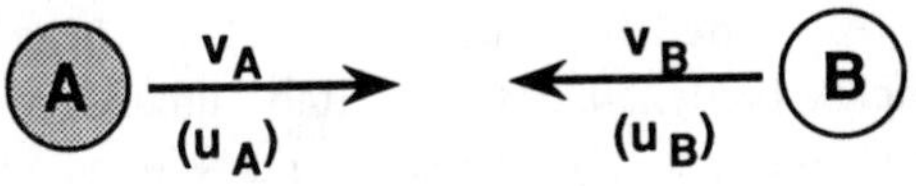

Relative weight: $$p = \frac{v_B - u_B}{(v_B - v_A) - (u_B - u_A)}, \quad q = 1 - p$$

Damping factor: $$e = \frac{v_A - v_B}{u_B - u_A}$$

Figure 16.1. KSD of a linear collision. Ball A and ball B approach with precollision velocities v_A and v_B, respectively. Their postcollision velocities are u_A and u_B. The relative mass of ball A is defined as p; the relative mass of ball B is q, where $p + q = 1$. The equations defining relative masses and the damping factor, e, of the collision are shown in the figure.

advanced the idea that humans are able to extract information from motion that is unavailable in the static stimuli. Furthermore, both hold that our perceptual system is designed for the extraction of motion from visual stimuli; much of our neural structure is tuned to specific motion parameters (e.g., speed and orientation). Motion is thus considered not as a complication, but as a fundamental. Motion information can uniquely specify object structure, spatial relationships of objects, and self-motion through the environment. Could motion also specify event dynamics?

The kinematic specification of dynamics view

One of Johansson's students, Sverker Runeson, proposed that (in theory) motion *could* specify dynamics. Runeson's dissertation (1977) was a formal demonstration that the motion equations of a simple linear equation (i.e., ball A and ball B approach and collide along a direct line) could be rearranged such that the relative weights of the balls and the damping factor of the collision were fully specified by equations involving only the pre- and postcollision velocities of the balls (Figure 16.1). If the human visual system were able to perceive these velocities veridically and combine them in the appropriate ratios, we could in fact directly perceive critical dynamic aspects of the collision. This was an extremely exciting concept. Causality need not be inferred; it could (in principle) be directly perceived.

As will be discussed in the section on empirical studies, initial investigations of Runeson's thesis were promising. Not only were observers able to make relative mass judgments when viewing collisions, they were also able to judge which of two boxes lifted by a human actor was heavier. This latter event involved a complex biodynamic system (the human body), yet observers appeared quite comfortable making a relative mass judgment. In fact, human observers seemed competent in making judgments concerning the dynamics of observed events in a number of contexts. This stood in marked contrast to findings emerging from cognitive psychologists' studies of people's naive beliefs about mechanics (Caramazza, McCloskey, & Green, 1981; McCloskey, Caramazza, & Green, 1980); the cognitive research suggested that well-educated individuals often gave erroneous responses to even trivial motion problems (e.g., predicting the path of a ball exiting a curved tube or the path of a bomb dropped from an airplane). People clearly seemed to possess a perception-based competence with event dynamics that did not depend on, nor generalize to, their representational understanding of the underlying mechanics.

However, the empirical studies also raised some issues that were problematic from the kinematic specification of dynamics (KSD) viewpoint. Of greatest concern was the fact that people still made some errors in dynamical judgments when viewing ongoing events. In fact, for certain classes of events, viewing the event did not aid dynamical judgments at all. Then too, there was the problem of defining the actual mapping between event dynamics and optical variables. Formal mappings had been derived for only the most simple events (e.g., two-body collisions, pendular motions). Researchers were claiming perceptual competence for event dynamics with only vague descriptions of the mappings among optical, kinematic, and dynamical parameters. Without an explicit statement of the KSD mapping, how could one empirically test whether observers were, in fact, utilizing the veridical visual information for their dynamic judgments?

The perceptual heuristics view

These critical issues became the principal arguments of the perceptual heuristics (PH) view. Researchers holding this view argue that the dynamics of most events are too complex to be directly penetrable to human observers. All but the simplest events require the integration of multiple dimensions of visual information. The human visual system cannot perform this integration, so instead it operates on individual dimensions. Driven by the salience of the dimension, or using some simple combinatory rule, observers' judgments are therefore heuristic in nature. Thus, judgments will be correct for large classes of events (in which the heuristic is valid) but will be based on simpler rules that utilize only a subclass of the information required by a proper KSD analysis (Gilden, 1991; Gilden & Proffitt, 1989; Kaiser, Proffitt, Whelan, & Hecht, 1992; Proffitt & Gilden, 1989; Proffitt, Kaiser, & Whelan, 1990).

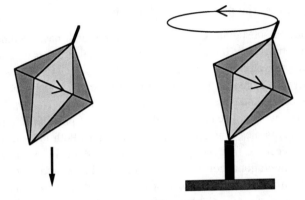

Figure 16.2. A spinning top in free fall (left) and on a pedestal (right). In free fall, the top's motion can be adequately described by particle dynamics. The top on the pedestal acts as a gyroscope, and an adequate motion description requires extended-body dynamics.

From the PH viewpoint, many classes of event dynamics are perceptually impenetrable. The classes of events whose dynamics are and are not perceptually penetrable map roughly onto the physical complexity distinction of particle and extended-body systems. Events that can be described in terms of the motions of objects considered as a single point are particle systems. An example of a particle system is a body in free fall. Events that require that the mass distribution of the object be included in the motion description are considered extended-body systems. This distinction can be appreciated if one considers the two tops shown in Figure 16.2. The top on the left is in free fall. Here the top's motion can be adequately described (and predicted) in terms of the displacement of its center of mass (a point-particle) over time. The speed at which the top rotates about its axis is irrelevant to the trajectory of its center of mass. The top on the right, however, must be considered as an extended-body system. Here the rotation about its axis creates gyroscopic forces that cause the top to precess. The extended-body dynamics results in object orientations that would be deemed unstable by a particle system analysis; the top pictured on the right would fall by such an analysis (and indeed would fall if not rotating). Our inability to appreciate the complexity of the extended-body system perceptually makes the gyroscope's motion appear magical and accounts for its enduring charm. This wonder persists, the PH position argues, despite the fact that the relevant dynamics of the system are fully instantiated in the kinematics of the events.

Although the KSD and PH views have significant theoretical differences, it is often difficult to disprove or support either model empirically (Hecht, 1996). Let us now examine the dynamical perception literature to better understand why definitive evidence is so hard to obtain.

Empirical research on the perception of dynamics

In the past decade, a substantial body of empirical research has examined the perception of dynamics. My discussion is limited to the visual perception literature, although a fair amount of the KSD-motivated research examines acoustic and haptic events (Jenkins, 1985; Solomon & Turvey, 1988) and a few studies deal with cross-modal sources of dynamic information (Warren, Kim, & Husney, 1987). The work I discuss covers three classes of phenomena: gravity, collisions, and biodynamics. The area of gravity concerns both motions caused by gravity (e.g., objects in free fall, pendulums) and systems in dynamic equilibrium reflecting gravitational constraints (e.g., balance beams and bridges). The work on collisions includes both the dynamics of two-body collisions and single bodies impacting on surfaces (i.e., bouncing). The biodynamic research focuses on visual appreciation of forces acting on or being exerted by animals performing purposeful actions (walking, climbing, etc.). Before discussing these three problem domains, it is useful to review the paradigms and methodologies common to all areas.

Methods of investigation

Research on the perception of dynamics can be classified fairly well on the basis of three factors: the experimental task, visual stimulus generation, and the nature of the required response. Differences on these three factors often reflect theoretical biases, and the impact these factors have on performance fuels the KSD–PH debate.

Experimental tasks consist of requiring an observer either to detect a dynamic anomaly or to make a dynamic judgment regarding a canonical event. The dynamic anomaly paradigm necessitates altering the natural dynamics of the event. Researchers seek to determine the degree or type of anomaly required for detection. The dynamic judgment paradigm assumes that people will be most adept at processing dynamical information when viewing canonical, undistorted events. Here the data are used to assess sensitivity to changes in a dynamic parameter. Both approaches measure sensitivity in a manner analogous to threshold research in other psychophysical domains. But the approaches differ in whether observers are required to detect distortions of natural dynamics or extract relevant dynamic parameters from natural events.

The manner by which the visual stimuli are generated is another important factor defining research paradigms. Some studies allow observers to view the actual physical system or use stimuli that consist of film or video recordings of actual events. Anomalies are introduced by surreptitious mechanisms (e.g., a pendulum is driven by a hidden weight) or via film/video editing (e.g., the preimpact motions of one collision are spliced to the postimpact motions of another). Whereas some perceptual artifacts (e.g., lack of binocular information) are introduced if film or video presentations are used, it is usually assumed that the dynamically relevant kinematics of the natural event are fully preserved. Alternately, visual stimuli can be computer generated. In this case, objects move according to the motion equations specified by the experimenter. This allows the experimenter precise control over the motion parameters. Such control is critical if one is to determine whether altering kinematics affects dynamical judgments in predicted ways. Even for simple events, however, formal motion descriptions require simplification. For example, colliding balls and pendulums are considered to be point masses. These simplifying assumptions render the events computationally tenable, but the kinematics differ somewhat from those of natural events. The two methods of stimulus generation, then, trade off in terms of control of motion parameters and realism of event kinematics. It is not surprising that some researchers insist that they would never use computer-generated stimuli because they do not instantiate completely natural event kinematics, whereas other researchers insist that they would not use a stimulus that was not computer generated because it is impossible to determine precisely the stimulus parameters that impact observers' judgments. Most researchers, of course, utilize both types of stimuli.[1]

Finally, there are paradigmatic differences in how observers are asked to respond to the visual stimulus. In studies of adults' perception of dynamics, people can be asked either to make a passive judgment or to actually interact with the physical system and control some dynamic aspect of it. Researchers concerned with perception–action coupling contend that verbal judgment tasks can underestimate people's sensitivities; they argue that people are more likely to "pick up" the relevant dynamical information in an interactive context. Researchers utilizing verbal judgments counter that such paradigms are extremely useful for establishing whether or not basic sensitivities exist. Further, data from active control studies are difficult to analyze because control behavior can be influenced by a number of factors (e.g., task strategies, limits in motor precision) that are extraneous to the perception of dynamical information.

Both verbal judgment and active control paradigms have been used with children. Active control studies are rarely performed with infants (although, in a related domain, von Hofsten [1983] has performed reaching studies with pre-crawling babies). Because infants are (by definition) preverbal, nonverbal responses are collected in the passive judgment paradigm. Most common are the preferential looking (or habituation) measures. It is assumed that babies look longer at novel events. Thus, an event that is recognized as different from the one previously shown will elicit longer gazes (dishabituation). Similarly, an event that is novel by virtue of violating the babies' expectations (e.g., an object that should fall but doesn't) should elicit preferential looking. Occasionally, perceived novelty is also assessed by physiological indications of surprise (e.g., increased heart rate, pupil dilation). Generally, data from infants and young children are noisier, with many extraneous factors affecting subjects' responses.

These three paradigmatic factors have been fairly well crossed in research methodologies and can be fully crossed in principle. People can be asked to interact with systems whose dynamics are anomalous.[2] Actual physical systems can be tampered with to distort dynamics. And advances in computer graphics allow the real-time generation of realistic objects and motions for active control tasks. The choice of experimental task, stimulus generation, and subject response most often reflects theoretical biases and the capabilities (or limitations) of particular laboratories. However, these factors create important paradigmatic differences across studies, which complicates the task of integrating (or even reconciling) findings from various laboratories.

Perception of gravitational constraints

Gravitational acceleration is a constant in our terrestrial environment. Our actions seem so finely honed to the movement of objects in this gravitational field that people appear clumsy and comical in their initial encounters with altered gravitational environments such as the micro-gravity of orbit. To what extent, however, can people draw on this constraint when judging the structure and motion of objects? Do we recognize whether objects are adequately supported, whether they are in dynamic equilibrium, or whether they accelerate at the rate defined by gravity?

Support and balance.   Our perceptual appreciation of the need for structural support is fairly keen and, moreover, is present at a very early age in life. Infants as young as 3 months of age demonstrate systematic visual preferences for events in which a visible object loses all support yet does not fall (Needham, 1990). During the first year of life, infants show increasing sensitivity to subtle distinctions between adequately and inadequately supported structures (Baillargeon, 1990; Baillargeon & Hanko-Summers, 1990). Watching a young child play with blocks underscores the child's appreciation of required structural support (and his or her delight in removing such support).

But this competence does not appear to extend to a full appreciation of dynamic equilibrium. Roncato and Rumiati (1986) showed that adults were unable to distinguish stable from unstable orientations of an object about a pivot (Figure 16.3). People demonstrated several important misunderstandings. First, in cases of neutral equilibrium (e.g., a body suspended by its center of gravity [CG], as in the left portion of Figure 16.3), people often thought that the object needed to be symmetric about the vertical axis. Second, when the rod was suspended away from its CG (see the right portion of Figure 16.3), people often responded that equilibrium would occur when "arm" height was inversely proportional to

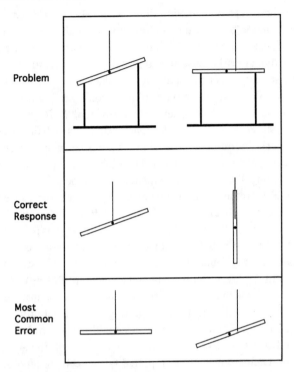

Figure 16.3. Two examples of balance problems from Roncato and Rumiati (1988). The top panel shows the problem presented to subjects. They were to predict the final, stable orientation of the bar if the support was removed. The middle panel shows the correct response. The bottom panel shows the most common erroneous response. In the problem presented on the left, the bar is suspended by a pivot at its center of gravity (CG – indicated by a dot). On the right, the pivot is displaced from the CG.

weight rather than when the CG was under the point of suspension. Unlike judging gravitational supports, people have difficulty judging when an object is stably balanced about a pivot.

Free and constrained falling. Objects can demonstrate gravitational acceleration in a number of motion contexts. Most simply, an unconstrained object can fall freely, accelerating due to gravitational forces. Or an object's motion can be subjected to constraints while exposed to gravitational force. Examples of constrained motion include pendulums and wheels rolling down incline planes. As previously explained, the object in free fall is a particle-motion system. The pendulum and rolling wheel are extended-body motion systems. As such, people may be sensitive to different aspects of these systems' dynamics.

At sea level, gravity causes a constant acceleration of 9.8 m/sec², but an object's air resistance creates counteracting drag forces. However, because drag forces increase as a function of the square of velocity, it usually plays a minimal role in the initial interval of free fall. This initial interval is of greatest concern to the perception of dynamics because it is unusual (in the terrestrial environment) to be able to see an object fall much longer than a second (4.9 meters) or so. In theory, gravitational acceleration of objects could serve as an absolute scalar for the visual scene (Watson, Banks, von Hofsten, & Royden, 1992). Also, Chapman (1968; see also Todd, 1981) suggested that a ball player can position himself properly by moving so as to null the visual image acceleration of the ball. But are people sensitive to whether objects fall with appropriate gravitational acceleration? The empirical evidence is equivocal.

The psychophysical literature suggests that observers are relatively insensitive to object motion acceleration (Calderone & Kaiser, 1989; Gottsdanker, Frick, & Lockard, 1961; Schmerler, 1976), and Shannon (1976) found that many college students hold the Aristotelian belief that objects fall at a constant velocity. But Johansson and Jansson (1967) found that subjects were able to adjust film speed to make jumping and diving events appear natural (although subjects might have been reacting to other biomechanical motion rates as well as, or instead of, to gravitational acceleration). Todd (1981), testing the tenability of the acceleration-nulling strategy, found that observers could not determine whether an object would land in front of or at their eye point based on image acceleration. But Babler and Dannemiller (1993) reported fairly accurate landing point judgments (which they attributed to the use of longer-duration stimuli and velocities more representative of actual ball-game events), and Michaels and Oudejans (1992) found catchers' position adjustments to be fairly consistent with an acceleration-nulling strategy. However, there are several proposed strategies for field-positioning which do not require the use of acceleration as a control variable (McBeath, Shaffer, & Kaiser, 1996; McLeod & Dienes, 1996). Further, recent studies indicate that people use average image speed, not acceleration per se, to judge size and distance (Hecht, Kaiser, & Banks, 1996).

Objects that are attached to a tether also move under gravitational acceleration. Although pendular motions are far more complex than free fall, certain systematic relations might be perceptually appreciated. The period of the pendulum's swing is a function of the square of the tether's length. The bob achieves greatest velocity at the nadir and minimal (zero) velocity at the apex. Pittenger examined whether observers could estimate the length of a pendulum from its motion (Pittenger, 1985) and recognize when the period had been surreptitiously altered (Pittenger, 1990). His studies on length estimation indicate that people generally appreciate that there is a monotonic relationship between tether length and period, but their estimation is more consistent with a linear mapping (rather than with the correct quadratic) between period and length. Observers could likewise recognize substantial deviations from natural periods

(Pittenger, 1990), but their response distributions indicated that pendulums with periods approximately 10% slower than veridical appeared most natural. These findings are consistent with those reported by Bozzi (1958), who asked people to adjust the speed of a pendulum such that the motion appeared natural; subjects tended to set the frequency lower than was correct. People can also correctly recognize the trajectory a pendulum bob takes if the tether is severed (Kaiser et al., 1992). This perceptual competence is notable because people often erroneously predict the trajectories (Caramazza et al., 1981); similarly, many people respond to verbal questions that period is either unrelated or inversely related to tether length (Pittenger, 1991).

Taken together, these findings suggest that observers do not veridically extract dynamic invariants of pendular motion. Rather, they possess a qualitative, or heuristical, appreciation of certain motion dimensions (Pittenger, 1991) and appreciate the motion of the bob only when it is severed from the pendulum system and moves as a point particle (Kaiser et al., 1992). However, proponents of the KSD view can argue that passive observation of pendulums is not sufficiently interactive to evoke optimal perceptual processing. And factors that have minimal impact on motion period (e.g., arc magnitude) can profoundly influence factors of relevance to our interactions with such systems (e.g., the speed at which a playground swing moved through the air).

Like a pendulum, a wheel rolling down an incline plane must be considered an extended-body motion system. In order to predict the velocity of the wheel at any point on the ramp, one needs to know not only the position of the wheel's CG (in terms of its vertical displacement from its starting point), but also the distribution of mass on the wheel itself. The more compact a wheel, the faster will be its rate of descent. Thus, a solid disk will descend a ramp at a faster rate than will a rim.[3] People do not appreciate this dynamic aspect of wheel motion (Proffitt, Kaiser, & Whelan, 1990). Instead, they often believe that irrelevant facts, such as wheel mass or diameter, affect velocity. As with other extended-body systems, people's judgments reflect only a heuristical appreciation rather than veridical processing of dynamical invariants.

Collisions

As previously stated, collisions were the first exemplars of potential KSD mappings. Following Runeson's derivation of the motion equations, several empirical studies examined people's ability to make relative mass judgments. Todd and Warren (1982) asked observers to make relative mass judgments for linear collisions and found above-chance performance for each of four mass ratios employed (the smallest of which was 1:1.25). Kaiser and Proffitt (1984) used only one mass ratio (approximately 1:3) and found above-chance performance for observers ranging in age from 7 years old to adults; the 5-year-olds they tested did not perform significantly better than chance. Kaiser and Proffitt (1984, 1987) also asked children and adults to judge whether collisions were canonical and anomalous; children recognized gross violations of momentum conservation, and adults (tested parametrically) demonstrated high sensitivity to violations of momentum conservation or temporal continuities. Warren, Kim, and Husney (1987) examined people's ability to judge the elasticity of a ball from observing it bounce. Judgments (i.e., mean "bounciness" ratings) were highly correlated with the balls' physical elasticity.

But despite the seeming support these findings lent to the KSD view, several aspects of the findings indicated that observers may not have been utilizing the appropriate kinematic variables to make their judgments. Todd and Warren noted that observers' judgments were consistent with strategies that only considered postcollision velocities. Gilden and Proffitt (1989) expanded this analysis in their examination of relative mass judgments for oblique collisions. They concluded that judgments were based, not on an analysis of the full set of dynamically relevant kinematics, but rather on simpler kinematic heuristics: Balls with significantly greater postcollision impacts or deflection angles were judged as lighter. Gilden (1991) similarly argued that the observers' judgments in the Warren et al. study were better explained by a heuristic based on the ratio of relative bounces.[4] Collisions continue to be an excellent paradigm in which to test the relative merits of the KSD and PH views. More will be said about this in the section on the state of the current debate.

Biodynamics

Most of the research on the perception of biodynamics has been performed by researchers who hold, or are favorably disposed toward, the KSD view. To a large extent, this work can be viewed as an extension of early event perception research on biological forms. Once Johansson (1973) demonstrated that we can recognize human forms and actions from point-light displays, it seemed logical to examine KSD in that domain, to wit: Can observers make judgments about the forces acting on people from visual observation?[5]

Runeson and Frykholm (1981, 1983) created point-light films of actors lifting boxes of different weights. Observers could not only see that the sequences showed people lifting weights, they could also estimate the weights of the lifted boxes with reasonable accuracy. Kaiser and Proffitt (1984) similarly showed that both adults and children could judge the relative weights of lifted boxes when watching the ongoing event, but only older children and adults could judge relative weight from static sequences, and their performance was greatly degraded. Similar findings were reported by Valenti and Costall (1997). Bingham (1987) performed a more detailed analysis of motion functions in these lifted-weight events in an attempt to better formalize the KSD mapping. Warren (1984) demonstrated that observers could view sets of stairs varying in tread and riser dimension and accurately pick the dimensions that require least effort to climb. Finally, Shaw and Pittenger have proposed that there might be a cardioidal shape invariant for growth, with perceived age associated with the degree of cardioidal strain present in the object's form (Pittenger, Shaw, & Mark, 1979; Shaw & Pittenger, 1979).

These biomechanical examples of potential KSD are intriguing, but often the kinematics proposed as the basis of dynamical judgments are ill defined or highly correlated with far simpler visual parameters that might serve as the basis of judgments (Gilden, 1991). This confounding of dynamically veridical kinematics and heuristically useful visual cues returns us again to the KSD–PH debate.

The KSD–PH debate: Current status

The essence of the debate between the KSD and PH views is not unique to the study of perception of dynamics. This tension exists throughout the domain of perceptual psychology and reflects the theoretical differences between the ecological and cue-based theories of perception. The ecological school holds that visual perception involves the direct pickup of structural invariants in the optic array. These invariants are sufficient to fully specify the organism-relevant "affordances" of the environment. Perception occurs transparently, without cognitive constructions, and (given a nonimpoverished environment and an observer who has become attuned to the relevant invariants) is error-free. The ecological approach can be contrasted with a broad class of theories that hold that visual perception has its own unique logic or organizing principles. Combining available visual cues (and, to varying degrees, internalized constructs and expectations), perception constructs a representation of the environment.

The same arguments debated in the perception of dynamics are recapitulated in the domain of visual information for vehicle control. Here researchers from the ecological school argue that optical invariants exist that fully specify such control parameters as heading, speed, time to impact (or pass) objects in the environment, and whether one's current rate of deceleration is sufficient for safe braking. Cue theorists counter that these optical variables are not always sufficient for vehicle control. Some variables are valid only if certain restrictive assumptions are made (e.g., time to contact assumes constant linear velocity). Others appear to be corrupted if extraneous motion is introduced and require extravisual information for proper interpretation (e.g., extracting heading in the presence of vehicle yaw). Empirically, given performance data that are *consistent* with the use of a proposed optical invariant, there is the same difficulty of determining whether behavior is actually controlled based on the invariant or on some other, correlated, visual cue.[6]

Given the breadth of this debate in the visual perception literature, it is all the more critical to assess its intellectual merit. Has the field created a tempest in a teapot or are genuine issues to be resolved in order to achieve an understanding of how we perceive our environment? I argue that there are two sets of issues to be considered. The first set concerns our theoretical models and approaches. The second set concerns the pragmatic application of our understanding of the visual perception of dynamics to real-world problems.

Theoretical issues

The impact that Gibson and Johansson have had on the field of visual psychology is tremendous and invigorating. Their work, and the work spawned by their writings, have completely revised how perceptionists regard motion. Once thought to be a complication and distraction to "normative" perception, motion is now viewed as an integral, perhaps primal, component of perceptual experience. Gibson, in particular, also provided great energy and excitement to the field by boldly rethinking the meaning of *information* and redefining where information resides: not "in our heads" or "in the world," but in the interaction of organism and environment. These bold new constructs liberated researchers to consider entirely new domains of perceptual competence. As I alluded to earlier, the idea that dynamics could be visually perceived was not at all obvious prior to event psychology and the ecological approach.

However, the excitement such new ideas engender should not justify a loss of rigor in the empirical validation of models and theories. Many of the early studies on the visual perception of dynamics had more of the flavor of Gestaltist "demonstrations" than of empirical experimentation. Even now, there is a tendency to present performance findings that are consistent with the use of a proposed optical invariant as strong evidence for its usage, without a clear demonstration that systematic (and unconfounded) variation in that parameter affects performance in the predicted manner (Gilden, 1991). KSD proponents counter that PH researchers, in their attempts to isolate potential motion cues, impoverish the visual array. Observers forced to make judgments about such events resort to inappropriate heuristical strategies that fail to represent their performance with natural, perceptually rich events (Runeson & Vederler, 1993).

But in addition to these questions of what constitutes empirical validation, there is the larger question of whether the KSD or PH models are testable. In fact, both models are difficult to test because, as currently instantiated, both are difficult to falsify. Also, given Runeson's concept of an incomplete invariant, the theoretical distinction between the two views becomes blurred.

Can a heuristical model of dynamical perception be disproved? As a general principle, it is very difficult (Hecht, 1996). As has been shown in the field of artificial intelligence, heuristical models can resemble analytical processes given a sufficiently complex set of heuristics. A *particular* heuristical model can be validated or falsified because the model makes specific predictions concerning when performance will be correct and when errors will occur. However, the model must be explicit about the rules that are utilized and the conditions under which each rule is evoked. Thus, Gilden and Proffitt's (1989) model for collision heuristics properly defines specific rules for relative weight judgments (e.g., the ball with the greater postcollision velocity is lighter). However, their model might be faulted for not adequately describing the conditions for evoking the two rules; whether the angle or velocity rule is used depends on the salience of the parameters, but *salience* is only loosely defined. To summarize, if a heuristical model is sufficiently specified, it is empirically testable; the model then predicts specific patterns of performance errors.

At first blush, it might seem that KSD models are equally testable. If the KSD model posits that judgments are based on invariants, and invariants provide (by definition) veridical information about the ecological dynamics, performance should be error-free. However, KSD researchers are (rightfully) unwilling to accept such stringent empirical criteria for several reasons. First, observers must learn to attend (become attuned) to the relevant optical invariants. Novices may attend to extraneous information, and even experts may perform poorly if there is insufficient time to process relevant information. Related to this point, there will be sensitivity limits; some differences in velocity or changes in acceleration will be too small for the observer to notice (*subthreshold*, in psychophysical parlance). Finally, there is Runeson's concept of incomplete invariance (Runeson, 1989). This idea holds that certain invariants will exist only in certain local regions of the environment. If the organism is required to perform outside of this domain (where the invariant is no longer valid), errors will occur. Although Runeson contends that there are significant theoretical differences between an incomplete invariant and a heuristic, these differences may prove difficult to operationalize.

Given these explanations for error, how is it possible to falsify a KSD model? As with PH, one must address a specific model. Any particular visual KSD model must posit a relationship between an optical variable and a dynamic parameter of an event. This relationship must be operationalized into a statement that specifies how altering the optical variable will impact an action or a verbal judgment. Probably the most difficult aspects of this operationalization are (1) decoupling the proposed optical variable from other naturally correlated optical variables (or cues) that might also be influencing behavior and (2) establishing reasonable criteria for determining whether the optical variable/behavior mapping is demonstrated (Kaiser & Phatak, 1993).

Pragmatic issues

Interestingly, some of the factors that are most problematic for a theoretical reconciliation of the KSD and PH views have minimal implications for how our understanding of the perception of dynamics is applied to real-world problems. Both views recognize that visual motion can provide observers with critical information concerning dynamic events. Both views encourage the delineation of optical variables that can be used by human operators to control dynamic systems. The need to understand the perceptual learning associated with the acquisition of expertise is recognized by both views. And both views appreciate that the same information sources useful to human observers might be exploited for the development of artificial guidance/control system (Sridhar, Suorsa, & Hussien, 1993).

Research on the perception of dynamics is highly relevant to the development of advanced motion displays used in the control of vehicles and systems. Researchers from both the KSD and PH schools (and other researchers less theoretically aligned) have greatly advanced our understanding of what visual information is necessary and sufficient for these control tasks, where motion displays do and do not aid our understanding of system dynamics, and how displays can be formatted to aid the acquisition of expertise by focusing visual attention on relevant parameters. Despite theoretical disagreements (or perhaps due to the intellectual synergism caused by their debate), KSD and PH researchers can continue to advance our understanding of how people perceive dynamics in visual events, and how this understanding can lead to the design of better interfaces between human operators and dynamic systems.

Notes

1. One of the best examples of how natural and computer-generated visual stimuli can complement one another comes from research on gender recognition with point-light walkers. First, Kozlowski and Cutting (1977, 1978) demonstrated that observers could reliably discriminate males from females by the motion of point lights attached to the major joints of human walkers. Hypothesizing that differences in men's and women's center of moment accounted for the judgments (Cutting, Proffitt, & Kozlowski, 1978), Cutting then created computer-generated point-light walkers that differed on this motion parameter (Cutting, 1978). These cumulative findings provide convincing support for the center-of-motion model.
2. In fact, the process of validating flight simulators is largely concerned with determining whether the nonveridicalities of platform motion, visual scene, and control dynamics are sufficiently intrusive to interfere with training transfer and/or cause the pilot to experience simulator sickness (McCauley, 1984).
3. In a similar vein, people do not appreciate the role of mass distribution in the conservation of angular momentum. As the mass distribution becomes less compact (e.g., a twirling ice skater extends her arms or a rotating satellite extends its solar panels), the angular velocity will decrease. Observers viewing animated satellites extending and retracting their panels showed no appreciation of these dynamics. So long as the rotation did not stop or reverse direction, observers judged all angular velocity changes (including no change) to look natural (Kaiser et al., 1992).

4. There are three redundant sources of kinematic information that specify the elasticity of a bouncing ball. First, using the equation shown in Figure 16.1 (and assuming the floor surface to be stationary), elasticity (*e*) is defined by

$$e = v_B / u_B \qquad (1)$$

where u_B is the preimpact velocity of the ball and v_B is the postimpact velocity. Elasticity is also specified by the duration of successive bounces because, for free-fall trajectories, duration of flight is proportional to launch velocity:

$$e = t_2 / t_1 \qquad (2)$$

Finally, elasticity is specified by the square root of the ratio of the maximum height reached between successive bounces:

$$e = (h_2 / h_1)_{1/2} \qquad (3)$$

Warren et al. (1987) demonstrated that observers could not reliably judge elasticity based on the kinematic information described in Equations 1 and 2 (displays were masked such that each of the three sources could be presented in isolation) and concluded that judgments must reflect the information described in Equation 3. Gilden (1991) re-analyzed Warren et al.'s data and found that a heuristical model based on the ratio of successive bounce heights (i.e., h_2/h_1) fit the response data better. Thus, as Pittenger found for period/length judgments with pendulums, the simpler linear heuristic was more consistent with observers' judgments than was the veridical quadratic function.

5. In fact, Bertenthal and Pinto (in press) propose that observers perceive biomechanical motions by detecting dynamical constraints inherent in their production (e.g., the motions of the limbs of a walker have the same frequency and are either in phase or counterphase). Thus, biomechanical motions have a special perceptual status based on the detection of regularities specific to the mechanical motions of such systems.

6. The distinction between kinematics and dynamics becomes somewhat blurred when studying the perception of self-motion. Although parameters of ego motion (e.g., heading, velocity, acceleration) are, strictly speaking, kinematic, the control of these parameters requires the consideration of human biodynamics (or vehicle dynamics). Because this chapter is limited to the perception of dynamics for events in which the observer is neither the agent nor the object, I do not discuss the self-motion research literature. A good overview of this domain is provided by Warren and Wertheim (1990).

References

Babler, T. G., & Dannemiller, J. L. (1993). Role of image acceleration judging landing location of free-falling projectiles. *Journal of Experimental Psychology: Human Perception and Performance, 19*, 15–31.

Baillargeon, R. (1990). *The development of young infants' intuitions about support*. Presented at the International Conference on Infant Studies, April, Montreal.

Baillargeon, R., & Hanko-Summers, S. (1990). Is the top object adequately supported by the bottom object? Young infants' understanding of support relations. *Cognitive Development, 5*, 29–54.

Bertenthal, B. I., & Pinto, J. (in press). Complementary processes in the perception and production of human movement. In E. Thelan & L. Smith (Eds.), *A dynamic systems approach to development: Applications*. Cambridge, MA: MIT Press.

Bingham, G. P. (1987). Kinematic form and scaling: Further investigations of the visual perception of lifted weight. *Journal of Experimental Psychology: Human Perception and Performance, 13*, 155–177.

Calderone, J. B., & Kaiser, M. K. (1989). Visual acceleration detection: Effect of sign and motion orientation. *Perception & Psychophysics, 45*, 391–394.

Caramazza, A., McCloskey, M. & Green, B. (1981). Naive beliefs in "sophisticated" subjects: Misconceptions about trajectories of objects. *Cognition, 9*, 117–123.

Chapman, S. (1968). Catching a baseball. *American Journal of Physics, 36*, 868–870.

Cutting, J. E. (1978). Generation of synthetic male and female walkers through manipulation of a biomechanical invariant. *Perception, 7*, 393–405.

Cutting, J. E., Proffitt, D. R., & Kozlowski, L. T. (1978). A biomechanical invariant for gait perception. *Journal of Experimental Psychology: Human Perception and Performance, 4*, 357–372.

Gibson, J. J. (1950). *The perception of the visual world.* Boston: Houghton Mifflin.

Gibson, J. J. (1966). *The senses considered as perceptual systems.* Boston: Houghton Mifflin.

Gibson, J. J. (1979). *The ecological approach to visual perception.* Boston: Houghton Mifflin.

Gilden, D. L. (1991). On the origins of dynamical awareness. *Psychological Review, 98*, 554–568.

Gilden, D. L., & Proffitt, D. R. (1989). Understanding collision dynamics. *Journal of Experimental Psychology : Human Perception and Performance, 15*, 372–383.

Gottsdanker, R. M., Frick, J. W., & Lockard, R. B. (1961). Identifying the acceleration of visual targets. *British Journal of Psychology, 52*, 31–42.

Hecht, H. (1996). Heuristics and invariants in dynamic perception: Immunized concepts or nonstatements? *Psychonomic Bulletin & Review, 3*, 61–70.

Hecht, H., Kaiser, M. K., & Banks, M. S. (1996). Gravitational acceleration as a cue for absolute size and distance? *Perception & Psychophysics, 58*, 1066–1075.

Heider, F., & Simmel, M. (1944). An experimental study of apparent behavior. *American Journal of Psychology, 57*, 243–259.

Johansson, G. (1950). *Configurations in event perception.* Uppsala, Sweden: Almqvist & Wiksell.

Johansson, G. (1973). Visual perception of biological motion and a model for its analysis. *Perception & Psychophysics, 14*, 201–211.

Johansson, G., & Jansson, G. (1967). *The perception of free fall.* Seminar paper, University of Uppsala, Sweden.

Kaiser, M. K., & Phatak, A. V. (1993). Things that go bump in the light: On the optical specification of contact severity. *Journal of Experimental Psychology: Human Perception and Performance, 19*, 194–202.

Kaiser, M. K., & Proffitt, D. R. (1984). The development of sensitivity to causally-relevant dynamic information. *Child Development, 55*, 1614–1624.

Kaiser, M. K., Proffitt, D. R., Whelan, S. M., & Hecht, H. (1992). Influence of animation on dynamical judgments. *Journal of Experimental Psychology: Human Perception and Performance, 18*, 669–690.

Kozlowski, L. T., & Cutting, J. E. (1977). Recognizing the sex of a walker from a dynamic point-light display. *Perception & Psychophysics, 21*, 575–580.

Kozlowski, L. T., & Cutting, J. E. (1978). Recognizing the gender of walkers from point-lights mounted on ankles: Some second thoughts. *Perception & Psychophysics, 23*, 459.

McBeath, M. K., Shaffer, D. M., & Kaiser, M. K. (1995). How baseball outfielders determine where to run to catch fly balls. *Science, 268*, 569–573.

McCauley, M. E. (1984). *Research issues in simulator sickness: Proceedings of a workshop.* Washington, DC: National Academy Press.

McLeod, P., & Dienes, Z. (1996). Do fielders know where to go to catch the ball or only how to get there? *Journal of Experimental Psychology: Human Perception and Performance, 22*, 531–543.

McCloskey, M., Caramazza, A., & Green, B. (1980). Curvilinear motion in the absence of external forces: Naive beliefs about the motion of objects. *Science, 210*, 1139–1141.

Michaels, C. F., & Oudejans, R. R. D. (1992). The optics and actions of catching fly balls: Zeroing out optical acceleration. *Ecological Psychology, 4*, 199–222.

Michotte, A. (1963). *The perception of causality* (T. R. Miles, Trans.). London: Methuen. (Original work published 1946)

Miller, J. (1988). Discrete and continuous models of human information processing: Theoretical distinctions and empirical results. *Acta Psychologica, 67,* 191–257.

Needham, A. (1990). *3.5-month-old infants' knowledge of support relations.* Presented at the International Conference on Infant Studies, April, Montreal.

Pittenger, J. B. (1985). Estimation of pendulum length from information in motion. *Perception, 14,* 247–256.

Pittenger, J. B. (1991). Cognitive physics and event perception: Two approaches to the assessment of people's knowledge of physics. In R. R. Hoffman & D. S. Palermo (Eds.), *Cognition and the symbolic processes: Applied and ecological perspectives.* Hillsdale, NJ: Lawrence Erlbaum Associates, Inc.

Pittenger, J. B. (1990). Detection of violations of the law of pendulum motion: Observers' sensitivity to the relation between period and length. *Ecological Psychology, 2,* 55–81.

Pittenger, J. B., Shaw, R. E., & Mark, L. S. (1979). Perceptual information for the age level of faces as a higher order invariant of growth. *Journal of Experimental Psychology: Human Perception and Performance, 5,* 374–382.

Proffitt, D. R., and Gilden, D. L. (1989). Understanding natural dynamics. *Journal of Experimental Psychology: Human Perception and Performance, 15,* 384–393.

Proffitt, D. R., Kaiser, M. K., & Whelan, S. M. (1990). Understanding wheel dynamics. *Cognitive Psychology, 22,* 342–373.

Roncato, S., and Rumiati, R. (1986). Naive statics: Current misconceptions on equilibrium. *Journal of Experimental Psychology: Learning, Memory, and Cognition, 12,* 361–377.

Runeson, S. (1983). *On visual perception of dynamic events.* (Acta Universitatis Upsaliensis: Studia Psychologica Upsaliensia, Serial No. 9). (Original work published 1977)

Runeson, S. (1989). A note on the utility of ecologically incomplete invariants. *International Society for Ecological Psychology Newsletter, 4*(1), 6–9.

Runeson, S., & Frykholm, G. (1981). Visual perception of lifted weight. *Journal of Experimental Psychology: Human Perception and Performance, 7,* 733–740.

Runeson, S., & Frykholm, G. (1983). Kinematic specification of dynamics as an informational basis for person and action perception: Expectation, gender recognition, and deceptive intention. *Journal of Experimental Psychology: General, 112,* 585–615.

Runeson, S., & Vedeler, D. (1993). The indispensability of precollision kinematics in the visual perception of relative mass. *Perception & Psychophysics, 53,* 617–632.

Schmerler, J. (1976). The visual perception of accelerated motion. *Perception, 5,* 167–185.

Shannon, B. (1976). Aristotelianism, Newtonianism, and the physics of the layman. *Perception, 5,* 241–243.

Shaw, R., & Pittenger, J. (1979). Perceiving change. In H. Pick, Jr. & E. Saltzman (Eds.), *Modes of perceiving and processing information* (pp. 187–204). Hillsdale, NJ: Lawrence Erlbaum Associates.

Sridhar, B., Suorsa, R., & Hussien, B. (1993). Passive range estimation for rotorcraft low-altitude flight. *Machine Vision and Applications, 6,* 10–24.

Todd, J. T. (1981). Visual information about moving objects. *Journal of Experimental Psychology: Human Perception and Performance, 7,* 795–810.

Todd, J., & Warren, W. H. (1982). Visual perception of relative mass in dynamic events. *Perception, 11,* 325–335.

Valenti, S. S., & Costall, A. (1997). Visual perception of lifted weight from kinematic and static (photographic) displays. *Journal of Experimental Psychology: Human Perception and Performance, 23,* 181–198.

von Hofsten, C. (1983). Catching skills in infancy. *Journal of Experimental Psychology: Human Perception and Performance, 9,* 75–85.

Warren, R., & Wertheim, A. H. (1990). *Perception & control of self-motion*. Hillsdale, NJ: Lawrence Erlbaum Associates, Inc.

Warren, W. H. (1984). Perceiving affordances: Visual guidance of stair climbing. *Journal of Experimental Psychology: Human Perception and Performance, 10*, 683–703.

Warren, W. H., Kim, E. E., & Husney, R. (1987). The way the ball bounces: Visual and auditory perception of elasticity and control of the bounce pass. *Perception, 16*, 683–703.

Watson, J. S., Banks, M. S., von Hofsten, C., & Royden, C. S. (1992). Gravity as a monocular cue for perception of absolute distance and/or size. *Perception, 21*, 69–76.

17 Perceptual learning

Merav Ahissar and Shaul Hochstein

Defining perceptual learning

Eleanor J. Gibson defined perceptual learning as the "increase in the ability to extract information from the environment, as a result of practice and experience with stimulation coming from it" (1969, p. 3). This definition encompasses only improvement in performance and is thus somewhat restricted but appropriate in the context of this chapter, where we refer only to phenomena of improvement. Included in Gibson's phrase "increase in the ability to extract information" are the abilities to extract a larger amount of information and to select task-relevant information. In addition, we would add an increase in the *rate* of information extraction and a more efficient extraction of information in order to explicitly include in learning improvement in speed and reduction in required effort. This extension is meant to include in learning any measurable improvement in performance, regardless of its underlying mechanism, compared to the original Gibsonian focus on gradual feature discovery.

Note, however, that perceptual performance improvement is not necessarily an outcome of improved information gathering from the external environment. A person may improve his or her decision mechanism based on the same perceptual information. An analysis of the pattern of responses would reveal that right from the start, the person could have done better had he or she optimized the criterion. Given the Gibsonian definition, it is an open question whether this should be considered *perceptual* learning. We feel that if there is a long-term improvement in decision making, this mechanism should not be excluded from perceptual learning. This is because, in our view, the information-gathering, information-processing, and decision-making elements in the visual system are intertwined. For example, in a cascade of visual processing stages (see Figure 17.5), the input to each subsequent stage may be seen as information extraction from the internal environment of results of decision making in the preceding stages.

We thank Anne Treisman and Howard Hock for many helpful suggestions in critically reviewing the manuscript. We thank the authors and publishers of the figures reprinted or adapted for reprinting here. Work on this review was supported by the U.S.–Israel Binational Science Foundation (BSF), the Israel Science Foundation, and the National Institute of Psychobiology in Israel.

In the following discussion, we confine ourselves to the consequences of extensive practice, ranging from several dozen trials to many thousands, also termed *skill acquisition*. Thus, repetition priming and its relation to the discussed phenomena are beyond the scope of this chapter, although the same mechanisms may underlie both and there may be a continuum of training phenomena between them (Logan, 1990; Treisman, Vieira, & Hayes, 1992; for a description of different learning types, see Squire, 1992; for other definitions, see Schwartz & Hashtroudi, 1991).

Range and limits of perceptual learning

What are the limitations of improvement? The traditional notion, expressed by James (1890), was that encoding basic elements of the stimulus is fixed. However, the task-specific readout mechanism, the process whereby higher, more task-specific structures acquire information sensed or processed by more basic elements, is modifiable and additional task-related memory traces may be accumulated. This view is easily reconciled with consistent findings of substantial improvement in numerous *complex* perceptual tasks (Gibson 1953, 1969).

However, James also knew that practicing simple tasks that involve only basic elements, and even changes along a single dimension, may also yield dramatic long-term effects. For example, the just noticeable difference (j.n.d.) in the spatial position of two points touching the skin can be greatly reduced. This paradigm was initially studied by Volkman (1858), who found that within several hours of practice, the minimal distance for which subjects distinguish between single and double stimulation may be halved, as illustrated in Figure 17.1. Subsequent studies found that in some areas of the skin, the threshold may be reduced to as little as 1% of its initial level by extensive practice over several weeks (Tawney, 1897).

Experimental results thus show that the distinction between tasks that are amenable to practice effects and those that are not does not reside in their apparent complexity. Perhaps the difference lies in their relevance during subjects' prior experience. Thus, if subjects have already learned to utilize efficiently the most suitable strategies, with the same range of parameters, then not much additional improvement will be seen. The effect of prior experience is especially prominent because learning curves follow a ubiquitous power law (note, however, that this law typically relates to the time needed to perform a task; see Newell & Rosenbloom, 1981).[1] Therefore, the initially measured position on the learning curve has a dramatic effect on the subsequently measured slope of improvement.

According to this view, the difference between tasks that can be trained and those that cannot does not lie in an intrinsic task property, but rather in whether the task has already been learned. Thus, there are almost no simple tasks in the

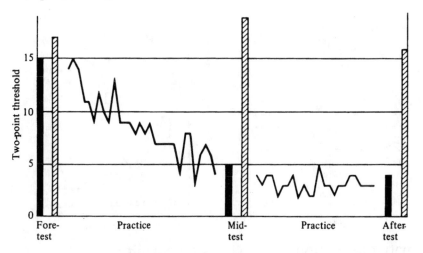

Figure 17.1. The first published perceptual learning curve. Subjects showed substantial reduction in two-point discrimination j.n.d. on the tip of the middle finger following extensive practice. There is complete transfer of the learning effect to the homologous finger on the other hand (black bars) but none to other skin regions, such as the forearm (striped bars). Adapted from Volkman (1858) after Gibson (1969, p. 166, figure 9–1.)

sense of unimprovable tasks, only tasks that have already been maximally improved. This is because initial performance in most conditions seems not to be limited by the information of the components, but instead by task-specific selection and decision-making mechanisms. Therefore, extensive practice can improve performance even on simple tasks.

We illustrate this point in the visual and somatosensory domains. Practicing foveal discrimination between sine-wave gratings does not yield improvement in resolution, as shown in Figure 17.2, top left, in the curves of four subjects for 0° eccentricity (Johnson & Leibowitz, 1979; see also Bennet & Westheimer, 1991; Fiorentini & Berardi, 1980, 1981), whereas discrimination between complex gratings improves substantially, as shown in Figure 17.8, middle right (Fiorentini & Berardi, 1980, 1981). However, even visual resolution improves in the periphery, as demonstrated in the curves for peripheral vision of Figure 17.2, top left (Johnson & Leibowitz, 1979; see also Bennet & Westheimer, 1991). Similarly, stereoacuity undergoes substantially greater improvement in the periphery, as shown in Figure 17.2, top right (Fendick & Westheimer, 1983). The difference between peripheral and central vision in their malleability to practice effects may be due to the difference in their use in daily life. Foveal visual resolution is crucial, so information processing resources there may be exhausted. Peripheral vision, on the other hand, is generally used to induce foveation, and therefore information processing capabilities there may not be

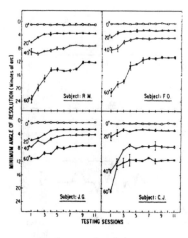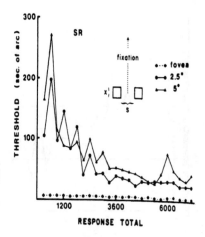

spatial resolution   stereo acuity

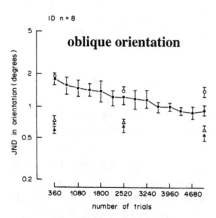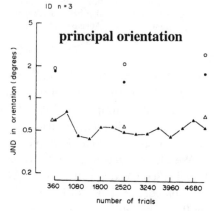

orientation discrimination

Figure 17.2. Limits of learning in simple visual tasks. Top: There is substantial improvement in spatial resolution (left) and stereo acuity (right) for peripheral stimuli but not
for foveally presented stimuli. Visual resolution thresholds (minimum angle of resolution,
period of sinusoidal grating, in minutes of arc) as a function of the number of practice
test sessions at 0°, 20°, 40°, and 60° of visual eccentricity (left) or stereoacuity (in reporting the relative perceived depth of the outlines of two squares presented at different
disparities) at 0°, 2.5°, and 5° deg. eccentricity along the vertical meridian (right). Bottom:
Orientation discrimination improves around an oblique standard (circles) but not around
the cardinal, horizontal, and vertical axes (closed and open triangles, respectively). Mean
of eight or three subjects. Note that training-induced improvement reduced but did not
eliminate the advantage of central vision and vision along the cardinal axes. From Johnson and Leibowitz, (1979, Figure 2), Fendick and Westheimer (1983, Figure 1), and
Vogels and Orban (1985, Figures 2 and 3.)

stretched to their limits. This line of explanation may also account for the differences between orientation judgment for oblique orientations versus orientations around the principal axes. Resolution may be poorer for oblique orientations partly because of their lower importance compared to the principal axes. Indeed, practice induces improvement for oblique orientations but not for principal orientations (Vogels & Orban, 1985), as seen by comparing Figure 17.2, bottom, left and right. By the same token, we would expect the proportion of practice-induced threshold reduction in touch resolution to be greater for the middle finger than for the index finger, which is typically used for tactual exploration.

A related question is whether training effects can eliminate initial biases, for example, between central and peripheral vision or between vision along oblique and principal axes. It is expected that practice cannot make peripheral vision improve to the extent that it reaches central vision levels due to the known difference in magnification factor (Figure 17.2, top). Vogels and Orban claimed that the difference between oblique and principal axis vision also derives partly from the sparser cortical representation of the oblique axes. They assumed that this representational difference at early processing stages cannot be eliminated with practice. In agreement with this assumption, they found that even following extensive practice that yielded a substantial threshold decrement, oblique discriminations remained inferior to discriminations around the principal axes (Figure 17.2, bottom).

A complementary aspect of the interpretation that controlled practice will improve whatever has not previously been extensively practiced is that some more complex tasks will not be amenable to great modification if they are overtrained by daily use. Wolford and Kim (1992) point out some tasks in which they found little improvement during several training sessions. These include accuracy in detection of tachistoscopically presented letters, a whole report paradigm, and lateral masking. Lateral masking, for example, may be utilized extensively for reading, and thus will be at a point where practice will have only a small incremental effect. Indeed, improvement was found to occur at a slower rate for lateral masking and for the whole report paradigm than in the less naturally occurring backward-masking condition (Wolford, Marchak, & Hughes, 1988), as illustrated in Figure 17.3. It would be interesting to test the prediction that for illiterate subjects, whether young or old, this relation of slower improvement in lateral masking compared to backward masking may not hold and lateral masking would improve at higher rates.

Note that in addition to the difficulty in further improving a well-trained task, it is difficult to change ingrained habits, that is, to learn a modified task. For example, in a study aimed at changing the reading habits of dyslexics, Geiger, Lettvin, and Zegarra-Moran (1992) employed an intensive training procedure for several months and succeeded in altering the distribution of lateral masking.

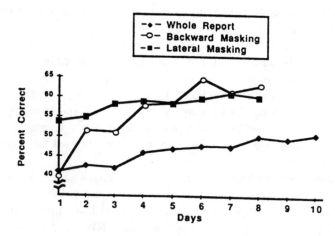

Figure 17.3. Different rates of improvement in more complex perceptual tasks. For all these tasks, stimuli were letters, presentation was brief, and initial performance was about 50%. Graph shows the percent correct as a function of days of learning in tasks of whole report (report of as many consonants as possible from briefly presented four-letter strings above and below the fixation point), backward masking (mask presented following a fixed stimulus onset asynchrony [SOA] chosen as that which gave close to 50% performance on the first session), and lateral masking (masks presented simultaneously but spatially offset from the stimulus). From Wolford et al. (1988, Figure 3.)

Some differential results, however, are hard to account for on the basis of this interpretation. For example, although foveal vernier hyperacuity substantially improves as a function of practice (Fahle & Edelman, 1993; McKee & Westheimer, 1978), three-point alignment hyperacuity does not (Bennet & Westheimer, 1991), as shown in Figure 17.4, bottom. Possibly, these seemingly similar hyperacuity tasks are used differently in regular vision. Alternatively, perhaps the tests were performed differently. Indeed, Fahle and Edelman (1993) studied improvement in both types of hyperacuity with the same training procedures and found similar trends toward initial improvement for the two, as demonstrated by comparing their results for three-point alignment shown in Figure 17.4, top, with their results for vernier acuity, shown in Figure 17.8, bottom, left. However whereas vernier acuity learning continued at a slow rate even after nearly 10,000 presentations, improvement in three-point alignment did not continue after 5,000 presentations.

Theories and experiments on perceptual learning

Several theories focused at the conceptual level have attempted to describe and elucidate the processes underlying perceptual learning. The basic questions addressed by the theorists are these: At what processing stages does learning oc-

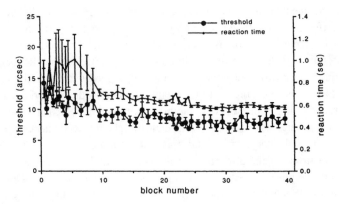

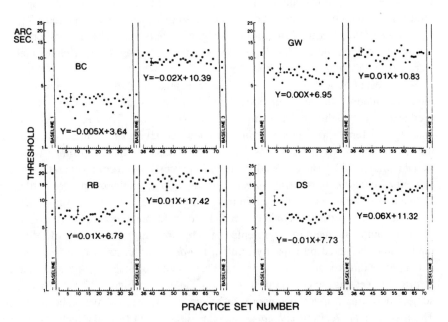

PRACTICE SET NUMBER

Figure 17.4. Practice effects for three-point vernier acuity tasks. Observers reported whether the middle point was offset to the right or left of an imaginary line through the other two points. The threshold was significantly reduced, and the reaction time somewhat reduced, during the first 20 blocks of 240 trials each (upper graph). Spacing of 10 min arc between adjacent points; means and S.E. for six observers. Lower graphs: similar experiment, results for four subjects, with vertical spacing between adjacent points of 4–5 min arc (circles) or 18 min arc (squares). Here there was no sign of improvement. Different results may depend on the use of subjects who are either naive or experienced in making psychophysical judgments. From Fahle and Edelman (1993, Figure 8) and Bennet and Westheimer (1991, Figure 2).

cur? What are the mechanisms operating at these stages? However, different theorists had different concrete ranges of phenomena that they attempted to explain (and a different world of associations), so that their various theories focused on different aspects of learning. Although several different mechanisms may be operating under different conditions and for different tasks, and even for any given task, it is desirable and more parsimonious to describe them all within a general learning framework to facilitate comparison. Such a general description, which separates the theories from their initial contexts, is necessarily the outcome of personal interpretation and biased selection.

It is hard to construct a general-purpose processing hierarchy in which arrows may point to putative plasticity sites. First, too little is known about the underlying representation. Second, the processing cascade of various tasks may be very different. Third, a major component of learning is described as a reduction in the need for top-down attentional resources, and incorporation of that behavioral finding within a stimulus-dictated processing sequence is not obvious. We try to bypass these basic difficulties by suggesting only a sketchy, general processing scheme, on the one hand, and by explicitly referring to experiments that were commonly addressed, on the other.

A suggested basic processing scheme is presented in Figure 17.5. Upon stimulus presentation, initial input nodes are of *stimulus features or components* (perhaps corresponding to the primal sketch; Marr, 1982). They interact and/or converge to form a preliminary *stimulus encoding* level, which includes basic transformations of initial stimulus features (analogous to the 2 ½-dimensional sketch; Marr, 1982). The encoded stimulus is processed to form a general *memory representation* or several *object representations* (perhaps an object file; Kahneman & Treisman, 1984) within this processing network or at a subsequent network stage. Various *algorithms* may be carried out utilizing the encoded stimulus and/or its memory representation. The bottom-up processing of information may be gated by capacity-limited, *top-down selection mechanisms* that may operate directly at the memory object representation stage, but perhaps also at prior processing stages (gray arrows on the left in Figure 17.5). When a subject performs a given behavioral task, specific decisions have to be made. The *task-specific decision category* stage has direct input from the memory object representation level, as basic decisions involve comparisons between memory or object representations. However, task-specific category decisions may also receive direct input from prior processing stages.

According to this general scheme, we may introduce learning effects in numerous ways. Learning may involve different types of connections: the readout connections to the task-specific decision category (black horizontal arrows in Figure 7.5) or the direct, bottom-up connections from stage to stage. Either change may be directed by the top-down selection mechanisms. Learning may

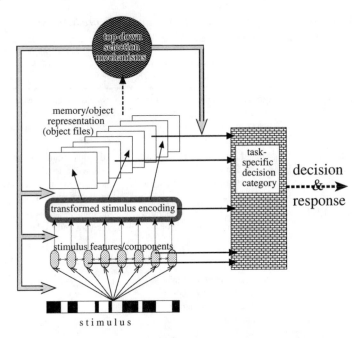

Figure 17.5. Schematic representation of basic perceptual processing mechanisms. Bottom-up path flows from stimulus presentation and encoding in initial *stimulus feature or component* nodes, via a preliminary *stimulus-encoding* level including basic transformations of the initial stimulus features, to a general *memory representation*, or several *object representations* or object files. Various *computations* may be carried out utilizing the encoded stimulus and/or its memory representation. *Top-down selection mechanisms* may gate the processes of this bottom-up path at various points (gray arrows, applied to all transitions [arrows] to each of the three levels, left, or from all levels to the category decision stage, right). The *task-specific decision category* stage has direct input from the various levels of the bottom-up path. Not shown are nonretinal inputs, especially to the *top-down selection mechanisms*, including vestibular and limbic inputs, as well as inputs from other senses. This diagram is, of course, only schematic and should be viewed generally. Its main purpose is to allow discussion of the basic learning mechanisms within a unified framework.

also involve different processing stages, either early (stimulus features or components), middle, or late. Note that learning at the input to the task-specific decision stage may occur at either early or late stages of the processing hierarchy.

We review several learning theories in the context of this general scheme, pointing out where and what type of learning takes place according to each theory and briefly describing experiments to which the theorists have referred. These theories and their predictions for specificity or transfer are summarized in Table 17.1.

Table 17.1. *Theories of perceptual learning and their predictions*

	Author	Theory	Transfer/Specificity Prediction
A.		Automatization Theories	
1.	LaBerge (1976, 1983)	formation of new "hard-wired" specific complex feature detectors, at stimulus-encoding level.	should affect processing of same objects for other tasks; could be stimulus specific.
2.	Shiffrin & Schneider (1977)	strengthening stimulus-response association at decision category stage and increasing priority at memory stage.	stimulus specificity; automatized task will interfere with performance of other tasks due to increased priority.
3.	Logan (1988)	associating patterns of features via memory representation directly with results of previously performed computations; item-based memory replaces process-based mechanism; specific traces in memory for each stimulus episode.	no transfer across stimuli of task-relevant and irrelevant features.
B.		Improved Discrimination	
4.	Boring (1942)	choice of best-suited criterion; fine-tuning decisions for response.	should transfer across stimuli.
5.	James (1890)	optimizing category evaluation by *enrichment* of memory; extending input population on basis of experience-based assumptions.	should affect performance of other tasks.
6.	Gibson (1953, 1969)	increase in correspondence between perception and external stimulus; exploration for cues best suited to *differentiation* needed. encoding only of task-specific discriminating features.	transfer to other tasks with same discriminating features; affect only task-relevant features.
C.		Increased Efficiency	
7.	Crossman (1959)	choice of more suited algorithm. testing for best results using condition-specific "tricks."	degree of specificity/transfer will depend on type of alternative strategy.

Table 17.1. *(cont.)*

	Author	Theory	Transfer/Specificity Prediction
8.	Anderson (1982)	algorithmic improvements: chunking adjacent procedural steps; using constants rather than variables; strengthening each product to facilitate its execution; parameter specific schemes.	transfer of algorithmic enhancement; specificity of automatization.
9.	Cheng (1985)	strategy shift; memory reorganization; decision-making at task-appropriate level (e.g. category rather than item level).	see Appendix.

I. Automaticity in search tasks with complex stimuli

One of the most prominent properties of perceptual learning and skill acquisition is automatization. Introspectively, automatization has the property of a change from initially effortful and demanding task execution to easy and effortless performance. It is therefore usually associated with a reduction in the need for attentional resources. Although this may not constitute a formal definition, it agrees with experimental findings in concurrent task paradigms, indicating a reduction in interference by an automatized task with the simultaneous performance of another, nonautomatized task.

In fact, automatization refers to one of the central puzzles of brain research. The neural circuits of the brain seem to be parallel processing structures, yet we are generally incapable of doing two things at the same time. The limiting resource has been termed *attention* (top-down selection mechanisms in Figure 17.5), and its role was emphasized in relation to object identification in binding outputs of local detectors (middle left gray arrow in Figure 17.5; e.g., Treisman & Gelade, 1980; see also Treisman, 1986) or in relation to mechanisms connecting detection to decision-making stages (gray arrow on the right in Figure 17.5; e.g., Deutsch & Deutsch, 1963; Shiffrin, 1975). Automatization was generally viewed as the gradual withdrawal of the need for the limited-capacity attentional mechanisms together with their consequent forced seriality. Recently, the whole concept of attention as a limiting resource has been questioned (for a recent review, see Allport, 1993). In parallel, it was argued that the common view of automatization as the gradual withdrawal of attention is meaningless if no learning mechanism is specified (Ryan, 1983). Moreover, it was pointed out that serial versus parallel performance may not be equivalent to attentive versus automatic processing, particularly because some mechanisms that increase efficiency or discrimination may mimic the effects of automaticity by specifically replacing serial, multistage processing with unitary processing (Cheng, 1985).

Experimental results. Search tasks have been used extensively in studying automatization because they naturally differentiate between apparently serial (attended) and parallel (automatic) processing by their dependence on set size. In *memory search*, initially studied by Sternberg (1966), a subject is first presented with a list of the target set. Then a single item is presented and the subject has to decide whether this item is a member of the target set. Sternberg found that the time needed to make a decision depends linearly on the size of the target set, with a typical slope of 40 ms per item. In a *visual search* task, a subject has to look for a single target element among a set of various displayed items. In most conditions, for a small number of elements, search time depends linearly on the number of elements in the display (e.g., for digits and letters, the slope is typically 40 ms). The two search tasks appear to be similar, and the slope in both tasks was interpreted as the time needed for attentional shifts through the list of target set (memory search) or displayed elements (visual search) to reach a decision. In special cases, in which the target greatly differs from a relatively homogenoeus distractor element field (Bergen & Julesz 1983; Duncan & Humphreys, 1989; Treisman & Gelade, 1980), the target "pops out" effortlessly, without dependence on the number of distractor elements – slope zero equated with parallel search.

Learning may transform an initially serial search into a parallel search, as first studied by Neisser, Novick, and Lazar (1963). They trained subjects in a letter cancellation task using columns of 50 strings. Following 13 sessions, subjects needed the same scanning time for target set sizes of 1–10 items (although the number of mistakes increased with practice). Shiffrin and Schneider (1977) used a hybrid of the memory and visual search tasks. Subjects scanned for one of a target set (letters or digits) on a card with a number of displayed elements (letters or digits). The target set size was varied, as was the number of displayed elements on each card. Following several consistent training sessions on mapping (see the later explanation), the initially hard, effortful search becomes easy, and performance is nearly independent of both target set size and number of display elements, as shown in Figure 17.6, top. In other cases, however, improvement is only partial. For example, Salthouse and Somberg (1982) studied learning of memory search with unfamiliar dot patterns. Although reaction time was reduced with practice, the slope did not reach zero even after more than 45 practice sessions, as shown in the slopes of Figure 17.6, bottom. Interestingly, the fraction of improvement was not age dependent. Older subjects (aged 62 to 73 years) improved even more than younger subjects (aged 19 to 27 years), although they never achieved the same asymptotic performance; compare Figure

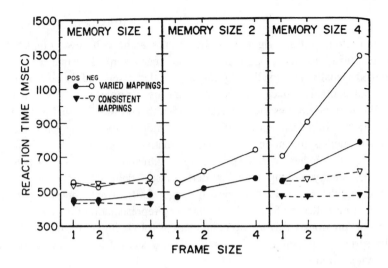

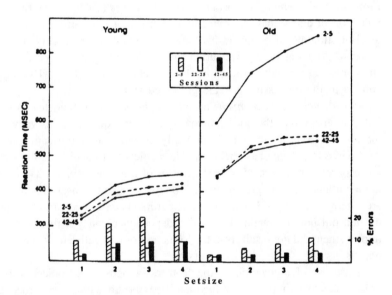

Figure 17.6. Practice effects in visual and memory search tasks. Top: Subjects were trained on this hybrid visual and memory search task, reporting whether one of the elements in the frame was from the memory set. Under the consistent mapping condition, elements were not transferred between the memory set (either digits or consonants) and distractor (consonants or digits, respectively) sets (triangles), and there was only a small reaction time dependence on either memory set size or frame size. For the alternative, varied mapping condition (where elements were letters only), large set size dependencies are seen (circles). Filled and open symbols are for trials with and without a target element, respectively. Bottom: Subjects improved in memory search for complex novel dot patterns. Interestingly, old subjects showed greater improvement, although they did not reach the same asymptotic level as younger subjects. Note that even following the 45th session, reaction time still depended on memory set size. From Schneider and Shiffrin (1977, Figure 6) and Salthouse and Somberg (1982, Figure 7).

17.6, bottom, left and right sides. In visual search, with new, complex figures or combinations, the slope also does not reach zero. Treisman et al. (1992) studied visual search for line figures or three-letter sets and found that the slope was substantially reduced (from 100 to 20 ms per item) but not eliminated.

We now briefly describe several theories that were suggested to account for the gradual shift from serial, effortful to parallel, effortless performance. These include models for automaticity and alternative suggestions. Models for automaticity include hard-wiring specific complex feature detectors (La Berge, 1976, 1983), directly linking stimulus detection to behavioral response category (avoiding the serial decision-making stage; Shiffrin & Schneider, 1977) and associating patterns of features via memory representation directly with the results of (previously performed) computations (obviating performance of the usually serial computation itself; Logan, 1988; discussed later in the section titled "Memory Retrieval").

Formation of complex feature detectors. La Berge (1976, 1983) suggested that reduction of attentional requirements is achieved by forming new nodes at the level of stimulus encoding. In his view, features that are initially combined by dynamic grouping through attention may, following practice, be combined by strengthened (or newly formed), hard-wired connections (1976). His suggestion, applied to the processing scheme presented in Figure 17.5, would be that the *top-down selection mechanisms* are no longer needed to bind features (middle left gray arrow – as the bottom arrow was never required, in his view). In fact, the level of basic features is functionally extended as initial combinations are hard-wired to become basic features. He predicts that under conditions in which all resources are allocated to performance of a single task, so that attention is not a bottleneck, no improvement will be found once the discriminating features are discovered (1983). However, the experiments described earlier, showing reduction but not elimination of set size dependence, suggest that in these cases improvement did not result from the formation of unitized detectors for the novel objects.

A process of unitization of the features composing an object (forming an object detector) should either facilitate or interfere with future processing for other tasks involving the same unitized object. Treisman et al. (1992) directly showed that this prediction is not valid. They gave subjects 16 sessions of visual search practice with novel stimuli composed of line patterns. Following training, the target almost "popped out" (see earlier). Yet, the performance of other tasks using the same target object was hardly affected. These include attention span, coherent motion, parts in the whole, and mental integration, which are illustrated in Figure 17.7, top and left. Thus the benefit of training seems to be task specific. Perhaps specificity derives from new nodes to which alternative tasks do not have access. Interestingly, learning was also stimulus specific. Changing the

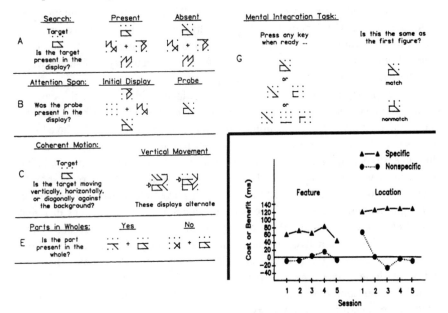

Figure 17.7. Top and left: Learning task specificity. Tasks and stimuli used to study transfer effects for complex random line patterns. If these complex forms become simple features during training with the search task, not only should the search task itself (A) be speeded up, but these forms should be easier to detect in the attention span (B), coherent motion (C), and mental integration (G) tasks and more difficult to break up in the "parts in a whole" task (E). However, trained elements did not behave as simple features: there was almost no transfer between tasks. Bottom right: Conjunction search learning specificity to apparently irrelevant features. Mean costs and benefits of frequent feature and frequent location (triangles, *specific*), relative to control trials with other features and locations. Subjects performed visual search for one of two targets defined by feature conjunctions (e.g., color and orientation) when for one target, a third feature (e.g., texture), and for the other, the target location, was fixed in 60% of trials. There was a significant performance increase for these frequent trial types and a greater benefit for frequent location than for frequent feature. On the first session only, the reaction time benefit of the location where one target appeared more frequently was shared by the second target; the location benefit was not target specific (circles, *nonspecific*). Adapted from Treisman et al., (1992, Figures 1 and 7).

display from the trained green elements on a black background to black on green greatly hampered performance.

Stimulus–response mapping. *Shiffrin* and *Schneider* (1977) assumed that object identification is essentially automatic even without learning (the gray arrows on the left in Figure 17.5 are not needed), and the attentional bottleneck is at the subsequent stage of decision categorization (Deutsch & Deutsch, 1963; Shiffrin, 1975). They emphasized the acquired association between stimulus representation and response category. Strengthening these connections requires consistent stimulus–response (S–R) mapping. Thus, the critical limitation for automatization is not the complexity of the physical stimulus but the consistency of training conditions. Following consistent training, stimulus presentation triggers a bottom-up process that flows until the decision category is reached, without the need for the gray arrow at the top right in Figure 17.5.

Cheng (1985) noted that the substantial reduction in slope, in the case of memory search tasks, may not reflect automatization at all but rather a strategy shift and memory "reorganization." In visual search, however, displayed elements must be addressed serially, and memory reorganization should not suffice. In this case, perhaps a different strategy is used to strengthen the differentiation between visual categories. Indeed, Schneider and Shiffrin (1977) only showed elimination of the slope as a function of the displayed elements in visual search for digits among letters, which perhaps are defined, even initially, as different visual categories (Duncan, 1983). Strengthening this category difference by exploration of the distinctive discriminating features may be sufficient to allow parallel detection of the odd element. Cheng's interpretation denotes the limitation of the expected apparent parallelism in visual search. When distinctive visual features cannot be exploited, search will not become parallel. (One cannot automatize any arbitrary topology within the stimulus space.) For example, search for three-letter sets among other letters (Treisman et al., 1992) and search for color–shape conjunctions (Treisman & Gelade, 1980) never become completely parallel, although the slope is substantially reduced.

Thus, we can account for the learning-dependent reduction of the dependence on both visual search display size and memory search set size by strategy shifts or improved discrimination, as further described later, rather than by automatization in the sense of eliminating attentional demands (Figure 17.5, gray arrows).

II. Improved discrimination

Learning may be confined to improvement in the choice of response: the output level of the decision category (black horizontal arrows, Figure 17.5). That is, based on the same inputs and input strengths, response criteria may be adapted to optimize decisions. This was in fact *Boring*'s interpretation of Volkman's result on improvement in spatial j.n.d. for touch on the skin (see Figure 17.1 and the earlier description; Boring, 1942, pp. 480–483). He stressed the importance of attention and motivation for applying a best-suited criterion. Learning replaces attention in fine-tuning decisions between vaguely different sensations.

Alternatively, learning could occur within the bottom-up sequence constituting the input level to the task-specific decision stage. If learning involves changes along this general path, it will affect the stimulus representation regardless of the behavioral context, and therefore other computations utilizing a common input stage will be drastically affected. On the other hand, if learning involves the task-specific decision stage, it will be revealed only under related behavioral contexts utilizing the same stimuli. As we have seen, Treisman et al. (1992) did not find such cross-task transfer.

Changes in either of these processing stages may involve extension of the utilized data base or, alternatively, a decrease by improved selection of information. Gibson and Gibson (1955) called distinction *enrichment* versus *differentiation*. Enrichment and differentiation both lead to increased discrimination (Postman, 1955). If learning involves only the input to the decision stage, differentiation may be realized either by discarding noninformative input connections or by strengthening the most informative ones within a previously viewed input population. Enrichment, on the other hand, could be achieved by extending input connections beyond the initial input population. If learning occurs within the bottom-up processing stream, it may be achieved by shrinking or proliferating the representation at the modified level.

Eleanor J. Gibson supported the differentiation principle. She associated enrichment with incorporation of experience-based assumptions that would improve inference and strengthen its component in decision making. Thus, in some cases, enrichment might lead to nonveridical perception of the stimulus. But this is true mainly if learning involves retrieval of extended prior representation, as suggested, for example, by James. Instead, Gibson described the process of perceptual learning as a gradual increase in the correspondence between our perception and the external stimulus. Learning is delineated by active exploration for cues within the stimulus that are the best bases for discriminations for the performed task. Such a process was demonstrated by Hock, Webb, and Cavedo (1987), who trained subjects on categorization of dot patterns. Subsequently, subjects were required to segment fields of dots into common patterns. The categorization training enabled them to notice increasingly larger common patterns of dots, suggesting that they gradually discovered initially nonsalient features. The Gibsons suggested that the same underlying principle may also account for apparently simple tasks, such as Volkman's skin spatial j.n.d. experiments (Gibson & Gibson, 1955). Their interpretation is that touch is actually a complex stimulus, and initially unnoticed cues are gradually discovered. Although stating this general principle, they do not specify the physical cues that are gradually noticed.

E. J. Gibson's notion of *direct perception* implies that discrimination is based on directly encoded, task-relevant discriminating features, so that we may expect some difficulty in switching to new tasks requiring a choice of previously disregarded stimulus features. Thus, interference is expected when the same stimuli are presented in a context that requires different discriminating features. On the other hand, Gibson suggests that the discriminating features are gradually abstracted (rather than using a template-matching scheme), so that the *principle of discrimination* may be transferred to untrained stimuli (such as across size and position; Gibson, 1969). Because the emphasis is on cues within the external stimulus, discriminating features are dictated by physical difference and not by different internal representations. Therefore, this hypothesis may be tested experimentally (see the transfer studies discussed later and the Appendix).

One of the advocates of the enrichment principle, even before it was so named, was *James* (1890), the first theorist to address Volkman's findings. He assumed that discrimination could be acquired only between stimuli that were vaguely different before practice. Experience produced a more accurate image of doubleness by "filling the memory with past differences of similar direction as the present one, but of more conspicuous amount" (p. 515). Although James's terminology does not fall directly into the previously suggested scheme, he obviously suggests task-specific improvement, achieved by proliferation of memory representation, leading to increased distinctiveness of cues.

Improved discrimination (versus automatization) may also be the mechanism of learning in visual search. In this case, one expects that learning would be specific only to task-relevant features (see the preceding discussion of Gibson). However, in her studies of conjunction search, Treisman found that learning was specific to both task-relevant and seemingly irrelevant features. For example, in the search for a target different in conjunction of color and orientation, learning was specific not only to color and orientation, but also to target location and texture. However, in terms of internal representation, the dissociation of relevant and irrelevant features is complex because location, orientation, color, and texture may be coupled at the level of modifications. For example, at a retinotopic stage, learning is expected to be location specific even if it occurs by strengthening of connections of the most informative conjunction units.

III. Increased speed and efficiency

Although the preceding theorists emphasized increased resolution, others focused on the gradual increase in speed expressed by the fact that the same performance is achieved in less time. Tasks composed of several calculation steps may be speeded up either by using a faster algorithm for answering an equivalent computational question or by improving the algorithm and/or facilitating its implementation. (Another radical possibility, replacing computation by memory retrieval, is discussed later.)

Crossman (1959) thought that all skill acquisition is the outcome of better choice, not of algorithmic improvement. All improvement originates from the choice of the best-suited preexisting strategy.

The notion of changing the strategy instead of facilitating the one initially utilized may also apply to simple perceptual tasks. For example, according to Cheng (1985), improved efficiency in memory search tasks results from taking decisions at the category level rather than from initial comparisons at the item level. Subjects use a preexisting category, if possible (e.g., when searching for a digit among letters) or attach a new task-specific category tag (e.g., searching for specific letters among others). Thus, identifying the displayed element becomes sufficient, regardless of target set size. Cheng's hypothesis was generally supported by a variety of experimental studies (see the description in the Appendix). These ideas refer partly to processes beyond the scheme of Figure 17.5, but *memory organization* is also partly reflected in the content, size, and order of the rectangles at the *memory/object representation* stage.

Conjunction search (visual search for a target that differs only by feature conjunction, e.g., orientation and color) may also gain from strategy shifts. It has been seen as a typical case of serial search in which attention is shifted serially from one element to another (Treisman & Gelade, 1980), resulting in a much longer search time than parallel search. However, when the target features are highly discriminable and the targets are consistent, conjunction search is performed with a speed approaching that of feature search and with a slope (dependence on element number) approaching zero (Treisman & Sato, 1990; Wolfe, Cave, & Frauzel, 1989). Training, which also reduces search time and slope (Treisman, 1992; Treisman et al., 1992; see also the data of Wolfe et al., 1989), may do so by increasing target discriminability, for example by allowing subjects to tune in to specific features. Another condition in which the slope is highly reduced involves displays with a large number of distractors, perhaps due to search by groups of elements rather than one by one (Wolfe et al 1989; Zohary & Hochstein, 1990). Learning could also reduce search time by a shift to search by groups of elements. Finally, other cases of serial search can be speeded, for example, search for a *T* among *L*'s (see the data of Wolfe et al., 1989) and several cases of search for difficult-to-discern features (Sireteanu & Rettenbach, 1993).

Anderson (1982) suggested a theory for acquisition of cognitive skills starting from the initial phases of interpreting the task and culminating in automatization and fine tuning. Following the initial declarative verbal stages, improvement is the outcome of both process enhancement by *unitizing products* (combining unitary operations) that are used in sequence and also by instance-specific automatization in a procedural stage where trained constants replace variables in the procedure, so that the capacity-limited short-term memory is no longer needed. Thus, algorithmic enhancement occurs through chunking of previously applied procedures and by automatization, and not through a change in strategy. Various patterns of learning transfer are accommodated by this model. There should be a general transfer component derived from algorithmic enhancement, but in addition, instance specificity is expected at the automatization stage. Another prediction is that in training with a consistent procedure, initial improvement will be algorithmic, and thus will generalize over different parameters, whereas only subsequent improvement will be stimulus specific. Although the theory is general, it is more interesting when applied to complex perceptual tasks composed of several processing stages.

Memory retrieval. Logan (1988) hypothesized that automatization is the outcome of a change in strategy whereby calculation is replaced by memory retrieval or, in his terms, a process-based mechanism is replaced by one that is item-based. Specifically, Logan suggests that each stimulation episode leaves a separate trace in memory (perhaps equivalent to the object file of Kahneman and Treisman [1984]), namely, proliferation of the number of rectangles at the *memory/object representation* stage of Figure 17.5. In subsequent encounters with the same stimuli, these traces are retrieved together with the results of related computations. The use of a specific long-term memory trace is similar to Anderson's (1982) concept of automatization. However, according to Anderson, a single set of specific processes is unitized and strengthened in long-term memory, whereas according to Logan, separate memory traces are formed by each stimulus presentation. Both theories predict item-specific automatization.

The applicability of Logan's theory was demonstrated with a numerosity task (Lassaline & Logan, 1993) in which subjects reported the number of elements in a display. With practice, response time did not depend on element number. However, in their experiment, a different global structure was associated with each number of elements. This association was learned, and learning was specific to the global structure of the display. The important point is that parallelization was not the outcome of more efficient or parallel, element-by-element construction of the same process, but rather of replacement with detailed, perhaps cued, facilitated perception of the global structure. To test whether, in addition to the strategy change (to global structure memory association), there is also facilitation of global structure perception, an additional probe task should be employed with the same global structures.

The applicability of Logan's model of automaticity to practice effects in search tasks is questionable both for memory (Logan & Stadler, 1991) and for visual search. In particular, if seriality in visual search is induced by attentional requirements at early prestimulus encoding stages (Treisman & Gelade, 1980), then theories of modifications at the poststimulus encoding memory stage will not make visual search parallel.

In summary, we have discussed putative mechanisms underlying improved efficiency, discriminability, and automatization – three manifestations of practice effects. Although they are measured differently, they may be the outcome of the same mechanisms. The role of active exploration of alternative strategies in addition to memory reorganization was emphasized for each of them. The straightforward assumption of automatization as the gradual elimination of the need for top-down enhancement of bottom-up processing due to strengthening of the repeated path at the weak links (La Berge, 1976; Schneider, 1985; Shiffrin & Schneider, 1977) was strongly questioned. The consequent limitations on the extent of improvement were also stressed. Taken together, the experimental results and theoretical considerations may seem to suggest that perhaps early processing stages do not retain plasticity. The following section presents data that refute this hypothesis.

Transfer studies using simple stimuli

Studying the extent of performance improvement with simple stimuli and tasks is very important in extending our understanding of what processing levels and mechanisms are modifiable. Both experimental findings and theories focusing on more complex tasks suggested that perhaps perceptual learning may be explained by modifications restricted to the stage of memory representation or with strategy shifts. If performance of simple tasks that require relatively little computation may be substantially improved, then perhaps early processing mechanisms are also modifiable. Changes related to the representation of basic features were either not suggested (e.g., by Logan and Cheng) or not supported experimentally (by Treisman).

In addition, our understanding of the mechanisms underlying improvement in simple tasks may be more comprehensive for the following reasons. First, we know more of the underlying representations utilized by simple tasks because their input is not very remote from the externally applied physical stimulus. For example, we understand more clearly the elementary components, and the task-relevant and task-irrelevant features, depending on the characteristics of the task representation (see the earlier discussion). Second, simple tasks are processed at a physiological level, namely, the level of processing for which there is accumulated physiological data and understanding. Thus, a behavior–neural network correlation may be attempted. This correlation may guide our search for the underlying neuronal site that may be associated with a specific processing stage (*stimulus feature/components* compared with *object representation* of Figure 17.5). Third, some simple tasks are performed automatically even before training and may yet be amenable to substantial improvement. Characterizing learning effects in these tasks may reveal the separation between effects of repeated task processing and requirements for plasticity. In addition, explaining improvement in these tasks is challenging for most learning theories.

The first controlled study which found substantial improvement in a simple task was performed 140 years ago (Figure 17.1). The drastic improvement found in skin spatial discrimination was subsequently addressed by several theorists. However, lacking knowledge of the internal representation, they did not elaborate on putative mechanisms and formulated them only in broad general terms. The various interpretations shared the notion that the underlying changes do not affect the nature of representation of the most basic perceptual elements, but rather affect the related memory/object representation or output connections to a task-specific decision stage (Figure 17.5; however, see Gibson, 1969, and the earlier discussion of Gibson). This basic notion may perhaps be addressed when integrating behavioral and physiological data.

Over the past 20 years, experiments have been conducted characterizing improvement in a variety of simple visual tasks and studying the extent of transfer across stimulus changes along various dimensions. Table 17.2 summarizes the studies of learning in simple tasks that tested their transfer/specificity characteristics. Substantial improvement was found for the following behavioral tasks: acuity tasks such as peripheral spatial resolution (Johnson & Leibowitz, 1979; Figure 17.2, top left); hyperacuity tasks including stereo acuity (Fendick & Westheimer, 1983; Figure 17.2 top, right), vernier acuity (Fahle & Edelman, 1993, McKee & Westheimer 1978; Figure 17.4, top), and stereopsis (Ramachandran & Braddick, 1973); discrimination tasks such as discrimination of orientation (Schoups, Vogels, & Orban, 1993; Shiu & Pashler, 1992; Vogels & Orban, 1985, Figure 17.2, bottom), of motion direction (Ball & Sekuler, 1982, 1987; Figure 17.8, bottom right), of complex wave gratings (Fiorentini & Berardi, 1980, 1981; Figure 17.8, top right; Berardi & Fiorentini, 1987; Figure 17.8, middle right), and of global aspect orientation (Ahissar & Hochstein, 1993, Figure 17.11, bottom, open circles); texture segregation (Karni & Sagi, 1991; Figure 17.8, top left); feature detection (Ahissar & Hochstein, 1993; Figure 17.8, middle left); and detection of a laterally masked Gabor patch (Polat & Sagi, 1994). Performance in all these tasks was subject to substantial improvement, although the rate of advance varied. In all cases, the fastest progress occurred within the first several hundred trials, but in those studies that continued training, additional improvement was obtained for several thousand trials. Fast and slow components showed stimulus specificity (although not necessarily equally so; see Karni & Sagi, 1993).

I. Specificity implications for learning site

Characterizing stimulus specificity may clarify the processing and anatomical site underlying improvement. For example, in all cases where oriented elements were used, learning was specific to the trained orientation (see Table 17.2 and Figure 17.8, bottom, left, for example). Orientation specificity suggests a learning site not prior to orientation-specific units, that is, not before the primary cortex (area V1). When sinusoidal gratings were used (Fiorentini & Berardi, 1980), improvement was specific to spatial frequency (Figure 17.8, middle right). When element size was greatly reduced (Ahissar & Hochstein, 1993), performance deteriorated toward initial values (Figure 17.8, middle, left). These findings suggest that learning in these cases is not located at an extremely high

Table 17.2. *Studies of simple task-learning specificities*

Task	Transfer characteristics	Training	Authors
Stereopsis	orientation specific		Ramachandran & Braddick (1973)
Complex grating relative phase discrimination	specific to orientation; spatial frequency; location (1°) except across hemifields; transfer across eyes.	one session 200 trials	Berardi & Fiorentini (1987) Fiorentini & Berardi (1980, 1981)
Orientation discrimination	no transfer from around oblique to around principal axes; some transfer to other obliques	several sessions 5000 trials	Vogels & Orban (1985)
Motion direction discrimination	specific to movement direction & speed; retinal location	several sessions	Ball & Sekuler (1982, 1987)
Bar pattern discrimination	specific to retinal location	one session	Nazir & O'Regan (1990)
Texture discrimination (for orientation)	specific to background orientation; retinal location; trained eye (but first session not eye specific)	several sessions	Karni & Sagi (1991, 1993)
Vernier acuity	specific to location and orientation	several sessions	Fahle et al. (1992, 1993, 1994, 1995)
Orientation discrimination	specific to orientation and retinal location	one session and more	Shiu & Pashler (1992); Schoups et al (1995)
Feature search for orientation	specific to orientation element size; retinal location (within 0.7°); almost no eye specificity	several sessions	Ahissar & Hochstein (1993, 1995, 1996)
Array orientation discrimination	specific to array size not to element size	several sessions	Ahissar & Hochstein (1993)
Detecting Gabor-patch flanked by two others	specific to retinal location and eye	several sessions	Polat & Sagi (1994)

visual area (e.g., the inferotemporal cortex [IT]) because, at that level, there is abstraction of viewpoint-specific properties such as object size (Gross & Mishkin, 1977).

In all tasks that tested specificity to a consistently trained retinal location,

eye

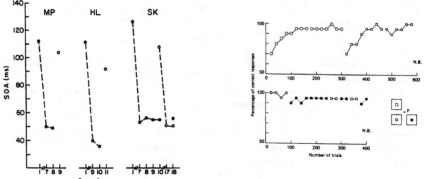

retinal location

size

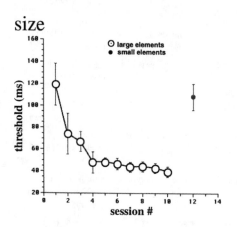

spatial frequency

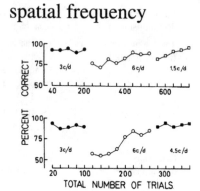

orientation

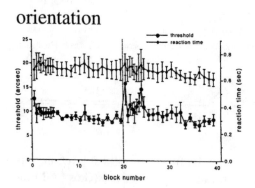

motion direction

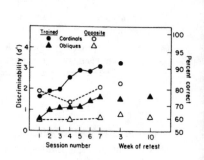

Figure 17.8. Stimulus specificities in simple perceptual tasks. Learning in various simple perceptual tasks is specific to a variety of stimulus dimensions. *Eye*: Texture discrimi-

substantial or nearly complete specificity was found. Various studies tested different spatial resolutions. Karni and Sagi (1991) found that there is almost no transfer of texture discrimination when moving from about 3° above and to the right of fixation to the same distances below or to the left of fixation. Schoups et al. (1993) found almost no transfer when shifting a grating patch location by 5° in an orientation identification task. Berardi and Fiorentini (1987) found complete specificity when moving a 1° complex grating patch from 1° to 2° from fixation to 2° to 3° (although there was transfer across the midline; see Figure 17.8, top, right). Recently, Polat and Sagi (1994) found that practice-induced increase in the range of lateral interactions is specific within 0.5° of the position of flanker elements.

Spatial specificity may be particularly important in elucidating the anatomical site of changes underlying behavioral improvement because there is a monotonic increase in the average receptive field size along the anatomical and processing hierarchy of cortical areas, with higher-stage neuronal receptive fields extending to nearly a hemifield (Gross, Roch-Miranda, & Bender, 1972). However, no specific cortical area can be uniquely indicated on the basis of the behaviorally tested spatial resolution of any of these psychophysical studies (e.g., there are neurons in area V4 with 1° diameter receptive fields; see Desimone & Schein, 1987; for a review, see Desimone & Ungerleider, 1989). Spatial resolutions that unequivocally point to the earliest cortical stage (area V1) have not been tested

Figure 17.8 *(cont.)*

nation is specific to the trained eye (filled circles, first trained eye; open circles, other eye). Learning is also eye specific in detecting a laterally masked Gabor patch, vernier acuity, and somewhat specific in motion direction discrimination. *Size*: Training orientation pop-out detection with large elements (22' length) does not transfer to half-length elements, although it does transfer in the reverse direction (not shown). Learning global orientation discrimination of a rectangular array of elements is also global size specific. *Orientation*: Learning vernier acuity with horizontal lines does not transfer to vertical lines or vice versa (not shown). All other studies, including texture discrimination, pop-out detection, phase discrimination, orientation discrimination, and Gabor detection, also showed orientation specificity. *Retinal location*: Learning to discriminate relative spatial phase between components in a compound grating patch located 1° from the vertical meridian in the upper quadrants of the visual field (circles) did not transfer to performance to the lower quadrant (squares) but did to the homologous quadrant across the vertical meridian (filled squares). Learning was also location specific for texture discrimination, pop-out detection, vernier acuity, motion direction discrimination, orientation discrimination, and detecting a Gabor patch. *Spatial frequency*: Relative spatial phase discrimination, as earlier, practiced previously at 3 cycles per degree (c/d), did not transfer to 6 or 1.5 c/d but did transfer from 3 and 6 c/d to 4.5 c/d. *Motion direction*: Learning discrimination of the direction of motion of a field of random dots around a cardinal or oblique direction (filled symbols) did not transfer to discriminations around the opposite direction, nor did it interfere with such discriminations (open symbols). Adapted from Ahissar & Hochstein (1995), Ball & Sekuler, (1987, Figure 1); Berardi and Fiorentini (1987, Figure 6); Fahle & Edelman (1993, Figure 6); Fiorentini and Berardi (1981, Figure 7); Karni & Sagi (1991, Figure 4).

(see Dow, Snyder, Gautin, & Bauer, 1981, for a discussion of foveal resolution in area V1). At this level, moving the stimuli by less than half a degree at the center of the fovea will excite a completely nonoverlapping population of neurons (disregarding long-range lateral interactions that seem to have only a secondary effect). Thus, although complete transfer across this distance would suffice as evidence against area V1, learning specificity is not a sufficient indication that modulations are confined to this area. However, behavioral testing with these fine spatial resolutions is very hard.

A related finding is that attention cannot be restricted to an area less than 1° in diameter (at least when tested for letters and words, for example by LaBerge, 1989), indicating perhaps that spatial attention cannot be confined to a single V1 unit. If learning can be shown to be specific to the sub-1° level, it may indicate that learning involves more than improved top-down spatial selection mechanisms because its resolution is dictated by bottom-up stimulus activation.

One reservation concerning the behavioral determination of anatomical site using learning spatial specificity resolution derives from the questionable consistency of the neural receptive field size when measured in different behavioral contexts. Spatial tuning may be modified dynamically, depending on the behavioral context. For example, Moran and Desimone (1985) found that the functional receptive field in area V4 and the IT may be narrowed when a monkey is engaged in a task demanding spatially selective attention.

Note that the increasingly larger receptive field sizes with increasing complexity of processing and abstraction predicts that the more basic the required processing, the finer the expected spatial specificity resolution. For example, improvement in identification of faces or other complex objects is expected to transfer completely across retinal locations (in agreement with some physiological observations in the anterior IT). Treisman (1992) compared the benefits of consistent relative location in training and testing of feature search (pop-out) and of conjunction search. As discussed earlier, the latter requires a combination of features and should be subsequent to feature search. It is thus expected to have a more crude spatial specificity. Treisman, however, found that whereas conjunction search showed substantial benefits from consistent target location (Figure 17.7, bottom, right), feature search was not substantially affected. Similarly, Nazir and O'Regan (1990) found location specificity for subjects learning to discriminate between complex spot patterns.

Treisman models this finding in the following way: When the subject attends an object, a "file" is opened and fine details, including location, are registered and encoded in memory. A subsequent presentation retrieves this information (see the earlier discussion of Logan). Because an object file is opened only with attention, it is opened for each element in conjunction search, whereas only one object file (if any) need be opened for feature search. Thus, detailed information will be registered for conjunction search and may not be registered for feature search. The implicit assumption is that learning in both tasks does not occur in an early visual area (Figure 17.5: *stimulus feature/components*), but rather in a subsequent non-retinotopically constrained cortical stage that stores detailed, multidimensional, object-related information (*memory/object representation*). However, in Treisman's reaction time studies, eye movements account for the lack of retinal location specificity in feature search. Furthermore, detection of conjunctions (and Nazir and O'Regan's spot patterns) could be performed and learned at a somewhat lower processing stage that retains retinotopic architecture.

In view of the complexity of deriving the site of learning from spatial specificity, the strongest indications of plasticity as early as V1 are the findings of ocular specificity. A single neuron collects input from the two eyes at the early stages of V1. In addition, under most conditions, we have no conscious access to purely monocular information. Training effects in texture discrimination with one eye covered are almost completely specific to the trained eye (Karni & Sagi, 1991; see Figure 17.8, top, left). This is also the case with lateral masking of a gabor patch (Polat & Sagi, 1994). Improvement in vernier acuity also shows ocular specificity (Fahle, Poggio, & Edelman, 1992). Relying on anatomical and physiological data, Karni and Sagi concluded that the underlying changes occurred as early as the primary visual cortex. This conclusion may be questioned, however. Although neurons at higher visual areas are typically binocular, they may receive different amounts of input from the two eyes; thus, monocular information may be reconstructed. Although formally this may be true, there is a correlation between the complexity of the task (in terms of the underlying neural representation) and its amount of interocular transfer, even with simple tasks (see, e.g., Ball & Sekuler, 1987; Fiorentini & Berardi, 1981).

Determining whether the learning in these cases is the outcome of modifications at the level of V1 is extremely important for understanding the learning process. Involvement of V1 would mean that learning changes in adults may occur even at the earliest processing and feature encoding stages. Involvement of V1 does not, however, directly determine whether these changes involve basic bottom-up processing architecture or task-specific selection mechanisms that may be directly connected to the earliest processing stages (i.e., to the black horizontal arrows at the bottom of Figure 17.5).

II. Changes underlying learning

Concluding that modifications can occur early does not necessarily indicate that they involve the encoding of basic stimulus elements. Can behavioral studies discriminate between changes within the stimulus representation stages (bottom-up processes in Figure 17.5) and changes at their output, task-specific decision stages (black horizontal arrows of Figure 17.5)? Findings of improved orientation discrimination were recently interpreted as originating from improved selection mechanisms among units representing an orientation-selective population vector (Seung & Sompolinski, 1993). The same general principle may underlie the finding of Hock et al. (1987) that category training increased the salience of previously low-salience complex subunits. As long as the task-specific decision stage resides at a level that has direct access to the level that retains stimulus specificity, then improvement will substantially follow this specificity. Improvement was interpreted as originating from an improved exploitation of information within orientation-selective units by an increase in weighting assigned to the most informative units. Optimization was sought only at the highest, task-specific stage. This interpretation is supported by the fact that training oblique orientations (which have an initially higher threshold than the principal axes) induces substantial learning, but not to the level of the principal axes. If the basic representation could be modified (e.g., by increasing representation of the oblique axes), then intensive training should lead to uniform thresholds.

Improvement in a vernier task was interpreted and modeled in two different ways. In vernier, the system interpolates between trained examples. One interpretation assumed that each different trained example is registered, adding more centers between which interpolation occurs and creating new perceptual modules (Poggio, Edelman, & Fahle, 1992a; Poggio, Fahle, & Edelman, 1992b). The other assumed that learning reassigns weights applied in a linear combination of oriented units so that the inputs of the most informative units are strengthened (Weiss, Edelman, & Fahle, 1993). The degree to which training may eliminate initial orientation biases was also tested for vernier acuity (McKee & Westheimer, 1978). However, in this case, the direction of the bias is not consistent between subjects and neither are the training effects. Therefore, it has no direct implications for choosing between the two previous interpretations.

Improvement in detection of a short light bar target element whose orientation differs from that of surrounding distractors by 30° (Ahissar & Hochstein, 1993; see Figure 17.11, top, right) is hard to account for on the basis of an improved task-specific selection mechanism. The target differs greatly from the distractors, so there is no apparent need for increased discrimination. In fact, the target initially pops out effortlessly and preattentively (Bergen & Julesz, 1983; Julesz, 1981). Models of the underlying plasticity assume a specific representation and mechanism. An often suggested mechanism is lateral interaction between similar distractor elements with the target being least inhibited and a "winner-take-all" mechanism producing pop-out (Koch & Ullman, 1985). An increase in lateral inhibition would make the odd element more prominent and improve detection. Such modifications should affect the basic orientation-representation architecture and the processing of the same stimulus under different behavioral contexts. However, improvement in pop-out may be interpreted differently. Applying consistent stimuli of both target and distractor orientations, a specific selection mechanism may gradually be tuned to this pair of orientations and thus avoid potential false alarms by distractor elements. Learning effects are indeed specific to both distractor and target orientations (indicating that modifications are not confined to connections between similar distractors). However, learning transfers almost completely to left–right reversed orientations (Ahissar & Hochstein, 1995). Perhaps the learning mechanism is related to improved tuning to a more complex orientation category (see Wolfe, Friedman-Hill, Stewart, & O'Connel, 1992). Transfer across left–right reversal casts further doubt on the suggestion of changes within stimulus encoding (see Figure 17.5) because transfer is evident for nondirectly activated orientations.

Ocular specificity challenges the hypothesis of changes at a task-related decision mechanism, implying that either these changes have direct access to the very early monocular processing stage or that training modifies the basic architecture. This later explanation may be substantiated by demonstrating training effects in other related behavioral contexts. An interesting point is that in texture discrimination (Karni & Sagi, 1991), subjects were instructed to perform two tasks. The emphasized one was at the fixation point and was aimed at forcing the subject to fixate. Learning in a dual-task condition may be different from learning in a single-task paradigm (see, e.g., Gopher, 1993) and may select earlier mechanisms.

Ocular specificity in texture discrimination was found only in the slower learning component, not in the fast within-session component (Karni & Sagi, 1993). However, the initial fast component was orientation and location specific. These results were interpreted as suggesting different learning mechanisms – an initial one that sets a task-specific routine to solve the perceptual problem and a slow one of ongoing, long-term modifications within these basic perceptual modules. The implication of that interpretation, namely, that stimulus specificities will increase with training (or at least will not decrease), has not been systematically studied with simple stimuli. With more complex stimuli, which perhaps follow different learning schemes, several studies reported decreased specificities with an increased training period (Rabbit, Cummings, & Vyas, 1979; Salthouse & Somberg, 1982, in visual search; but see Figure 17.7, bottom, right – location specificity).

Constraints from physiological studies of learning

Physiological studies focused on the same questions asked earlier: Where do changes occur? What is their nature? However, the "where" refers specifically to the anatomical site. Linking the anatomical site with a processing stage requires knowledge of processing at different physiological sites and thus can be addressed only in general terms, as discussed earlier. The "what" question was addressed physiologically either at the level of the local learning rule (e.g., Is it Hebb-like?); at the level of implementation by single neurons (e.g., Is there an increase in single neuron firing rate? Is the coherence between firing of different neurons increased? Is the preferred stimulus shifted toward the trained parameters?); or at the level of neural population recruitment for the processing needed to perform the task. Correlating between the physiological level and learning models requires understanding the internal representation and its encoding. This missing link is perhaps the reason that the potential relevance of these findings to the various models described earlier has not been addressed. We briefly describe recent physiological findings and then discuss their possible relation to the learning theories presented earlier.

Following the experiments of Hubel and Wiesel (1970), it was assumed that plasticity within the early cortical stages is not retained past an initial, brief critical period. However, recent experiments have found that even in adult animals, selective input deprivation yields substantial modifications of receptive field properties and functional architecture (Kaas, Merzenich, & Killackey, 1983; Merzenich et al., 1983). Deprivation was induced either by a restricted surgical cut of incoming fibers or by functional deprivation (see the review by Gilbert, 1993). Under both conditions, within minutes, receptive field sizes of the unstimulated area increased to include surrounding regions of the visual field. These changes are spatially restricted (e.g., 1–2 mm in the visual cortex), but the spatial shift is increased in the following weeks (4–5 mm; see Gilbert & Wiesel, 1992; Kaas et al., 1990), during which the initially silenced cortical area regains activity. Within the lateral geniculate nucleus, a large silent area remains.

The idea that the preference of single neurons may shift toward experimentally enhanced stimuli was directly demonstrated at the single-cell level in the primary visual cortex. If a given visual stimulus, not initially preferred by the neuron, is coupled with increased activation (either directly by applying current [Fregnac, Shultz, Thorpe, & Bienenstock, 1988, 1992; Shultz & Fregnac, 1992] or by the use of neuromodulators [Greuel, Luhman, & Singer, 1988]), then the neuronal tuning shifts toward that stimulus. This was demonstrated for both ocular dominance and orientation, as illustrated in Figure 17.9, left. What would underlie the increased activation of units with a different stimulus preference under physiological conditions? They are not particularly activated by the retinal input because they initially prefer a different stimulus. Their activation must derive specifically from an extraretinal component, perhaps *selective attention*, whose role would be to increase the underlying representation of the stimulated parameters (by particularly strengthening the response of differently tuned neurons). These studies implicitly assumed that learning involved enrichment of representation. Alternatively, the role of selective attention is to differentiate and select a best-suited neuronal population rather than to recruit neurons from the fringes.

In any case, these findings demand a revision of the "hard-wired V1" view and constitute firm evidence of continued plasticity. They suggest that the apparent specificity of receptive fields is the outcome of dynamic competition among broad-range inputs. However, because these results are from anesthetized animals,

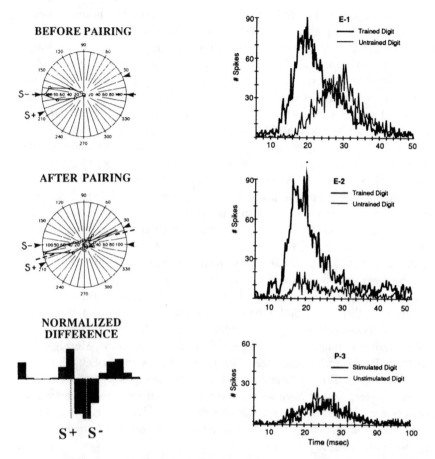

Figure 17.9. Physiological studies of perceptual learning. Left: Orientation tuning changes in adult cat striate cortical neurons. Following pairing (iontophoretically) of the initially nonpreferred orientation with a "high" response level, S+, and the initially preferred orientation with a "low" response level, S−, orientation preference shifted by 18° from the S− orientation toward the S+ orientation. The histogram shows a gain (loss) of responsiveness around the S+ (S−) orientation. Right: Monkeys were trained to discriminate tactile stimuli on a single digit in the 20- to 30-Hz range. Following training, responses were recorded in the anesthetized preparation. Histograms are shown for 20-Hz stimuli (50-ms cycle) summed across a population of area 3b neurons, superimposed for stimulation of previously trained and untrained digits. There was an overall increase in magnitude of response (monkeys E-1, E-2) and a shorter rise time (E-1) for the trained digit. No differences were found for a third previously passively stimulated monkey (P-3) between previously stimulated and unstimulated digits. From Fregnac et al. (1992, Figure 8) and Recanzone et al. (1992d, Figure 11).

they do not suffice as proof that such modifications occur under normal training conditions. Recently plasticity was demonstrated for behaving monkeys (Rosenthal, 1997) in the primary visual cortex, as it was demonstrated in other primary sensory areas (Ahissar et al., 1992; see the recent review by Weinberger, 1993).

Plasticity directly correlated with perceptual learning was shown only in the somata-sensory cortex. Recanzone, Jenkins, Hradex, and Merzenich (1992a) trained owl monkeys in a tactile frequency discrimination task and found threshold reduced to about one-third after a few dozen sessions. The neural representation of the behaviorally stimulated spatial area was substantially increased, as was the representation of the stimulated frequencies (Recanzone, Merzenich, & Jenkins, 1992b; Recanzone, Merzenich, Jenkins, Grajski, & Dinse, 1992c). Thus, representation expansion indeed occurs under behavioral conditions. But is this expansion the essential underlying mechanism for learning? Interestingly, substantial changes occurred only for behaviorally stimulated animals, not for passively stimulated animals. However, Recanzone et al. found that the extent of expansion, the magnitude of increased response, and the degree of neuronal receptive field size modification for the various animals trained, and for their different fingers, were not highly correlated with the amount of behavioral improvement. Rather, behavioral changes were strongly correlated with distributed neuronal response coherence for individual cycles of the vibratory frequencies applied during training, as seen in Figure 17.9, right (Recanzone, Merzenich, & Schreiner, 1992d; for reviews, see Merzenich & Sameshima, 1993; Ahissar & Hochstein, 1994). Thus, although related to the training process, increased representation seems not to have been the direct cause of improved performance. Recanzone et al. studied only the stimulus-related passive effects of behavioral practice because recordings were performed when the previously trained monkeys were anesthetized.

The few studies that examined practice effects during task performance recorded neuronal responses in higher cortical areas. Their results emphasize the importance of task-related modifications, at least for higher cortical areas. The modified representation was consistently related to the behaviorally trained task, although the extent of task specificity was not studied. Following practice, responses were more affected by the behaviorally trained context. This was the case when recording in the IT following training on orientation discrimination (Vogels & Orban, 1992). Interestingly, Vogels and Orban could not find stimulus-dictated effects such as increased response strength, sensitivity, or reduced variance, although the IT area does carry trained, stimulus-specific visual associations (Sakai & Miyashita, 1991). Similarly, following training on visual discrimination, task-specific effects were found in the higher prefrontal area (Kubota & Komatsu, 1985). Practicing motor responses (frontal cortex; Mann, Thau, & Schiller, 1988) and associations (premotor cortex; Mitz, Godschalk, &

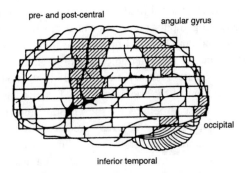

Figure 17.10. Regional cerebral glucose metabolic rate (GMR) quantified by PET measured before and after practice on the visuo-spatial-motor game Tetris. Regions showing a significant decrease in GMR with practice are shaded. These include the left and right post- and precentral cortex, left angular gyrus, left posterior temporal cortex, and left area 17 of the occipital cortex. Adapted from Haier et al. (1992, Figure 4).

Wise, 1991) also induce neuronal responses that are associated only with task-relevant movements.

The task-related effects found at higher cortical areas compared with the stimulus-specific effects found at primary sensory areas may reflect a cortical distribution of hierarchical processing. However, it also reflects the research, which did not study task-related responses at early areas and did not focus on characterizing stimulus-specific effects in higher cortical areas, perhaps due to the a priori conviction that such a hierarchy indeed exists.

The global distribution of activity at various cortical and subcortical areas as a function of learning was studied using positron emission tomography (PET) scans. A comparison was made between glucose metabolism before and after several weeks of training on the computer game Tetris (which combines perceptual and motor components). Energy consumption decreased in both motor and perceptual areas, including area V1, as shown in Figure 17.10 (Haier et al., 1992). No area was found to increase its activity significantly. However, in a different PET study, at the initial learning phase of rotor movement pursuit, the activity in restricted areas (premotor, pulvinar, and supplementary motor) was increased. This discrepancy may be attributed either to the different tasks or to the different stage of learning that was measured. There may be an initial increase in representation at the hard, exploratory, strategy-seeking stage of learning, followed by a decrease and confinement (Fitts, 1964; but see the discussion in the previous section and results of Karni et al., 1995). However, the physiological single-unit results of increased representation were also taken following a very large number of training sessions with perhaps overtrained animals.

The question of whether perceptual learning is largely due to increased representation for highly trained stimuli (and perhaps the task) or to refinement and selection among preexisting inputs relates to the distinction made by Gibson between discrimination and enrichment. Enrichment models at the various processing levels include James's ideas, Poggio's incorporation of additional examples, and Logan's separate memory traces. All these models predict an increase in the representation of the trained stimuli. Discrimination models, on the other hand, such as those proposed by the Gibsons and the one recently applied by Seung and Sompolinski (1993), may predict the use of a better-tuned and more informative subpopulation of neurons chosen from the initial one. Enrichment may be related to recruitment of an increased neuronal population, achieved perhaps by shifting the best response toward intensively trained stimuli. In contrast, discrimination may be implemented by a bias toward the most informative units (which are typically not those that respond maximally; see Seung & Sompolinski, 1993).

Can the physiological findings dissociate between changes within the general bottom-up processing scheme and their outputs to the task-specific decision mechanism? Increased representation, specifically at early processing stages, suggests that a larger capacity is dedicated. However, it is not clear whether this is increased computational power (Poggio), and thus perhaps more general, or increased storage capacity (Logan), and thus task specific.

Addressing the relation between the behavioral learning mechanism and the physiological implementation is highly important – perhaps even more so the more complex this relation is. For example, if learning of even simple tasks is achieved by changing strategies (as discussed earlier), studying the physiological correlate would be rather perplexing. Changes may occur at an early cortical stage and may still not be implemented by local stimulus-dictated mechanisms. The alternative straightforward hypothesis, that the consistently repeated stimulus response associations are strengthened with practice and eventually become automatic, was at least strongly questioned by behavioral findings.

The role of selective attention

Do all types of perceptual learning require gating of top-down selection mechanisms? And, if so, how specific are these mechanisms? Studying the role of attention in learning may elucidate the conditions for learning, the underlying mechanisms, and the possible physiological sites.

Wolford studied letter identification with backward masking. A three-letter target followed by a mask appeared 2° into the left or right visual field. The likely location of the target (and mask) was indicated by a precue (a left- or right-pointing arrow; see Posner, 1978). Improvement occurred only for trials with the target appearing in the predicted, and therefore attended location, indicating that spatial attention is a necessary factor for perceptual learning (reported in Wolford & Kim, 1992).

When one uses relatively complex stimuli whose identification may require attention, the need for selective attention may not be surprising. However, when considering simple tasks, it was not obvious a priori that selective attention is necessary for improvement. Recently, the requirement for selective attention was shown also for simple tasks. Shiu and Pashler (1992) used a dual-task paradigm in which the same stimuli, line bars, were used for two tasks. In an orientation discrimination task, the subjects had to decide whether bars had the same or different orientations. In a brightness discrimination task, subjects had to judge whether the bars had the same brightness. Practicing brightness discrimination improved orientation discrimination between the same line segments (for groups trained with easy or hard brightness discrimination tasks), as shown in Figure 17.11, top, left, but this improvement was not statistically significant. In addition, the improvement due either to direct training in orientation discrimination or to the limited transfer from brightness discrimination training was location specific in both cases, though the degree of specificity of cross-task transfer was again not statistically significant. Another finding of task-specific improvement was reported in a double task with vernier acuity and color discrimination (Moller, Crabb, & Hurlbert, 1993).

Surprisingly, selective attention is necessary even for improvement in preattentive tasks whose processing probably does not require selective attention. Ahissar and Hochstein (1993) also applied a dual task paradigm. The stimuli were arrays of 5×6 or 6×5 line segments with all elements either of the same orientation or with one element's orientation differing by 30° from the others, as illustrated in Figure 17.11, top, right. One task involved discrimination of the global array orientation (horizontal or vertical), and the other involved detection of the odd element (the highly studied automatic pop-out task; Treisman & Gelade, 1980). Parameters were chosen so that the two tasks had very similar thresholds. The curves of Figure 17.11, bottom, illustrate the course of improvement for two groups trained first with the local pop-out task (C) or the global orientation discrimination task (D) and then tested (and trained) on the other task. Practicing the pop-out detection task had no effect at all on array orientation discrimination, and practicing orientation discrimination had only a small effect in improving the detection of the odd element. Because detection is processed even without attention (or control), this finding shows that unattended processing and even focal attention are insufficient for learning. Thus we must differentiate between repeated performance and learning.

If pop-out learning occurs as early as V1 (Julesz, 1990; see the discussion by Ahissar & Hochstein, 1994), this means that specific attentional control is necessary even for plasticity at this early stage. Such studies have not yet been

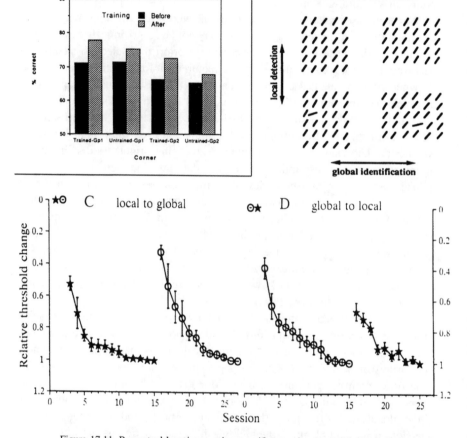

Figure 17.11. Perceptual learning requires specific attentional control. Top left: Percentage of correct orientation discrimination between two light bars of 7° and 10° tilt and orthogonally varied brightness before (filled bars) and after (striped bars) practice on brightness judgment using the same bar stimuli. Results are shown for trained and untrained retinal locations. Although orientation learning was location specific, the graph shows that the (insignificant) cross-task transfer was not location specific. Top right: Four stimuli used to test cross-task learning transfer. Subjects reported the presence or absence of the odd orientation element, or whether the array of elements was aligned vertically or horizontally. A mask stimulus (containing a square array of asterisk-like elements) was presented following a variable SOA. From the resulting performance versus SOA psychometric curve, the threshold SOA for 82% correct performance was determined and plotted as a function of training. Bottom: Learning curves showing the relative threshold change due to learning the "local" pop-out task and subsequent training on the "global" array orientation task (C) or learning first the global task and subsequently the local task (D). Note that learning in both cases was task specific, although there was a small degree of global to local task transfer. Thus, although learning is stimulus specific (e.g., Figure 17.8), it is also task specific, suggesting involvement of top-down attentional control mechanisms (see Figure 17.5). Adapted from Shiu and Pashler (1992, Figure 4) and Ahissar and Hochstein (1993, Figures 1 and 4).

undertaken at the physiological level. However, when subjects are tested at a postlearning stage, neuronal responses at higher visual areas (V4 and above) are affected by the behavioral context (e.g., Maunsell & Hochstein, 1992; Moran & Desimone, 1985), whereas neuronal responses at the level of V1 are not sensitive to attentional demands (Haenny & Schiller, 1988; Wurtz, Goldberg, & Robinson, 1982; except focal attention [Motter, 1993]). This implies that if learning does occur at the level of V1, then it involves additional separate mechanisms that are not apparent in neuronal responses.

To test whether practiced S–R correlation is sufficient for improvement, another experiment was conducted by Ahissar and Hochstein (1993). Here only two stimuli were applied: a vertical array with an odd element and a horizontal array with no odd element (top right and bottom left in Figure 17.11). Now the correct responses for the two tasks were correlated. However, again, practicing the pop-out task did not improve performance in array orientation discrimination. This indicates that experienced contingencies are not sufficient for improved performance. Task-specific attention needs to be allocated.

To what processing stage is attention allocated to facilitate improvement? Salthouse and Somberg (1983) studied improvement in a video game composed of several components. Interestingly, task improvement was due not to more efficient processing of the individual task components but rather to revision of the processing operations. This is in agreement with improvement at the top task-specific processing stage. General reinforcement learning would "highlight" the entire activated and trained processing path and would thus cause an improvement in the performance of the components.

Do these findings of improvement as an active exploration process indicate a specific mechanism? It seems that the visual system actively searches for a hypothesized underlying rule at a level that is discriminately activated by the displayed stimuli in correspondence with the task being performed. Perhaps selective attention is expressed by the choice of the task-relevant stage or neuronal assembly, and this choice affects network plasticity.

Although the importance of selective attention is not proof, it supports the suggestion that even in early automatic and very simple tasks, improvement is derived from an active search for task-specific modifications, and repeated performance itself will not do. Interestingly, this is in agreement with physiological findings. Long-term modifications depended on selective attention (Recanzone et al., 1993b – d), in spite of the fact that performance itself did not alter the measured neuronal responses (Mountcastle, Steinmetz, & Romo, 1990). However, selective attention was a prerequisite even for changes that were not correlated with improvement. It will be of interest to study whether attended practice changes the representation of unattended properties that show no behavioral improvement. For example, a monkey may train for the global array discrimination with a fixed element orientation. Then the question is whether there will be a change in the representation of the elements even though they were not relevant for the attentively performed task.

Appendix: Conclusions and findings of studies of learning in search tasks

A. Specificity of learning in memory search to physical properties while maintaining semantic categories: A change from uppercase to lowercase letters had a small but significant effect in disrupting performance (Graboi, 1971; Ross, 1970; see also Kolers, 1976). Doubling the probe size somewhat improved performance (Ross, 1970).

B. Cheng's model (1985) is consistent with the findings of the following effects:

1. In scanning for letter targets among lists of strings, the dependence on memory target set size is gradually eliminated (Neisser et al., 1963), but dependence on viewed string length is not (six compared with two letters; Neisser, 1963; see also Rabbit et al., 1979).

2. *Category effects* disappear when practicing visual search but not memory search. Subjects performing memory search tended to either have more false alarms or slower correct rejections on catch trials where members of the target category that were not part of the target set were presented. This category effect did not decrease with practice at least during 768 trials (Logan & Stadler, 1991). This agrees with the performance of *memory search* at the category level. On the other hand, in a similar study with *visual search* (Hock, Rosenthal, & Stenguist, 1985), the digit-letter category effect was eliminated within 400 trials, implying that here learning is element specific.

3. Some findings from transfer studies in memory search support a shift to a category-based decision. Complete transfer was found to either the new background letter set (Rabbit et al., 1979) or the new positive set (Kristofersson, 1979). Thus tagging is of categories and not of specific items.

Other findings are in agreement with either category shift or stimulus response association strengthening. There is complete transfer when the combination of separately practiced target and distractor sets is changed (Prinz, 1979). However, replacing all elements causes large decrements (Madden & Nebbes, 1980). Worst of all is the reversal condition in which negative and positive sets are interchanged (Graboi, 1971; Shiffrin & Schneider, 1977; see the discussion in Kristofersson, 1979; Prinz, 1979; Salthouse & Somberg, 1982).

Note

1. The generally accepted form for learning is (not an exponential-decay type function but) a power law with a negative exponent. That is, the time needed to perform a task as a function of the

number, n, of practice trials is $RT = RT(\text{asymptote}) + b \circ n^{-c}$, so that the rate of learning decreases with past achievement, and learning is bounded (the second term approaches zero, and RT approaches its asymptotic value as n gets very large).

References

Ahissar, M., & Hochstein, S. (1993). The role of attention in early perceptual learning. *Proceedings of the National Academy of Science of the U.S.A. 90*, 5718–5722.

Ahissar, M., & Hochstein, S. (1995). How early is early vision? Evidence from perceptual learning. In T. V. Papathomas (Ed.), *Early vision and beyond* (pp. 23–37). Cambridge, MA: MIT Press.

Ahissar, M., & Hochstein, S. (1996). Learning pop-out detection: Specificities to stimulus characteristics. *Vision Research 36*, 3487–3500.

Ahissar, E., Vaadia, E., Ahissar, M., Bergman, H., Arieli, A., & Abeles, M. (1992). Dependence of cortical plasticity on correlated activity of single neurons and on behavioral context. *Science, 257*, 1412–1415.

Allport, A. (1993). Attention and control: Have we been asking the wrong questions? A critical review of twenty five years. In D. E. Meyer, & S. Kornblum (Eds.), *Attention and performance* (Vol. XIV, pp. 183–218). Cambridge, MA: MIT Press.

Anderson, J. R. (1982). Acquisition of cognitive skill. *Psychological Review, 89*, 369–406.

Ball, K., & Sekuler, R. (1982). A specific and enduring improvement in visual motion discrimination. *Science, 218*, 697–698.

Ball, K., & Sekuler, R. (1987). Direction specific improvement in motion perception. *Vision Research, 27*, 953–965.

Bennet, R. G., & Westheimer, G. (1991). The effect of training on visual alignment discrimination and grating resolution. *Perception & Psychophysics, 49* (6), 541–546.

Berardi, N., & Fiorentini, A. (1987). Interhemispheric transfer of visual information in humans: Spatial characteristics. *Journal of Physiology, 384*, 633–647.

Bergen, J. R., & Julesz, B. (1983). Parallel versus serial processing in rapid pattern discrimination. *Nature (London), 303*, 696–698.

Boring, E. G. (1942). *Sensation and perception in the history of experimental psychology.* New York: Appleton-Century.

Cheng, P. W. (1985). Restructuring versus automaticity: Alternative accounts of skill acquisition. *Psychological Review, 92*, 414–423.

Crossman, E. R. F. W. (1959). A theory of the acquisition of speed-skill. *Ergonomics, 2*, 153–166.

Desimone, R., & Schein, S. J. (1987). Visual properties of neurons in area V4 of the macaque: Sensitivity to stimulus form. *Journal of Neurophysiology, 248*, 835–868.

Desimone, R., & Ungerleider, L. G. (1989). Neural mechanisms of visual processing in monkey. In F. Boller & J. Grafman (Eds.), *Handbook of neuropsychology* (Vol. 2, pp. 267–299). Amsterdam: Elsevier.

Deutsch, J. A., & Deutsch, D. (1963). Attention: Some theoretical considerations. *Psychological Review, 70*, 80–90.

Dow, B. M., Snyder, A. Z., Gautin, R. G., & Bauer, R. (1981). Magnification factor and receptive field size in foveal striate cortex of the monkey. *Experimental Brain Research, 44*, 213–228.

Duncan, J. (1983). Category effects in visual search: A failure to replicate the "oh-zero" phenomenon. *Perception & Psychophysics, 34*, 221–232.

Duncan, J., & Humphreys, G. W. (1989). Visual search and stimulus similarity. *Psychological Review, 96*, 433–458.

Fahle, M., & Edelman, S. (1993). Long term learning in vernier acuity: Effects of stimulus orientation, range and of feedback. *Vision Research, 33*, 397–412.

Fahle, M., Edelman, S., & Poggio, T. (1995). Fast perceptual learning in hyperacuity. *Vision Research, 35*, 3003–3013.

Fahle, M., Poggio, T., & Edelman, S. (1992). Fast perceptual learning in hyperacuity. *Perception, 21* (Suppl), 69a.

Fendick, M., & Westheimer, G. (1983). Effects of practice and separation of test targets on foveal and peripheral stereoacuity. *Vision Research 23*, 145–150.

Fiorentini, A., & Berardi, N. (1980). Perceptual learning specific for orientation and spatial frequency. *Nature (London), 287*, 43–44.

Fiorentini, A., & Berardi, N. (1981). Learning in grating waveform discrimination: Specificity for orientation and spatial frequency. *Vision Research, 21*, 1149–1158.

Fitts, P. M. (1964). Perceptual-motor skill learning. In A. W. Melton (Ed.), *Categories of human learning* (pp. 243–285). New York: Academic Press.

Fregnac, Y., Shultz, D., Thorpe, S., & Bienenstock, E. (1988). A cellular analogue of visual cortical plasticity. *Nature, 333*, 367–370.

Fregnac, Y., Shultz, D., Thorpe, S., & Bienenstock, E. (1992). Cellular analogs of visual cortical epigenesis. I. Plasticity of orientation selectivity. *Journal of Neuroscience, 12*, 1280–1300.

Geiger, G., Lettvin, J. Y., & Zegarra-Moran, O. (1992). Task-determined strategies of visual process. *Cognitive Brain Research, 1*, 39–52.

Gibson, E. J. (1953). Improvement in perceptual judgements as a function of controlled practice and training. *Psychological Bulletin, 50*, 401–431.

Gibson, E. J. (1969). *Principles of perceptual learning and development*. New York: Appleton-Century-Crofts.

Gibson, J. J., & Gibson, E. J. (1955). Perceptual learning – differentiation or enrichment? *Psychological Review, 62*, 32–41.

Gilbert, C. D. (1993). Rapid dynamic changes in adult cerebral cortex. *Current Opinion in Neurobiology, 3*, 100–103.

Gilbert, C. D., & Wiesel, T. N. (1992). Receptive field dynamics in adult primary visual cortex. *Nature, 356*, 150–152.

Gopher, D. (1993). The skill of attention control: Acquisition and execution of attention strategies. In D. E. Meyer & S. Kornblum (Eds.), *Attention and performance* (Vol. XIV, pp. 298–322). Cambridge, MA: MIT Press.

Graboi, D. (1971). Searching for targets: The effect of specific practice. *Perception & Psychophysics, 10*, 300–304.

Greuel, J. M., Luhman, H. J., & Singer, W. (1988). Pharmacological induction of use dependent receptive field modifications in the visual cortex. *Science, 242*, 74–77.

Gross, C. G., & Mishkin, M. (1977). The neural basis of stimulus equivalence across retinal translation. In S. Harned, R. Doty, J. Jaynes, L. Goldberg, & G. Krauthamer (Eds.), *Lateralization in the nervous system* (pp. 109–122). New York: Academic Press.

Gross, C. G., Roch-Miranda, C. E., & Bender, D. B. (1972). Visual properties of neurons in inferotemporal cortex of the macaque. *Journal of Neurophysiology, 35*, 96–111.

Haenny, P. E., & Schiller, P. H. (1988). State dependent activity in monkey visual cortex. 1. Single cell activity in V1 and V4 dependence on visual tasks. *Experimental Brain Research, 69*, 225–244.

Haier, R. J., Siegel, B. V., Jr., MacLachlan, E., Soderling, E., Lotenberg, S., & Buchsbaum, M. S. (1992). Regional glucose metabolic changes after learning a complex visuo-spatial/motor task: A positron emission tomography study. *Brain Research, 570*, 134–143.

Hock, H. S., Rosenthal, A., & Stenquist, P. (1985). The category effect in visual search: Practice effects on catch trials. *Perception & Psychophysics, 37*, 73–80.

Hock, H. S., Webb, E., & Cavedo, L. C. (1987). Perceptual learning in visual category acquisition. *Memory & Cognition, 15*, 544–556.

Hubel, D. H., & Wiesel, T. N. (1970). The period of susceptibility to the physiological effects of unilateral eye closure in kittens. *Journal of Physiology, 206*, 419–436.

James, W. (1890). *Principles of psychology*. New York: Holt.

Johnson, C. A., & Leibowitz, H. W. (1979). Practice effects for visual resolution in the periphery. *Perception & Psychophysics, 24*, 218–224.

Julesz, B. (1981). Textons, the elements of texture perception and their interactions. *Nature (London)*, 290, 91–97.

Julesz, B. (1990). Early vision is bottom up except for focal attention. In *Cold Spring Harbor symposia on quantitative Biology* (Vol. LV, pp. 973–978). Cold Spring Harbor, NY: Cold Spring Harbor Laboratory Press.

Kaas, J. H., Krubitzer, L. A., Chino, Y. M. Langston, A. L., Polley, E. H., & Blair N. (1990). Reorganization of retinotopic cortical maps in adult mammals after lesions of the retina. *Science, 248*, 229–231.

Kaas, J. H., Merzenich, M. M. & Killackey, H. P. (1983). Reorganization of somatosensory cortex following peripheral nerve damage in adult and developing mammals. *Annual Review of Neuroscience, 6*, 325–356.

Kahneman, D., & Treisman, A. M. (1984). Changing view of attention and automaticity. In R. Parasuraman & D. R. Davies (Eds.), *Varieties of attention* (pp. 29–61). New York: Academic Press.

Karni A, Meyer, G., Jezzard, P., Adams, M. M., Turner, R., Ungerleider, L. G. (1995). Functional MRI evidence for adult motor cortex plasticity during motor skill learning. *Nature 377*, 155–158.

Karni, A., & Sagi, D. (1991). Where practice makes perfect: Evidence for primary visual cortex plasticity. *Proceedings of the National Academy of Science of the U.S.A., 88*, 4966–4970.

Karni, A., & Sagi, D. (1993). The time course of learning a visual skill. *Nature, 365*, 250–252.

Koch, C., & Ullman, S. (1985). Shifts in selective visual attention: Towards the underlying neuronal circuitry. *Human Neurobiology 4*, 219–227.

Kolers, P. A. (1976). Reading a year later. *Journal of Experimental Psychology: Human Learning and Memory, 2*, 554–565.

Kristofferson, M. W. (1979). The effect of practice with one positive set in memory scanning task can be completely transferred to a different positive set. *Memory & Cognition, 5*, 177–186.

Kubota, K., & Komatsu, H. (1985). Neuron activities of monkey prefrontal cortex during the learning of visual discrimination tasks with GO/NO-GO performances. *Neuroscience Research, 3*, 106–129.

La Berge, D. (1976). Perceptual learning and attention. In W. K. Estes (Ed.), *Handbook of learning and cognitive processes* (Vol. 4, pp. 237–273). Hillsdale, NJ: Erlbaum.

La Berge, D. (1983). Spatial extent of attention to letters and words. *Journal of Experimental Psychology: Human Perception & Performance, 9*, 371–379.

La Berge, D. (1989). Theory of attentional operations in shape identification. *Psychological Review, 96*, 101–124.

Lassaline, M. E., & Logan, G. D. (1993). Memory-base automaticity in the discrimination of visual numerosity. *Journal of Experimental Psychology, 19*, 561–581.

Logan, G. D. (1988). Towards an instance theory of automatization. *Psychological Review, 95*, 492–527.

Logan, G. D. (1990). Repetition priming and automaticity: Common underlying mechanisms? *Cognitive Psychology, 22*, 1–35.

Logan, G. D., & Stadler, M. A. (1991). Mechanisms of performance improvement in consistent mapping memory search: Automaticity or strategy shift? *Journal of Experimental Psychology: Learning, Memory & Cognition, 17*, 478–496.

Madden, D. J., & Nebbes, R. D. (1980). Aging and the development of automaticity in visual search. *Developmental Psychology, 16*, 377–384.

Mann, S. E., Thau, R., & Schiller, P. H. (1988). Conditional task-related responses in monkey dorsomedial frontal cortex. *Experimental Brain Research, 69*, 460–468.

Marr, D. (1982). *Vision*. New York: W. H. Freeman.

Maunsell, J. H. R., & Hochstein, S. (1992). Effects of behavioral state on the stimulus selectivity of neurons in area V4 of the macaque monkey. In B. Blum (Ed.), *Channels in the visual* nervous system: Neurophysiology, psychophysics and models (pp. 447–470). London & Tel Aviv: Freund.

McKee, S. P., & Westheimer, G. (1978). Improvement in vernier acuity with practice. Perception & Psychophysics, 24, 258–262.

Merzenich, M. M., Kaas, J. H., Wall, J., Nelson, J., Sur, M., & Felleman, D. (1983). Topographic reorganization of somatosensory cortical areas 3b and 1 in adult monkeys after restricted deafferentiation. Neuroscience, 8, 33–51.

Merzenich, M. M., & Sameshima, K. (1993). Cortical plasticity and memory. Current Opinion in Neurobiology, 3, 187–196.

Mitz, A. R., Godschalk, M., & Wise, S. P. (1991). Learning dependent neuronal activity in the premotor cortex: Activity during the acquisition of conditional motor associations. Journal of Neuroscience, 11, 1855–1872.

Moller, P., Crabb, T., & Hurlbert, A. C. (1993). Color specific learning in vernier acuity and colour discrimination tasks. Perception, 22 (Suppl), 37a.

Moran, J., & Desimone, R. (1985). Selective attention gates visual processing in the extrastriate cortex. Science, 229, 782–785.

Motter, B. C. (1993). Focal attention produces spatially selective processing in visual cortical areas V1, V2 and V4 in the presence of competing stimuli. Journal of Neurophysiology, 70, 909–919.

Mountcastle, V. B., Steinmetz, M. A., & Romo, R. (1990). Frequency discrimination in the sense of flutter: Psychophysical measurements correlated with postcentral events in behaving monkeys. Journal of Neuroscience, 10, 3032–3044.

Nazir, T., & O'Regan, J. K. (1990). Some results on translation invariance in the human visual system. Spatial Vision, 5, 81–100.

Neisser, U. (1963). Decision time without reaction time: Experiments in visual scanning. American Journal of Psychology, 76, 376–385.

Neisser, U., Novick, R., & Lazar, R. (1963). Searching for ten targets simultaneously. Perceptual and Motor Skills, 18, 785–793.

Newell, A., & Rosenbloom, P. S. (1981). Mechanisms of skill acquisition and the law of practice. In J. R. Anderson (Ed.), Cognitive skills and their acquisition (pp. 1–55). Hillsdale, NJ: Erlbaum.

Poggio, T., Edelman, S., & Fahle, M. (1992a). Learning in visual modules from examples: A framework for understanding adaptive visual performance. CVGIP: Image Understanding, 56, 22–30.

Poggio, T., Fahle, M., & Edelman, S. (1992b). Fast perceptual learning in visual hyperacuity. Science 256, 1018–1021.

Polat, U., & Sagi, D. (1994). Spatial interactions in human vision: From near to far via experience dependent cascades of connections. Proceedings of the National Academy of Science of the USA. 91, 1206–1209.

Posner, M. L. (1978). Chronometric explorations of mind. Hillsdale, NJ: Erlbaum.

Postman, L. (1955). Association theory and perceptual learning. Psychological Review, 62, 438–446.

Prinz, W. (1979). Locus of the effect of specific practice in continuous visual search. Perception & Psychophysics, 25, 137–142.

Rabbit, P., Cumming, G., & Vyas, S. (1979). Improvement, learning and retention of skill at visual search. Quarterly Journal of Experimental Psychology, 31, 441–459.

Ramachandran, V. S., & Braddick, O. (1973) Orientation specific learning in stereopsis. Perception, 2, 371–376.

Recanzone, G. H., Jenkins, W. M., Hradex, G. T., & Merzenich M. M. (1992a). Progressive improvement in discriminative abilities in adult owl monkeys performing a tactile frequency discrimination task. Journal of Neurophysiology, 67, 1015–1030.

Recanzone, G. H., Merzenich, M. M., & Jenkins, W. M. (1992b). Frequency discrimination training engaging a restricted skin surface results in an emergence of a cutaneous response zone in cortical area 3a. Journal of Neurophysiology, 67, 1057–1070.

Recanzone, G. H., Merzenich, M. M., Jenkins, W. M., Grajski, A., & Dinse, H. R. (1992c). Topographic reorganization of the hand representation in cortical area 3b of owl monkeys trained in a frequency discrimination task. *Journal of Neurophysiology, 67,* 1031–1056.

Recanzone, G. H., Merzenich, M. M., & Schreiner, C. E. (1992d). Changes in distributed temporal response properties of S1 cortical neurons reflect improvement in performance on a temporally based tactile discrimination task. *Journal of Neurophysiology, 67,* 1071–1091.

Rosenthal, O. (1995). Behavioral Effects in the Primary Visual Cortex. M.Sc. thesis, Hebrew University, Jerusalem, Israel.

Ryan, C. (1983). Reassessing the automaticity–control distinction: Item recognition as a paradigm case. *Psychological Review, 90,* 171–178.

Sakai, K., & Miyashita, Y. (1991). Neural organization for the long term memory of paired associates. *Nature, 354,* 152–155.

Salthouse, T. A., & Somberg, B. L. (1982). Skilled performance: Effects of adult age and experience on elementary processes. *Journal of Experimental Psychology, General, 111,* 176–207.

Schneider, W. (1985). Toward a model of attention and the development of automatic processing. In M. I. Posner & O. S. Marin (Eds.), *Attention and performance* (Vol. XI, pp. 475–492). Hillsdale, NJ: Erlbaum.

Schneider, W., & Shiffrin, R. M. (1977). Controlled and automatic human information processing. I. Detection, search, and attention. *Psychological Review, 84,* 1–66.

Schoups, A. A., & Orban, G. A. (1996). Interocular transfer in perceptual learning of a pop-out discrimination task. *Proceedings of National Academy of Science USA, 93,* 7358–7362.

Schoups, A. A., Vogels, R., & Orban, G. A. (1995). Human perceptual learning in identifying the oblique orientation: Retinotopy, orientation specificity and monocularity. *Journal of Physiology, 483.*3, 797–810.

Schoups, A. A., Vogels, R., & Orban, G. A. (1993). Lack of transfer of perceptual learning in orientation discrimination task. *Perception, 22* (Suppl), 123b.

Schwartz, B. L., & Hashtroudi, S. (1991). Priming is independent of skill learning. *Journal of Experimental Psychology: Learning, Memory and Cognition, 17,* 1177–1187.

Seung, H. S., & Sompolinski, H. (1993). Simple network models for reading neuronal population codes. *Proceeding National Academy of Science USA, 90,* 10749–10753.

Shiffrin, R. M. (1975). The locus and role of attention in memory systems. In A. Rabbit & S. Dormic (Eds.), *Attention and performance* (Vol. V, pp. 142–169). New York: Academic Press.

Shiffrin, R. M., & Schneider, W. (1977). Controlled and automatic human information processing: II. Perceptual learning, automatic attending, and a general theory. *Psychological Review, 84,* 127–190.

Shiu, L., & Pashler, H. (1992). Improvement in line orientation discrimination is retinally local but dependent on cognitive set. *Perception & Psychophysics, 52,* 582–588.

Shultz, D., & Fregnac, Y. (1992). Cellular analogs of visual cortical epigenesis. II. Plasticity of binocular integration. *Journal of Neuroscience, 12,* 1301–1318.

Sireteanu, R., & Rettenbach, R. (1993). Serial visual search can become parallel with practice. *Perception, 22* (Suppl), 36a.

Squire, L. R. (1992). Mechanisms of memory. *Science, 232,* 1612–1619.

Sternberg, S. (1966). High speed scanning in human memory. *Science, 153,* 652–654.

Tawney, G. (1897). Ueber die Wahrnehmung zweier Punkte mittelst des Tastsinnes, mit Rucksicht auf die Frage der Uebung. *Philosofische studien, 13,* 163–222.

Treisman, A. (1992). Perceiving and reperceiving objects. *American Psychologist, 47,* 862–875.

Treisman, A., & Gelade, G. (1980). A feature integration theory of attention. *Cognitive Psychology, 12,* 97–136.

Treisman, A., & Sato, S. (1990). Conjunction search revisited. *Journal of Experimental Psychology: Human Perception and Performance, 16,* 459–478.

Treisman, A., Vieira, A., & Hayes, A. (1992). Automaticity and preattentive processing. *American Journal of Psychology, 105,* 341–362.

Vogels, R., & Orban, G. A. (1985). The effect of practice on the oblique effect in line orientation judgements. *Vision Research, 25,* 1679–1687.

Vogels, R., & Orban, G. A. (1992). Changes in response properties of inferotemporal cells during orientation discrimination learning. *Perception, 21* (Suppl), 68c.

Volkman, A. W. (1858). Ueber den Einflus der Uebung. Leipzig Berichte. *Math.-phys. Classe, 10,* 38–69.

Weinberger, N. M. (1993). Learning induced changes of auditory receptive fields. *Current Opinion in Neurobiology, 3,* 570–577.

Weiss, Y., Edelman, S., & Fahle, M. (1993). Models of perceptual learning in vernier hyperacuity. *Neural Computation, 5,* 695–718.

Wolfe, J. M., Cave, K. R., & Franzel, S. L. (1989). Guided search: An alternative to feature integration model for visual search. *Journal of Experimental Psychology: Human Perception and Performance, 15,* 419–433.

Wolfe, J. M., Friedman-Hill, S. R., Stewart, M. I., & O'Connel, K. M. (1992). The role of categorization in visual search for orientation. *Journal of Experimental Psychology: Human Perception and Performance, 18,* 34–49.

Wolford, G., & Kim, H.-Y. (1992). The role of visible persistence in backward masking. In A. F. Healy, S. M. Kosslyn, & R. M. Shiffrin (Eds.), *From learning processes to cognitive processes. Essays in honor of William K. Estes* (Vol. 2, pp. 12–31). Hillsdale, NJ: Erlbaum.

Wolford, G., Marchak, F., & Hughes, H. (1988). Practice effects in backward masking. *Journal of Experimental Psychology: Human Perception and Performance, 14,* 101–112.

Wurtz, R., Goldberg, M., & Robinson, D. L. (1982). Brain mechanisms of visual attention. *Scientific American 246* (6), 100–107.

Zohary, E., & Hochstein, S. (1989). How serial is serial processing in vision? *Perception, 18,* 191–200.

18 The history of size constancy and size illusions

Helen E. Ross and Cornelis Plug

Introduction

Discussions of size perception and size illusions have a long history that predates the rise of experimental psychology. Meyering (1989) distinguishes three developmental phases in the history of perception, which we describe.

The first phase is represented by the view, held during ancient times and by many medieval authors, that perceptual knowledge is directly impressed on the senses by stimulus objects. The study of perception was mainly concerned with the problem of how a distal stimulus produces a sensory response; the proximal stimulus (retinal image) was not recognized, and the origin of perceptual knowledge was largely ignored. Perceptual theories during this phase were implicitly based on the so-called identity postulate (Meyering, 1989, p. 15): the assumption that reality is perceived directly and accurately by the eye. This view implied that illusions were physical in origin, as the postulate does not allow for perceptual illusions. Also, the term *apparent size* and its synonyms had the unambiguous meaning of visual angle, a usage that survives in astronomy to the present.

The second phase began as soon as the optical functioning of the eye was understood, and concentrated on the epistemological problem of how a sensory response gives rise to perceptual knowledge – a problem first tackled in earnest by Descartes (1637/1956) and later by Berkeley (1709/1948) and others. Most authors saw perceptual knowledge as resulting from the cognitive processing or decoding of stimulus information assumed to be *sufficient* to ensure veridical perception.

The third phase began with Helmholtz (1867/1962), when perceptual knowledge came to be seen as a hypothetical construction based on *insufficient* stimulus information. For Helmholtz, perception was an *unconscious inference (unbewusster Schluss)*.

The preceding scheme is not entirely accurate, as the distinction between perceived size and visual angle was introduced by Ptolemy during the first phase (2nd century A.D.). It was further developed in the 11th century by the Arab physicist Ibn al-Haytham, who clarified size constancy and discussed perceptual

499

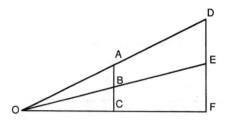

Figure 18.1. Angular size, linear size, and target distance. The apparent enlargement of AC compared to EF is an example of the Ponzo illusion.

illusions. Thus the second phase had early beginnings that overlapped the first phase.

We shall now discuss some terms used for size perception. It is easy to show in geometric terms that the angular size of an object is approximately halved when its viewing distance is doubled, although its linear size remains constant. This is illustrated in Figure 18.1, where the line AC subtends the angle AOC at distance OC but the same line length EF subtends the smaller angle EOF at distance OF.

It is less easy to illustrate what happens to *perceived size* when viewing distance changes. Much of the literature is ambiguous as to whether perceived size should relate to angular size or to linear size, or possibly to some hybrid between the two. The *classic* form of the *size-distance invariance (SDI)* hypothesis equates perceived size with linear size, and states that perceived size is a function of the true angular size and the perceived distance. Thus, in Figure 18.1, the angular size AOC could give rise to a perceived linear size AC at the perceived distance OC or the larger linear size DF at the further perceived distance OF. According to this argument, angular size is correctly encoded by the brain, and all misperceptions of linear size are caused by misperceptions of distance. An alternative version of SDI uses *phenomenal* measures for all the variables and states that perceived linear size is a function of the perceived angular size and the perceived distance (e.g., McCready, 1965). In this version there are two types of perceived size, angular and linear, and misperception of perceived linear size may occur through misperceptions of either angular size or distance or both. Thus, in Figure 18.1, the length BC may be perceived as enlarged to AC because its angular size is incorrectly perceived as AOC rather than BOC, and not purely because of a mistake in distance perception.

The ambiguity in defining perceived size creates ambiguities in defining illusions. If angular size is intended, then all departures from angular size, including the phenomenon of *size constancy,* should be classed as illusions or misperceptions. If linear object size is intended, then size constancy is veridical and the other size phenomena are illusions. Explanations for size illusions are often the same as one or the other of the standard explanations given for size constancy. We therefore describe the history of size constancy before the various other size effects.

Size constancy

The phenomenon we now call size constancy was described by Ptolemy in the 2nd century A.D. but was not discussed in detail until the 11th century. This is probably because the conceptual framework was insufficiently developed until then. In addition, it is not a phenomenon that attracts much attention. At close distances, constancy is so effective that there is little change in perceived size with distance – and it took Euclid (c. 300 B.C.) to point out that the visual angle does diminish with distance. At far distances objects certainly appear smaller, but the diminution can easily seem to be explained by the reduction in visual angle. It is only when perceived size is measured at various distances and compared with the visual angle that the discrepancy between the two becomes obvious.

Some early speculations and experiments relating to size constancy concerned a perspective phenomenon that later came to be called the *alley problem*: If one looks along a path with regularly spaced trees or pillars forming parallel rows, the two rows appear to converge in the distance. The phenomenon has been known since at least the time of Leonardo da Vinci (1452–1519), who noted that horses running away from an observer on parallel tracks appear to converge in the distance (*Works*, 1956, Vol., 1. p. 113). The problem ultimately derives from one of Euclid's propositions, namely, that "parallel lines, when seen from a distance, appear not to be equally distant from one another" (Burton, 1945, p. 358). Euclid simply meant (and proved) that the *angular* separation between parallel lines decreases with distance. This fact does not, of course, constitute a perceptual problem if it is thought that perception follows the retinal image. However, the alley problem acquired a new meaning when stated in terms of perceived rather than angular convergence. It was discussed at length during the 18th century but was first investigated experimentally in 1902 by Hillebrand, who found perceived parallelity to be a compromise between angular separation and objective parallelity (Boring, 1942, p. 294).

The term *size constancy* was introduced by the Gestalt psychologists in the 1920s as one of their laws of visual form perception. The term is perhaps unfortunate, as it incorrectly suggests that objects always appear the same size, regardless of distance or other variables. Because constancy is incomplete, Thouless (1931) named it *phenomenal regression to the real object*, and Brunswik (1933) called it *transformation to the intermediate object (Zwischengegenstand)*. Not surprisingly, the shorter name survived. Much effort was devoted to the measurement of size constancy, and both Brunswik (1929) and Thouless (1931)

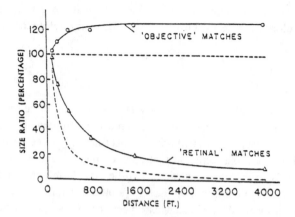

Figure 18.2. Gilinsky's size ratios, based on the linear sizes of standard and comparison stimuli, for linear size matches (upper curve) and angular size matches (lower curve). Constant object size is shown by the upper broken line and visual angle by the lower broken line. From Gilinsky (1955).

developed formulae for constancy ratios. These ratios ranged from 0 for complete conformity with angular size to 1.0 for complete conformity with linear size.

Following the letter symbols of Hochberg (1971), Brunswik's ratio is given by $(S' - s)/(S - s)$, where S is the linear size of the standard object (set at a given distance), S' is the linear size of the matched comparison object (set at a different distance from S), and s is the linear size of the comparison object that would match the angular size of the standard object. The Thouless ratio has the same form, except that the logarithm of each variable is used.

Some of the difficulties with these and other ratios are discussed by Sedgwick (1986). For example, the degree of constancy can appear very different, depending on the formula used, and (for the Brunswik ratio) on whether the far or near object is taken as the standard. An instructive case is the classic experiment of Gilinsky (1955). She conducted an outdoor field experiment in which a variable triangle at a distance of 100 ft was matched for either linear or angular size to more distant standard targets of different sizes. She found "overconstancy" (ratios greater than 1.0) for linear matches and some overestimation of angular size for the angular matches. She presented her data as percentages derived from simple ratios of the linear sizes of the variable and standard targets (Figure 18.2). The upper half of the figure clearly illustrates overconstancy, but it is difficult to calculate the overestimation of angular size from the linear ratios in the lower half of the figure.

Sedgwick presents Gilinsky's angular matching data as Thouless ratios and as two versions of Brunswik ratios, and shows how deceptively different the results can look (Figure 18.3).

It has been argued (e.g., Joynson, 1949) that these formulae are flawed: They involve a conflation of angular and linear measures, which are logically (and perhaps perceptually) different in kind and ought not to be merged mathematically. We therefore present a simplified version of Gilinsky's angular matching data, showing the ratio of the matched to the standard angular size at different target distances (Figure 18.4). This figure shows clearly that the overestimation of angular size increases linearly with the logarithm of the target distance, reaching a factor of 4 at 4,000 ft (0.76 mile or 1.2 km). If the data are extrapolated in the same manner, a factor of 5 is reached at a distance of about 12,000 ft – farther than one is likely to see discrete objects with normal horizontal viewing.

Several explanations for size constancy have been proposed, of which the dominant one has been classical SDI, or the scaling of perceived linear size for perceived distance. The other main accounts were relative size (now espoused by Gibsonians), the learning of various proprioceptive and visual cues (Berkeley), and oculomotor theories. The history of these accounts will now be outlined.

Scaling by distance

Euclid's *Optics* (c. 300 B.C.) deals with the question of apparent size in a geometric manner. Euclid pointed out that the nearer of two objects of equal physical size subtends a larger visual angle. Ptolemy's *Optics* (2nd century A.D.) was based on Euclid's *Optics*, but it contains a long discussion relevant to size and shape constancy (II, 53–63, and several other sections). These passages state that perceived size is determined by angular size in conjunction with perceived distance. A typical passage, referring to Figure 18.5, reads:

Suppose there are two lengths, AB and GD, which have the same inclination and subtend the same angle, E. When the distance of AB is not equal to that of GD, but shorter than it, AB will never appear longer than GD when determined by its true distance. Instead it will appear either shorter, which would happen when the difference in distance of the two lines is distinguishable; or equal, if the difference in distance is indistinguishable. (*Optics* II 56, our translation)

A clearer statement of SDI comes from Ibn al-Haytham (Latinized to Alhazen), who wrote his *Optics* around 1030. Alhazen based his *Optics* on Ptolemy's *Optics*. He had access to Ptolemy's original Greek text, now lost to us (Sabra, 1987), and he specifically referred to the preceding passage by Ptolemy. Alhazen discussed size constancy at great length, but a typical passage runs as follows: "When human vision perceives the size of visible objects, it perceives it from

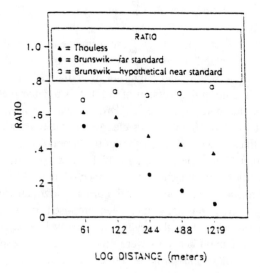

Figure 18.3. Gilinsky's (1955) angular matching data shown as Thouless ratios and as two interpretations of the Brunswik ratio. These ratios vary widely in their apparent conformity with linear size or with visual angle. From Sedgwick (1986).

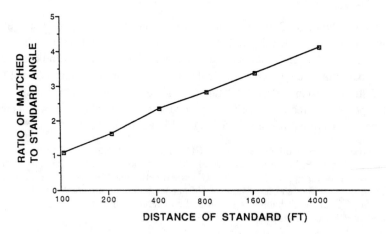

Figure 18.4. Gilinsky's (1955) angular matching data redrawn as the ratio of matched to standard angular size. The ratio increases linearly with the logarithm of the viewing distance.

the size of the angles that visible objects project to the center of vision, and from the degree of intervening space, and by comparing the angles with the intervening space'' (our translation, from Reimann, 1902a, p. 2).

The same point was later made by Descartes (1637, in the Sixth Discourse,

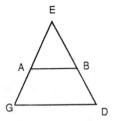

Figure 18.5. The diagram for angular and linear size in Ptolemy's *Optics* (II, 56). The observer's eye is at E.

trans. in Gregory, 1981, p. 361). Since that time, SDI was often described and was widely accepted. Desaguiliers (1736) demonstrated the phenomenon experimentally before the Royal Society of London and showed that it varied with distance cues and the observer's hypothesis about the distance. Helmholtz (1821–1894) believed in SDI, and his influence may have been one reason why the theory has dominated perceptual thinking for the past century. Also, it is hard to get away from the underlying idea that the options open to perception are defined by an optical array of lines of projection. The evidence for SDI was reviewed by Epstein, Park, and Casey (1961), with only mixed support. As Joynson (1949) pointed out, a correlation between size and distance judgments need not imply a causal connection because both factors could be processed independently. However, many modern authors have continued to produce mathematical models of size perception that rely on some type of distance scaling (e.g., Gilinsky, 1955, 1971, 1989) or *inverse geometric transformation* of the retinal image (e.g., Wagner, Baird, & Fuld, 1989).

A striking phenomenon that is often taken to support SDI is Emmert's law of afterimages. Benedetto Castelli (1557–1664) was probably the first to describe the effect (Ariotti 1973a, 1973c). Later, Emmert (1881) reported that an afterimage (which has a constant retinal size) appears to grow in proportion to the distance (or perceived distance) of the surface against which it is seen. Emmert's exact explanation is unclear, and he may not have intended to implicate SDI (see the review by Epstein et al., 1961). An alternative account can be given in terms of relative size because the image occupies a greater proportion of the background scene at farther distances. For example, in Figure 18.1, if a retinal image of angle BOC is projected onto a screen of height AC it occupies half of the screen, whereas if it is projected onto a screen of the same height (EF) at twice the distance, it occupies the whole of the screen. Afterimages viewed in darkness are also reported to shrink in perceived size when the observer moves his or her head towards the perceived location of the image (Gregory, Wallace, & Campbell, 1959; Taylor, 1941) – an observation that rules out relative size as the only factor and may be taken to implicate perceived distance.

However, the perceived size change occurs only if there is a concomitant convergence response (Taylor, 1941), so it is more likely that oculomotor factors are implicated.

It was also reported in the 19th century that certain figures, such as the Necker cube (1832) and the Schroeder staircase (1858), are perceptually reversible in perspective. Similar patterns occur in the tiling of medieval churches and other ancient buildings, so it is likely that the phenomena were observed long before they were reported. It was later noted that when the perspective reverses, the figures appear to change shape, with the part apparently at the front seeming smaller than the part at the back (e.g., Sanford, 1898, p. 256). This size effect has been taken to support SDI. Necker himself suggested that the reversal of perspective was related to changes in fixation, and there is some recent evidence that such reversals are accompanied by changes in accommodation (Enright, 1987). Oculomotor factors may therefore contribute to the apparent size changes in two-dimensional figures. The apparent size change is much larger for three-dimensional objects such as wire cubes (Gregory, 1970), and this larger effect may be related to the larger oculomotor involvement.

Scaling by size

Acceptance of size-distance scaling was not universal. The main competitor theories involved some form of size contrast or relative size, but their date of origin is uncertain. An early theory that may be an example of relative size was that of Plotinus (c. 203–270), who argued that size scaling was given by the details within objects, and that size constancy fails at great distances not because the angular size is small but because the details are lost. He wrote (Second Ennead, VIII):

But the phenomenon [of size scaling] is more easily explained by the example of things of wide variety. Take mountains dotted with houses, woods and other land-marks; the observation of each detail gives us the means of calculating, by the single objects noted, the total extent covered: but, where no such detail of form reaches us, our vision, which deals with detail, has not the means towards the knowledge of the whole by measurement of any one clearly discerned magnitude. . . . It was the detail that prevented a near object deceiving our sense of magnitude: in the case of the distant object, because the eye does not pass stage by stage through the stretch of intervening space so as to note its forms, therefore it cannot report the magnitude of that space. The explanation by lesser angle of vision has been elsewhere dismissed. . . . (Trans. by S. MacKenna and B. S. Page in Plotinus, *The Six Enneads*, 1952, p. 65)

Leonardo da Vinci (1452–1519) also commented on relative size (*Notebooks*, 1956, Vol. 1, pp. 238–239). He wrote: "And as [the pupil] varies its size the same object when seen by it will appear of different sizes, although it often happens that the comparison with surrounding things does not allow this change to be discerned when you look at a particular object."

A clearer statement about relative size was made by Castelli around 1639. He wrote: "After having reflected much and carefully it came to my mind that this business of the large and the small [of the constellations] is by our mind managed always in relation to some other magnitude better known to us than that which is the magnitude of the object about which we must form an idea of whether it is large or small" (Ariotti, 1973c, pp. 15–16). Castelli was clearly convinced that perceived size is mainly determined by comparison with known objects or extents. However, he then went on to accept the flattened sky explanation of the celestial illusion: The moon looks larger on the horizon because it seems farther away there (p. 17). This change of view came about as a result of discussing the problem with his teacher, Galileo, who convinced him of the SDI explanation.

Relative size theories remained current in the literature at the same time as SDI. Hering (1834–1918) – the nativist competitor of Helmholtz's empiricism – espoused such a theory (Boring, 1942, p. 292). More recently, Gibson (1950) stressed the importance of the texture gradients and size invariants present in the visual scene. A more general size recalibration theory that incorporates past experience has been developed by Andrews (1964).

Size cues

Berkeley (1709/1948) disbelieved in both SDI and relative size, and maintained that size perception was learned from various *cues*. These cues included the two for which he is best known: *aerial perspective* and the *angle of regard*. Berkeley is widely misquoted on his size theory. Most psychologists know that he held a cue theory of distance perception but falsely assume that he believed that size was derived through SDI (e.g., Boring, 1942, pp. 223, 298). Berkeley rejected SDI firmly:

What inclines men to this mistake (beside the humour of making one see by geometry) is, that the same perceptions or ideas which suggest distance, do also suggest magnitude. . . . I say they do not first suggest distance, and then leave it to the judgement to use that as a medium, whereby to collect the magnitude; but they have as close and immediate a connexion with the magnitude, as with the distance; and suggest magnitude as independently of distance, as they do distance independently of magnitude. (Berkeley, 1709/1948, Section 53)

An excellent discussion of Berkeley's position and a critique of SDI can be found in Schwartz (1994).

Berkeley also argued that tactile impressions of size possessed an intrinsically spatial quality that was absent in vision, and that this quality was transferred to visual size by experience (Berkeley, 1709/1948, Sections 49–54). The question of whether tactile and visual size (or shape) were innately linked was discussed by Molyneux and became known as *Molyneux's question* (Morgan, 1977), and many inconclusive investigations were made of formerly blind people who re-covered their sight. The relation between visual and bodily size has continued to be investigated by a few recent authors. Rock (1966, pp. 145–152) discussed the effect of remembered size when revisiting childhood scenes or when wearing magnifying lenses; Sedgwick investigated eye height and the horizon ratio rule for the size of objects apparently cutting the horizon (Gibson, 1979, pp. 164–165; Sedgwick, 1973, 1986); and Warren (1984) and Warren and Whang (1987) have investigated body-scaled information in relation to various physical actions. It is a topic likely to receive renewed attention in the field of computer vision and robotics: If a robotic hand is to grasp an object, the computer image of the object must be scaled to the size of the hand.

Cue theories were further elaborated in the probabilistic functionalism of Egon Brunswik (1944, 1956) and Taylor's behavioral theory (1962). Recent evidence for cue theory has been provided by Morgan (1992), who showed that relative size judgments for line lengths could be conditioned to the arbitrary cue of the line's orientation. Similarly, McKee and Welch (1992) showed that ob-servers could maintain a consistent size scale when the association between retinal size and binocular disparity was reversed from its usual direction.

Accommodation-convergence scaling

Observations on binocular eye movements date back to the invention of the stereoscope by Wheatstone (1938) and Brewster (1849). It was noted that changes in convergence, accommodation, and retinal disparity produced changes in perceived size without a corresponding change in retinal image size. Mc-Cready (1965) calculated from data of Heinemann, Tulving, and Nachmias (1959) that a perceptual shrinkage of about 25% was caused by an accommo-dation and convergence increase equivalent to 5 diopters (or a change in the far point from infinity to 0.2 m). The changes in perceived size are not always accompanied by an appropriate change in perceived distance (Wheatstone, 1852), so it is arguable whether the effects are consistent with SDI. An alter-native account is that changes in perceived angular size are mediated indepen-dently of perceived distance by the oculomotor system, probably by the efferent command signal (see the review by Enright, 1989). A mechanism of this sort could contribute significantly to size constancy.

The Celestial Illusion

The celestial illusion – the apparent enlargement of celestial bodies near the horizon in comparison with their appearance near the zenith – is so striking that it has been discussed since antiquity (Plug & Ross, 1989). Its explanation par-allels the development of various branches of science: astronomy, physics, optics, physiology – and, most recently, psychology. The classical astronomers suggested that refraction of rays by the Earth's atmosphere caused magnification of the sun's image. Aristotle (384–322 B.C.) held this view, as did Poseidonius, Cleomedes, and, later, Ptolemy (c. 142 A.D.). The refraction theory was unclearly expressed, mainly because refraction was poorly understood. The theory was also complicated by the view that vision is caused by visual rays that leave the eye through the pupil and return after encountering an object, bringing a visual image back to the observer. The idea of outgoing visual rays was gradually given up, but the refraction theory was not explicitly rejected until the 17th century, when it was understood that refraction caused a distortion of shape rather than size (e.g., Gregory, 1668). Nevertheless, the refraction theory is still believed today by many otherwise well-educated persons (Walker, 1978).

A quite different explanation, also based on outgoing visual rays, was given by Ptolemy in his *Optics*. He stated that, even though objects subtend equal angles, the visual ray produces a reduced sensation of size and distance for objects on high because of the unusual conditions and the difficulty of the action. This passage is hard to interpret (Ross & Ross, 1976; Sabra, 1987). A possible forerunner of this idea is to be found in Vitruvius (1st century B.C.) who stated (1931, Book III, Chap. 5 [9]): "For the higher the glance of the eye rises, it pierces with the more difficulty the denseness of the air; therefore it fails owing to the amount and power of the height, and reports to the senses the assemblage of an uncertain quantity of the modules."

Arab scientists translated and absorbed many classical works during the 8th and 9th centuries. They tended to accept Ptolemy's refraction theory of the moon illusion. However, Alhazen (c. 1030) produced the first clear psychological theory, defining the illusion in terms of perceived size rather than a change of image size. He believed that the size of an object is judged by combining its visual angle with its judged distance. Distance to the horizon can be judged through the intervening objects, but there are no intervening objects when looking up. The sky appears as a flat plane, seeming closer overhead than at the horizon. The celestial bodies move in this plane, and thus appear further away and larger on the horizon. This account by Alhazen has often been incorrectly ascribed to Ptolemy (Ross & Ross, 1976). The confusion may have arisen because Ptolemy described SDI in relation to noncelestial objects and because of an obscure passage in the *Planetary Hypotheses* in which he mentioned the difficulty of judging the sizes and distances of planets (translated in Sabra, 1987). One of the earliest comprehensible diagrams illustrating the flattened sky theory dates back to Robert Smith (1738, Plate 20, Figure 273); it is reproduced as Figure 18.6.

Alhazen's flat-sky theory consisted of two parts: (1) Lack of intervening objects causes the sky to appear flattened and (2) the flattened sky causes the sun to appear farther away on the horizon and therefore larger. These two parts

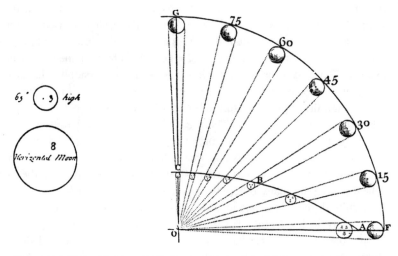

Figure 18.6. Robert Smith's (1738) diagram for the flattened sky and size-distance invariance account of the moon illusion. His illustration on the left shows the ratio of the perceived diameters of the horizontal and raised moons as 8:3 (an enlargement of 2.7).

gradually gave rise to separate theories, one concerning intervening objects (which contributed both to perceived distance and to relative size theories) and the other the flattened sky. Many measurements (begun by Robert Smith, 1738) were concerned with the apparent shape of the sky, and many more (begun by Zeno, 1862) dealt with the apparent size of afterimages viewed against different parts of the sky.

Alhazen's theory, and the earlier refraction theory, were absorbed into the scientific tradition of medieval Europe through Latin translations (Lindberg, 1976; Van Hoorn, 1972). Particularly influential were the 13th-century Latin works on optics by Roger Bacon, John Pecham, and Witelo, all of which were based on Alhazen. When the refraction theory was abandoned psychological theories came to predominate, but the illusion continued to be investigated as part of physiological and meteorological optics until about 1920.

Along with the change of disciplines went a change in the method of investigation. At first, informal observations and speculative explanations predominated. During the 17th century astronomic measurements were used to reject the refraction hypothesis, but other theories were not rigorously tested. Around 1900 there was an explosion of interest in the illusion, which involved naturalistic observation, field experiments, and laboratory experiments. This broad attack allowed some hypotheses to be rejected, but no generally accepted explanation was found. The position has changed little since then (e.g., Hershenson, 1989).

There is a subset of theories, lying within physiological optics rather than psychology, that ascribes the illusion to an enlargement of retinal image size within the eye when viewing horizontally. Pierre Gassendi (1592–1655) believed that the sun and moon were dimmer on the horizon than at the zenith (due to the Earth's atmosphere), and that this caused the pupils to dilate, which in turn increased the perceived size. The view that perceived size is increased by dilation of the pupil was expressed earlier by Leonardo da Vinci (*Works*, par. 31; *Notebooks*, 1956, pp. 211, 238). No satisfactory explanation was given for a relation between pupil size and perceived size, although various later authors made attempts. Some explanations involved changes in accommodation, which were believed to affect image size. Accommodation has been favored by a few modern authors (Enright, 1975; Iavecchia, Iavechia, & Roscoe, 1983), but the supposed mechanisms were unclear. Some authors (Enright, 1989; Lockhead & Wolbarsht, 1989; Roscoe, 1989) now accept a perceptual version of oculomotor theory, in which changes in the effort to convergence and/or accommodation evoke changes in perceived size – a theory that dates back to Zoth (1899).

All other modern theories are clearly perceptual. Berkeley (1709/1948) maintained that the moon illusion was due to the size cues of aerial perspective and the angle of regard. Aerial perspective has continued to be listed by many authors as a contributing factor. The angle of regard is much more controversial. It includes the convergence effort and other possible effects of raising or lowering the eyes in the head (e.g., Holway & Boring, 1940a, 1940b), changes in bodily posture, and vestibular stimulation. Several so-called vestibular experiments were conducted during the 1960s and 1970s (e.g., Wood, Zinkus, & Mountjoy, 1968), but none has shown a clear vestibular effect independent of such factors as head tilt and eye elevation. It is probable that all the factors relating to angle of regard cause changes in the oculomotor responses, which in turn affect perceived angular size.

It has become clear that the SDI explanation of the illusion cannot hold in its classic form. The vast majority of observations and experiments agree that the moon (and afterimages) appear both larger and nearer on the horizon than at the zenith, whereas the theory demands that they appear farther away. Belief in SDI has led to paradoxical explanations such as the *farther-larger-nearer* theory (Reimann 1902a, 1902b), in which there are two levels of size and distance perception: At an unconscious level the moon appears farther away and larger, but at a conscious level the large apparent size causes the moon to appear nearer. In the first inference, perceived size is supposed to behave like linear size, increasing with distance for a constant visual angle. In the second inference, it is supposed to behave like angular size, increasing as an object approaches.

The size of the illusion varies with the visual scene, the measurement method, and other factors: The sun's or moon's diameter is usually found to be enlarged by a factor of about 1.5 to 2.0 when its horizon and zenith appearances are compared. This illusion is larger than most other size illusions, and it is often argued that only size constancy (meaning SDI) is large enough to account for it. However, this argument does not hold if it is accepted that size constancy is itself the sum of several effects.

Currently, more authors are coming to accept that the celestial illusion entails a misperception of angular size (e.g., Enright, 1989; McCready, 1986; Reed, 1984; Roscoe, 1989; Suzuki, 1991) and that it may have many components (Coren, 1989; Leibowitz & Owens, 1989; Robinson, 1972), including a sizable oculomotor component (Enright, 1989; Leibowitz & Owens, 1989; Roscoe, 1989; Suzuki, 1991). The strength of the various components is outlined by Plug and Ross (1994).

Aerial perspective, brightness, and color

Aerial perspective

The apparent enlargement of objects in a mist is an obvious phenomenon that was reported in classical times. Aristotle wrote in his *Meteorologica* (1923, 6, 373b): "So promontories in the sea 'loom' when there is a south-east wind, and everything seems bigger, and in a mist, too, things seem bigger: so, too, the sun and stars seem bigger when rising and setting than on the meridian." Aristotle believed that the enlargement was physical, caused by what we would now call refraction. Ptolemy made similar comments (*Optics*, 1956, Book II, paragraphs 124–125).

It was later accepted that the enlargement was perceptual, and was related to the changes in color and brightness that affect distant objects seen through the atmosphere. Atmospheric effects have always been of special interest to land-scape painters, so it is not surprising that Leonardo da Vinci discussed them (*Notebooks*, 1956, Vol. 2, p. 237) and is said to have introduced the term *aerial perspective* (Boring, 1942). Leonardo used the term to describe the increasing blueness and faintness of objects in the distance. He seems to have believed that aerial perspective could explain the sun illusion. He denied that the sun illusion was due to refraction, and added: "for the things seen through the mist are similar in colour to those which are at a distance, but as they do not undergo the same process of diminution, they appear greater in size" (*Notebooks*, 1956, Vol. 1, pp. 262–263). It is unclear from this passage whether Leonardo thought that aerial perspective was an example of SDI or perhaps of relative size or expected size.

Most later authors, including Helmholtz (1867/1962, Vol. 3, p. 283), backed SDI. For example, Burnet (1773, pp. 30–31) wrote:

Another proof of this [SDI] is what happens when we are deceived with respect to the distance, as when we see things through a fog: for from the dimness of the image upon the retina, we infer, that the object is at a considerable distance; and from this supposed distance, compared with the greatness of the image upon the retina, we conclude, that the object is much greater than it truly is. And in this way, a dog seen through a mist appears as big as a horse, and an ordinary man looks like a giant.

There were a few dissenting authors. One was Myers (1911, pp. 282–283), who wrote: "But this [SDI] explanation is quite inadequate; for, owing to the exaggerated size of familiar objects seen through a fog, they appear to us as nearer, not further, than they actually are." However, Myers went on to "rescue" SDI by invoking the idea of an unconsciously registered far distance (c.f. Reimann's explanation of the celestial illusion). A more fundamental dissenter was Berkeley, who proposed that "faintness" was an important learned cue to both size and distance independently (1709/1948, Sections 55–58).

There appears to be little empirical evidence on the question. Ross (1967) found that the diameters of target discs were overestimated in a fog by an average factor of 1.2 and their distances were overestimated by a factor of 1.8, and there was a poor correlation between size and distance overestimation at different distances. Goeters (1975) found that linear sizes were overestimated by an average factor of 1.03, and distances by 1.08, in murky water compared to clear water: He concluded that SDI did not hold in murky water.

Aerial perspective is not described in detail in current psychology textbooks. Gibson (1950, p. 141) even maintained that aerial perspective was not a precise geometric correlate of distance and was only an approximate cue. In fact, it was defined mathematically in the 1940s (e.g., Fry, Bridgman, & Ellerbrock, 1947). The omission of quantitative accounts from recent texts may have occurred because the early psychological literature was unquantitative and often confused, and much of the later quantitative work was conducted by atmospheric and underwater scientists (e.g., Woods & Lythgoe, 1971) and was not published in the standard visual perception journals.

The main effects contributing to aerial perspective are a loss of luminance contrast and color contrast between the object and its background. With increasing distance, all reflecting objects take on the color and luminance of the sky background. Luminance contrast is probably more important than color contrast, yet dictionaries and textbooks highlight the effects of color. Troscianko, Montagnon, Le Clerc, Malbert, and Chanteau (1991) have shown that isoluminant hue gradients are an ineffective monocular cue to depth, but that luminance gradients and isoluminant color saturation gradients are indeed effective.

Brightness and color

The early literature on the effect of perceived brightness on perceived size is confusing regarding the relative importance of absolute luminance or of luminance contrast. Leonardo da Vinci noted that a dark object against a bright background appears smaller and a bright object against a dark background larger than usual (*Works*, 1939, Vol. 1, p. 214) – an illusion that seems to have been known to the ancient Greeks (Fletcher, 1963). Plateau (1839) and Helmholtz (1881/1968, p. 160) proposed that this was due to *irradiation* (the diffusion of light within the eye) – although the effect of this is rather small. However, at low contrasts the effect reverses, darker targets appearing larger than brighter targets of the same contrast (Weale, 1975). Other observers since Ptolemy in the 2nd century A.D. (Hirschberg, 1898) have reported that bright objects appear nearer than dim ones (Ashley, 1898). Ames (1946) showed that a circle of light appears to shrink and recede or expand and advance as its luminance contrast is changed by altering the luminance of a surrounding circle of light. Such findings contradict SDI, which requires an object of constant angular size to appear smaller if it appears nearer. An alternative account is that luminance contrast increases the perceived angular size, which then acts as a cue to closer distance. Luminance can increase apparent size by a factor reported to range from 59% (Holway & Boring, 1940c) to as little as 4% (Robinson, 1954).

The literature concerning the effects of color on perceived size or distance is even more confusing. There is a large literature on distance effects both for *advancing and retreating colors* (Luckiesh, 1918; Pillsbury & Schaeffer, 1937) and for binocular *color stereoscopy* (Oyama & Yamamura, 1960). It has been observed that blue colors generally appear farther away than red ones. This is sometimes explained as a learned effect of the changes in hue that occur with distance (Haenel, 1909); or as an effect of luminance, brighter colors appearing nearer (Taylor & Sumner, 1945); or as an effect of color or luminance contrast, blues generally having lower contrast with the background than reds (Ross, 1975); or as an effect of color stereoscopy involving binocular disparity (Donders, 1868, in Oyama & Yamumura, 1960).

The binocular stereoscopic effect varies with the illumination and with whether the eyes are crossed or uncrossed. It cannot be used to explain the monocular effects of advancing and retreating colors. There is a shortage of monocular experiments on the effects of color on apparent size. Quantz (1895) used a distance adjustment technique to match the perceived angular size of colored discs and found an effect of only about 1%. Over (1962) used a similar technique and found red targets to be judged about 20% larger than blue targets. Bevan and Dukes (1953) had their subjects make linear size matches for colored targets outdoors; it is not stated whether the subjects used one or both eyes, but they judged red targets to be about 6% larger than blue targets. However, there is little monocular evidence for an independent effect of hue because most studies failed to control for the effects of luminance or luminance contrast.

Geometric illusions and figural aftereffects

Geometric illusions

Detailed accounts of the history of geometric illusions exist elsewhere (e.g., Coren & Girgus, 1978; Robinson, 1972), so only a few points will be highlighted here.

The Greeks and other early architects were clearly aware of perspective and certain geometric illusions, because they took care to counteract the effects (Johannsen, 1971; Mayer-Hillebrand, 1942; Raymond, 1909). Vitruvius (1st century B.C.) stated that the slope of the upper parts of columns must be altered to counteract perspective effects.

The study of geometric illusions started in earnest in the 1850s with the work of Oppel in Germany (Johannsen, 1971; Zehender, 1899). Oppel coined the term *geometric-optical illusions* (*geometrisch-optische Täuschungen*) and described several different illusions including the horizontal-vertical (in which vertical lines appear longer than horizontal lines) and the filled-unfilled space (in which a space divided into small segments appears longer than an undivided space). The former illusion was, he claimed, well known to geometry teachers. The latter (later named the *Oppel–Kundt illusion*) was probably known to Aristotle, although his description of it appears to be the wrong way around (Johannsen, 1971).

There followed a plethora of illusions and their explanations. Some explanations were so vague as to be untestable. Some were very precise and involved optical or retinal processes that could cause a change in image size: These were mainly disproved. Others involved processes familiar from size constancy, such as SDI, relative size, and oculomotor factors.

Although a relation between the celestial illusion and depth perception was suggested as early as Alhazen, a similar explanation for geometric illusions of size apparently did not arise until the end of the 19th century (Brentano, 1892; Sanford, 1898; Thiéry, 1986). This later date coincides with a burst of theorizing about the geometric illusions. Many illusions – particularly the horizontal-vertical, the Müller–Lyer, and the Ponzo – can be interpreted as perspective figures, and the parts that appear enlarged are those with a more distant perspective: The enlargement could therefore be due to SDI. Versions of perspective theories were given renewed popularity in the second half of this century (Day, 1972; Gregory, 1963; Segall, Campbell, & Herskovitz, 1966; Tausch, 1954), when there was another surge of interest in geometric illusions. Insofar as these theories maintain that different parts of the figure actually appear to be at different depths, they are clearly mistaken. The figures usually appear to lie flat in the plane of the paper on which they are drawn. According to McCready (1985), some observers may report that the truly smaller or converging parts of the figure appear farther away (as required by the theory), but they may also report that the perceptually enlarged segment appears nearer (contrary to classical SDI). This contradiction has led some authors to invoke the idea of an unconsciously registered distance (e.g., Myers, 1911, pp. 282–283). Alternatively, some authors regard such illusions as resulting from misperceptions of angular size (e.g., McCready, 1985). One theorist who circumvented this difficulty was Gregory (1963), although he is frequently misquoted in this respect. He argued that there were two types of size-constancy scaling: *primary* and *secondary* (1963) or, in current terminology, *bottom-up* and *top-down* (e.g., 1986, p. 72). Primary scaling is automatic and occurs at an early stage, whereas secondary scaling is cognitive and involves scaling for apparent distance. Gregory argued that geometric illusions represent the first type: Size changes are triggered by typical depth features, without the necessity to see the figures in depth. Gregory's description appears to be equivalent to that of McCready insofar as it denies a role to the *classical* form of SDI.

If geometric illusions are caused by learned perspective cues, adults should be more susceptible than children, and people brought up in different visual environments should be differentially susceptible to certain illusions. For example, people living in a built-up city environment should be more susceptible to the Müller–Lyer illusion, whereas people living in a flat open environment should be more susceptible to the horizontal-vertical one. Investigation of these ideas began with the work of the anthropologist Rivers (1901, 1905), who studied the sensory perception of European and non-European people. This was followed by many cross-cultural studies in the 1950s and 1960s, of which the most famous was that of Segall et al. (1966). In general, the environmental hypothesis was upheld, although some authors found contradictory results. However, most studies were flawed because the groups differed in racial and educational background in addition to visual environment. Furthermore, developmental studies tended to show that perspective illusions *decreased* rather than *increased* with age (Coren & Girgus, 1978). For these and other reasons, support for perspective theories has waned in recent years.

Explanations based purely on relative size do not seem to have been explicitly stated until the latter part of this century. The ideas of contrast and assimilation were mentioned by Helmholtz (1856, cited by Robinson, 1972). Many authors discussed relative size as a cue to depth and then used it as part of a perspective theory (e.g., Day, 1972). Even Gibson (1950, p. 182) did so, giving Figure 18.7 the title "Size as determined by distance" – although he later specifically stated that size could be determined by units of texture gradients, without taking distance into account (1979, p. 163). Much Japanese work was conducted in the 1960s on contrast/assimilation illusions such as the Delboeuf and Titchener circles and divided lines (see Robinson, 1972). Neurological models based on spatial frequency analyzers were mainly developed for figural aftereffects, but they have also been

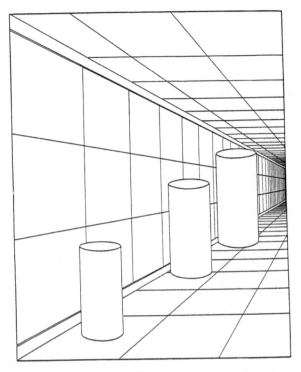

Figure 18.7. A perspective or relative-size illusion. From Gibson (1950, p. 182) with permission (Houghton Mifflin Co).

applied to simultaneous contrast effects (Gillam, 1980; Klein, Stromeyer, & Ganz, 1974). Such models are restricted to gratings at specific orientations and are not applicable to most illusion configurations. Current explanations of size contrast or assimilation concentrate on high-level cognitive comparisons (e.g., Coren & Enns, 1993) or on various computational approaches (e.g., Morgan, Hole, & Glennester, 1990; Redding, Winston, & Temple, 1993).

As described earlier, oculomotor theories of convergence effort were developed to explain size constancy and the moon illusion. It has also been argued that changes in accommodation and vergence occur when viewing perspective pictures and figures and are related to changes in perceived size (Enright, 1987). Another type of oculomotor theory was developed to explain geometric illusions, based on the idea that the eye scans the image and that the muscular effort is somehow taken into account. The early history of scanning theories is described by Scheerer (1984) and Coren (1986). Bain (1855) promulgated a view of this type, although he believed that "muscular consciousness" was additional to the visual information derived from the retinal image. Scanning theories assume that we have accurate information about eye movements, which is unlikely. Such theories also fail to explain size perception in the absence of eye movements, and simultaneous size perception in different parts of the visual field. Further- more, erroneous movements are followed by corrective saccades, showing that veridical retinal information is available. It could be that erroneous movements are caused by, rather than causing, misperceptions of size.

A different scanning theory is that movement effort, or intended effort, de- termines perceived size. Lotze (1852) developed a theory of *local signs*, invok- ing the reflex tendency of the eyes to move so as to bring to the fovea any stimulated point that comes under attention. Every retinal point thus becomes associated with a particular intensity of movement. Spatial extent is recon- structed from these intensities. Once local signs are acquired, actual eye move- ments are unnecessary: Tendencies toward eye movements will suffice. Misperception of angular size can be explained by changes in the sense of effort. Thus vertical eye movements are said to require more effort than horizontal movements (because they work against gravity), and this could explain the hor- izontal-vertical illusion. Wundt (1897) developed a neurological account of the sense of effort based on efference copy, but the details changed over the years (Ross & Bischof, 1981). In some modern theories, *efferent readiness* rather than efference copy or actual eye movements is said to determine perceived angular size (e.g., Coren, 1986; Festinger, White, & Allyn, 1968; Virsu, 1971). In these theories, a set of eye movements is computed and is held in readiness to be emitted across the visual display. However, efferent readiness has the status of an intervening variable that cannot be measured directly.

Geometric illusions can produce size distortions of up to about 30%. Many authors now accept multicomponent explanations, with the extent of the illusion varying with the components (e.g., Coren & Girgus, 1978; Robinson, 1972).

Figural aftereffects

Many geometric illusion figures can be separated into an inducing background component and a test component that appears distorted. If these components are presented sequentially, the test component appears distorted after the observer has stared at the background for a few seconds. Such aftereffects are generally called *figural aftereffects*. They are reviewed by McEwen (1958) and Robinson (1972). The earliest type of aftereffect was described by Gibson (1933) and involved the *normalization* of curved lines with a subsequent negative afteref- fect. Later, Köhler and Wallach (1944) described a more general type of spatial aftereffect that did not depend on normalization of the inspection figure. Ap- parent size changes can be induced that are very similar in kind and extent to those in the simultaneous displays of geometric illusions. For example, Oyama (1953) used a successive version of the Delboeuf figure, in which the inspection figure and test figure are circles of different sizes. Some of the explanations are similar to those given for geometric illusions. For example, perspective effects may be invoked for both. At a neurological level, simultaneous contrast effects (as in geometric illusions) are often explained by the inhibition of neighboring feature-detecting cells, whereas contrast aftereffects are explained by the fatigue of one type of cell.

Since the 1960s, size adaptation has been studied through the use of gratings, or spatial frequencies (e.g., Blakemore & Sutton, 1969). These stimuli are usually expressed in terms of cycles per degree subtended at the eye and thus relate to angular rather than linear size. The stimulus figures were not discovered by accident, as seems to have been the case with many earlier geometric illusions: They were deliberately created to test theories concerning spatial frequency-analyzing mechanisms. It remains unclear how such orientation-specific analyzers could encode the angular size subtended by the outline of an object and thus provide a mechanism for size perception.

Another class of sensory aftereffect arises from moving rather than static displays. Movement aftereffects and simultaneous contrast effects are obvious natural phenomena: The linear aftereffects of staring at moving water were reported by Aristotle, Lucretius, and others (Johanssen, 1971), and simultaneous induced motion was described by Ptolemy in his *Optics* (Hirschberg, 1898, p. 336). Travel in vehicles provides aftereffects of both size and movement-in-depth, as was noted by Thompson: "Thus, if from a rapid railway train objects from which the train is receding be watched, they seem to shrink as they are left behind, their images contracting and moving from the edges of the retina towards its centre. If after watching this motion for some time the gaze be transferred to an object at a constant distance from the eye, it seems to be actually expanding and approaching" (1877, p. 32). Rotary aftereffects are less likely than linear aftereffects to occur in a state of nature, and Plateau (1849) is generally credited with providing the first experimental account of the rotating spiral aftereffect. It was noted that the aftereffect of spiral expansion is combined with a depth effect of approach, and contraction with retreat (e.g., Szily, 1905). Such combinations contradict the conventional form of SDI, although they are consistent with the form in which a change in perceived angular size determines a change in perceived distance (McCready, 1965). The latter relationship has been termed *kinetic* SDI by Hershenson (1982). Presumably the display stimulates and fatigues "looming detectors," which jointly serve both changing distance and changing angular size.

Adaptation to optical distortion

After the invention of magnifying glasses, telescopes, and binoculars, observers noted that the perceived size change of objects viewed through these devices was not as great as the angular magnification (e.g., Wallis, 1687, p. 326). Many authors noted (or repeated the notes of others) that objects look nearer rather than larger and implied that the relationship was consistent with SDI. Burnet (1773, p. 29) made this point, as did Loiselle (1898) and Helmholtz (1867/1962, Vol. 3, p. 283). Unlike earlier authors, Thouless (1968) measured perceived size and distance through binoculars and concluded that SDI did not hold: Objects appeared to be slightly *reduced* in size and to be located at about twice their optical distance.

An alternative interpretation to SDI is that there is some rapid perceptual adaptation to angular size distortion. Stratton (1903, pp. 150–151) predicted that adaptation to a size-distorted image should occur:

As for the size of visual objects – that in spite of the minuteness of the image in the eye, the object looks no smaller than it feels – doubtless some enthusiast will one day try the experiment of wearing glasses that make all things appear twice or thrice or half as large as they normally do. . . . We can pretty safely say what the outcome of such an experiment would be. At first the visual report of things would contradict the report as given by the hand, but in time the disparity would begin to pass away and . . . things would seem to be of the same size whether seen or touched. For the amount of surface that an object covers in the eyes has but little to do with the extent of the object as we see it. . . . The all-important thing is not the absolute size of visual images or of touch-perceptions, but that the relations should be kept intact – that when touch reports a thing to be half the size of another, sight should tell the same story.

It was not until 1965 that Rock confirmed that adaptation occurred for a minified image seen in a convex mirror. Shortly afterward there was a spate of experiments on underwater magnification.

The "bent stick" phenomenon was well known to the ancients and was understood to be due to refraction (Hirschberg, 1898). Similarly, Ptolemy reported that objects appeared enlarged in water, although his understanding of refraction was limited (Ross & Ross, 1976; Sabra, 1987). After the invention of modern face masks and the development of underwater swimming, researchers became interested in the perceptual effects of the magnification caused by the face mask in water. The apparent angular magnification is generally less than the optical magnification, and the apparent linear magnification is less than would be predicted from SDI. Apparent size also decreases with viewing time in the water, and there is an aftereffect on leaving the water, when objects appear minified for a short time (Ross, Franklin, Weltman, & Lennie, 1970). The size of these adaptation effects is variable but is probably not more than about 20–25% (Kinney, 1985). Underwater magnification is accompanied by a diminution of the optical distance, and adaptation to distance distortion may also occur. SDI requires an increase in perceived distance to be accompanied by an increase in perceived linear size (and vice versa), so simultaneous adaptation to both the size and the distance distortions implies a breakdown of SDI (if size is interpreted as linear rather than angular). Many subjects adapt to size but countera-

Table 18.1. *Size illusions and their explanations*

Phenomenon	Explanation					
	Classic SDI	Relative size	Cue	A-C scaling	Image size	Scan
Constancy	−	+	+	+	−	−
Celestial	−	+	+	+	−	
Aerial P	?		+		−	
Color	−		+		+	
Luminance	−		+		+	
Geom. Ill.	−	+	+	+	−	−
Fig. AEs	−	+	+	+	−	−
Opt. Dist.	−	+	+	+	?	?

Note: A plus sign indicates a plausible explanation (even if unproven), a minus sign implausible or tested as negative, a question mark that the explanation is inadequately tested, and a blank that the explanation is irrelevant.

dapt to distance, or the reverse, which suggests that at least a weak form of SDI is upheld (Franklin, Ross, & Weltman, 1970). However, trading between the different dimensions is incomplete, so some degree of angular adaptation (about 10–17%) can be said to occur (Ross & Lennie, 1972). As with vision through binoculars, the underwater size effects are more simply interpreted as adaptation to angular size distortion.

Most laboratory studies of optical distortion used prisms that caused a lateral angular shift, and they were concerned with changes in eye–hand coordination (see Welch, 1978). Adaptation was frequently explained by a shift in felt arm position rather than a shift in visual perception. It is not as easy to produce a motor explanation for changes in perceived size, but it has been attempted. Stratton, as quoted earlier, took the Berkeleyan view that touch educates vision. Others have relied on versions of eye movement theory in which corrective eye movements are related to perceived size. For example, the vestibulo-ocular reflex (VOR) is designed to cancel head movements with compensatory eye move-ments. If the VOR gain is 1.0, the system is accurate. If optical magnification is introduced, the gain must increase so that a given angle of head movement is accompanied by a larger compensatory eye movement. The system takes time to adapt (Gauthier & Robinson, 1975). On first exposure to magnification the VOR gain is too small, and a corrective increase is necessary: This correction might be the source of objects that appear to be enlarged. When the gain is correct, objects appear to be of normal size. However, there need be no causal connection between perceived size and corrective saccades: The time scale of adaptation may fortuitously be similar for both. This eye-movement account also fails to explain how size is determined in the absence of corrective saccades.

Summing up size perception

The main explanations that have been advanced for the various size illusions are summarized in Table 18.1. There is, of course, some difficulty in deciding what should be classified as a phenomenon versus an explanation. Once an effect is understood, it may be used as an explanation for other effects. Thus constancy has often – prematurely – been used as an explanation, whereas effects that are probably low in level, such as luminance contrast, may soon rate as explanations.

Acknowledgments

We are grateful to the following people for comments on early drafts of this chapter: Roddy Cowie, Ben Craven, Mike Morgan, Robert O'Shea, Nick Wade, Vin Walsh.

References

Ames, A. (1946). *Some demonstrations concerned with the origin and nature of our sensations. A laboratory manual.* Dartmouth, NH: Dartmouth Eye Institute.

Andrews, D. P. (1964). Error-correcting perceptual mechanisms. *Quarterly Journal of Experimental Psychology, 16,* 102–115.

Ariotti, P. E. (1973a). On the apparent size of projected after-images: Emmert's or Castelli's law? A case of 242 years anticipation. *Journal of the History of the Behavioral Sciences, 9,* 18–28.

Ariotti, P. E. (1973b). Benedetto Castelli and George Berkeley as anticipators of recent findings on the moon illusion. *Journal of the History of the Behavioral Sciences, 9,* 328–332.

Ariotti, P. E. (1973c). A little known early 17th century treatise on vision: Benedetto Castelli's Discorso sopra la vista (1639, 1669). *Annals of Science, 30,* 1–30.

Aristotle. (1923). *Meteorologica* (Trans. E. W. Webster). Oxford: Clarendon Press.

Ashley, M. L. (1898). Concerning the significance of intensity of light in visual estimates of distance. *Psychological Review, 5,* 595–615.

Bain, A. (1855). *The senses and the intellect.* London: Longmans, Green.

Beare, J. I. (1906). *Greek theories of elementary cognition from Alcmaeon to Aristotle.* Oxford: Clarendon Press.

Berkeley, G. (1709/1948). *An essay towards a new theory of vision.* In A. A. Luce & T. E. Jessop (Eds.), *The works of George Berkeley bishop of Cloyne,* Volume 1. London: T. Nelson & Sons.

Bevan, W., & Dukes, W. F. (1953). Color as a variable in the judgment of size. *American Journal of Psychology, 66,* 283–288.

Blakemore, C., & Sutton, P. (1969). Size adaptation: A new after-effect. *Science, 166,* 245–247.

Boring, E. G. (1942). *Sensation and perception in the history of experimental psychology.* New York: Appleton-Century-Crofts.

Brentano, F. (1892). Über ein optisches Paradoxen. *Zeitschrift für Psychologie, 3,* 349–358.

Brewster, D. (1849). Account of a new stereoscope. *Report of the British Association, Transactions of the Sections* (pp. 6–7). Reprinted in N. J. Wade (Ed.), *Brewster and Wheatstone on vision* (pp. 135–137). London: Academic Press. 1983.

Brunswik, E. (1929). Zur Entwicklung der Albedowahrnemung. *Zeitschrift für Psychologie, 109,* 40–115.

Brunswik, E. (1933). Die Zugänglichkeit von Gegenständen für die Wahrnehmung. *Archiv für die gesamte Psychologie, 88,* 377–418.

Brunswik, E. (1944). Distal focussing of perception: Size constancy in a representative sample of situations. *Psychological Monographs, 254* (whole number).

Brunswik, E. (1956). *Perception and the representative design of psychological experiments.* Berkeley: University of California Press.

Burnet, J. (1773). *Of the origin and progress of language,* Volume 1. Edinburgh: Kincaid & Creech. (Reprinted 1967, Menston, Scotland: Scolar Press Ltd.)

Burton, H. E. (1945). The optics of Euclid. *Journal of the Optical Society of America, 35,* 357–372.

Coren, S. (1986). An efferent component in the visual perception of direction and extent. *Psychological Review, 93,* 391–410.

Coren, S. (1989). The many moon illusions: An integration through analysis. In M. Hershenson (Ed.), *The moon illusion* (pp. 351–370). Hillsdale, NJ: Erlbaum.

Coren, S., & Enns, J. T. (1993). Size contrast as a function of conceptual similarity between test and inducers. *Perception and Psychophysics, 54,* 579–588.

Coren, S., & Girgus, J. S. (1978). *Seeing is deceiving: The psychology of visual illusions.* Hillsdale, NJ: Erlbaum.

da Vinci, Leonardo. (1939). *The literary works of Leonardo da Vinci* (2nd ed.), compiled and edited by J. P. Richter. Oxford: Oxford University Press.

da Vinci, Leonardo. (1977). *The literary works of Leonardo da Vinci: Commentary,* by C. Pedretti. Oxford: Phaidon Press.

da Vinci, Leonardo. (1956). *The notebooks of Leonardo da Vinci,* Volumes 1 and 2 (Trans. Edward MacCurdy). London: Jonathan Cape.

Day, R. H. (1972). Visual spatial illusions: A general explanation.*Science, 175,* 1335–1340.

Desaguiliers, J. T. (1736). An attempt to explain the phaenomenon of the horizontal moon appearing bigger than when elevated many degrees above the horizon. *Philosophical Transactions of the Royal Society of London, 39,* 390–394.

Descartes, R. (1637/1956). *La dioptrique* In C. Adam & P. Tannery (Eds.), *Oeuvres de Descartes,* Volume 6. Paris: Librairie Philosophique J. Vrin.

Emmert, E. (1881). Grossenverhaeltnisse der Nachbilder. *Klinische Monatsblatter für Augenheilkunde und für augenartzliche Fortbildung, 19,* 443–450.

Enright, J. T. (1975). The moon illusion examined from a new point of view. *Proceedings of the American Philosophical Society, 119,* 87–117.

Enright, J. T. (1987). Perspective vergence: Oculomotor responses to line drawings. *Vision Research, 27,* 1513–1526.

Enright, J. T. (1989). The eye, the brain, and the size of the moon: Toward a unified oculomotor hypothesis for the moon illusion. In M. Hershenson (Ed.), *The moon illusion* (pp. 59–121). Hillsdale, NJ: Erlbaum.

Epstein. W., Park, J., & Casey, A. (1961). The current status of the size-distance hypotheses. *Psychological Bulletin, 58,* 491–514.

Festinger, L., White, C. W., & Allyn, M. R. (1968). Eye movements and decrement in the Müller–Lyer illusion. *Perception & Psychophysics, 3,* 676–682.

Fletcher, B. (1963). *A history of architecture on the comparative method,* London: Athlone Press.

Franklin, S. S., Ross, H. E., & Weltman, G. (1970). Size–distance invariance in perceptual adaptation. *Psychonomic Science, 21,* 229–230.

Fry, G. A., Bridgman, C. S., & Ellerbrock, V. J. (1947). Effect of atmospheric scattering upon the appearance of a dark object against a sky background. *Journal of the Optical Society of America, 37,* 635–641.

Gassendi, P. (1964). Epistolae quattuor de apparente magnitudine solis humilis et sublimis (1636–1642). In *Opera Omnia.* Stuttgart: Friedrich Fromann.

Gauthier, G. M., & Robinson, D. A. (1975). Adaptation of the human vestibuloocular reflex to magnifying lenses. *Brain Research, 92,* 331–335.

Gibson, J. J. (1933). Adaptation, after-effect and contrast in the perception of curved lines. *Journal of Experimental Psychology, 16,* 1–31.

Gibson, J. J. (1950). *The perception of the visual world.* Boston: Houghton-Mifflin.

Gibson, J. J. (1979) *The ecological approach to visual perception.* Boston: Houghton-Mifflin.

Gilinsky, A. S. (1955). The effect of attitude upon the perception of size. *American Journal of Psychology, 68*, 173–192.

Gilinsky, A. S. (1971). Comment: Adaptation level, contrast, and the moon illusion. In M. H. Appleby (Ed.), *Adaptation level theory* (pp. 71–79). New York: Academic Press.

Gilinsky, A. S. (1989). The moon illusion in a unified theory of visual space. In M. Hershenson (Ed.), *The moon illusion* (pp. 167–192). Hillsdale, NJ: Erlbaum.

Gillam, B. (1980). Geometrical illusions. *Scientific American, 242*, 86–95.

Goeters, K.-M. (1975). *Die viso-motorische Orientierung des Tauchers im Greifraum in Abhängigkeit von der Erfahrung und den Sichtbedingungen im Wasser. DLR-FB 75–35.* Cologne, Germany: DLR, Linder Höhe, Porz-Wahn.

Gregory, J. (1668). *Geometria Pars Universalis* (pp. 141–142). Trans. by J. D. Mollon & H. Ross (1975) as Gregory on the sun illusion. *Perception, 4*, 115–118.

Gregory, R. L. (1963). Distortion of visual space as inappropriate constancy scaling. *Nature, 199*, 678–680.

Gregory, R. L. (1970). *The intelligent eye.* London: Weidenfeld and Nicolson.

Gregory, R. L. (1981). *Mind in science: A history of explanations in psychology and physics.* London: Weidenfeld and Nicolson.

Gregory, R. L. (1986). *Odd perceptions.* London: Methuen.

Gregory, R. L., Wallace, J. G., & Campbell, F. W. (1959). Changes in the size and shape of visual after-images observed in complete darkness during changes of position in space. *Quarterly Journal of Experimental Psychology, 11*, 54–55.

Haenel, H. (1909). Die Gestalt des Himmels und Vergrösserung der Gestirne am Horizonte. *Zeitschrift für Psychologie, 51*, 161–199.

Heinemann, E. G., Tulving, E., & Nachmias, J. (1959). The effect of oculomotor adjustments on apparent size. *American Journal of Psychology, 72*, 32–45.

Helmholtz, H. von. (1867/1962). *Treatise on physiological optics* (J. P. C. Southall, Ed.). Translation of the 3rd German ed. New York: Dover.

Helmholtz, H. von. (1881). On the relation of optics to painting. In *Popular scientific lectures* New York: Appleton, being the substance of a series of lectures delivered in Cologne, Berlin, and Düsseldorf, 1871–1873 (Trans. E. Atkinson). Reprinted in *Helmholtz on perception: Its physiology and development* (R. M. Warren & R. P. Warren, Eds.). New York: Wiley, 1968, p. 160.

Hershenson, M. (1982). Moon illusion and spiral aftereffect: Illusions due to the loom-zoom system? *Journal of Experimental Psychology: General, 111*, 423–440.

Hershenson, M. (Ed.). (1989). *The moon illusion.* Hillsdale, NJ: Erlbaum.

Hirschberg, J. (1898). Die Optik der Alten Griechen. *Zeitschrift für Psychologie, 16*, 321–351.

Hochberg, J. (1971). Perception II: Shape and movement. In J. W. Kling & L. A. Riggs (Eds.), *Woodworth and Schlosberg's experimental psychology* (3rd ed., pp. 147–196). New York: Holt, Rinehart & Winston.

Holway, A. H., & Boring, E. G. (1940a). The moon illusion and the angle of regard. *American Journal of Psychology, 53*, 109–116.

Holway, A. H., & Boring, E. G. (1940b). The apparent size of the moon as a function of the angle of regard: Further experiments. *American Journal of Psychology, 53*, 537–553.

Holway, A. H., & Boring, E. G. (1940c). The dependence of apparent visual size upon illumination. *American Journal of Psychology, 53*, 587–589.

Iavecchia, J. H., Iavecchia, H. P., & Roscoe, S. N. (1983). The moon illusion revisited. *Aviation, Space, and Environmental Medicine, 54*, 39–46.

Johannsen, D. E. (1971) Early history of perceptual illusions. *Journal of the History of the Behavioral Sciences, 7*, 127–140.

Joynson, R. B. (1949). The problem of size and distance. *Quarterly Journal of Experimental Psychology, 1*, 119–135.

Kinney, J. A. S. (1985). *Human underwater vision: Physiology and Physics* Bethesda, MD: Undersea Medical Society.

Klein, S., Stromeyer, C. F., & Ganz, L. (1974). The simultaneous spatial frequency shift: A dissociation between the detection and perception of gratings. *Vision Research, 14*, 1421–1432.

Köhler, W., & Wallach, H. (1944). Figural after-effects: An investigation of visual processes. *Proceedings of the American Philosophical Society, 88*, 269–357.

Leibowitz, H. W., & Owens, D. A. (1989). Multiple mechanisms of the moon illusion and size perception. In M. Hershenson (Ed.), *The moon illusion* (pp. 281–286). Hillsdale, NJ: Erlbaum.

Lindberg, D. C. (1976). *Theories of vision from Al-Kindi to Kepler.* Chicago: University of Chicago Press.

Lockhead, G. L., & Wolbarsht, M. L. (1989). The moon and other toys. In M. Hershenson (Ed.), *The moon illusion* (pp. 259–266). Hillsdale, NJ: Erlbaum.

Loiselle, A. (1898). (Grandeur apparent de la lune.) *L'Intermediare des Biologistes, 1*, 352.

Lotze, R. H. (1852). *Medicinische Psychologie oder Physiologie der Seele.* Leipzig: Weidmann.

Luckiesh, M. (1918). On "retiring" and "advancing" colors. *American Journal of Psychology, 29*, 182–186.

Mayer-Hillebrand, F. (1942). Die geometrische-optischen Täuschungen als Auswirkungen allgemein geltender Wahrnehmungsgesetze. *Zeitschrift für Psychologie, 152*, 126–210, 292–331.

McCready, D. (1965). Size-distance perception and accommodation-convergence micropsia – a critique. *Vision Research, 5*, 189–206.

McCready, D. (1985). On size, distance, and visual angle perception. *Perception & Psychophysics, 37*, 323–334.

McCready, D. (1986). Moon illusions redescribed. *Perception & Psychophysics, 39*, 64–72.

McEwen, P. (1958) Figural after-effects. *British Journal of Psychology Monograph Supplement*, 31.

McKee, S. P., & Welch, L. (1992). The precision of size constancy. *Vision Research, 32*, 1447–1460.

Meyering, T. C. (1989). *Historical roots of cognitive science: The rise of a cognitive theory of perception from antiquity.* Dordrecht: Kluwer.

Morgan, M. J. (1977). *Molyneux's question: Vision, touch and the philosophy of perception.* Cambridge: Cambridge University Press.

Morgan, M. J. (1992). On the scaling of size judgements by orientational cues. *Vision Research, 32*, 1433–1445.

Morgan, M. J., Hole, G. J., & Glennester, A. (1990) Biases and sensitivities in geometrical illusions. *Vision Research, 30*, 1793–1810.

Myers, C. S. (1911). *A text-book of experimental psychology* (2nd ed.), Part 1: Text-book. Cambridge: Cambridge University Press.

Necker, L. A. (1832). Observations on some remarkable phenomena seen in Switzerland; and an optical phaenomenon which occurs in viewing a figure of a crystal or geometrical solid. *Philosophical Magazine*, 3rd series, *1*, 329–337.

Over, R. (1962). Stimulus wavelength variation and size and distance judgments. *British Journal of Psychology, 53*, 141–147.

Oyama, T. (1953). Experimental studies of the figural after-effect: 1. Temporal factors. *Japanese Journal of Psychology, 23*, 239–245.

Oyama, T., & Yamamura, T. (1960). The effect of hue and brightness on the depth perception in normal and color-blind subjects. *Psychologia, 3*, 191–194.

Pillsbury, W. B., & Schaeffer, B. R. (1937). A note on "advancing and retreating" colors. *American Journal of Psychology, 49*, 126–130.

Plateau, J. (1839). Note sur l'irradiation. *Bulletin de l'Académie Royale des Sciences, des Lettres et des Beaux-Arts de Belgique, 6*, 501–505.

Plateau, J. (1849). Quatrième note sur des nouvelles applications curieuses de la persistance des impressions de la rétine. *Bulletin de l'Académie Royale des Sciences, des Lettres et des Beaux-Arts de Belgique, 16*, 254–260.

Plotinus. (1952). *The six Enneads* (Trans. S. MacKenna & B. S. Page). Encyclopaedia Britannica great books of the western world (Vol. 17). Chicago: Encyclopaedia Britannica (p. 65).

Plug, C., & Ross, H. E. (1989). Historical review. In M. Hershenson (Ed.), *The moon illusion* (pp. 5–27). Hillsdale, NJ: Erlbaum.

Plug, C., & Ross, H. E. (1994). The natural moon illusion: A multi-factor angular account. *Perception, 23*, 321–333.

Ptolemaeus, Claudius. (1956). *L'Optique de Claude Ptolème* (A. Lejeune, Ed.). Louvain: Publications Universitaires de Louvain, 1956.

Quantz, J. O. (1895). The influence of the color of surfaces on our estimation of their magnitude. *American Journal of Psychology, 7*, 26–41.

Raymond, G. L. (1909). *Proportion and harmony of line and color in painting, sculpture, and architecture* (2nd ed.). New York: Putnam.

Redding, G. M., Winson, G. D., & Temple, R. O. (1993). The Müller–Lyer contrast illusion: A computational approach. *Perception and Psychophysics, 54*, 527–534.

Reed, C. F. (1984). Terrestrial passage theory of the moon illusion. *Journal of Experimental Psychology: General, 113*, 489–500.

Reimann, E. (1902a). Die scheinbare Vergrösserung der Sonne und des Mondes am Horizont, I. Geschichte des Problems. *Zeitschrift für Psychologie, 30*, 1–38.

Reimann, E. (1902b). Die scheinbare Vergrösserung der Sonne und des Mondes am Horizont, II. Beobachtungen und Theorie. *Zeitschrift für Psychologie, 30*, 161–195.

Rivers, W. H. R. (1901). Vision. In A. C. Haddon (Ed.), *Reports of the Cambridge anthropological expedition to the Torres Straits,* Volume II, Part I. Cambridge: Cambridge University Press.

Rivers, W. H. R. (1905). Observations on the senses of the Todas. *British Journal of Psychology, 1*, 321–396.

Robinson, E. J. (1954). The influence of photometric brightness on judgements of size. *American Journal of Psychology, 67*, 464–474.

Robinson, J. O. (1972). *The psychology of visual illusion*. London: Hutchinson.

Rock, I. (1965). Adaptation to a minified image. *Psychonomic Science, 2*, 105–106.

Rock, I. (1966). *The nature of perceptual adaptation*. New York: Basic Books.

Roscoe, S. N. (1989). The zoom-lens hypothesis. In M. Hershenson (Ed.), *The moon illusion* (pp. 31–121). Hillsdale, NJ: Erlbaum.

Ross, H. E. (1967). Water, fog and the size-distance invariance hypothesis. *British Journal of Psychology, 58*, 301–313.

Ross, H. E. (1974). *Behaviour and perception in strange environments*. London: Allen & Unwin.

Ross, H. E. (1975). Mist, murk and visual perception. *New Scientist, 66*, 658–660.

Ross, H. E., & Bischof, K. (1981). Wundt's views on sensations of innervation: A reevaluation. *Perception, 10*, 319–329.

Ross, H. E., Franklin, S. S., Weltman, G., & Lennie, P. (1970). Adaptation of divers to size distortion under water. *British Journal of Psychology, 61*, 365–373.

Ross, H. E., & Lennie, P. (1972). Adaptation and counteradaptation to complex optical distortion. *Perception & Psychophysics, 12*, 273–277.

Ross, H. E., & Ross, G. M. (1976). Did Ptolemy understand the moon illusion? *Perception, 5*, 377–385.

Sabra, A. I. (1987). Psychology versus mathematics: Ptolemy and Alhazen on the moon illusion. In E. Grant & J. E. Murdoch (Eds.), *Mathematics and its applications to science and natural philosophy in the Middle Ages* (pp. 217–247). Cambridge: Cambridge University Press.

Sanford, E. C. (1898). *A course in experimental psychology.* Part 1: *Sensation and perception.* London: Heath.

Scheerer, E. (1984). Motor theories of cognitive structure: A historical review. In W. Prinz & A. F. Sanders (Eds.), *Cognition and motor processes* (pp. 77–98). Berlin: Springer-Verlag.

Schroeder, H. (1858). Ueber eine optische Inversion bei Betrachtung verkehrter, durch optische Vorrichtung entworfener physischer Bilder. *Poggendorff's Annalen der Physik und Chemie, 105*, 298–311.

Schwartz, R. (1994). *Vision: Variations on some Berkeleian themes*. Oxford: Blackwell.

Sedgwick, H. A. (1973). The visible horizon: A potential source of visual information for the perception of size and distance. *Dissertation Abstracts International, 34,* 1301B–1302B.

Sedgwick, H. A. (1986). Space perception. In K. R. Boff, L. Kaufman, & J. P. Thomas (Eds.), *Handbook of perception and human performance* (pp. 21-1–21-57). New York: Wiley.

Segall, M. H., Campbell, D. T., & Herskovits, M. J. (1966). *The influence of culture on visual perception.* Indianapolis: Bobbs-Merrill.

Smith, R. (1738). *A complete system of optiks.* Cambridge: Crownfield.

Stratton, G. M. (1903). *Experimental psychology and culture.* New York: Macmillan.

Suzuki, K. (1991). Moon illusion simulated in complete darkness: Planetarium experiment reexamined. *Perception and Psychophysics, 49,* 348–354.

Szily, A. von. (1905). Bewegungsnachbild und Bewegungskontrast. *Zeitschrift für Psychologie und Physiologie der Sinnesorgane, 38,* 81–154.

Tausch, R. (1954). Optische Täuschungen als artifizielle Effekte der Gestaltungsprozesse von Grössen- und Formenkonstanz in der natürlichen Raumwahrnemung. *Psychologische Forschung, 24,* 299–348.

Taylor, F. V. (1941). Change in size of the after-image induced in total darkness. *Journal of Experimental Psychology, 29,* 75–80.

Taylor, I. L., & Sumner, F. C. (1945). Actual brightness and distance of individual colors when their apparent distance is held constant. *Journal of Psychology, 19,* 79–85.

Taylor, J. G. (1962). *The behavioral basis of perception.* New Haven, CT: Yale University Press.

Thiéry, A. (1896). Über geometrisch-optische Täuschungen. *Philosophische Studien, 12,* 67–126.

Thompson, S. P. (1877). Some new optical illusions. *Report of the British Association for the Advancement of Science. Transactions of the Sections, 32.*

Thouless, R. H. (1931). Phenomenal regression to the 'real' object. I. *British Journal of Psychology, 21,* 339–359.

Thouless, R. H. (1968). Apparent size and distance in vision through a magnifying system. *British Journal of Psychology, 59;* 111–118.

Troscianko, T., Montagnon, R., Le Clerc, J., Malbert, E., & Chanteau, P.-L. (1991). The role of colour as a monocular depth cue. *Vision Research, 31,* 1923–1930.

Van Hoorn, W. (1972). *As images unwind: Ancient and modern theories of visual perception.* Amsterdam: University Press of Amsterdam.

Virsu, V. (1971). Tendencies to eye movement and misperception of curvature, direction and length. *Perception & Psychophysics, 9,* 65–72.

Vitruvius Pollio. (1931). *De architectura,* 2 vols. (Trans. Frank Granger). New York: Putnam.

Wagner, M., Baird, J. C., & Fuld, K. (1989). Transformation model of the moon illusion. In M. Hershenson (Ed.), *The moon illusion* (pp. 147–165). Hillsdale, NJ: Erlbaum.

Walker, B. H. (1978). The moon illusion: A review – Part 1. *Optical Spectra, 12,* 68–69.

Wallis, J. (1687). Comments on Molyneux, 1687. *Philosophical Transactions of the Royal Society of London, 16;* 323–329.

Warren, W. H. (1984). Perceiving affordances: Visual guidance of stair climbing. *Journal of Experimental Psychology: Human Perception and Performance, 10,* 683–703.

Warren, W. H., & Whang, S. (1987). Visual guidance of walking through apertures: Body-scaled information for affordances. *Journal of Experimental Psychology: Human Perception and Performance, 13;* 371–383.

Weale, R. A. (1975). Apparent size and contrast. *Vision Research, 15,* 949–955.

Welch, R. B. (1978). *Perceptual modification: Adapting to altered sensory environments.* New York: Academic Press.

Wheatstone, C. (1838). Contributions to the physiology of vision – Part the first. On some remarkable, and hitherto unobserved, phenomena of binocular vision. *Philosophical Transactions of the Royal Society, 128,* 371–394. Reprinted in N. J. Wade (Ed.), *Brewster and Wheatstone on vision.* London: Academic Press, 1983, pp. 65–93.

Wheatstone, C. (1852). Contributions to the physiology of vision – Part the second. On some remarkable, and hitherto unobserved, phenomena of binocular vision. *Philosophical Transactions of the Royal Society, 142,* 1–17. Reprinted in N. J. Wade (Ed.), *Brewster and Wheatstone on vision.* London: Academic Press, 1983, pp. 149–168.

Wood, R. J., Zinkus, P. W., & Mountjoy, P. T. (1968) The vestibular hypothesis of the moon illusion. *Psychonomic Science, 11,* 356.

Woods, J. D., & Lythgoe, J. N. (Eds.). (1971). *Underwater science.* London: Oxford University Press.

Wundt, W. (1897). *Outlines of psychology* (Trans. C. H. Judd). Leipzig: Engelmann.

Zehender, W. von. (1899). Die Form des Himmelsgewölbes und das Grösser-Erscheinung der Gestirne am Horizont. *Zeitschrift für Psychologie, 20,* 353–357.

Zeno, T. (1862). On the changes in the apparent size of the moon. *Philosophical Magazine, 24,* 390–392.

Zoth, O. (1899) Ueber den Einfluss der Blickrichtung auf die scheinbare Grösse der Gestirne und die scheinbare Form des Himmelsgewölbes. *Pflüger's Archiv für Physiologie, 78,* 363–401.

Author index

Note: Italicized page numbers refer to citations in references.

Abramov, I., 235, *257*
Ackles, P.K., 233, *257*
Adams, R., 240, *257*
Adams, R.J., 238, 243, *257*
Adelson, E., 262, 277, 278, 279, *279*
Ahissar, E., 486, *493*
Ahissar, M., 476, 477, 479, 482, 483, 489, 490, 491, *493*
Allan, L.G., 39, 40, 47, 54, 55, 57, *60*, *61*
Allen, D., 230, 237, *257*
Allport, A., 465, *493*
Altmann, L., 166, *168*
Ames, A., 514, *521*
Amit, D.J., 166, *169*
Anderson, B.L., 424, *432*
Anderson, C.H., 153, *169*
Anderson, J.R., 465, 473, 474, *493*
Andrews, D.P., 57, 58, 59, *61*, 373, *405*, 507, *522*
Anstis, S.M., 59, *61*
Antell, S.E., 9, *28*
Arend, L.E., 2, *4*, 262, 265, 268, 273, 275, 276, 277, *279*
Ariotti, P.E., 505, 507, *522*
Aristotle, 512, *522*
Ashley, M.L., 514, *522*
Atick, J.J., 55, *61*
Atkinson, J., 8, *28*
Attneave, F., 110, 111, *116*
Autrum, H.J., 325, *348*

Babler, T.G., 444, *451*
Bagnara, S., 110, *116*
Baillargeon, R., 27, *28*, 442, *451*
Bain, A., 517, *522*
Bajcsy, R., 308, 318, *320*
Ball, K., 476, 477, 479, 481, *493*
Banks, M.S., 231, 232, 235, 236, 237, 238, 239, 240, 241, 247, 256, *257*
Barlow, H.B., 55, 59, 60, *61*, 114, *116*, 144, 146, 151, 152, *169*

Bartram, D.J., 99, 100, *116*
Baylor, D.A., 352, *368*
Beare, A.C., 245, *257*
Beck, J., 262, 275, 276, 279, *279*, *280*
Bedford, F.L., 32, *61*
Bedford, R.E., 247, *258*
Bennet, R.G., 457, 460, 461, *493*
Benson, D.F., 217, *225*
Benton, A.L., 212, 223, *225*
Berardi, N., 476, 477, 479, *493*
Bergego, C., 212, *225*
Bergen, J.R., 466, 482, *493*
Berk, L., 23, *28*
Berkeley, G., 499, 507, 511, 513, *522*
Berlin, B., 358, *368*
Bertenthal, B.I., 11, 13, 14, *28*, *29*, 451n5, *451*
Berti, A., 224, *225*
Besner, D., 196, 197, *206*
Bevan, W., 514, *522*
Bevington, P.R., 375, *405*
Biederman, I., 72, 73, 74, 75, 78, 84, 91, 92, 93, 94, 98, 102, 103, 104, 113, 115, *116*, *117*, 124, 125, 131, 134, *141*, 197, 198, 205, *206*
Bienenstock, E., 153, *169*
Binford, T.O., 130, 131, *141*
Bingham, G.P., 446, *452*
Blake, A., 294, 296, 299, *320*, 428, *432*
Blake, R., 33, 34, 60n3, *61*, 392, *405*
Blake, T., 36, *61*
Blakemore, C., 31, 54, *61*, 519, *522*
Bomba, P.C., 15, 16, *29*
Borges, C., 263, *280*
Boring, E.G., 373, 379, *405*, 464, 470, *493*, 501, 507, 512, *522*
Bornstein, M.H., 244, 245, 246, 247, *258*, 372, *280*, 352, 358, *368*
Bottini, G., 215, *225*
Bower, T.G.R., 7, 20, 27, *29*
Bowmaker, J.K., 331, 333, 335, *348*, 352, *368*
Boynton, R.M., 273, *280*, 358, *368*

Bradshaw, M.F., 420, 424, *432*
Brady, M., 129, *141*
Brainard, D.H., 256, *258*, 276, *280*
Braine, L.G., 70, *117*
Bramwell, D.I., 285, *320*
Braunstein, M.L., 426, *432*
Breitmeyer, B.G., 41, 54, *61*
Brelstaff, G., 294, *320*
Brentano, F., 515, *522*
Brewster, D., 508, *522*
Brill, M.H., 256, *258*, 262, 263, 264, *280*, 291, 304, 313, *320*
Broerse, J., 38, 39, 40, 52, 53, 54, 60, *61*, *62*
Brown, A.M., 235, 237, 240, 241, 254, 256, *258*
Brown, J.F., 396, *405*
Bruce, C.J., 164, *169*
Bruce, V., 87, *117*, 198, *207*
Brunswik, E., 269, *280*, 501, 508, *522*, *523*
Buchholz, C., 339, *348*
Buchsbaum, G., 262, 264, *280*, 286, 291, 295, 303, 304, *320*
Budesen, C., 916, 197, *207*
Buhmann, J., 153, *169*
Bulla-Hellwig, M., 211, 216, *225*
Bullier, J., 167, *169*
Bülthoff, H.H., 73, 74, 105, 115, *117*, 138, 139, *141*, 153, *169*, 426, 427, 428, 432, *433*
Burbeck, C.A., 376, 381, 386, *405*
Burkamp, W., 331, *348*
Burkhalter, A., 359, *368*
Burnet, J., 512, 520, *523*
Burnham, D.K., 27, *29*
Burns, J., 132, *141*
Burton, H.E., 501, *523*
Buser, P., 33, *62*
Bushnell, E.W., 242, *258*
Bushnell, I.W.R., 8, *29*
Butter, C.M., 219, *225*
Butterworth, G., 18, *29*
Byth, W., 56, *62*

Calderone, J.B., 444, *452*
Campbell, F.W., 41, 47, *62*, 377, *406*
Campion, J., 217, *225*
Caramazza, A., 438, 445, *452*
Carlson, V.R., 376, *406*
Caron, A.J., 21, 24, *29*
Carpenter, P.A., 111, *117*
Cavanagh, P., 74, *117*, 262, 277, 279, *280*
Cavill, J., 45, *62*
Chapman, S., 444, *452*
Chen, Y., 398, *406*
Cheng, P.W., 465, 466, 470, 472, 492, *493*
Chugani, H.T., 236, *258*
Churchland, P.S., 141*n*6, *142*
Clark, J.J., 426, 428, *433*

Clavadetscher, J.E., 240, *258*
Cohen, J., 252, *258*, 264, *280*
Cohen, L., 199, *207*
Cohen, L.B., 242, *258*
Collett, T.S., 176, *190*, 415, 416, 419, 421, 422, 430, *433*
Collewijn, H., 421, *433*
Conel, J.L., 236, *258*
Cook, M., 412, 414, 416, 417, *433*
Coolen, A.C.C., 153, *169*
Cooper, E., 198, *207*
Cooper, L.A., 92, 95, 96, 97, 104, 111, 115, *117*
Corballis, M.C., 69, 80, 92, 106, 110, 111, 112, 115, *117*
Coren, S., 385, *406*, 512, 515, 516, 517, 518, *523*
Cornsweet, T.N., 343, 345, *348*
Courtney, S., 301, *320*
Craven, B.J., 251, *258*
Creuzfeldt, O.D., 55, *62*
Crocker, R.A., 339, *348*
Crossman, E.R.F.W., 464, 472, *493*
Cumming, B.G., 415, 523, *433*
Cummins, R., 140, *142*
Cutting, J.E., 11, *29*, 110, *117*, 450*n*1, *452*
Cutzu, F., 86, 88, 89, 91, 103, *118*

Dannemiller, J.L., 233, 241, 243, 244, 249, 250, 251, 252, 253, 254, 255, 256, *258*, *259*, 262, 279, *280*, 292, *320*
Daumer, K., 324, *348*
Davidoff, J., 220, *226*
da Vinci, L., 501, 506, 511, 512, 514, *523*
Dawson, B.M., 56, *62*
Day, R.H., 22, 23, 25, *29*, 41, 54, 60*n*1, *62*, 515, 516, *523*
Dayan, P., 151, *169*
Dean, P., 360, *368*
Dearborn, G.V.N., 70, *118*
de Courten, C., 236, *259*
Delius, J., 182, *190*
de Monasterio, F.M., 359, *368*
Dennett, D.C., 141*n*10, *142*, 168, *169*
De Renzi, E., 211, 212, 217, 223, *226*
Derrington, A.M., 357, *369*
DeSa, V.R., 168, *169*
Desaguiliers, J.T., 505, *523*
Descartes, R., 499, 504, *523*
Desimone, R., 34, *62*, 192, 193, 199, 202, *207*, 360, 363, *369*, 479, *493*
Deutsch, J.A., 465, 469, *493*
De Valois, K.K., 42, *62*
De Valois, R.L., 201, *207*, 352, *368*
DeYoe, E.A., 354, *369*
Diamond, B.J., 223, *226*
Dickerson, J.A., 196, *207*
Diener, H.C., 398, *406*

Dimentman, A.M., 332, 333, 334, *348*
Dodd, B., 18, *29*
Dodwell, P.C., 43, 44, 46, 47, 48, 49, 51, 52, 53, 55, 57, 58, *62*
Dörr, S., 345, 348, *349*
Dosher, B.A., 427, *433*
Douglas, R.H., 331, *349*
Dow, B.M., 354, *369*, 479, *493*
Dricker, J., 214, *226*
Duncan, J., 466, 470, *493*
Duncker, K., 110, *118*
Dzhafarli, M.T., 343, *349*
D'Zmura, M., 252, 256, *259*, 286, 291, 295, 302, 303, 306, 310, *320*

Edelman, S., 73, 74, 75, 76, 77, 78, 79, 88, 105, 115, *118*, 134, 138, 139, 141n7, *142*, 153, *169*
Eley, M.G., 80, 115, *118*
Ellis, R., 99, 100, 101, 102, *118*, 196, 198, *207*
Ellis, S.R., 32, *62*
Ellison, A., 4, *4*
Emerson, P., 277, *280*
Emerson, V.F., 45, 46, 49, 50, 51, *62*
Emmert, E., 505, *523*
Endler, J.A., 347, *349*
Engel, A.K., 43, 60, *62*
Enright, J.T., 506, 508, 511, 512, 517, *523*
Enroth-Cugell, C., 41, *62*
Epstein, W., 2, *4*, 373, 387, 388, 394, 395, 398, 400, *406*, 505, *523*
Erkelens, C.J., 418, *433*
Evans, R.M., 296, *319n6, 320*
Everitt, B., 151, *169*
Ewert, J.-P., 173, 174, 175, 177, 184, 189, *190*

Faglioni, P., 211, *226*
Fahle, M., 460, 461, 476, 477, 479, 481, *493*
Fairchild, M.D., 252, 256, *259*, 285, *320*
Fantz, R.L., 230, *259*
Farah, M.J., 214, 222, 225, *226*
Favreau, O.E., 54, 56, *63*
Feldman, J.A., 110, 111, *118*, 150, 158, *169*
Felleman, D.J., 354, *369*
Fendick, M., 457, 458, 476, *493*
Ferrera, V.P., 354, *369*
Festinger, L., 518, *523*
Fidell, L.S., 60n4, *63*
Field, D.J., 41, *63*
Field, T.M., 8, *29*
Finke, R.A., 38, *63*
Finlayson, G., 285, 291, 293, 302, *320*
Fiorentini, A., 457, 476, 477, 479, 481, *494*
Fischler, M.A., 126, *142*
Fisher, C.B., 110, *118*
Fitts, P.M., 487, *494*
Fletcher, B., 514, *523*

Földiák, P., 151, 160, 162, *169, 170*
Foley, J.M., 377, *406*, 415, 418, 419, *433*
Forde, E.M.E., 221, *226*
Foreit, K.G., 40, *63*
Forsyth, D.A., 141n4, *142*, 291, 293, 295, 305, 320, *321*
Foster, D.H., 303, *321*
Fox, R., 13, 14, *29*
Franklin, S.S., 392, *406*, 521, *523*
Freeman, W.T., 130, 131, *142*
Fregnac, Y., 484, 485, *494*
Friedman, A., 105, *118*
Frisby, J.P., 425, *433*
Fromme, F., 54, *63*
Fry, G.A., 513, *523*
Fujita, I., 202, *207*
Fukushima, K., 156, 158, *170*
Funt, B.V., 290, 295, 309, 314, 317, 318, *321*

Gallant, J.L., 48, *63*
Gårding, J., 423, 424, *433*
Gardner-Medwin, A.R., 152, *170*
Garey, L.J., 236, *259*
Gassendi, P., 511, *523*
Gauthier, G.M., 521, *523*
Gegenfurtner, K.R., 164, *170*
Geiger, G., 459, *494*
Geisler, W.S., 238, *259*
Georgeson, M., 1, *5*
Gerhardstein, P.C., 74, 76, *118*
Gershon, R., 309, 310, *321*
Ghim, H.-R., 10, 12, *29*
Gibson, E.J., 18, 21, *29*, 455, 456, 457, 464, 472, 476, *494*
Gibson, J.J., 43, 57, *63*, 70, *118*, 380, 383, *406*, 436, *452*, 471, *494*, 507, 508, 513, 516, 517, *523*
Gilbert, C.D., 167, *170*, 484, *494*
Gilchrist, A., 262, 269, 271, 276, 279, *280*
Gilden, D.L., 438, 446, 447, 448, 449, 451n4, *452*
Gilinsky, A.S., 376, 381, *406*, 502, 504, 505, *523, 524*
Gillam, B., 384, 385, *406*, 424, *433*, 517, *524*
Glasser, L., 268, *280*
Glennerster, A., 416, 418, *433*
Gnadt, J.W., 421, *433*
Gnyubkin, V.F., 337, *349*
Gochin, P.M., 153, *170*
Goeters, K.-M., 513, *524*
Gogel, U., 249, *259*
Gogel, W.C., 420, *433*
Goodale, M.A., 37, *63*, 199, 200, 206, *207*, 411, 429, *433*
Gopher, D., 483, *494*
Gordon, I.E.G., 28, *29*
Gottsdanker, R.M., 444, *452*
Gouras, P., 354, 356, *369*

Graboi, D., 492, *494*
Granrud, C.E., 23, *29*
Green, M., 42, *63*
Gregory, J., 509, *524*
Gregory, R.L., 373, 384, 388, *406*, 505, 506, 515, 516, *524*
Grether, W.F., 345, *349*
Greuel, J.M., 484, *494*
Grobstein, P., 177, *190*
Gross, C.G., 164, *170*, 193, 202, *207*, 362, 363, *369*, 477, 479, *494*
Grossberg, S., 51, 55, 60, *63*, 148, *170*, 276, 277, 279, *280*
Grzywacz, N.M., 402, *406*

Haapasalo, S., 41, 56, *63*
Haenel, H., 514, *524*
Haenny, P.E., 192, *207*, 491, *494*
Haier, R.J., 487, *494*
Haller, U., 110, *118*
Hamer, R.D., 232, 240, *259*
Hamsher, K. DeS., 214, *226*
Harnad, S., 272, *280*
Harries, M.H., 87, 88, *118*
Harris, C.S., 32, 54, 55, *63*
Harris, J.P., 59, *63*
Harvey, L.O., 388, *406*
Hasselmo, M.E., 193, 194, *207*
Hawryshyn, C.W., 331, *349*
Healey, G., 288, 289, 295, 309, 310, 312, *321*
Hebb, D.O., 6, *29*, 147, *170*
Hecht, H., 439, 444, 448, *452*
Heeger, D.J., 402, *406*
Heeley, D.W., 47, *63*
Heggelund, P., 54, *63*
Heider, F., 436, *452*
Heinemann, E.G., 422, *433*, 508, *524*
Held, R., 56, *63*
Hell, W., 388, *406*
Helmholtz, H. von, 275, *280*, 283, *321*, 409, 419, 424, *433*, 499, 512, 514, 520, *524*
Helson, H., 57, *63*
Henneman, R., 276, *280*
Heppler, N., 54, *64*
Hering, E., 275, *280*
Hershenson, M., 54, *64*, 510, 519, *524*
Hertel, H., 347, *349*
Herter, K., 185, *190*, 344, *349*
Hertz, J.A., 149, *170*
Heywood, C.A., 236, *259*, 360, 361, *369*
Hickey, T.L., 236, *259*
Hildreth, E.C., 138, *142*
Hinton, G.E., 110, 111, *118*, 151, 153, *170*
Hirschberg, J., 518, 519, 520, *524*
Hochberg, J., 383, 393, *406*, 502, *524*
Hock, H.S., 111, *118*, 471, 482, 492, *494*
Hoffman, K.-P., 167, *170*
Hoffman, W.C., 43, 46, 47, *64*

Holmes, W.R., 166, *170*
Holway, A.H., 379, 380, 382, *407*, 511, 514, *524*
Horn, B., 277, *280*
Horn, B.K.P., 131, *142*, 294, 296, 299, *321*, 367, *369*
Houck, M.R., 34, 54, *64*
Hubel, D.H., 53, *64*, 164, 166, *170*, 354, *369*, 484, *494*
Huber, J., 378, *407*
Hummel, J.E., 113, 115, *118*, 136, 137, *142*, 198, *207*
Humphrey, G.K., 35, 36, 37, 40, 45, 46, 47, 48, 49, 50, 52, 56, 60*n*1,*n*5, *64*, 75, 76, 77, 85, 90, 91, 92, 100, 105, 110, 113, *118*, *119*, 219, *226*
Humphrey, N.K., 384, *407*
Humphreys, G.W., 84, 89, 90, 110, 113, 114, *119*, 213, 214, 217, 218, 219, *226*
Hunt, R., 284, *321*
Hurlbert, A.C., 252, *259*, 294, 295, 296, 299, 300, 302, 307, 309, *321*, 367, *369*

Iavecchia, J.H., 511, *524*
Ingle, D.J., 173, 174, 176, 177, 178, 181, 182, 185, 186, 189, *190*, *191*, 334, 336, *349*
Ingling, C.R.J., 240, *259*
Ito, M., 164, *170*, 203, *207*

Jaaskelainen, T., 292, *321*
Jacobs, G.H., 338, 339, *349*
James, W., 456, 464, 472, *494*
Jameson, D., 3, *5*, 244, 248, *259*, 275, *280*, 300, *321*
Jeannerod, M., 199, *207*
Jenkins, B., 39, *64*
Johannsen, D.E., 515, 519, *524*
Johansson, G., 11, *29*, 436, 444, 446, *452*
Johnson, C.A., 457, 458, 476, *494*
Johnson, C.J., 249, *259*
Johnston, E.B., 377, *407*, 415, 416, 419, 427, 428, 429, 430, 431, *433*
Jolicoeur, P., 72, 75, 80, 81, 82, 83, 84, 92, 93, 95, 104, 106, 107, 109, 111, *119*, 196, *207*
Jones, P.D., 53, *64*
Joynson, R.B., 503, 505, *524*
Judd, D.B., 252, *259*, 292, *321*, 352, *369*
Judge, S.J., 421, *434*
Julesz, B., 34, *64*, 114, *119*, 482, 489, *494*
Juola, J.F., 115, *119*
Just, M.A., 111, *119*

Kahneman, D., 462, 474, *495*
Kaiser, M.K., 438, 445, 446, 449, 450*n*3, *452*
Kalfin, K., 54, *64*
Kanizsa, G., 10, *29*
Karnath, H.O., 224, *226*

Karni, A., 476, 477, 479, 481, 483, *495*
Kaski, S., 148, *170*
Kato, H., 158, *170*
Katz, D., 249, *259*, 275, *280*, 338, *349*
Kaufman, J.H., 38, *64*
Kaus, J.H., 484, *495*
Kelly, D.H., 41, 42, *64*
Kelter, S., 100, *119*
Kerschensteiner, M., 211, *226*
Kezeli, A.R., 339, 340, 343, *349*
Kien, J., 347, *349*
Kimura, D., 91, *119*
Kirk, J.T.O., 347, *349*
Klein, S.A., 376, *407*, 517, *525*
Klinker, G.J., 310, 312, 319, *321*
Kobatake, E., 192, 193, 202, *207*
Koch, C., 482, *495*
Koenderink, J.J., 43, 44, *64*, 127, *142*
Koffka, K., 279, *280*
Kohler, I., 54, *64*
Köhler, W., 337, 342, *349*, 518, *525*
Kolers, P.A., 69, *120*, 492, *495*
Komatsu, H., 359, 363, 364, 367, *369*
Koriat, A., 80, 107, 108, 111, *120*
Kosslyn, S.M., 105, *120*
Kovács, GY., 152, *171*
Kozlowski, L.T., 450n1, *452*
Krauskopf, J., 50, *64*, 257, *259*, 365, *369*
Krinov, E., 292, *321*
Kristofersson, M.W., 492, *495*
Kubota, K., 486, *495*
Kühn, A., 324, 344, *350*
Kulikowski, J.J., 41, *65*, 201, *207*
Kunen, S., 38, *65*

La Berge, D., 464, 468, 475, 480, *495*
Ladavas, E., 110, *120*
Lamdan, Y., 126, 127, *142*
Land, E.H., 275, 276, 277, 279, *280*, *281*, 286, 294, 295, 296, *321*, *322*, 366, 367, *369*
Landis, T., 89, *120*, 220, *226*
Landy, M.S., 377, 378, *407*
Langlois, J.H., 17, *29*
Lansdell, H.C., 211, *226*
Larsen, A., 196, 197, *208*
Lassaline, M.E., 474, *495*
Lawson, R., 101, 104, 115, *120*
Layman, S., 89, *120*, 211, 213, 214, 215, 216, 219, *226*
LeCun, Y., 158, *171*
Lee, H.-C., 288, 289, 295, 303, 310, 311, 319n8, *322*
Leeuwenberg, E., 278, *281*
Legge, G.E., 377, *407*
Lehmkuhle, S.W., 60n3, *65*
Leibowitz, H.W., 381, *407*, 421, *434*, 512, *525*
Lennie, P., 355, 357, 364, 365, 366, *370*
Lester, R.A.J., 166, *171*

Lettvin, J.Y., 174, *191*
Leventhal, A.G., 53, 56, *65*
Levine, C., 91, *120*
Levine, M., 111, *120*
Levy, W.B., 166, *171*
Lewis, D.A., 37, *65*
Lichten, W., 380, *407*
Liebman, P.A., 337, *350*
Lindberg, D.C., 510, *525*
Lippmann, R.P., 148, *171*
Lissauer, H., 217, *227*
Livingstone, M.S., 56, 57, *65*, 354, 356, 357, 367, *370*
Locke, N.M., 342, *350*
Lockhead, G.L., 511, *525*
Logan, G.D., 456, 464, 468, 474, 492, *495*
Logie, R.H., 87, *120*
Logothetis, N.K., 153, 163, *171*
Logue, N.A., 56, *65*
Loiselle, A., 520, *525*
Lombardi, C.M., 182, *191*
Longuet-Higgins, H.C., 409, *434*
Loomis, J.M., 410, 411, 412, 413, *434*
Lotze, R.H., 518, *525*
Lovegrove, W.J., 32, 41, 54, *65*
Lowe, D.G., 126, 130, 131, 136, *142*, 197, 208
Lucassen, M., 262, 264, 265, 269, 270, 279, *281*, 303, *322*
Luckiesh, M., 514, *525*
Lueck, C.J., 236, *259*
Lueschow, A., 202, 203, 205, *208*
Lund, J.S., 353, *370*

McBeath, M.K., 444, *452*
McCann, J.J., 265, 266, 268, 269, 276, *281*, 295, 303, *322*
McCarter, A., 55, *65*
McCauley, M.E., 450n2, *452*
McCleary, R.A., 182, 189, *191*, 332, *350*
McCloskey, M., 438, *453*
McCollough, C., 31, 32, 40, 51, 53, 59, *65*, 66
McCready, D., 500, 508, 512, 515, 516, 519, 525
McEwen, P., 518, *525*
Mach, E., 111, *120*
MacKay, D.M., 42, 47, 53, *65*
McKee, S.P., 376, 378, 388, 389, 390, 392, 396, 398, 399, 400, 401, 402, *407*, 460, 476, 482, *495*, 508, *525*
McKenzie, B.E., 22, *29*, 248, *260*
MacKintosh, N.J., 186, *191*
McLeod, P., 444, *452*
MacLeod, R., 276, *281*
McLoughlin, N.P., 60, *66*
McMullen, P.A., 83, 109, 110, 111, 112, 113, 120
Madden, D.J., 492, *495*

Maguire, W.M., 59, *65*
Maki, R.H., 81, 109, *120*
Maloney, L.T., 231, *260*, 262, *281*, 286, 291, 292, 295, 304, 305, 306, 319*n*5,*n*7, *322*, 426, *434*
Malsburg, C.V.D., 148, *171*
Mandriota, F.J., 396, *407*
Mann, S.E., 486, *495*
Marill, T., 129, *142*
Marks, L.E., 54, *65*
Marks, W.B., 333, *350*, 352, *370*
Marr, D., 69, 75, 80, 89, 90, 100, 110, 111, 113, *120*, 139, *142*, 198, *208*, 213, 221, 227, 277, *281*, 426, *434*, 462, *495*
Masland, R.M., 54, *65*
Matuzawa, T., 352, 358, *370*
Maunsell, J.H.R., 354, 360, *370*, 491, *495*
Maurer, D., 243, *260*
Maximov, V.V., 338, *350*
May, J.G., 42, 43, *65*
Mayer, M.L., 166, *171*
Mayer-Hillebrand, F., 515, *525*
Mayhew, J.E.W., 34, 54, 56, *65*, 422, *434*
Mays, L.E., 421, *434*
Mazokhin-Porshnjakov, G.A., 325, *350*
Meesters, A., 185, *191*
Meister, M., 167, *171*
Meltzoff, A., 18, *30*
Menzel, R., 325, 347, 348, *350*
Merigan, W.H., 353, *370*
Merzenich, M.M., 484, 486, *495, 496*
Meyer, G.E., 39, *66*
Meyering, T.C., 499, *525*
Michael, C., 354, 355, 356, 368, *370*
Michael, C.R., 53, *66*
Michaels, C.F., 444, *453*
Michotte, A., 436, *453*
Mikaelian, H.H., 54, *66*
Miller, E.K., 205, *208*
Milliken, B., 72, 93, *120*
Milner, A.D., 37, *66*, 199, *208*
Milner, B., 211, *227*
Minsky, M., 154, *171*
Mishkin, M., 362, *370*
Mitsumoto, H., 130, *142*
Mitz, A.R., 486, *496*
Miyashita, Y., 165, 168, *171*, 362, *370*
Moericke, V., 344, *350*
Mohan, R., 128, *142*
Moller, P., 489, *496*
Mollon, J.D., 53, *66*, 283, *322*
Monk, A.F., 111, *120*
Montalvo, F.S., 55, 60, *66*
Moore, A., 294, 299, 303, *322*
Moran, J., 480, 491, *496*
Morant, R.B., 47, *66*
Morgan, M.J., 373, 390, *407*, 429, *434*, 507, 508, 517, *525*

Mori, T., 110, *120*
Moses, Y., 132, 141*n*4, *142*
Motter, B.C., 491, *496*
Moulden, B., 33, *66*
Mountcastle, V.B., 491, *496*
Murch, G.M., 33, 50, 51, 54, 55, 60*n*1, *66*
Murray, J.E., 83, 103, 109, 115, *120*
Myers, C.S., 513, 516, *525*

Nakayama, K., 383, *407*, 410, *434*
Nayatani, Y., 284, *322*
Nazir, T., 477, 480, *496*
Necker, L.A., 506, *525*
Needham, A., 442, *453*
Neisser, U., 466, 492, *496*
Neumeyer, C., 326, 327, 330, 331, 335, 338, 344, 346, *350*
Newcombe, F., 211, 217, 218, *227*
Newell, A., 456, *496*
Newell, F., 91, *120*
Norman, J.F., 377, 378, 388, *407*, 428, *434*
Nowlan, S.J., 150, *171*

Ogle, K.N., 424, *434*
O'Leary, A., 425, *434*
Olshausen, B.A., 153, *171*
Ono, H., 419, *434*
Oram, M.W., 153, 161, 163, *171*, 192, *208*
Orban, G.A., 396, *407*
O'Reilly, R.C., 166, *171*
Over, R., 36, 54, *66*, 380, *407*, 514, *525*
Owens, D.A., 420, *434*
Oyama, T., 352, *370*, 514, 518, *525*

Packer, O., 240, *260*
Paivio, A., 91, *121*
Palmer, S.E., 86, 87, 88, 98, 105, 110, 111, *121*, 134, *142*, 197, *208*
Parker, A.J., 432, *434*
Parkkinen, J., 264, *281*, 292, *322*
Pasternak, T., 402, *407*
Peeples, D.R., 239, 240, *260*
Perrett, D.I., 88, 89, *121*, 163, 165, 167, *171*, 192, 193, 194, 203, *208*, 210, *227*, 363, *370*
Philbeck, J.W., 410, 412, 425, *434*
Piaget, J., 6, 7, *30*
Pillsbury, W.B., 514, *525*
Pinker, S., 111, *121*
Pittenger, J.B., 444, 445, 447, *453*
Plateau, J., 514, 519, *525*
Plendl, H., 236, *260*
Plotinus, 506, *525*
Plug, C., 508, 512, *525, 526*
Poggio, G.F., 354, *370*
Poggio, T., 78, *121*, 129, 138, *143*, 150, *171*, 482, *496*
Polat, U., 476, 477, 479, 481, *496*

Porrill, J., 197, *208*, 422, *434*
Posner, M.L., 488, *496*
Postman, L., 471, *496*
Pouget, A., 420, *434*
Prinz, W., 492, *496*
Proffitt, D.R., 438, 445, *453*
Przyrembel, C., 337, *350*
Ptolemy, C., 503, 505, 512, *526*
Pulos, E., 256, *260*
Putnam, H., 141*n*9, *143*
Pylyshyn, Z.W., 59, *66*, 140, *143*

Quantz, J.O., 514, *526*
Quinn, P.C., 15, *30*

Rabbit, P., 483, 492, *496*
Ramachandran, V.S., 476, 477, *496*
Ratcliff, G., 89, *121*, 214, *227*
Raymond, G.L., 515, *526*
Recanzone, G.H., 485, 486, 491, *496*
Redding, G.M., 517, *526*
Reed, C.F., 512, *526*
Reid, R., 276, *281*
Reimann, E., 504, 511, *526*
Reingold, E.M., 93, *121*
Rey, A., 221, *227*
Rhodes, P.A., 166, *171*
Richards, W., 130, *143*, 262, *281*, 421, 430, *435*
Richmond, B.J., 363, *370*
Riddoch, M.J., 213, 217, 218, 219, 221, *227*
Riehle, A., 347, *350*
Riggs, L.A., 53, *66*
Rivers, P., 126, *143*
Rivers, W.H.R., 516, *526*
Rivest, J., 422, *435*
Robertson, L.C., 111, *121*
Robinson, E.J., 514, *526*
Robinson, J.O., 512, 515, 516, 518, *526*
Rock, I., 69, 70, 71, 72, 73, 75, 95, 104, 111, 112, 113, 114, *121*, 134, *143*, 279, *281*, 383, 384, 393, 398, *407*, 508, 520, *526*
Rogers, B.J., 378, *407*, *408*, 422, 423, 424, 432, *435*
Rogers, D., 263, 277, *281*
Rolls, E.T., 165, 168, *171*, *172*, 202, 203, 205, *208*
Roncato, S., 442, 443, *453*
Roorda, J., 59, *66*
Rosch, E., 75, *121*
Roscoe, S.N., 511, 512, *526*
Ross, H.E., 392, *408*, 509, 513, 514, 518, 520, 521, *526*
Rovee-Collier, C., 243, *260*
Roy, J.-P., 427, *435*
Roy, M.S., 241, *260*
Rubens, A.B., 218, *227*
Rubin, J.M., 308, 309, *322*, 368, *370*

Rudge, P., 212, 220, *227*
Rumelhart, D.E., 148, 158, 161, 168, *172*
Runeson, S., 437, 446, 448, 449, *453*
Ryan, C., 465, *497*

Saayman, G., 242, *260*
Sabra, A.I., 503, 509, 520, *526*
Sakai, K., 138, *143*, 165, 168, *172*, 486, *497*
Sakata, H., 200, *209*
Sällström, P., 262, 264, *281*, 292, 304, 319*n*5, *322*
Salthouse, T.A., 466, 467, 483, 491, 492, *497*
Samuels, C.A., 17, *30*
Sandell, J.H., 352, *370*
Sanford, E.C., 506, 515, *526*
Sáry, GY., 152, *172*
Sato, T., 363, *370*
Saul, A.B., 60, *66*
Saund, E., 151, *172*
Savoy, R.L., 33, 37, 55, 56, *66*
Schacter, D.L., 92, 94, 95, 115, *121*
Scheerer, E., 517, *526*
Schein, S.J., 359, 360, 367, *371*
Schiemenz, F., 331, *350*
Schiller, P.H., 361, *371*
Schirillo, J., 262, *281*
Schmerler, J., 444, *453*
Schnapf, J.L., 352, *371*
Schneider, W., 467, 470, 475, *497*
Schoups, A.A., 476, 479, *497*
Schroeder, H., 506, *526*
Schwartz, B.L., 456, *497*
Schwartz, E.L., 165, *172*, 192, *209*, 363, *371*
Schwartz, R., 507, *526*
Schwarz, U., 412, *435*
Seaber, J.H., 33, 57, *66*
Sedgwick, H.A., 376, 383, 385, 387, 404*n*2, *408*, 421, 425, *435*, 502, 504, 508, *526*, *527*
Segall, M.H., 515, 516, *527*
Sergent, J., 214, 220, 223, *227*
Servos, P., 37, *66*
Seung, H.S., 481, 488, *497*
Shafer, S.A., 287, 288, 310, 312, *322*
Shallice, T., 90, *122*
Shannon, B., 444, *453*
Sharpe, L.T., 54, 56, *67*
Shashua, A., 128, *143*
Shaw, R., 447, *453*
Shepard, R.N., 83, 84, 85, 104, 105, 106, 108, 110, 111, *122*, 134, 141, *143*, 197, *209*
Shepard, S., 136, *143*
Sheridan, J., 221, *227*
Shiffrin, R.M., 464, 465, 466, 468, 469, 475, 492, *497*
Shimojo, S., 410, *435*
Shinoda, H., 363, *371*
Shipp, S., 353, 354, *371*

Shiu, L., 476, 477, 489, 490, *497*
Shultz, D., 484, *497*
Shute, C.C.D., 47, 55, 56, *67*
Siegel, S., 40, 54, 55, *67*
Simion, F., 107, 110, *122*
Sireteanu, R., 473, *497*
Skowbo, D., 32, 53, 54, 55, *67*
Slater, A.M., 8, 9, 15, 21, 24, *30*, 248, *260*
Smith, A.T., 398, 402, *408*
Smith, F.D., 42, *67*
Smith, O.W., 398, *408*
Smith, R., 509, 510, *527*
Snodgrass, J.G., 81, 85, 106, *122*
Sobel, E.C., 411, 423, *435*
Solms, M., 221, *228*
Spehlmann, R., 56, *67*
Spelke, E.S., 18, 19, *30*
Spitzer, H., 167, *172*
Squire, L.R., 456, *497*
Sridhar, B., 450, *453*
Srinivas, K., 98, 99, 104, 115, *122*
Steinfeld, G.J., 72, *122*
Stephen, D., 102, *122*
Stephens, B.R., 248, *260*
Sternberg, S., 466, *497*
Stewart, F., 221, *228*
Stone, J., 167, *172*
Stratford, K., 166, *172*
Stratton, G.M., 520, *527*
Stromeyer, C.F., III, 32, 47, 54, 60n1, *67*
Stryker, M.P., 168, *172*
Sung, K.-K., 309, *322*
Sutton, R.S., 160, *172*
Suzuki, K., 512, *527*
Szily, A. von, 519, *527*

Takahama, K., 262, *281*
Takano, Y., 107, *122*
Tanaka, K., 163, *172*, 193, 202, *209*, 363, *371*
Tarr, M.J., 69, 82, 83, 84, 85, 87, 103, 104,
    105, 109, *122*, 134, 135, *143*
Tausch, R., 515, *527*
Tawney, G., 456, *497*
Taylor, A.M., 218, 221, *228*
Taylor, F.V., 505, 506, *527*
Taylor, I.L., 514, *527*
Taylor, J.G., 508, *527*
Teller, D.Y., 230, 232, 235, 237, 238, 239,
    240, 245, *260*
Terry, R., 56, *67*
Teuber, H.L., 218, *228*
Thiéry, A., 515, *527*
Thomas, S., 87, *122*
Thompson, P., 33, 34, 35, 36, 41, *67*
Thompson, S.P., 519, *527*
Thomson, J.A., 410, *435*
Thorell, L.G., 355, *371*
Thouless, R.H., 379, *408*, 501, 520, *527*

Timney, B.N., 56, *67*
Tiplitz-Blackwell, K., 265, *281*
Tittle, J.S., 430, *435*
Todd, J.T., 444, 445, *453*
Tominaga, S., 312, 317, *322*
Tootell, R.B.H., 354, 357, *371*
Tovee, M.J., 165, *172*
Treisman, A., 34, 35, *67*, 456, 465, 466, 468,
    469, 470, 471, 473, 474, 480, 489, *497*
Tritsch, M., 339, *351*
Trojano, L., 223, *228*
Troost, J.M., 2, *5*, 262, 263, 264, 265, 269,
    272, 273, 274, 275, 276, 277, *281*
Troscianko, T., 513, *527*
Trotter, Y., 421, 422, *435*
Ts'o, D.Y., 56, *67*, 355, 357, 359, *371*
Turnbull, O.H., 214, 222, *228*
Tyler, C.W., 42, *67*

Uchikawa, H., 273, *281*
Uchikawa, K., 273, 275, *281*, 358, 363, *371*
Uhlarik, J., 38, 39, *67*
Ullman, S., 57, 59, *67*, 104, 105, 115, *122*,
    126, 128, 129, 136, *143*, 153, *172*, 197,
    209, 409, 430, *435*
Ungerleider, L.G., 199, *209*, 354, 362, *371*

Valberg, A., 2, *5*, 265, *267*, 273, 276, *28*

Valenti, S.S., 446, *454*
Valeton, J.M., 365, *371*
Van Essen, D.C., 354, 359, *371*
Van Hoorn, W., 510, *527*
van Trigt, C., 262, 264, *281*
Varner, D., 232, 238, 240, *260*
Vautin, R.G., 358, *371*
Verfaillie, M., 225, *228*
Vidyasagar, T.R., 33, *68*
Viola, M., 54, *68*
Virsu, V., 56, *68*, 518, *527*
Vitruvius Pollio, 509, *527*
Vogels, R., 192, *209*, 458, 459, 476, 477, 486,
    497
Volbrecht, V.J., 237, *260*
Volkman, A.W., 456, 457, *497*
Volpe, B.T., 224, 225, *228*
von Bonin, G., 362, *371*
von Campenhausen, C., 323, 324, 341, *348*
von Frisch, K., 324, 331, *349*
von Helversen, O., 325, *349*
von Hofsten, C., 441, *454*
von Kries, C., 409, 415, 419, *434*
von Kries, J., 262, 264, *282*

Wachsmuth, E., 152, *172*, 194, 203, *209*
Wagner, M., 505, *527*
Walker, B.H., 509, *527*
Walker, J.T., 54, *68*

Walker, W.D., 45, 48, 50, 51, *68*
Wallach, H., 397, 400, *408*
Wallis, G., 161, *172*
Wallis, J., 520, *527*
Walsh, V., 236, 257, *260*, 360, 361, 362, *371*
Walton, G.E., 8, *30*
Warren, R., 451n6, *454*
Warren, W.H., 411, 425, *435*, 440, 446, 451n4, *454*, 508, *527*
Warrington, E.K., 3, *5*, 89, 90, *122*, 141n8, *143*, 211, 212, 213, 214, 215, 216, 217, 218, 220, 222, 223, *228*
Watanabe, T., 39, 40, *68*
Watson, J.S., 444, *454*
Weale, R.A., 514, *527*
Webster, M.A., 366, *372*
Webster, W.R., 33, 42, 43, *68*
Weinberger, N.M., 486, *497*
Weinshall, D., 128, 130, 132, 136, *143*
Weiskrantz, L., 200, *209*
Weiss, Y., 482, *498*
Welch, M.J., 242, *260*
Welch, R.B., 521, *527*
Wenderoth, P., 384, *408*
Werner, A., 330, *351*
Werner, J.S., 237, 241, 247, *260*, *261*
Wertheimer, M., 18, *30*
West, G., 302, *322*
Wheatstone, C., 418, *435*, 508, *527*
White, K.D., 33, 34, *68*
White, M.J., 80, 115, *122*
Whiteley, A.M., 223, *228*
Wild, H.M., 361, *372*
Wiser, M.A., 111, 114, *122*

Witkin, A.P., 130, 136, *143*
Wolfe, J.M., 47, 54, *68*, 473, 483, *498*
Wolff, H., 331, *351*
Wolford, G., 459, 460, 489, *498*
Wong, R.O.L., 167, *172*
Wood, R.J., 511, *528*
Woods, J.D., 513, *528*
Worthey, J.A., 256, *261*, 262, 264, *282*, 301, *322*
Wundt, W., 518, *528*
Wurtz, R., 491, *498*
Wyszecki, G., 264, *282*, 292, *322*, 347, *351*

Yamane, S., 363, *372*
Yasuda, K., 45, 51, *68*
Yoskioka, T., 357, 358, 359, *372*
Young, A.W., 91, *122*, *123*
Young, J.M., 80, *123*
Young, M.J., 391, *408*, 429, *435*
Young, R.A., 336, *351*
Yuille, A.L., 148, *172*, 304, *322*, 377, *408*
Yuodelis, C., 235, 236, *261*

Zehender, W. von, 515, *528*
Zeki, S.M., 33, *68*, 236, *261*, 354, 359, 360, *372*, 426, *435*
Zemel, R.S., 153, *172*
Zeno, T., 510, *528*
Zhang, Y., 421, *435*
Zhou, H., 38, 42, *68*
Zipse, W., 337, *351*
Zohary, E., 398, *408*
Zoth, O., 511, *528*

Subject index

accommodation
  celestial illusion explanation, 511, 517
  in depth scaling, 418–422
  in distance estimation, 377, 410–411
  perceived size scaling, 508
accuracy
  distance estimation, 377–379, 410–414
  precision difference, 375
  in size constancy judgments, 375–383
advancing colors, 514
aerial perspective cues, 507, 512–513
affine representation, 127–128
aftereffects, 31, 518–519; see also McCollough
  effect
afterimages
  apparent size judgments, 388
  Emmert's law, 388, 505–506
  geometric figures, 518–519
aging, and practice effects, 466–467
agnosia, 216–225
  definition, 217
  and object constancy, 216–226
  plane rotation studies, 221–223
  types of, 217–218
Alhazen
  celestial illusion theory, 509–510
  size-distance perception theory, 503
alignment approach
  geometric hashing comparison, 127
  shape constancy computation, 126–127, 135–
    136
  size transformation, 197
alley phenomenon, 501
Alzheimer's disease, McCollough effect, 37–
  38
analog transformations, 104
analytical color view, 272
angle of regard, 507
angular size
  disparity cues, 388
  distance effects, 502–504
  versus linear size, perception, 500, 502
  moon illusion explanation, 512

neural calculations, 393–394
in objective size estimations, 382–383
psychophysical measurement, 376, 378;
  precision, 378
recalibration, 391–392
and relational cues, 386
in speed constancy estimation, 394–396,
  402, 404
"anti-constancy" conditions, 391–392
aperture color
  brightness in, 276
  definition, 275–276
  and Mondrian patterns, 277
aperture discrimination, frogs, 176–178
aphid, successive color contrast, 344
apparent motion effects, 104–105
apparent size effects, 499
apperceptive agnosia, 217–218
associative agnosia, 217–218
asymmetric matching paradigm
  color constancy studies, 266–272
  retinex theory test, 266–268
atmospheric effects, 512
attention
  and automaticity, 465–466
  McCollough effect independence, 34–36
  pop-out tass, 489–491
  serial versus parallel processing, 465–
    466
  single-cell changes, learning, 484
  in size perception, 394–395
automatization, 464–470
  and attention, 465–466
  definition, 465
  feature detector formation, 468–469
  models, 468
  in perceptual learning, 464–470, 488
  specificity of, 468–469
  stimulus–response mapping in, 469–470
axis of elongation
  and frame of reference, 109–110
  object recognition role, 89–91
  and right-hemisphere damage, 90, 213

backward alignment, rotating objects, 108–109
backward-masking tasks
   attention role, 488–489
   practice effects, 459–460
balance perceptions, 442–443
bar detectors, 41–43
"barrier blindness," 176–177
"bent stick" phenomenon, 520
Berkeley, George
   aerial perspective explanation, 513
   moon illusion theory, 511
   perceptual learning theory, 6
   size cue theory, 507
bilateral symmetry assumption, 129–130
binocular parallax
   object distance cue, 377, 379–380
   precision of, 377, 379
binocular viewing
   and color constancy, 269–272
   and color-size effects, 514
   size constancy accuracy, 379–380
   speed constancy, 397
   vertical disparities, depth scaling, 422–426;
      horizontal disparities comparison, 424–
      425
binoculars, optical distortion, 519–520
biodynamics; *see also* dynamical constancy
   age-related changes, 14
   infants, 11–15; research paradigms, 441–442
   kinematic specification, 446–447
   knowledge-based constraints, 14–15
bipartite test patterns, 49–50
blind spots, reconstruction, 141n10
"blind" walking, 411–412
blobs
   area V1 subregion function, 356–357
   color selective neurons, 357
   visual pathway organization, 353
blue color
   early infancy discrimination, 238
   honeybee compensation, 347
   and perceived size, 514
blue–green boundary, infants, 246
Bower's conditioning experiments, 20–21
brain damage; *see also* right hemisphere
      lesions
   canonical view effects, 89–90
   McCollough effect perception, 36–38
brightest is white assumption, 298–299
brightness
   in aperture color, 275–276
   and minimal-effort principle, 278
   perceived size effects, 513–514
Brunswik ratio, 502–504
Bufo bufo
   color constancy, 337
   shape constancy, 184
bug detectors, 174

canonical view, 86–92
   axis of elongation role, 89–91
   brain damage effects, 89–90
   computational approach, 138
   familiarity role, 87
   hemifield effects, 90–91
   three-dimensional objects, 86–92
   unfamiliar faces, 87
   variations among subjects, 88
cardioidal shape invariant, 447
Castelli, Benedetto, 505, 507
categorization
   in infancy, 15–17
   memory search task performance, 492
   and right-hemisphere lesions, 211–215
   transfer of training, 482
cats
   color-blind/lightness–contrast test, 341–342
   color constancy, 338–342
   color vision dimensionality, 339
causality perception, 437–438
celestial illusion, 508–512
   contemporary theories, 512
   farther-larger-nearer theory, 511
   historical perspective, 508–512
   perceived size theory, 509–510
   refraction theory, 509–510
chromatic adaptation
   color constancy mechanism, 256, 347, 364–
      366
   cortical stage, 366
   honeybees, 347
   opponent stage, 365–366
   receptor level, 364–365
chromatic discrimination
   early infancy, 237–241
   spatial factors, 240–241
chromatic opponency, 240
chromatic signature algorithms, 285, 318
chromaticity convergence algorithm, 311–312
classical conditioning, McCollough effect, 54–
      55
cognitive control
   color constancy, 285–286
   McCollough effect, 38–39
   size and shape constancy, 25–26
collision dynamics, 445–446, 449
color, and perceived size, 513–514
color aftereffects, *see* McCollough effect
color-blind/lightness-constancy, cats, 341–342
color categorization
   V1 area, 358
   V4 area, 362
color constancy
   in amphibians, 337
   in analytical viewing, 272
   assessment methods, 229–233
   asymmetric matching paradigm, 265–272

in birds, 337–338
in carp, 332–334
central mechanisms, 279
in chicks, 249
in chimpanzees, 342
chromatic adaptation mechanism, 256
chromaticity convergence algorithm, 311–312
color naming method, 272–275
comparative aspects, 323–351
computational models, 283–322
in cyprinid fishes, 331–336
development of, 254–256
empirical studies, 249–255, 262–282
and figural organization, 269–272
in fish, 331–336
and global view, 272–273
in honeybees, 324–331
and hue categorization, infants, 243–248
infants, 229–257; in newborn infants, 237–242
instruction effects, 268–269
Lambertian model, 290–291
matrix equation, 291–295
minimal effort principle, 278
in monkeys, 342–343
monocularly versus binocularly viewed figures, 269–272
mutual reflections role, 313–319
neural network transformation, 307
perceptual models, 284–285, 307–319
physiological substrates, 352–373; mechanisms, 364–368
psychophysiological response function, 269
sensory models, 284–285
simulation methods, 263–264
in song birds, 338
in toads, 337
V4 area, 257
color naming task, 272–275
color opponency
  chromatic adaptation mechanism, 365
  lightness algorithm problem, 303, 308
  and mutual reflections, 318
  segmentation algorithm, 308–309
  V1 area processing, 354–356
color segmentation algorithms, 285, 308–310
  goal, 308
  and opponent colors, 308–309
  ordinality in, 309
  single-source assumption, 309
color spreading
  inferotemporal cortex, 367
  McCollough effect, 50–51
color vision
  assessment methods, 229–235
  early infancy, 237–242
  evolutionary purpose, 12

in frogs, 337
infants, 229–242
maturation, 235–237
colorimetrics, 263–264
competent infant conception, 7
competitive learning model
  limitations, 150
  in neural networks, 148–150
  nonlinearity, 149–150
complexity
  color sensation factor, 276, 278–279
  and Mondrian patterns, 276–277
computational approaches
  color constancy, 283–322; perceptual model, 313–319; physiology, 366–368
  feature detectors in, 140–141
  invariant recognition, 153–168; hierarchical model, 153–159
  lightness algorithms, 294–303
  multiple view models, 124, 135–139
  normalization methods, 126–128, 135–136
  versus phenomenological models, color, 284
  reconstruction model, 124–131, 139–141
computer simulations, color constancy, 263–264
conditioning
  McCollough effect explanation, 54–55
  size and shape constancy, infants, 20–21
cones; *see also* photoreceptors
  chromatic adaptation mechanism, 365
  infant anatomy, 235
  in lightness algorithms, 300–303
  long-wavelength sensitive cones, early infancy, 238
  nonlinear signal transmission, 291
conjunction search, 473, 480–481
connectionism, *see* synaptic learning
conscious processing, 224–225
contingent aftereffects; *see also* McCollough effect
  conditioning model, 54–55
  fatigue explanation, 53–54
  functional role, 57–59
convergence; *see also* binocular parallax
  celestial illusion explanation, 511
  in depth perception, 418–422
  in distance estimation, 378, 411
  neural signals, 421–422
  perceived size scaling, 508
  viewing distance effects on, 421
co–occurrence rule, synapses, 147–148
cooperative representations
  discrimination and generalization in, 164
  in neural networks, 150–151
  specialization and generalization, 151–152
cooperative vector quantization, 151
corpus callosum lesions, 212
cortical blindness, 38

cross-cultural studies, illusions, 516
cue-based theories
    dynamic constancy, 447–450
    size constancy, 507
cue combination
    cooperation and supplementation in, 429–431
    in depth estimation, 426–432
    disambiguation function, 432
    linear models, 427–429
    modular designs, 426–427
cultural factors, geometric illusions, 516
cyprinus carpio, 332–334

da Vinci, Leonardo, 506, 511–514
daylight
    linear basis model assumption, 292
    and monochromatic animals, 323–324
    spectral composition, 347
Delboeuf figure, 518
depth estimation; 69–123, 409–423; *see also*
        three-dimensional rotation
    binocular vertical disparities in, 422–425
    and cue combination, 426–432
    in depth comparison tasks, 416–418
    distance cues, 418–426
    image size cues, 421
    modular designs, 426–427
    and object recognition, principal axis, 90–92
    perceptual measures, 415–416
    perspective cues, 425
    precision, 410–414
    and priming, 101–102
    and relational size information, 386–387
    retinal elevation cues, 425
    single- versus multiple cue judgments, 378
    size constancy contribution of, 379–380,
        383, 386–387; in natural circumstances,
        383
development
    color constancy, 254–256
    color vision, 235–237
    and learned perspective illusions, 516
DF case, 37, 199–200
diagonal matrix equation, 303
dichromacy, early infancy, 239–240
Dichromatic Reflection Model, 312
differentiation principle, 471
direct perception, 471–472
disambiguation, and cue combination,
        432
discrimination
    and chromatic adaptation, 365
    enrichment models comparison, 488
    generalization compatibility, cooperative
        networks, 164
    infant preferential looking, 231–232
    mechanisms, 470–472, 488

newborn infant studies, 238–240
    size constancy judgments, 382, 389–390;
        disparity mechanisms, 389–390
    somatosensory cortex plasticity, 486
    speed judgments, 396
    V4 area lesions, monkeys, 360–361
dissociation, memory systems, priming, 92–104
distance estimation/scaling
    accuracy, 375–379, 410–414
    amphibians, 173–178
    cues, 377–379, 410–414
    in motor tasks, 410–414
    multiple cues, 410–414
    in objective size judgments, 379–383
    precision, 375–379
    psychophysical studies, 375–376
    size constancy role, 388–391, 505–507
    and speed constancy, 400–402
dorsal pathway, and size information, 199–200
double opponency
    computational approach, 367
    V1 area role, 354–357
dual-task conditions
    attentional mechanisms, 489–490
    learning specificity implications, 483
dynamic equilibrium, 442–443
dynamical constancy, 436–454
    anomaly paradigm, 440
    collision judgments, 445–446
    ecological- versus cue-based theories, 447–450
    empirical research, 440–447
    gravitational constraints, 442–445
    infants, 11–15; research paradigms, 14
    judgment paradigm, 440
    kinematic specification, 437–438, 447–450
    natural versus computer-generated stimuli,
        441
    perceptual heuristics view, 438–439, 447–450

ecological theories
    dynamical constancy, 447–450
    McCollough effect, 43–44
efferent readiness, 518
Emmert's law, 388, 505–506
enrichment principle, 471–472, 488
error correction device
    McCollough effect role, 57–59
    schematic model, 58
Euclid's propositions, 501, 503
European tiger salamander, 337
evolution
    color vision cause, 373
    rotational invariance, 187–188
existence constancy, infants, 26–27

explicit memory
  implicit memory dissociation, 92–104
  priming studies, shape representations, 92–104
extended-body dynamics, 439
extinction, visual, 224–225
eye–hand constancy, evolution, 188
eye movements
  in distance scaling, 412–414
  geometric illusions explanation, 517–518
  and McCollough effect, 51–52

face perception/recognition
  canonical views, 87
  infants, 8, 17
  priming effects, 198
  prosopagnosia, 223–224
  prototype effects, infants, 17
Face Recognition Units, 198
face-selective neurons
  invariance learning, 167
  orientation generalization, physiology, 193–196
  temporal cortex, size effects, 203–205
familiarity
  canonical view role, 87
  and infant biomechanical motion perception 14
  and intermodal perception, newborns, 18
farther-larger-nearer theory, 511
feature detectors
  hierarchical arrangement, 156–159
  in perceptual learning, 468–469
  shape constancy computation, 140–141
figural aftereffects, 31, 518–519
figure–ground relationship, color encoding, 243–244
flat-sky theory, 509–510
fluorescent illuminants
  color constancy studies, infants, 249–254
  versus incandescent illuminants, 249–250, 254
Forced Choice Preferential Looking Technique
  double psychophysics in, 231–232
  either/or questions, 232
  procedural overview, 230–233
foreshortened views
  and frame of reference, 113
  object identification effects, 89–91
  Ponzo illusion, 385–387
  priming representations, 102
  and right-hemisphere lesions, 90, 211–215, 219–220
form perception
  McCollough effect, 56
  newborn infants, 8, 10–12
Fourier analysis
  invariant recognition limitations, 154
  McCollough effect, 41–43

frame of reference, 109–114
  and axes, 109–110, 113–114
  in foreshortened views, 113
  and left–right discrimination, 112
  in pattern recognition, 112
  viewer- versus object-centered, 110–114
"free-floating" stimuli, 103, 106
frontal cortex, task-specific effects, 486
Fukushima network, 156–159

Gabor patch detection, 476–479
generalization
  in competitive networks, 151–152
  discrimination compatibility, cooperative networks, 164
  and multiple neural unit layers, 154–159; hierarchies, 156–159
  object orientation physiology, 192–206
  single-cell studies, 193–196, 201–206; size changes, monkeys, 201–205
geometric hashing
  advantages, 127
  shape constancy normalization, 126–127
geometric illusions, 384–387, 515–518
  aftereffects, 518–519
  cross-cultural studies, 516
  developmental effects, 516
  effort theory, 518
  historical perspective, 515–518
  oculomotor theory, 517–518
  perspective theory, 515–516
  relational size misjudgments, 384–387, 516–517
  scanning theory, 517–518
geons, 75–77, 131
  nonaccidental shape properties, 181
  in recognition by components theory, 136–137
Gestalt theory
  color perception, 279
  size constancy, 373–374, 501–502
global color view, 272–273
grating patterns, McCollough effect, 48–53
gravitational constraints, 442–445
gray-world assumption, 298–300
  linear-basis algorithm, 304–307
  retinex algorithm, 298–299
green–yellow boundary, infant response, 246

habit effects, 459–460
habituation (infants)
  color constancy, 249–254
  hue categorization, 245–247
  size constancy, 22–26
  visual attention, 233–235
Hebb's rule, 146–147

heuristic models
  dynamic constancy perception, 438–439
  ecological theories comparison, 447–450
  theoretical issues, 448–449
hierarchical networks
  invariance recognition, 156–159, 161
  Neocognitron model, 156–159
  shift invariance simulation, 161
horizon ratio rule, 508
horizontal–vertical illusion, 515, 518
hue categorization, infants, 243–248
hue discrimination, V4 neurons, 360–361

identification
  rotated shapes, 80–86
  selective attention role, 489
identity constancy, infants, 26–27
illuminants
  in asymmetric matching paradigm, 265–272
  chromatic adaptation mechanism, 364–365
  color constancy studies, infants, 249–254
  color simulation models, 263–264
  computational models, 286–319
  fluorescent versus incandescent, 249–250, 254
  Lambertian model, 290–291
  linear-basis algorithm assumptions, 304–307
  matrix model, 291–294
  and minimal-effort principles, 278–279
  perceptual models, 307–319
  reflectance separation, computation, 286–295
  specular highlights, 310–313
image irradiance equation, 286–289
  direct and indirect illumination in, 287–288
  and Lambertian model, 290–291
  and lightness algorithms, 300
  and mutual reflections, 313–315
  surface reflectance assumption in, 288
implicit memory
  explicit memory dissociation, 92–104
  priming studies, shape representations, 92–104
incandescent illuminants
  color constancy studies, infants, 249–254
  versus fluorescent illuminants, 249–250, 254
infancy, 6–28; *see also* newborn infants
  achromatic channel, 240
  categorization in, 15–17, 243–249
  chromatic adaptation, 256
  color constancy, 229–257
  dynamic constancy, 11–15; research paradigms, 441–442
  face perception, 8, 17
  form perception, 8, 10–12
  gravitational support perception, 442
  identity constancy, 26–27
  intermodal perception, 17–19
  knowledge-based perception, 14–15

point-light displays, 11–15
prototype effects, 15–17
size and shape constancy, 20–26
subjective contour perception, 10–12
visual organization, 6–28
inferotemporal cortex
  color selectivity, 363–364
  color spreading neuron response, 367
  face-selective cells, size effects, 203–205
  general organization, 362–363
  nonlinear summation cone inputs, 363–364
  orientation-specific cells, 192–193
  short-term memory effects, 205
  and size changes, single cells, 202–205
  size generalization, monkeys, 200–201
  task-specific practice effects, 486
inhibitory processes, McCollough effect, 55–56
interface reflection
  computational models, 287–289
  determinants, 287
  and image irradiance equation, 287
intermodal perception, infants, 17–19
interocular transfer, 33–34
intraretinal invariance, fish, 189–190
irradiance, 286–289, 319n2

just noticeable difference
  practice effects, 456–457, 470

kinematic specification of dynamics, 437–438
  collision studies, 445
  problematic issues, 438
  testability, 448–449
  theoretical issues, 448–449
knowledge-based constraints, 14–15

Lambertian reflectance model, 289–291
  color constancy computation surfaces, 289–291
  and image irradiance equation, 288–291
  mutual reflections problem, 290
  single-source assumption, 290
Land's model
  physiological substrate approaches, 366–368
  retrinex algorithms, 296–299
lateral geniculate nucleus
  chromatic processing, 353
  development, 236
lateral masking tasks, 459–460
learning constancies, 144–172; *see also* perceptual learning
  competitive models, 148–149
  co–occurrence models, 147–148
  cooperative representations, 150–159
  multilayered hierarchical networks, 156–159
  simulation, 160–163
  spatial, in monkeys, 386

specialization and generalization in, 151–159
synaptic connections, 146–148
trace mechanisms, 159–168
left–right discrimination
and frame of reference, 112
mental rotation, 106–107
LG case, 222
Lie operators
McCollough effect role, 44–48
visual constancy function, 44
Lie Transformation Group Theory of
Neuropsychology
"ecological" interpretation, 43–44
McCollough effect interpretation, 43–53
light adaptation
and color constancy, 256, 364–365
photoreceptor mechanisms, 364–365
lightness
algorithms, 285–286, 294–304
cat perception, 341–342
cyprinid fish perception, 332
and figural organization, 278
monkey perception, 342
photoreceptor scaling, 300–303
retinex theory, 276, 296–299
sensory models, 285–286
in surface color, 275–276, 278
von Kries's model, 300–303
line drawing recognition, agnosia, 218–219
line length perception, cue theory, 508
linear models
assumptions, 286, 292–294
color constancy, 291–294, 303–307
depth cue combinations, 427–429
versus light algorithms, 304
and matrix equation, 292–294, 303–307
McCollough effect, 41–43
neural network techniques, 307
neural unit factor, 146–147
shape reconstruction, 128–129
weighting factor assignment, 428
linear grating patterns, 48–53
linear size
angular size matches comparison, 502–504
perceived size influence, 500
local signs theory, 518

macaques, *see* color constancy, in monkeys
McCollough effect, 31–68
adaptation mechanism, 53–57
and attention, 34–36
brain-damaged subjects, 36–38
cognitive organization role, 38–39
color spreading, 50–51
computer simulations, 60
conditioning model, 54–55
edge detector mechanism, 41–43
error-correcting mechanism, 57–59

and eye movements, 51–52
fatigue hypothesis, 53–54
functional role, 57–59
global mechanisms, 43–53
indirect, 47–48
inhibitory processes in, 55–56
interocular transfer, 33–34
linguistic factors, 39–40
mechanisms, 40–53
as mind–brain problem, 32
spatial frequencies analysis mechanism, 41–43
test pattern differences, 48–53
magnocellular system, 353–354
memorial agnosias, 221
memory, *see* recognition memory
memory search tasks
automatization, 466–468, 470
category effects, 492
learning specificity/transfer issue, 492
practice effects, 466–468, 492
strategy shifts in, 470
mental rotation
analog nature of, 104–105
apparent motion similarity, 104–105
computational approach, 136, 138
normalization function of, 104–107
orientation effects, 105–107
plane rotated object perception, 221–223
and right-hemisphere lesions, 214
three-dimensional object representation, 85–86, 104–107
two–dimensional object representation, 83–84, 104–107
metamers, 264
middle-wavelength sensitive cones
early infancy, 238
infant anatomy, 235
lightness algorithms, 301–302
mind-brain problem, 32
minimal-effort principle, 278
and Gestalt theory, 279
surface color perception, 278–279
minimal-feature views, 219–220
mirror images, 96–97
model-based invariant operator, 132
modules, and depth cues, 426–427
Molyneux's question, 507–508
Mondrian patterns
in asymmetrical matching paradigm, 265–268
color simulation methods, 263, 276–277
and complexity, 276–277
goldfish color constancy, 334–336
honeybee color constancy, 330–331
lightness factor, 276, 297
retinex algorithm, 297
V4 neurons, 360, 367–368

monocular viewing
  and color constancy, 269–272
  and color-size effects, 514
  ocular specificity, learning, 481
  reconstruction of, visual areas, 481
  size judgment accuracy, 379–380
  speed constancy, 397
moon illusion, *see* celestial illusion
motion aftereffect, 31, 519
motion cues
  depth cue weighting, 429
  dynamical constancy specification, 437–438
  and gravitation forces, 443–445
  and speed calculation, 395–396
  stereo cues cooperation, 427, 429–430
motion parallax
  binocular disparity combination, 429
  and depth scaling, 422, 429
  disambiguation, 432
  in distance estimation, 378, 411
  size constancy role, 388
movement aftereffects, 519
Müller–Lyer illusion, 515
Munsell colors, 264–267
mutual reflection
  in body color determination, 313–319
  color-opponency interpretation, 318
  in Lambertian model, 290
  one-bounce model, 314–315

natural illuminants; *see also* daylight
  assumptions, 292
  computational approach, 292
Neocognitron, 156
neural networks
  color constancy transformation, 307
  competitive learning in, 148–150
  cooperative model, 150–151, 164
  Hebb's rule, 147–148
  linear summation, 146–147
  multiple unit layers, 154–159; hierarchies, 156–159
  shift invariance learning simulation, 160–163
  spatial constancy, frog, 181–182
  specialization and generalization in, 151–159
  stereo depth scaling, 420–421
neural plasticity, *see* plasticity
neuronal response, *see* single-cell studies
neutral interface model, 288–289
  assumptions, 288–289
  and real images, 313
"neutral point" judgments, 57
neutral point test, 239–240
newborn infants
  existence concept in, 27
  intermodal perception, 17–19
  visual organization, 7–19

normalization
  in computation of shape, 126–128, 135–136
  in lightness algorithms, 294, 298–299, 301
  mental rotations role, 104–107
  multiple stored views approach, 135–136
  retinex algorithm, 298–299
  rotated object representations, 104–109
  size transformations, 197
  visual code in, 108
novel objects
  dynamical constancy research, 441
  newborn infant preference, 9–10, 441
  and right-hemisphere lesions, 215

object-centered representations; *see also* orientation
  frame of reference, 109–114
  and priming, 100–102
  and rotation, 69–123
object concept, development of, 27
object constancy
  in agnosia, 216–226
  and canonical views, 86–92
  dual systems theory, 107
  face stimuli, 223–224
  learning, 144–168
  memory system dissociation, 92–104
  and mental rotation, 104–107
  neuropsychology, 210–228
  orientation effects, 69–123
  priming representations, 92–104
  right-hemisphere lesions, 211–216
object-naming tasks, 106–107
objective perception
  generalization physiology, 192–209
  neural unit models, 146–147
  size change effects, 196–206
oblique orientation judgments, 458–459
oblique patterns, infant perception, 15
ocular specificity, learning, 481, 483
oculomotor theory, geometric illusions, 517–518
one-bounce model, 314–315
Oppel–Kundt illusion, 515
opponency, *see* color opponency
optical distortion, adaptation, 519–521
optical illusions, *see* size illusions
optokinetic nystagmus, 232–233
orbits
  McCollough effect role, 48
  perceptual constancy function, 44–45
ordinality, color segmentation algorithms, 309
orientation
  and backward alignment, 105–106
  contextual effects, 103–104
  and evolution, 187–188
  face-selective neurons, 167
  in frame of reference, 110–114

and infant perception, 15
and McCollough effect coding, 55–56
and mental rotation, 83–84, 105–106
priming studies, 92–104
rotated shapes, 69–123; in fish, 185–190
single-cell studies, 192–196, 484
and size constancy, in monkeys, 200–206
orientation-congruency effect, 111
orthogonal gratings, 50–51, 60*n*4
overconstancy, 376

pale stripes, area V2, 354
parallax judgments, *see* binocular parallax
parallel processing
and automaticity, 465–468
practice effect studies, 466–468
parietal cortex
size generalization, monkeys, 200
three-dimensional orientation coding, 206
particle dynamics, 439
parvocellular system, 353–354
pattern recognition
and frame of reference, 112
hierarchical network models, 158–159
memory system dissociation, 92–104
opportunistic nature of, 81
orientation null effects, 81
priming studies, 92–104
young infant color encoding, 242–243
PB case, 37
pendular motions, 444–445
perceptron units
hierarchies of, 156–159
and invariant recognition, 154
pattern recognition, 158
perceptual categorization, *see* categorization
perceptual color models, 285
perceptual heuristics, *see* heuristic models
perceptual learning, 455–498
automaticity theory, 465–470, 488
definition, 455–456
distance estimation, 429
improved discrimination theory of, 470–472
memory and visual search tasks, 466–468, 492
neural plasticity, 484–486
physiology, 483–488
positron emission tomography, 487
range and limits of, 456–460
selective attention mechanism, 484, 488–491
specificity implications, 476–481
speed and efficiency theory of, 472–475
theories of, 460–475
transfer of, simple stimuli, 475–483
peripheral vision, practice effects, 457–459
phenomenological model
color constancy, 284
versus computational models, 284

phosphor luminances, 264–265
photoreceptors
chromatic adaptation, 256, 364–365
early infancy chromatic discrimination, 238
infant anatomy, 235
lightness algorithm scaling, 300–303
picture matching, and priming, 99–102
plane rotation effects
and agnosia, 221–223
mental rotation role in, 222–223
plasticity
and neural deprivation studies, 484
selective attention role, 488–491
V1 area, 481, 484–486
Plotinus's size scaling theory, 506
point-light perception
age-related changes, 14
infants, 11–15
point of subjective equality, 376
polyhedral scenes, computation, 129
Ponzo illusion
perspective theory, 515
relational size in, 384–387, 516–517
pop-out learning, 482–483
attentional control, 489–491
interpretation of, 482–483
pose computation, 125–127
practice effects; *see also* perceptual learning
and aging, 466–467
attention role in, 491
limits of, 456–460
physiology, 486–488
rotated object recognition, 85
precision, 375–376
accuracy difference, 375
depth estimates, 410–414
in distance estimations, 375–379, 410–414
objective size judgments, 379–383
preferential looking
assessment in infants, 230–233
dynamical constancy research, 441
prefrontal area, task-specific effects, 486
premotor cortex, task-specific effects, 486
presynaptic mechanism, trace learning, 160, 166
priming, 92–104
and foreshortened views, 102
mirror-image reversal effects, 96–97
object category similarity effects, 102–103
picture-matching tasks, 99–102
semantic representation role, 93–94, 99–101
size perception memory, 92–104, 197–199
viewpoint-invariant claims, 92–104
visual component, 93
prosopagnosia, 223–224
prototypes, infant perception, 15–17
Ptolemy
apparent size theory, 503, 505
celestial illusion theory, 509

Rayleigh discrimination, 232, 237–238
recognition by components theory
  implementation, 136–137
  multiple-view interpolation comparison, 137–138
  shape constancy computation, 136–137
recognition memory
  priming studies, 92–104
  rotated objects, 69–80, 85–86
  size change effects, 196–197
reconstruction of shape
  computational approach, 124–135, 139–141
  model-based approaches, 125–126
  model-free approaches, 129–131
  normalization, 126–128
reference frame, *see* frame of reference
reflectance; *see also* spectral values
  color simulation methods, 263–264
  computational models, 286–319
  illumination separation, computation, 286–294
  matrix equation, 291–294
  and minimal-effort principle, 278
  perceptual models, 307–319
  retinex theory, 267–268, 297–298
  separability assumption, 288–289
  tristimulus models comparison, 264
refraction theory, celestial illusion, 509–512
regularization, object shape recovery, 130
relational size
  depth judgment contribution, 386–387
  and geometric illusions, 384–387, 516–517
  size constancy estimation, 383–388
reliability, *see* precision
retina, developmental changes, 235–237
retinal image
  and rotated shape memory, 71–72
  and size constancy, newborns, 22–26
retinex theory, 296–299
  assumptions, 286, 296–297
  asymmetric matching paradigm test, 266–268
  brightest as white assumption, 298–299
  in color sensations prediction, 276, 286
  goldfish color constancy, 334–336
  gray-world assumption, 298–299
  implementation, 297–299
  lightness algorithm, 296–299
  spatial decomposition constraints, 297–299
retreating colors, 514
Rey figure, 221
rhesus monkeys, *see* color constancy, in monkeys
right-hemisphere lesions
  depth perception deficits, 214, 219
  face recognition, 223–224
  versus left-hemisphere damage, object constancy, 220

novel object perception, 215
object constancy, 89–91, 211–216
  and perceptual categorization, 211–214
  plane rotation perception, 222
  and principal axis extraction, 90–91
  unusual view tasks, 89–91, 211–215, 219–220
  visual extinction, 224–225
  visual function matching tasks, 215–216
rotary aftereffects, 519
rotational invariance, 69–123; *see also* mental rotation
  and agnosia, case studies, 221–223
  in amphibians, 187–188
  backward alignment normalization, 108–109
  canonical views, 86–92
  dual systems theory, 107
  evolution, 187–188
  in fish, 185–190
  frame of reference, 109–114
  identification time, 85–86
  normalization operations, 104–109
  orientation effects, 69–124
  priming studies, 92–104
  right-hemisphere lesions, 214
rotor movement pursuit, 487
RT patient, 222–223

salamanders, color constancy, 337
Sällström–Buchsbaum model
  theoretical constraint, 264
  tristimulus model comparison, 264
scanning theories, 517–518
Schroeder staircase, 506
scotoma, 141n10
segmentation algorithms, *see* color segmentation algorithms
selective attention
  perceptual learning role, 488–492
  pop-out tasks, 489–491
  simple tasks role, 489
  and single-cell learning shifts, 484
semantic representations
  decay, 101
  visual priming role, 93–94, 99–101
sensory color models, 284–285
serial processing, practice effects, 466–468
shading, and depth cue weighting, 428
shadows, and color segmentation, 308–310
shape constancy; *see also* size constancy
  cognitive control in, 25–26
  computational approaches, 124–143, 153–159
  and evolution, 187–188
  eye–hand constancy relationship, 188
  feature detectors in, 140–141
  fish and amphibians, 182–190
  infant perception, 20–26

multiple-view approach, 135–139
reconstruction approach, 124–131
in toads, 184
transitional equivalence, fish, 189–190
shape recognition, in fish, 189–190
shift invariance, 167
short-wavelength sensitive cones
early infancy, 238
infant anatomy, 235
lightness algorithm, 301–302
silhouette recognition, 218–219
simultaneous color contrast
in animals, 343–345
definition, 343
physiological models, 366–368
underlying mechanisms, honeybees, 345–347
single-cause classification models, 150
single-cell studies
object orientation, 192–196
perceptual learning shifts, 484
selective attention influences, 484
and size changes, monkeys, 201–206
sinusoidal grating stimuli, 457–458, 476–478
size constancy, 373–408
accuracy and precision in, 375–383
amphibians, 182–190
attention role, 394–395
cognitive control in, 25–26
definition, 373
distance effects, 379–383, 388–391, 505–507
explicit–implicit memory dissociation, 92–104
fish and amphibians, 182–190; functional dissociation, 184
frogs and toads, 173–178; epistemology, 177–178
Gestalt interpretation, 373–374
historical perspective, 499–528
illusions, 384–387, 499–528
learning of, 391–392
measurement error, 375–376
in monkeys, 201–206
neural dual calculations, 392–394
neuropsychology, 199–200
in newborn infants, 20–26
physiology, 192–206
Ponzo illusions, 384–387
priming studies, 92–104, 197–199
recalibration, 391–392
and recognition memory, 196–197
relational determinants, 383–388
and retinal size, infants, 22–24
single-cell studies, 201
size invariance distinction, 196
Structuralist interpretations, 373–374
ventral and dorsal pathways, 199–200

size-distance invariance hypothesis, 500, 505–507, 512
size illusions, 499–528
size invariance
models, 197–198
size constancy distinction, 196
skill acquisition, *see* plasticity or perceptual learning
slant perception, infants, 21–22
Smith, Robert, 510
somatosensory cortex, 486
spatial representation
frogs, 178–182
learning transfer/specificity, 479–481
neural network, 181–182
newborn infants, 9–10
somatosensory cortex plasticity, 486
split-brain subjects, 178, 181
specialization and generalization
in competitive networks, 151–152
and multiple neural unit layers, 154–159; hierarchies, 156–159
spectral sensitivity, development, 237
spectral values; *see also* reflectance
illuminant color contribution, 310–313
lightness algorithms, normalization, 294
mathematical models, simulations, 264
segmentation algorithms, 308–310
speed constancy, 394–405
angular distance scaling in, 400–402
calculation, 395–396
depth cues, 398–400
motion signals, 395–396
neural algorithm, 403–405
relational effects, 397–398
and spatial scaling, 396–400
temporal frequency in, 398, 402, 405
split-brain subjects, 178, 181
stereoscopic vision, *see* three-dimensional vision
stimulus compounds, 9–10
stimulus–response mapping
attentional control in, 491
and automatization theory, 469–470
stripes
color selective neurons, 358–359
V2 area, 354, 358–359
Structuralism, 373–374
successive color contrast
in animals, 343–345
definition, 343
sun illusion, 512
superior temporal sulcus
color-selective neurons, 359
face selective cells, size effects, 203–205
orientation generalization, 193–196
surface color
definition, 275–276

surface color (cont.)
  Lambertian model, 289–291
  lightness in, 276
  minimal-effort principles, 278
  and Mondrian patterns, 277
  reflectance recovery, computation, 286–303
  V1 area neuron response, 358
surface reflectance assumption, 288
surface reflection
  computational assumptions, 291–292
  determinants, 287
  and illuminant color, 310–313
  and image irradiance equation, 287–288
  and inhomogeneous materials, 288
  and mutual reflections, 313–319
synaptic learning
  competitive model, 148–150
  co-occurrence in, 147–148
  cooperative model, 150–151
  Hebb's rule, 147–148
  hierarchical multilayered model, 156–159
  linear summation model, 146–147
  trace mechanism, 160, 164–168

tactile size, 507–508
temporal frequency judgments
  imprecision of, 402
  in speed perception, 398, 402
text-contingent color aftereffects, 39–40
texture gradient
  discrimination, 477–479, 483; dual-task
    conditions, 483
  in distance estimation, 378, 387; precision,
    378
  in linear cue combination, 427–429
  in size constancy estimation, 374–375,
    383
thin stripes
  color selective neurons, 358–359
  V2 area, 354, 358–359
Thouless ratio, 502–504
three-dimensional rotation, 69–123
  canonical views, 86–92
  and frame of reference, 113–114
  normalization, 104–109
  priming effects, 92–104
  viewpoint-dependent representation, 73–80,
    85–92
three-dimensional silhouettes, 213–214
three-dimensional vision
  binocular vertical disparity in, 422–425
  cue combination, 426–432
  depth constancy, 409–432
  distance cues, 418–426
  modular designs, 426–427
tilt aftereffects, 31, 47
time averaging
  biological relevance, 163–168

in learning constancies, 159–168
top-down processing
  geometric illusion, 516
  perceptual learning, 462–464
trace learning rule
  biological relevance, 163–168
  fundamental assumptions, 165–167
  object constancy, 160–168
  postsynaptic version, 160
  presynaptic version, 160
  simulation, 160–163
training, *see* perceptual learning
transfer of learning, 475–483
  simple stimuli studies, 475–483
  underlying mechanisms, 481–483, 492
  unitizing products in, 473–474
transparency, and McCollough effect, 39
transretinal equivalence, fish, 189–190
trichromacy
  honeybees, 324–325
  infant development, 237
  matrix equation, 292–293
tristimulus ratio model, 263
  color simulation studies, 263–264
  reflectance model comparison, 264
tritan pair discrimination, 240
two–dimensional rotation, 69–123
  and frame of reference, 71–72, 113–114
  identification time, 80–84
  levels of representation, 71–72
  normalization, 104–109
  priming effects, 92–104
  recognition memory, 69–72, 80–84

ultraviolet light, 331
unconscious processing
  geometric illusion explanation, 516
  Helmholtz's theory, 499
  visual extinction studies, 224–225
underwater magnification, 520–521
unusual views task, 211, 213, 219–220

visual cortex
  development, 236–237
  V1 area: and attention, pop-out learning,
    489, 491; blob regions, 356–357; color
    categorization, 358; color processing, 354–
    358; double opponent neurons, 354–357;
    general organization, 353–354;
    McCollough effect, 32–35, 56; plasticity
    in, 481, 484–486; spatial specificity
    neurons, 479–480; surface color response,
    358
  V2 area: color representation, 358–359;
    general organization, 354
  V4 area: 359–362; color constancy role,
    257, 361–362, 367–368; color

discrimination, 360–361; color-selective neurons, 359–360; development, 236–237; general organization, 353–354, 358; Mondrian stimuli, 360, 366–367; neuron suppression surround, 360, 364, 367–368; orientation-specific cells, 192–193; size change effects, monkeys, 201–202
vectorfield, 44
  McCollough effect role, 44–46, 52
  perceptual constancy function, 44
velocity transposition, 397
ventral pathway, size processing, 199–200
vernier acuity
  ocular specificity, 481
  training effects interpretation, 482
  transfer/specificity characteristics, 477–479
vestibulo-ocular reflex, 521
viewpoint-dependent representation. *See* orientation
visual agnosia, 216–225
visual angle, *see* angular size
visual extinction, 224–225
visual preference, infants, 230–233
visual search tasks

automatization studies, 466, 492
  discrimination mechanism in, 472
  learning specificity/transfer issue, 492
  practice effects, 466–469, 492
  strategy shifts in, 470
von Kries's model, 300–303, 365
  calculation, 264, 301
  and chromatic adaptation, 365
  color constancy, photoreceptor scaling, 300–303

wavelength
  cat sensitivity, 339–340
  cortical substrates, 354–355, 359
  habituation studies, 245–248
  honeybee sensitivity, 325
  infant vision, 235–236, 238, 240–241, 245–248, 256
  retinex algorithm, 301–302
Weber's law, 365, 376
weighted averaging, *see* linear models
wheel motion dynamics, 445
word stimuli, 39–40